Clinical
Child Psychology

THE WILEY SERIES IN CLINICAL PSYCHOLOGY

Series Editor

Fraser N. Watts
MRC Applied Psychology Unit
Cambridge

Severe Learning Disability
and Psychological Handicap
John Clements

Cognitive Psychology
and Emotional Disorders
J. Mark, G. Williams, Fraser N. Watts,
Colin MacLeod and Andrew Mathews

Community Care in Practice
Services for the Continuing Care Client
Edited by Anthony Lavender and Frank Holloway

Attribution Theory in
Clinical Psychology
Freidrich Försterling

Panic Disorder:
Theory, Research and Therapy
Edited by Roger Baker

Measuring Human Problems
A Practical Guide
Edited by David Peck and C. M. Shapiro

Clinical Child Psychology
Social Learning, Development and Behaviour
Martin Herbert

Further titles in preparation

Clinical
Child Psychology

Social Learning,
Development and Behaviour

Martin Herbert
University of Leicester

With specialist contributions from

Clive R. Hollin, *University of Birmingham, UK*
Chrissi Ioannou, *Brookside Family Consultation Clinic, Cambridge, UK*
Neville J. King, *Monash University, Australia*
Thomas H. Ollendick, *Virginia Polytechnic Institute and State University, USA*
William Yule, *Institute of Psychiatry, University of London, UK*

JOHN WILEY & SONS
Chichester · New York · Brisbane · Toronto · Singapore

1991

Other Wiley Editorial Offices

John Wiley & Sons, Inc., 605 Third Avenue,
New York, NY 10158-0012, USA

Jacaranda Wiley Ltd, G.P.O. Box 859, Brisbane,
Queensland 4001, Australia

John Wiley & Sons (Canada) Ltd, 22 Worcester Road,
Rexdale, Ontario M9W 1L1, Canada

John Wiley & Sons (SEA) Pte Ltd, 37 Jalan Pemimpin #05-04,
Block B, Union Industrial Building, Singapore 2057

Library of Congress Cataloging-in-Publication Data:
Herbert, Martin.
    Clinical child psychology : social learning development, and
behaviour / Martin Herbert ; with contributions from Clive R. Hollin
. . . [et al.].
        p.   cm. — (The Wiley series in clinical psychology)
    Includes bibliographical references and index.
    ISBN 0-471-92166-1 (ppc)
    ISBN 0-471-92907-7 (paper)
    1. Clinical child psychology.   I. Hollin, Clive R.   II. Title.
III. Series.
    [DNLM: 1. Child Psychology. 2. Psychology, Clinical — in infancy &
childhood.   WS 105 H537c]
RJ503.3.H47   1991
    155.4 — dc20
DNLM/DLC
for Library of Congress   90–12947
                                                               CIP

British Library Cataloguing in Publication Data:
Herbert, Martin
    Clinical child psychology : social learning, development
    and behaviour – (Wiley series in clinical psychology).
    1. Clinical child psychology
    I. Title
    155.4

    ISBN 0-471-92166-1 (cloth)
    ISBN 0-471-92907-7 (paper)

Typeset by APS, Salisbury, Wilts.
Printed and bound by Courier International Ltd, Tiptree, Essex

Contents

Series Preface

The Wiley Series in Clinical Psychology includes authoritative, up-to-date texts relating to the core fields of clinical psychology. Wherever possible such books are written by a single author, to ensure that they have the coherence which is often lacking in edited books.

Though Clinical *Child* Psychology is a well developed professional sub-speciality within clinical psychology, and though it has been the focus of considerable research activity, there is a surprising dearth of texts which present a coherent and comprehensive overview of the field. In this situation, I am confident that the present book will meet a real need amongst practitioner and trainee clinical psychologists whose clients include children. The author, Martin Herbert, is already well known and respected for his more specialized books on clinical psychological work with children. The present book, like his previous work, is authoritative, not only displaying an impressive grasp of the research literature but also being informed by his considerable practical clinical experience. It is also highly readable.

The book takes a broad 'social learning' approach, retaining the concreteness and practicality of behavioural approaches to child problems, without neglecting a broad understanding of social factors in the child's environment. Indeed, one of the themes of this book is the value of a 'triadic' approach in which the psychologist works with the child *and* a significant adult figure in the child's life (parent, teacher, or whoever is relevant).

The early chapters of this book set out the general approach taken to childhood problems, showing how they should be assessed and how a developmental history can be relevant to understanding the presenting problem. Next, the book turns to common childhood problems, beginning with preschool children, and continuing through the problems of school-age children and early adolescents. With this background, the range of available psychological interventions to help children is reviewed. The book concludes with more detailed reviews of five common or representative childhood problems four of which are written by invited experts.

Clinical psychology is a field with close links with many other professions in scientific disciplines. I hope that the series will have a broad appeal to all those concerned with the application of psychological knowledge to clinical problems. This particular book should interest clinical, developmental and educational psychologists, child psychiatrists, and social workers specializing in work with children.

FRASER WATTS
Series Editor

Preface

It is a daunting task to attempt to convey the flavour, and something of the substance, of contemporary clinical child psychology theory and practice — such is the present-day range of the practitioners' activities and diversity of their approaches. With regard to the latter, I shall focus largely on a social learning theory and developmental perspective, although, heaven knows, this is a broad enough remit. In the case of the former (the range of problems to be found in the clinical child psychologist's caseload) I am forced to make some invidious choices. The awkward questions are: which subjects to leave out, which to mention in a somewhat cursory fashion (with some compensatory suggestions for further reading), and which to treat at some depth? Inevitably my choice will not be everyone else's, but the coverage is comprehensive enough to include most of the major disorders.

As this is a clinical psychology not a psychiatric text on childhood, the positioning of problem areas may differ somewhat from more conventional books. What has guided my organization of problems for discussion, broadly speaking, is a consideration of the life- or developmental-tasks that are salient at particular ages and stages in the child's progression toward maturity. Certain kinds of problems peak at these times and reflect the tensions associated with transition and change. Other problems, like severe learning disabilities, have their effect throughout the life-span, but are particularly to the forefront of parents' consciousness when they first learn about their child's handicap. At such a time a psychologist's knowledge and understanding could be invaluable. So handicap is placed early in the chronological time-span (from conception to early adolescence) around which the later chapters are organized. A framework of normal development and learning is, in my view, central to the understanding of a child's and his or her family's problems. The scope for this framework is life-span development, as parents and grandparents are also coping with significant developmental tasks, and their experiences have an influence on the child and other members of the family. Indeed, the family has a dynamic of its own, a life-history and life-tasks to perform. For these reasons the book is systemic, family-orientated in its approach.

Part One begins with the referral to a clinical child psychologist of a child with problems. This raises the question of the nature of psychological disorders in childhood, and leads on to the wider context of problems in parents and the family system. It poses the 'what' question: the complex issues of assessment, diagnosis and classification. The 'why' question — the matter of causation — introduces the theme of social learning theory and its applications. This is the particular but not exclusive emphasis of this book.

Part Two introduces the reader to the areas covered in a typical case history: biological/physical factors intrinsic to the child (e.g., genetic factors, physical anomalies, prematurity, resilience) and extrinsic (environmental influences) on the pre-, peri- and postnatal periods of the child's life.

Part Three is about preschool children and describes some of the crucial developments and associated problems — cognitive, emotional, linguistic, social and moral — one might expect, as the child moves from infancy to early childhood. It ends with a discussion of the emotional (internalizing) and conduct (externalizing) problems which beset parents, and which are likely to be a major concern of teachers as the child comes of school-going age.

Part Four deals with developmental tasks, events and associated difficulties of middle childhood and early adolescence. It examines a variety of school and classroom difficulties of the social, intellectual and behavioural kind. This means looking at specific learning difficulties, problems of attention, hyperactivity, motor-incoordination, perceptual problems and deficits in social skills. The section also addresses the question of what *special* skills the clinical psychologist brings to the area of health care. Among the subjects dealt with here are concepts of primary, secondary and tertiary prevention; psychophysiological disorders (e.g., bronchial asthma, diabetes mellitus, anorexia nervosa), and, of course, assessment and treatment.

Part Five provides a review of clinical psychology interventions ranging from psychological therapies (such as structural family therapy, behavioural family therapy and family-style residential treatment) to rehabilitation strategies for children with (say) head injuries. Special attention is paid to the consultation or triadic model of intervention. This includes a critical review of theories and methods of teaching social skills and problem-solving.

Part Six deals with five major clinical problems: my own on antisocial, disruptive disorders, and four invited contributions covering delinquency (Clive Hollin); fears and phobias (Tom Ollendick and Neville King); acute pain (Chrissi Ioannou) and post-traumatic stress (William Yule). The authors of the invited chapters provide stimulating and critical accounts of the present 'state of the art' in their chosen fields. The problems they elucidate were chosen because they are among the most challenging difficulties dealt with by contemporary clinical child psychologists. They also illuminate in different ways the social learning and developmental perspective that has proved so fruitful in its theoretical and practical implications.

It is my hope that this book will provide a useful and thought-provoking introduction to the fascinating subject of clinical child psychology for undergraduate students of psychopathology, trainees on clinical psychology courses, and practitioners in the many and varied health services, social services and educational settings in which children and their families receive psychological help.

MARTIN HERBERT
Clinical Psychology Department
University of Leicester 1990

Introduction

In the early 1960s when I worked in the Children's Department and the Adolescent Unit at the Institute of Psychiatry, Maudsley Hospital, in London, the role of the clinical psychologist was very different from, and certainly more restricted than, today. Although things were beginning to change with the advent of behaviour therapy, much of our time was spent as part of a multidisciplinary team, answering requests from psychiatrists for a variety of investigations and assessments: tests of I.Q., tests of personality, tests of brain-damage, and tests of goodness knows what else. Psychometric testing was our bread-and-butter, and a boring diet it seemed to be.

Compare the situation today; psychologists who work with children do so in a variety of settings which include the homes and schools of their clients, social services day nurseries, community settings, general practice surgeries, in-, out- and day-patient facilities in departments of child psychiatry and paediatrics, units for children with terminal illnesses, renal and burns units, neurological and neurosurgical and head injury facilities. They are involved in assessment, treatment, rehabilitation, remedial work, teaching, planning and research.

Fraser Watts (1990) observes that their clients span the age range from infancy to the late teens and come from differing social and ethnic backgrounds. They will have been referred for any of a multitude of problems, ranging from common disorders such as bed-wetting, sleeping and eating difficulties to more serious emotional and behavioural disorders such as autism or anorexia nervosa. The referral might be for difficulties in peer or other social relationships; for developmental disorders of language and learning; or for profound impairments of mental and physical functioning. Other children will be referred because of problems relating to physical health. These could include (a) difficulties such as failure-to-thrive, persistent headache, abdominal pain, asthma, eczema, faecal incontinence or chronic constipation, (b) management problems such as noncompliance with medical prescriptions, fear of injections or, (c) assistance in the management of head injuries, terminal illness or chronic pain, among many other primary physical conditions where there are important psychological components. Table 1 gives you an idea of the range and variety of the work of clinical child psychologists and the many settings in which it is conducted.

Several factors have contributed to the dramatic extension of the child clinical

Table 1. Settings in which clinical child psychologists work and examples of their work. (Source: Fielding, 1987, reproduced by permission of the Oxford University Press).

Setting	Example
(a) *Health*	
(i) Community	
Child welfare clinics	Liaison/consultation with health
Health centres	visitors
GP practices	Parents groups for behavioural, sleeping, feeding problems of under-fives
(ii) Hospital	
Ante-natal clinics	Counselling of mothers with suspected handicapped child
	Counselling of adolescents deciding about termination of pregnancy
Intensive care neonatal units	Counselling for staff and parents
Paediatric assessment clinics	Assessment and remediation of development delays
Paediatric hospital wards	Preparation of parents/children for hospitalization
	Counselling of parents/staff dealing with terminally ill children
Casualty wards	Crisis counselling for adolescents who have taken overdoses
Psychiatric in-patient and out-patient units	Assessment and treatment with families of children showing emotional and behavioural problems
	Consultation/training of psychiatric child care staff (in psychological procedures)
(b) *Social services*	
(i) Local authority nurseries	Advice to nursery nurses concerning problems of child abuse
	Assessment of development delays
(ii) Community homes	Consultation with staff concerning management of difficult behaviour problems
	Counselling foster parents
(c) *Voluntary organizations*	Drop-in clinics for adolescents with drug taking or alcohol problems (e.g., Samaritans, Adoption Societies, Brook Advisory Centres, Grapevine, etc.)

psychologist's role. The major influences according to Fielding (1987) are (a) the reorganization of the clinical psychology services into health district departments which has meant greater access for a variety of professionals (e.g., GPs, health visitors, voluntary and social workers in the community, paediatricians, surgeons and nurses in general hospitals); (b) changes in legislation concerning child care and education and the publication of influential governmental reports which have drawn clinical psychologists with their particular expertise into areas of treatment, consultation and policy making; (c) advances in research and clinical practice which have broadened the skills of clinical psychologists and reinforced their relevance; (d) changes in patterns of health and disease within the population of children.

Watts (1990) observes that with the reduction of infectious diseases and other physical ailments, emotional and behavioural disorders have become the particular concern of parents. They constitute the 'new morbidity'. For this reason they are also a major preoccupation of this book although I will naturally be paying attention to many of the other problems referred to above. The generic term 'emotional and behavioural problems' refers to a large and heterogeneous collection of disorders ranging from depression, anxiety, inhibition and shyness to non-compliance, destructiveness, stealing and aggression. In essence, these problems represent exaggerations, deficits or disabling combinations of feelings, attitudes and behaviours common to all children.

Despite the absence of an agreed-upon set of criteria for defining childhood dysfunction there has been a remarkable consistency in the investigations of the prevalence of psychological problems in children. It has been estimated on the basis of epidemiological studies in the United Kingdom and United States, that some 12 % of children manifest significant emotional or behavioural problems (Gould, Wunsch-Hitzig and Dohrenwend, 1980). Indeed, approximately 90 % of all childhood psychiatric disorders fall into these categories, conduct disorders being the most prevalent (see Chapter 16). Sadly, only 20–33 % of children with clinically significant problems are thought to receive treatment (Knitzer, 1982); furthermore, the more seriously disturbed are less likely to obtain such help than those with milder dysfunctions (Sowder, 1975).

The knowledge base for understanding the wide range of childhood problems and the skills required for assessment and intervention have obviously been extended to an extraordinary extent over a relatively short period of time. All of this has implications for training clinical child psychologists, a matter discussed by Yule (1983) and Routh (1985). It is worth noting that the training of psychologists, with its emphasis on empiricism and experimental method, has resonances with the present concentration in the health service on accountability and effectiveness of service delivery. The empiricism of psychologists, the methods of checking and evaluation built into many of their assessments (e.g., functional analysis, psychometrics) and clinical interventions (e.g., behaviour therapy) provides a model which other professions are increasingly interested in learning (Hollin, Wilkie and Herbert, 1987).

Although clinical child psychology builds upon a generic or core knowledge base of general psychology and psychopathology, it is a specialism with features that give the work of the child psychologist a distinctive flavour, one which is neatly captured in a quotation from Yule (1983):

> Children *are* different from adults. Working with children is more demanding in many ways. Not only are they developing rapidly, but they are also inextricably involved in a variety of social networks. Therein lies one of the challenges for an applied child psychologist.

One of the most interesting — perhaps significant — developments in the last fifteen years or so in the field of child treatment has involved psychologists in the altruistic task of 'giving away' or (as I prefer it) 'sharing', their skills with others who can then mobilize them to help others and/or themselves. The triadic model, as it is called, has built into it the objective of making the therapist redundant as soon as possible in the life of a particular case or client. Hopefully, such an approach is not subversive to the profession; far from making the psychologist's role surplus to requirements, it provides an additional and powerful focus for his or her expertise.

The use of the triadic model of intervention for treatment, training or remedial work began from an assumption that parents, surrogate parents, teachers and other caregivers have a profound effect on children's development and mental health. Because they exert such a significant foundational influence during the impressionable years of childhood, they are usually in a strong position to facilitate prosocial learning, and moderate the genesis of behaviour disorder. Here then is a theme that will recur in this book. The approach, based as it often is, on social learning theory, has crucial implications not only for the way in which the psychologist works, but also for the location of that work. The child's natural environment (be it home, classroom or playground) becomes another setting to add to the consulting room or playroom, for the therapeutic endeavour. The parents — it could also be teachers or care staff — are drawn into the therapeutic alliance, but on the basis of a very *active* partnership. Indeed, the partnership model of practice (be it with other professions or caregivers) will be another theme in the chapters that follow.

One of the many advantages of an applied social learning theory approach, as I see it, is its breadth. It is the major perspective of this book because of its firm roots in empirical evidence, and its heuristic value for theory and practice in clinical child psychology. In my own work with parents, children and adolescents, I have found the marriage of behavioural and cognitive theory in this model (awkward and dissonant though it is at times), invaluable for problem-solving, giving advice, and designing interventions.

Social and developmental psychologists with a cognitive orientation have a fruitful literature to share with clinical child psychologists about the ideas parents bring to the task of parenting: the nature of these ideas, their sources, and their consequences (e.g., Goodnow, 1984; 1988). The behavioural paradigm — or at least an early version of it — tended to deflect the attention of behaviour therapists away from cognitive processes in parents in deference to an exclusive preoccupation with their *actions* and the details of contingencies in their transactions with their children. This disparaging neglect seemed to imply that parents were not thinking beings like therapists. Parke (1978) was moved to assert that psychologists often credit mothers with about as much cognitive complexity as they do babies. Fortunately the credit given to both parties seems, of late, to be on the up-and-up.

I will attempt, where relevant, to address the issue of the ideologies, schemas, constructs, images, perceptions or scripts which inform many parental actions. It is certainly time to redress the balance, given the long-standing willingness of many theorists (e.g., Aronfreed, Bruner, Kohlberg and Piaget) to explain the behaviour of their offspring (in social situations) in terms of their interpretations of events, as well as their cognitive maturity and capacity to assimilate information.

The convergence of these cognitive perspectives directed towards adults *and* children makes sense as a way of integrating theories (e.g., cycles of disadvantage) linking the experiences and actions of succeeding generations. There are theories, for example, which interpret the effects of early experience or later personal actions and personality attributes in terms of the 'internal models' that people develop about the nature of relationships, and these models are based on their own childhood experiences, carried forward in time and functioning as 'filters' through which the behaviour of their own offspring are perceived (Belsky, 1984; Crowell and Feldman, 1988).

Part One

The Nature of the Problem

THE REFERRAL

Parents and teachers tend to become worried about the children in their care when their behaviour appears (a) to be out of control, (b) to be unpredictable, or (c) to lack sense or meaning. If these tendencies are extreme and/or persistent they are likely to be thought of as 'problematic' or 'abnormal' and the growing concern they engender may result in a referral (usually through a social worker or general practitioner) to a clinical child psychologist or child psychiatrist.

Another concern arises from an expectation (not always accurate) of *what* an infant should be doing, and *when* — the notion of a developmental timetable in the parent's mind. When some activity (e.g., talking, relating to people) seems to be delayed or 'odd' in some way, it is quite likely that the chain of referrals (including now a paediatrician) will lead, among others, to a clinical psychologist. He or she might carry out an assessment alone, or in partnership with other specialists. It all depends on the nature and location of the referral. Their findings could lead to a reassuring ('there is nothing untoward') sort of statement; perhaps some advice; or in the case of a serious problem, an intervention — a therapeutic or remedial programme. The assessment leads to a formulation (a set of hypotheses about the nature and causes of the difficulties) which, in turn, leads directly and logically to a plan of action, possibly discussed and debated by members of a multi-disciplinary team, and designed to help the child and family. The action could be a multi-level, broadly based programme involving several members of the team (e.g., the speech therapist, group worker, social worker). It might consist of a focused treatment for which the psychologist or psychiatrist takes responsibility.

The process is very much like the moves in an experiment, and involves three vital questions:

(i)   *What* is the nature of the problem and what constitutes its parameters?

(ii) *Why* has this problem come about? (a statement on causation, a set of explanatory 'hypotheses').

(iii) *How* can the psychologist (where necessary with others) intervene in a way that allows him or her to help the client and (at the same time) test the validity of the explanation of the case?

This, on the face of it, looks fairly straightforward; in reality it isn't so. I have put forward my preferred way of looking at assessment, but there could be, and are, disagreements about what the focus should be in asking the 'what' question (in other words, what information is relevant), about the causes of problems covered by the 'why' question, and the means of helping clients. Indeed some psychologists might reject the sequence I have described as overly mechanistic.

For example, psychologists like Maslow (1954) whose ideas have been seminal in the Human Potential Movement and the humanistic branch of psychology, view individuals as organisms with an inherent need to grow or change. This is their intrinsic motivation, i.e., growth or abundance; it does not derive from other needs, namely 'deficiency motivation'. This reveals itself in the process called self-actualization, a facet of human nature which receives scant attention in any clinical assessment of the child. These issues and debates reveal themselves in the vital area of assessment, my first topic. Some of the theoretical and practical aspects of assessments are dealt with in Appendix I.

Chapter 1

Clinical Assessment

Assessment, and its conceptual partner, intervention, are major activities in the professional life of clinical child psychologists. How they go about them — the objectives and goals they set, the procedures they use, the information they focus on, the meaning they impose on it — will vary according to the 'model' of psychopathology that informs their practice. And in uttering (or writing) that word 'psycho-*pathology*' we receive our first hint of the pervasiveness of medical conceptualizing in the area of childhood psychological problems. Table 2 shows a list of terms child psychiatrists (and many clinical psychologists) use, ones which other professionals (and, to be fair, some psychiatrists) studiously avoid.

Are these distinctions academic, indeed pedantic; or are they ideologically important, not merely reflecting significant theoretical but also metatheoretical perspectives, i.e., ways of thinking about the nature of human action and of valuing people? Whatever one's point of view, it is difficult — and in many instances inappropriate — to avoid (as you will see in this text) medical concepts.

In clinical child psychology research, matters of definition are inextricably enmeshed with issues of classification and measurement. Clinical judgements of whether a child is

Table 2.

Medically-orientated Terminology	Alternative usage
Patient	Client/Resident
Psychopathology	Psychological problems, surplus behaviour,
Illness/disease	deficits, difficulties
Symptom	Target behaviour/problem/difficulty
Treatment/therapy	Intervention
Causation	Antecedents
Cure	Reduction in X or increase in Y behaviours/skills
Diagnosis	Assessment
Mental handicap	Learning difficulty/disability

manifesting a psychological problem involve two important and distinguishable processes:

- *Assessment*, which aims to differentiate, operationalize and measure those behavioural, cognitive, and affective patterns that are considered to be problematic.
- *Classification*, which aims to group individuals according to their distinguishing problematic behavioural, cognitive, and affective patterns.

ASSESSMENT

Operational definitions of psychological problems in the literature on childhood psychopathology are many and varied and these variations often influence clinical decisions concerned with diagnosis (assessment) and classification. Achenbach and Edelbrock (1989), in a useful review of these issues, acknowledge that there is little agreement about the proper nature and role of diagnosis with respect to child psychopathology. At a practical level Schwartz and Johnson (1985) illustrate how assessment can vary depending on the practitioner's preferred theoretical model:

> ... assessment procedures may be employed in an attempt to determine the personality characteristics of the child and the underlying nature of his or her psychological problems so that the cause of the disorder can be determined and treated. Or assessment procedures can be directed toward observable behaviors rather than underlying causes. In the latter case the clinician may focus on the specific behaviors that have led to the child's referral, the context in which these behaviors are displayed, and the factors in the child's natural environment that reinforce and maintain these problem behaviors.

The second example represents very much a psychological perspective, although there is nothing cut-and-dried about these distinctions.

Nowhere is the influence of medical thinking in child clinical psychology more pronounced than in the attention paid to the classification and diagnosis of children's psychological problems. Underlying the creation of classificatory systems (e.g., the DSM-III-R described below) and taxonomies of 'symptoms', is the assumption that specific syndromes (disease patterns) with identifiable and specific causes (aetiologies) can be diagnosed. The terminology is resonant with that found in physical and psychiatric illness. And certainly it is important to look carefully at such schemes, especially in the light of the consistency of definition of childhood disorders required by researchers, among others. Uninformed, emotive rhetoric about the medical model in clinical child psychology simply brings its practitioners into disrepute. This is not to suggest that one should not adopt a clear position (and I shall state mine shortly); the point is to be clear about *why* one has adopted a particular orientation, model or perspective, and *what* the underlying assumptions and the implications of that choice happen to be. Another point is the necessity to understand the conceptual language and theoretical framework of those with whom one works even if you disagree with some of their ideas — a not unlikely scenario in a multi-disciplinary Child and Family Psychiatry Unit.

THE AMERICAN PSYCHIATRIC ASSOCIATION CLASSIFICATION SYSTEM: DSM-III.

This is the best known and most widely accepted system in use. The letters DSM stand for Diagnostic and Statistical Manual of Mental Disorders. The most recent, third, edition (American Psychiatric Association, 1980) has already given birth to a revised version: the DSM-III-R (American Psychiatric Association, 1987). (A training manual has been published by Reid and Wise, 1989.) It provides criteria for making diagnostic judgements about a number of specific disorders, criteria that are more objective than previous editions and more often based upon observable behaviour.

The DSM-III contains a section on children with 40 specific diagnoses gathered in nine general groups (major categories). The various editions of the DSM were compiled by committee discussion — something of an irony given that the 'S' stands for 'statistical' and the process of derivation is scarcely that. The Task Force on Nomenclature chaired by Robert Spitzer set out to define each disorder for the third edition of the DSM without assumptions about the aetiology of the disorder, a feature much criticized in earlier versions. For all its medical 'flavouring' DSM-III is not essentially a categorical taxonomy, but a *multiaxial* system of classification (see Reid and Wise, 1989). It provides more than a diagnostic label; it adds a set of independent dimensions (axes) which are coded or rated along with the psychiatric diagnosis: Axes I and II are used to describe the patient's current condition, i.e., clinical conditions.

Axis I includes (inter alia) the following:

- Disruptive behaviour disorders
- Anxiety disorders of childhood or adolescence
- Eating disorders
- Gender identity disorders
- Tic disorders
- Elimination disorders
- Speech disorders.

Axis II lists personality or developmental disorders. Disorders usually first evident in infancy, childhood or adolescence are coded on this axis when they fall within the following categories:

- Mental retardation
- Pervasive developmental disorders
- Specific developmental disorders.

Axis III. Here the clinician lists all physical disorders or conditions, e.g., hypothyroidism, epilepsy, bronchial asthma.

Axis IV contains a 'severity of psychological stressors scale' for children and adolescents (there is also one for adults).

Axis V. Here the clinician estimates the patient's level of function at the time of evaluation and the patient's highest level of function during the past year.

A good deal of discussion, positive and critical, and a mixture of both, has been generated by the publication of the DSM-III manual (e.g., Cantwell, 1985; Garmezy, 1977; Quay, 1984; Rutter and Shaffer, 1980). Although, as we have seen, it follows a multi-axial system on which behavioural descriptions of the presenting problems are coded on the major axis, and includes ratings of psychosocial stressors and levels of adaptive functioning, it still refers to its target phenomena as 'illnesses' and gives rules for deciding in a yes-or-no manner which illness(es) a person has (see Achenbach, 1982). With the exception of the use of I.Q. tests for classifying 'mental retardation', multiaxial systems do not specify operations for the assessment of disorders. The use of diagnosis is important in American clinical psychology because of the requirements of medical and insurance schemes. It is helpful (or convenient), given the antipathy of so many psychologists to making categorical diagnoses, that both systems accept that disorders are defined in terms of the interaction between the child and his or her environment — a notion with which social learning theorists feel at ease.

Psychiatrists appear not to be happy with the system as a whole. A survey by Jampala, Sierles, and Taylor (1986) of the use of, and satisfaction with, the DSM-III among 1000 qualified American psychiatrists and psychiatric trainees (residents) indicated that 48 % of the psychiatrists 'did not believe in the validity of the DSM-III criteria' and 55 % of the sample surveyed would cease to use it if it were not required. The diagnostic categories failed to accommodate almost half of their patients.

Whatever the reliability and validity of this and other schemes, there is an objection raised by many psychologists (and psychiatrists) to what they see as invidious 'labelling' and stigmatizing of individuals. While there may be good policy, planning and resource-mobilizing reasons for diagnostic labels, there is concern about how parents', teachers' and children's attributions, perceptions and actions are affected by having an individual called hyperactive, dyslexic, disruptive or whatever (see Chapter 9). More damning, from a more detached technical point of view, is the absence of a clear relationship between most global diagnostic classifications applied to particular children and any clear aetiology or focused therapeutic/remedial programme of action (Herbert, 1964).

There is another area of terminology where the question 'what's in a name?' has very important implications for the named/labelled — the 'mentally handicapped' — and their parents. Of all the attributes of human beings, 'mind' is usually thought of as the quintessence. So to be found wanting in mental capacity or intellectual ability is an awful stigma. And it is a devastating shock for parents to learn that their child is mentally handicapped.

Fryers (1984) observes that there are many confusing terms in use, serving different traditions or different purposes. Currently, 'mental handicap' appears to be most favoured internationally by parents, and 'mental retardation' or 'severe learning difficulties' by service professionals. But handicap and mental retardation are not medical diagnoses, although doctors frequently refer to them in this manner. They are administrative categories from educational traditions.

It has taken over a decade of debates before terminology relating to abnormality, dysfunction, and disadvantage could be codified in the World Health Organization's

(WHO) 'International Classification of Impairments, Disabilities and Handicaps' (1980). Fryers is of the opinion that there is hope now that in scientific writing and serious discourse the confusion brought about by a plethora of terms and concepts can be overcome.

The WHO definition of impairment incorporates a functional as well as a structural component:

- 'Impairment: in the context of health experience, an impairment is any loss or abnormality of psychological, physiological or anatomical structure or function.'
- Disability is seen as the limitation of personal activity consequent upon impairment: '... any restriction or lack (resulting from an impairment) of ability to perform an activity in the manner or within the range considered normal for a human being.'
- Handicap is the resulting personal and social disadvantage: '... a disadvantage for an individual, resulting from an impairment or disability, that limits or prevents the fulfilment of a role that is normal (depending on age, sex and social and cultural factors) for that individual.'

This terminology is adopted, where appropriate, in this book.

As this is a textbook on clinical child psychology (not child psychiatry or child psychopathology), it should come as no surprise that my preferred framework for conceptualizing psychological problems of childhood is mainly in terms of quantitative deviations of cognition and behaviour from developmental and social norms, rather than as a taxonomy of symptomatically distinct diseases. For this reason my location and grouping of problems does not always coincide neatly with the DSM categories. The fact is that despite interesting correlations between childhood problems, the vast majority of 'disorders' (it is difficult to escape from medical usage) cannot be viewed — except figuratively — as disease states or entities (Graham, 1980; Yule, 1981). Nevertheless, it *is* useful to distinguish between those clusters of unacceptable behaviours ('symptoms') that tend to co-vary and to interfere with adaptive functioning, and *isolated* behaviours that may be characteristic of both 'normal' and 'disturbed' children. The former tend to come into the clinical or psychiatric realm because of their ramifications.

Childhood signs of psychological abnormality are, by and large, manifestations of behavioural, cognitive and emotional responses common to all children. Their quality of being dysfunctional lies in their inappropriate intensity, frequency and persistence (see Figure 1). It seems to me that there is no point in splitting too many hairs over classification, or of being precious about the so-called 'medical model'. Certainly it is shortsighted to reject medical knowledge and practice as some psychologists do, especially when it comes to problems like enuresis and encoprésis (to mention only two) which can figure large in clinical child psychologists' caseloads.

In any event, there are exceptions (fortunately rare) to the generalization about quantitative deviations from the norm, made earlier on. The psychoses of childhood and behavioural aberrations brought about by brain injury are conditions that do not seem to fit that category. Of course, the view that most childhood disorders differ in degree,

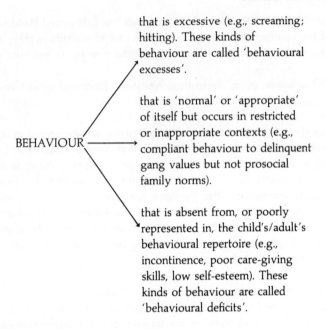

that is excessive (e.g., screaming; hitting). These kinds of behaviour are called 'behavioural excesses'.

that is 'normal' or 'appropriate' of itself but occurs in restricted or inappropriate contexts (e.g., compliant behaviour to delinquent gang values but not prosocial family norms).

BEHAVIOUR

that is absent from, or poorly represented in, the child's/adult's behavioural repertoire (e.g., incontinence, poor care-giving skills, low self-esteem). These kinds of behaviour are called 'behavioural deficits'.

Figure 1. Three categories of problematic behaviour.

rather than kind, from normal behaviour, leaves us with rather embarrassing questions about definition: 'when precisely is a problem a problem?'; 'at what point do we demarcate the "normal" from the abnormal?'.

The relativity of criteria

These questions are embarrassing not only because they are extremely difficult to answer, but because they are open to value judgements — a potential Pandora's box of personal and cultural (not to mention theoretical) bias and prejudice. After all, the word 'norm' from its Latin root means a standard, rule or pattern. Thus 'abnormal' applied to children's behaviour implies (with the prefix 'ab' meaning 'away from') a deviation from a standard. An analysis of these standards, in public and professional usage, makes it clear that they are *social standards* (rules, expectations, codes, conventions) and comparisons made with patterns of *normal child and adolescent development* (Herbert, 1987a). Psychological problems are seen as having unfavourable social and personal consequences for the child himself or herself, for the family, and, sometimes, for the wider community. Wright (1971) distinguishes between antisocial acts, the adverse repercussions of which are felt primarily by others, and antiascetic acts, forms of pleasurable self-indulgence judged by others to be harmful to those who engage in them.

A good example of the difficulties of judgement and definition is provided by the conduct disorders (see page 270) which are among the most common problems dealt with by clinical child psychologists. Arguably they contain what society would see as a moral dimension, and thus require a familiarity with the literature on moral development. Fundamental questions about the nature of the person are central to investigations in this area. An excellent starting point for psychologists is the work of Piaget. He devoted a considerable part of 'The Moral Judgement of the Child' (1932) to a discussion of the relative value for society of behaviour based on reciprocal relations of affection, trust and respect, and behaviour based on obedience to authority, arguing the superiority of the former and asserting the importance of an education which fosters mutual respect between student and teacher, as well as cooperation and affection between pupil and peers. He was of the opinion that the concept of 'good' comes not from a sense of obligation based on learned obedience, but from 'a conscious realisation of something which is the primary condition of moral life — the need for reciprocal affection'.

For Piaget morality involves a strong cognitive element. Moral behaviour depends on the consistent action of the mind, the cognitive framework supplied by recognition of the principle of reciprocity, which gives form to an emotional response to a particular situation. As he puts it, 'morality is the logic of action, as logic is the morality of thought' (Piaget, 1932).

Other psychologists, less concerned with philosophical issues, take the accepted moral code of society as the starting point for their research. They have studied children in choice situations where the behavioural alternatives are either desirable or undesirable, and the factors which lead to children learning to make one response rather than the other. It is not meaningful in this context to make a distinction between moral development and other aspects of socialization. It may also be meaningless to distinguish between social conformity and morality. Because behaviour is heavily influenced by previous learning experiences in similar situations the idea of the individual's control over his or her behaviour assumes a different meaning. Control is consequent, to a significant extent, on the internalization of learned rules, rather than an untrammelled and active freedom to choose between behavioural alternatives. It is precisely on this issue that a fascinating, if inconclusive, debate takes place between those who take up somewhat polarized views of the individual as *proactive agent* (e.g., Bannister, Harre, Kelly) shaping and constructing his or her world, and those who emphasize the person as *reactor*, being 'pushed' and 'pulled' to a large degree passively by the contingencies in his or her environment (e.g. Skinner). These views *do* affect the way clients are assessed and worked with (see page 260).

The clinical child psychologist's essential interest — whether he or she is ideologically at one extreme or the other, or somewhere in the middle — is the cognitive and emotional aspects of behavioural choice in situations where the child's behaviour is likely to impinge adversely on self and other people. There will be no problem in designating self-injurious (self-mutilating) behaviours as abnormal; but where does one draw the line between assertive and aggressive actions? The context or (more accurately) contexts for such actions become critical in making judgements. And it is the dynamic, transactional and individualized process of assessment to which this requirement gives rise, that gives a *broadly-based* functional analysis, in my view, an advantage over traditional classification (see page 64).

None of the problems of subjectivity and relativity of social judgement should prevent us from attempting to derive cut-off points — rigorous, objective operational criteria — for what constitutes 'abnormal' behaviour (Haynes, 1978; Mash and Terdal, 1988; Ollendick and Hersen, 1984). This can be done in terms of the measurable impact of behaviour on self, on interpersonal relationships, and on social settings. And certainly it is feasible to compare children's behaviour and other attributes with norms from the many studies, longitudinal and cross-sectional, that now enrich the psychological literature.

Settings must be taken into account in a clinical assessment; for example the findings of several studies (e.g., Fergusson and Horwood, 1987, 1989; Goddard, Brodge and Wenar, 1961; Rutter, Tizard and Whitmore, 1970) suggest that maternal and teacher accounts of child behaviour are only modestly correlated. This is possibly due to the effects of situational factors; it has been suggested that since mothers and teachers see children in different contexts governed by different rules, there is no strong reason to expect that their ratings of behaviour should be identical.

While maternal and teacher ratings of particular children are only modestly correlated, there is quite marked stability in their ratings over time; in other words their individual judgements tend to be consistent, even if they do differ somewhat. There is evidence to suggest that rater-specific as well as situation-specific factors may influence behaviour ratings. In particular, maternal mood and notably maternal depression appear to influence the mother's ratings of the child. This result strongly suggests that some component of ratings of child behaviour reflects variability between the perspectives of raters rather than variability in child behaviour (Fergusson and Horwood, 1987). More generally, their results suggest that maternal and teacher ratings of, say, conduct disorder are not unalloyed measures of the child's generalized propensity to aggressive disruptive behaviour but reflect also the effects of other rater-specific and situation-specific factors.

The continuities of child behaviour in a given situation and the discontinuities across situations appear to derive, in large part, from the various social roles children imitate or have thrust upon them. Even by 6 or 7 years of age, children begin to adopt behavioural roles which vary with the context in which they are functioning. Thus a given child may exhibit difficult behaviour at home but modulate his or her behaviour at school. Such a behavioural repertoire would result in there being relatively stable behaviour within a given situational context but relatively little agreement between behaviour in different situations (Fergusson and Horwood, 1987). Yule (1989) has a caveat against rejecting the concept of personality traits and leaving them out of an assessment. There is increasing evidence that introverted children respond differently from extraverted children to different regimes in the classroom and even to different styles of therapeutic intervention. He adds that evidence is mounting that personality (or temperamental characteristics) affect how a child will respond to a particular situation.

> Once one recognizes that a child is extremely introverted, one interprets his or her lack of
> many friends in a different light. Provided he or she has a few close friends and can use

appropriate social skills when he or she wants to, such a child would not be considered a candidate for social skills treatment. A measurement of the child's degree of introversion coupled with a knowledge of the total constellation characterized as extremely introverted are combined to judge the abnormality or, in this case, normality of the child's behaviour. Having only two friends may be statistically abnormal; but it is clinically normal in the examples given.

When it comes to 'abnormal' aspects of personality, there seems to be a minority of children whose behavioural characteristics generalize in their maladaptive aspects, over both time and situation; these are among the children who turn out to cause most concern in the wake of their 'high profile' behaviour disorders. The presence of such children would account for the fact that parent and teacher ratings do show some modest positive correlation.

Implications for assessment

These considerations suggest that the interpretation of parent and teacher reports of child behaviour is a complex matter and that probably relatively little information can be gained about a child's behavioural tendencies from a *single* measure taken at one particular time using a solitary source of information. Moral behaviour is a good example. Parents and teachers like to make judgements about the moral standards of children and adolescents. A reified concept of morality is simplistic. We know that moral behaviour is not unidimensional (Wright, 1971); each of its facets is complex, and they do not intercorrelate in any simple way.

The classic study of some 12 000 subjects (aged 11 to 16) by Hartshorne and May (1928–1930) showed that there was very little correlation among situational cheating tests; children's verbal moral values about honesty had little to do with how they acted. The decision to cheat was largely determined by expediency. Even when honest behaviour was not dictated by concern about punishment or detection, it was largely determined by immediate situational factors of group approval and example. The child's perception of risk of detection appeared to be a better predictor of his or her behaviour than any measure of moral maturity. The authors concluded that the educator's task must be to teach acceptable social habits in specific situations. The concept of moral 'character' was not, however, finally abandoned; Hartshorne and May's conclusions have been challenged by the use of their own data with more sophisticated techniques of analysis. Vernon (1964) factor-analysed the results of the tests, and found a small but distinct 'morality' factor operating across situations.

Much weight has been given to the development (or failure of development) of conscience, or the internalization of behavioural inhibitions and controls, in prosocial and antisocial children (Aronfreed, 1968; Hoffman, 1970). Our growing awareness of the importance of situational control and reinforcement of conduct disordered and delinquent behaviour (Chapter 16) does not necessarily contradict the theory of a central control 'mechanism'. Bowers (1973) concludes from a review of empirical studies, that both trait theorists and situationists have overstated their case.

We can expect some sort of consistency to be attached to the concept of a mature social/moral being, whether it be consistency in the application of a sophisticated cognitive framework such as the principle of reciprocity across situations, or the operation of a fully internalized set of rules for behaviour, freed from the control of external reward/punishment contingencies. But clearly a crucial (if inconvenient) clinical implication of these findings is that the evaluation of children referred for an alleged conduct disorder should include consideration not only of the child's behaviour, but of the situation in which, and the persons with whom, this behaviour occurs. It is important also to know something of the characteristics of the individual(s) complaining about the conduct disorder.

The preoccupation with objective operational criteria for childhood disorders should not blind the psychologist to his or her obligation to assess the quality of the child's parenting. And here is another terrain with its share of mines and booby traps in the shape of judgements of 'good' mothering and fathering (see Sluckin and Herbert, 1986). This difficult subject is tackled in Chapter 4. But spare a thought — a long and careful consideration — for the predicament of parents, and more particularly, mothers. Schutze's (1987) analysis of standards for the 'good mother' demonstrates how the standards advocated by experts make success more and more difficult to achieve. An example is a concept of mother-love which insists that the essential prerequisite of a child's healthy development is a warm, confident attitude during pregnancy, conveyed to the child in utero and beyond. Schutze observes that this kind of prescription moves influence away from fathers *at any point in time*, and away from mothers' *later* feelings. How can the mother recover from an ambivalent start and become a good mother after the birth is over? The standards become all the more unattainable if, in addition to the requirement of proper attitudes during pregnancy or during the first hour, a 'boundless giving of oneself' and a sense of personal enrichment is demanded? Schutze states that 'the mother of the second half of the twentieth century can carry out her duties until she drops with exhaustion, and yet she is culpable if she does not have the feeling of personal enrichment, or if she has even unconscious negative feelings'.

Emmerich (1969) has shown that dissatisfaction with oneself as a parent turns out to be the highest when a child's characteristics are seen as open to influence in principle, open to influence by others in practice, but — for one reason or another — not susceptible to influence stemming from one's own efforts. In effect, the unhappiness springs both from not meeting one's own standards and from an attribution pattern that provides little comfort for not doing so. There is evidence that parents' definition of problems and referral of their children to clinics, may reflect as much a problem in themselves as in their offspring (e.g., Conger et al., 1984).

MULTIVARIATE APPROACHES

Statistical (and particularly factor analytic) methods have proved popular in the search for clusters, patterns or syndromes of problems which might lend support to the classifications built upon clinical observation and experience. What is advocated is an empirical approach which involves a minimum of assumptions and constructs regarding the causation of behavioural disorders. It endeavours to tease out, from masses of data culled from clinic records and epidemiological surveys, dimensions of disturbed behaviour which are explicit and operational.

Many instruments have been constructed to describe and classify the behaviour of children, particularly in the last decade or so. Alongside this development of methods for measuring behaviour, many dimensions of child behaviour have been identified. Despite the range of instruments that is available and the number of dimensions measured by these instruments, two major dimensions emerge from most analyses: those of emotional and conduct disorders.

For example, Achenbach and Edelbrock (1983) collected data on 2300 American children referred to 42 mental health settings, based upon the parents' (or surrogate parents') observations of the children in their care. The Child Behaviour Checklist (CBCL) was used for this purpose. Factor analysis of scores uncovered several syndromes, described parsimoniously by two broad dimensions: 'internalizing' behaviours and 'externalizing' behaviours. The former included emotional problems such as anxiety, phobias, inhibitions, fearfulness, worrying, somatic difficulties, while the latter included aggression, fighting, noncompliance and hyperactivity. What is impressive is that these behaviour clusters suggesting a bipolar dimension of excess approach behaviour (antisocial aggression) and excess avoidance behaviour (inhibition/social withdrawal), have emerged in several empirical studies conducted on children in a variety of schools, child guidance clinics and residential institutions, beginning with the well-known study by Peterson (1961) and continuing through two decades of research to the present time (see Dreger, 1982, for a review of the evidence).

The various researchers find, despite further diversity in subjects, nationalities, raters, and statistical analyses, that empirical investigations consistently elicit problems of an *undercontrolled* type (variously referred to as conduct disorder, aggressive, externalizing, acting out) and an *overcontrolled* type (emotional disturbance, personality disorder, inhibited, internalizing, anxious). There is a convergence between clinical and factor analytical studies with regard to these dimensions. Fischer *et al.* (1984) focused on the two kinds of psychological maladjustment: the 'internalizing' and 'externalizing' dimensions with a study of 541 children. They were first seen when they were between 2 and 6 years of age and then again seven years later. At both ages parents were asked to complete a behaviour checklist, comprising about 100 items dealing with the frequency with which specific kinds of behaviour occurred and indicating the presence and severity of problems, with particular reference to those falling into the internalizing and externalizing categories.

Of these two, the externalizing dimension appears to be the more stable. For both sexes externalizing symptoms found during the preschool period showed a significant continuity with externalizing symptoms seven years later. No such stability over age was found for internalizing behaviour. The same conclusion emerged when a clinically disturbed group was selected from the total sample on the basis of their deviant score on either of the two dimensions: the results show that preschool children with severe internalizing symptoms are no more likely still to be showing such severe shy, withdrawing behaviour seven years later than are other children. On the other hand children with severe behaviour problems of the externalizing kind early on are much more likely to persist with the same kind of disturbance after this long interval.

Not surprisingly, of the various 'syndromes' described in the literature, conduct disorder is particularly significant because of its long-term and far-reaching ramifications. Peterson (1961) demonstrated that conduct disorder is a cluster (or constellation) of problems characterized by non-compliance, restlessness, irresponsibility, boisterousness, and aggression. It is often associated with hyperactivity and might include, especially in older children, delinquent activities. The common theme running through this rather heterogeneous collection of problems is antisocial disruptiveness, and the social disapproval they earn because they flout society's sensibilities and rules and because their consequences are so disturbing or explicitly harmful to others. Chapter 16 contains a detailed description of the assessment and treatment of this disorder. The group of emotional problems which includes childhood fears and phobias, depression, social inhibition (shyness), tends (although there are exceptions) to be more benign and transient in nature. Chapter 18 deals at length with some of these difficulties.

In practice, a sizeable proportion of children have behaviour problems which, to an important extent, share characteristics of both emotional and conduct disorders. In other words, there is a category of 'mixed disorders' which, in many respects, has most in common with the conduct disorders, but in other respects occupies an intermediate position. It has been suggested that emotional disorders should be separated into depressive and non-depressive types (Puig-Antich, 1986). Clearly, a social criterion is being applied to certain categories of behaviour. When, for example, is a child's fearfulness or irresponsibility not a legitimate by-product of his or her immaturity, but a sign of emotional disturbance? Any definition — particularly of conduct problems — must involve a critical consideration of the social value judgements that lead to certain behaviours being labelled in this way, and their appropriateness, given the child's age and intellectual level.

Multivariate approaches to classification undoubtedly have advantages; but there are also disadvantages. Although they provide empirical evidence for the existence of patterns or clusters of behavioural problems, and make possible the reliable and valid assessment of such clusters, the emergence of patterns depends on the data that goes into the analysis. Obviously, a cluster cannot be uncovered if its constituent behaviours are not included in the data processed through the computer. Then there are several approaches to factor analysis and results often depend on the method chosen by the researcher. For instance, Peterson (1961) reported evidence for a 2-factor model of preschool behavioural functioning, but he also found a 5-factor solution. He decided to reject it on theoretical grounds.

The various questionnaires and interview protocols used to assess childhood behavioural function and dysfunction in clinical research measure a bewildering variety and number of specific behaviours. There may be differences in the behaviours explored by the various instruments, depending on the expected source of information (say, parents, teachers or peers), the context of assessment (for example, children in a general population study as opposed to children referred to a clinic), the choice of methodology made by the researcher (say, observational ratings as opposed to interview ratings), and the theoretical perspective of the research (e.g., 2-factor versus 3-factor models of behavioural dysfunction).

Quay's review of 55 factor analytic investigations (Quay, 1984) elicited seven behavioural dimensions (each with its cluster of associated characteristics) that had been replicated in as many as ten separate studies. Essentially they are (with the exception of number (vii)) refinements of the two major categories mentioned above.

  (i) Conduct disorder.
 (ii) Socialized aggression.
(iii) Motor overactivity.
(iv) Problems of attention.
 (v) Anxious-depressed.
(vi) Somatic complaints.
(vii) Psychotic disorder.

Each of these 'syndromes' will be considered later. But as Schwartz and Johnson (1985) observe, they have implications for the validity of existing classification systems such as the DSM-III. While there is some agreement between the empirically derived patterns and certain DSM-III diagnostic categories, *most* DSM categories have no empirically derived counterparts (see Table 3).

CONTINUITIES OF BEHAVIOUR

We have looked at correlations across behaviours (clusters) but what of associations between behaviour patterns over time — in other words, continuities? Several retrospective and longitudinal studies have investigated the intercorrelations among behavioural or personality ratings over the years — an exercise fraught with methodological and interpretive problems.

The fixity of the child's psychological attributes at a tender age — an article of faith in the early Freudian canon — seem to have been exaggerated (Clarke and Clarke, 1986). As Brim and Kagan (1980), following their edited review of this important subject, put it:

> The view that emerges from this work is that humans have a capacity for change across the whole life span. It questions the traditional idea that the experiences of the early years, which have a demonstrated contemporaneous effect, necessarily constrain the characteristics of adolescence and adulthood ... many individuals retain a great capacity for change, and the consequences of the events of early childhood are continually transformed by later experiences, making the course of human development more open than many have believed.

Table 3. Empirically derived dimensions of behaviour set against DSM-III–R categories.

Behavioural Dimension	Co-varying Characteristics	DSM-III Category
CONDUCT DISORDER	Disobedient, defiant Fighting, hitting Destructive Uncooperative, resistant	CONDUCT DISORDER (312 xx) (Group Type (312.20)) (Solitary Aggressive Type (312.00)) (Undifferentiated Type (312.90))
SOCIALIZED AGGRESSION	Has 'bad' companions Truants from school/home Loyal to delinquent friends Steals in the company of others	
MOTOR OVERACTIVITY	Restless, overactive Overtalkative Excitable, impulsive Squirmy, jittery	
ATTENTION PROBLEMS	Poor concentration, short attention span Daydreaming Preoccupied, stares into space Impulsive	ATTENTION-DEFICIT HYPERACTIVITY DISORDER (ADHD) (314.01) Without Hyperactivity
ANXIOUS-DEPRESSED WITHDRAWAL	Anxious, fearful, tense Shy, timid, bashful Depressed, sad, disturbed Feels inferior, worthless	ANXIETY DISORDERS Overanxious Disorder (313.00) Separation Anxiety Disorder (309.21) Avoidant Disorder (313.21)
SOMATIC COMPLAINTS	Stomach aches Vomiting, nausea Headaches	
PSYCHOTIC DISORDER	Bizarre, odd, peculiar Incoherent speech Visual hallucinations Strange ideas and behaviour	PERVASIVE DEVELOPMENTAL DISORDERS Autistic Disorder (299.00) Pervasive Developmental Disorder not otherwise specified (299.80)
		OTHER DISORDERS (inter alia) Reactive Attachment Disorder of Infancy (313.89) Identity Disorder (313.82) Elective Mutism (313.23) Oppositional Defiant Disorder (313.81) Gender Identity Disorder (302.60)

For normal children, personal characteristics and, indeed, most areas of behaviour, do not begin to crystallize or stabilize until the early school years are reached. And even then, only modest correlations with adult behaviours emerge (Herbert, 1980). The view, commonly held by workers in the mental health field, that early characteristics remain relatively unchanged seems to be true only of a specially vulnerable section of the population.

Certainly, in the case of the emotional problems — fears, phobias, inhibitions, and so on, of childhood — they tend to be relatively short-lived, although, again, not always as transient as stated in the literature (see Chapter 18). Nevertheless, children who attend clinics for such problems are impossible to distinguish as adults from persons who were not referred in their youth for such problems (Herbert, 1980). These optimistic findings about 'spontaneous remission' are not repeated elsewhere. There is general agreement that it is those disorders involving disruptive, aggressive, or antisocial behaviour that are most likely to persist into adolescence (Robins, 1966); there are also links between childhood and adult life in the area of antisocial personality (Farrington, 1978).

In the Rutter studies (e.g., Rutter, Tizard and Whitmore, 1970), Isle of Wight children who were diagnosed initially at 10 years old were followed up at 14 or 15 years. Three-quarters of those diagnosed earlier as having a conduct disorder still manifested a handicapping disorder at adolescence. More specifically, aggression — of problematic proportions — has been shown to persist (from as early as 8 years to the middle and late teens) in British and American studies (Farrington, 1978; Lefkowitz, *et al.*, 1977). Overactivity is another specific behaviour with worrying prognostic implications, especially when it shows the sort of generality that is rated high by both parents and teachers (Herbert, 1987b).

General population surveys show that just under half of adolescent disorders have an onset before adolescence, whereas clinic-based studies suggest that the majority of adolescent psychiatric disorders have been manifesting themselves from early or middle childhood (Rutter, 1979b). There is a degree of continuity between early conduct disorder and juvenile delinquency. West and Farrington's (1973) study of London boys indicates the marked relationship between troublesome, difficult and aggressive behaviour in boys aged 8 to 10 (combined ratings by teachers and social workers on a measure of 'combined conduct disorder', also combined ratings by peers and teachers on a measure of 'troublesomeness') and later juvenile delinquency. These measures powerfully predicted severe and persistent delinquency continuing into adult life.

Robins (1966), in her longitudinal studies of American males, demonstrates that most adult antisocial behaviour is antedated by similar behaviour in childhood. The behaviour of childhood, and in particular the *extremeness* and *variety* of antisocial actions, provided better predictors of adult functioning — and, in particular, antisocial adult life style — than the family background, social class of rearing, or particular types of childhood behaviour.

All of this has implications for preventative work and/or effective interventions (see Chapter 16). It also provides an added justification for emphasizing a developmental perspective.

A developmental framework

Children are not homunculi — that is to say, small, less complicated versions of adults. Their problems, to be understood, are best looked at within the context of the 'growing up' process: that kaleidoscope of poignant and sometimes painful experiences, which adults so quickly forget, and which scientists make bland by the phrase 'normal development'. Charles Darwin (1877) was one of the earliest scientists to publish a detailed account of the development of an infant. He wrote 'A Biographical Sketch of an Infant' which contained detailed observations of the development of one of his own children. Over a hundred years on, the normal development of the infant is well documented (see Bremner, 1988; Kaye, 1982), and yet still a closed book to many of the professionals who would find this data base invaluable.

The most dramatic transformations take place in the first years of life, the child acquiring skills in many different ways: physical growth, the development of gross motor movements, the development of vision and fine motor movements, social relationships, cognition and the understanding and use of language. We shall be looking at some of these skills in later chapters. Undoubtedly, this developmental literature has enriched, of late, the clinical study of childhood problems. After all, some 'problematic behaviours' are *characteristic* of a particular developmental stage and often prove to be transient; others are developmental problems and reflect *exaggerations* of age-appropriate behaviours or awkward *transitions* from one stage of development to the next.

During the last 15 years or so, several theorists (e.g., Achenbach, 1974, 1982; Cicchetti, 1984a,b; Herbert, 1974; Sroufe and Rutter, 1984) have urged the necessity for underpinning the study of child psychopathology with principles and findings from developmental psychology — an approach which has been referred to as the 'developmental psychopathology movement' (Gelfand, Jenson and Drew, 1988). This developmental framework has been applied to research and clinical practice in the form of a broad-based, interdisciplinary knowledge-base, incorporating works as diverse as that of ethologists, developmental neurologists, cognitive anthropologists, cognitive-development theorists and social learning theorists. The essence of this work, in the words of Susan Campbell (1989), is 'a transactional and ecological view that assumes the coherence and predictability of development and adaptation, despite change and transformation ... and that emphasizes the importance of family and social environmental factors in understanding the nature and direction of that change'.

For Cicchetti and his colleagues (Cicchetti, Toth and Bush, 1988) normal behaviour and abnormal patterns of behavioural adaptation — as represented by clinical problems such as hyperactivity and failure-to-thrive — are most fruitfully construed as a series of stage- and age-related 'tasks'. The issue of 'competence' is common to all of them and, as the child gets older, his or her self-esteem. If the child fails to develop skills and social competence he or she is likely to suffer a sense of inadequacy which has spiralling ramifications. There is evidence, not only of the power of parents to facilitate the child's mastery of developmental tasks or hinder him or her, but to do this unwittingly. Dubin and Dubin (1965) have shown that children accept into their self-image what they *believe* is their parents' view of them, even though their appraisal may be a misreading of their attributes.

Cicchetti, Toth and Bush (1988) suggest that the developmental tasks (or issues) that emerge at particular stages during the child's progress through life remain critical to the child's continuing adaptation even when their centrality has been superseded by new issues. This is somewhat different from the construction of the ontogenetic process (by theorists like Erikson, 1965) as a series of unfolding tasks that must be accomplished but which then decrease in importance. Cicchetti and his colleagues suggest that each developmental task has to be coordinated and integrated — as a continuing process — into the overall scheme of the child's adaptation to his or her environment.

They list seven stage- and age-related tasks that take the individual from birth to the school-going period (see Table 4).

The authors make the point that there are corresponding roles for caregivers which increase the probability that their children will successfully resolve each stage-related task. This is a transactional model and Cicchetti, Toth and Bush (1988) provide empirical evidence for the manner in which parents facilitate or impede their offspring's development. These are children drawn from five 'high-risk' groups: Down's syndrome; failure-to-thrive; childhood depression; children of depressed parents; and a child abuse sample.

Their review of the evidence provides confirmation of the difficulties these high-risk groups of children have in negotiating the developmental tasks of the early and middle years of childhood. All of the groups except Down's syndrome children manifested failures to resolve these developmental tasks, listed in Table 4.

A developmental knowledge base

The evaluation of normality and abnormality within a developmental framework requires a familiarity with *general principles* of development with particular reference to personality and behaviour. It necessitates a comprehensive knowledge of children — how they look,

Table 4. Life-span age-related tasks. (Source: Cicchetti, Toth and Bush, 1988, reproduced by permission of Plenum Publishing Corp.)

Approximate Ages	Developmental Tasks
1. 0–3 months	Homeostatic regulation and the development of a reliable signalling system.
2. 4–6 months	Management of 'tension' (cognitively produced arousal) and the differentiation of affect.
3. 6–12 months	Development of a secure attachment.
4. 18–24 months	Development of an autonomous self.
5. 24–36 months	Symbolic representation of further self–other differentiations.
6. Early childhood	Establishing peer relationships.
7. Middle childhood	Adapting to school.

think and talk, their skills and limitations at various ages, their typical repertoires of behaviour and the life-tasks and crises that they confront. Such a normative or comparitive approach needs to be complemented by an idiographic assessment which takes into account biographical and social-contextual influences. The latter should take into account the proposition that parental actions *structure* a child's environment rather than directly framing a particular action. This view of parental action comes mainly from anthropologists, notably Beatrice Whiting (1963). As she points out, the most significant actions taken by parents, significant in the sense of having the most impact on children, have to do with their assignment of children to various niches or settings in a society: from creches and nurseries to private schools, apprenticeships, helping sell produce in the market, or tending animals. Each of these settings has flow-on effects upon the people children encounter, their opportunities for play with peers, and their opportunities to acquire informal cognitive skills. What we do not know are the expectations parents have of these various settings, the degree of influence they feel they have over what happens to them; nor do we know much about the inferences children draw from a parent's approach to placing children in different settings: approaches that may range from a sudden immersion into the 'deep end' to a cautious 'shallow end' method — a series of transitional activities and transitional placements. These many and varied influences give the child his or her *unique* quality.

'Development' is typically defined as a progressive series of orderly, coherent changes leading to the goal of maturity. This may be the grand design, but as many long-suffering parents and teachers know to their cost, children's progress through life is often disorderly and incoherent, and the changes (when change is not being resisted) are not always in the direction of maturity.

The value of a developmental framework for clinical work does not cease after adolescence. We do not stop developing as adults. It is short-sighted to try to understand, say, an adolescent's misdemeanours without considering the preoccupations and attitudes characteristic of his or her parents' stage of life (Herbert, 1987a). For this reason I will be 'shadowing' the discussion of the child's development where relevant, with an account of changes in adult caregivers' development.

LIFE-SPAN DEVELOPMENT

Paul Baltes, a German psychologist, has played an important part in emphasizing the life-span nature of development and the importance of historical influences (Baltes, Reese and Lipsitt, 1980). Baltes is at pains to stress that age-related trends, the 'bread-and-butter' of developmental psychology, is only one of three major influences operating on development throughout a person's life. These are:

(i) *Normative age-graded influences* These influences are quite powerfully correlated with chronological age. Like the other two categories, age-graded influences are determined by an *interaction* of biological and environmental forces, varying in their predominance. The onset of puberty — age-related — has a string of biological components; entry into British schools at 5 years of age has not.

(ii) *Normative history-graded influences* These are historical events which affect most members of a particular generation or cohort. One can think of wars, famine, the advent of television, and the 'one child per couple' family policy of China in the early 1980s, as examples. Famine in, say, Ethiopia would have significant biological implications for a cohort of children; the advent of TV provided a major environmental influence which has lost none of its impact during the second half of this century.

(iii) *Non-normative life-events* These are events that occur outside the range (for most people) of the influences described above. Serious head injuries sustained in a car accident would have powerful biological repercussions; the reverberations for the child caught up in a messy divorce would be mainly psychological. Figure 2 illustrates how the three major systems of influence in life-span development interact and differ in their combinations for different individuals and for different behaviours.

The main emphasis and organization of this book will be on, and around, categories (i) and (iii). We cannot (unfortunately) appeal to a general, i.e., integrated, holistic,

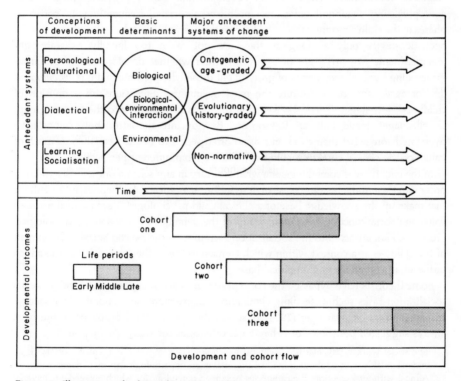

Figure 2. Illustration of relationships among life-span development, cohorts, and three major influence systems: ontogenetic (age-graded), evolutionary (history-graded) and non-normative (nondevelopmental). (Source: Baltes *et al.*, 1980, reproduced, with permission, from the *Annual Review of Psychology*, vol. 31, © 1980 by Annual Reviews Inc).

conceptually coherent, theory of normal child development as our touchstone for understanding and assessing clinical abnormality. There simply is *no* single or agreed explanation of the processes of normal growth and development. Developmental theories range from the psychoanalytic (e.g., Freud's stages of psychosexual development), the ethological (e.g., Bowlby's attachment theory), behavioural (e.g., Bandura's social-learning theory) to the structural-developmental (e.g., Kohlberg's theory of moral development). Each of these theoretical perspectives provides a particular methodology and conceptual framework for viewing the specifics of developmental processes. Conceptions of individual characteristics also vary from those postulating stability to those assuming constant change. For example, trait theorists investigate relationships between characteristics (e.g., temperament, intelligence) across various ages, while those favouring an idiographic approach examine the individual's unique organization of trait attributes across various ages.

On the other hand, stage-sequential approaches do not assume trait stability; rather, they investigate sequences of change which may be conceptualized as variant or invariant stages of development. The notion of developmental 'stages' provides one means of conceptualizing childhood difficulties: problems associated frequently with particular phases in the child's progress through life form the basis of the analysis. But this is a useful heuristic device only as long as they are not taken too literally as watertight 'compartments'; theorists are not only uncertain whether development is *continuous* (proceeding by small increments of growth) but those who presume that it is *discontinuous* do not agree on what constitute the most meaningful dimensions for a division of childhood into stages. Theorists like Bijou or Staats fit broadly into the former group; Gesell, Piaget, Freud, Sullivan, Erikson and Bowlby into the latter. Both camps have overstated somewhat their cases and, as so often seems to be the case, there is much of value for the clinical child psychologist to derive from different perspectives.

In the end, there is something somewhat arbitrary in any schema one chooses to bring order into the untidy, teeming mass of descriptions, empirical data, theories, interventions that make up the knowledge base of a clinical child psychologist. Because of the social-value and social-function basis of so many of the definitions of children's psychological problems, I am attracted to the socialization literature — the psycho-social development of the child — as a context within which to make sense of the subject. It has the added virtue of a generally sound empirical base.

Some theorists have bypassed the concept of stages and focus on critical and universal socialization tasks such as feeding, elimination-, aggression-, sex-, moral-, dependency-training and so on. Danziger (1971) observes that the practical problems of life have always suggested the choice of behavioural categories for study. As he puts it:

> The social worker, psychiatrist or clinical psychologist, acting as the agent of society, is understandably worried about individual aggressiveness or pathological forms of dependency. Almost without exception, the categories of human behaviour for which antecedents have been sought in childhood are categories that define current social problems ....

I will follow this tradition and consider the problems associated with various important socialization tasks. Wherever possible, they will be considered in the light of developmental events and schemata regarded in the literature as significant.

Developmental tasks

Developmental tasks have been defined as tasks which arise at a certain period of life of an individual, successful achievement of which lead to a sense of satisfaction or achievement, and to more likely success with later tasks; failure leads to distress, disapproval by society and difficulty with later tasks. Among the tasks I will be examining are the following:

  (i) Become attached to caregivers.
 (ii) Learning to talk.
 (iii) Learning control over elimination.
 (iv) Developing self-control (e.g., over aggressive outbursts).
  (v) Restraining sexual inclinations.
 (vi) Developing moral attitudes.
 (vii) Mastering social and other life-skills.
(viii) Adjusting to school.
 (ix) Mastering academic competencies.
  (x) Becoming increasingly independent, self-directed.

The developmental tasks postulated by Erikson (1965) centre very much on attitudes and behaviour that feed into the child's evolving personality, and more particularly his or her sense of identity. Erikson's writings occupy a somewhat ambiguous position in developmental and clinical psychology. He is widely quoted, his work in my opinion has been of significant heuristic value, and it has face validity for many practitioners as a way of thinking about children and their families. At the intuitive (not always a respectable term in some psychological circles) and descriptive level, there are interesting similarities between his ideas about key events in infancy and a disparate group of theorists, including Freud, Piaget, Mary Ainsworth and Seligman. Their views are couched in different language but seem to be alluding to similar significant developments in the progress of the child toward maturity. Let us take an example of what looks like an interesting conceptual convergence between cognitive and social developments.

Erikson (1965) regards early personality development as a series of stages in the development of patterns of reciprocity between the *self* and *others*. At each stage (see Table 5) a conflict between opposite poles of this relationship has to be resolved. These are psychosocial events in the sense that they represent biological developmental processes interacting with facilitative or hindering influences in the environment, notably the family. There is potentially a sense of identity 'crisis' between trust and mistrust, confidence and doubt, initiative and guilt, and other crucial attitudes which the child will internalize as he or she grows up. Although the stages are described as if the two alternatives are complete opposites, Erikson would see persons occupying positions between the extremes, depending on the persons with whom, and situations in which, they are interacting. Generally, however, they would tend to show a predominance of one attitude if they'd been exposed to certain kinds of experience (see Table 5).

Danziger (1971) sees a connection between these bi-polar pairs and Piaget's concepts of *assimilation* and *accommodation* (Piaget, 1953). Assimilation occurs when children alter

Table 5. Developmental tasks: facilitative and adverse influences (based on Erik Erikson's theorizing).

Approximate age periods	Characteristics to be achieved	Major hazard to achievement	Facilitative factors
Birth to 18 months or so	Sense of trust or security.	Neglect, abuse or deprivation of consistent and appropriate love in infancy; harsh or early weaning.	If parents meet the preponderance of the infant's needs, the child develops a strong sense of trust.
Around 18 months to about 3 years	Sense of autonomy — child viewing self as an individual in his/her own right, apart from parents although dependent on them.	Conditions which interfere with the child's achieving a feeling of adequacy or the learning of skills such as talking.	If parents reward the child's successful actions and do not shame his or her failures (say in bowel or bladder control) the child's sense of autonomy will outweigh self-doubt/shame/guilt.
3 to 5 years or so	Sense of initiative — period of vigorous reality testing, imagination, and imitation of adult behaviour.	Overly strict discipline, internalization of rigid ethical attitudes which interfere with the child's spontaneity and reality testing.	If parents accept the child's curiosity and do not put down the need to know and to question the child's sense of initiative will be enhanced.
5/6 to 11 years	Sense of duty and accomplishment — laying aside of fantasy and play; undertaking real tasks, developing academic and social competencies.	Excessive competition, personal limitations, or other conditions which lead to experiences of failure, resulting in feeling of inferiority and poor work.	If the child encounters more success than failure at home and at school he or she will have a greater sense of industry than of inferiority.
12 to 15 years	Sense of identity — clarification in adolescence of who one is, and what one's role is.	Failure of society to provide clearly defined roles and standards; formation of cliques which provide clear but not always desirable roles and standards.	If the young person can reconcile diverse roles, abilities, and values and see their continuity with past and future, a sense of personal identity will be developed and consolidated.

the environment to meet their own needs; accommodation occurs when they modify their own behaviour in response to environmental (say parental) demands. Piaget gives 'play' and 'imitation' as examples of cognitive activity marked by a lack of balance, in one direction or the other, between assimilatory and accommodatory processes. Danziger suggests that it is feasible to view Erikson's bi-polar pairs as involving a similar lack of balance or conflict between ego and alter in the development of *social reciprocity* — a key item, as it happens, in the assessment of any child's 'psychological adjustment'.

This conflict assumes qualitatively different forms at different stages of development. Erikson provides descriptive terms to describe what is happening to the child, and he also takes us into young adulthood and beyond that to old age. The first of the three adult stages is intimacy and 'distantiation' — the ability to stand up for oneself — set against self-absorption and isolation. The options are forming a mature and intimate relationship with a partner of the opposite sex and defending one's interests, versus a retreat into isolation and weakness. The next stage is generativity (having children or in other ways looking beyond oneself to a concern for the world around us, and its future). This is set against stagnation and absorption in one's own little world and personal welfare. The final stage puts integrity (accepting the validity of one's life) against despair, or even disgust, with one's life-style.

The family-life map is a useful visual device for bringing together the life-events, transitions and developmental (life) tasks of different members of a family living together (see Figure 3). All the elements are there, not only for generating potential conflict (the clash of discordant goals), but also for mobilizing the emotional support that empirical studies tells us is so critical in helping individuals overcome their difficulties (Brown and Harris, 1978).

THE FAMILY: A SYSTEMS APPROACH

Mention of the family is my cue for introducing another major strand of this book: the development and dynamics of family life. The simpler forms of behavioural theory are reductionist and linear: a direct link is sought between cause and effect, between stimulus and response; children are described in terms of their responses to environmental forces impinging on them. Contrasted with this model is the *systems* version of family therapy. The perspective, influenced by a General Systems or Cybernetic paradigm was originally conceived by Bertalanffy in the late 1920s in an attempt to understand living organisms in a holistic way, but it was many years later that Jackson (1957) and others in the 1970s applied it to work with families. The systems approach embraces the concept of circular/ reciprocal causation. What we have is a recursive sequence in which each action can be considered as the consequence of the action preceding it and the cause of the action following it. No single element in the sequence controls the operation of the sequence as a whole because it is itself governed by the operation of the other elements in the system.

Thus any individual in a family system is affected by the activities of other members of

TIM: 22 months	ANNE: age 10 years	PETER: age 14	MOTHER: age 38	FATHER: age 45	GRANNY: age 66
LIFE TASKS	*LIFE TASKS*	*LIFE TASKS*	*LIFE TASKS*	*LIFE TASKS*	*LIFE TASKS*
• develop motor skills	• cope with academic demands at school (underachieving)	• adjust to physical changes of puberty	• review her life and commitments	• review commitments in mid-life	• deal with increasing dependence on others
• develop self-control	• developing her sense of self	• and to sexual awareness	• adjust to loss of youth and (in her perception) 'looks'	• develop new phase in relationship with wife	• come to terms with old age/ death
• elaborate vocabulary	• learn to be part of a team	• cope with the opposite sex (shyness)	• cope with an adolescent as a patient and caring parent	• face physical changes — some limitations on athletic/ sexual activity	• cope with loss of peers
• explore his world — make 'discoveries'		• deepen friend-ships (intimacy)			
LIFE EVENTS	*LIFE EVENTS*	*LIFE EVENTS*	*LIFE EVENTS*	*LIFE EVENTS*	*LIFE EVENTS*
• parents insist on obedience now	• afraid to go to school (cannot manage maths)	• worried about his skin (acne) and size of his penis	• coping with late child — an active toddler	• threat of redundancy	• poor health
• adjust to temporary separations when mother works	• bullied by a girl in her class	• has a girlfriend — his first	• has taken part-time job to relieve feeling trapped	• high blood pressure	• gave up home when bereaved (may have made a mistake!)
• not the centre of attention and 'uncritical' deference	• jealous of attention Tim gets (calls him a spoiled brat)	• upset by his parents' quarrels	• feels guilty	• worried about drifting apart from his wife	• enjoys the little one, but
	• worried about father's health	• complains that his mother is always watching him	• bouts of depression	• had a brief affair	• feels 'claustrophobic' with all the activity/squabbles
			• no longer enjoys sex	• feels unattractive	

Figure 3. Illustration of a family-life map.

the family, activities which his or her actions or decisions (in turn) determine. An individual's behaviour is both stimulus and response. Such considerations have influenced the way in which casework is conceptualized by today's practitioners of behaviour modification — especially that brand that finds its intellectual sustenance in social learning theory (Bandura, 1977; Herbert, 1987b,c).

Systems theorists in contemporary behavioural practice — those who work within a behavioural family therapy modality — are agreed in focusing not only on the individual but on the system of relationships in which he or she acts out his or her life. Whereas the traditional treatment model tended to identify the nominated client or patient as the unit of attention (for example, the child referred to the child guidance clinic) the focus of assessment in the light of this interactional frame of reference is far more broadly conceived. Thus the focus of help is not necessarily prejudged as only the child (say) who was referred to the clinic. The unit of attention may now be defined as the family (or one of its subsystems). It goes beyond the kind of 'lip service' which treats the child in the context of the family.

Behavioural and systems approaches to family therapy are often viewed as being incompatible. Despite their epistemological differences there are several significant similarities. Both approaches:

(a) focus on interactional rather than intrapsychic causation, i.e., how the problem behaviour of one person meshes with the behaviour of others;
(b) seek to discover regularities or repetitive sequences in interpersonal processes;
(c) emphasize observable behavioural events rather than unobservable subjective events;
(d) view the presenting problem as representative of broader classes of interactional patterns;
(e) utilize behavioural interventions aimed at changing dysfunctional patterns of interpersonal behaviour.

The family as a small group can be observed and assessed on a variety of dimensions: patterns of communication, processes of decision making, cohesion, dysfunctional patterns, to mention only a few of clinical significance (Lask, 1980; Vetere and Gale, 1987).

The family has its own life-cycle from 'infancy' to 'old age'. With the birth (or adoption) of the first child to a couple, they become a new 'infant' family. The tasks of the parents, the roles they occupy, the 'rules' (or expectations) they must now take note of, particularly in their responsibility to a baby, all change profoundly. These changes for the partners alter their routines and relationships and may put great stresses on them until a new equilibrium can be established in their lives. There are quite likely to be reverberations in all of this for the infant and his or her well-being.

The concept of 'equilibrium' is a commonly used idea in systems theory. The family has been likened to a physical system with many of its properties; the individuals (members of the family) are seen as interacting sub-units or elements. What happens to one part of the system (say a mother's clinical depression) affects the other parts (children, husband) and the functioning of the system (family) as a whole. The robust system can accommodate setbacks and change, will have feedback and self-corrective properties; the 'healthy' family, likewise, has adaptive mechanisms that allows it not only to survive and protect its members, but also to 'bounce back'.

Let us look at some of these systemic properties of the family:

Adaptability

This indicates that a family can modify its roles and relationships in response to influences for change.

An investment in more than one relationship

Belsky, Rovine and Fish (1989) take as their starting point the system as a set of intersecting relationships: mother/father, mother/child, father/child, sibling/sibling, etc. It follows, from such a definition, that to be closely involved with, say, one's wife, but uninterested in one's child, or with one's child but not one's partner, is a sign that the family is not functioning well as a system. The goal for a family may be some 'proper' balance of investments.

A sense of boundaries

Boundaries are defined by 'rules' which specify individuals' roles, what subsystem he or she belongs to, and the appropriate behaviours which such membership entails. Boundaries can be *clear* (easily recognized and acceptable rules), *diffuse* (ambiguous and chaotic because rules are unstable or absent), or *rigid* (inflexible, unadaptable). Family therapy is often especially concerned with families that contain weak boundaries or reversed territories between generations. Parent plays child, for instance, and/or child moves into the role of parent (e.g., Minuchin, 1974). Family members define boundaries and base these (inter alia) on prescriptions for generation and gender.

Boundaries apply also in distinctions between 'family' and 'not-family'. Family systems theories again offer an example of this dimension as a way of defining a family that is functioning well: namely, that 'family relationships should neither prevent outside contact nor force outside contact as an escape' (Walsh, 1981). The attitude toward the outside society should be 'open and hopeful'.

Homeostasis

This term describes the 'steady state' of the 'organism' (for our purposes the family) — indicating that the various subsystems are in balance and the whole system is in harmony with the environment. To achieve and maintain homeostasis in the face of change and stress, a system (it is hypothesized) must be:

- *Open*, which means that family members have a high level of exchange with the outside community, as compared with systems which are
- *Closed*, which have very little exchange with the community outside its boundaries.
- *Feedback* processes are believed to characterize social systems and reflect the ability of (say) the family to 'recognize' its own output as input at some later stage. For example, the family that is functioning well is capable of monitoring its progress toward family goals and correcting (modifying) its actions to bring itself back on track, if necessary.

THE PARENT–CHILD ATTACHMENT SYSTEM

There is another application of the term 'system', this time to 'dyadic' relationships. Theorists have found it useful to conceive of, say, the mother and child, while they are interacting with each other, as a single 'attachment system'. This system is almost always at work, especially in the early part of a child's life. Mother and baby are seldom out of each other's minds; what happens to one has its 'ripple' effect on the other: matters that strongly affect a mother usually have some sort of repercussion on her baby. We cannot analyse a child's so-called problems, for example, without also describing the mother's behaviour towards her child. I can illustrate this in a very simple manner, by describing a little incident in the waiting room at the Child and Family Centre where I used to work. I had gone there to fetch 5-year-old Colin to the playroom. He was referred (as a 'timid, clingy, nervous child') by the family doctor for our help. As I extended my hand, explaining to Colin who I was, where we were going, and where his mother would be, Colin came forward smiling at me. As we turned to go his mother jumped up, saying anxiously, 'Oh I don't think he'll go on his own; he doesn't like leaving me'. Colin immediately turned to his mother, hung on to her legs and began to cry.

Chapter 2

The Analysis of 'Causes'

A consistent theoretical framework is of vital importance to the clinical child psychologist trying to make sense of, predictions about, and intervention plans for, the dysfunctional behaviours and interactions of children and/or their parents. Social learning theory, with its emphasis on the active nature of learning, the social context in which it takes place, and the role of cognition and meaning, is well-suited to such a remit in clinical work (Bandura, 1977).

The view put forward here is that abnormal behaviour in children and adults (our particular concern is their caregivers) does not differ, by and large, from *normal* behaviour in its development, its persistence and the way it can be changed. It follows the same laws and principles from experimental psychology, notably the areas of learning theory, social and developmental psychology (Herbert, 1985a). As several varieties of learning are so central to the applied social learning theory paradigm, it is worth reviewing — albeit briefly — some of the main issues.

LEARNING BY DIRECT REINFORCEMENT

This perspective begins from a focus on the behaviour of an organism in a stimulating environment; the stimulus impinges on the organism, the organism responds with behaviour. Learning may be said to have taken place when a given stimulus regularly elicits a given response. The stimulus-response association is generally established by reinforcement which may be stimulus-contingent or response-contingent, providing two different learning paradigms: stimulus-contingent reinforcement and response-contingent reinforcement.

Stimulus-contingent reinforcement provides a learning paradigm developed by the Russian physiologist, Pavlov (1927), and referred to as classical conditioning. A stimulus (the 'unconditioned stimulus') is presented to the organism which reflexly elicits a response (e.g., salivation to the presentation of food). A previously neutral stimulus is repeatedly paired with the first and gradually acquires its response-eliciting properties. The response of the organism has been — in technical parlance — 'conditioned' to the second stimulus (the 'conditioned stimulus').

Response-contingent reinforcement is termed instrumental or operant conditioning. The organism engages in random, trial-and-error behaviour motivated by a state of arousal (e.g., hunger or thirst). Its behaviour is 'shaped' by reward whenever it approximates to that particular response or response sequence which the researcher has chosen to be learned. When this response has been emitted it may be elicited repeatedly by making reinforcement contingent on its performance.

Considerable discussion has hinged on the possibility of integrating these two paradigms into one superordinate theory of learning (Mowrer, 1960a, b). Mowrer's theory is a combination of classical and instrumental conditioning principles and has had wide influence, not least on the clinical field. Aversive stimulation produces a state of emotional arousal in the organism which becomes classically conditioned by contiguity to external and/or proprioceptive cues immediately preceding the punishment. This conditioned autonomic response functions as a 'drive', leading the organism to produce an increased level of activity. Its behaviour will generally include responses which are instrumental in escaping the aversive stimulation and thus in reducing the 'fear' or 'anxiety' drive.

As a consequence, and over time, these responses are selected and stabilized, being regularly elicited whenever the organism receives the warning cues from the stimulus situation. The escape or avoidance behaviour is learnt whether the organism is directly stimulated until the adaptive response is discovered, or suffers unavoidable aversive stimulation and is allowed to discover escape only under the motivation of conditioned anxiety. This theory has been applied persuasively to phobic behaviour in humans.

The importance of these ideas becomes apparent when the stability of learned behaviour is a matter of concern. Under either set of learning conditions, the learned response will normally diminish in frequency or intensity on a gradual basis, when reinforcement ceases to be forthcoming. Fears acquired by children are thought to remit 'spontaneously' through this process. It is necessary to know the conditions under which stability and maintenance of learning are maximized, that is, the case where behaviour persists without external or overt reinforcement. Such stability is obviously crucial to the socialization of the child, and may be used to define what is meant by 'internalization'. Aronfreed (1968) considers an act to be internalized to the extent that its maintenance has become independent of external outcomes — that is, to the extent that its reinforcing consequences are internally mediated, without the support of external events such as reward and the avoidance of punishment.

It has been found that stability is increased by *intermittent* positive reinforcement, that is, by rewarding the learned response, but not on every occasion it is manifested. A variable-ratio intermittent reinforcement schedule (where the number of responses per reward is varied randomly around a given average) produces maximum stability (Ferster and Skinner, 1957).

It should be noted that researchers like Aronfreed (1968) have demonstrated that under optimum conditions (which depend upon such factors as strength and timing of punishment, ease of discrimination among preceding stimuli and availability of non-punished alternative forms of behaviour) aversive stimulation can produce rapid and highly stable learning. This could be either the inhibition of on-going behaviour (passive avoidance learning) or the performance of behaviour leading to escape (active avoidance learning).

All forms of learning generally functional in their effects — they help children to adapt to life's demands — can, under certain circumstances, contribute to maladjustment. In that sense learning is dysfunctional in its effects. Thus a youngster who learns usefully on the basis of classical and operant 'conditioning' processes to avoid dangerous situations, can also learn in the same way (maladaptively) to fear and avoid school or social gatherings. A parent may unwittingly reinforce immature behaviour by attending to it. The operant equation — commonly discussed with parents in training groups — is a simple but powerful one:

Acceptable behaviour + reinforcement   = more acceptable behaviour

Acceptable behaviour + no reinforcement = less acceptable behaviour

Unacceptable behaviour + reinforcement   = more unacceptable behaviour

Unacceptable behaviour + no reinforcement = less unacceptable behaviour

LEARNING BY INDUCTION

In mature beings, much instrumental behaviour and more especially a great part of verbal behaviour is organized into higher-order routines and is, in many instances, better understood in terms of the operation of rules, principles, strategies and the like. Proven (1990) makes the point that although conditioning principles are excellent when used to teach targeted learning in specific situations, in the real world they are of less value when the child needs to extrapolate from a general principle to particular instances. Consider for example (she suggests) the 3-year-old who, having been rebuked for throwing water over the floor out of a plastic bucket, and having within a few seconds emptied more water over the floor from a different receptacle, sobs with indignation at further chastisement: 'I didn't throw it out of my bucket, I threw it out of my tortoise'.

She adds that this is not to argue that specific skills training is without merit; quite the contrary, because the adult as well as the child needs to know specifically which behaviours are functional, say personally or socially desirable, and which are not. But it is not usually enough. Whether training parents or children, a more fundamental change in perception may be necessary to bring about the sort of change in behaviour which is self-monitoring and self-adjusting. The subject may possess firmly entrenched beliefs about his or her functioning which learning based on conditioning alone would not change.

Inductive methods, giving reasons and explanations to the child, have been demonstrated to facilitate the internalization of rules and principles. These methods are elaborated on page 98.

LEARNING BY OBSERVATION (IMITATION)

The speed and complexity that a child demonstrates in learning is difficult to explain in terms of direct reinforcement or punishment. It became apparent to many psychologists that social experience and the opportunity to observe another's behaviour are of crucial importance in human learning and that paradigms drawn solely from animal studies are simply too restrictive, especially in accounting for the appearance of 'novel responses' in children.

Most complex and novel behaviour (be it adaptive or maladaptive) is acquired by watching the behaviour of exemplary models. These may be people children observe in their everyday life or they may be symbolic models that they read about or see on television. This is called 'observational learning'. It is considered by social learning theorists to be the cornerstone of learning for socialization, and a significant basis for therapeutic interventions. As with the forms of learning mentioned above, what are normally functional processes can sometimes be perverse in their consequences. Thus an immature child who learns by imitating an adult will not necessarily understand when it is undesirable (antisocial/dysfunctional) behaviour that is being modelled.

The growth of interest in learning by imitation led to attempts to integrate the concept of imitation into the general stimulus-response framework (e.g. Miller and Dollard, 1941). Their account was not seriously questioned for nearly twenty years until Mowrer's (1960a, b) theory which associated imitation with the principles of classical rather than instrumental conditioning. Guided initially by an interest in the Freudian theory of identification and, in particular, anaclitic identification, he proposed that imitative behaviour occurred when responses of the model were associated with affective changes in the subject by contiguity, because the model either performs an act and simultaneously rewards the subject, or alternatively, the subject *observes* the model both acting and being rewarded. In each case the subject experiences some of the same sensory consequences of the model's behaviour. In other words he or she experiences reinforcing proprioceptive feedback. Therefore, in the model's absence he or she may attempt to reproduce the responses in order to experience again the pleasant sensations which have become classically conditioned to them.

An example in real life might be the mother talking to her young child as she feeds him or her; in her absence, the child babbles to himself or herself, trying to imitate the sounds associated with the comforting experience. Although Mowrer's theorizing represented an advance it did not satisfactorily account for the performance of imitative responses when neither the subject's nor the model's behaviour appears to generate positive consequences, nor the discrimination learning apropos the stimulus situation for which a response is appropriate.

Bandura and Walters (1963) made the acquisition of novel responses through the process of 'observational learning' the foundational principle of their theory of social learning. Their concept of vicarious conditioning was of central importance. As Bandura puts it:

> Virtually all learning phenomena resulting from direct experience can occur on a vicarious basis, through observation of other persons' behaviour and its consequences for them. Thus,

for example, one can acquire intricate response patterns merely by observing the performance of appropriate models; emotional responses can be conditioned observationally by witnessing the affective reactions of others undergoing painful or pleasurable experiences; fearful and avoidant behaviour can be extinguished ... (Bandura, 1969)

The vicarious conditioning of those responses usually elicited by classical conditioning techniques — gross emotional and 'autonomic' responses — was established as a possibility in a number of experiments. Bandura describes what happens when the observer performs no overt imitative response at the time of observing the model. He or she can acquire the behaviour only in cognitive representational form. As Bandura puts it:

Observational learning involves two representational systems — an imaginal one and a verbal one. After modelling stimuli have been coded into images or words for memory representation, they function as mediators for subsequent response retrieval and reproduction. Imagery formation is assumed to occur through a process of sensory conditioning ... modelling stimuli elicit in observers perceptual responses that become sequentially associated and centrally integrated on the basis of temporal contiguity of stimulation. (Bandura, 1969)

Performance is thought to be influenced by the observed consequences of responses, or more generally operant conditioning. Bandura demonstrated the separability of these two processes in an experiment where children observed a film-mediated model perform aggressive acts, with rewarding, punishing or no consequences (Bandura, 1969). While response consequences for the model clearly affected subsequent imitative behaviour in the children, attractive incentives offered to them to reproduce the aggressive behaviour completely wiped out these performance differences, revealing an equivalent amount of learning or acquisition.

Aronfreed (1968) in trying to deal with the acquisition of imitative behaviour rejects those simple 'learning by contiguity' explanatory models which do not take into account the affective value of the stimulus context in which the model's behaviour is observed. He makes a distinction between two major types of contingency for observational learning; those in which affective value is directly transmitted in the observed behaviour, and those in which affective value is transmitted by outcomes of the behaviour. Aronfreed observes that when the affective value of observed behaviour is inherent in the behaviour, then the child's affectivity will be governed quite closely by intrinsic stimulus features of the behaviour itself, rather than by the instrumentality of the behaviour in producing outcomes. He uses the term 'cognitive template' to refer to the child's apparent ability to form a rapid symbolic or representational structuring of the observed behaviour, to which the affective value of the stimulus situation becomes attached. The problem of observational learning is to account for the motivation to form a cognitive representation of behaviour and the degree of fidelity with which it is reproduced. The concept of imitation (according to Aronfreed, 1968) has maximum utility when it is restricted to the type of observational learning which produces a high degree of fidelity in the child's replication of another individual's behaviour.

There is growing evidence of the role of exposure to antisocial models as antecedent influences in the young person's entry into a delinquent life-style. Belson (1975) found in his survey of London boys that the onset of stealing was highly correlated with exposure to social models of offending — that is, associating with boys already stealing (see also Knight and West, 1975). Feldman (1977), after reviewing the evidence, concludes that failures in *learning not to offend* during childhood are not as exclusively significant as suggested by earlier research. As he puts it, 'certain social settings favour the positive acquisition of criminal behaviours by exposure to relevant persuasive communications and social models, as well as by direct experience'.

Berkowitz *et al.* (1978) report three experiments that demonstrated that a diet of aggressive films increased aggression in adolescent male juvenile delinquents during the movie week and in the following period as well. Some of this influence was clearly imitative in nature. The controversy over the effects of television viewing on conduct problems such as aggression continues. However, the evidence (e.g., Bandura, 1973) would seem to be tilting in the positive direction, that is, that exposure to certain categories of television violence occurring in particular settings increases the likelihood of violent actions from already vulnerable observers.

SOCIAL LEARNING

Learning occurs within a *social context*: rewards, punishments and other contingencies and events are mediated by human agents and within attachment systems, and are *not* simply the consequences of behaviour. Bandura (1977) underlines the reciprocal influence and relationship between behaviour and environment when he suggests that the dictum 'change behaviour and you change contingencies' should be added to the better known 'change contingencies and you change behaviour'. By their *actions* (and humans are *active* agents not simply passively reacting organisms) people play a positive role in producing the reinforcing contingencies that impinge upon them. It is often said that operant theorists pay insufficient attention to the element that comes in between antecedents (A) and consequences (C), namely the learner's own behaviour (B). This behaviour is not simply something *elicited* by a stimulus and strengthened or otherwise by the nature of the reinforcement that follows: it is in fact a highly complex activity which involves three major processes, namely (a) the acquisition of information, (b) the manipulation or transformation of this information into a form suitable for dealing with the task in hand, (c) testing and checking the adequacy of this transformation. Again we see an emphasis on the active role of the learner.

FROM THEORY TO PRACTICE

The emphasis on the learned aspects of maladaptive behaviour has led to the application of a variety of behavioural methods including life skills (e.g., social, parenting, problem-solving) training, which are based on an assumption that dysfunctional behaviours and cognitions are learned and can therefore be unlearned or modified directly. Likewise adaptive behaviours, cognitions and skills which have not been acquired can be encouraged in, and/or taught to, the individual.

Functional analysis

A behavioural assessment concentrates initially on identifying target clinical problems (behaviours) which are then measured or specified in the following terms:

 (i) Their frequency   :   how often they occur.

 (ii) Their duration   :   the duration of the responses.

 (iii) Their amplitude   :   the intensity of the responses.

 (iv) Their topography   :   the physical description of the response.

Behaviourists adopt a *functional* stance as opposed to a *topographical* perspective. A topographic approach specifies the physical attributes of the behaviour (e.g., the physical details of a phobia). Functionalists would see these as relatively unimportant as two physically different phobias are 'equivalent' because they serve the same function. For example: phobic avoidance of parties might be equivalent to the phobic avoidance of school, because they both remove the child from the fear-provoking stimulus — having to mix with other children. A functional analysis (or applied behaviour analysis) would be concerned only with the terms (i), (ii) and (iii) above.

Responses or behaviours are viewed as samples of what a child *does* in particular settings or situations, not as signs of what he or she *has*, nor as symptoms of some *underlying* cause, be it complex or conflict. Inferred qualities such as drives or emotional trauma tend to be looked upon with distrust by radical behaviourists because of their 'hidden' attributes, their inaccessibility to direct observation. To address the question of *why* certain self-defeating or others-offending behaviours are initiated and maintained (the issue of causation) behaviourally oriented psychologists conduct a functional analysis of the child's behaviour relating it to events and contingencies in its environment.

Cognitive assessment

Cognitively orientated psychologists, on the other hand, accept as primary data the phenomenology of problems: verbal reports of *internal* cognitive states, such as the child's descriptions of his or her fears or temptations to transgress rules. An example of a cognitive approach is Ellis's (1982) RET (Rational Emotive Therapy) with its notion that certain core irrational ideas are at the root of much emotional disturbance, and that such dysfunctional cognitions can be altered. The basic ABC paradigm described in Figures 4 and 5 becomes ABC-DE in the RET model: antecedents, beliefs, consequences: disputation and effect — the last two referring to the intervention.

The clinical formulation

Figure 4 illustrates the complexities of a clinical formulation. It shows in diagrammatic form the multilevel and multidimensional nature of causal influences on problem behaviour.

It is useful, in a clinical formulation — the putting forward of hypotheses to explain clinical problems — to draw a distinction between proximal and distal, direct and indirect causal influences. These are explained below:

Direct causal influences

Proximal (current) influences are direct in their effects and close in time to the actions they influence. They are *functionally* related to behaviour and can thus — as hypotheses about causation — be tested in therapy using single case experimental designs (Herbert, 1990; Morley, 1989).

In the behavioural canon the relative temporal relationships of the elements can be specified in terms ($S \rightarrow O \rightarrow R \rightarrow C$) of the Stimulus, Organismic factors, Response, and Consequences, the influence of each, and their *interaction* one with the other. The formulation is directed towards the precise identification of the antecedent, outcome and symbolic conditions which control the problem behaviour. Behaviour theorists often refer to their assessment — as a simple mnemonic for clients — in ABC terms (see Figure 5).

A stands for antecedent events.
↓
B stands for behaviour(s) — the *target behaviour(s)* or interactions.
↓
C stands for the consequences that flow from these behaviours/interactions.

Target behaviours and/or interactions are chosen for analysis because of their hypothesized significance as problems in the child's (possibly the parents') repertoire, or in their relationship. Wilson and Evans (1983) studied the reliability of target behaviour selection in behavioural assessment by asking 118 members of the Association for Advancement of Behaviour Therapy to assess three written case descriptions of (a) fearfulness, (b) conduct disorders, (c) social withdrawal in children. Granted that the means of assessment is somewhat artificial there was nevertheless a surprisingly low agreement (38 %) between clinicians in selecting a first-priority behaviour for treatment. There was considerable variability in selecting behaviours for intervention and, perhaps surprisingly, a substantial (22 %) tendency to introduce psychodynamic and intrapsychic terminology such as 'internalized hostility', 'poor self-concept' and 'insecure child'.

From a behavioural perspective, a child who indulges in frequent, intense temper tantrums would be observed in order to determine the specific circumstances and conditions in which the tantrums occur. Such conditions may involve antecedent organismic (O) and/or environmental stimulus events (A) which precipitate or set the scene as discriminative stimuli, for the temper outbursts and the consequent events (C) that maintain them. The functional relationship (behaviourists tend to avoid the term

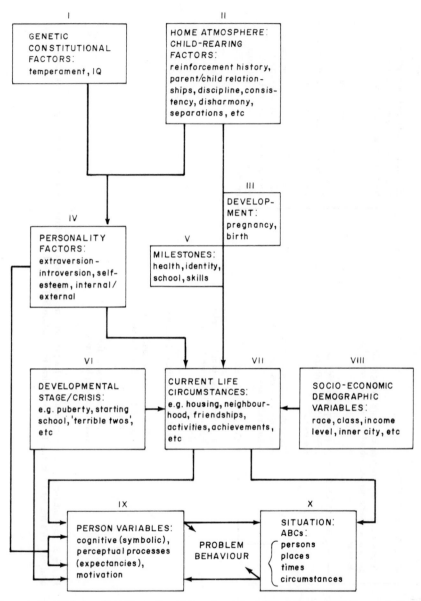

Figure 4. The 10-factor clinical formation of causation (adapted from Clarke 1977, by permission of the British Psychological Society).

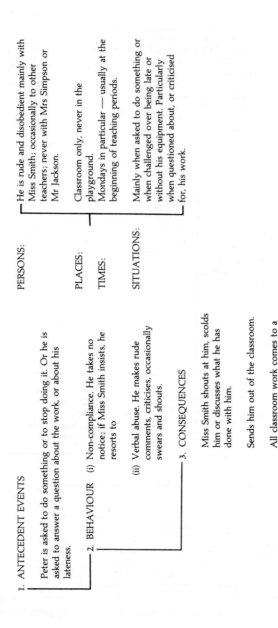

1. ANTECEDENT EVENTS

Peter is asked to do something or to stop doing it. Or he is asked to answer a question about the work, or about his lateness.

2. BEHAVIOUR (i) Non-compliance. He takes no notice; if Miss Smith insists, he resorts to

(ii) Verbal abuse. He makes rude comments, criticises, occasionally swears and shouts.

3. CONSEQUENCES

Miss Smith shouts at him, scolds him or discusses what he has done with him.

Sends him out of the classroom.

All classroom work comes to a stop; all the pupils watch the confrontation.

The original cause of the confrontation is forgotten.

PERSONS: He is rude and disobedient mainly with Miss Smith; occasionally to other teachers; never with Mrs Simpson or Mr Jackson.

PLACES: Classroom only, never in the playground.

TIMES: Mondays in particular — usually at the beginning of teaching periods.

SITUATIONS: Mainly when asked to do something or when challenged over being late or without his equipment. Particularly when questioned about, or criticised for, his work.

Figure 5. Lay-out for a preliminary analysis of a problematic classroom situation. (Here we see a simple linear causal analysis. This fits into X in the 10-factor clinical formulation in Figure 4.)

'causation') would be formulated in hypothetical form. Thus an assessment and clinical formulation might indicate particular *antecedent conditions* which directly *elicit* or *signal the reinforcing potential* of problematic responses. Other conditions involve some lack of appropriate stimulus control over the person's behaviour (see Figures 5 and 6):

(a) *inappropriate stimulus control of behaviour* A situation in which a normally neutral stimulus configuration (e.g., boarding a bus) acquires the capability of eliciting a dysfunctional response like anxiety. This might arise — in part — from a history of classical conditioning (e.g., a fearful experience while taking a bus journey);

(b) *defective stimulus control over behaviour* This means the inability of a stimulus, normally associated with a pattern of behaviour, to cue this pattern in a person. The fact that it is an essentially vulnerable infant, crying insistently from distress, for example, does not inhibit an enraged parent from administering a violent beating. Another example might be the child who reacts invariably to imagined 'provocation' from peers by acts of aggression. This pattern of defective control in children might stem from inconsistent discipline, *laissez faire* parenting, extreme permissiveness, or the lack of outcomes to actions — such as to make discriminating between socially desirable or undesirable behaviour irrelevant or unimportant.

There could be 'outcome conditions' which either reinforce problem behaviour, or punish desirable responses. Aversive behavioural repertoires, such as violent actions or extreme dependency behaviours, could well originate from learning conditions such as these.

Any of these inappropriate forms of antecedent or outcome control might be operating in the person's symbolic processes, rather than in his or her external environment or as a function of physiological changes. In the case of 'aversive self-reinforcing systems' the person sets high standards in evaluating himself or herself, thus leading to self-depreciation and criticism rather than self-approval. Such punitive cognitions may have originated from an early history in which the individual was taught to rely on stern standards of self-appraisal. An example might be found in the depressed, suicidal individual, or the youngster who badly lacks self-confidence and self-esteem.

A clinical formulation might also reveal:

(a) *defective incentive systems* which are characterized by the failure of rewards, normally capable of acting as incentives, to influence a youngster. Defective incentive systems are to be seen in the aloof and isolated child, the child who is indifferent to achievement and learning; inappropriate incentive systems are to be found in the cross-dresser and some delinquents. These developments may have their origins in peculiarities in the early reinforcement history of the individual;

(b) *behavioural deficits* which are observable in the absence of skills normally expected in a child of a particular age or, indeed, the parent. There could also be an impairment in the child's (or caregiver's) problem-solving capacity. These deficits stem, sometimes, from physical disability, the absence of appropriate parental models, the suppression of prosocial behaviour through punitive attitudes, or the lack of encouragement of social and problem-solving skills.

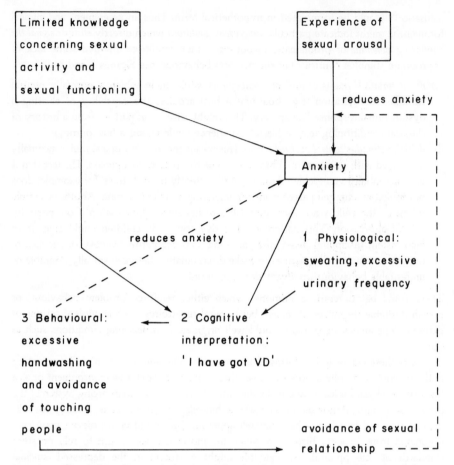

Figure 6. Clinical formulation of obsessional handwashing in a 16-year-old male adolescent. (Source: Fielding, 1983, reproduced by permission.)

Contemporary indirect (contextual) influences

These influences include the peer group, neighbourhood values and the school ethos. Differences in the performance of schools (according to the findings of Rutter *et al.*, 1979) are not a matter of buildings, available space or the size of the school. In other words, they are not due to physical factors, even when seemingly unpromising. Rather, they owe their favourable or unfavourable outcomes to their attributes as social institutions:

(a) teacher actions in lessons;
(b) the availability of incentives and rewards;
(c) good conditions for pupils;
(d) opportunities for pupils to take on responsibility;
(e) an emphasis on academic work.

The cumulative effect of various social factors is greater than the effect of any of the individual influences taken alone: the individual actions, approaches or measures combine to create a special ethos, or set of values, attitudes and behaviours which could be said to be characteristic of the school as a whole. The qualities of schools as social institutions really matter (Rutter, *et al.*, 1979). To give an example of specifics: the researchers found outcomes for pupils to be better when both the curriculum and approaches to discipline were agreed and supported by the staff acting together. Thus, attendance was better and delinquency less frequent in schools where courses were planned jointly. Group planning provided opportunities for teachers to encourage and support one another. In addition continuity of teaching was facilitated.

Much the same was found with regard to standards of discipline. Examination successes were more frequent and delinquency less common in schools where discipline was based on general expectations set by the school (or house or department), rather than left to individual teachers to work out for themselves. School values and norms appear to be more effective if it is clear to all that they have widespread support.

Indirect predisposing influences

These include genetic factors, family upbringing, intellectual ability and health. These are dealt with in later chapters.

Historical (distal) influences

These are factors distant in time from the current life-situation, but significant as predisposing causes, e.g., early learning, traumatic experiences and so on. These are the subject (inter alia) of Parts 2 and 3. Such influences obviously cannot be modified or manipulated directly.

An analysis of these factors is not necessarily a condition of successful interventions. It is not possible to change history. Nevertheless they are worth considering. Haynes (1978) lists four reasons for obtaining a history:

(a) it may suggest conditions under which the behaviour problem may reappear after successful modification;
(b) it may provide clues concerning controlling variables;
(c) understanding of how behaviour problems begin is very instructive to clients;
(d) the historical information may be relevant to behaviour theory and to the development of preventative programmes.

It may not be possible to reverse history but people bring their past into the present through their attitudes and attributions; they *can* be 'liberated' (it is suggested) by cognitive restructuring and therapeutic conversations from the hold their past has on their present. In that sense therapists set out to help clients to 'rewrite' history. Or, to change the metaphor, ghosts can be put to rest.

A typical history would take account (inter alia) of the following information:

- *Prenatal and perinatal factors* (see Chapter 5)
- *The home background*
   (i) family composition
   (ii) living conditions
   (iii) financial position

- *The child's background*
   (i) health
   (ii) growth and development
   (iii) school
   (iv) life events
   (v) interests
   (vi) friendships

- *The family background*
   (i) parents   (a) personal details
   (ii) siblings   (b) attitudes to child
   (iii) extended family   care/discipline
   (iv) cohesion in the family   (c) problem areas

The role of such factors in particular disorders is the subject of subsequent chapters; the basis of the information is often reports from retrospective studies. Take the conduct disorders mentioned in Chapter 1. Typically the children with serious conduct problems come from families where there is discord and quarrelling; where affection is lacking; where discipline is inconsistent, ineffective and either extremely severe or lax; where the family has broken up through divorce or separation; or where the children have had periods of being placed 'in care' at times of family crisis. Parents, especially fathers, have high rates of psychological disorder. These generalizations are useful in guiding the psychologist toward particular lines of enquiry, so long as they don't become 'blinkers' which exclude other causal possibilities.

While it is acknowledged that the social environments of children — notably their caregivers — have a crucial role in shaping and maintaining their actions, the emphasis on intrinsic dispositions (motives, traits, attitudes, etc) in individual parents gives a misleadingly one-sided picture of events. The common observation that young children *initiate* a substantial proportion of the interactions with their parents helps explain the paucity of reliable generalizations about parent–child transactions based on the traditionally unidirectional (parent-to-child) account of what occurs. Interpretations of socialization in terms of social reinforcement shared a common model of the child as a 'tabula rasa' — an essentially passive organism under the control of a socializing agent (e.g., caregiver or teacher) who dispenses rules, rewards and punishments. This preconception resulted in the neglect of those factors which are not under the control of external agents: maturational processes, as well as hereditary and congenital conditions. Among the latter are the temperamental attributes found in certain 'difficult' children (so-called) which make them highly resistant to socialization (see page 57). Even the simplest training requirements could seem, to the hapless parent, an uphill struggle. Bell and Harper (1977), in an important review, showed how children's behaviour could have as much effect on their parents' actions as parental behaviour had on them. The point is that children are not 'empty vessels'. We need to know what is happening within the organism.

ORGANISMIC VARIABLES

A child's unique pattern of development represents a complex interaction of biological factors and experience. Congenital factors may limit the individual or predispose him or her to certain behavioural styles, but they do not of themselves shape the content of particular problems. For example, the minimally brain-damaged child may suffer from difficulties such as short attention span, restlessness, and other difficulties which have a parallel with the deficits of the child with poor ego-control. But these difficulties are not sufficient, of themselves, to cause behaviour problems; rather it is their *interaction* with a judgemental environment which produces dilemmas for all concerned.

Neuropsychological influences

It is clear from the evidence that will unfold in subsequent chapters that children with organic complications are more likely than nondamaged youngsters to suffer from conduct disorders or other psychological problems. There is a smattering of rather global and unhelpful generalizations of this kind to be found in the clinical child psychology literature. Neuropsychological studies of fairly precise relationships between the nervous system and psychiatric disorders in adults are fairly commonplace, but it is a more recent phenomenon for there to be a systematic application of neurophysiological methods to psychological disorders of childhood (McGuffin and Gottesman, 1985).

Gray (1982), in particular, has developed a neuropsychological theory to explain some of the relationships between brain and behaviour. His theory suggests that different subsystems of the brain control responsivity to external stimuli. Gray proposes that reward learning, active avoidance and escape learning are under the control of the so-called *behavioural activation/reward system*, while passive avoidance and extinction are under the control of the *behavioural inhibition system* in the brain. He suggests that noradrenaline (as well as serotonin) is a principal neurotransmitter involved in the activation of the behavioural inhibition system, while dopamine seems to be the principal neurotransmitter in the reward system pathway.

Gray's theory has been studied in relation to responsivity to reward and punishment. Patterson (1982), in a review of empirical studies of conduct disordered children, demonstrates that antisocial children show less of a tendency to delay gratification and a greater propensity for impulsive behaviour. He points out that it is during the preschool years that much of the training for responsiveness to social stimuli takes place. In the light of these findings it is of interest that Quay, Routh and Shapiro (1987) are persuaded that conduct disordered children show lower levels of the essential enzyme responsible for dopamine or noradrenaline conversion. This is consistent with over-activity of the reward mechanism and an underactivated inhibitory system, as a physiological predisposition in conduct disorders.

At a behavioural level it was claimed much earlier by Patterson (1965), that antisocial children are less responsive to social stimuli than normal children. Patterson and Bank (1986) suggest that a parent's verbal punishment of aversive behaviour was more effective in normal than in antisocial children. The proposition that children are not equally responsive to social reinforcers (Gray's theory predicts oversensitivity to rewards, insensitivity to punishments in conduct disordered children) or to aversive social stimuli leads to the prediction that they would show different rates of socialization, i.e., the acquisition of social behaviour. Patterson suggests that the more responsive children are to social reinforcers the more likely they are to display the kinds of behaviour that are valued and reinforced by culture.

Hyperactive children — often indistinguishable from conduct disordered children — have also come under scrutiny. Parry and Douglas (1983), using a concept identification task, found that under continuous reward there were no significant differences between hyperactive children and controls, but when rewards were given on an intermittent basis, the performance of hyperactive children was significantly inferior. It was suggested that hyperactive children may be overly sensitive to reward, to loss of reward, and to the failure of expected rewards to appear.

Cognition

Bandura (1977) points to a therapeutic paradox, when he comments that '... explanations are becoming more cognitive. On the other hand, it is performance based treatments that are proving most powerful in effecting psychological changes. Regardless of the method involved, the treatments implemented through actual performance achieve results consistently superior to those in which fears are eliminated to cognitive representations of threats'.

Interestingly, behavioural procedures seem to be among the most powerful methods of activating cognitive processes. Not surprisingly they are recruited for the remediation of a wide range of intrapersonal and interpersonal problems. There is an irony in the burgeoning literature on the cognitive aspects of behaviour therapy. Nowadays the approach encompasses a plethora of techniques that depend upon those mediating processes and private events which were once so passionately repudiated as 'ghosts in the machine'. Thus self-verbalizations, illogical thoughts, misperceptions and misinterpretations, attributions and self-appraisals (in other words what the client thinks, imagines, and says to himself or herself prior to, accompanying, and following their overt behaviour, become a primary focus for a therapeutic intervention. (See Hewstone, 1989, for a theoretical account of causal attribution.)

What, essentially, is being claimed is that people can be taught to eliminate some of their maladaptive behaviours by challenging their irrational beliefs and faulty logic or by getting them to instruct themselves in certain ways, or to associate wanted behaviour with positive self-statements, and unwanted ones with negative self-statements. (See Chapter 17 for a detailed account of cognitive behaviour modification applied to deviant behaviour.)

There is another aspect to the issue of cognitive processes which is a matter of concern in the psychologist's assessment. It has to do with what are called 'mutual cognitions'. Maccoby and Martin (1983) observe that if we are to study the effect of ideas on parenting and on parent–child interactions, we shall need to come to terms with the ideas held by both parents and children. If we are to do so, we shall certainly need to ask about the causes and consequences of a lack of match in their ideas and expectations which may arise from differences in conceptual level. With regard to the consequences of a lack of congruence in ideas about the way a relationship should proceed, the consensus is that smooth interactions require that both parent and child must act from the same 'script' (Hinde, 1979; Maccoby, 1984). Mismatches are thought to promote conflict (e.g., Damon, 1989; Selman, 1980). Further information comes from a study by MacKinnon and Arbuckle (1989). Mothers and their 7–9-year-old sons were observed while working together on an Etch-a-Sketch task. Each person controls one of the two knobs. Interactions were rated for their overall coerciveness. Mothers and sons were also asked, when given stories where the intent of one party was ambiguous, to describe how the situation may have come about. These descriptions, and other comments, were then coded for the extent to which the situation was seen as brought about by the other's negative intentions, as opposed to a prosocial intention or an accidental outcome. The highest incidence of coercive interactions occurred within dyads where both individuals were inclined, on the vignettes, to attribute negative intent to each other. The next highest incidence of coerciveness occurred with dyads where the mother's attributions (but not the son's) were predominantly negative.

Damon (1989) and Selman (1980) have argued that the child's lower level of conceptual development contributes to a mismatch between adults' and children's concepts of relationships and, thus, to their scripts for how interactions should proceed. The sources of difference may lie also in a child's changing sense of what he or she is entitled to. For example, a script whereby children make self-disclosing statements to parents, but parents do not disclose private information about themselves to children, may be typical and tacitly shared during early and middle childhood, but not in adolescence. At this older age, children are likely to withhold certain information about themselves and to recognize the parents' right to do the same. Parents may also move to a script of mutual privacy, or they may continue to expect the one-sided self-disclosure of earlier years (Miller, 1986; Selman, 1980). This brings us neatly to the next organismic variable, age.

Age

Piaget's theories of cognitive development indicate how intellectual processes change qualitatively as the child grows up. It is important to know about these processes in order to understand what sense and meaning the child is able to make of the physical, social and moral world he or she inhabits — at different ages and stages of development. As physical skills develop, mental capabilities also expand allowing for the deployment of the new physical skills in an intelligent way. Thus the development of motor skills and the growth of mental abilities are closely interwoven.

Piaget's theories are concerned with a description of the way children conceptualize a view of the world and their reactions to it (Piaget, 1932, 1953). There are several concepts in Piaget's theory that illuminate the manner in which children process information and deal with the world. To mention one for the moment: 'schemata' are the internal processes that the child uses in conceptualizing experiences. Young children have only a few schemata with poorly defined boundaries. For example, if the child has learned to call one man 'daddy', he or she will categorize other men as 'daddy'. With experience the number of schemata increases with more precise boundaries, so that 'daddy' becomes a particular person and 'daddies' a reference to fatherhood.

The guiding principle of cognitive-developmental theorists like Piaget is that children structure the environment by the route of internal experiencing and that cognitive structures and functions unfold in a regular developmental sequence. This is an interactional point of view in the sense that enduring and significant behavioural trends are the product of the interaction of certain structuring tendencies within the organism and the structures of the external environment.

Variations in parent's ideas are, in part, a function of the child's age. An example comes from an analysis of longitudinal data by Roberts, Block and Block (1984). During the period in which their children grew from age 3 to age 12, parents increasingly emphasized childrearing values and goals related to achievement and independent behaviours. Poresky and Hendrix (1989), in another longitudinal study, show that changes in goals and in methods are more pronounced over the 3–24 month span of a child's life than over the 36–60 month span.

Such variations suggest the value of adding information about age to an assessment of a child's problems, a procedure illustrated in the study by Dix *et al.* (1986) of adults' responses to hypothetical misbehaviours by children and adolescents. The older the child, the more likely parents were to infer that the child understood that certain actions are wrong, that the transgression was intentional, and that the behaviour indicated 'negative dispositions' in the child. Furthermore, when parents inferred that the child was capable of self-control and that the misbehaviour was intentional, they were more upset with the child, and they thought punishment, rather than discussion and explanation, was a more appropriate response.

Parents' ideas are also influenced by an interaction of the age and sex of their children (Zebrowitz-MacArthur and Kendall-Tackett, 1989). In their interesting variant of the design mentioned earlier (the MacKinnon/Arbuckle study), photographs were added to vignettes describing various transgressions, so that the children now varied not only in age (4 years vs 11 years old) but also in the extent to which they were 'baby-faced' or 'mature-faced'. The parents were parents of 10–12-year-olds, and the results show intriguing effects from both the gender of parent and child, and from the child's age. Mothers and fathers perceived less intentionality for misdeeds of baby-faced children of the opposite gender, regardless of whether the children were 4 or 11 years old. Gender was the critical variable rather than age. In contrast, age influenced the severity of punishment recommended. Parents recommended more severe punishments for mature-faced than for baby-faced four-year-olds. The reverse was true for 11-year-olds, especially for acts of commission. The results may have something to do with the current age of the parents' own children (10–12 years). What is proposed is that some actions are sharp violations of the expectation that baby-faced adolescents (and adults) will have 'benign' dispositions. They may be forgiven for forgetting to act in approved fashion, but not for acting 'out of character'.

Sex

It would seem clear that an assessment of children's psychological problems needs to take account of age and gender, not only with reference to what has been shown empirically to be normal or abnormal, but also with regard to parents' subjective expectations for, and interpretations of, their offsprings' behaviour. Restlessness, for example, is extremely common at age 5, and in that sense is 'normal'. At the age of 15 restlessness is fairly uncommon and may prove — in its social and academic ramifications — rather problematic. Girls are much less likely to be restless than boys at this age (see Table 6). Whatever the norms some parents may refer a child to the doctor at age 5 because they find it aversive and worrying.

Temperament

Parental effectiveness depends almost as much on the infant's 'goodwill' as on their own resourcefulness. It is self-evident that children do not start life as nonentities. Their response to the environment, as we have seen, is more than a simple or passive reaction to the environment: they are actively engaged in reaching out to shape and influence the world. Erikson (1965) observed that a family brings up a baby by being brought up by him or her. From the beginning then, children have an individuality such that a caregiver's initial task is not to create something out of nothing. It is rather to dovetail his or her behaviour to that of the child. Early differences in temperament set the stage for varying patterns of interaction with the environment, leading to the shaping of personality along lines which are *not* predictable from knowledge of the environment alone.

Table 6. Percentages of children recorded as showing 'extreme' types of behaviour at each age from five to fifteen. (Source: Shepherd, Oppenheim and Mitchell, 1971, reproduced by permission of Hodder & Stoughton for the University of London Press.)

GIRLS (age in years:)	5	6	7	8	9	10	11	12	13	14	15
Very destructive	2	–	1	–	*	*	–	*	–	1	–
Fear of animals	5	5	3	3	3	1	2	2	1	1	7
Fear of strangers	1	*	2	2	*	2	1	1	1	2	–
Fear of the dark	11	5	8	7	8	8	6	5	4	5	4
Lying	2	2	1	1	3	1	3	1	1	3	2
Dislike of school	1	3	2	4	3	2	3	3	5	7	4
Stealing	1	–	–	–	*	–	–	*	–	1	–
Irritability	10	9	9	10	12	10	12	10	11	16	11
Food fads	20	19	20	22	21	23	17	17	15	17	09
Fear of other children	–	*	1	1	*	1	*	1	*	1	–
Always hungry	5	6	6	10	9	10	10	13	15	11	16
Small appetite	21	17	21	18	13	12	12	8	7	8	5
Worrying	5	7	4	4	6	4	7	5	1	4	5
Whining	7	5	5	3	6	2	5	4	3	5	–
Restlessness	20	16	20	16	13	13	13	11	11	10	4
Underactivity	–	2	1	1	2	3	3	4	7	7	5
Jealousy	8	4	5	5	6	3	4	3	3	6	4
Wandering	*	*	–	1	1	*	1	2	1	2	4
Withdrawn	2	1	2	2	3	2	2	3	2	3	7
{ Disobedient	10	10	8	8	11	7	10	10	12	14	14
{ Always obeys	8	7	7	9	9	8	14	11	12	10	12
Truanting — at all	*	1	1	*	1	*	*	1	1	3	4
Tics	1	–	1	1	1	*	–	*	–	1	–
Mood change	5	2	4	3	5	3	5	5	7	7	14
Reading difficulty	5	7	14	14	10	13	10	11	5	7	4

The 'problem' infant

Thomas, Chess and Birch (1968) carried out research with New York families which was to prove highly influential. They demonstrated just how important these inborn or constitutional aspects of personality — the temperamental qualities of the child — can be in the unfolding of normal behaviour and behaviour problems. An intensive study of 136 children measured temperament in terms of nine descriptive categories: activity level; rhythmicity; approach and withdrawal; adaptability; intensity of reaction; threshold of responsiveness; quality of mood; distractibility/attention span; and persistence. They classified babies according to clusters of temperamental characteristics; these groupings were referred to as 'difficult', 'easy' and 'slow to warm up' babies.

The authors found that 65 % of their original babies could be assigned to one of the general 'types' of temperament. Some 40 % of the children fell into the easy category, while 10 % were difficult. Another 15 % of the children were slow to warm up. That left about 35 % of children who showed a mixture of characteristics not fitting into any of the

Table 6 (continued)

BOYS	(age in years:)	5	6	7	8	9	10	11	12	13	14	15
Very destructive		3	2	2	—	2	1	1	1	2	1	2
Fear of animals		3	3	2	1	1	2	2	1	1	1	—
Fear of strangers		2	1	1	1	—	*	*	1	2	*	4
Fear of the dark		9	6	8	8	10	7	6	5	2	2	2
Lying		5	3	5	2	3	3	3	5	4	2	2
Dislike of school		4	5	5	3	5	5	5	6	7	10	4
Stealing		—	1	1	1	1	*	1	1	2	1	—
Irritability		10	7	13	11	12	14	11	14	11	9	16
Food fads		19	20	22	22	22	18	23	19	17	17	16
Fear of other children		1	*	—	—	*	1	1	1	1	*	—
Always hungry		11	10	10	14	16	13	16	19	15	23	39
Small appetite		11	13	17	14	11	10	13	9	7	5	—
Worrying		4	5	5	7	6	5	3	3	5	4	5
Complaining		7	6	8	5	4	3	4	4	3	2	2
Restlessness		23	19	25	21	22	19	20	18	15	17	20
Underactivity		1	2	1	1	1	2	2	4	3	6	2
Jealousy		6	2	4	4	4	5	3	4	2	3	2
Wandering		3	1	2	3	3	3	3	4	4	8	2
Withdrawn		2	2	4	3	3	3	2	3	3	2	7
⎰ Disobedient		17	11	14	12	12	13	13	14	11	12	9
⎱ Always obeys		8	7	7	8	7	6	7	7	9	9	16
Truanting — at all		1	—	1	—	*	2	—	2	1	4	16
Tics		*	1	1	2	1	2	1	2	2	1	2
Mood change		4	3	3	2	5	3	4	4	2	2	2
Reading difficulty		7	18	21	27	25	17	21	22	13	13	9

Note * = less than 0.5 %

three main groups. The temperamental make-up of the majority ('easy') group of children is such that it usually makes early care remarkably rewarding. They are mainly positive in mood, very regular, low or mild in the intensity of their reactions, rapidly adaptable and unusually positive in their approach to new situations. These children frequently enhance their mothers' sense of well-being and of being 'good' and effective parents. Even these easy children, who generally thrive on the widest variety of life situations and demands, can, under special circumstances, find themselves vulnerable to adverse influences; when they adapt to inconsistent and unpredictable parental demands, their easy adaptability, usually a temperamental asset, becomes a liability.

The difficult children (referred to colloquially as 'mother killers') have inborn characteristics — irregularity in biological functions (feeding, sleeping, passing motions), unadaptability, hypersensitivity, a tendency to withdraw in the face of new situations, powerful and frequent bad moods — which make them particularly troublesome to rear (Earls, 1981; Graham, Rutter and George, 1973)

Infants who are 'slow to warm up' combine negative responses of mild intensity to new stimuli with slow adaptability after repeated contact. Infants with such characteristics differ from the difficult child in that they withdraw from new situations quietly rather than loudly. They do not usually exhibit the intense reactions, predominantly negative mood and biological irregularity of difficult children.

Temperament should not be reified in the sense of being conceptualized as a fixed unmodifiable 'entity'. Environmental factors shape the manner in which temperament is displayed as the child gets older and, indeed, changes in temperament over time have been shown to be correlated with parental characteristics (Cameron, 1978). Having said this, there does seem to be a genetic component. Identical twins are more like each other in several of the nine attributes than are the two children in a non-identical pair (Torgerson and Kringlen, 1978).

Goodness of fit

The significance of differences in temperament (or behavioural style) is underlined by research which demonstrates the releasing effect and initiating role exerted by the behaviour of the child on his or her parents (Bell, 1971). The reciprocal interactions of parent and child are in a state of constant adjustment as each reinforces the other positively or negatively. Rewardingness or punitiveness, for example, are not qualities inherent in the parent but are called out by a particular child and its behaviour. Children's characteristics interact with parental attributes — a concept referred to as 'goodness of fit'. A mismatch of temperament can result in an extended series of mutually unrewarding interactions. They can also lead to depression in mothers (in particular) and faulty or incomplete socialization in children (Herbert, 1987b; Herbert and Iwaniec, 1981).

Quite apart from the emotional distress experienced by the parents, they have to cope with a child whose disorganized condition makes his or her signals more difficult to interpret and whose unusual demands cause confusion and inappropriate reactions in the parents. Pathological crying, disturbed sucking patterns, unusual waking-sleeping rhythms, distractability — these are but some of the infant characteristics with which some parents are confronted.

There is evidence (Thomas, Chess, and Birch, 1968) that even as early as the second year of life, and before the manifestation of symptoms, children who were later to develop behaviour problems requiring psychiatric attention showed particularly difficult temperamental attributes (70 % of the so-called 'difficult' category). Only 18 % of the easy children developed such problems.

Health (see Sarafino, 1990)

Good health is vital if a child is to be successful at school. It is the basis for the stamina demanded by long hours of concentration in the classroom. Regular attendance at school depends upon it, and effective learning, in turn, depends upon reasonably consistent presence at lessons. Children who miss a series of lessons (particularly those who have chronic recurrent illnesses) may experience great difficulty in catching up. Even regular attenders may not be able to learn efficiently if they are tired or apathetic. The clinician needs to be alert to physical and intellectual limitations such as short-sightedness, deafness, epilepsy, slow learning and impairment of intellect, and the referral services available for dealing with these disabilities.

Physical problems are not only responsible for undermining scholastic endeavours; they may themselves be the consequence of emotional disturbance. If a child shows physical lethargy and a lack of interest, he or she may be depressed. In its milder forms, depression may show itself as a lack of physical energy and well-being. In its more severe manifestations, the child tends to be irritable and bad-tempered, and when it is at its worst, he or she sleeps poorly, lacks an appetite and is always dejected, apathetic and lifeless. Children who are (for whatever reason) depressed refuse or are unable to meet the challenges of life; they cease to strive and to use their full effectiveness in whatever sphere of activity they find themselves. An essentially affective problem like this is often mistaken for a purely physical one.

Activity level

Activity level is a temperamental attribute which tends to be stable over time. Parents tends to react to a child with a high activity level in a different manner than to a child with a low activity level (Barkley, 1982).

The 'overactive infant'

High rates of activity and high intensities of emotional expression in the repertoire of children tend to be aversive to adults, and, indeed, are among the most frequent complaints made by adults in referring children to out-patient clinics (Herbert, 1987b). Hyperactivity is one of the specific problems dealt with in a later section of the book.

Although it might seem to be a statement of parental exculpation (or scapegoating) to propose that the stimulus characteristics of the child can constitute a sufficient or necessary provocation to maltreatment, studies do indicate that abnormal attributes in the child are at least as substantial a factor in explaining incidents of abuse as deviance in the parents (Gil, 1970). It has been reported that abused children have been ill-treated in a foster home, transferred, and then abused in another foster home.

Episodes of persistent, intense crying, or screaming by the infant, bouts of bladder or bowel incontinence in the older child (not always that old), and defiance, are frequently cited as 'immediate antecedents' of parental violence. It is important to remember that most of these incidents occur in the context of what parents (rightly or wrongly) perceive as 'disciplinary' encounters (Wolfe, 1987). Many of the abnormal attributes referred to above have their roots in biological aspects of the child's makeup; and this is a subject examined further in Part 2.

Chapter 3

Applied Social Learning Theory: Behaviour Therapy/Modification

Behavioural interventions play an important role in alleviating problems of childhood. Watts (1990) observes that several factors contributed to their impact: (a) they represent a distinct and novel addition to the range of treatment techniques available for clinical problems; (b) they were developed by the deliberate application of well-established psychological principles; and (c) they are accompanied by a sustained and rigorous attempt to evaluate their effectiveness.

Behaviour therapy represents a theory (indeed, a philosophy) of treatment rather than a technology or collection of 'ad hoc' techniques. As we have seen, it is based upon a *broad* and empirically-based theory of normal and abnormal behaviour. This is not simply a nice academic distinction but a defining attribute of good practice having, as it does, implications for the expertise, training and supervision of those who implement behavioural programmes, as well as the aims, objectives and methods (and their ethical acceptability) of the programmes that are designed. One aspect of behaviour therapy in particular, the view that abnormal behaviour differs mainly in degree rather than kind from normal behaviour, and is acquired by similar processes of learning and influence, leads to misunderstandings about its boundaries. The confusion arises not only in the public mind but also in the minds of many in the therapeutic/helping professions. The term is sometimes applied inappropriately to methods of social control, for example the punitive use of seclusion in residential settings, which have nothing to do with therapeutic work in its technical or ethical sense.

THE SCIENTIFIC STATUS OF BEHAVIOUR THERAPY
(see Masters *et al.*, 1987)

Traditional psychotherapy is not a natural science, even though the value of its methods may often have been empirically evaluated. But it is the proud claim of many behaviour therapists that *behavioural* psychotherapy (behaviour modification) enjoys a scientific status which stands in sharp contrast to alternative psychological therapies, such as psychoanalysis. This *is* a critical issue, since explanations dealing with complex aspects of human functioning have tended, in the past, to be intuitive, literary or semantic, rather than scientific (see Farrell, 1970; Rycroft, 1970). For the first time, it is claimed (Beech, 1981; Kazdin, 1978) viable, testable and *successful* theories of human behaviour (adaptive and maladaptive) have been developed and applied to a wide variety of child and adult psychopathological phenomena (see Erwin, 1979, for a critical view).

Kazdin (1978) observes, in his history of behaviour therapy, that the discipline has grown and diversified out of all recognition since its formal beginnings in the late 1950s and early 1960s. It is no longer the monolithic entity it once was, and certainly is not tied by an 'all-sustaining' behaviouristic umbilical cord. Indeed, as he acknowledges, behaviour therapy has become so variegated in its conceptualizations of behaviour, research methods, and techniques, that no unifying schema or set of assumptions can incorporate all extant techniques. He states that although behaviour therapy emphasizes the principles of classical and operant conditioning it is not restricted to them; it draws upon principles from other branches of experimental psychology such as social and developmental psychology. The importance of 'private events' or the cognitive mediation of behaviour as we saw in Chapter 2, is recognized; and a major role is attributed to vicarious and symbolic learning processes, for example modelling.

The behavioural treatment of children (specifically) can be traced back to some innovative (but strangely isolated) work carried out by Mary Cover Jones in the early 1920s. Where Little Hans with his fear of horses became the much quoted hero of the psychoanalytic paradigm, Little Peter (aged 2 years 10 months at the beginning of his treatment for a fear of rabbits) became the hero of the behavioural paradigm (see Jones, 1924). In this he was to join Little Albert, victim of a distasteful experiment — the deliberate attempt to 'engineer' an experimental neurosis in the hapless infant — by John Watson and Rosalie Rayner (Watson and Rayner, 1920). By the application of conditioning methods they claimed to convert his fondness for white rats into phobic anxiety; and by stimulus generalization, they engendered milder aversive reactions to a fur coat, a dog and a Santa Claus mask.

Little Peter was treated for his phobia by Mary Cover Jones by methods which foreshadowed contemporary methods (see Chapter 18). Apart from some isolated studies, this experimental work (based upon learning theory) seemed to be forgotten; its humane potential certainly did not catch on within mainstream child therapy — which was mainly psychodynamic and very often play therapy (Axline, 1947). It is worth mentioning the studies of Holmes who conducted a survey of children's fears and the most effective ways they were dealt with by parents and the sufferers themselves. She advocated encouraging the child to cope actively with the feared situation, following the attempt with a reward (Holmes, 1935). In effect, she was putting forward an operant conditioning paradigm combined with exposure training.

The really dramatic developments in the behavioural approach have taken place in the last 25 years or so. The 1960s saw a revival of interest in behavioural theory and it derived much of its impetus from operant work ('behaviour modification') with mentally handicapped and autistic children (e.g., Baer, Wolf and Risley (1968)), and respondent work ('behaviour therapy') with phobic children (e.g., Rachman, 1962). The terms behaviour modification and behaviour therapy nowadays tend to be used synonymously, and they are applied (as we shall see in later chapters) to a wide variety of specific problems generated by the interaction of children's social environments with their particular difficulties.

Applied behaviour analysis has a 30-year history of experimental research; the experimental analysis of behaviour provided, and continues to provide, a technology which has been applied to disabilities, such as mental and physical handicap, autism and psychosis (see Hemsley et al., 1978; Yule and Carr, 1980).

Behaviour therapists insist on carefully monitored pretreatment assessments — often along the lines of the conceptual framework provided in Figure 7, or some variation of it. They believe that the client — and here we may be considering adults (e.g. parents) as well as children — is best described and understood by determining what he or she thinks, feels and does in particular life situations. The goal is eventually to help the client to control his or her own behaviour and achieve self-selected goals.

BEHAVIOUR: IDENTIFYING TARGET PROBLEMS (see 1, Figure 7)

A behavioural assessment of childhood, parenting or other disorders is likely to encompass a broad spectrum of problems:

- An avoidance of situations/people/objects one should not have to avoid.
- A sense of emotional turmoil (anger, fear, anxiety, dread, guilt, depression, disgust).
- A feeling of helplessness, of not being fully in control of one's life; or in control of one's child/teenager.
- Feelings of unhappiness, distress, misery.
- Vague feelings that life is not being lived as meaningfully, effectively or joyfully as it should be.
- A feeling of having lost a sense of direction as a parent; of not enjoying or liking one's child.
- A loss of the ability to make decisions.
- A loss of the ability to make choices.
- A loss of the feeling of being real, vital, committed to or enthusiastic about life.
- A sense of conflict, apathy, aimlessness.
- A sense of alienation (with self and/or society/or from one's child/parent).
- A sense of being compelled to do things against one's will.
- Unrestrained, uncontrollable outbursts (e.g., aggressive, punitive behaviour).

It is crucial in behavioural assessment and treatment to reformulate these complaints in operational terms, i.e., in overt terms of what the client says and does, and in a manner that lends itself to quantifying the problem (Herbert, 1987c).

For the purposes of this review it is useful to group problems according to whether behavioural excesses and deficits are involved (see 3, Figure 7). Behavioural excesses refer

64

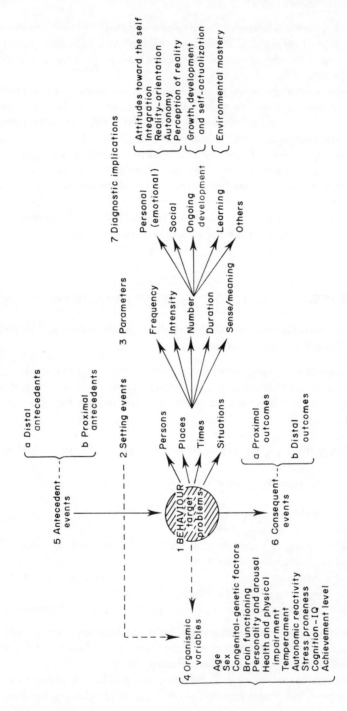

Figure 7. A conceptual framework for an assessment of behaviour problems.

to behaviours which the client (and it could be child and/or parent), with the help of the therapist, wishes to reduce or eliminate (see Table 8, page 69). In the case of deficit behaviours there is a need to increase them (see Table 7, page 68). Behavioural anomalies constitute a third target for modification.

Violent, persistent temper outbursts in an adolescent constitute an *excess* problem. Extreme shyness would be an example of a *deficit* problem in, say, an adolescent boy or girl. An instance of *anomalous* behaviour is the uncontrollable utterance of obscene words — a problem associated with Gilles de la Tourette's syndrome.

Situation specificity (see 2, Figure 7)

The situation specificity of normal behaviours has been well documented (Mischel, 1968); maladaptive behaviours are no exception. The problems of a client suffering from phobic fears, to take one example, are not unidimensional (Rachman, 1978); each of the facets is complex, and they do not intercorrelate in any simple way. With regard to the particular components of a child's anxiety disorder, they are likely to consist of verbal reports of distress, cognitive, autonomic and motor phenomena which display a degree of specificity with regard to persons, places, times and situations/circumstances, and indeed, with regard to each other. The specificity of a phobic disorder must be carefully assessed in order to plan an effective programme of treatment.

If the major component of the problem is behavioural then the treatment might focus on modifying the behaviour directly. Alternatively, if the predominant feature of the client's difficulties is the intensity of his or her physiological reaction then a direct concentration on the physiological overreaction might be indicated. Cognitive treatment would be given for problems with a prominent cognitive component (Bandura, 1977).

Parameters (see 3, Figure 7)

What separates behaviours defined as 'neurotic' from the anxiety, avoidances, fears, indecisiveness and obsessions shown by all children (and parents) at one time or another, is the frequency (rate), intensity and persistence (duration) with which they are manifested, the sheer number of problems with which they are associated, also their implications for the well-being and the 'effective' functioning of the individual.

These parameters are matters for careful individual assessment in any child or adult with a psychological disorder. They are important not only for the understanding of the nature and ramifications of the problems, but also for the highlighting of the ethical issues inherent in deciding whether to use a powerful change-oriented approach like behaviour therapy. The meaning of the problems for the client — the sense made of them, the 'pay-off' they provide — and, indeed, his or her family, also constitutes a vital element of the overall assessment.

Formulation: identifying controlling variables (see 4, 5, 6, Figure 7)

In identifying controlling variables two categories are generally considered: current environmental variables (antecedent and consequent events — 5 and 6 Figure 7) and organismic variables (see 4, Figure 7). The contemporary causes of problem behaviour may exist in the client's environment or in his or her own thoughts, feelings or bodily processes (organismic variables) and they may exert their influence in several ways: as eliciting or discriminative antecedent stimuli or as outcomes (consequences) of a reinforcing kind. Excellent accounts of the experimental derivations of these ideas are to be found in Rimm and Masters (1989).

Organismic variables include individual differences produced by age, sex, genetic constitution, physiology and by past learning. Behaviour therapists tend to adopt a transactional position — the view that behaviour results from a (still poorly understood) interaction of the current situation and individual differences (biological and psycho-social).

Proximal antecedents (see 5b, Figure 7)–Contemporary influences

A distinction is made (as we saw in Chapter 2) between the direct and vicarious learning experiences that contribute to the acquisition of problematic behaviour and those contemporary influences which determine whether the client will perform the behaviour he or she has acquired. For example, in the conduct disorders — which are discussed in Chapter 16 — some antisocial action which has been acquired by imitation or modelling, may not be performed, either because appropriate instigating conditions do not occur, or because its consequences are likely to be unrewarding or unpleasant.

Proximal consequences (see 6a, Figure 7)

Turning to the maintenance of problematic behaviour, this is postulated to be largely dependent on its consequences. Maladaptive actions that are rewarded tend to be repeated, whereas those that are unrewarded or punished are generally discarded. The reinforcement which strengthens an adolescent's disruptive behaviour — to take an increasingly typical example from the contemporary classroom — may be in terms of direct external reinforcement, vicarious or observed reinforcement or self-reinforcement.

Distal consequences and 'diagnostic implications' (see 6b and 7, Figure 7)

While it is true to say that clinicians delineate certain 'symptoms' as pathognomonic of particular psychiatric disorders the fact is that in our chosen area of disorders of childhood, we are dealing mainly with social rather than medical criteria of what is problematic. It is important to look, not only at the immediate consequences of a client's behaviour, but also at the longer term implications (distal outcomes). What are the likely consequences of nonintervention in the problem for the person and his family? Problem behaviours are usually so called, because they have a variety of unfavourable short-term and long-term outcomes. They are therefore referred to as maladaptive actions or dysfunctional thoughts and feelings; they are inappropriate in terms of several criteria which are assessed by the therapist. The 'diagnostic' criteria are listed as Distal Outcomes (see 6b, Figure 7) and Diagnostic Implications (see 7 in Figure 7). They are concerned with the a) social, b) personal, c) developmental, d) work and learning implications of the child's behaviour and life-style.

Ultimately, the professional judgement of a client's behavioural/pyscho-social/mental status is made in individual terms, taking into account his or her particular circumstances. It involves an estimate of the consequences that flow from the clients' specific thoughts, feelings and behaviours and general approach to life, with particular reference to their personal and emotional well-being, their ability to form and maintain social relationships, their ongoing development toward (rather than away from) maturity and self-actualiza-tion, their ability to work effectively and (in the case of children) learn academically, and their accessibility to socialization. All are subject to disruption in emotional and behavioural disorders, and are gravely affected in the conduct disorders of childhood and adolescence. Other factors to be considered are youngsters' self-esteem and competence (see Chapter 7, page 125).

THE CHOICE OF PROCEDURES/TECHNIQUES

Procedures are chosen on the basis of one's knowledge of their therapeutic effects and acquaintance with the literature on the modification of particular problems (see Tables 7 and 8). The choice of therapeutic approach will depend not only on the nature of the target behaviour to be modified and the stimuli which maintain it, but also on the circumstances under which the child manifests the problem behaviour, and the aspects of the environment which are subject to the therapist's influence. There are two basic learning tasks that are commonly encountered in child therapy:

(a) the acquisition (i.e., learning) of a desired behaviour in which the individual is deficient (e.g. compliance, self-control, bladder and bowel control, fluent speech, social or academic skills);

(b) the reduction or elimination, of an undesired response in the child's behavioural repertoire (e.g. aggression, temper-tantrums, stealing, facial tics, phobic anxiety, compulsive eating) or the exchange of one response for another (e.g., self assertion in place of tearful withdrawal).

Each of these tasks may be served, as we have seen, by one or a combination of four major types of learning: (a) classical conditioning; (b) operant conditioning; (c) observa-tional learning; and (d) cognitive learning. Furthermore, they can be analysed (and a therapeutic intervention planned) in terms of antecedent events, consequent events, organismic and self variables.

Methods for increasing behaviour

The methods shown in Table 7 are designed for the child (and sometimes parent or teacher) whose responses and/or skills are absent from his or her behavioural repertoire, or too weakly, too inappropriately represented.

Methods for reducing behaviour

When a particular behaviour occurs at a high rate (with excessive frequency) or with surplus intensity and magnitude, or where a response is emitted under inappropriate conditions, the therapeutic task is to bring the behaviour within a range that is more socially acceptable.

The setting for treatment

There are three main settings in which behavioural work with children takes place. Therapy based on the dyadic (one-to-one) model tends to take place in the clinic;

Table 7. Methods for increasing behaviour.

Procedure	Method
Positive reinforcement.	Present a positive stimulus (a rewarding event or object) following the desired behaviour.
Negative reinforcement.	Remove a stimulus (an aversive or noxious event) following the desired behaviour.
Contingency management in the token economy.	
Differential reinforcement (including discrimination training and method of successive approximations).	Reinforce appropriate behaviours in the presence of the S^D leave them unreinforced in the setting of inappropriate circumstances, S^Δ
Provide an appropriate model.	Get someone suitable to model the desired behaviour.
Remove interfering conditions (e.g., aversive stimuli).	Remove stimuli that are incompatible (interfere) with the desired behaviour.
Stimulus control and change (including cueing and prompting).	Determine (or develop) appropriate discriminative stimuli for the desired behaviour.

Table 8. Methods for reducing behaviour.

Procedure	Method
Extinction	Withhold reinforcement following inappropriate behaviour.
Stimulus change	Change discriminative stimuli (remove or change controlling antecedent stimuli).
Punishment	Present mildly aversive/noxious stimuli contingent upon (following) inappropriate behaviour.
Time out from positive reinforcement (TO)	Withdraw reinforcement for X minutes following inappropriate behaviour.
Response-cost (RC)	Withdraw X quantity of reinforcers following inappropriate behaviour.
Overcorrection	Client makes restitution plus ...
Positive reinforcement:	
(a) Reinforcing incompatible behaviour (RIB)	Reinforce behaviour that is incompatible with the unwanted one.
(b) Differential reinforcement of other behaviours (DRO)	Reinforce behaviour other than the undesired one on a regular schedule.
Skills training	Various approaches.
(e.g., behaviour rehearsal)	Simulate real-life situation in which to rehearse the child's skills and to improve them.
Gradual exposure to aversive stimuli (e.g., desensitization)	Expose child gradually to feared situation while secure and relaxed.
Avoidance (e.g., covert sensitization)	Present (in vivo or in imagination) to-be-avoided object with aversive stimulus.
Modelling	Demonstrate behaviour for child to copy.
Role-playing	Script a role so client can rehearse behaviour and/or a situation.
Cognitive control (cognitive restructuring including problem solving)	Teach alternative ways of perceiving, controlling, solving problems.
Self-control training	Various approaches.

treatment on the triadic model (using significant caregivers or teachers as mediators of change) takes place in the home or in the school.

The treatment of 'neurotic' and stress disorders is likely to occur in the clinic, although there is nothing absolute about such a demarcation. These problems tend to be of relatively short-term duration. Although the distinction between treatment and training is, at times, indistinct, the training model is most appropriate to the longer-term disorders and handicaps of childhood. These problems (and others) tend to be dealt with in interpersonal or transactional (systemic) terms these days, using comprehensive, multi-modal treatment packages, rather than as isolated bits of childish behaviour on which to focus one's techniques. I return to this theme in Part 5.

Part Two

Taking a History: Early Influences on Behaviour

We have seen in Part 1 that a child's and family's history is an essential component of a clinical assessment. In Part 2 I shall review the kinds of data that inform a comprehensive history — one that will give depth to the formulation of causes in a particular case.

Behaviour problems may be apparent immediately after birth, stemming from prenatal or perinatal complications of one kind or another. They may appear in infancy, taking the form of feeding or sleeping difficulties or excessive crying, reflecting biological dysfunction and/or deficiencies in the care babies receive, *or* the sheer absence of affection. Problems may emerge during the preschool years, reflecting emotional and social difficulties such as fears, excessive temper tantrums or shyness; they may be manifested as conduct problems like aggressiveness, hyperactivity or poor concentration. In any particular case they are likely to reflect the influence of psychosocial factors interacting with inborn factors of the kind described in the previous chapter.

The question is often asked whether trauma, privations and deprivations that occur in the early stages of development are persistent in their effects and therefore of predictive significance? If so, does this indicate a fundamental 'weakness' (a vulnerability) created in the child, such that adverse experiences give rise to disproportionate psychological difficulties later in life. Does a child's early status forecast later adolescent, even adult, maladjustment?

Our knowledge base is as yet limited. This is not surprising in view of the methodological difficulties inherent in the longitudinal studies which are required to provide credible results. Such studies are time consuming and expensive and therefore relatively rare.

The implications for the provision of services are considerable. If early problems are not generally transient but do have predictive significance then intervention at an early stage could be effective in preventing or mitigating subsequent difficulties. It is important to identify the kinds of problem that are most likely to persist and the conditions that are conducive to maintaining them, if one is going to target interventive action more effectively. This raises issues regarding children's capacity for coping, their flexibility and adaptability. There is surprising variability in children's (and, for that matter, parents') response to stress. Some individuals are completely overcome by circumstances which leave others relatively unscathed.

The question formulated in the earlier stress literature was as follows: 'what makes for a vulnerable child?' Of late this question has been turned on its head in the following manner: 'what makes for a resilient child?' At one time attention focused exclusively on victims — those children who succumbed to deprivation, maltreatment, neglect and other life stresses. Later it became apparent that not every maternally deprived child — to take a well-researched example — becomes an affectionless character. As clinical impressions and anecdotal evidence gave way to empirical studies it became apparent that the *probability* of psychological pathology in institutionalized children is greater than it is in family reared individuals. This modification of the stark 'either-or' claims of the early maternal deprivation literature (see Rutter, 1981a) parallels the situation that exists with respect to contemporary theories about other pathogenic stress factors. Their impact is moderated by many social and personal factors.

We cannot predict with certainty that a particular child will develop this or that disorder merely from a knowledge of his or her history; the moderating variables have to be added to the predictive formula before one can anticipate who will succumb and who will survive. It is the search for these other factors that increasingly occupies those concerned with children's reactions to stresses of various kinds, and it is their efforts that I will be discussing in subsequent chapters (see Chapter 5 in particular). There are, on the one hand, biological and psychosocial factors that make some individuals particularly susceptible; on the other hand there are protective influences that serve a buffering function. They may be 'inside' the child (temperament, sex, birth condition, and so forth) or 'outside' (e.g., poverty, unsettled life style, family discord). (See Rutter, 1979a.)

By and large it is a combination of biological and social factors that is most successful in differentiating children according to vulnerability (Werner and Smith, 1977). In the Werner and Smith study, a longitudinal investigation to which I shall return, birth complications were consistently related to later impaired physical and psychological development, but *only* when combined with persistently poor environmental circumstances. The authors stress, however, that one should not underestimate the self-righting tendencies within the make-up of children; they produce normal development in all but the most intractable adverse circumstances.

In Chapters 4 and 5 we examine some of the biological and social factors that predispose children to problem behaviour.

Chapter 4

Biological Foundations of Childhood Problems

As a bio-social organism the child's development can be impaired by inherited and/or acquired biological defects, as well as harmful psycho-social experiences. The impact of maturational factors, those neurophysiological and biochemical changes which are a function of time and age, are so complex and many-sided that a book like this cannot hope to do the subject justice. What I can offer is a 'broad canvas' of what I believe to be important.

Maturational changes are in the direction of ever greater complexity and are qualitative shifts which allow a structure to begin functioning or to function at progressively higher levels. The disruption of such processes can have devastating effects on a child's well-being, and, in turn, the parents' peace of mind. In looking at some of these influences the logical place to begin, therefore, is at the very beginning, 40 weeks before the birth.

GENETIC INFLUENCES (see Rutter *et al.*, 1990a and b; Vandenberg and Crowe, 1989)

From the moment of conception — the entry and fusion of the father's spermatozoon with the ovum produced by the mother — the new individual takes possession of a genetic blueprint containing all the information that determines the genetic aspects of development for the rest of his or her life. From conception on, the child's inherited capacities *interact* with influences emanating from the environment (the first being the mother's womb) to produce a complete and unique human being.

This individuality, a uniqueness about which human beings are so proud (and about which they can also seem so ambivalent) begins with the 'lottery' whereby we receive our genetic constitution. This is the 'genotype' — the total set of genes. The 50 000 or so genes in that original cell (zygote) — a barely visible particle of matter — turn up in all of the many millions of cells that eventually constitute the neonate, and years later, the adult. Normally the genes remain unaltered throughout life and are transmitted to the individual's offspring in the same form. These genes, which have been likened to minute chemical factories, produce substances (the nucleotides) which influence behaviour. In essence they are strands of the chemical deoxyribonucleic acid (DNA) which exist in the nucleus of the cell in the form of a double helix. The nucleotides make up the four 'letters of the alphabet' of the genetic code: A for Adenine, C for Cytosine, G for Guanine and T for Thymine. With this four-letter alphabet and combining the letters in groups of three, the number of nucleotide sequences in a typical cell adds up to some 3000 million. The code 'instructs' every cell in the way it develops. The genes are responsible for inherited traits, and are strung together on compact threads of material, the chromosomes, each of which carries thousands of these units. The paternal germ cell — the fertilizing sperm — contributes 23 *single* chromosomes (each parent has 23 pairs of chromosomes) to the child-to-be; the mother's contribution likewise is 23 *single* chromosomes. In this manner the baby begins life with a complement of 23 *pairs* of chromosomes (i.e., 46, half of his or her heredity from the mother, half from the father). In either parent's case, which chromosomes of which pair go into which sperms or ova is a matter of chance. One pair of chromosomes — the so-called sex chromosomes — determines the gender of the child. Females have two X chromosomes (XX) and males an X and a Y chromosome (XY).

No two children (except MZ, monozygotic twins) receive the same assortment of genes. Siblings will, on average, be identical in 50% of their genetic background. The fertilized zygote brings together various combinations of parental chromosomes and in this way different genes are given to each child of the same parents. The genes on the chromosomes in the sex cells are the one which get transmitted to successive generations. They always work in pairs, each gene being paired with a gene on the corresponding chromosome. Thus one member of the gene-pair comes from the father, the other from the mother.

Genes are sometimes identical in a pair (homozygous) sometimes different (heterozygous). Those which are 'dominant' (e.g., for brown eyes) determine which characteristic will show up when 'recessive' genes (e.g., blue eyes) are paired with them. Genes may make themselves felt late in life (e.g., in the presenile and senile dementias); they may produce their effect early on in the person's development (as we've seen with sex differences). Genes have two basic functions: they must be able to replicate themselves and they must be able to determine the architecture of protein molecules. Protein and enzyme synthesis is controlled by genes.

INTELLECTUAL IMPAIRMENT

A multiplicity of causes — hereditary and enviromental — contribute significantly to severe intellectual impairment and its sequelae, disability and handicap.

To take one example, the Lesch–Nyhan syndrome which occurs in about 1 in 50 000 babies is produced by a deficiency of an enzyme essential for purine metabolism. From about 3 years of age the child's behaviour (e.g., self-mutilation, biting, head-banging) becomes more bizarre and extreme. Prevention (detection before birth) is possible, but tragically there is no known cure for the undetected disorder.

There are many other rare conditions involving metabolic defects; over 50 have been described and they continue to be discovered. Phenylketonuria (PKU), Tay Sachs disease, Neiman-Pick disease, and Hurler's disease (Gargoylism) are among the better known (see Table 11, page 162). In the overall scheme of things these conditions are so rare that they contribute minimally to the overall incidence of mental handicap.

Children may be born with abnormalities of the chromosomes. A single chromosome or part of a chromosome may be absent, duplicated, or have moved out of place. Obviously a large number of genes can be affected, a fact often incompatible with the continuing viability of the foetus. However, some do survive to birth. One of the most common examples of a chromosome abnormality and a relatively easily recognized condition — the largest single contributor to severe intellectual impairment — is Down's syndrome. It is the result of a genetic anomaly that occurs because one pair of the mother's chromosomes fails to separate during meiosis, giving her offspring 47 rather than 46 chromosomes, the extra one at position 21. This form of mental handicap is described in Chapter 9.

Other, rarer, conditions, such as Klinefelter's syndrome, Turner's syndrome, and the Fragile X syndrome, occur because of an abnormality of the sex chromosomes.

Phenylketonurea (PKU) provides us with an example of how an environmental intervention (dietary control) can mitigate an inherited defect. In PKU — a form of mental handicap — an enzyme necessary for normal development is not produced, owing to the abnormality of a crucial gene. (One gene is responsible for the synthesis of one enzyme.) In this case the absence of an enzyme required to convert phenylalanine into tyrosine means that phenylalanine accumulates in body tissue. This results in the interference with cerebral functioning and development. Fortunately the condition can be detected by a routine test in the first weeks of life. If the identified infant is put on a phenylanaline-free diet he or she will not become intellectually impaired.

INTERACTION OF HEREDITY AND ENVIRONMENT

A normal set of genes and an appropriate, facilitative environment are each needed for satisfactory development and the acquisition of adaptive behaviour. What appears to be the same effect can be produced by different genes (e.g., a type of blindness called retinitis pygmentosa, also schizophrenia); the same genotype may produce different effects due to the influence of other genes ('modifiers') and of differing environmental experiences. This variation is termed the 'penetrance' of the gene.

In the case of epiloia (tuberous sclerosis), a form of mental handicap accompanied by epilepsy, the condition is brought about by a single abnormal gene. Because of variation in the penetrance of this gene, children could be (a) mentally handicapped but not epileptic; (b) epileptic but not mentally handicapped; or (c) neither epileptic nor handicapped but manifesting other signs of the disorder such as rashes and tumours.

Environmental factors can set limits on (or enhance) the individual's achievement of all his or her genetic potential. A youngster well endowed with intellectual potential may well be cognitively 'stunted' if starved of stimulation and the opportunity to learn.

A large number of degenerative conditions of the central nervous system are hereditary (e.g., certain types of ataxia) as are degenerations of the neuromuscular system. These disorders are determined by a variety of single genes — dominant and recessive, autosomal (non-sex) and sex-linked.

Many characteristics in which there is quantitative variation, particularly complex ones like intelligence, temperament, stature, longevity and athletic ability, depend on the action of many genes (called 'polygenic' inheritance). Polygenic inheritance is of much greater significance to those working with behaviour problems, learning difficulties and developmental problems than are chromosomal or single-gene abnormalities. Polygenic mechanisms are believed to produce attributes which are continuous and approximately normally distributed, e.g., height, weight, blood pressure and intelligence. Hereditary theories of natural selection usually posit that a large contribution to evolutionary advance is produced by the accumulation of physiological genes which cause minor differences in such biologically crucial variables as fertility, intelligence, stature and longevity.

The term phenotype is used to describe all the observable features or characteristics of an individual at any given time. Personality is an example of a phenotype. It is the end product of an interaction between all that the individual has inherited and all the environmental influences which have moulded him or her. The same sort of interaction — but on a more restricted basis — is thought to occur in the evolution of the so-called 'personality problems'. Specific problems acquired by parents through their life-experiences can only be transmitted via psycho-social mechanisms; their germ cells are not affected by what they learn with their brain cells. Thus, the father cannot transmit his fear of confined spaces (claustrophobia) to his daughter through genetic mechanisms. What the individual inherits is the potential for behaving in certain ways. In the present example she might inherit a predisposition (in the form of a labile autonomic nervous system and an introverted personality-type) to acquire neurotic fears (see page 170). There is a well-established genetic component in the predisposition to depressive illness and schizophrenia; polygenic inheritance is the preferred hypothesis for accounting for variation in the predisposition to neurotic reactions (Slater and Cowie, 1971).

In the psychiatric field then, what is inherited is usually a susceptibility to develop a particular problem. Whether or not this disorder is manifested depends to some extent on the experiences and supportive networks a person has during his or her life (Brown and Harris, 1978). Certain genotypes will manifest themselves without regard to the nature of the environmental experience. The abnormal gene producing Huntington's Chorea is an example of this exception. A single dominant gene is the necessary and sufficient cause of this psychosis.

GENETIC ACCIDENTS

The mechanism of heredity is remarkably reliable, and the vast majority of infants are born within the normal range of variation. The basic chemical structure of the chromosomes appears to be particularly stable. However, genetic errors do sometimes occur and they take many different forms. The cause of abnormalities in the inherited material may be a defect of the genes or of the chromosomes as a whole.

The first type of genetic error concerns the effects of mutation. Any deviation from the norm in genetic information is called a mutation. The DNA structure of the gene may be wrongly copied. Gene changes occur in exceptional circumstances such as excessive radiation from x-rays or nuclear fallout. They can occur spontaneously but this is rare — about once in 50 000 generations for any particular gene. A mutant gene can be passed on from one generation to the next in exactly the same way as a normal gene. It becomes a permanent characteristic. On the whole the effects of mutation are deleterious. The resultant pathological condition is often self-limiting owing to its severity and the inability of the affected individual to reproduce. Although deleterious genes arise by mutations or changes in the chemical structure at specific points in chromosomes, these changes cannot be conceptualized in the same way as gross morphological changes in chromosomes. This brings us to the second type of genetic error.

In the second case the abnormality is in the structure or number of chromosomes due to translocations and deletions. Errors may occur in the processes of forming sex cells and fertilization, which cause chromosomal anomalies with important consequences for development and behaviour. Chromosome abnormalities are found in approximately 1 in every 200 live births. Most, though, are found in spontaneous abortions (miscarriages).

PHYSICAL GROWTH

Growth and development are not necessarily smooth, continuous processes; in the early months of life weight and height increase rapidly, followed by a constant rate of increase until puberty when there is another growth surge (see Tanner, 1978). Body proportions also change considerably from birth to adulthood. A newborn infant has a large head which reflects the early development of the brain as compared with other body tissues.

Tanner (1978) urges caution when measurements of growth and development are interpreted. It is important that they are looked at with reference to a *normal range* so that reliable deductions about the individual's well-being can be made. It is necessary to distinguish between *normal* and *average*. Growth is monitored from serial measurements, a single measurement only being useful if it is clearly abnormal. It is useful to know the average weight of a one-year-old, the average age at which a child walks unaided. However it is also vital to know how far from average a measurement can deviate and yet remain within what is considered the range of what is normal (for example a standard deviation from the mean).

It is generally considered that the potential for physical growth after birth is determined largely by genetic factors, i.e., maturational changes occurring regardless of practice or training. The extent to which this potential is achieved may be influenced by nutrition, disease and emotional factors, e.g., a change in physical size may be due to dietary change rather than just a maturational effect of muscle and bone growth. Failure of normal physical growth is usually recognized in infants by unsatisfactory weight gain, a condition called 'failure-to-thrive' (see page 136).

PHYSICAL ANOMALIES

The importance of biological factors is demonstrated in another direction by Bell and Waldrop (1982). They have recorded a relationship between behaviour problems in general, temperament in particular, and minor physical anomalies. The latter are slight irregularities or deviations in the child's physical make-up. They include small or large head circumference, slightly malformed ears, high steepled palate, no ear lobes, curved fifth finger, wide gap between first and second toes — all cumulative indications of deviant embryological development.

Theorists often stress the importance of a healthy physical constitution as a prerequisite for sound psychological adjustment. This applies particularly to the physical integrity of the brain (normally a remarkably sturdy and reliable 'instrument') (Herbert and Kemp, 1969). There is a brief section on neuropsychological issues in Chapter 8; psychologists are likely to be called upon to assess neuropsychological deficits in children and also the adverse sequelae that contribute to a child's behavioural difficulties. They play a large part in designing and facilitating rehabilitation programmes for head-injured and other disabled children.

Neurological damage has been implicated in mental handicap, specific learning difficulties, infantile autism and cerebral palsy, to mention only some of the areas we will be considering. It is less common today to refer to brain-damaged or neurologically impaired children as if they comprise a homogeneous group, which they are certainly not. The popular stereotype of the brain-damaged child was a cluster of symptoms made up of over-activity, motor-incoordination, impulsiveness, distractibility and perceptual disturbance. In fact the symptoms resulting from different types of brain injury are, not surprisingly, very diverse (Herbert, 1964); and the stereotype — the unitary syndrome — applies to only a very small proportion of the cases of brain injury in the general population.

Cerebral palsy provides a good example of the diversity shown by children covered by a single diagnosis associated with lesions to the central nervous system. Several different motor disorders are referred to under that generic term. These disorders are the result of lesions that can occur at a number of levels within the system of motor control. For example lesions in the cortex or in its projections into the corticospinal tracts produce spasticity; the associated musculature lack voluntary control and are usually hypotonic. In contrast, lesions in the basal ganglia may produce either athetosis (slow writhing movements) or choreiform movements (irregular, jerky muscular contractions).

For psychologists a major concern is that such motor disorders do not occur in isolation; cerebral palsied children tend to show intellectual deficits. The assessment of the children is therefore essential to establish suitable educational provision. Not surprisingly their motor deficits make reliable and valid intelligence testing extremely difficult (Cruickshank, Hallahan and Brice, 1976). In the wider context and for the purposes of clinical assessment, there is a variety of brain-injured children with many quite different problems. Each of these calls for intensive individual analysis and remediation.

PERINATAL INFLUENCES

In any analysis of causes (for a case history) particular attention is paid to the vital period before and after birth: the perinatal period, as it is called. The term *perinatal* applied to causal influences refers to those that arise between the 28th week of pregnancy and the end of the first week after birth. Causes in this time-frame are often those associated with prematurity.

PREMATURITY

Prematurity is a rather imprecise concept. Infants who weigh less than 2000 grammes (four-and-a-half pounds) are referred to as 'low birthweight' babies. Those who are born prematurely — i.e., after a short prenatal period — are known as 'short-gestation period' babies. Babies who are small considering the duration of their gestation are called 'small for dates'.

Generally speaking, this last group gives rise to most concern, but all infants who are born prematurely are likely to have some developmental delay compared with non-premature babies, at least in the first year of life. With proper care, most catch up the lost ground by the time they start attending school.

Prematurely born infants are particularly susceptible to brain injury during birth. The skull does not provide as effective a protection to brain-tissue as is provided in the case of an infant born at full term. Serious nervous system injuries may occur. Pressure during birth may cause the fracture of bones. Should this happen in the vicinity of nerve centres, there may be temporary or permanent injury to some of them, or to the sense organs, particularly the ears and eyes (Pratt, 1954). Babies who are of low birth weight for their gestational age (more than two standard deviations below the mean) are found to have more abnormalities of the nervous system than the normal population. Prematurity at birth is correlated with various later complications such as excessive distractibility, hypersensitivity to sound, personality disturbance and reading difficulties (Knoblock and Pasamanick, 1966).

Drillien (1964a) studied (longitudinally) the sequaelae of premature births in over 1000 mothers. Using the Bristol Social Adjustment Guide, she tested the school-going children at ages 6 and 7. She found that the proportion of youngsters considered maladjusted or unsettled increased as birth weight decreased. Obstetric difficulties — severe complications of pregnancy and/or birth — were associated with an increased risk of disturbed behaviour in the offspring. An intensive investigation of 112 babies whose birth weight was three pounds or less, revealed defects of vision in 37 % of those who were of school-going age. Eight % had some degree of congenital defect. Other defects included cerebral diplegia (18 %), epilepsy (7 %) and speech defects (8 %). At five years or more, one-third of this subgroup were below the fifth percentile for mature controls in weight; nearly one-half were behind in height and over one-quarter in both weight and height. Over one-third were likely to be ineducable in ordinary schools for reasons of physical or mental impairment or both. Only 30 % of the school-age children could be described as manifesting no behaviour disturbance.

Drillien (1964b) found that the most common behaviour problems associated with very severe prematurity (birth weight of three pounds or less) were hyperactivity and restlessness. These problems, and distractibility, are probably the only types of childhood behaviour disorder which can be associated (with any degree of confidence as to causality) with perinatal factors. However, it would not be surprising if other behaviour disorders of a reactive nature (e.g., delinquency) followed on the educational and social failures frequently experienced by hyperactive, restless and distractible children (see Chapter 16).

The complexity of disentangling cause and effect from the masses of correlations in the literature is illustrated by the range of problems associated with prematurity. They include primiparity, maternal age, malnutrition, multiple births, vaginal bleeding, prolonged rupture of membranes, habitual abortion, previous history of infertility, acute infections, and toxaemia during pregnancy. If we consider only the last of the factors — toxaemia — we find that cases involving behaviour problems reveal a greater incidence of this complication of pregnancy in their antenatal histories than control cases (Herbert, 1974). Toxaemia can produce anoxia which, in turn, can engender a variety of cerebral dysfunctions ranging from mild behavioural-control problems to cerebral palsy. The point is that an interlacing network of prenatal influences robs umbrella concepts like 'prematurity' of their explanatory value, unless precise links in the causal chain are elaborated. The other point to bear in mind is the technological advance in the care of premature babies available today. This, and improved antenatal care of pregnant women, does much to mitigate the risks of yesteryear.

The abnormalities of pregnancy and birth which seem to be important in the large scale, retrospective studies made by the Baltimore (Pasamanick) group of researchers involve infection, malnutrition and other forms of stress which in turn are related to low socio-economic status. It is worth remembering that mothers from the low socio-economic stratum of society also tend to receive less intensive medical care during pregnancy and delivery.

BIRTH TRAUMA

Much has been made in the past of the translation of the neonate from the 'tranquility' of the womb to the busy world outside this sheltered environment. The notion of a *psychological* 'birth trauma' (Greenacre, 1945) has not proved susceptible to proof or disproof, although this has not deterred many people from employing a form of therapy based upon liberation from the prolonged and allegedly traumatizing influence of the birth process. The emotional trauma is seen as the prototype for later anxiety attacks.

Leaving aside the psychological ramifications of being born, there is little doubt that the birth process is the most hazardous single event in a person's life. Many factors can affect the outcome. The neonate may show acute signs of distress, the effects varying according to the duration and difficulty of birth. Physicians in the delivery room usually make a rapid assessment of the newborn, using the so-called Apgar Score named after the anaesthetist Virginia Apgar. A numerical value from 0–2 is assigned to each of five dimensions:

- Heart rate
- Respiration
- Muscle tone
- Response to stimulation
- Skin colour

Scores range from the perfect 10 to the very low scores (3 or 4) usually associated with intensive care for the infant. Less than perfect, middle-range scores may require further investigation.

Babies who are in a very poor condition after birth, take a long time to give their first cry, and subsequently develop distressed breathing or convulsions are at some risk of slow development later on. The seriousness of their difficulties can be gauged by the length of time they require special care; over three or four days would indicate a matter of serious concern. Fortunately most, on recovery, will develop normally.

Complications in the process of being born that may result in damage to the central nervous system include:

- A difficult passage through the birth canal (prolonged/precipitate).
- Delivery by instruments.
- Breech delivery (where the foetal head is the last part of the body to emerge).
- Accidental twisting of the umbilical cord.

Each of these complications can disrupt the supply of vital oxygen to the brain ('anoxia'), the resulting degree of damage depending on the duration of oxygen starvation. The Ancient Chinese, with their aphorism 'difficult birth, difficult child' were aware of the psychological sequelae of birth complications. Several studies (e.g., Pasamanick and Knoblock, 1961) have highlighted the correlations between complications of pregnancy and birth and behaviour disorders in later childhood. These would occupy a position along a dimension referred to by Pasamanick and his colleagues as a 'continuum of reproductive casualty'. The continuum ranges from the extremes of foetal or neonatal death, through a graded series of neuropsychological disorders (e.g., cerebral palsy, epilepsy and mental handicap), to behaviour and other difficulties. The latter could include *some* cases of clumsiness and hyperactivity, also reading difficulties. These theorists are concerned that in the eagerness to find psycho- or socio-genic factors to explain behaviour problems, constitutional influences may be overlooked.

AUTONOMIC RESPONSE PATTERNS

The control system responsible in large part for so-called 'psychophysiological' (see page 227) reactions is the autonomic nervous system (ANS). This network of motor nerve cells plays a large part, not only in maintaining the individual's internal environment and homeostasis, but also in determining his or her level of arousal, particularly their emotional state. It regulates the work of:

(a) the glands;
(b) the blood vessels;
(c) heart muscle;
(d) stomach muscles;
(e) intestines;
(f) bladder;
(g) lungs.

The autonomic nervous system not only controls the day-to-day 'vegetative' functions of the body, but also operates to change the economy of the body when the person is faced with stress. Disturbance of this function sometimes leads to pathological conditions referred to as psychophysiological or psychosomatic illnesses.

Individuals who score high on the dimension of personality called 'neuroticism' are thought to have inherited the properties of an excessively reactive ANS, one that is biased toward sympathetic predominance (Eysenck, 1967). This bias is thought to contribute to the acquisition of emotional problems. The integrating processes which regulate the balance between the sympathetic and parasympathetic divisions of the autonomic nervous system are located in the brain.

The nerves from the spinal cord have branches to the sympathetic ganglia, which they control; the parasympathetic ganglia are controlled by branch nerves at the lower end of the spinal cord and by a nerve from the medulla known as the vagus ('wandering') nerve because it connects with most of the organs of the body, including the heart, lungs, liver, stomach, and much of the digestive tract.

The sympathetic and parasympathetic systems tend to have opposed actions. The sympathetic nervous system acts to adjust the body to states of alarm or emergency, and the main role of the parasympathetic nervous system is to organize the normal activity of the body's organs. The two systems are not simply opposed; in many instances they act in a coordinated pattern. For example, if a corrosive poison is swallowed, there is sympathetic arousal, with dilation of the pupils and sweating, together with vomiting, which is organized by the parasympathetic system.

Interest in the relationships between the psychology of the person (e.g., attitudes, traits, stress-proneness), a variety of illnesses (e.g., ulcers, asthma) and ANS activity has led to a number of correlational studies. Indices of ANS activity can be measured quite readily: heart rate (speeded by the sympathetic system, slowed by vagal activity); the electrical resistance of the skin; the temperature of the skin; and blood pressure. Unfortunately many of the psychophysiological studies make simplistic assumptions about the unitary nature of ANS reactions.

Lacey (1964) lists the following forms of autonomic response stereotypy:

(i) Intra-stressor stereotypy — which refers to idiosyncratic response patterns which are reliably reproduced by a single form of stressor.

(ii) Inter-stressor stereotypy — which refers to patterns of responding which are reproduced to a similar extent by different types of stressor.

(iii) Symptom stereotypy — which refers to the constancy of the physiological measure in which maximum activation is induced by stressful experience in patients with psychosomatic disorders — the area of maximal activation being consistent with the somatic complaint.

(iv) Situational stereotypy — which refers to changes in average response pattern which are produced by changes in stressors or which accompany different affective experience.

An individual's response hierarchy itself may vary. Some subjects may exhibit an almost random pattern of responding, showing one response hierarchy to one stimulus, another to another stimulus and so on (Lacey and Lacey, 1958). At the other extreme are individuals who seem not to be flexible, as can be observed in their production of the same response hierarchy on the same measures in situation after situation. Lacey and Lacey (1962) provided evidence for response stereotypy over a four-year period, but only one stimulus situation was applied (the cold pressor test).

What one is left with is a highly complex and somewhat contradictory picture; certainly a single model of a generalized arousal level causing *uniform* changes is inappropriate. Lacey has stated that the notion of generalized arousal (e.g., Eysenck, 1967) may have arisen, in part, because of the very limited nature of the experimental situations used. Anxiety-provoking stimulation, aversive physical stimuli, intellectually challenging tasks, and certain types of perceptual-motor problems may have features in common which determine the homogeneity of autonomic nervous system patterning.

While there does seem to be a degree of generality *and* specificity in autonomic responding, the studies do suggest that as the number of stimulus and response variables are increased, individual response stereotypy is harder to demonstrate; and the reliability of responding when stimulus situations are repeated is greatly diminished.

Chapter 5

Prenatal and Early Postnatal Influences

The child's first 'home' is within the mother's uterus, an environment which is not always hospitable, a fact given witness to by the neonates born with a drug addiction, with acute foetal alcohol syndrome, syphilis or infected by HIV, the AIDS (Acquired Immune Deficiency Syndrome) virus. Having said that, *most* women in our society enjoy the kind of health and environmental conditions during their pregnancy which allow for a good outcome for their baby. These are vital requirements as the nine months between conception and birth present more risks to the developing individual than any similar span up to the ninth decade. It is, of course, a period of rapid growth and development. The child-to-be faces trials which begin with fertilization and implantation; they continue with the development of the organs of the body and the establishment of the mechanisms required for the regulation of the internal environment; they come to an end with the birth process.

INTRAUTERINE INFLUENCES

The first trimester of pregnancy is the most crucial in the child's development. The major organs and basic tissues are being laid down and developed during the first eight weeks after conception.

Montagu (1964) puts it in this way:

> During this critical period, the development of the human body exhibits the most perfect timing and the most elaborate correlation that we ever display in our entire lives ... development proceeds in an orderly manner and at a regular rate, with specific changes occurring at specific times. Every organ and every tissue — in fact, every cell — has its own timetable for coming into existence, for developing, for taking its place in the machinery of the body, and for beginning to carry out its functions. And every small timetable is meshed with every other timetable. The whole process is so orderly, in fact, that embryologists have been able to draw up a schedule that accounts for all parts of the human body and shows how each part fits into the whole.

During its critical period in the timetable, a particular organ system is both highly sensitive to growth enhancing agents and vulnerable to deleterious influences. If the organ system does not develop normally during its critical period, it does not have another chance to get things right.

Courts of law have given recognition to the fact that the foetus, developing and growing inside the mother, is always a distinct individual. The unborn baby is never actually a part of the mother's body despite its tenancy of her womb. It has its own unique pattern of genes, and processes its own nervous system and bloodstream. There is no direct nerve connection between the mother and infant. Their bloodstreams are separated by a semipermeable barrier, the placenta. As Scheinfeld (1967) puts it, '... the mother's blood, which carries the nourishment, stops on one side of the wall and the blood elements are broken down and strained through it. There is therefore no more direct blood tie between a mother and a child than between a father and child.' Nevertheless, there are several physical and psychological factors which, by severely distressing the mother, can have a disruptive effect on the embryo or foetus. The most likely route for the effects of maternal stress on the foetus is via neuro-endocrinal changes in the mother, with concomitant effects on the chemical composition of her blood.

Active substances are transmitted to the foetus by transplacental transfer and these may be capable of affecting its neural, endocrinal or other structures (Sontag, 1966). They include vitamins, hormones, antigens, antibodies, blood proteins, oxygen, amino acids, drugs and viruses. Those physical agents that are capable of altering the design or morphology of the organism have their most disruptive effect during the germinal period (first two weeks) and the embryonic phase (2–8 weeks) when the organ systems are first emerging. From about the beginning of the third month to birth (the foetal stage) various illnesses, such as German measles, and toxins, like alcohol, can produce permanent damage, but they no longer change the basic structural design of the organism. The embryo has all the vital external and internal features of a human being. The more damaging agents are diseases in the mother such as German measles (rubella), AIDS and syphilis; drugs like alcohol, nicotine, thalidomide and barbituates; heavy dosages of radiation from x-rays; poor diet (malnutrition) and blood-type incompatibility.

Social (and therefore widespread) activities like smoking and drinking carry their risks. The damaging effects of excessive intrauterine alcohol exposure on the child's behaviour and development have been documented in a variety of studies (e.g., Steinhausen and Spohr, 1986). 'Foetal alcohol syndrome' is characterized by intrauterine and postnatal retardation, microcephaly, mental handicap and craniofacial anomalies. Maternal activities like smoking are less devastating but, in their ability to lower birthweight, potentially harmful. Mothers who smoke during pregnancy run the risk of giving birth to a baby who is about half a pound lighter than one born to a non-smoking mother. Babies with low birthweight are more at risk of infection, handicap and death. Nor do these babies catch up quickly with other children; at 10 years of age they are still likely to be smaller than normal. Women who smoke during pregnancy are also more likely to lose their babies through miscarriage. Mothers-to-be who are unable to give up smoking might find psychological counselling plus a behavioural programme helpful in reducing or eliminating the habit.

Despite the potential hazards, the vast majority of babies emerge into the world as reasonably intact beings. The total incidence of fairly serious malformations — abnormalities of structure — due to faulty intrauterine developments is variously estimated at between one-half and two % of all births.

It remains a moot question as to whether, and to what extent, maternal stress can convey itself to the unborn child, that is, to a degree that has long-term adverse consequences. Much of the work on the relationship between maternal attitudes and emotions and *significant* effects on the child-to-be, is beset by serious methodological problems which make it difficult to arrive at confident generalizations (Joffe, 1968).

Bonding in utero

Modern technology has raised some interesting issues. For example, does parental viewing of the early foetus (before 'quickening') by means of ultrasound imagery accelerate the mother's attachment to her child-to-be, in other words her bonding with the foetus? MacFarlane (1977) asked 97 mothers, who had their first infants delivered two months previously, when they had first felt love for their babies. Forty answered that it was during pregnancy, 23 said it was at birth. Winnicott (1957) describes the very early 'identification' of the mother with her infant, of which there are (he claims) increasing signs as the pregnancy advances; the primary feature of this is her willingness, as well as ability, to withdraw interest from herself and her surroundings and focus them on the unborn child. He termed this attitude the 'primary maternal preoccupation'. Winnicott believes that this identification has adaptive functions for mother and child, although it is difficult for some women to attain.

POSTNATAL INFLUENCES

Physical factors

Severe trauma, which can markedly affect the physical, and consequentially the child's psychological well-being, tend to occur particularly in road accidents, accidents in children's playgrounds, sportsfields, and in the context of family violence (child abuse).

Between the ages of 1 and 14, accidents constitute the greatest single cause of death, 40 % of these being head injuries. Each year in Britain, 4 children in every 10 000 will die from a head injury. Over 40 000 children were admitted to hospital following a head injury in 1985 and in the UK the figures are going up each year. A mildly as well as a severely injured brain can cause subtle long-term cognitive, emotional and behavioural problems — even alongside the semblance of physical normality. The problems for the child or adult with a head injury and for their family do not go away.

The relatively small number of severe injuries has been acknowledged to produce profound and long-term effects. There is no room for complacency simply because the majority of injuries are relatively mild. Mild injuries were once thought not to produce significant congitive or psychological sequelae; the evidence, in fact, suggests that there are subtle repercussions that show themselves in children's behaviour at home and at school (McCabe and Green, 1987; Rutter, Chadwick and Shaffer, 1984). Clinicians like McCabe and Green (1987) have written about children's reporting of their own experience of head injury: the sense of loss of competence, the grief, the restriction of personal freedom, the anger and sorrow that follow in the wake of such injuries. (An account of the possibilities of rehabilitation can be found in Chapter 14.)

A particular environmental hazard for children — by causing damage to the immature brain — is the presence (inter alia) of lead in the atmosphere. Just what exposure to particular levels of lead in the atmosphere produces harmful effects (e.g., on intellectual functioning) via brain damage is a matter of some controversy (see Rutter, 1980). What is not in doubt is the harm that can be caused by infections of the brain (e.g., encephalitis and meningitis) which are fortunately uncommon these days. Pertussis produces an encephalopathy, presumably by some immunological mechanism.

A controversial issue is the influence of diet on children's behaviour, notably the effect of colourings and additives such as tartrazine and salicylates in their food. This is a topic that raises the emotional temperature, generating more heat than light, especially in discussion of hyperactivity. Controlled trials suggest that food additives are important in the problem behaviour of only a small percentage of children (e.g., Weiss, 1984). High-solute artificial milk is considered hazardous to the developing brain, especially in the presence of fever and increased fluid loss.

Psychosocial factors

The family is much venerated as the bedrock of a stable society; stability within the family is rooted in the mutual attachment of parents and their children. Before looking at dyadic relationships it is necessary to be aware of the faulty patterns in family functioning — taken at a systemic level — that can undermine the well-being of the members. Lask (1980) lists some of them as follows:

(a) an inability to resolve conflicts, make decisions, or solve problems;
(b) poor organization and therefore a chaotic response to change or stress;
(c) too rigid an organization, which leads to an inability to respond at all to change or stress, or to a stereotyped and therefore impoverished reaction;
(d) overcloseness to the point that family members lose any sense of individuality;

(e) such distance between family members that emotional and physical needs are not met;

(f) a failure of the parents to work together, to the detriment of the children, or unresolved marital conflict which has repercussions on other family members;

(g) alliances across generations which interfere with the smooth running of the family;

(h) feelings of being responded to inappropriately;

(i) open communication being inhibited or blocked or so excessive that the speaker is not heard, is interrupted, or is always spoken for.

The origins of such problems have been reviewed from different perspectives by family process theorists like Lidz (1968), Rapoport, Rapoport and Strelitz (1977) and Vetere and Gale (1987). Their implications will be explored later. At the personal level the first attachments are important because they are foundational. A bond of mutual respect and affection fuels the 'pact' between parent and child which, in a sense, is what socialization is all about — a loving but exacting quid pro quo. The nature and conditions of 'attachment' (as it is called when discussing infant love) and 'bonding' (as it is referred to when speaking of adult love) have received a great deal of attention, especially when children present problems.

MOTHER-TO-INFANT BONDING

Put briefly, this 'doctrine', which is what it has become, owing to the very persuasive writings of Klaus and Kennell (e.g., Klaus and Kennell, 1976), proposes that in some mammalian species, including our own, mothers become bonded to their infants through close (e.g., skin-to-skin) contact during a short critical period, soon after birth. This is an awesome claim considering that no other adult human behaviour, and a complex pattern of actions and attitudes at that, is explained in such 'ethological' terms. It also seems demeaning to women as the bonding process is not, apparently, a requirement for paternal love. The rejoinder to this observation would be that mother love is different *and* special. The suggestion is that sensory stimulation from the infant soon after its delivery is essential if the mother is to fall in love with her baby. During the critical hours following birth, tactile, visual and olfactory stimulation of the mother by her baby are thought to be particularly significant. A great deal is at stake. Bonding theory suggests that when all goes well an attachment is cemented between a mother and her baby which underpins a relationship of unconditional love, self-sacrifice and nurturant attitudes. These, on the mother's part, will probably last a lifetime.

Mothers are, of course, crucial for the care and protection they offer the young during their relatively prolonged state of dependency. (I will come to fathers shortly.) Significantly 'mothering' is a feminine word and reflects the mother-centred connotations of child care. It is still women — despite the feminist movement — who bear generally the burden of child care and see themselves as having a special responsibility for the children. Whatever the lip-service paid to changes of attitude in men, this still seems (with some sub-cultural variations and individual exceptions) to be the reality (Lewis, 1986). When there is a showdown it is the mother who is expected to stay (and usually does) with the children. She is made aware by the mass media, the books she reads and the experts she consults, that the child's growth, indeed well-being and future, depend upon her love and competence as a caregiver. Much of the rhetoric about, and mystification of, motherhood is misleading and has proved oppressive to women (see Boulton, 1983; Chess, 1964; Sluckin, Herbert and Sluckin, 1983).

The practical consequences of the bonding concept for women as reflected in hospital policy have been beneficial *and* potentially harmful. In the past, when maternity hospital routine tended to be rigid, mothers were separated from their infants for long periods — and not always for good reasons. Currently, in the UK and the USA, more than 90 % of all babies are separated after birth for at least brief periods. More prolonged separations are likely if the baby has to receive special care or requires intensive care, e.g., prolonged oxygen therapy with close monitoring, etc. Special care is an eventuality affecting some 14 % of all British babies. The policy on many special-care baby units and, indeed, ordinary maternity wards, has in the past been antipathetic to incipient maternal feelings and sensibilities. The critique of policy by Klaus and Kennell (1976) was a potent influence for change in obstetrical practices at a time when these practices were being criticized by mothers and nurses who objected to the pervasive view that childbirth was the surgical culmination of a nine-month-long illness. Margison (1982) makes the point that their work appeared to provide the scientific support needed to convince a sceptical medical establishment to accept changes that should have been welcomed on humanitarian grounds alone.

The aim of Klaus and Kennell in their writing and teaching was to minimize the separation of the ill or premature infant and mother, and thus minimize the putative risk of a later disorder of maternal bonding. The steps they recommended are summarized by Margison (1982) as follows:

(i) The mother should be allowed brief contact and the baby should be nursed in the same hospital if possible.
(ii) If the baby has to be moved, the father should accompany the baby to the special-care unit in the other hospital.
(iii) The mother should be given a photograph of the baby.
(iv) As soon as possible the parents should be encouraged to make physical contact with the baby. Eye contact should be established as soon as possible.
(v) Even when the baby is severely ill pessimistic remarks should be avoided because they may delay attachment if the baby does survive. If the baby dies, Klaus and Kennell see it as the responsibility of staff to help the parents with mourning.
(vi) A particularly important recommended action is the keeping of a 'contact diary' in which all contacts by the mother are recorded. The staff, therefore, record all telephone and personal contacts. If a mother telephones or visits less than three times in two weeks the baby is identified as being at high risk of non-accidental injury, failure to thrive or rejection.

These suggestions have been applied particularly to sick babies, but the general principles were thought to be applicable in other situations, for example, during the mother's physical or mental illness.

Unforeseen implications

It can be seen from these prescriptive items that some of the implications of bonding are very far-reaching indeed. There is mention not only of attachment but of rejection and child abuse. The bonding doctrine has been very influential in the health *and* social services. Obstetric and nursing procedures sometimes provide for skin-to-skin contact between a mother and her newborn at almost any cost — even if the baby is ill or the mother depressed, exhausted or in pain.

Due to the bonding doctrine there has been a policy of discharging low-weight babies very much earlier than was the practice in the past. Sometimes going home early is a good move; but it may not always be in the best interest of the child, and may not allow social workers to assess the home situation correctly. The view has been taken, particularly with handicapped babies, that unless the mother is allowed to have the baby as soon as possible she may not want it later. Like much of the received wisdom directed at hapless mothers, these decisions (if based on bonding notions alone) emerge from a rationale that is a gross oversimplification.

It is difficult to imagine a more daunting prospect to hold before an expectant mother than the possibility that a fortuitous separation from her infant might put a blight on her motherly love. If she believes that there is a period when she is optimally receptive to processes which will bind her to the baby, then that belief and conversely her fear could be influential (if her baby has to be separated from her), in 'determining' future events, whatever the reality of the existence (or non-existence) of a critical period might be. In the light of what we know about the workings of self-fulfilling prophecies and their disruptive consequences, one would be hard put to think of a theory that offers more 'hostages to fortune' for a mother with a sick or premature infant, than this widely publicized view of mother-to-child attachment. It is unfortunately the case that many mothers have been led over the years, to believe that failures or distortions of maternal bonding could lead to all sorts of ills, such as infantile autism, unsuccessful adoptions, failure-to-thrive, and, especially, child abuse. The last three indicate the source of Social Services interest in the bonding concept.

Sad to say, liberalizing ideas in the field of child care — for example, bonding and 'maternal deprivation' theory — can become oppressive when elevated into dogmas. The eminently realistic and humane idea of allowing a mother and her new baby to get to know one another early on, by means of frequent and intimate social interactions, becomes intrusive and unrealistic when the permissive 'ought' of physical contact is transformed into an authoritarian 'must' — a decision which takes no account of the condition of the mother or her offspring.

Evidence for maternal bonding

There is insufficient space here for a detailed review of the evidence on bonding, in any event this has been done elsewhere (Chess and Thomas, 1984; Herbert, Sluckin and Sluckin, 1982). However, a summary of the present position may prove helpful to the paediatric-based practitioner.

Evidence from the most recent, carefully controlled studies suggest that close contact soon after birth makes no difference to mothering effectiveness or to mother-love, as reported by mothers or as inferred from their behaviour. There seems to be no reliable evidence that skin-to-skin contact is necessary for the development of mother-love; and, what is more significant, mother-to-infant attachment does not depend on such contact occurring during a sensitive period of short duration after the birth of the baby (see Chess and Thomas, 1984; Sluckin, Herbert and Sluckin, 1983).

This is not to assert a counter doctrine that early human contact and relationships are of no consequence. Far from it! Close mother-infant contact is decidedly desirable whenever possible. Mothers tend to like it and lactation is facilitated. Where better to begin than at the very beginning, with a newborn child placed in its mother's arms? Mutual awareness and familiarity have an opportunity to develop. What we are talking about is foundational learning, learning how to relate to (and love) a stranger, a baby. It would seem that this learning comes quickly for some but for others more slowly. The range of individual differences is wide. The wider family is also participant in these events; the period after birth, with its heightened emotional arousal and excited expectation and fulfilment of a new family member, are likely to have tremendous significance not only for the mother, but also the father, siblings and others. (We leave grandparents out of clinical calculations at our peril.) Parental bonds and relationships have their own complex, many-sided developmental histories, stretching over many years. It is simplistic, and a disservice to a mother, to trace the development of her love and its positive and negative outcomes, solely to the amount of contact that occurs in the postpartum minutes and hours. Most of the differences in maternal behaviour associated with early contact fade away with the passage of time. There is no hard evidence that post-partum contact is a necessary or sufficient condition for the development of mother-love or mother-to-infant bonds.

Among the factors which can influence the way a mother behaves and relates to her offspring are her own cultural and social background, her own experience of being parented, her personality, her previous experience with babies and her experiences during pregnancy and birth. Also important are the sex and temperament of her baby. In general, the mother's previous experience of having infants is a potent influence on her actions with a new baby. Multiparous women appear more efficient in managing their child than primiparous women, and are less likely to be influenced by outside disturbances. They respond more quickly to their babies' crying and are more likely, subsequently, to feed them. They are less likely than primiparae to feel an initial indifference to the newborn baby — a not uncommon but disconcerting experience for first-time mothers (Robson and Powell, 1982).

CHILD ABUSE AND BONDING

Some theorists (Lynch, Roberts and Gordon, 1976) have suggested that mothers prone to child abuse are mothers who have not been bonded to their babies soon after delivery.

> Evidence for the absence, weakness or distortion of the usual affectional bond between parent and child, can be found in virtually every case of child abuse ... (Lynch et al., 1976)

While it is understandable that professionals err on the side of making 'Type 1 errors' (asserting relationships falsely) in a fraught area like child abuse, the implications of Type 1 errors may also be harmful to clients. Interventions which, at best, are ineffectual, at worst demoralizing, may be the cost. In any event there are several problems connected with the findings on which the child abuse prognostications are based. It is always difficult to be sure about the validity of retrospective information obtained from mothers about their pregnancy, the child's birth, the neonatal period and the youngster's early development. Granted that some studies rely on clinical records (perhaps more reliable than parental reports, although also at times somewhat suspect), far too much data is drawn from retrospective research designs to allow for confident generalizations. Research samples also tend to be relatively small in number.

In a study, unusual for its large numbers, Gaines et al. (1978) investigated the circumstances of 240 mothers, drawn from known-abuse, neglect and normal control populations. The multivariate analysis included twelve variables, of which six discriminated the abusing, neglecting and normal mothers at a high level of significance. Infant risk, determined on the basis of neonatal complications requiring hospitalization, was not a successful discriminator. According to the authors, the hypothesized relationship between mother–neonate bonding and maltreatment was not supported.

Clare Hyman, a NSPCC (National Society for the Prevention of Cruelty to Children) researcher into child abuse, reporting on a number of recent significant research projects which corrected for social class differences and maternal age, stresses that neither prematurity nor handicap (often associated with periods of separation immediately after birth) play a significant part in the causation of child abuse. She further adds that these findings hardly support the idea that abuse is due to 'impaired bonding' and it is therefore worrying that this issue has received so much attention (Hyman, 1980).

Bonding is frequently used in a manner that is suggestive of a mechanical thing. If successful, the mother is 'tied' figuratively to her offspring. This mechanical model seems to suggest an all-or-nothing 'fixing' phenomenon; yet there is no evidence that caring is really like that. It seems more likely to involve many facets of loving and nurturance. People love and become attached in different ways. Nevertheless, many of the clinical discussions of 'bonding' fail to specify precisely what such a global term means or, indeed, ways of assessing the significance of those component behaviours thought to be indices of bonding. Mothers who feel little or no affection or sense of belonging towards their offspring have been known to care meticulously for their welfare. Mothers who love their children have also been known to hurt their children in moments of despair and in fraught situations arising from various causes (Iwaniec, Herbert and McNeish, 1985).

FATHER-TO-INFANT BONDING

The father's responses to his newborn infant very strongly resemble maternal behaviour. Likewise, attachment, resulting from exposure to the baby and from other forms of learning, develops in the father if he is closely involved in child rearing, just as it develops in the mother (Herbert and Sluckin, 1985). Most human fathers develop a strong love for their offspring, even if they were nowhere near the delivery room when they were born. The study of 30 first-time fathers by Greenberg and Morris (1974) suggests that they began developing a bond to their newborn by the first three days after the birth and often earlier. They tended to develop a feeling of preoccupation, absorption and interest ('engrossment'). There were indications that the early contact by the father with the newborn facilitated this engrossment.

At present, the situation with regard to the division of domestic duties between males and females appears to be changing, but fathers still appear to be 'superpals' to their offspring rather than primary caregivers (Lewis, 1986). Nevertheless, there is no apparent reason why a father cannot be a good 'mother' – in society's gender-biased sense of being the main caregiver – and do an adequate job.

Variations in child care

It has to be remembered for the purpose of clinical assessments that there have been striking variations in perinatal practices within Western culture. At one time there was a widespread belief that labour pains were conducive to the growth of motherly love for the baby; hence the opposition to the administration of pain-killing drugs during labour. In Victorian times ladies who could afford it were advised to rest after giving birth by staying in bed for several weeks. Women are nowadays expected to be up and about as soon after the birth as possible.

The methods of feeding newborn babies also vary not a little. Breast-feeding by the natural mother is the traditional way. However, the fashion for bottle-feeding which set in several decades ago is still prevalent in many parts of the world, but is now on the wane among the middle classes in the West. Breast feeding is once again thought to be best both for the mother and her baby.

The newborn baby

It is not only in infant care that we find cultural variations; child care practices with older children have varied throughout history and vary a great deal at the present time (Aries, 1973; Liddiard, 1928). It is important for the practitioner to remember that ethnocentricity in clinical practice can lead to much individual suffering if methods offend against cherished cultural and/or religious beliefs. For some ethnic groups the bonding doctrine, if applied insensitively by doctors and nurses, may have disturbing repercussions. In some

Asian families, for instance, birth is a less personal event than in European families. An Indian baby is thought to be bonded to the family group rather than to the mother in particular. In some Asian communities mothers are considered unclean for the first three days after birth and close physical contact with the baby is avoided. The infant is handled by a close relative of the mother or father, depending on local custom. Unless hospital staff are sensitive to ethnic differences in behaviour and attitudes after birth, immigrant parents could feel intense conflict over 'bonding procedures' which are alien to their values.

Cross-cultural studies indicate that human beings vary enormously in their ideas of what is the 'right' way to deal with newborn babies and to bring up children. For example, a woman in labour in Ghana is said to 'lie between life and death' (Kaye, 1962). The period of confinement is regarded as an anxious time. In some tribes excessive pain is attributed to infidelity. It is widely believe in Ghana that a newborn baby may in fact be a spirit and not a human child at all. If it is a spirit child it will return to the spirits before a week is out; thus for the first seven days (in some areas, three days for a boy, or four for a girl) mother and child are confined to the room in which the birth took place. If the child dies during that time it is assumed that it was a spirit child. The parents are not allowed to mourn its loss but should show signs of joy at being rid of such an unwelcome guest.

It is possible to see an 'adaptive' element in such cultural beliefs; they may help parents to come to terms with death, especially in areas where there are high rates of infant mortality.

VARIETIES OF PARENTING

It is useful to draw a distinction between generalized caregiving behaviour and specific parental behaviour. Adult human beings tend to exhibit some degree of caregiving towards young children in general. Women and men often act as temporary substitute 'parents', carrying out this role most effectively. In contrast, *parental behaviour* is concerned with caring specifically for one's own, or one's adopted, children. It implies parental feelings of love and an affectional attachment by parents to their children.

In our society it is generally agreed that parents have the prime responsibility for meeting the basic physical and emotional needs of their children by caring for them. These responsibilities are shared with others but the extent to which others are allowed to intervene is limited. To complicate matters, the term 'parent' contains at least three components:

- *Birth-parents* give the child life, physical appearance, intellectual potential and certain personality characteristics and special talents.
- *Legal parents* carry responsibility for the child's maintenance, safety and security, and make decisions about the child's residence, education, medical treatment and so on.
- *Parenting parents* provide the day-to-day love, care, attention and discipline.

For many children the three components of parenting are embodied in one set of parents. Adopted and fostered children, however, are likely to have more than one set of parents: the birth parents and the substitute parents.

STYLES OF CHILD REARING

Despite extensive research, there is much doubt as to how different styles of child rearing influence the development of the child's personality. Thus, we do not really know whether the psychological development of children is affected by feeding methods (breast feeding versus bottle feeding, or fixed-interval feeding versus on-demand feeding) or by early or late weaning, and so on. The available evidence suggests negligible effects for these early events (Caldwell, 1964; Yarrow, Campbell and Burton, 1968).

Notwithstanding variations in family pattern and style of parenting, all societies seem to be broadly successful in the task of transforming helpless, self-centred infants into more or less self-supporting, responsible members of their particular form of community. Indeed, there is a basic 'preparedness' on the part of most infants to be trained — that is, an inbuilt bias toward all things social (Stayton, Hogan and Ainsworth, 1971). The baby responds (for example) to the mother's characteristic infant-orientated overtures in a sociable reaction. He or she also initiates social encounters with vocalizations or smiles directed to the mother which cause her in turn to smile back and to talk to, tickle or touch him or her. In this way she elicits further responses from the baby. A chain of mutually rewarding interactions is thus initiated on many occasions (Schaffer and Collis, 1986; Stern, 1977; 1985). Parents and child learn about each other in the course of these interactions; they develop attachments.

Schaffer and Collis (1986) observe that

> ... it is curious that reciprocal influence suffered so long from neglect as a topic of empirical investigation, as even extreme environmentalist theories of development involve two-way processes. For example, Skinnerian principles imply, on the one hand, that the behaviour of the child is conditioned by virtue of contingent responsiveness on the part of the parent ... and on the other hand that parental behaviour can be conditioned by virtue of contingent responsiveness on the part of the child.

However, as Hinde (1979) makes clear the principle of two-way responsiveness goes beyond the boundaries of conditioning theory. It is the essence of *social interaction* that individual X does something to individual Y who in return does something back to X and so on and on. What happens at one point of the interaction influences subsequent interactions between X and Y and probably also the interactions of X and Y with other individuals.

A few studies have indicated that the mother's attitudes, measured before the child's birth, can affect mother–child interaction. Positive attitudes toward infants have been found to be related to maternal responsiveness to the baby's crying and to his or her social behaviour in the early months of life. Mothers who are highly anxious during the pregnancy have also been evaluated as having less satisfactory interactions with their babies at eight months than mothers who had been low in anxiety (see Robson and Powell, 1982, for a review of studies).

We have seen that infants are not passively reactive to stimulation; they are proactive, reaching out to affect their environment. Individual differences in temperament and styles of behaving affect parents markedly, and thus, in the course of myriads of interactions, the direction of development (Thomas and Chess, 1977).

Psychologists sometimes have to explore the social and emotional context in which the infant or child feeds, for example in cases where they fail to thrive (Iwaniec, Herbert and McNeish, 1985). Parental responsiveness is important in something as apparently basic as providing growth-enhancing sustenance to a baby. Typically, feeding times must be adapted to the cycles of hunger and satisfaction expressed by the infant and responded to by the parent. During the feeding sessions parents should preferably be calm, and sensitive enough to respond from moment to moment to changes in the baby's behaviour. For example, they commonly respond to pauses in the child's sucking at the breast by nudging the baby. They will gaze back at the baby and talk to it. They will be alert to the child's changing needs for nourishment as it matures, by altering its diet.

PARENT–INFANT RELATIONSHIPS

The interactions between parents and children (particularly the early ones involving communication between mother, 'mother-figure' and baby) are of crucial significance in the child's development (Hinde, 1979; Trevarthen, 1977). Personal factors can interfere with these intricate processes. To take the extreme case: a mother suffering from depression may find it difficult to 'tune in' to her child in a sufficiently sensitive manner to be able to construct with him or her a mutually beneficial and stimulating sequence of interactions (e.g., Cohn and Tranick, 1983).

It is argued (Belsky and Nezworski, 1988) that the past decade has witnessed a 'virtual revolution' in our understanding of early development, and in particular a recognition that individual differences measured within the first year of life are predictive of later development. Evidence suggests that individual differences in information processing capabilities — speed of discrimination between familiar and novel stimuli — from the third through to the sixth month of life (and possibly earlier) — are predictive of variations in I.Q. measured as far forward as the eighth year of life (see Bornstein and Sigman, 1986).

With regard to socio-emotional development it is the measurement of security of infant-to-mother attachment (at the end of the first year of life) that has come into its own as a predictor of competence as far forward as the early school years (see Bretherton, 1985). The basic assumption is not that the relationship between mother and baby *inevitably* influences later development, but rather that the infant's initial (and founda- tional) experience of his or her relationship with the mother predicts later social development because it affects his or her expectations and attributions about other relationships, feelings about self, and social skills mobilized in other social contexts.

LATER PARENT–CHILD RELATIONSHIPS

What about later relationships and interactions between parents? Given the intimate, protracted and highly influential nature of parents' relationships with their children, it seems self-evident that the quality of such relationships, the power and reach of early experiences must have a vital bearing on the development of the child's personality and general adaptation. The scientific inquiry into these matters has produced disappointingly meagre results. The reasons are not difficult to find: the sheer complexity of the subject, a daunting number of methodological problems, and some quirky biases in scientists' approach to this area of research. Leaving aside the complexity issue which is self-evident, there are particular doubts about many of the studies of human parenting due largely to flawed research designs, biases in sampling, and a tendency for social-class and ethnocentric values to determine the questions asked and the assumptions made in various investigations (Herbert, 1974, 1980). Despite the many methodological hurdles researchers have reached a consensus about a predictable structure underlying parental and other interpersonal transactions (e.g., Schaefer, 1959): two major dimensions, with orthogonal axes ascribed as warm–hostile and control–autonomy (see Figure 8).

Schaefer's dimensions in Figure 8 have been combined with the table describing the sort of behaviour and problems produced by different combinations of parental attitude (as summarized by Becker, 1964). The nature of these combinations — trends, of course — appear at the foot of the figure.

Another useful source of information about child care and development is the research carried out on prosocial behaviour in children. It is possible to summarize the major factors which foster prosocial behaviour (Staub, 1975):

(a) parental affection and nurturance;
(b) parental control (setting limits);
(c) induction — the use of reasoning in disciplinary encounters;
(d) modelling;
(e) assigning responsibility.

The balancing of these components is perhaps best illustrated in the philosophy of what (on the basis of her investigations) Baumrind (1971) calls the 'authoritative' mother. This kind of parent attempts to direct her child's activities in a rational manner determined by the issues involved in particular disciplinary situations. She encourages verbal give-and-take and shares with the child the reasoning behind her policy. She values both the child's self-expression and his or her so-called 'instrumental attributes' (respect for authority, work and the like); she appreciates both independent self-will and disciplined conformity. Therefore, this kind of mother exerts firm control at points where she and the child

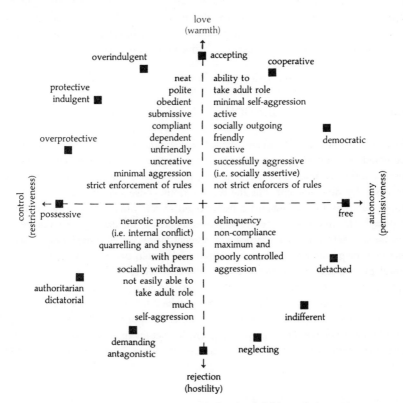

Figure 8. Range of parental behaviour types with details of children's behaviour.

The combination of *loving and controlling* attitudes is indicated by behaviours which are restrictive, over-protective, possessive or over-indulgent in content: *loving and permissive* attitudes are shown by actions which are accepting, co-operative and democratic. The combination of *rejecting and controlling* attitudes is indexed by behaviours which are authoritarian, dictatorial, demanding or antagonistic; *rejecting and permissive* attitudes are indicated by actions which are detached, indifferent, neglectful or hostile. Children's reports of their parents' behaviour suggest an additional factor: a dimension of firm versus lax control. It is possible for children to perceive their parents as firm but allowing independence at one and the same time; or indeed, lax but still controlling.

diverge in viewpoint, but does not suppress him or her with endless restrictions. She recognizes her own special rights as an adult, but also the child's individual interests and special ways. (We should not forget the values that give direction to or, at least, set the presumptions, for this kind of research — valuable though it is.)

DISRUPTION OF SOCIALIZATION

Although it is not usually made explicit, substantial deviations from this ideal as represented by authoritarian parenting at one 'extreme' and permissive (*laissez faire*) parenting at the other, are regarded, if not as pathological, at least as entailing risks for the child's healthy development. But the most serious consequences result from punitive methods persistently used against a background of rejecting, hostile parental attitudes. These methods are often referred to as power-assertive; the adult asserts dominant and authoritarian control through physical punishment, harsh verbal abuse, angry threats and deprivation of privileges. There is a positive relationship between the extensive use of physical punishment in the home by parents and high levels of aggression in their offspring outside the home (Becker, 1964). It would seem that physical violence is the least effective form of discipline or training when it comes to moulding a child's behaviour. Violence begets violence. What the child appears to learn is that might is right. Delinquents have more commonly been the victims of adult assaults — often of a vicious, persistent and even calculated nature — than non-delinquents (Herbert, 1987b).

Part Three

Preschool Children

INTRODUCTION

A feature of much problem behaviour in childhood is its transitoriness. So mercurial are some of the changes of behaviour in response to the rapid growth and successive challenges of childhood, that it is difficult to pinpoint the beginning of serious problems. According to a long-term American longitudinal study (Macfarlane, Allen and Honzik, 1954), the problems which decline in frequency with age are elimination (toilet training) problems, speech problems, fears, and thumb sucking. Problems such as insufficient appetite and lying reach a peak early and then subside. Many problems show high frequencies around or just before school-starting age, then decline in prevalence and later rise again at puberty. Among these are restless sleep, disturbing dreams, physical timidity, irritability, attention demands, over-dependence, sombreness, jealousy and, in boys, food-finickiness. Only one 'problem' increases systematically with age — nail-biting. This habit reaches a peak and begins to subside only near the end of adolescence. Among the problems which show little or no relationships to age is oversensitiveness.

PREVALENCE RATES OF BEHAVIOUR PROBLEMS

Richman, Stevenson and Graham, (1975), using a screening questionnaire and interview with the mothers of over 800 preschool children, found that 7 % had moderate to severe and 15 % a mild category of behaviour problems. Similar prevalence rates were reported by Richman, Stevenson and Graham (1982) in 705 non-immigrant 3-year-old children — a 1 in 4 random sample from a borough in London — again using a parent screening questionnaire and interview with parents. These problematic children were more likely than the 'normal' children to attend a child clinic, were more accident prone and showed more signs of developmental delay. The rate of language delay was found to be in the region of 2 to 3 %. Children with such delays were more likely to come from large families and the families were more likely to have suffered stressful circumstances over the previous year.

The quality of the parents' marital relationship was associated with the presence or absence of behaviour problems in the children. In the control group, nearly one in five children had parents whose marriage was rated as poor, while in problem children the rate was nearly twice as high (37 %). The proportion of women working (about 20 %) was almost exactly the same in both the problematic and non-problematic children.

Earls and Richman (1980a) compared the prevalence of behavioural problems in 3-year-old children of West Indian-born parents with children of British-born parents, using a semi-structured interview with parents, together with a 12-item behaviour screening questionnaire. The children of West Indian-born parents were all born in the UK and the parents were all working in the UK for less than 20 years. The children of West Indian families were living in poorer housing and had experienced more separations but did not show higher rates of behaviour problems. A one year follow-up (Earls and Richman, 1980b) showed that the prevalence and pattern of behaviour problems were very similar in the two groups. The global rating of severity of behaviour adjustment suggests that behaviour problems might be more frequent as well as more severe for the children of British-born parents.

In an American epidemiological study of 110 3-year-olds, using the same behaviour screening instruments while applying a correction formula, Earls (1980) estimated a prevalence rate of 16.5 % with a cut-off score of 11.

THE RANGE OF PROBLEMS

With regard to individual problems in 3-year-olds, Richman, Stevenson and Graham, (1982) reported that 37 % exhibited nocturnal enuresis more than three times per week; over 10 % displayed eating problems, sleeping problems, overactivity and restlessness, several fears, poor sibling and peer relations, difficulty in being controlled, and encopresis. Less than 10 % of 3-year-olds were reported to exhibit poor concentration, high dependency, frequent temper tantrums, unhappy moods, and several worries. Earls (1980) reported similar patterns for an American sample; however, the American 3-year-olds were less likely to display eating problems, overactivity, and worries.

Of course, babies can be 'difficult' as we have seen in the section on temperament; but it is not until about the age of 3 that epidemiological studies begin to report the behaviour problems of children as belonging, in a sense, to them as individuals. During the earliest stages of life — say the first year or two — problems are not so much *of* them, but rather problems created *for* them, difficulties — organismic and environmental — which can impede their development and blight their contentment. At this stage they're absolutely dependent and, as such, to be viewed in clinical assessments (if there is to be an understanding of what is going wrong) as part of caregiver-infant attachment systems. This is not to deny that they are individuals in their own right, or to forget that they *have* rights, as the UN Charter is at long last acknowledging in a formal sense. The point is often made that dependence means *power* for caregivers, and power can be (and very often is) abused (see Chapter 6). The parent-infant system continues to be important as the child gets older but is not as all-embracing as it was during infancy. This leads to a seeming paradox that a discussion of the problems of infants is, in large part, a discussion of adults, their attitudes to, and interactions with, their babies.

HANDICAP

Knowledge of child behaviour and development enables a clinical psychologist to be sensitive to the timetable of 'achievements' (walking, talking, etc.) about which parents become so proud or worried. Where an infant is mentally handicapped, a dawning awareness that something is 'not right' may be so gradual that parents cannot say when they began to worry. It would not be surprising if at some time during a pregnancy parents asked themselves: 'Will the baby be all right?' For most parents these anxieties are somewhat submerged in the activity of the last few months of the pregnancy. They become apparent again at the birth, but despite such apprehensions parents are never really prepared for the birth of a handicapped child.

Adjustment to the fact of handicap — if the baby is impaired physically and/or intellectually — may continue over many years, depending (to some extent) on whether the handicap was apparent at birth, or only became clear later, and whether the parents were told clearly and several times about the probable extent and nature of the child's handicap. Parent's reactions to their handicapped child are frequently formulated in the literature, in terms of a series of stages: shock or denial, guilt, despair, depression, disappointment and eventual acceptance or adjustment. However Blacher (1984) and Allen and Affleck (1985) argue on the basis of their findings that by no means all parents experience emotional reactions to the birth of a handicapped child in such an ordered sequence; nor are they necessarily affected adversely over the longer term.

Whatever the outcome over the medium- or longer-term, the early period of adapting to the arrival of (or revelation about) a handicapped child, is fraught with difficulty. Adapting their lifestyle to the advent of a normal baby can be difficult enough for parents. Here, then, is a time when an expert and sensitive psychological intervention could make a lot of difference to that outcome.

DEVELOPMENTAL TASKS

Life's demands (referred to by theorists as developmental tasks) put a heavy burden on children's adjustive skills or coping strategies (be they handicapped or not) as they make progress toward maturity. The newborn infant (to take one example) is said to need to develop a sense of trust and later, a growing capacity for independence. A lasting sense of trust, security, confidence or optimism (as opposed to distrust, insecurity, inadequacy or pessimism) is thought to be based upon affection, a degree of continuity of care-giving and the reasonably prompt satisfaction of the infant's needs. Some parents may be too immature or too preoccupied by personal problems to manage this.

The chronological ages quoted as guidelines to the stages (and the youngsters' capabilities) are somewhat arbitrary because rates of maturation and development vary from child to child and, indeed, between the sexes. Each stage of development corresponds to a particular social demand, and yet again, the timing of demands by caregivers is marked by individual and cultural differences. Certain types of emotional and behavioural problem tend (although not exclusively) to be associated with these stages and with the mastering of specific socialization (or developmental) tasks. In other words difficulties such as shyness, mood swings, food finickiness, lying, temper tantrums and disturbing dreams can occur at almost any age; however, they tend to peak at particular phases of the child's life (see Table 9).

The relatively high prevalence rate for behavioural dysfunction during the preschool period is suggestive of management problems for parents and caregivers — an area in which psychologists can provide empirically-based advice. To establish the developmental significance of such problems, one needs to investigate their continuity into subsequent developmental stages.

THE STABILITY OF PROBLEM BEHAVIOUR

It is difficult to make confident statements with regard to longer term prediction as there have been too few methodologically sound studies. Follow-back designs are the most common but they can be somewhat unreliable in their inferences; they involve methodological weaknesses which limit the conclusions researchers can safely make (see Yarrow, Campbell and Burton, 1968).

Generally, estimates of the continuity of preschool behavioural dysfunction vary according to the definition of dysfunction, and the age, sex, and/or environment of the child. Specific behavioural problems, symptoms, or disorders appear to vary in their rates of continuity and extent of prediction of later behavioural outcomes. Predictions become more unreliable as the period separating predictor and outcome increases. At best, preschool behavioural dysfunction exhibits low correlations with outcomes in late adolescence or adulthood, low to moderate correlations with outcomes during early adolescence, and moderate correlations with outcomes at school entry.

Recent evidence from prospective studies suggests that although many problem behaviours are *transient*, children who develop *significant* behaviour problems during the preschool period are more likely to exhibit problems at a later stage. For instance, Richman, Stevenson and Graham, (1982) concluded that 61% of problematic 3-year-olds still displayed significant difficulties on a clinical rating at age 8 years. Chazan and Jackson (1974) found that 42.5% of children rated as poorly adjusted on entering school also presented with behaviour problems at around 7 years of age. Coleman, Wolkind, and Ashley (1977) found moderately high correlations for parental reports of children's home

Table 9. Behaviour problems shown by one-third or more of normal boys and aged $1\frac{3}{4}$–14 years at each age level (adapted from MacFarlane *et al.*, 1954.)

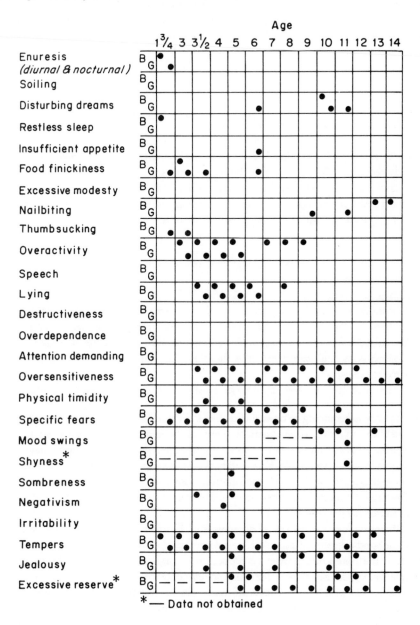

* — Data not obtained

behaviour between the ages of 3–4 years, 4–5 years, and 3–5 years. However, there was generally a poor correlation between parent-reported behaviour at home and teacher-rated reports of children's school behaviour, particularly for boys, suggesting that issues of contextual specificity need to be considered. Predictors which include information about family, stress, child-rearing, or temperamental characteristics, in addition to early behavioural data, may offer higher rates of prediction concerning later developmental outcomes (Barron and Earls, 1984).

RESILIENCE (see Werner and Smith, 1982)

An interesting aspect of children's reactions to the tasks and stressors of childhood, which has only received critical attention in the last decade, is the issue of *resilience*; most studies of deprived or disadvantaged children have noted wide variations in response. Despite the most difficult homes and stressful experiences some children come through apparently unscathed with a healthy personality. Rutter (1981a) postulates the operation of protective factors which he considers under six headings:

● The number of stresses (single, isolated stresses as opposed to multiple stresses carry no appreciable psychiatric risk).
● Changed circumstances.
● Factors in the child (sex in favour of girls, temperament, and genetic background).
● Factors in the family (good parent-child relationships, adequate caring, well-structured family environment with well-understood rules and effective supervision).
● Coping skills (the manner in which the individual responds to his or her hazardous circumstances).
● Factors outside the home (the impact of schooling, the area in which families live).

The evidence is beginning to make it clear that such ameliorating or protective factors can do much to aid normal development even in the worst circumstances. So far, our knowledge of these factors is somewhat sketchy, but it could eventually have very substantial policy, preventative and therapeutic implications. There is evidence, for example, that social and family characteristics such as those listed above can act to cushion the individual child from the effects of adverse life events (Quinton and Rutter, 1976; Rutter, 1979a, 1980).

Furthermore, there are *individual* differences in the extent to which negative life events and childhood adjustment are associated. Garmezy, Masten and Tellegen, (1984) have indicated the potentially protective properties of high ability levels in the face of an adverse family environment. There is also evidence to suggest that boys are more vulnerable than girls to the effects of stress (Dunn, Kendrick and MacNamee, 1981) although these findings may not generalize to all stress situations (Wolkind and Rutter, 1985). Rutter, Tizard and Whitmore, (1970) reported that, while the proportion of 10-

year-old children rated by their teachers as exhibiting behavioural disturbance was related to marital discord, there was a significant tendency for children who had a warm, positive relationship with at least one parent, to be less likely to develop behavioural adjustment problems.

Rutter (1981a,b) describes moderating factors which by themselves may have little or no impact on behavioural adjustment, but which may interact with both chronic and acute stress to increase the risks of poor developmental outcomes. Vulnerability variables act as catalysts to increase the influence of stressors. These stressors are usually divided, for research purposes, into the following categories:

(a) *acute stress*, which is associated with specific life events such as divorce, bereavement, hospitalization, and birth of a sibling;
(b) *chronic stress*, which is related (inter alia) to long-term physical illness, low social status, a family characterized by psychopathology in the parents, and parental rejection and abuse.

Early research was concerned with identifying the kinds of stress that made children vulnerable to the development of behavioural problems. For example:

● *Hospitalization* has been linked to a concurrent increased incidence of disturbance in preschool children. Longer term effects are rare, particularly for short-term hospital admissions of less than one week (Quinton and Rutter, 1976; Rutter, 1981a).
● *Birth of a sibling* has been found to be related to increased preschool behavioural difficulties such as sleeping and toileting problems, and increased tearfulness (Dunn, Kendrick and MacNamee, 1981).

Chronic stress such as that associated with low social status, poor housing conditions, and parental psychopathology has long been associated with childhood behavioural problems. The evidence (Rutter 1981a,b) suggests that children with only one chronic stress factor do not exhibit an increase in the risk of disturbance compared with children without stress factors operating in their lives. If two or more stressors are present concurrently, the risk of developing behavioural problems is raised over and above the rate that would be expected on the basis of a simple additive model of risk. Chronic stressors exhibit a potentiating or multiplicative influence on each other, in the sense that the effects of two or more stressors experienced simultaneously can exert more influence on the individual than the effects of those same stressors experienced separately.

Rutter refers to a 'family adversity index' which combines six variables associated with childhood behavioural problems:

(a) severe marital discord;
(b) low social status;
(c) overcrowding or large family size;
(d) paternal criminality;
(e) maternal psychopathology;
(f) child admission into the care of welfare services.

Table 10. Family environment factors that are related to children's dysfunctional behaviours. (Source: Sines, 1987, reproduced by permission of Plenum Publishing Corp.)

	I.Q.		Somatic		Depression		Aggression		Hyperactivity	
	Boys	Girls	Boys	Girls	Boys	Girls	Boys	Girls	Boys	Girls
SES	+	+	?	?	0	0	?	?	−	−
Pressure for achievement	+	+	?	?	−	?	−	0	−	−
Family sociability	?	?	?	?	−	0	−	−	−	0
Parental rejection	?	?	+	?	+	?	+	+	+	+
Parental aggression	?	?	+	+	+	?	+	+	+	+
Marital conflict	?	?	+	+	0	0	+	+	+	+
Broken home	?	?	0	0	0	0	+	+	+	+
Loss	?	?	+	+	0	0	0	0	0	0
Change	?	?	+	?	+	+	+	+	+	+
Same behaviour in parents	+	+	+	+	+	+	+	+	?	?
Family deviant	−	−	−	−	+	+	+	+	+	+

+ = positive correlation
− = negative correlation
0 = not associated
? = inconclusive data

Sines (1987) has reviewed the evidence of socially undesirable environmental conditions which are positively correlated with dysfunctional behaviours of all kinds. This is summarized in Table 10.

ASSESSMENT

Among the better known life stress measures for younger age groups are the 'Life Events Record' (Coddington, 1972) and 'Life Events Checklist' (Johnson and McCutcheon, 1980).

Chapter 6

Problems Associated with Infancy
(Birth to Approximately Eighteen Months)

So much happens to the infant in this time-span, he or she is so dramatically transformed in physical appearance and psychosocial skills from the somewhat amorphous neonate (that was) to a distinct personality of a year-and-a-half, that it seems naïve to treat infancy as a unified period. The justification for doing so is the extent of the dependency of human infants during this time, and the implications this has in terms of the ability to enhance development, which is in the gift of their caregivers. The converse, of course, is the power to disrupt development.

Babies are more competent than was once realized, or capable of being realized, by the research methodology of earlier times (Bower, 1977; Bremner, 1988; Kaye, 1982). Normal infants are born with all sensory systems functioning; they are capable at birth of engaging in reciprocating relationships with other persons. The most important aspect of infant development in the first months is the capacity for learning (Oates and Sheldon, 1987). All of the developmental milestones involve an immense input and appreciation by the baby of sensory stimulation, the registration of that stimulation in memory, and the alteration of behaviour style as a function of experience. The rate of acquisition of behaviour is stunning. Parents, the source of much of the infant's experience, are often concerned about the competency and rates of development of their offspring.

INDIVIDUAL FACTORS

Let us take a *sample* — only a narrow range is possible — of the knowledge required as a background to assessment by clinical child psychologists. The longer term consequences of maldevelopments are discussed in Chapters 8 and 9.

Perceptual development (vision and fine motor movement) (see Bower, 1977)

Newborns can turn their eyes with approximate accuracy towards a sound source presented to the left or right of them. Studies of eye movements (Mackworth and Bruner,

1970) have shown that infants fixate specific features of the environment from birth. Babies prefer to look at things that are somewhat novel. They tend to be attracted to areas of greater contrast or discontinuity in a visual stimulus, for example patterns. As they get older scanning becomes broader in scope and progressively larger amounts of information are sought.

At 8 weeks babies will observe with a convergent gaze a dangling toy held 9 to 12 inches from their face, and will move their head in order to follow it. At around 4 to 5 months infants show a strong preference for looking at faces and can 'identify' the human face and discriminate between different people on the basis of facial information. With experience the infant acquires knowledge about sizes of different objects and depth perception emerges. The increased mobility (and consequent exploration) of infants helps them to gain a better appreciation of the spatial characteristics of the environment. There is now a wealth of fascinating research which makes use of film and video to analyse the function of intricate and intricately related perceptuo-motor skills in infants, as they strive to make sense of, and master, their environment.

As both vision and motor skills improve, hand-eye coordination develops. At 6 months infants use a clumsy palmar grasp; by 9 months a scissor grasp is used to pick up objects, and at 12 months they will pick objects up precisely between the ends of the thumb and index finger in a pincer grasp (M. D. Sheridan, 1975). Further development consists of increased selectivity and organization of the infant's world — a function, in large part, of the growth of knowledge about the perceptual environment.

Motor development

According to M. D. Sheridan (1975), motor development is effectively completed in infancy. When pulled to sitting, the head comes up in a line with the trunk by 3 months, and is then held steady as the child is supported sitting. The child will sit unsupported for a minute or so at 7 months, and for ten minutes by 9 months. At 6 months a child will start to take weight on his or her legs and at 9 months he or she bounces or stamps when supported. By 13 months a child will take about 10 steps unsupported.

Thus in infancy the sequence from lying, to sitting, to standing, to walking takes place. Of course there are variations between infants — an important fact to convey to parents — in the timing of particular changes. For example, 50 % of children can walk ten steps unaided at 13 months, but a few can do this at 8 months, and others do not manage this until 18 months (Frankenburg and Dodd, 1967). The changes in motor ability which follow walking tend to be consolidations and refinements of existing abilities rather than the emergence of completely new skills. Walking gradually becomes more competent and running becomes fluent and controlled. More complex skills such as skipping, riding a bike and throwing a ball and catching, tend not to develop until around the school-going age. In general children cannot reach a particular milestone without achieving the previous ones, e.g., they do not run until they can walk or walk until they can stand.

Because of the regularity and predominantly self-contained nature of motor develop-ment it is usually assumed that it involves a genetically programmed sequence. Although the rate of development varies, the sequence is virtually the same for all children, even those with marked physical or mental handicaps. For all that, it is still possible for specific environmental influences to alter the rate at which change takes place. Some practice is necessary for the child to develop motor skills. Dennis (1960) demonstrated that when opportunities for exercise and movement are greatly restricted there is some retardation in motor development. An adequate diet and good health are also critical (Bee, 1981).

In Down's syndrome motor development is typically slower than normal; nevertheless it moves through the sequence from sitting, to standing, to walking, in the normal order (Carr, 1975). However, with the use of intervention programmes specifically aimed at giving large amounts of practice in sensory-motor tasks, it is possible to accelerate motor development to almost normal levels.

Speech and language development (see Schacter and Strage, 1982)

Language development is a critical component of social development: so much teaching and learning is facilitated by verbal communication (see Trevarthen, 1977). The advent of speech and language enhances the ability to solve problems without acting them out concretely on objects in the child's world. The development of language passes through distinct stages beginning with the infant who demonstrates an ability to distinguish between different speech sounds (Mussen, Conger and Kagan, 1984). Babbling begins at about 5 or 6 months and appears to be 'pre-programmed', as it is produced by congenitally deaf children who have no experience of hearing sounds produced by themselves, or by others. The sounds produced are the first combination of vowels and consonants, typically 'bababa' and 'dadada'.

Progression to the next stage occurs 'naturally' only in hearing infants. Throughout the following stages, children's *understanding* of language is far ahead of their ability to express themselves — not infrequently the source of frustration and outbursts of temper. Between 9 and 11 months the infant will begin to inhibit an activity in response to the word 'no', although he or she will not generally be using the word himself or herself (M. D. Sheridan, 1975). The first recognizable spoken word appears at about one year, and from this, single word labels are used for familiar objects and people (Nelson, 1973).

In the single word stage the meaning attached to words may differ markedly from the conventions of adulthood, e.g., 'cat' may mean any four-legged furry animal, an overextension of meaning (Mussen, Conger and Kagan, 1984). The single word stage lasts several months, speech being used increasingly for specific effects, and, as more words are added, used with increasingly precise and adult-like meaning. Sentence development comprises the next stage. At approximately 18 months — when children have some 50 words in their speaking vocabularies — words begin to be combined in pairs to convey ideas, e.g., 'Dadad gone', and not long after there is a steady increase in sentence length and complexity. Even those first two-word sentences show systematic regularity of word order and from the very beginning express the basic grammatical relationships of subject, predicate, and object. Children from different nations with different languages express essentially the same range of meanings in their earliest sentences, including such basic semantic relations as identification, location, negation, attribution, agent-action and agent-object. By this stage infancy has come to an end; but language-development continues apace.

From 3 years, sentences are used to describe past and present happenings. The average adult length of sentence (6–7 words) is achieved by school-going age, reflecting important changes in the development of grammatical ability which appear to be closely linked with the development of cognitive and intellectual capacities. As these increase in capacity and sophistication, children can learn more complicated grammatical rules. By the age of 5 or 6 years, children can use several thousand words in complex adult-like sentences and are able to understand complex meanings. Their speech is fluent with few remaining infantile substitutions (M. D. Sheridan, 1975). Improved verbal ability often facilitates cognitive functions such as memory, thinking, reasoning and problem-solving. (Problems of speech and language are dealt with in Chapter 8.)

EARLY LEARNING

The objective of skills (e.g., social) training, to put it grandly, is the preparation of the child for life. Caregivers, and later teachers, are required to teach and train; children need to learn. There has been much speculation about the special quality of early experience and learning. In fact, there is little reason to suppose that infant learning is acquired more easily than later learning, and there is no indication that it is better retained or more resistant to forgetting. In fact, experiments suggest that infants and young children are strikingly inferior to adults in many dimensions of learning (Clarke and Clarke, 1976). Studies do suggest that early learning is of importance for its foundational nature, but there is good reason to be sceptical about the rigid structuring of character which the early Jesuits and Freudians thought to crystallize during infancy and just beyond. The fixity of the child's psychological attributes at a very tender age — looked at in the light of longitudinal studies — has been exaggerated (Clarke and Clarke, 1976). Early learning experiences do not appear to set the child on an inevitable 'tramline route' for his or her later development. Of course one can trace certain continuities from early childhood to adulthood, but these depend, in large part, on whether certain experiences — be they benign or malignant — are *reinforced* over and over again, also on the nature of what constitute 'core' learning situations.

CORE LEARNING/TEACHING SITUATIONS (see Dunn, 1988)

Observations of preschool children and their mothers at home show that a great many of the encounters between mother and child, in the course of any one day, can be characterized as 'core teaching situations' (Schaffer and Collis, 1986). This means that the adult has the opportunity of influencing the child's behaviour in ways that can contribute towards his or her development. However, children who develop a relatively high degree of competence generally have mothers who tend to demonstrate and explain things at the *child's* instigation rather than their own, thus providing help and guidance orientated around the child's interests and at times determined by the child himself or herself. Children of lower developmental competence, on the other hand, experience rather more didactic handling from their mothers, whose respect for the child's own interests is thus more limited and more discouraging. Certain parents, and particular kinds of interactive situation (e.g., play and storytime) lend themselves well to the provision of facilitative input. Abusive parents, on the other hand, tend to display disruptive, intrusive tendencies in their interactions with their infants and older children (Browne, 1986).

SYSTEMIC FACTORS: PARENT–CHILD INTERACTIONS

Parenting skills

Parenting is made up of a series of far-from-simple skills, part commonsense, part intuition and part empathy, the ability to see things from another's point of view. An assessment of caring parenthood might take account of the following provision:

(a) safety;
(b) shelter;
(c) space (which includes space to play, and, particularly in older children, privacy);
(d) food;
(e) income;
(f) physical care;
(g) health care.

In addition to basic survival functions, responsible parents meet vital psychosocial needs, including the child's requirements of

(a) love;
(b) security;
(c) attention;
(d) new experiences;
(e) acceptance;
(f) education;
(g) praise;
(h) recognition;
(i) belongingness.

Infants and children — if they are to survive — must also acquire vast amounts of information about the environment they inhabit. The transmission by adults of information of various kinds from one generation to another is referred to as socialization.

Effective parents tend to be those who care for their children with a sense of confidence in themselves as caregivers, doing what, at the time, the community by and large believes is best for the child (Behrens, 1954; Kallarackal and Herbert, 1976). Such mothers and fathers tend to feel supported by their community and are thus relaxed and confident in their parenting. There is a risk that mothers will become anxious when they are dogmatically instructed about the *details* of their mothering activities.

Contemporary women (and men) are frequently inexperienced at child care. They may be unaccustomed to small children because they were brought up in small families and were not given responsibilities for caring for the young ones, as older sisters of yesteryear had to do. This is only remedied when they have children themselves. They need to learn mothering and fathering skills very quickly. And here is a danger: the potentially explosive situation of a socially isolated, inexperienced single parent, living often in poor accommodation and trying to manage a persistently difficult, crying baby.

Parents acquire ideas about the nature of children and child development, including a developmental timetable of expectations, against which their offspring's actions and progress are measured, even though these expectations may not be rational or accurate. It is therefore important to ensure as far as is possible that parental beliefs are realistic, and that they are aware of their own child's abilities and interests. If this is achieved parents will be less likely to confront the child with environments posing either unstimulating, boring undermatches, or impossibly high and therefore distressing levels of aspiration.

Parents tend to assess the progress of their children by calling on criteria and norms drawn from multiple sources: cultural norms, observations of other children, opinions from health care personnel, or their own ideas about what is appropriate for a given chronological age. Parents have their own boundaries of normal behaviour, with upper and lower limits. If the child's behaviour falls outside these limits parents may then intervene, adjusting their teaching according to their own conceptions of how the child should be behaving. If the parent does not consider that the child should be able to fulfil a given task at a particular time, he or she will not encourage the child.

Parents *can* enhance the development of their children if they have some understanding of the developmental processes taking place (Goodnow *et al.*, 1984). But how much knowledge and understanding of child development do parents actually possess? Shaner (1985) found a poor level of knowledge in female undergraduates, who both under- and over-estimated children's abilities. McCune (1985) found that 80 % of parents under 20 years of age scored low on knowledge of child development and none of them scored high, whereas 30 % of older parents (aged 26–31 years) did achieve high scores. Comparing income levels, 68 % in the low income bracket had a low score, whereas over 40 % with a high income had a medium score. None of the parents who had left school before college achieved a high score, compared to 35 % of parents who had been to college. Goodnow (1984) did not find any evidence of socio-economic status having any impact on child development knowledge, but she states that 'age expectations at pre-school level seem especially sensitive to ethnic or national differences'.

Ninio (1979) found that mothers in a group of Asian-African origin differed from mothers of European origin in the ages at which they expected babies to show various perceptual and cognitive achievements although they did not differ in judgements about when it is best to stop breast-feeding or begin toilet training. The latter finding is probably the result of similar advice from the same well baby clinics. Ninio believes that parents' timetables represent one facet of a culture's 'naïve theories' about the nature of childhood and development.

Somewhat surprisingly, McCune (1985) found that 'experience' as indexed by the number of siblings with whom parents grew up, their birth order, or the age of their own children, did not correlate with knowledge of child development. Fry (1985) found that young teenage mothers had less knowledge of child development, less mature expecta-tions of the maternal role and tended to be more 'controlling' and 'nonverbal' than older teenage mothers who not only had more knowledge but whose interactions with their children were more stimulating.

Parents may be unskilled for reasons other than inexperience (e.g., mental handicap). Then again, some parents who have demonstrated skill early on, become *de-skilled*, losing their self-confidence because a later child has proved 'unmanageable' (Iwaniec, Herbert and McNeish, 1985).

Trust vs distrust

From the time of birth infants can signal information about their needs. Where the mother perceives the signals accurately and responds appropriately, the mother–infant relation-ship is said to be characterized by 'synchrony' which facilitates the baby's development and is a source of satisfaction to the mother. It is postulated that those children whose parents respond to their signals and communications *promptly* and *appropriately* through-out infancy develop confidence in their parents' availability and will have the security to use them as a base from which to explore their environment (see Belsky and Niezworski, 1988). Insecure children, on the other hand, tend to be anxious about their parents' availability and show little confidence in their reactions to the world.

Erikson (1965) theorizes that during the early months and years of life a baby learns whether the world is a good and satisfying place to live in or a source of pain, misery, frustration and uncertainty. Because human infants are so totally dependent for so long, they need to know that they can depend on the outside world. If their basic needs are met by the significant people in their lives, they are thought to develop a 'basic trust' in the world, and thus to evolve a nucleus of self-trust, which is indispensable to later development. But how does trust show itself in behavioural terms at this early stage of life? According to Lowe (1972) it is demonstrated in the ease with which babies feed, in the depth of their sleep, and in the relaxation of their bowels. Later on it is shown when infants will let their mother out of their sight without undue anxiety or rage. Babies who smile easily are also thought to demonstrate trust in Erikson's sense.

Major obstacles to the development of a perception of a benign and predictable world in which children initiate independence-seeking and perceive their own actions as having meaningful consequences are neglect, abuse and indifference (see Table 5, page 30). Such influences are likely to produce a child who behaves in a very troubled and troublesome manner.

Incidentally, handicapped children are statistically overrepresented in the population of youngsters with behaviour problems; but there is good reason to believe that if such children can be helped to become more competent, and if they are not excepted from the 'rigours' of socialization out of misplaced pity, they might have less recourse to problem behaviour. Seligman says of the earliest caregiver–infant interactions:

> The infant begins a dance with his environment that will last throughout childhood ... it is the outcome of this dance that determines his helplessness or mastery. When he makes some response, it can either produce a change in the environment or be independent of what changes occur. At some primitive level, the infant calculates the correlation between response and outcome. If the correlation is zero, helplessness develops. If the correlation is positive the response is working, the infant learns either to perform that response more frequently or to refrain from performing it, depending on whether the correlated outcome is good or bad. But over and above this, he learns that responding works, that in general there is synchrony between responses and outcomes. When there is no synchrony and he is helpless, he stops performing the response, and further, he learns that in general responding doesn't matter. Such learning has the same consequences that helplessness has in adults: lack of response initiation, negative cognitive set, and anxiety and depression. But this may be more disastrous for the infant since it is foundational: it is at the base of his pyramid of emotional and motivational structures. (Seligman, 1975)

To take an example from day-to-day child care of how sensitive parenting facilitates the youngster's development, it has been shown that maternal speech occurring in the context of joint attention to pictures and books is particularly rich in those features thought to be important in rapid language development. In such a situation the mother's speech is likely to be especially closely tied to the child's interests and to what he or she is trying to communicate, and the extent to which such situations occur in the daily lives of mothers and children may well have considerable implications for the child's mastery of linguistic skills (see Lock and Fisher, 1984).

The father's role in child care

We frequently take the role of mothers in child care (to their extreme annoyance) for granted; but what of fathers? Women, it is often claimed, are biologically pre-adapted for child care in a psychological as well as physical sense, with the consequence that their responsiveness and attachment to their offspring are greater than these attributes in men. Recent work on early paternal sensitivity to children has employed scientific procedures in order to examine relevant areas in detail (see Lamb, 1981; Lamb, Pleck and Levine, 1985; Lewis, 1986; for reviews of the evidence).

Researchers have been keen to see whether babies trigger the same responsiveness in males and females. They usually show men and women films of babies crying and measure their psychophysiological responsiveness, in terms of heart rate, blood pressure and skin conductance. In general men and women appear to react in similar ways.

Researchers have also examined the ways in which parents greet their newborns, since in many species parental behaviour is programmed to protect neonates and enhance responsive behaviour toward the young. Studies show few differences between parents in the ways they greet their new children. Mothers and fathers alike, also tend to exhibit stereotypical patterns of handling their young, starting with the trunk and proceeding to their limbs and faces (Schaffer and Collis, 1986).

The popular notion that maternal care is under the control of hormonal mechanisms that are triggered by the process of birth (and therefore not operative in men) receives no support once one also takes into account the effects of different kinds of socialization pressure on males and females. Indeed, studies provide little evidence that mothers are more responsive than fathers during the period following birth. It is therefore unlikely that hormonal factors, on their own, can in some simple mechanical fashion account for variations in responsiveness. The evidence suggests that cultural factors are more important in producing those differences that do exist between males and females than are hormonal factors (Herbert and Sluckin, 1986).

Of all the factors listed by Staub (1975) in his review of the development of prosocial behaviour, the establishment of responsive, sensitive parenting fuelled by an affectional bond between parent and child is perhaps the most critical foundation on which all social training is based (see also Hoffman, 1970). Rejection of the child, for whatever reason and at whatever level, is therefore likely to have far-reaching and harmful effects. The factors which make for a 'loving' or a 'good enough' parent do not lend themselves easily to objective assessment, a circumstance which can bring little comfort to the psychologist whose opinion is sought in a case involving a care order or the breakdown of a fostering arrangement.

ASSESSMENT CRITERIA OF ATTACHMENT

Parental love (for example) is inferred by the 'person-in-the-street' from particular aspects of maternal or parental behaviour such as fond gazing, cooing and other vocalizations, smiling, touching and fondling the infant. And, of course, it is judged by many other such actions. Unfortunately, from the clinician's or researcher's point of view, these activities do not have a necessary or sufficient link with the concept of a specific emotional bond. Most normal women (for example) have a predilection to smile, touch and tickle other people's babies and speak to them in an 'odd' manner, when they come into contact with them. They do this naturally and in spite of the fact that they are in no sense tied to them (Stern, 1977).

A more focused criterion might be the mother's own report of her feelings towards her child. Thus, she might be thought to be attached to her child if she consistently, over a number of months and years, reports that she loves her child. The clinician would also be impressed — perhaps more impressed — by her deeds and would assess attachment in terms of her actions. By this token a mother would be considered to be 'bonded' to her child if she looked after it well, gave it much attention, and showed affection for it in the form of 'fondling, kissing, cuddling, and prolonged gazing' (Klaus and Kennell, 1976). Thus we have come nearly full circle.

Even caring, nurturant activities (say, by a good foster mother or nurse) need not imply a loving bond as such; it might reflect a creditable professional attitude only. Even if we decide to use several of the action-indices of attachment, they are not always easy to quantify; they are dependent to some degree upon the clinician's interpretations of observed behaviour. Most deal simply with the amounts of physical contact with the baby (a feature of the bonding literature) and it is by no means self-evident that this has got anything to do with specific bonding. Appropriate scales of attachment should be helpful, but would such a scale of attachment yield a global measure of bonding, rather like a composite I.Q. score?

Dunn and Richards (1977) conducted a longitudinal investigation of 77 mother–child pairs (from birth to five years) to see if a number of categories of behaviours that have been used as indices of affection did indeed intercorrelate. Correlations between measures were not high and they were unable to demonstrate a unitary attribute reflecting 'warm' mothering. The analysis of early feeding interactions indicated that measures of maternal affectionate behaviour do not co-vary in any simple way. The different facets of maternal style are associated with different infant and delivery factors; success and coordination of the feed, for instance, are affected by labour and delivery variables. Total sucking, another example, is correlated with differences in the infant's reactivity (latency to cry on removal of teat) and not with the measurement of affectionate style and contact. Touching the baby — often used as an index of maternal feeling — did not correlate with the other measures of maternal 'affection'. A complicating factor in the attempt to verify attachment as a characteristic of the mother alone, was the finding that the baby was a vital contributor to the early differences in mother–child interaction.

It takes two to form a relationship. We are dealing with an 'attachment system' — an interacting couple — not simply a mother's feelings or a baby's feelings. Both must be considered in arriving at an assessment of attachment. Dunn (1975) demonstrated the significance of the child's role in the formation of bonds. She found continuities over time in her longitudinal study of mothers and infants (70 pairs) which she concludes are best described in terms of interactional styles rather than of exclusively maternal behaviour. It was not possible to assume that a correlation between measures of maternal responsiveness was independent of infant characteristics.

Sequences of mother–child/father–child interactive behaviours are likely to provide a better measure of the parent–infant relationship than a one-sided account; both mother and child are active concurrently, each for part of the time; the 'good' mother is *responsive* to her baby and continues to respond until it is satisfied; she also *initiates* activities. The notion of a dialogue (or 'conversation') between two individuals has been used as an indicator of the quality of attachments, and gives rise to a definition of 'good' relationships expressed in terms of the reciprocity of interactions between the partners.

According to Klaus and Kennell (1976) the intimate mother–infant contact in the post partum 'sensitive period' gives rise to a host of innate behaviours; in their own words, 'a cascade of reciprocal interactions begins between mother and baby (which) locks them together and mediates the further development of attachment'.

In the case of infant-to-mother attachment, Ainsworth (1969), on the basis of extensive studies, recommends the use of multiple criteria to describe the way in which such behaviour is organized and manifested. Surely it would be logical to require as much sophistication in quantifying such mature human behaviour as mother-to-child or father-to-child attachment in clinical child psychology practice.

Twins

Bearing in mind the strength and flexibility of mother love it should make no difference to the mother's feelings towards each child whether she gives birth to a singleton or twins or triplets. However, one must remember that in the case of multiple births the babies are often premature and underweight at birth, and need very special attention, if not special care, during their first few weeks. Even in the case of a normal delivery, one of the babies may be more vulnerable than the other. It could be argued that in multiple births synchrony is more difficult to achieve as the mother may be too exhausted physically and emotionally to adapt herself to the rhythms of two or more babies. Since the advent of fertility drugs, multiple births have become somewhat more common and many of these mothers tend to be older.

Certainly, problems can arise if a mother finds herself spending more time initially with the weakly baby. She may experience a sense of guilt and may blame herself for not giving each an equal amount of attention, thinking that this may adversely affect present and subsequent relationships.

CHILD-TO-PARENT ATTACHMENT (see Ainsworth, 1970)

In the development of attachments, the entire first year of life is a crucial one. Within 12 months, almost all babies have developed strong ties with the mother, or a mother-figure. Bowlby (1969) sees attachment behaviour as the operation of an internal control system. The child is biologically predisposed to form attachments. It could be said that he or she is biased to respond to social situations; almost every baby enjoys human company. Babies display social forms of behaviour (e.g., smiling, crying, clinging, and so on) from the beginning of their existence, up to and beyond the point in time that they make focused attachments to parental figures.

The human face in movement, for example, 'triggers' a smile in young babies. Even in the first days of life, as Bowlby points out, a baby is soothed and quietened by social contact — being caressed, rocked, talked to, or just picked up. A baby attracts and keeps his or her parents' attention by crying, smiling, babbling and laughing. And the more attention they get, the more they babble and smile. They respond to people even though they can't discriminate one from another. If anyone approaches, they change their position, track them with their eyes, grasp a finger, reach out, and stop crying when they catch sight of a face or hear a voice. The rate of emission of smiling behaviour in infants can be increased by reinforcing it with social contact (Brackbill, 1958). All these kinds of interaction encourage attachment.

What is new when a child becomes attached, in Bowlby's account, is not the display of new forms of behaviour or new intensities of social responses, but a pattern of organization of these responses in relation to one significant person. Virtually all the elements in the child's behaviour repertoire become capable of being functionally linked to a controlling system or plan which is hierarchical in its organization and target-seeking in its effect. The 'target' is defined as the maintenance of proximity to mother (or father), and the hierarchical nature of the organization is revealed in the fact that a particular response can serve a number of different functions in maintaining this proximity.

Bowlby's conceptualization of attachment seems to offer the clinician fruitful ways of looking clinically at attachment; it stresses such features of attachment as its goal-seeking qualities, the way in which almost any behaviour can be enlisted in its service, and the fact that behaviours compensate each other and can be alternative routes to the same goal. It suggests new ways in which attachment systems can be compared. Instead of thinking of children as simply being more or less attached ('dependent'), their attachment systems can be compared according to the nature of the favoured strategies they employ, how strongly they are established, the degree of elaboration of alternative strategies, and the nature of their setting, i.e., the closeness of the proximity they are set to maintain (see Chapter 10).

INSECURE BEHAVIOUR IN INFANTS

The longer term implications of attachment have been investigated in laboratory situations in which infants (usually under 18 months) and their parents enter a strange room with toys in it. The infant is observed (often using video) with a parent, then with a stranger, and finally when the parent leaves the room and returns (Ainsworth et al., 1978; Lee, Wright and Herbert, 1972). Some are secure in this. Other infants show extreme distress when (say) their mothers return after the brief separation, and cling to them but are inconsolable. These babies are said to demonstrate 'anxious or insecure attachment'. Others ignore mother on her return and react to her no differently than to the stranger. They are described as displaying 'avoidant attachment behaviour'. There are other subgroups, particularly one in which infants display both heightened avoidance of the mother when reunited with her as well as heightened resistance. Crittendon (1988) has shown that these infants can be judged erroneously as 'secure'. What is of particular interest about them is that they are disproportionately likely to have been abused and/or neglected.

Two investigations (Erickson, Sroufe and Egeland, 1985; Lewis *et al.*, 1984) have established a clear link between early insecure attachments and later development of behaviour problems, bringing attachment research into the domain of the clinic. It is hypothesized that many 'conduct problems are strategies for gaining the attention or proximity of caregivers who are unresponsive to the child's pro-social communications' (Greenberg and Speltz, 1988). This is a theme we shall return to in Chapter 16.

It is important to remember that the patterns of behaviour described above do not necessarily persist and they are not necessarily indicators of a serious rift in the relationship between parent and child. However, they are worthy of following up in an assessment.

BEHAVIOURAL PROBLEMS FOLLOWING DISRUPTION OF ATTACHMENTS

Not surprisingly, much attention has been paid by researchers over the years to the subject of parental (and in the research literature this usually means maternal) separation or deprivation (see Rutter, 1981a, for a review). What we now know is that the effects of early maternal separation are not always predictable, and certainly not necessarily (as was once thought), permanent (e.g., Hellman, 1962). Each and every separation is a unique, complex and many-sided matter, requiring painstaking analysis. The outcome is heavily dependent on the substitute care and support — their quality and continuity — that are available (Herbert, 1988).

In an institution, the child commonly suffers other kinds of deprivation which add to the burden of his or her grief over a separation. Frequently a shortage of residential staff means that the intensive care required by each child cannot be given. And the rapid turnover of staff means that children's experiences of separation are repeated over and over again until they cannot trust themselves (or adults) to make the emotional commitments most people take for granted.

DIVORCE/SEPARATION

Studies of the effects of separation, though they tend to support the assumption of an increased risk of later disturbance, raise a number of problems. It is difficult to isolate the effects of separation from other adverse side-effects. To what extent are the ill-effects of a child's experience of separation (brought about by, say, a divorce) the result of the discord between his or her parents, or the disruption of bonds, or both? The highest risk or likelihood of a divorce (at present) occurs in the fourth year of marriage. In other words, it is very likely to be *young* children who are involved in the lead-up to, and aftermath of a divorce. Separation — the event that really hits children — is likely to precede divorce by several years.

It is often said that children hold themselves responsible for the break-up of their parents' marriage and feel very guilty about this. In fact such reactions do not seem to be very widespread; much more common is anger towards the parents for separating. Children of all ages frequently express the wish that their parents be reunited, and they blame either, or both, of them for the breakup (Hetherington, 1979; Richards and Dyson, 1982).

Most children do not want their parents to separate and they may feel that their father and mother have not taken *their* interests into account. A marital separation may result in children reappraising their own relationships with their parents and, indeed, questioning the nature of all social relationships. For younger children in particular, there is the painful realization that social relationships do not last forever. Preschool children usually appear to be very sad and frightened when their parents separate, and they become clinging and demanding. Bedtime fears and a refusal to be left alone, even for a few minutes, are not uncommon. Children attending school or nursery may become very anxious about going there, and may protest strongly when left. Vivid fantasies about abandonment, death of parents, and similar themes, are encountered. Such children often express aggression towards other children.

Many childish reactions at such a time are expressions of the child's fear of being abandoned by one or both parents. Such fears are likely to be most acute if contact has been lost with a parent. If, however, relationships between parents and child can remain intact and supportive, these fears are usually short-lived (Richards and Dyson, 1982).

With somewhat older children, grief and sadness remain a prominent feature but anger becomes more marked. This is usually directed at the parents, especially the one with whom the child is living — which more often than not means the mother.

These are the immediate reactions to parental separation. Usually they are seen in an acute form for a matter of months and then (hopefully) begin to subside. Unfortunately, the evidence concerning long-term consequences is very meagre and difficult to evaluate. Researchers have found that those people who experience a broken home in childhood have only a slightly higher risk of developing psychiatric problems compared with those from unbroken homes. For those from a comfortable economic background, there is no difference at all in the risk factor (Herbert, 1974).

There is a close relationship between fatherlessness and poverty, and many of the unfavourable consequences of deprivation of a father are primarily the consequences of financial difficulties. Many worries may deplete the last emotional resources of the mother left alone. Young children need special attention and care, but she may have to seek employment and finding substitute caregivers can be expensive. Housing, too, is a common and costly problem.

From the professional's point of view, if called on to work with a disintegrating family, it is vital to appreciate how an atmosphere of strife and turmoil in the home, prior to separation, is one of the most corrosive of influences. This quarrelling is something that children describe as very damaging — especially episodes of hostility between mother and father.

Of the factors that are significant to a benign outcome for children — after all the misery of divorce — three are of the utmost significance:

- Communication about separation.
- Continued good relationship with at least one parent.
- Satisfaction with custody and access arrangements.

Children who consider themselves most damaged are:

- Those whose parents are not able to talk to them about divorce (apart from blaming their ex-spouse).
- Those who do not get on well with at least one parent after separation.
- Those who are dissatisfied with custody and access arrangements, whatever these happen to be.

Most children would like two happily married parents, but most would prefer to live with a single parent rather than two unhappily married ones. It is a natural wish on the part of workers to keep parents and children together; but there are times when 'heroic' work to maintain an intact family is counter to the best interests of all concerned.

RESILIENCE AND VULNERABILITY

We have examined various influences that have a bearing on the quality of an infant's life in the here-and-now and on the direction of his or her development over a relatively short period of time. But what of the longer term? Who copes and who 'goes under' when adverse circumstances prevail? Werner and Smith (1977) conducted a longitudinal study over a 30-year period of an infant cohort born on the island of Kauai, Hawaii. The cohort was characterized by high levels of perinatal stress, poverty, family instability, low parental education, and parental psychopathology in some cases. The researchers compared a group of resilient children with non-resilient peers. They found that resilient children were rated in infancy and childhood as being more active, socially responsive, and autonomous than the non-resilient youngsters. The family environment of the resilient children was characterized by parental support, family closeness, rule setting, discipline, and a respect for individuality. Thus, a positive social orientation, a positive personal disposition, and a positive family environment were related to resilience in the face of stress. Factors that increased vulnerability included late birth order, poor integrity of the central nervous system, prolonged mother–infant separation, repeated childhood health problems, family and parental discord, a high cumulative number of stressful life events, and low parental intelligence.

Werner and Smith reported that, amongst the stress factors that were associated with serious learning and/or behaviour problems in childhood, family disruptions (e.g., prolonged absence of the father, the departure of an older sibling from home, death of a sibling, and replacement of the natural father by a stepfather (following divorce), marital discord, maternal mental health problems, and low social class were the most salient. Early predictors of serious coping problems in the short and longer term included a low level of maternal education, poor living standards, family instability, low levels of maternal psychological functioning, moderate-to-severe perinatal stress, congenital defects, a significant physical handicap, poor intellectual ability, and negative temperamental characteristics during infancy (i.e., very low or high activity level and low social responsiveness).

Garmezy and colleague (Garmezy, 1987; Garmezy, Masten and Tellegen, 1984), using parent, teacher, peer, and clinical ratings to study resilience and competence, found that the influence of stress on competence varied as a function of sex, intelligence, family attributes, as well as the criterion of competence. Disadvantaged children, characterized by low social status, low intelligence, and less positive family attributes, were less competent and were more likely to be disruptive at high stress levels. Boys were less socially competent than girls, and at high stress levels were less likely to be protected by positive family attributes.

Despite burgeoning research in this area, causal relations have been difficult to specify precisely because most studies are correlational in nature, and because of the shortage of adequate prospective studies. Most life stress research has been univariate in nature, with little concern for interactional or transactional processes. The use of multivariate analytic techniques by Garmezy, Masten and Tellegen (1984) generated three generic models. They take the form of regression equations, which vary in the extent to which stress and personal attributes predict quality of adaptation or competence. A 'compensatory' model suggests that personal qualities can compensate for severe stress. Hence, as stress levels increase, so can the manifestation of a protective personal attribute. This model is best summarized by the familiar simple linear multiple regression model. A 'challenge' model suggests that stress is a potential enhancer of competence, provided that stress levels are not too excessive. This model is reflected in a curvilinear relationship between stress and competence. An 'immunity-versus-vulnerability' model suggests an interactional relationship between stress, personal attributes and competence. The presence of protective personal attributes may lead to a weakened influence of stress on competence. On the other hand, the presence of personal vulnerability may lead to a strengthened influence of stress on competence. Alternatively, a personal attribute may become more or less salient under increasing stress levels. The three models are not mutually exclusive, and may be combined.

Chapter 7

Problems Associated with Early Childhood (The preschool period from 18 months to about 5 years)

The major developmental task during this period is hypothesized by Erikson (1965) to be the achievement of 'initiative': vigorous reality testing, imagination, and imitation of adult behaviour.

The psychoanalytic (Freudian) concept of identification, in which the child 'incorporates' his or her parents as an ego-ideal, finds a close parallel with an increase in the child's global 'imitation' of the parent followed by more selective attention to 'good' and 'role-appropriate' attributes (Lee and Herbert, 1970). In the Freudian canon the resolution of the Oedipus complex brings in its wake the formation of the super-ego, establishing both the child's sex-role identification and his or her moral standards. These events are thought to occur around the age of five.

Kohlberg's account is similar in its timing (Kohlberg, 1976; 1978). In the case of cognitive developmental theory, however, identification is not a fixed, rigid personality structure which depends on a specified relationship with the parents. Kohlberg suggests that children's behaviour is motivated by an intrinsic need for mastering the environment; adult approval for their behaviour is an indication that a satisfactory level of competence has been reached. Children seek and are increasingly dependent on adult approval. Kohlberg (1978) states that:

> ... it is more correct to say that the child wants to secure rewards or approval as a sign that he has performed the task competently rather than to say that the child wants to perform competently in order to obtain situational rewards and approval.

Before the age of two, children largely fail to differentiate what *they* do, from what an *adult* does, in other words causal agency. The cognitive development of the ability to differentiate between 'self' and 'other' leads to a recognition of causal relationships transforming, in turn, the assimilation of the interesting into a desire for control over things and people. It is suggested that this differentiation and motivation constitute the prerequisites of the perception and imitation of modelled behaviour. When the adult does something interesting, children want to see if they can do it too.

THE NEGATIVISTIC CRISIS

This increasing awareness of self-identity typically leads to a 'negativistic crisis' around the age of 2 — the 'terrible twos'. Children who have previously accepted assistance in their efforts without fuss insist on doing things themselves and displaying their own competence; they also resist parental requests and commands.

Patterson (1975) states that by the age of 2 most toddlers have advanced to the point of possessing an important range of verbal and motor strategies to replace their more coercive responses of former times (crying and screaming). He traces the developmental history of coercive behaviours. They display a steady decline in performance rates from a high point in infancy down to more moderate levels at the age of school entrance. The highest rates of negativistic-disruptive behaviours occur before the age of 3; 2- and 3-year-olds display high rates of whining, crying, yelling, and high frequency behaviours, as well as high rates for most other coercive actions. By the age of 4, there are substantial reductions in negative commands, destruction, and attempts to humiliate. By the age of 5, most children used less negativism, non-compliance, and negative physical actions than younger siblings (Reynolds, 1982). Hartup (1974) also notes a significant decrease in aggression from the ages of 4 through to 8 in his study of classroom behaviour. The 'aggressive' boy or girl — identified as 'problematic' — displays coercive behaviours at a level commensurate with a 3- to 4-year-old child and in this sense are exemplars of arrested socialization (Patterson, 1975). With increasing age, certain coercive behaviours are no longer acceptable to parents. The behaviours then become the target for careful monitoring and punishment which in turn is accompanied by reductions in their rate.

NON-COMPLIANCE AND TEMPER TANTRUMS

The display of non-compliant behaviour is often associated with temper tantrums and aggression. The origin and development of oppositional behaviour in children has been the subject of considerable theoretical speculation. Patterson (1982) suggests that oppositional behaviour is a learned 'coercive' strategy by means of which the child exerts control over parental behaviour. The oppositional child if commanded by an adult in authority is quite likely to react with rage — a frightening display of temper. The parent insists, so the child escalates the aggravation. A vicious circle can be set in motion. If the tantrum is intense or persistent enough, the parent or teacher may concede to the child. Giving in to the child's non-compliance tends not to occur on every occasion, producing what is, in effect, an intermittent schedule of reinforcement for coercive, non-compliant actions. The parent's capitulation is also reinforced by the termination of the child's tantrum. This process of reciprocal reinforcement by the removal of aversive stimuli has been described as the 'negative reinforcer trap' (Wahler, 1969). The implications of this theory for practice are discussed in Chapters 10 and 16.

CONFORMITY AND IMITATION

As children approach 5 years, and become increasingly aware of the relativity of competence and their own limitations, imitation and conformity to suggestion or instruction increases, adults being selected for imitation apparently on some generalized notion of power usually associated with physical size. After 5 there is a decline in the amount of imitation which bears witness to a child's increasing differentiation of aspects of the adult's behaviour. 'Good' and 'skilful' behaviour is selected, showing a movement away from physical to psychological notions of relative competence.

The increasing ability to abstract aspects of behaviour and, in particular, to abstract 'role-appropriate' behaviour, is related to changes in interaction with the parents. The child is made aware that there is something beyond conformity to the parents' wishes; that the parents themselves conform to a set of rules which are not embodied in the actions of any one person. At this stage children become capable of acting and assessing their own competence in relation to principles of 'good' and 'right'.

A major hazard at this stage of development is thought to be overly strict discipline and the concomitant internalization of rigid ethical attitudes which interfere with the child's spontaneity and reality testing, and lead to excessive guilt (Erikson, 1965). Guilt is but one of several facets of moral behaviour. It is the emotional discomfort or remorse we ascribe to our consciences when we have transgressed the rules. Prior to the present stage of development the child has certainly felt 'bad' when he or she has transgressed, but primarily because of fears of external parental punishment or disapproval. Now, at about 4 or 5 years of age, the locus of anxiety or fear comes from within and the child feels guilt when he or she has transgressed. Hoffman (1970) observes that:

> ... the guiding concept in most moral development research is the internalization of socially sanctioned prohibitions and mandates. One of the legacies of Freud, and the sociologist Durkheim as well, is the assumption now prevalent among social scientists that the individual does not go through life viewing society's central norms as externally and coercively imposed pressures to which he must submit. Though the norms are initially alien, they are eventually adopted by the individual, largely through the efforts of his early socializers — the parents — and come to serve as internalized guides so that he behaves in accord with them even when external authority is not present to enforce them. That is, control by others is replaced by self-control.

Over- and under-socialized behaviour

In a clinical context children are sometimes referred to as being 'over-' or 'under-socialized' in their style of behaviour. Reasonable conformity (contrasted with slavish or blind conformity) enables the child to learn the patterns of prosocial behaviour that will guarantee social acceptance, which in turn leads to good personal and social adjustments (Herbert, 1974). Nonconformity, on the other hand, is as prejudicial to good adjustment as extreme conformity. The child who refuses to conform to the accepted standards of the group is likely to find himself or herself a social outcast. This is serious for social development because he or she is deprived of the satisfactions of belonging to a group and of the learning experiences which come from a sense of belonging and the feelings that go with comradeship.

A sometimes precarious balance is required by society — a balance which is often difficult to perceive, and difficult to achieve for the child. It is difficult enough for adults. In a series of experiments carried out by Asch, he found evidence that adult human subjects conformed to a judgement that they knew was contrary to fact, contrary to what they perceived, or both (Asch, 1956). Children, also, bend to these group pressures or feel anxious when they try to resist them (Berenda, 1950).

THE DEVELOPMENT OF CONSCIENCE

Hoffman (1970) makes the point that all disciplinary encounters that contribute to social and moral development have a great deal in common, regardless of the specific techniques used. The techniques have three components, one or the other of which may predominate:

Power assertion

Hoffman contends that the most reliable finding in the parent–child area of research is the negative relationship between power assertion and various indices of moral behaviour. It holds up for both sexes and the entire age range of childhood.

Love withdrawal

Anxiety about threatened withdrawal of parental love or approval is not (according to the evidence which runs counter to 'received wisdom') the major contributing factor to the child's internalization of parental values. However, there is evidence that love withdrawal may contribute to the inhibition of anger (Hoffman and Saltzstein, 1967). It produces anxiety which leads to the renunciation of hostile and possibly other impulses. While it may contribute to making the child more susceptible to adult influence, this does not necessarily have a bearing (in Hoffman's view) on moral development (i.e., guilt and internal moral judgement).

Induction

This is the type of discipline which is most conducive to moral development; it involves pointing out the effects of the child's behaviour, giving reasons and explanations. (The cognitive structuring of wrong acts is elaborated on page 180.)

Learning theorists (e.g., Mowrer, 1960a,b) base their investigations of conscience-development upon the assumption that there is nothing about moral learning to distinguish it qualitatively from other forms of learning. Principles which derive from the study of anxiety conditioning on the one hand, and instrumental learning on the other, are used to explain resistance to temptation (see page 181). Learning theorists consider that behaviours indicative of guilt such as confession, self-criticism and apology, are learned responses which have been found to be instrumental in reducing post-transgression anxiety. Within the theory, there is no basis for differentiating punishment and reward mediated by *human agents* from those which are the impersonal consequences of behaviour. Yet it appears that the nature of the reinforcing agent, and of the individual's relationship to this agent, are crucial factors in moral development. Additional principles like imitation (Bandura and Walters, 1963) and identification (Kagan, 1958a) as we saw earlier, have been introduced.

OVER-CONTROLLED BEHAVIOUR

It is a fairly reliable generalization that punishment leads to self-control only when children are on the side of the person doing the punishing. Since they love their parents the children are on their side. Because of this identification they join in with the parental disapproval of the behaviour. Although such attachment is a condition which makes the development of conscience possible, it also gives parents a power which can be detrimental to the child. And this brings us to one of the problems of oversocialization. If children are strongly and exclusively attached to parents who set impossibly high standards and are deeply 'hurt' when their offspring fail to live up to them, it is quite likely that they will acquire a sense of conscience so severe and restrictive that their spontaneity and emotional life will be crippled, and much of their creative energy remain unused (Wright, 1971).

The risk comes particularly from authoritarian, restrictive parenting (Baumrind, 1966). Authoritarian parents attempt to shape, control and judge the behaviour and attitudes of their children according to unbending standards of conduct, usually absolute standards, often determined by theological considerations (Baumrind, 1966). Such parents value obedience for obedience's sake, in other words as a virtue; they favour punitive, forceful measures to curb self-will at those points where the child's actions or beliefs conflict with what they think is proper conduct. Children should be indoctrinated with such values as respect for authority, respect for work, and respect for the preservation of traditional order. They do not encourage verbal give and take, believing that the child should accept unquestioningly that *they* know best. Kagan and Moss (1962) have demonstrated that maternal restrictiveness with older boys is associated with high levels of aggression but this does not hold for young boys or for girls. In the case of paternal punishment, Eron *et al.* (1963) have shown that the consequences depend on their occupational level. Punitive fathers with high-status appear to be much more likely to have aggressive sons than low-status punitive fathers.

REALITY TESTING

The preschool and early school years of 4 to 7 coincide with a phase of 'intuitive thinking' (Piaget, 1953), during which children wrestle with problems regarding the interpretation of the environment. They are using language (as we saw on page 112) in a more complex and subtle manner. The parents transmit to the child the essential adaptive techniques of the culture including this uniquely human one of language. Youngsters learn the basics of communication — language and logic — at their mother's and father's knees. That is to say, children obtain their fundamental training in 'consensual meanings' — the concepts and symbols used by society, the generally accepted meanings of words, nuances of expression such as emotional gestures and glances, and other forms of communication — within the family. A great deal is at stake as we saw above.

The child is intuitive about relationships because he or she cannot give reasons for them. He or she is still without true concepts. There are still many limitations to his or her development of logical thinking, consistent explanations and coherent arguments. He or she is susceptible to conflict and confusion caused by the illogicality of communications from parents who are irrational in their thinking and behaviour. The child is also vulnerable, in a stage of intense imitation and identification, if parents are indifferent or hostile to their children, thereby creating poor 'models'.

Lidz (1968) observes that interference with children's attempts to satisfy their curiosity by exploring their world and by trying to find solutions to problems can retard the development of language. Discouragement of the free play of discussion also impedes development. Lidz has this to say about the child's reality testing:

> ... the child's trust in language — and what can be conveyed verbally and what responses his words will elicit — develops in the home setting. Here he learns how effective words will be: whether they concur with the unspoken communications; whether they are apt to match the feelings that accompany them; whether they subserve problem solving or are just as often a means of masking the existence of problems. The child's trust in verbal communication depends upon whether the words of the persons who are essential to him help solve problems or confuse, whether they prove more consistent signals than nonverbal cues, and whether the child's use of words can evoke desired responses. Difficulty can arise when parents' words contradict their nonverbal signals, as, for example, when the mother's words of affection are accompanied by irritable and hostile handling of the child; or when the mother's instructions for the child to obey his grandmother are accompanied by her obvious delight when the child disobeys and becomes a nuisance to the grandmother. The value of words is diluted or negated when erroneous solutions are habitually imposed, and when the child who cries because he wants attention is told that he is hungry and is fed. Predictive values of communication are undermined when promises rarely materialize.

DECENTRING

There is reason to think with regard to social development, that the end of the phase we are considering — approximately 5 years of age — is something of a watershed. After 5 there is a decline in the amount of imitation and a change in the child's interactions with his or her parents. According to Piaget (1953), the age of 5 to 7 marks the transition from preoperational thinking to operational thinking, and hence the decline in social as well as perceptual and cognitive 'egocentricity'. The child is being exposed to wider cultural influences through the mass media, visiting friends' homes and (perhaps) attending a playgroup or nursery school.

The number of friendly contacts between children becomes more pronounced between the ages of 2 and 5; attachments to friends and the peer group begin to evolve. During these years, the first friendships are generally, but not exclusively, with others of the same sex. Friendship patterns change dramatically with age. Between the ages of 2 and 5 the number of friends increases; after this age the development is towards closeness of attachment to a few special children.

In studies of nursery school children, affiliation is a predominant tendency of the little girls. They spend the greatest proportion of time in social interaction of one kind or another, while boys are more frequently engaged in some physical activity (running, chasing, etc.). The girls are also more cooperative especially with younger children. Hutt (1972) observes that these differences reflect the predominant tendency of the girls to perform a care-taking and protective role — aiding younger infants in carrying heavy objects, helping button pinafores or tie aprons, and so on.

Popular children can actually be distinguished as early as the nursery-school phase. The popular children are frequently sought out as playmates, while others are consistently avoided and shunned by their peers. The interactions of these preschool or nursery school children are more characteristically friendly and cooperative than hostile, competitive or unfriendly. The friendships at this age are casual, transient and unstable, and in the view of Mussen (1963) they probably have few important or enduring effects on a child's personality. The implications of friendlessness are much more serious when the child is older (see page 213). Sociometric devices are useful for assessing children's interactional and friendship patterns (Herbert, 1990).

PARENTAL PATHOLOGY

Rutter in his 1966 study found that, of children with neurotic and behaviour problems attending a child psychiatric clinic, one in five had a psychiatrically ill parent. This was three times the incidence found in the parents of a control group consisting of children attending a dental clinic. Also, the children under psychiatric treatment whose parents had a history of psychiatric disorder had more severe and extensive difficulties than other problem children at the same clinic. However, not all, by any means, of the children of mentally ill parents develop emotional problems; many grow up to be healthy adults. Nevertheless, children in this situation are at risk.

The problems of those members of families who are genetically predisposed to some psychiatric or psychosomatic disorder, or those who are recovering from illness or trauma, are mitigated when they can look to a cohesive family for support (Brown and Harris, 1978; Orford, 1980). Childhood problems are more likely to be associated with psychiatric illness in the mother than in the father. When both parents are psychiatrically disturbed, the child is particularly vulnerable as there is no one, except possibly brothers and sisters, to act as a buffer between himself or herself and the mental illness of his or her parents (Rutter, 1966).

The children of psychotic parents are less vulnerable than those with psychopathic parents. There is little relationship between the specific type of mental illness in the parent and the type of problem displayed by the child. What does seem to make children most susceptible is direct involvement in the mother's or father's symptoms. They are particularly at risk, for example, if the parent has delusions about the child, paranoid feelings, obsessional fears of harming them, morbid anxiety concerning their development, or hostile feelings towards them. Affective symptoms (that is to say, disturbed emotions such as hostility and depression) are particularly associated with the development of problems in the offspring (Rutter, 1966).

MATERNAL DEPRESSION

Puckering (1989), in a review of this important subject, highlights the 'alarmingly high' incidence of major depression among young women, reaching possibly 9%. The most vulnerable women are the non-working mothers of preschool children, among whom the rate can reach 40% (Brown and Harris, 1978; Richman, Stevenson and Graham, 1982). Rutter (1988) has collated evidence pointing up the association between parental mental disorder and children's cognitive (as well as emotional) development. The consequences for the child of maternal depression, in particular, depend on the age at which he or she is exposed to the disorder and, of course, the parenting style (e.g., availability of mother, her irritability, and the other difficulties that flow from fatigue and a depressed state of mind) (see Puckering, 1987).

Puckering (1989) concludes that those who work clinically with children should give careful consideration to depression in the parents 'and to seek points in the cycle which might have an impact'. As she puts it:

> There may be a necessity to treat maternal depression in tandem with tackling behavioural problems in the child, if either condition is to be relieved. Those who deal with depression in adults too must look beyond their immediate client, as problems with spouse, children and the community may have powers to undo whatever good work they can effect.

PARENTAL REJECTION

What is difficult for any child to cope with is palpable, ongoing parental rejection. Some fathers and mothers did not want the pregnancy in the first place; others may become rejecting for a variety of reasons: their babies are perceived as unresponsive or, indeed, in some of their attributes, quite 'unlovable' (Herbert and Iwaniec, 1977). The infant's mere presence may lead to disharmony between the mother and a pathologically jealous partner. In cases where there are serious child-management problems disagreements could give rise to the eventual disintegration of a marriage. Of course, rejection is not a *fixed* characteristic — feelings can and do change.

An understanding of 'affectionless' parents requires a more general understanding of so-called affectionless personalities in people who are described often as psychopathic personalities. It is quite likely that adults who are capable only of relating to other adults (spouses for example) in a superficial, exploitative and hostile manner, show similar relationships with their children (Gil, 1970).

There is certainly a relationship between child abuse and psychological disorder, notably the kind that involves alcohol abuse. This is significant on account of the facilitating, releasing effect of alcohol upon violence of all varieties, but in the case of a drunken parent, particularly the risk of attacks directed toward a convenient child victim.

The most popular theory of active, aggressive, paternal and maternal rejection, attributes the predisposition to neglect or abuse their offspring to experiences of a similar nature (or the absence of critical learning opportunities) in their own childhood: the so-called 'cycle of disadvantage' (Rutter and Madge, 1976). The modelling of violent behaviour by a parent or parents, the reinforcement by parents of the child's (and thus parent-to-be's) aggressive actions, are among the explanations put forward. For some, rejection means callous and indifferent neglect or positive hostility from the parents; but it may also be emotional and subtle (Iwaniec, Herbert and McNeish, 1985). Children come to believe that they are worthless, that their very existence makes their parents unhappy. The term 'emotional abuse' has been added to the concept of 'physical abuse'; more than any other category of abuse this area is beset with value judgements and subjective opinion (see Garbarino, 1978; 1988), which makes it difficult to assess.

EMOTIONAL ABUSE

Emotional abuse is 'signposted' by parental indifference. The child is ignored, there may be inadequate physical care, the child lacks stimulation, physical contact, security; he or she is thus denied emotional warmth and love and may not receive protection, support and discipline. Overall negative attitudes may lead to abusive threats, constant criticism and scapegoating. With older children this is sometimes accompanied by ridicule and denigrating all the child's efforts to please. Parents tend not only to neglect the child's need for nurturance, but also to punish manifestations of that need (Iwaniec, Herbert and Sluckin, 1988).

DAMAGE TO THE SELF-CONCEPT

The potential for harm of these parental attitudes and actions resides in large part in the sensitivity of this and earlier stages of life for the emergence of the self-concept (Ausubel and Sullivan, 1954). Between birth and the ages of about 2 or 3 there is no apparent evidence in infants of any *clearly defined* self awareness, whereas it is plainly discernible in the child of 4 or 5. Until this age, there is good reason to think that the child's own perception of his or her personal identity is unstable (Herbert, 1966). The role of the mother (and other important persons close at hand) by providing verbal input, warmth, comfort and nurturance, and relief from discomfort, helps the very young child to discriminate the qualities of objects and the significance and separateness of self and others. The child comes to see that its behaviour works (Seligman, 1975). The imposing of routine, predictability and thus meaning, on the infant's early experiences are of key importance in the process of self-awareness. The child develops an intense relationship to the responsive parent. Loevinger (1966) designates this later phase of infant ego-development as symbiotic. The damage that can be inflicted on an evolving self-image of a child by dereliction of parent responsibility is discussed in Chapter 12.

Chapter 8

Developmental Disorders

Now that psychologists are so involved with paediatric assessment clinics, general practice, and well baby clinics, they are required to assess and intervene in a wide variety of developmental problems. Particularly in the early preschool years, young children present a wide range of difficulties in sleeping, eating, and elimination. Delays in speech and language are likely to be brought to the notice of family doctors and are likely to be referred on for specialist help. By their very nature, many of such developmental difficulties disappear over time, but they can cause untold worry in the interim. And it is worse when the advice 'Just ignore it, it'll go away' or 'He'll grow out of it' proves to be incorrect. The ability to differentiate short- and long-term problems is crucial. In 1977 1.8 % of the school population of England and Wales was attending special schools or special classes designated as such by the local educational authorities. However, it is estimated that about 1 in 6 children of school age have a significant physical educational or psychological handicap, and most of these are educated in ordinary schools (Rutter, Tizard and Whitmore, 1970).

Developmental disorders are coded on Axis II in the DSM-III-R classification because some of them are chronic and may persist into adult life without remission. Their essential feature is a disturbance — general or specific — in the acquisition or retention of motor, language, cognitive or social skills. They include (inter alia):

- Elimination disorders (functional encopresis: code 307.70)
                  (functional enuresis: code 307.60).
- Developmental receptive language disorder: code 315.31.
- Developmental expressive language disorder: code 315.31.
- Pervasive developmental disorder (Autistic disorder: code 290.00).
- Speech disorders (not elsewhere classified) (elective mutism: code 313.23)
                      (stuttering: code 307.00).
- Gender identity disorders   code 302.60.

These problems of developmental deviation or delay are so called because they are an explicit application of a statistical paradigm. Large deviations from the norm are regarded as abnormal. The first problem we shall consider involves abnormal growth — a failure on the part of the child to thrive.

FAILURE-TO-THRIVE

Failure-to-thrive is described in the literature as a failure to grow and develop healthily and vigorously. The child's weight (inter alia) is significantly below the norms on developmental charts. Only a few decades ago, when growth began to be studied scientifically, was it realized that failure-to-thrive is not a clearcut disease but a symptom (or more accurately a syndrome) which has many causes; they include inadequate nutrition, malabsorption, chronic infection, major structural congenital abnormalities, metabolic and endocrine defects. However, there are some infants and young children who fail to thrive, in whom none of the above factors is obvious and whose present management and well-being is problematic.

A search of the literature on failure-to-thrive reveals a paucity of good studies (see Woolston, 1984). The term failure-to-thrive (once referred to as marasmus), has been applied to conditions caused by organic illness and those due (allegedly) to failure of the environment to provide appropriate nurturing, i.e., psychosocial causes. The more specific term 'non-organic failure-to-thrive' as a diagnosis becomes significant in the sort of society in which one can presume that food will be available to all its children, and where knowledge of paediatric disease and normal growth and development have become sufficiently precise to define the reasons for growth failure

The hypothesis of a psychological aetiology for the non-organic failure-to-thrive syndrome has its historical roots in the extensive literature on the effects of institutionalization (hospitalism) and 'maternal deprivation' in infants. The early descriptions of the failure-to-thrive syndrome (but by a different name) were those of Spitz (1945, 1946). The disorder of 'hospitalism' as Spitz termed it, occurred in institutionalized children in the first year of life, and the major manifestations involved emotional disturbance, failure to gain weight, and developmental retardation. The term 'anaclitic depression' was applied to the sad, bereaved and apathetic demeanour of these infants, one of extreme mourning and melancholia (see Bowlby, 1980; Freud, 1917). A significant aetiological factor according to Spitz, was the quality of maternal love and nurturance available to the infant; and, in particular, its discontinuation.

The early studies of failure-to-thrive were conducted in hospitals and institutions. The investigation of failure-to-thrive in the child's own home is a more recent phenomenon (e.g., Iwaniec, Herbert and McNeish, 1985). Of course it is taken for granted these days that a baby needs a close, confident and caring physical and emotional contact with the parent, be it mother (or mother surrogate), or father, in order to be healthy and develop vigorously. The absence of such continuing nurturance and physical intimacy can bring about anxiety in the child, fretting and disruption of biological functions.

Pollitt, Eichler and Chan, (1975) conducted a study to determine whether the mother of a failure-to-thrive child is likely to be psychologically 'maladapted', and whether she creates adverse environmental conditions that interfere with the child's physical growth and psychological development. Results of this detailed study of the economic, social, family, nutritional and medical causes of failure-to-thrive, based upon 38 mothers of children selected from an Outpatients Paediatric Clinic, indicated that the behaviour of the mothers of the failure-to-thrive group did not show overt psychopathology. Their pattern of stressful childhood experiences seemed to suggest that they would have a higher chance of becoming maladjusted during childhood and later life, yet (at least with regard to marital history and mental health) they did not differ from the controls. The largest between-groups statistical differences were found in the scores drawn from the mother–child interaction check-list. The mothers in the experimental group showed less frequent verbal and physical contacts with their children, were less positively reinforcing and warm. These differences in verbal interactions were noted on various socialization tasks. Substantial differences were also noted in maternal affection, described as 'inoperant' in many cases.

Pollitt and Eichler (1976) investigated the eating, sleeping, elimination, autoerotic and self-harming behaviours of 19 preschool failure-to-thrive children; their behaviour was compared with a group of 19 children growing normally for their chronological age. The most noticeable differences in behaviour between the two groups of children occurred in the area of eating. There was no difference in the incidence of problems when each of the behavioural areas was examined separately (sleeping, elimination, autoerotic and self-harming). However, a significant number of failure-to-thrive children presented more than one of the above problem behaviours.

Assessment

A summary of the main features of the non-organic, failure-to-thrive syndrome is provided in Figure 9.

Causation

It is notoriously difficult (not to say dangerous) to infer causal relationships from retrospective data, and from largely correlated antecedents. Correlations do not necessarily imply causation although they may be suggestive. One can speculate on the basis of findings carried out at the University of Leicester, on a series of 34 organic and non-organic failure-to-thrive children and their families (and a control group of normally developing ill children), that there are several routes to the failure-to-thrive disorder (Iwaniec, Herbert and McNeish, 1985). An original organic lesion may heal but the subsequent emotional overlay continues to disrupt eating, which in turn, affects the mother–child relationship because of the worry and conflict that ensues. Maternal resentment and ambivalence is, in a sense, secondary. Maternal rejection — when it is primary — is quite likely to be expressed in rough, hostile feeding patterns which lead to phobic avoidance (food aversion) on the part of the child. A child with aversive temperamental attributes is predisposed to biological irregularity and resistance to socialization. Here, too, may lie a precursor to fraught feeding situations, anxiety and

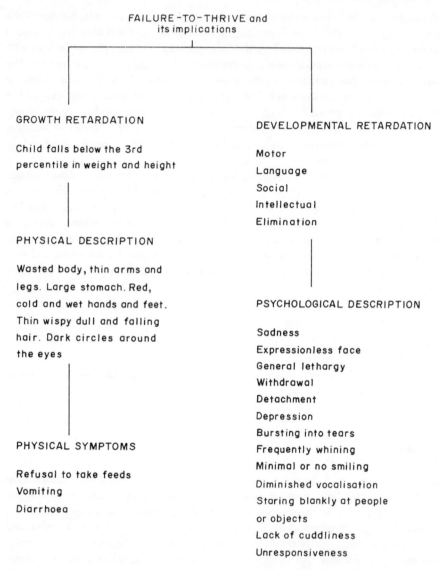

Figure 9. A summary picture of the main features of the nonorganic failure-to-thrive syndrome.

mutual hostility by mother and child. The point is that an acute feeding difficulty, no matter how it originates — for organic reasons, as a function of temperament, maternal hostility, etc. — will, if it persists over a considerable time, result not only in the child's poor growth and development but also (in some circumstances) distort, or more often, exacerbate the mother–child relationship.

Treatment

A method of treating failure-to-thrive children, based on the approach developed at the Leicester University Centre for Behavioural Work with Families, is detailed in Iwaniec, Herbert and McNeish (1985).

Bladder control

Wetting, a feature of all babies, becomes a 'problem' (or a potential problem) referred to as enuresis, at a cut-off point somewhere between 3 or 4 years of age. At this stage of development the estimated incidence of bedwetting is 10–15 % of that cohort (Baller, 1975). Daytime control of the bladder is established earlier than a 'dry bed'.

An important developmental task for the toddler (and one whose failure has been reported to lead to specific incidents of child abuse in some families) is the achievement of continence in toilet functions. The control of elimination means the inhibiting of processes which are, at first, completely involuntary. The baby's muscles must mature until they are strong enough and coordinated enough to hold back the waste products that are trying to emerge from his or her body. Of all the muscles in the trunk region, those which control the organs of elimination are the slowest to come under voluntary control. Children are expected to achieve satisfactory bladder control during the day by the time they start school. Parents and teachers may tolerate occasional lapses in the infant school but, thereafter, an incontinent child is likely to come under increasing social pressure. Bladder control comes somewhat later than bowel control.

There is, at the best of times, a wide (and normal) range of differences in the ages at which babies and toddlers develop control over their organs of elimination and communicate their needs. From birth onwards, children become dry for gradually increasing periods. At about 15 months they will point to wet pants and puddles. They may wake at night and cry to be changed. They usually have a word which is used for both urine and faeces. By between 18 months and 2 years of age most children report to mother when they have soiled themselves. Their vocabulary now distinguishes between urine and faeces. By two-and-a-half, about 90 % of girls and about 80 % of boys make known their need to urinate. By about 3 years of age, children commonly go to the toilet by themselves. The difficulty of the exercise in self-control depends on the child's degree of maturity when training begins. Once the child has had a dry night then we know that the necessary physical control mechanisms are present. After a month of completely dry nights it is fairly safe to assume that the maturational and training processes are complete. Delayed continence is one of the biggest problems encountered in mental handicap.

NOCTURNAL ENURESIS

Nocturnal enuresis is one of the commonest reasons for families seeking help from general practitioners and clinical child psychologists. The problem was referred to as early as the 16th century in 'The Boke of Chyldren' by Thomas Phaire, in a chapter with the delicate title 'Of pissing in the bedde'. Fortunately this ancient problem is very responsive to expert intervention today (Sluckin, 1989; Smith and Smith, 1987).

According to Baller (1975) nocturnal enuretics

(a) involuntarily wet the bed;
(b) show no evidence of urinary, organic pathology;
(c) are three and one half years of age or more;
(d) have simply continued the night time wetting habits of infancy ('primary enuresis') or have fallen into a pattern of bed-wetting ('secondary enuresis') that averages more than twice a week.

Morgan and Young (1972) say of enuresis that it is not only a source of embarrassment to the sufferer, often invoking ridicule or punishment, but it can place an intolerable burden upon intrafamilial relationships — especially in those large families living in overcrowded conditions, where several children may wet the bed. For the majority of enuretics, to be a bedwetter carries adverse emotional consequences, and they tend to exhibit some degree of reactive disturbance. They make the point that even when this is not apparently the case, enuresis imposes a limit on the child's choice of activities; few enuretics can happily go camping or stay with friends. In own-homes and residential establishments, the daily wash of bedlinen is unpleasant and onerous; all too often both natural parents and house-parents are forced into a fatalistic acceptance of enuresis as an inevitable correlate of child upbringing.

Prevalence

Nocturnal bedwetting (at least once a week) occurs in approximately 13 % or 14 % of five-year-old boys and girls respectively, 9 % or 7 % of 10-year-old boys and girls, 3 % or 2 % of 14-year-old boys and girls (Rutter, Tizard and Whitmore, 1970). The prevalence rate is 1 % to 2 % for youngsters over fifteen and adults. Enuresis is a very common occurrence amongst children in residential establishments, and many cases continue (if untreated) into late adolescence or even adulthood (Turner and Taylor, 1974). Daytime wetting (diurnal enuresis) is present in approximately one in ten nocturnal enuretics.

Assessment

This problem, when it represents a behavioural deficit is called 'primary enuresis'. The child has never gained control of nocturnal wetting. In 'secondary enuresis' he or she reverts to bedwetting after a period of being dry. The child's control may, anyway, have been tenuous at best. A period of stress may produce the regression; behaviours acquired under stress are particularly prone to break down under emotional strain. A further distinction can also be made between children who are 'regularly' and those who are 'intermittently' enuretic. In the latter case fluctuating control may point to a psychogenic aetiology. Some children wet the bed when under great pressure.

Causation

The origins of nocturnal enuresis would seem to be multifactorial. Enuresis may have its origins in faulty learning. Because the peak age range for the emergence of continence is between one-and-a-half and four-and-a-half years of age, it could be that there is a 'sensitive' period for the emergence of nighttime dryness. Harsh 'pressurizing' of the child or (conversely) complaisant neglect of training may lead to a failure of this development. Emotional problems are then superimposed when the child is made to feel acute shame at his or her 'babyish' ways. Only too often — a point made already — they have to endure punishment, scorn and ridicule at home and school. Among other contributory causal influences suggested (MacKeith, 1973; Smith and Smith, 1987) are urological and medical factors, deep sleep, small functional bladder capacity, genetics, maturation and developmental disorders, also a variety of psychological factors. As many as 10% of all cases of enuresis are the result of medical (physical) conditions, most commonly urinary tract infections. Approximately one in twenty female and one in fifty male enuretics have such an infection. Other uncommon physical causes are chronic renal or kidney disease, diabetes, tumours and seizures (Kolvin, MacKeith and Meadows, 1973). Such potentially important causes should make an expert physical examination a matter of routine.

Conscious modelling or imitation has been postulated as an explanation for the acquisition of diurnal continence. Children may learn appropriate behaviour by observing how other children ask to go to the toilet, adopt the correct position for urinating and arrange their clothing. Some children seem quite suddenly to become aware of the inappropriateness of their behaviour, especially when mocked by their peers. It is as if latent learning has occurred and performance awaits a final 'push' from the environment.

Treatment

Many physicians turn to medication to treat their enuretic patients. Their favourite drug is a tricyclic antidepressant, imipramine hydrochloride (Tofranil). Certainly, an increase in urinary control tends to occur in about 85% of cases in the first two weeks of treatment (Shaffer, 1973). But up to 95% relapse following the withdrawal of medication (e.g. Blackwell and Currah, 1973). More sure, but more bother, is the approach based on a training paradigm; treatment, in such cases, can be thought of as the teaching of new and more effective skills, more appropriate responses to stimuli.

The enuresis alarm

The enuresis alarm is intended to alleviate the problem of enuresis by creating an effective learning situation, on the assumption that whatever influences may have led to inadequate development or maintenance of bladder control, appropriate control may best be established through effective learning. Its use does not imply a parallel between the learning processes involved in treatment and the means by which bladder control is normally acquired.

In 1904, a German physician named Pfaundler devised an alarm system to alert nurses to wet beds in children's wards, and noticed that the children began to wet less as a result. The theory that awakening a child immediately he or she has begun to wet might have a therapeutic effect was put forward as long also as 1830 (Glicklich, 1951). However, it was in the 1930s that Mowrer and Mowrer (1938) provided the necessary impetus for the systematic treatment of enuresis by devising a special training pad which was placed under the child when he was tucked up in bed. The pad, when moistened (with urine) during the night, closed a circuit and rang a bell. It was arranged that when this happened, someone would wake the child, take him to the toilet, and change him. This 'conditioning' technique was very effective. The children were actually encouraged to drink water before going to bed as opposed to the old method of avoiding liquid.

The object of the alarm system is to train the enuretic to exercise in sleep exactly the same control over bladder function that he or she exercises during the day. The purpose is not, as is sometimes stated, to train the child to awaken easily to bladder pressure although this may occur during the training procedures. Once a stable conditioned response of inhibiting urination during sleep is established by means of the alarm, the buzzer is superfluous and the child reacts to bladder pressure like the normal person.

Effectiveness

The evidence for the superiority of the alarm method (with rates of remission between 80% and 90%) over no-treatment and other-treatment control procedures is well documented for nocturnal enuresis (Blackwell and Currah, 1973; Collins, 1973; Herbert and Iwaniec, 1981; Morgan, 1984). While Doleys' (1977) review of data based on over 600 subjects revealed an average relapse rate of 40%, nearly 60% of those returned to continence after booster sessions. A team from the Child Treatment Research Unit (now the Centre for Behavioural Work with Families) was able to demonstrate the effectiveness of the method in the difficult setting (dormitory living; many staff) of a community home (Jehu et al., 1977).

Despite the potential of these methods, it is common, in my experience, to meet professionals who are disillusioned because behavioural methods have not worked in such cases. Sometimes uncharitably, one suspects a lack of special skill or experience in the complainants, or a tendency to underrate the painstaking requirements of the assessment phase. Undoubtedly, the supervision of an enuresis alarm programme by parents (or staff of an institution) can be time-consuming. Many things can go wrong: problems of a technical nature, inconsistency on the part of the exhausted parents, insufficient expert monitoring of the programme; premature withdrawal of therapy and so on. Morgan (1984) in reviewing such problems, and counter-measures to relapse, acknowledges that professional supervision — adequate in both frequency and expertise — is a prerequisite of success.

The prediction of outcome

Much research has been conducted into the possibility that factors known prior to therapy might predict therapeutic outcome. A better prognosis has been reported for younger children and those with more frequent bedwetting by Gillison and Skinner (1958) among others. These reports have not been subsequently confirmed, age and frequency not emerging as prognostic factors in the studies of Turner, Young and Rachman (1970) and Young and Morgan (1973). The latter studies also found the sex of the patient to be irrelevant to outcome. Nor does intelligence appear to be relevant to outcome. Although Kolvin (1973) reports a superior response among primary enuretics, other investigators have reported similar results for both primary and secondary enuretics (Sacks and De Leon, 1973; Young and Morgan, 1973). In consequence of the above research findings, it is not considered that outcome can be predicted with any confidence from factors known at the outset of treatment.

In addition to specific learning processes involved in alarm treatment, there is evidence that impressive procedures and the expectation of being cured, may well contribute to treatment response in some unexplained manner (Peterson, Wright and Hanlon, 1969). This phenomenon is similar to the 'placebo' effect commonly observed in the use of some medical preparations. It does suggest, however, that careful and confident presentation and supervision of alarm treatment can reap dividends in terms of a 'non-specific' contribution to becoming dry.

In summary, alarm treatment of enuresis may be regarded as comprising the following components:

- The production by the alarm of (a) inhibition of urination and (b) waking, and the gradual association of these responses with bladder tension.
- The encouragement of these responses as alternatives to wetting when the bladder is full, by virtue of their different consequences.
- The establishment of bladder tension both as a stimulus for the production of these new responses, and as a signal that their performance may secure pleasant consequences while avoiding less pleasant ones.
- An increase in the quantity of urine which the bladder is capable of holding without emptying, many former enuretics thus becoming able to hold the entire night's output of urine without either wetting or waking.

The old cumbersome 2-mat systems for producing a sound (or vibration for deaf children) have been overtaken by the popular single-mat mini-alarms. The mini-alarm and small detector pad can be placed in a diurnal enuretic child's underpants as an aid to training. (See Berg, 1979 for a discussion of the treatment of diurnal enuresis.)

BOWEL CONTROL AND ENCOPRESIS

Ordinarily, bowel control comes before bladder control; after the child can walk. Most children develop bowel control within the first three years but there is considerable variation in their individual rates of development (Bellman, 1966). Night control usually precedes day control. Girls tend to be continent before boys. The total time required to complete bowel training has been found to be less when it is initiated relatively late. Sears, Maccoby and Levin (1957) were able to show that when mothers began bowel training before the child was 5 months old, nearly ten months (on average) was required for success. But when training was begun later (at 20 months or older), only about five months were required. Children whose toilet training was begun between 5 and 14 months or after 19 months, manifested fewest emotional reactions during training.

Soiling (encopresis) (see Doleys, 1978)

Soiling, or more technically encopresis, is a disturbance in the regulation of bowel evacuation, involving, usually, involuntary defaecation which is not directly attributable to physical illness. DSM-III (APA, 1980) defines the problem as '... repeated *voluntary or involuntary* passage of faeces of *normal or near normal consistency* into *places not appropriate* for that purpose in the individual's own sociocultural setting. It is *functional when not due to any organic disorder.*'

Occasionally, soiling is associated with the hiding of faeces or the smearing of the walls with excreta. Pringle, Butler and Davie (1966), found that 1.2% of the 1958 National Cohort of British Children were encopretic at the age of 7 years. The problem occurs more often in boys than in girls (Rutter, Tizard and Whitmore, 1970); at 10 to 12 years, 1.3% of boys and 0.3% of girls are soiling themselves at least once a month. The incidence of disturbance is high among the sort of children with whom clinical psychologists often work — those with physical handicap and/or intellectual impairment. They are also associated significantly with the ramifications of other aspects of behavioural disturbances (Rutter, Tizard and Whitmore, 1970).

Encopresis is usually a daytime problem and is manifested frequently in the later afternoon after school. The child goes to great lengths to hide dirty underwear. Encopretic children often smell and thus incur savage teasing and sometimes out-and-out rejection. The resulting shame and damage to self-esteem can well be imagined.

Encopresis is not a unitary disorder; it includes rather different soiling problems:

- *Retentive encopresis* is characterized by an excessive retention of faecal matter, often with soiling due to leakage around the hardened faecal material.
- *Non-retentive encopresis* involves involuntary expulsion of faeces (incontinence) resulting in soiling of clothing and bedding.

   There is another dimension:

- *Continuous or primary encopresis* refers to a situation where control has never been reliably established.
- *Discontinuous or secondary encopresis* refers to circumstances in which the child has acquired control in toileting and then lost it.

These distinctions are significant when it comes to a discussion of causation. The aetiology of encopresis is multifactorial. Bowel control, and its precise development, is poorly understood. It certainly involves complex processes of learning. As Anthony (1957) puts it, 'From the child's eye view, the toilet rituals as practised by the adults in our compulsive communities, must sometimes appear as an exacting and complex ordeal far removed from the simple evacuation into the nursery pot. It is his business with maternal prompting to become aware of defaecation cues in time, to stop his play in response to this, to suppress the desire for immediate excretion, to search for and find an appropriate place for the purpose, to ensure adequate privacy for himself, to unfasten his clothes, to establish himself firmly on the toilet seat, to recognize an end point to the proceedings and cleanse himself satisfactorily, to flush the toilet, to re-fasten his clothes, to unbolt the door and emerge successfully to resume his interrupted play at the point where he left off'.

It is postulated that many children in the continuous group have suffered neglectful training, and children in both the retentive and discontinuous categories tend to have had severe coercive training experiences. Either parents are too lax in their training methods, so that defaecation remains a pleasurable act, or they are too coercive, so that extreme disgust is associated with the act.

But what precisely leads up to the act? The walls of the rectum when stretched give rise to the sensation of the urge to defaecate. The strong peristaltic 'rush' and consequent urge to go to the toilet occurs daily in most people, usually in the morning, approximately 20 to 40 minutes after breakfast, although there are marked individual differences. Young children are so involved in their play that they sometimes leave it until too late to go to the toilet; others fail to respond to, or are fearful of, the signals from their bodies. A factor with important implications for treatment is that constipation and retention of faeces are found in a vast majority of cases of encopresis (Gabel, 1981). When a hard mass of faeces builds up the length of the colon, liquid waste finds its way around the blockage, seeping out and causing continual soiling, which is sometimes mistaken for diarrhoea. Such 'functional' or 'psychogenic megacolon' as it is called may be associated with extreme fear of the toileting situation because of the pain experienced by the child. He or she may also be accused of wilful soiling when, in fact, they do not get appropriate bodily signals that it is time to go to the toilet.

Treatment

Yates (1970) contends that the continuous encopretic suffers from a failure to acquire internal control of the defaecatory act whereas the discontinuous encopretic has lost internal control because of externally imposed environmental stress. It is suggested (Anthony, 1957) that the continuous encopretic is in need of habit training rather than therapy. The discontinuous encopretic is thought to have a more serious problem needing therapy for himself or herself and counselling for his or her parents.

Paediatric assistance is invaluable in the physical aspects of an intervention. The approach tends to involve the use of enemas, laxatives, stool softeners, together with dietary advice, all of importance in the case of retentive encopresis.

Doleys (1977), in his review of treatment studies, found that 93% of cases were successfully treated by the use of behavioural methods. Operant conditioning techniques have been used successfully in the treatment of the various types of encopresis. A combination of positive and negative reinforcement is used to modify the encopresis and smearing. (e.g., Bach and Moyland, 1975; Herbert and Iwaniec, 1981; Young, 1973). Sluckin (1973) successfully treated four cases of encopresis attending an out-patient child guidance clinic. Mothers of the children were instructed to reward them for passing a motion in the lavatory. Laxatives (senekot) were prescribed in order to ensure regular and painless bowel movements. A psychological *and* somatic approach is often required in the case of encopretic problems. Advice on dietary matters can also be helpful (Houts and Peterson, 1986).

PROBLEMS OF COMMUNICATION

Communication in spoken language is the latest, most complex and probably the most valuable of man's and woman's evolutionary achievements. To communicate is to convey meaning from one individual to another in an intelligible code. Such a code is provided by language. In learning a language, infants are assimilating their culture's conceptual categories for thinking, perceiving and reasoning. Given that the basic needs of children are fulfilled by interaction with adults and other children, it is not surprising that serious emotional problems flow from children's inability to express themselves meaningfully or to comprehend others. Cantwell and Baker (1985b) distinguish between:

- Pure speech disorder: 'impairment (including delay and deviance) in the articulation or fluency of production of speech sounds' and
- Pure language disorders: 'impairment (including delay and deviance) in the receptive or expressive use of words to convey meanings'. The relationship between speech and language dysfunction and behavioural disorder is substantial; the fact is that 50% of speech-and-language disordered children also display psychopathology of sufficient intensity to warrant a 'diagnosis' (Piacentini, 1987).

Selective mutism

The child who elects to remain silent in the presence of others, or (more accurately) selects to whom he or she will talk, is a phenomenon which was described a long way back in literature (Austin 1811), but relatively recently in clinical publications. Kratochwil (1981) gives good reasons why the earlier diagnostic term 'elective mutism', should be superseded by 'selective mutism' (SM). SM children are reported to have age-appropriate speech development, but appear 'stuck' at a stage children often pass through at about 2–3 years, which is characterized by excessive shyness. Selective silence tends to occur most frequently in school, presenting a formidable problem in the classroom (Baldwin, 1985). In 4–5 year olds, shortly after initial school entry, the prevalence of non-speaking in school is 7.2 per thousand among a Birmingham UK sample (Brown and Lloyd, 1975). However, a sharp decline in the number of non-speakers was noted over the next 20 months, after which only one child remained totally mute. The disorder represents less than 1% of child guidance and social work referrals in the USA, an incidence which nevertheless is sufficiently high to be problematic (Ollendick and Matson, 1983).

Several studies (e.g., Sluckin, Foreman and Herbert, 1990) have attempted to isolate individual and demographic factors associated with, and possibly predisposing children to, selective mutism. Of particular interest is the finding that SM children have been exposed to greater family discord and a greater number of environmental stressors than controls. Moreover, they frequently come from families with a history of some form of psychopathology (Kolvin and Fundudis, 1981).

Intervention

Treatment for SM has progressed through several identifiable phases. Early psychodynamic approaches stressed infant and childhood experiences which had interfered with the mother–child relationship, hence treatment had a relatively narrow focus and little effort was made to remove the 'symptom' of restricted speech itself.

Reed (1963) was possibly the first author to propose that SM might be a learned pattern of behaviour. Thus a child's differential pattern of communication might be subjected to a functional analysis (see Chapter 2) with respect to the frequency of talking (speech) in certain situations and/or to certain individuals. Using a behavioural analysis, Cunningham et al. (1983) point out that in response to a child's silence, adults (teachers in particular) often tend to adopt a pattern of verbal interaction which reinforced simple, non-verbal responses, while peers, in contrast, do not speak, or simply reduce their interaction with the SM child. The effectiveness of the child's non-verbal communication is said to be a major factor contributing to the persistence of the disorder. These authors found that the most fruitful treatment strategies were 'shaping' by rewarding an approximation to the goal in situations where a minimum of speech was present, by 'situation fading' and 'individual fading'. In situation fading, the child and the person he or she is willing to talk to are moved, step by step, from one place where speech is present, to another where speech is not as yet present. In individual fading, new individuals are gradually introduced into situations familiar to the child. A combination of fading and judicious reinforcement procedures leads to the child's being able to talk to an increasing number of people in a variety of situations, treatment duration positively correlating with degree of generalization of speaking. Procedures such as 'escape avoidance' and 'response cost', both of which are mildly punitive, are counter-productive since increasing anxiety might inhibit speech.

An alternative paradigm, described by Labbe and Williamson (1984) is 'reinforcement sampling'. This technique, based on incentive motivation, enables a child to sample or play with a reinforcer that can later be earned by speaking. In one case, a pet rabbit was used for this purpose. In another case, a 7-year-old SM was permitted to use a pair of skates for a period. Possession of the skates was made contingent on speaking in class and in the clinic. This procedure was said to be successful even when response shaping had failed.

Many case studies have appeared, reporting behavioural programmes and showing that such treatments are often successful not only with regard to increasing the speech, but also in improving the child's overall functioning (e.g., Sanok and Stiefel, 1979). The use of behavioural techniques does not always provide a quick solution to the problem.

Outcome studies evaluating particular techniques have tended to focus on the immediate post-treatment period; medium- and long-term follow-up studies of SM patients are few by comparison with those concerned with aetiology. This paucity of follow-up data is likely to reflect difficulty in keeping track of clients over a long period, the initially low incidence of the condition, and the sporadic way in which most therapists encounter it.

In a retrospective study by Sluckin, Foreman and Herbert (in press), 25 children, who had at one time been selective mutes, were followed up by means of questionnaires administered via their schools, two to ten years after referral. Eleven had been given individual therapy programmes with a behavioural content and home and school involvement. The remainder received remedial help from Special Needs teachers in the school setting, with routine Schools Psychological Service support and minimal home contact. Data were gathered on the following: number of school terms spent mute, age at referral and at follow-up, referral–follow-up interval, incidence of past and present mental illness in the family, social class, Rutter (B1) score, and whether they came from an indigenous or non-indigenous background. Stepwise multiple regression revealed the importance of a history of some form of mental illness in the family as a major determinant of non-talking at follow-up. Those children receiving individual behavioural programmes had made significantly greater improvements than those having had non-intensive, school-based programmes.

STUTTERING

This problem, an example of the first subcategory (page 146) is also referred to as 'stammering' and is a disorder of speech rhythms. Kanner (1953) states that 'the flow of speech is disrupted by blocks and tensions which produce hesitations and repetitions or prolongations of sounds. The continuity of diction is broken by clonic and tonic spasms of the muscles which participate in the mechanism of speech'. Stein and Mason (1968) are critical of definitions of stammering which emphasize the lack of fluency in speech because they see stammering as a disorder of communication not of speech. They define persistent stammering as a problem 'manifest in progressive dissolution of communication. The disorder is expressive of a disharmony in the interrelation between psychic processes and the linguistic encoding process irrespective of possible neuropathological conditions'. A majority of cases have their onset between the ages of 3 and 5 years. There are no onsets, apparently, after the age of nine. Andrews and Harris (1964) in a survey of over a thousand school children found an incidence of 3 %; this figure rose to 4.5 % if cases of transient stammering lasting up to six months were included.

It is well known that emotional factors can affect speech mechanisms; normal speakers occasionally stutter with strong emotion and stutterers may experience a particularly severe blockage in speech in times of distress. In fact, at the best of times, there is a considerable degree of overlap to be observed in the speech features of persons classified as stutterers and those classified as non-stutterers (Johnson, 1956). Three categories of stutterer have been identified by Andrews and Harris (1964):

(i) Developmental stuttering, being of early onset (2–4 years) but lasting only a few months.
(ii) Benign stuttering, characterized by late onset (mean age $7\frac{1}{2}$ years) but tending to spontaneous remission after about two to three years.
(iii) Persistent stuttering, with an onset between $3\frac{1}{2}$ and 8 years.

Treatment

There is a substantial literature on this topic (Beech and Fransella, 1968; Di Lorenzo and Matson, 1981; Ollendick and Matson, 1983) and a multiplicity of aetiological theories and therapeutic techniques are catalogued there. Behaviour therapists view stammering as learned behaviour, and, where there is no definite physical defect, as a behaviour pattern that may be directly and successfully retrained by a variety of behaviour-orientated techniques. These include aversive response-contingent procedures (Flanagan, Goldiamond and Azrin, 1958); contingency management (Burns and Brady, 1980); negative practice (Case, 1960); distraction (Cherry and Sayers, 1956); the correction of the negative habits or poorly developed speech patterns (Dalali and Sheehan, 1974) and systematic desensitization of anxiety about speaking (Boucheau and Jeffry, 1973).

DEVELOPMENTAL APHASIA

Disturbances in the ability to produce and comprehend speech are referred to as aphasic conditions (aphasia). The *aphasia* disorders are those that are thought to be directly linked to brain dysfunction in language processing. The *acquired aphasias* result from postnatal brain damage.

The distinction between congenital and developmental aphasias is usually based upon whether a family history is present (indicating developmental aphasia) or neonatal brain damage was indicated (congenital aphasia). The true developmental aphasias are rare; estimates of 1 in 10 000 for receptive developmental aphasia and 1 in 1000 for expressive developmental aphasia have been obtained in community surveys (Rutter, Graham and Yule, 1976).

Much of the information that enables the individual to understand or express himself or herself in speech appears to be stored in the left parietal cortex in right-handed people (Penfield and Roberts, 1959). The use and understanding of language may be impaired in several ways, and such impairments lead to associated difficulties in mastering that all-important skill of reading. Penfield and Roberts are of the opinion that there are no really pure forms of language defect. However they present evidence that relatively small lesions may in some cases produce impairments where one aspect of language is much more disturbed than others. The commonly quoted examples of this are expressive impairments of speech associated with lesions in the region of the Rolandic fissure, and dyslexia, usually accompanied by dysgraphia, associated with parieto-occipital lesions.

Executive aphasia

It is fairly common for there to be a developmental delay in language expression in the case of intelligent children with unimpaired comprehension and normal adjustment. There is usually a good prognosis in such cases of developmental speech retardation. Many of these children will enjoy normal speech by six years of age. However, this sort of problem shades into the more serious syndrome of executive aphasia. Here there is usually evidence of perceptual difficulties indicative of brain-injury. The comprehension of language may be normal or relatively less impaired than the ability to speak.

Receptive aphasia

This syndrome is rare in its more serious form. The milder form of impairment may involve an inability to localize sounds although the child can respond to some of them in an undifferentiated and gross manner. Such a deficit makes it impossible for the youngster to process the complex series of sounds which make up language. At the other extreme are those individuals who are 'word deaf' and, in fact, totally inattentive to sounds, although special techniques indicate that there is no peripheral or cochlear hearing loss to account for their deafness. The problem may occur in early childhood following or preceding a series of epileptic attacks.

These children with receptive and executive aphasia often have the kinds of language disorder and present other handicaps — perceptual and behavioural — which are reminiscent of infantile autism. There are children whose clinical features reveal them to be in the hinterland between autism and aphasia and there are aphasic children who, under stress, temporarily preoccupy themselves with the same obsessive rituals and avoid making interpersonal relationships in a manner analogous to autistic children. Aphasic children shed these habits on removal from stressful conditions, unlike autistic children.

The assessment and treatment of aphasic children requires the involvement of speech and language therapists. Estimates of the prevalence of such language delays vary, but a recent review of three separate epidemiological surveys suggested a prevalence figure in the range 3–5 % for 3-year-olds showing significant delay in their language development (Stevenson, 1984). Longitudinal studies demonstrate that children with language delays are markedly at risk for continuing educational or behavioural difficulties; many language problems (e.g., delay in speech) are linked with other basic disabilities (see Rutter, 1977). To take one example, children with profound hearing loss will require specialist help to acquire adequate communicative abilities. Children with partial transient hearing loss may also experience speech or language disturbances. Thus an audiological assessment should always be considered for children with language delays or speech abnormalities.

Many of the factors causing delays in the normal rate of language acquisition are broadly connected with psychosocial disadvantages including poor parent–child relationships, institutionalization, large sibships, deaf parents and maternal depression.

Intervention

The most appropriate treatment for children with language delays has not yet been established. Simply to provide these children with a remedial language programme will not offset the continuing adverse influences (in many cases) of their social and family situations.

Howlin (1984) has reviewed a number of schemes for parental involvement in the treatment of children with language delays. These ranged from those centred on children with delays associated with mental retardation and autism through to those involving expressive language delays primarily the result of inadequate or inappropriate stimulation at home. She found that although few of these approaches to treatment had been adequately evaluated, those that involved the parents in home-based activities as part of a structured programme of remedial help for the children were likely to show significant gains (see also Scaife and Holland, 1987).

Chapter 9

Handicap in Early Childhood and Beyond

I have chosen to group two wide categories of pervasive developmental disorder and mental handicap within one chapter on impairment, not because of their similarity (although they certainly 'touch' at several points), but because of the special needs they generate. They put heavy demands on the caregivers (that often means their parents) and they require careful planning and dedicated expertise (not to mention practical resources) when it comes to their education and ongoing welfare.

PERVASIVE DEVELOPMENTAL DISORDERS

This is a general classificatory category from DSM-III-R. It contains two conditions: infantile autism and childhood onset pervasive developmental disorder which are now thought to represent a single category called 'Autistic Disorder'. Childhood psychoses, schizophrenia and pervasive developmental disorders are essentially *generic* terms used to describe some of the most serious and pervasively disruptive of the disorders of childhood. A diagnosis called 'Childhood Onset Pervasive Developmental Disorder' was introduced in the USA to replace the earlier category called 'childhood schizophrenia'. Before being displaced it applied to children who were thought to have a form of schizophrenia which was simply an early version of adult schizophrenia. The evidence, as it emerged over the years, did not support the view that adult and childhood schizophrenia (as was) were closely related disorders.

Lockyer and Rutter (1969) in a five-to-fifteen-year follow-up of infantile psychoses failed to find that psychotic children (many of whom fulfilled the defining attributes of 'childhood schizophrenia') became adult schizophrenics. The attributes of 'childhood psychosis' or 'childhood schizophrenic syndrome' were formulated in the UK by a working party (Creak, 1961) and listed the following symptoms:

- Gross and sustained impairment of emotional relationships with people.
- Apparent unawareness of his own personal indentity to a degree inappropriate to his age.

- Preoccupation with particular objects or part of his own body.
- Sustained resistance to change in the environment or routine, and a striving to maintain or restore sameness.
- Apparent abnormalities of special senses in the absence of any detectable physical cause.
- Abnormalities and inappropriateness of mood, such as acute, excessive and seemingly illogical anxiety.
- Absence of speech or presence of speech disturbance.
- Disturbance of movements and the general level of motor activity (e.g., hyperkinesis, immobility, bizarre posturing, or ritualistic mannerisms).
- Apparent islets of ability against a background of varying degrees of intellectual retardation.

These criteria were not without their critics; but it was always stressed that no single behavioural item is diagnostic of psychosis when taken in isolation. Some of the items could be manifested in other emotional or organic disorders.

AUTISM

Leo Kanner (1943), the first person to describe this disorder precisely, saw 'infantile autism' as a variation of childhood schizophrenia.

The major characteristics of this syndrome as described by Kanner and his colleague (Eisenberg and Kanner, 1956) are as follows:

- A profound withdrawal of contact from other people ('aloneness').
- Failure to use language for communication.
- Obsessive maintenance of the status quo — 'sameness' — in the environment.
- Skill in fine motor movements, especially with regard to objects, as opposed to
- Inability to deal with people.
- Very high cognitive potential as manifested by 'islets' of performance.

Over the years two aspects in particular of Kanner's diagnostic characteristics have been questioned: one concerning the intelligence of these children, and the other concerning the primary symptom. The current view of autism is that the majority are intellectually impaired, and that in some children this coexists with isolated skills. The second question concerns which of the behaviours are most important, or primary, to the condition. Kanner held that the absence of any emotional response to people was of fundamental importance, the insistence on things staying the same. One of the problems with this position is that these behaviours cannot account for the other behaviours which go to make up the condition. More recently researchers suggest that the basic impairment is cognitive. They argue that a cognitive impairment leads to problems in communication and language, and that the behavioural and emotional difficulties are secondary to this. Rutter (1983) argued that autistic children have a basic cognitive deficit, basic in the sense that it is fundamental to their handicap, and a deficit in the sense that certain of their cognitive processes are damaged.

The reader will have noticed how confusing (confused?) these terminological issues prove to be. It would be easy (and eccentric, in the light of the relatively low priority given to classification in this book) to get bogged down in a differential diagnostic debate as to the precise meaning of autism and its boundaries relative to childhood psychosis in general or childhood schizophrenia, mental handicap and brain damage in particular (see Bender, 1969; Mahler, 1952; Rimland, 1964). Nevertheless psychologists work with people, and read research articles by investigators who do believe there is a place for rigorous taxonomies. The fact is that psychoses of the adult type (schizophrenia and manic depression) are extremely rare before puberty, but occur at a rate of about 1 per 1000 by mid-adolescence. In the opinion of Hermelin (1963) 'childhood psychosis' like 'mental subnormality' or 'brain damage' is too general a term to be of much value in planning precise experimental investigations. She points out that whereas 'schizophrenia' is the name given to a group of mental illnesses which usually develop after the age of puberty, and which have a characteristic pattern of clinical symptoms, and a characteristic course and outcome, there is no justification for finding analogies between it and between infantile autism — a condition of maldevelopment in childhood — which simply has as one of its features (like schizophrenia) social withdrawal. This characteristic is shared with many other psychotic conditions, and may be secondary in childhood autism to difficulties in language and communication.

Not all the children who are diagnosed as autistic show all of the supposedly 'pathognomonic' behaviours. The severity of the behaviours varies, and they generally tend to become less severe as the child gets older. This makes it hard to know where to draw the boundary, to say which children are autistic and which children are not. In Rutter's (1983) opinion, not enough is known about the processes underlying the behaviours which characterize autism; until more is known about the cognitive deficits in autism and how they relate to the behaviours which characterize autism, a definitive description of autism will not be possible.

It is interesting to examine the term 'autistic disorder' in DSM-III-R. The APA has combined the old infantile autism and childhood schizophrenia ('childhood onset pervasive developmental disorder'). It is applied when a child shows at least eight of the following attributes, two from A, one from B and one from C:

A   Qualitative impairment in reciprocal social interaction.
   (i)   Marked lack of awareness of the existence or feelings of others (e.g., treats a person as if he or she were a piece of furniture; does not notice another person's distress; apparently has no concept of the need of others for privacy).
   (ii) No, or abnormal, seeking of comfort even when ill, hurt, or tired; seeks comfort in a stereotyped way (e.g., says 'cheese, cheese, cheese' whenever hurt).
   (iii) No, or impaired, imitation (e.g., does not wave bye-bye; does not copy mother's domestic activities; mechanical imitation of others' actions out of context.

  (iv) No, or abnormal, social play (e.g., does not actively participate in simple
        games; prefers solitary play activities; involves other children in play only as
        'mechanical aids').
  (v)   Gross impairment in ability to make peer friendships (e.g., no interest in
        making peer friendships; despite interest in making friends, demonstrates lack
        of understanding of conventions of social interaction, for example, reads phone
        book to uninterested peer).
B   Verbal and nonverbal communication, imaginative activity.
  (i)   No mode of communication.
  (ii) Markedly abnormal nonverbal communication.
  (iii) Absence of imaginative activity (e.g., fantasies, acting out adult roles, interest
        in stories about imaginary events).
  (iv) Marked abnormalities in speech production.
  (v)   Marked abnormalities in form or content of speech (including stereotyped or
        repetitive speech).
  (vi) Marked impairment in the ability to initiate or sustain a conversation, despite
        adequate speech.
C   Repertoire of activities and interests.
  (i)   Stereotyped body movements.
  (ii) Persistent preoccupation with parts of objects.
  (iii) Marked distress over changes in trivial aspects of the environment.
  (iv) Unreasonable insistence on following routines in precise detail.
  (v)   Markedly restricted range of interests, with preoccupation with a narrow
        interest.
D   Onset during infancy or childhood.

The prevalence rate of childhood autism is three to four per 10 000 children (Lotter,
1966).

Communication problems

Many aspects of the causation of autism remain a mystery, but many theorists relate
much of the bizarre symptomatology to deficits and/or abnormalities of cognition (see
Rutter, 1983). This applies particularly to the autistic child's problems of communication.
Autistic children display deficits and abnormalities in communication prior to the period
when language is normally acquired. Babbling is infrequent and conveys less information
than that of non-autistic infants. However, they often cry and scream to indicate need.
They do not use gestures (as deaf children try to do) as a substitute for speech and it has
proved difficult to train them to do so (Bartak, Rutter and Cox, 1975). Their faces show
little expression.

   As they get older the language and non-verbal communication deficits of autistic
children become even more pronounced, with mutism a feature of some 50 % of all
autistic children. Even when speech is acquired there are many oddities such as 'pronoun

reversal' (e.g., the child referring to himself or herself as he or you) and the related problem of 'echolalia'. Echolalic speech is not speech for communication, but the echoing, often with notable fidelity and in a high-pitched monotone, of what has been said to him or her.

The ability to acquire speech appears to be a crucial prediction of later adjustment in autistic children. In a follow-up study of 80 autistic children, Eisenberg and Kanner (1956) reported that 50 % of the children who were able to speak by the age of 5 were rated as demonstrating fair or good adjustment while only 3 % of the nonspeaking children were rated in this way. This general finding of a close relationship between the ability to speak and later adjustment has been confirmed in several studies (e.g., Rutter, 1977).

Like the child with 'developmental aphasia' the autistic patient has a fundamental difficulty in the comprehension of language and in addition experiences disturbance in the organization of perception (Stroh and Buick, 1964). If the mechanisms in that part of the brain responsible for processing and structuring (i.e., integrating) the visual and auditory stimuli which enter the eyes and ears of the child were faulty, it would make sense of several observations concerning the autistic youngster. A failure to achieve order and meaningful structure from the incoming messages the child is receiving from the environment would explain his or her withdrawal, limited span of attention, intensely violent emotional reactions when he or she receives certain forms of stimulation, and obsession with sameness. Hermelin (1966), and Hermelin and O'Connor (1964) have conducted a series of experiments on the hierarchical organization of sensory systems and sensory dominance in the development of autistic children. The background to their work is explained as follows: the developing child goes through a number of sequences, in the course of which alterations in the nature of the hierarchical structure of the senses occur. Thus interoceptive and visceral sensations are dominant in the infant, and this dominance is gradually superseded first by tactile and kinesthetic, and then by auditory and visual sensory systems. Thus, in an organism in which vision represents the predominant sense mode, the other avenues of sensory input are utilized as background information against the pre-eminent visual stimulus. Once a certain stage of development has been reached, it is the meaning rather than the modality of stimuli which determines their place in the hierarchy. As Luria (1961) has put it, the second signalling system concerned with meaning and language comes to dominate and direct the first, which is concerned with the organization of direct sensory input. The hierarchical organization of sensory systems therefore functions to a very large extent to determine which aspects of the environment constitute figure and which aspects constitute background. One would expect that the organization of behaviour would depend on whether and how such a hierarchical structure of sensory systems has developed.

The experiments performed by Hermelin and O'Connor (1964) demonstrated that this development is relatively orderly in most nonpsychotic mentally handicapped children. At a mental age of about 4 to 5 years visual dominance is established in the sensory hierarchy of the first signalling system. However, this visual dominance is suppressed if it competes with meaningful verbal stimulation, which then in turn assumes dominance. In mentally undisturbed Down's syndrome children a hierarchical structure of sensory systems, with vision as the dominant sense avenue has also developed. However, even if words are the competing stimuli, Down's children remain primarily responsive to the direct visual signals coming to the first signalling system.

In autistic children, even within the first signalling system, the structural hierarchy seems to be insufficiently developed. Variables such as intensity or reinforcement schedules, rather than sensory modality seem to determine response behaviour. Their behaviour appears more random and less predictable than subnormal controls. In short, the authors demonstrated that less intellectually impaired children respond most often to words, Down's children to light and autistic children most often to the most intense signal regardless of its modality or meaning. Hermelin (1963) proposes that failure to achieve auditory dominance may be a factor in the impaired speech of autistic children.

There have been many brave efforts (see Kiernan's 1983 review) to teach autistic children non-vocal means of communicating. There is some evidence that even some of the most handicapped children can learn to communicate needs using signs and symbols that may assist the development of their spoken language.

Preservation of sameness

Autistic children become very disturbed over changes in their surroundings and alterations in their routines. Temper tantrums may greet the apparently most trivial change, for example, their 'regimented' toys accidentally pushed out of place. Obsessional attributes may be even more pronounced at adolescence.

Extreme tendency to autistic aloneness

From early in life the infants' preference to be alone — his or her inability to relate to persons and situations — becomes noticeable. At first this 'undemandingness' is construed by some parents as the behaviour of a 'good' baby. This self-absorption, the physical repudiation (drawing away) of cuddling, the lack of concern about the comings and goings of people, the preoccupation with things, soon begin to disturb his or her caregivers. This rejection of social interaction has its corollary in a retardation of development.

Reports of autistic children indicate the absence of the sorts of attachment behaviour which are characteristic of normal children. They tend not to keep close by their parent, and may not even show any acknowledgement of their parent's return after an absence, let alone any sign of greeting. They do not seem to use their parents for comfort, although they will enjoy a game of rough and tumble. Another characteristic of autistic children's social behaviour is their failure to seek bodily contact to gain comfort or security (see Rutter, 1983).

Wing (1971b) asked a group of parents about the early behaviour of their 6–15-year-old autistic children. Fourteen of the 17 children were thought to have been handicapped from birth. According to their parents, a number of these children failed to show various social behaviours at the appropriate age, or even when they were older: ten failed to lift their arms up when their parent came to pick them up; seven showed very little response to their mother's voice and eleven did not draw their parent's attention to things by pointing. All of these behaviours are part of normal social interaction.

Intervention

Under certain circumstances (with skilled encouragement) autistic children will interact with other people. Clark and Rutter (1981) found that, as the demands for a social response from autistic children are increased, the children are more likely to produce a social response. This kind of observation has encouraged psychologists and teachers to use behavioural methods to shape up social behaviour, skills and speech (De Myer, Hingten and Jackson, 1981; Ferrari and Harris, 1981; Lovaas, 1977; Weatherby and Baumeister, 1981). Harris and Handleman (1987) make the point that although treatment focuses primarily on the creative application of traditional operant procedures, interventions with parents and siblings extend to the full range of cognitive behavioural methods. A plethora of aversive procedures (water mist, nasty tasting substances, etc) have been used to suppress the unwanted and dangerous behaviour (e.g., aggression, self-injury, self-stimulation) characteristic of autistic children. Recent years have witnessed a welcome search for non-aversive alternatives, such as physical exercise (jogging).

Sadly, there is no treatment of autism that encompasses the notion of treating to bring about a cure. The clinical and educational work is essentially habilitative and remedial. The Warnock Report (1978), in the UK, made several recommendations for meeting children's special educational needs both in ordinary and special schools. The choice will be between a mainstream school, a special school catering for a range of handicaps and a specialist school for autistic children.

Lewis (1987) states that the main advantage of special schools catering solely for autistic children is that the teachers are aware of their characteristics and needs. However, because of the relatively low incidence of autism, many of these schools are residential, ranging from full-time residential to weekly boarding. Residential schools provide needed relief for families who cannot cope with the child at home. They will help accustom those autistic young people, particularly in adolescence, who will be unable to live in the community, to living away from home. She adds that the transition between home and school is likely to be difficult and far more disruptive when the child is residential than when the child attends school on a daily basis and lives at home.

SEVERE LEARNING DIFFICULTIES (see Clements, 1987)

Severe learning difficulty/disability, as many professionals and parents now prefer to refer to mental handicap, is such a vast and (in its rapidly changing theoretical and practical frameworks) controversial subject, that there is no possibility of doing it justice in a general text. Seriously handicapped children, no matter what the causes of their impairment, or from what specific syndrome they may be suffering, are individuals who learn more slowly than the average child. And professionals are emphasizing this in their choice of terminology, preferring to describe such children as children with moderate or severe learning difficulties. One of the main reasons for this appears to be that severely impaired children have difficulty in abstracting the general principles which describe their environment, and help them to organize actions, plan and solve problems of everyday life.

'Mental retardation' (as it is referred to in DSM-III-R) is characterized there as significantly subaverage general intellectual functioning and significant deficits or impairments in adaptive functioning, both of which present before the age of 18 (Codes 317.00–319.00).

The more severely impaired in intellect the child is, the more likely it is that he or she will be suffering from additional physical and sensory handicaps, although by no means all severe learning disabled children are so additionally handicapped. (Of course, physical or sensory handicap does not necessarily imply 'learning disability'.) However, the generalized learning difficulty, and consequent slow cognitive development of the child, does mean that mentally handicapped children remain dependent on parents, or parental substitutes, for longer than normal, that they move from stage to stage in child development more slowly, and that scholastic achievement will be slower than average. Just as a large proportion of the 'normal' child's behavioural, social and emotional development is dependent on learning, so is the disabled child's. The difference mainly lies in the *rate* of what is learned, not primarily (there are some exceptions) in how it is learned. Development may be slow, but every child is capable of learning, provided that the 'teaching' (e.g., playing with, talking to, and instructing) is appropriate to the child's level of comprehension.

For this, accurate and early assessment by a multidisciplinary paediatric team is a necessity; this should lead to a programme geared to the special needs of the individual child, taking into account his or her particular range of abilities and disabilities (see paediatric neuropsychology in Appendix II). Fryers (1984) makes the point that aetiological diagnosis is concerned very largely with specific pathology or patterns of structural impairment of chromosomes, tissues, or organs and their causal processes. This is of great importance for *primary prevention* and for helping parents to come to terms with their child's disorder without guilt or shame. Although biochemical and neurological diagnosis is also concerned with structure, the principal clinical focus is impairment of function. This is important for *secondary prevention*, limiting consequent disability, and controlling concurrent impairments such as cerebral palsy and epilepsy. The clinical team should be able to provide practical advice on general development and advice on behavioural problems displayed by the child within the family or school setting.

Part of the adjustment that some parents will have to make is in deciding whether or not to have more children. The possibility of future children being handicapped can be discussed with the genetic counselling service, but the degree of dependence of the handicapped child may prove a more persuasive factor for couples. A more general kind of counselling could assist parents to cope with a wide range of decisions.

IMPAIRMENT OF INTELLECT

The functional impairment has been operationalized by using measures of I.Q. — that most contentious quotient (see Appendix II). The I.Q. has been the foundation of most classifications of intellectual impairment, and in spite of doubts about comparability, has generally been the basis of much research and many policy decisions. An I.Q. under 70 has usually been accepted for 'mild' impairment, in conjunction with 'social criteria'. A level of I.Q. 55 divides 'mild' from 'severe'. An I.Q. of 55 is, in fact, 3 standard deviations below the mean. In practice, however, I.Q. 50 has proved more useful and is the most widely used convention in the epidemiological literature. Severe learning disability (I.Q. below 50) appears at a rate of about three children per 1000 (Fryers, 1984). The 'profound' category has achieved poorer agreement, coming into play for I.Q.s of under 25 or 20. Fryers (1984) makes the following wise observation:

> It is obvious that no set of categories and no single system of classification is satisfactory, nor can it ever be however defined, since the group of people with whom we are concerned suffer from a ragbag of disorders, difficulties, and needs, and a varying ragbag at that, and who have been brought together almost by historical accident of educational development. They do not, and cannot, constitute an entity except we make it so. Research workers in this field must be exceptionally wary and clearheaded; more epidemiological awareness would benefit much of the literature. Service planners should try to understand the conceptual problems before applying simple criteria. To study and to plan clearly defined standard categories is essential, but whatever system of classification is satisfying to the epidemiologist or convenient to the planner or administrator should not be allowed to determine the life-style and lifetime services for any individual. Taxonomies are for groups, categories serve the needs of professionals; individual clients require thorough, multidisciplinary assessment of their individual situation, constantly updated, and a service delivery system which can respond to their changing needs and those of the family.

Causes of intellectual impairment

Table 11 provides a synopsis of the major conditions leading to mental impairment.

Interventions

It is not possible to detach the discussion of the 'management' of mental handicap from an ideological–political context of civil rights expansion to handicapped persons. Radical changes are taking place under the impetus of the normalization and deinstitutionalization movements, more options being available as behavioural technology lifts the self-help skills and aspirations of this group. Clinical child psychologists have extended their

Table 11. Mental handicap and its ramifications (adapted from Fryers, 1984).

Handicapping disorder	Nature of disorder	Features	Detection/Prevention	Intellectual implications
1. Down's syndrome	chromosome aberrations, present at conception (i) Trisomy 21 (94 % of cases) (ii) Trisomy mosaics (3 % of cases) (iii) Translocation (3 % of cases)	Highest prevalence at birth/1000 in mothers of 45–49 (56.52) Primary disorder	Amniocentesis can indicate affected foetus	All likely to be intellectually impaired, a majority severely so (however, much variability in Trisomy mosaics)
2. Patau's syndrome (Tri. 13)	Autosomal anomalies present at conception	Prevalence at birth: Collectively 2/1000	Nil	Occasionally severe, or mild intellectual impairment
3. Edwards' syndrome (Tri. 17 or 18)	Autosomal anomalies present at conception	Primary disorder	Nil	Occasionally severe, or mild intellectual impairment
4. Cri du chat syndrome (anom. 5)	Autosomal anomalies present at conception		Nil	Occasionally severe, or mild intellectual impairment
5. Klinefelter's syndrome	Sex chromosome disorder	Prevalence at birth 3/1000	Nil	Occasionally severe, or mild intellectual impairment
6. Phenylketonuria (PKU)	Defect of protein metabolism	Prevalence at birth 0.05–0.2/1000	Screening programme after birth; special dietary regime prescribed	Extreme impairment if not treated
7. Galactosaemia	Defect of carbohydrate metabolism	Prevalence at birth 0.02/1000	Screening programme after birth; special dietary regime prescribed	Extreme impairment if not treated
8. Tay Sach's Disease	Defect of libid metabolism	Prevalence 0.04/1000, death in early childhood	No treatment available Genetic counselling	Extreme impairment
9. Epiloia (tuberous sclerosis)	Causal mechanisms are not clear	0.01/1000	No treatment available	Many severely impaired

interventions from the mental handicap hospitals out into the community where they work with handicapped children and adolescents in their own homes, in sheltered accommodation, hostels and training centres. Evans and Meyer (1985) propose a three-component model for the design of behavioural interventions with children who are mentally handicapped: interventions which either manipulate natural consequences (contingency strategies), teach alternative behaviours (curricular strategies), or modify environments (ecological strategies). All three levels are examined in Part 5 in detail. A good deal of attention has been given to speech training, the results of which have been somewhat disappointing (Ager, 1985). The success of many behavioural interventions which tend to be biased to the *non-verbal*, and the general preference of persons with severe learning difficulties for coding information in a *visuo-spatial modality*, has led to increasing use of non-vocal teaching strategies.

Intellectually impaired children learn maladaptive behaviours in the same way as children who are not handicapped, but there are some important differences:

(a) parents may consider the child to be 'ill' on a long-term basis, and so not expect more reasonable behaviour from their child — 'After all, he is mentally handicapped, we can't expect him to stop banging his head on the walls';

(b) because mentally handicapped children learn more slowly, procedures which would have been successful if continued, tend to be abandoned because there is so little improvement in the short term (i.e., the parallel situation to teaching new developmental skills).

Teaching the child new ways of behaving requires a more structured approach than is necessary with the normal child. This structure, natually enough, seems to go against the grain for many parents, who quite understandably prefer to rely on a less formal, more intuitive approach to their normal children.

PARENT TRAINING

For most parents, the idea of the expert handing out advice on child-rearing, 'ex cathedra', was always doomed to failure. It is now recognized that all parents have a considerable expertise which needs to be mobilized in cooperation with specialists so that a jointly agreed programme may be evolved. There are several schemes available providing help and support for parents of handicapped children. They may take the form of parent groups (e.g., Mencap) or training groups with specialist members, or home visits by specialists. The latter is of importance because intellectually impaired children, like all children, perform to their best when relaxed, and in familiar surroundings with familiar people present. Assessment in hospital, or clinic, can yield quite misleading results. The past history of a child's problem behaviour can also prove unreliable if relied on to the exclusion of the parent's record of the child's behaviour — as and when it occurs.

Parent training is now seen as a standard ingredient for early intervention programmes with mentally/developmentally handicapped children (Bidder, Bryant and Gray, 1975; Jeffree, McConkey and Hewson, 1977; Revill and Blunden, 1979). Home-based assistance is available through the Portage project which began in Wisconsin in 1969. A trained person visits the family at frequent intervals and works with the parents and child. During these visits, the parents and the Portage visitor agree on what skills the child needs to acquire next and how the parents can achieve this by working with the child each day (e.g., Daly et al., 1985); these methods have proved to be extremely valuable (Clements et al., 1979; Revill and Blunden, 1979; Scaife and Holland, 1987).

Another service of help is the Education of the Developmentally Young (EDY) project started by the Hester Adrian Research Centre at Manchester University. This was designed to teach those working with young handicapped children the skills for modifying the behaviours of these children (e.g., Farrell, 1982).

Hudson (1982) makes the point that very little research has focused on the issue of the most appropriate formats for training the parents of developmentally handicapped children. With this in mind he carried out a component analysis of a group training programme for parents in Melbourne, Australia. The sample consisted of the mothers of 40 developmentally handicapped children, who were randomly allocated to one of four treatment groups: verbal instruction, verbal instruction plus teaching of behavioural principles, verbal instruction plus the use of modelling and role-playing, and a waiting list control group. Using multiple outcome criteria it was found that (a) the inclusion of the teaching of general behavioural principles did not improve the performance of parents, and (b) it was necessary to include techniques that directly shaped the parent's behaviour (modelling and role playing) in order for them to learn to be effective teachers of their children.

Much of the literature and comment in the past emphasized the debilitating effect of a handicapped child on his or her home, upon the brothers and sisters (Gath, 1972) and even more upon the marriage. However, all is not gloom (see Allen and Affleck, 1985; Blacher, 1984; Hewett, 1970); many families meet the challenge of handicap with courage, resilience and common sense. Many of them are not 'just coping' but are positively happy. It is necessary to avoid the extremes, a panglossian view of handicap and its effects on everyone concerned, on the one hand, and a pessimistic or fatalistic view on the other. Many parents cope on their own, a few break down under the strain; others are supported by social workers from the local authority, or clinical psychologists with counselling skills and expertise in the ramifications (personal, practical and social) of having a child who is impaired in intellect. This is truly vital work.

(The DHSS Report 'Helping mentally handicapped people with special problems' is a particularly useful source booklet for bibliographies, resource names and addresses, and advice, for those working in the UK (DHSS, 1984).)

It is difficult to lay down guidelines on how best to aid and encourage a handicapped child at home. This is not the place to describe in full what is available to such parents. However, the bibliography contains references to helpful books. Parents are advised by the experts to strike a balance — giving the child every opportunity to make the fullest use of his or her abilities, while making allowance for his or her disabilities. Targets set to help them learn better speech, manual dexterity or social skills, must be realistic. The goal should be beyond the child's present attainment, so as to provide a challenge, but not so far ahead as to reinforce a sense of failure. Clear instructions and patience are required in any learning situation. Coercion should be avoided. Handicapped children are likely to encourage their parents to be too protective, both because they *are* more helpless and because they often like routine and letting things be done for them. If parents do too much for their children the message they are giving them is that they are incapable of doing things for themselves. They are teaching them to be helpless.

Although the problem of handicap has always been with us, a number of developments in our society have re-emphasized its importance. One is the increasing complexity of society and the demands it makes on its members, and another is the emphasis on compulsory education. Both of these have served to alter the definition of intellectual impairment and to bring within the category persons who would not previously have been considered handicapped. Recently, the growing realization by educators that more than 50 % of the jobs in our society do not require schooling beyond primary level has meant a growing emphasis on the integration of the less severely-handicapped youngsters into the community to which they rightly belong — a theory and, indeed, a policy referred to as 'normalization' (Wolfensberger, 1980).

Chapter 10

Internalizing and Externalizing Problems of Early Childhood

INTERNALIZING (EMOTIONAL) PROBLEMS

Studies of the internalizing or emotional problems of childhood (Herbert, 1974) indicate that some of them are so common that it might be said to be 'normal' for children to be fearful, worried or shy about one thing or another at different stages in their development. Many investigators (e.g., Lapouse and Monk, 1958) found that it was commonplace for a majority of their samples of non-clinic-attending children to report having one or more fears. Obviously, if a degree of fearfulness is widespread during childhood we have to judge the seriousness of a particular child's anxieties by the consequences they have in his or her day-to-day life. And the consequences are not necessarily adverse. There is a positive as well as negative aspect to fear. The subjective and physiological responses which children experience in times of challenge and stress can be adaptive. A modicum of fear could be functional in testing situations (examinations, athletic contests) which require peak efficiency.

CHILDREN'S ANXIETY DISORDERS (Last, Strauss and Francis, 1987)

The DSM-III-R classifies three anxiety disorders of childhood or adolescence: separation anxiety disorder, avoidant disorder, and overanxious disorder.

Separation anxiety disorder is characterized by 'excessive anxiety concerning separation from those to whom the child is attached' (APA, 1987, p.60). A child with separation anxiety disorder may be reluctant to go to school in order to stay near his or her mother or with some other important attachment figure. Headaches and stomach aches and other physical symptoms are also common. To warrant a diagnosis, the separation anxiety must go well beyond that manifested as part of normal development and also extend for a period of at least two weeks.

Avoidant disorder is characterized by 'excessive shrinking from contact with unfamiliar people that is of sufficient severity to interfere with social functioning in peer relationships' (APA, 1987, p.61). Such a child is likely to appear shy, socially withdrawn, embarrassed and timid when in the company of peers and adults. Of course, these behaviours may be appropriate at specific stages of development. For this reason the DSM-III-R diagnosis is not applied until the child is at least two-and-a-half-years of age; in addition the avoidant reaction must be extended in duration for at least six months.

Overanxious disorder is characterized by 'excessive or unrealistic anxiety or worry' (APA, 1987, p.63). An overanxious child tends to worry excessively about school work and future events, and usually appears nervous or tense. The child has an incessant need for reassurance or comfort. Further, he or she complains of a variety of physical complaints (e.g., nausea and dizziness), and shows frequent self-consciousness. The problem, to be defined as such, must be relatively long-lived (i.e., at least six months in duration). Developmental guidelines are not indicated, however, since pervasive anxiety is not expected to be typical of any age group.

In addition to these three primary types of disorders, the DSM-III-R recognizes the presence of phobic disorders in children that are not subsumed under the categories mentioned above. Simple or 'specific' phobias are defined as persistent fears involving circumscribed stimuli such as animals, blood, closed spaces, heights, and air travel. Chapter 18 describes in detail the fears and phobias of childhood and their management.

In addition to these phobic disorders, there are other anxiety diagnoses included in the DSM-III-R that may be applied to children and adults. For example, obsessive-compulsive disorder is characterized by recurrent obsessions (persistent thoughts and impulses) or compulsions (repetitive behaviours performed according to certain rules or in a stereotyped fashion). These obsessions or compulsions are 'sufficiently severe to cause marked distress, be time-consuming, or significantly interfering with the person's normal routine, occupational functioning, or usual social activities or relationships with others' (APA, 1987, p.245). Obsessive-compulsive disorder may begin in childhood, although it usually begins in adolescence or early adulthood (Flament *et al.*, 1990). It has a poor prognosis. Other anxiety disorders include agoraphobia, panic disorder, and post traumatic stress disorder (see Chapter 20).

SCHOOL REFUSAL (see Blagg, 1987)

I have chosen to touch on school refusal problems (sometimes referred to as school phobia) because they illustrate the far-reaching psychosomatic and social ramifications of fear — implications that tend to demand a multimodal, systemic approach to the many-sided problems that arise. The young person who is desperately afraid of some aspect of attending school usually has recurrent physical symptoms for which there is no adequate medical explanation. The school refusal crisis, well under way, is apt to affect the entire family.

Assessment

The breakfast scene (on school days) is likely to be harrowing. Parents display varying degrees of anxiety, anger or despairing resignation. If such children are being pressured to go to school, they are likely to present physical signs of intense distress. They may be pale and tremulous; they may have a frequent need to urinate, or they may suffer from diarrhoea. They usually complain of physical malaise and a variety of ailments, most particularly abdominal pains and headache. They are likely to be off their food — particularly breakfast — and to feel nauseous and perhaps have bouts of vomiting. The physical complaints are inclined to subside at weekends and during school holidays or, even, shortly after the parents have resigned themselves to keeping the youngster at home.

The onset of school refusal is most common around the age of 11. The beginning of the problem is usually rather gradual; a build-up of tension, in the form of irritability, restlessness, disturbed sleep, vomiting and abdominal pain precede the full manifestation of the problem. And from the youngster's initial attitude of unwillingness, hedged around by varying excuses and complaints, the problem escalates to an outright refusal to set out for school (Herbert, 1974). School refusal tends to follow, not infrequently, a child's legitimate absence from school, particularly if he or she has a chronic recurrent illness.

Causation

When it comes to causal theories of school refusal one finds a fairly wide range of views. As with other emotional problems, the aetiology of school refusal is probably multifactorial, which is to postulate that a variety of influences, a network of precipitating and predisposing factors, contribute to the development of the problem.

Given that many children are not enamoured of life at school, why do only certain children carry their reluctance to go to school right through to the point of adamant refusal? Much will depend on the intensity of the stresses in a particular school situation, but the normal range of stressful school situations, whatever they are, precipitates drastic reactions in a minority of children only. For most children school fulfils several important needs, providing a stimulating and reasonably happy environment most of the time. Despite the inevitable complaints and the occasional reluctance (expressed to suspicious — sometimes complaisant — parents) which are part of the ups-and-downs of any child's school-going career, surveys show that most children enjoy school life once the routine becomes established. Mitchell and Shepherd (1966) reported that in Buckinghamshire about 5 % of boys and 3 % of girls under the age of 12 disliked going to school; yet their attendance was very little different from those who liked school. They say that 'this would seem to indicate that, during the primary school years, children may achieve regular attendance under firm parental pressure and regardless of their own inclinations'.

The 50 school-refusing children Hersov (1960) studied gave different explanations for their refusal; the commonest (34 %) was a fear of some harm befalling mother while the child was at school; next in importance were fears of ridicule, bullying, or harm from other children (28 %); next, fear of academic failure (28 %); then — rather less frequently — the fear of a strict, sarcastic teacher (22 %). Hersov found overt anxieties about menstruation in six girls and concern about puberty and masturbation in three boys. Other reasons for absence were fear of vomiting or fainting during school assembly. In some children more than one of these reasons was given by the same child while others could not give a lucid explanation other than that 'something' stopped them from going to school. There was a high incidence of neurosis in the families of school refusers, the symptoms being most often those of an affective disorder. This factor might well have had an influence on the children in terms of genetic endowment and environmental rearing.

The reported incidence of emotional problems in the parents has important implications for the sensitization of the child to fear. It is crucial to investigate this factor in all cases of school refusal, as the development of fears in children is influenced by their history and the setting in which distressing stimulation occurs (Eysenck and Rachman, 1965). There is evidence of the social facilitation or inhibition of fear in children, brought about by the mother's emotional state at the time (Hagman, 1932).

Intervention

Chapter 18 deals fully with the treatment of childhood fears and phobias. It is very likely in cases of school refusal, that the family members (parents *and* siblings) will have to be involved, because of the way in which they become 'entangled' in the emotion, the legal implications, and all-round misery, that is generated by a persistent school-non-attendance disorder.

PSYCHOLOGICAL PROBLEMS DUE TO PERSONALITY EXTREMES

Eysenck (1964, 1967) puts forward several interlocking theories (biological and psychological) to explain the evolution of psychological disorders like school phobia and truancy (another, but very different problem involving non-attendance at school). His work — which in many respects has been contentious, but of undoubted heuristic value in the child psychiatric field — distinguishes between two broad categories of emotional disorder. According to the model as it applies to children (Figure 10) normal and abnormal subjects are distributed with respect to behaviour and test performance over a two-dimensional factor space. The continua normality–neuroticism and extraversion–introversion form the axes.

There is evidence (Collins, Maxwell and Cameron, 1962) to show that the introverted neurotic child (the child with very marked introversion and neuroticism) tends to be predisposed to manifest to so-called 'personality' or emotional problems — dysthymic

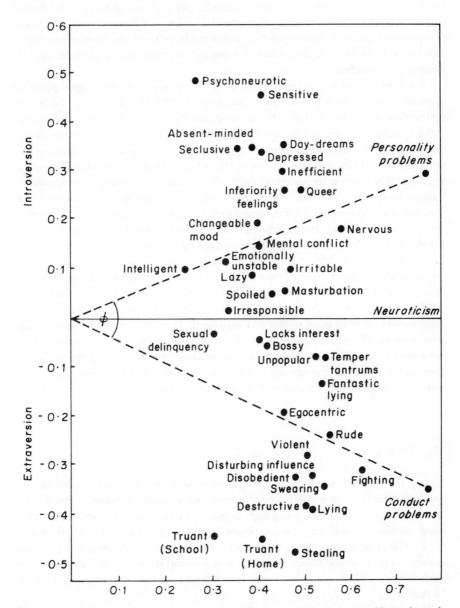

Figure 10. Results of a factor analysis of various conduct and personality problems shown by children. (From H. J. Eysenck, *The Biological Basis of Personality*, 1967, reproduced by permission of Charles C. Thomas, Publisher, Springfield, Illinois.)

disorders such as 'anxiety state'. This child tends to be depressed, seclusive, absent-minded, irritable, to have daydreams, inferiority feelings, mood swings and mental conflict. The extraverted neurotic child (the child with very marked extraversion and neuroticism) is liable to display 'conduct' problems; he or she is described as egocentric, rude, violent, disobedient, destructive, has temper tantrums, and is given to fighting, stealing, and truanting.

How does Eysenck explain such a taxonomy? According to his typological postulate (Eysenck, 1967), persons with weak 'excitory' potentials and strong 'inhibitory' potentials will tend to develop extraverted personality traits, and hysteric and psychopathic symptoms if subjected to neurotic breakdown. These constitutional attributes also contribute to the efficiency of conditioning. Eysenck (1964) goes on to propose that neuroticism and extraversion–introversion interact complexly to determine some of the individual differences in the success or failure of socialization. Training in socialization is thought to involve the acquisition of conditioned fear responses. If conditioning is as crucial in learning maladjusted (e.g., neurotic) behaviour as is claimed, then it would be very significant if human beings differed in their capacity to be conditioned.

Indeed, there seems to be some evidence according to Eysenck (1967) to suggest that there are individual differences in the speed and strength with which conditioned responses are formed. It follows from this that, other things being equal, the acquisition of a 'conditioned emotional response' like fear will be facilitated in children who form conditioned responses rapidly, strongly, and lastingly. Introverts do seem to form conditioned responses more swiftly and persistently than do extraverts. Those youngsters who condition ineffectually tend to be less susceptible to the impact of the environment; they are less likely to acquire maladaptive behaviour patterns such as phobias. However, being somewhat impervious to the impact of the environment is not without its risks, namely an antisocial outcome (see Chapter 16).

NEUROTICISM

Among the factors which are thought to predispose a child to develop psychological problems is the dimension (mentioned only briefly so far) called neuroticism, emotionality or instability. The child who has a high degree of this attribute is often referred to as being 'nervous', 'timid', 'emotional' or 'highly strung', because his or her emotions seem to be so labile, so volatile. He or she tends to be anxious, worried, unhappy, egocentric, quickly and easily aroused. Such traits set him or her apart from the 'calm' individual who tends to be persistent, steadfast, carefree, hopeful and contented according to experimental studies.

The child who shows intense emotionality and anxiety is susceptible to neurotic breakdown. Such a vulnerability implies a low tolerance for stress, whether it be physical as in painful situations, or psychological as in conflictual or frustrating situations. Eysenck's theories are examined further in Chapter 16.

NIGHTMARES AND NIGHT TERRORS

Nightmares and night terrors are often referred to as nocturnal anxiety attacks. The term 'night terror' is defined by Anthony (1959) as follows:

> At some late hour in the night, the child is found in a bizarre, crouching posture in bed or rushing about in a state of great agitation and apprehension, screaming in terror, and staring at something in front of him with wide open eyes and dilated pupils. He is not fully awake, does not recognize people and is disorientated in time and space. He will, however, reply to questions and gradually respond to soothing suggestions or reassurance. In the morning he has no recollection of the nocturnal event. The attacks tend to resemble each other and to show a periodicity. The condition does not appear to be related to other sleep disturbances, although it shares a similar background of anxiety, insecurity, instability, overstimulation and traumatization (reaction to shock).

Nightmares often set in for shortish periods when the child — particularly the sensitive child — is unsettled or worried by a change of school, a move to a new town or the trial of examinations. They may become a more persistent and worrying problem following a major trauma (see Chapter 21).

In the MacFarlane studies (MacFarlane, Allen and Honzik, 1954) disturbing dreams become something of a problem for boys and for girls at about the ages of 10 and 11. This means that one-third or more of the children in this American sample were manifesting the problem. There is another peak in the incidence of nightmares in the case of girls at 6 or 7 years of age. About one girl in ten, between the ages of 7 and 10, will experience disturbing dreams (not as severe as nightmares — but nevertheless distressing) two or three times a week. They diminish in frequency as the girl gets older. According to the Buckinghamshire study (Shepherd, Oppenheim and Mitchell, 1971) the proportion of British children with nightmares declines as they get older.

SEPARATION ANXIETY AND DEPENDENCY

Almost as soon as infants learn to seek help they begin to learn to manage without it. Independence becomes an end in itself. Young children take great pride in being able to do things for themselves. Rheingold and Eckerman (1970) note that the infant's separation from his or her mother is of crucial psychological importance, because it greatly widens their opportunities to interact with the environment. The universe can only be explored and understood if the infant becomes separated from the mother. As long as he or she is in physical contact with the mother, the infant's universe is limited to her person and the adjoining environment. There are limits to what even the most attentive and indulgent mother can bring to an infant. The authors observe that as soon as infants are able to move, they begin to separate themselves from their mother. It makes considerable difference whether the separation is voluntary or not. Human infants who are separated from their mothers after the age of 6 months or thereabouts manifest fear or resentment. They enjoy separation from their mothers only if they are in control so that they can initiate it and can return to home base (mother) at will (Lee, Wright and Herbert, 1972; Rheingold and Eckerman, 1970).

A second critical (or more accurately, 'sensitive') period is thought to come between the ages of 2 and 3 when children are expected to relinquish some of their dependent attitudes and behaviours. The human infant during the third year of life becomes fearful and anxious when the mother leaves him or her temporarily. By about three-and-a-half-years most children will separate from their mother, at least for a reasonably short time, and especially if they know the adults to whom they are entrusted. Before this age it is a somewhat hazardous matter labelling the child's dependent behaviours as maladjusted.

The object and intensity of a child's dependency may change with age. This raises the issue of the generality of dependency. Danziger (1971) puts it this way:

> The naive and unreflecting tendency of human beings is to see their interaction in terms of agents endowed with permanent and constant properties ... But if we want to gain some knowledge of the other as he really is, we need to step outside the confines of a particular relationship and look at the person in *all* his important relationships. We may find that a particular child is called 'overdependent' only by female teachers. In other words, we have no right to expect that the labels attached to individuals by particular classes of others correspond to any truly general personality characteristics that will reliably manifest themselves no matter what the circumstances.

Unfortunately there are circumstances powerful enough to affect even the child who is reasonably well adjusted. Such psychosocial stressors affect the well-being of young children because (in part) they disrupt their sense of security (see checklist below). The emotional disturbance is likely to derive from the threat to attachments to significant others. Garmezy (1983) and Goodyer (1990) provide valuable reviews of the interrelationships of life events, family relationships and psychopathology. The impact of life events depends on the good sense, support, and compensating stability provided by the significant persons in the child's 'world':

Life stresses (with a guide to some useful readings) (see Scaife and Frith, 1988):

- Separation (Ainsworth *et al.*, 1978; Bowlby, 1973; Rutter, 1981a,b,c).
     Hospitalization (Wolff, 1981; Wolkind and Rutter, 1985).
     Beginning playgroup/nursery/school.
     Taken into care.
- Birth of a sibling (Dunn and Kendrick, 1982).
- Divorce (Richards and Dyson, 1982; Richman, 1988).
- Bereavement (Black and Urbanowicz, 1987; Van Eerdewegh *et al.*, 1982; Van Eerdewegh, Clayton and Van Eerdewegh, 1985).
- Physical injury/pain (Eland and Anderson, 1977; see Chapter 18).
- Physical handicap (Wasserman and Allen, 1985).
- Illness (Eisser, 1985).
- Change in residence.

- Change in school/problems at school (Kelly, 1973; Trueman, 1984).
- Reconstituted family (Maddox, 1980).
    new 'parent'.
    new (step)siblings.
- Minor change in living conditions.
- Sexual difficulties (Green, 1974).
- Failure at school (Ausubel and Sullivan, 1954).
- Leaving home.
- Friendship difficulties (Goodyer, Wright and Altham, 1989).

Assessment

At what point does dependent behaviour become dysfunctional, a problem? A careful interview should reveal excessively dependent behaviour: it shows itself particularly in the needless seeking of help. Rather than showing initiative, the child keeps going to an adult for assistance. He or she requires aid not only when they come up against some real obstacle, but even when the task is of a routine nature. Physical proximity-seeking, the excessive need to stay close to an adult, is yet another behaviour suggestive of maladaptive dependency behaviour. The child clings or may always want to sit on his or her mother's lap. Attention-seeking behaviour is a further clue; here the child habitually wants the adult to watch him or her, talk to him or her, or look at something he or she has made. Finally, the child who seeks frequent reassurance and approval is manifesting an inability to rely on his or her own competence.

Separation and loss

Stendler (1952) states that there are two periods during which preschool children might become excessively dependent. The first period occurs near the end of his first year of life. Children, with their glimmering awareness of their absolute dependence on parents, test out their responses toward them. It is as if they are working out the extent to which they can rely on them. It is therefore thought essential to respond to the infant's needs for social and physical contact, also reliability (see Stayton, Hogan and Ainsworth, 1971) during this phase of development. During the early preschool years frequent hospital admissions can increase the risk of behavioural dysfunction in future, particularly in those children from disturbed families (Wolff, 1981).

Children from divorced families have higher rates of emotional and behavioural difficulties than those from intact families. Richman (1988) has described a variety of responses to parental divorce in preschool children, such as misery, withdrawal, disobedience, tempers, marked anxiety about the remaining parent going away, fears about separation, nightmares, sleeping and eating difficulties. She points out that boys remaining with their mothers are the most likely to present difficulties, and that they use various strategies to cope with separation from parents. Some deny the incident and some blame themselves; great anger may be expressed to the remaining parent, and finally, the child may be preoccupied with his or her absent parent's whereabouts and fate.

Children's reactions to bereavement are likely to be related to many factors such as family relationships, individual differences, social context, religious background of the family (Garmezy, 1983), the remaining parent's mental state and his or her personality (Wolff, 1981) etc. These reactions can be influenced by sex and age of the child at the time of the event and the time of the assessment (Garmezy and Rutter, 1985; Rutter, 1981b).

Stability of independent and dependent behaviour

What can be said about the stability over time of independent and dependent behaviour? There are social-emotional factors at one age which predict similar factors at another age despite changing social circumstances; early *secure attachments* provide a foundational learning experience through which children internalize or represent relationships (Sroufe and Fleeson, 1988). Such positive experiences help secure the long-term potential for independent development. Wider social influences also play their part. Kagan and Moss (1962) carried out a longitudinal study on 27 males and 27 females from birth through adolescence, at the Fels Research Institute. Their findings suggest that passive dependent behaviour remains stable over time for the dependent female but not for the dependent male. Their results are interpreted as supporting the importance of cultural influences which operate to reinforce gender roles. The social pressures work in such a way that the small boy is encouraged to become self-reliant and independent, while the small girl is directed toward the stereotype of relative passivity.

One of the child's major acquisitions on the road to becoming a social being (as we saw in Chapter 1) is the development of conscience. Erikson (1965) comments as follows on this momentous achievement:

> Man's childhood learning, which develops his highly specialized brain-eye-hand coordina-
> tion and all the intrinsic mechanisms of reflection and planning, is contingent on prolonged
> dependence. Only thus does man develop conscience, that dependence on himself which
> will make him, in turn, dependable; and only when thoroughly dependable in a number of
> fundamental values (truth, justice, etc) can he become independent and teach and develop
> tradition.

Reasonable conformity can be contrasted with unreasonable, or blind, conformity — as a socializing force that enables the child to learn the patterns of behaviour that will facilitate social acceptance. Erikson (1965) recognizes that there are risks attached to this vital aspect of socialization for the individual. As he puts it '... the immature origin of his conscience endangers man's maturity and his works: infantile fear accompanies him through life'.

Intervention

The diversity of the problems referred to as internalizing or emotional disorders requires planning on a case-by-case basis, treatment being decided on the basis of a broad spectrum functional analysis and a knowledge of the literature on particular problems.

Contingent attention

Shyness, the avoidance of, and timidity in social situations, has been tackled successfully (e.g., Walker *et al.*, 1979) by the use of contingent adult attention to increase peer interaction in preschool children. Peer mediated reinforcement, modelling and feedback have been shown (e.g., Furman, 1980) to be a useful adjunct to adult-mediated interventions.

Evers and Schwartz (1973) compared modelling — a 23-minute film — with modelling plus adult contingent reinforcement. They proved to be equally effective in reducing socially withdrawn patterns of behaviours by the increase of competing social responses. Both groups maintained their new and higher level of social interaction over a four-week follow-up period.

Desensitizing anxiety

Variants of systematic desensitization have proved useful in therapeutic work with (inter alia) socially anxious children. For example, rather than using muscular relaxation as the anxiety inhibitor, Lazarus and Abramovitz (1962) suggested the use of emotive imagery, i.e., the categories of imagery which are assumed to arouse feelings of self-assertion, pride, affection, mirth, and similar anxiety-inhibiting responses.

Methods used in work with children manifesting night-time fears include the use of engaging stories and images of heroic characters to build up a positive affect into which fear-eliciting stimuli are gradually interwoven (King, Cranstoun and Josephs, 1989).

EXTERNALIZING (CONDUCT) PROBLEMS

An assessment of externalizing (conduct) problems is likely to encompass a broad spectrum of childhood problems including (more particularly in the preschool child) moderately troublesome behaviours, as well as seriously antisocial acts — an increasing trend as the school-age child gets older. They range from the more or less involuntary forms of what are referred to as coercive or oppositional problems (commanding, screaming, crying, pestering, tantrums and negativism) to the legally defined delinquent activities. I will deal with the more serious conduct disorders when we get to the older child.

NON-COMPLIANT OPPOSITIONAL BEHAVIOUR (see Forehand and Peed, 1979).

The common theme running through this rather heterogeneous collection of problems is oppositional, disruptive behaviour and the parental disapproval it earns because it flouts parents' rules and because their consequences can be so annoying, even disturbing or explicitly hurtful to others. A tendency to disobey parents and other caregivers is one of the most common forms of behaviour problem of childhood (Johnson et al., 1973). Many children are disobedient, or go through disobedient phases (notably during toddlerhood). Some take to an extreme their antagonism to parental requests and commands. So intense is the resistance that at times it becomes quite clear that the child is not merely failing to comply, but is doing precisely the opposite of what is desired. This pattern is called negativism.

A child's oppositional behaviour is often maintained by the contingent application of positive social reinforcement in the form of parental attention. Such attention can come in a variety of forms, including verbal reprimands (scolding, nagging), reasoning with the child, or simply trying to be caring and understanding by discussing the misdemeanour at great length. In response to parental actions of this kind, the child may behave in a cooperative manner, thus reciprocally reinforcing the parental intervention. Wahler (1969) calls this process the 'positive reinforcer trap'. In most cases, oppositional behaviour is probably maintained by a combination of both positive and negative reinforcement (Gross, 1983).

Interestingly there is a fairly high correlation between overall *parental* negativism and child deviance. In an investigation of some of the processes involved Johnson and Lobitz (1974) were able to provide conditions (by instruction) in which parents in twelve families could manipulate the deviancy level in their children (aged from 4 to 6 years) according to prediction. They did this by increasing their rate of ignoring or commanding their offspring, and of being negative, restrictive, disapproving, and noncompliant.

In another study by the same researchers (Lobitz and Johnson, 1975) it was found that the best discriminating factor between 'normal' children and children referred for psychological treatment was a parental negativeness score. There was also a clear trend for parents of referred children to give more commands. Interestingly, there was a great deal of overlap in the distributions of deviancy rates in the referred and non-referred children, although the former showed significantly higher rates.

Noncompliance as a general trait

Johansson et al. (undated) made a study of the social and behavioural correlates of compliance and noncompliance in 33 'normal' children of 4–6 years of age and their families. The children and their families were observed in their homes on five separate occasions, for 45 minutes on each occasion. The behaviour of the target child and that of any family members who interacted with him was recorded with the use of a behavioural coding system designed for rapid sequential recording. It was found that there was significant consistency in children's compliance and noncompliance to their mothers and fathers. The authors found consistent evidence of a negative relationship between children's compliance ratio and the display of all other deviant behaviours; this suggests that noncompliance may be related to a more general tendency towards deviant activities. Although this finding provided some evidence for a general deviancy 'trait', the magnitude of the correlations is quite small; and although the correlations relating children's consistency of compliance across agents provided evidence for the generality of compliant behaviour, the correlations were at a low level.

Temper tantrums

Disobedient behaviour is often accompanied by a display of temper tantrums and aggression. The oppositional child, if coerced by his or her parents or teacher, can turn on a breathtaking display of hostility which, in its turn, is highly coercive. Patterson (1975) suggests that applications of pain control techniques (e.g., crying and screaming) by infants may be innate. Their yelling when in distress has obvious survival value. The use of these methods is maintained and, indeed, elaborated by many toddlers, and in some (further on in time) refined into coercive 'weapons' of great effectiveness in shaping parental behaviour (see page 283). The circular, or recursive, nature of negativistic behaviour in parent-to-child/child-to-parent interactions is central to the conduct problems and requires further analysis.

Resistance to social training

Patterson (1982) found that parents of 'anti-social' children issue more negative and vague commands than their 'normal control' counterparts. More recently Patterson and Bank (1986) confirmed this view by showing that such a parent's most common failure in parenting skills was inept discipline, scolding, threatening, and nagging (toward the child) and the use of frequent and intense physical punishment.

While Patterson emphasized the negative aspects of parent–child interactions, Gardner (1987) considered both positives and negatives in her study of preschool conduct disordered children. She found that relationships that subvert or negate socialization (when comparing problem and non-problem children) differ markedly not only with regard to the aversive interactions they have with their mothers, but also to the positive ones, as indicated by the amount of time spent in positive activities, and warmth during joint play.

It is not possible to describe, in anything but superficial detail, the reasons why certain children find it easier than others to conform to parental instructions and resist the temptation to break the rules. Fortunately this has been done very fully elsewhere (e.g., Aronfreed, 1968; Wright, 1971).

The strength of passive avoidance learning — the internalization of inhibition — has been demonstrated in a series of studies by Aronfreed and Reber (1965). These are worth describing in some detail as they have a bearing on the 'disciplinary encounters' which loom so large in the consciousness of parents and disobedient children.

In the initial experimental situation, each child was required to choose between two toys in each of nine trials. In each case, one toy was highly attractive, the other relatively unattractive. The child was told that certain toys were meant for older boys, and that he was not supposed to choose these toys. The choice involved picking up the toy he 'wished to tell about' and describing its function to the experimenter. When the attractive toy was chosen, the child was punished with verbal disapproval: 'No! — that's for the older boys'. Children quickly learned to discriminate, consistently choosing the unattractive toy after only two or three trials. Despite this narrow range of variance it was found that children who received punishment as they reached for the toy, that is at the initiation of transgression, learned inhibition of the prohibited behaviour significantly more quickly than children who were punished two or three seconds after they had lifted the toy. In a test for internalization directly following, where the child was left without surveillance with yet another pair of toys, a smaller incidence of transgression (touching the attractive toy) was found among the children punished at initiation of transgression. Twenty-five out of 34 of these children resisted the temptation to touch the forbidden toy, compared with ten out of 34 of the children punished at completion of transgression.

Aronfreed now intensified the punishment by adding deprivation of candy to verbal disapproval and giving cognitive structure ('toys for older children') to aid discrimination. Four variations in the timing of punishment were used. Timing of punishment did not have a significant effect on speed of learning although there was a tendency for inhibition to appear more slowly with increasing delay of punishment. However, timing directly influenced strength of internalization in the post-training test, in the expected direction. This suggests that 'suppression of the initiation of transgression is controlled by the anxiety that becomes attached to the intrinsic correlates of the incipient act' (Aronfreed, 1968). The typical post-training test behaviour of the children was picking up the unattractive toy, which also points to the role of non-punished behavioural alternatives in inducing stable inhibition. Non-punished behavioural choices may have anxiety-reducing functions in a situation where strong motivation to transgress conflicts with strong internalized inhibition. In naturalistic situations, acceptable behaviour alternatives to prohibitions may even be directly rewarded; failure to take into account the interaction of punishment and reward in such situations may account for the ambiguity of some research findings.

Since the temporal locus of punishment seems of crucial importance (yet one is aware that punishment under natural conditions is frequently far removed in time from the transgression) the role played by the child's ability to recall behaviour in representational and symbolic form is crucial. Aronfreed demonstrated the power of 'cognitive structure' in internalizing inhibition. When the child was told it would be punished for choosing toys which are 'hard to tell about' and therefore only appropriate for older children, this markedly facilitated suppression in the post-training test. But again, a reliable difference appeared between the situation in which the child received the verbal cognitive structure at the same time as the punishment, and the paradigm where the cognitive structure was presented between trials, this producing less stable internalization. It would seem that punishment attaches anxiety to cognitive representations according to the same temporal gradient observed in regard to the behaviour itself.

Finally a paradigm was designed which focused on the child's intentions (the child was told it would be punished for *wanting* to pick up a toy appropriate only for older children). This is of particular interest for a study of moral development — the role of intention in the acquisition of moral judgement. A verbalized cognitive structure focusing on the child's intention produced even stronger suppression than that which made no reference to intention. Even when the cognitive structure was changed to emphasize wanting to *tell* about the toy, so that the child actually picked up the prohibited toy before punishment, this was found to be equivalent — in strength of internalization produced — to the original condition where the child was punished immediately on reaching for the toy. But the effect disappeared when punishment occurred after both picking up and telling — thus underlining once more the importance of timing of punishment. It must be closely and distinctly linked to the intention itself *as it forms*.

Differential effects of the intensity of punishment on discrimination learning have been recognized for many years. Aronfreed and Leff (1963) — in demonstrations with children — have shown that if discrimination of the punished choice is difficult, intense punishment is actually *more likely* to lead to transgression subsequently. This finding has clear implications for child-rearing practices. A child who is unable to distinguish what aspect of his behaviour is being punished is unable to exercise control over the outcomes of its behaviour and is therefore subject to periods of prolonged anxiety and frustration. He or she will also fail to experience the anxiety-reduction associated with non-punished behavioural alternatives and so will not learn them.

It is suggested (Wright, 1971) that one of the most effective sanctions available to the mother is any action which threatens or implies the withdrawal of her approval. It provokes intense anxiety in the child, as distinct from aggression. There is evidence that punishments which evoke anxiety are likely later to result in self-control, while those producing an aggressive reaction are not — although they may well make a child wary of being caught.

Assessment

The most commonly used assessment procedures for noncompliance include the behavioural interview, rating scales, questionnaires and direct observation (see Gross and Wixtead, 1987; Lytton and Zwirner, 1975; Mash and Terdal, 1988; O'Brien and Budd, 1982; Quay and Peterson, 1983; Stiffman, 1983). A perennial problem for the psychologist assessing the seriousness of noncompliance is the ubiquity of disobedience as a 'problem' of childhood, a matter I touched upon on page 126. It is a 'normal' response to the 'rigours' of socialization (Forehand, Gardner and Roberts, 1978) although one that peaks at certain stages in the child's development, notably during the striving for independence which takes place in toddlerhood and adolescence (Haswell, Hock and Wener, 1981). Indeed, up to a point, disobedience is undoubtedly adaptive and its complete absence would be a matter of concern. But what is that 'point' at which noncompliance is thought to be excessive, counterproductive and thus maladaptive?

What is needed is normative data on rates of compliance in the population of children at large; and this is precisely what is lacking. Indeed, it is not an easy task to obtain norms. There are difficulties in finding a uniform definition of disobedient acts, and non-compliance rates vary according to criteria and means of measurement (Stiffman, 1983).

The interval method involves scoring compliance and noncompliance within an interval (say five or ten seconds) following a command. It is possible to count the number of, say, ten-second intervals (repeat instructions) it takes to obtain a compliant act. The total interval method compares the number of compliance or noncompliance intervals to the total number of intervals. One can take account of the *initiation* of a compliant act, or refrain from scoring until the *completion* of the required action as indicated by the parent's instruction (see Forehand and Scarboro, 1975; O'Brien and Budd, 1982).

The measure of compliance used by Hudson (1988) at the Psychology Clinic at the Phillip Institute of Technology in Melbourne, Australia, is such that to comply with a request or instruction the child must initiate a response within ten seconds of that request and complete it without repetition of the request. The rate of compliance (per cent compliance = instances of compliance/total requests) at which an intervention is considered necessary is something less than 50%. Current studies in the institute, establishing norms for Australia, indicate that the mean rate is approximately 60% with a range of 40–90%. Forehand's (1977) review of the normative data that is available indicates that compliance to parental commands for non-clinic normal samples range from approximately 60–80%. He makes the point that considering the range of experimental settings and compliance definitions employed, the agreement across studies provides a reasonable estimate of compliance norms.

Generic interventions for conduct problems

Developmental counselling on disciplinary issues should — in the light of the literature reviewed in Chapter 16 — have a preventative *and* 'remedial' function (Herbert, 1987a; 1989b).

The social-structural context within which conduct problems (particularly the severe variety) develop and thrive — poor housing, destitute inner city slum environments, physical and emotional deprivation — cannot be ignored in our desire to get on with individualized or family-based clinical interventions. Social and health policy issues represent another level of analysis and potential intervention which are of concern to community psychologists, which today also means a growing number of clinical psychologists. Family therapy has been used, but with less success than behavioural methods (see Chapter 16). Behavioural programmes for specific aspects of the conduct problem 'syndrome': noncompliance, aggression, disruptiveness, and a variety of antisocial, deceitful activities have been reviewed in detail by Herbert (1987b) and Kazdin (1987).

There is little doubt that parent training is the treatment of choice for oppositional behaviour. Several reports have been published of the successful modification in home settings (and other environments) of noncompliant-oppositional behaviour (e.g., Forehand and King, 1977; Forehand and McMahon, 1981; Forehand, Gardner and Roberts, 1978; Forehand, Wells and Griest, 1980; Peed, Roberts and Forehand, 1977; Webster-Stratton, Hollinsworth and Kolpacoff, 1989). They vary in the sophistication of their methodology (i.e., the extent to which they provide rigorous designs, precise base-line measurements and data, observer reliability figures, follow-up data, etc) and the extent to which the parents participate fully in the programme. They tend to use differential reinforcement: positive reinforcement plus extinction or time-out procedures.

In a typical intervention — which illustrates a time-series experimental design — Zeilberger, Sampen, and Sloane (1968) examined the effectiveness of time-out, extinction, and differential reinforcement in reducing a 5-year-old boy's aggressive behaviour and increasing his willingness to follow instructions. They successfully modified his severe screaming, fighting, negativism, teasing, and 'bossy' behaviour. Treatment was conducted at home with the mother as therapist. The authors trained the parents in the home, using daily one-hour sessions, showing them how to apply differential reinforcement. The procedures consisted of ignoring maladaptive behaviour, putting the boy in time-out, and giving social rewards paired with food or special toys for compliant behaviour. The parents did not have responsibility for making observations and recording data. Observations were made and recorded by two observers in the home. The training was apparently limited to specific techniques for dealing with the presenting problems rather than a broader theoretical framework which would allow them to deal with any subsequent problems in the child of their own accord. The authors incorporated a design for reinstating baseline conditions to demonstrate that the behaviour was in fact under the mother's control (see Figure 11).

The ABC of noncompliance: altering consequences

Most of the early behavioural work on non-compliance concentrated on the consequence side of the ABC equation, modifying (inter alia) parents' usual responses to the child's opposition by means of training in the employment of time-out from positive reinforcement (TO) and differential attention (DA). There have been reports of successful interventions along these lines (e.g., Goetz, Holmberg and Le Blanc, 1975; Tams and Eyberg, 1976) and reports of failure when DA was used on its own (e.g., Herbert *et al.*, 1973; Wahler, 1969). It is worth noting that the addition of DA was generally sufficient to bring about a positive outcome.

TO is a particularly potent aid to behavioural change and improvement in fiercely oppositional children (e.g., Day and Roberts, 1983; Roberts, Hatzenbuehler and Bean,

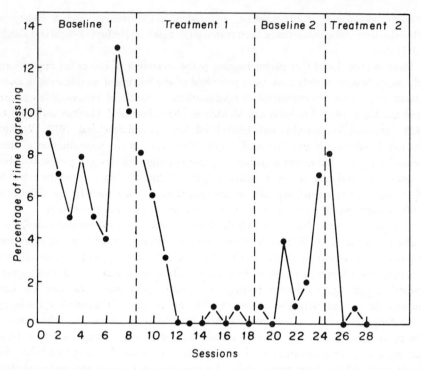

Figure 11. Rate of aggressive responding during treatment periods when positive responses were rewarded and injurious actions were punished by brief social exclusion. The figure shows the reductions in physical aggression achieved by a mother in her five-year-old son. (Source: Zeilberger *et al.*, 1968, reproduced by permission. © *Journal of Applied Behavior Analysis*.)

1981) and I have found it particularly valuable in cases of child abuse when non-compliance is a major complaint by parents. It allows parent and child the opportunity to 'cool down', and it tends to have face-validity for those parents (during the early stages of a programme) who demonstrate a punitive ideology of child-rearing and who find it difficult to engage in the positive aspects (so vital) of finding opportunities to encourage and praise their offspring. The essentially punitive quality of TO (sadly) gives it credibility for parents who have not yet moved on, in treatment, from an authoritarian view of discipline and power-assertive practices to more benign attributions as to why their children behave in the way they do. It is not simply an ethical matter of counterbalancing TO with positive attention (play, praise, additional contact) it is also good practice. Waller, Hobbs and Caldwell (1984) found that the best outcomes were obtained when both praise and time-out were employed (see also Hobbs and Forehand, 1977).

The ABC of noncompliance: altering antecedents

In recent years researchers/clinicians have paid more attention to the antecedent events that influence behaviour (e.g., Hudson and Blane, 1985), in the expectation that parents can preempt, by good anticipatory management, the child's antisocial repertoire. Several studies (e.g., Lutzker *et al.*, 1983) have pursued this reasoning with encouraging results.

There are several ways to alter proximal and distal antecedent events (see Figure 7, page 64) so as to increase (say) the parent's stimulus control in disciplinary situations:

(a) examining rules and expectations in the home (Herbert, 1987c, 1989b; McIndoe, 1989);
(b) assessing and altering setting events (Wahler and Fox, 1980; Wahler and Graves, 1983);
(c) attending to the nature of caregiver commands, instructions, requests (Roberts *et al.*, 1978);
(d) training caregivers in giving instructions (Forehand and McMahon, 1981; Hudson and Blane, 1985).

RULES

McIndoe (1989) makes the point that while a good deal of attention has been given to both verbal and non-verbal aspects of giving instructions, little attention has been given to more distal antecedents such as noncompliance to long-standing rules about expected behaviour. In a pilot study of parents' expectations of children's behaviour, she used a structured interview and questionnaire to obtain information about types of rules, methods of conveying rules, reasons for rules, frequency of rules being broken, and consequences for rules being followed and broken. Twelve categories of rules were established, two of which were meta-rules. One related to respect and cooperation (Meta-rule 1) and the other to compliance to rules (Meta-rule 2). The other categories related to manners, chores, behavioural prohibitions, safety and responsibility. Meta-rule 1, personal responsibility and chores were reported most often. Rules were conveyed verbally most frequently and three levels were established (Instructed, Reminded, Discussed).

Data on the frequency of rules being broken was not sufficient to draw many conclusions. However, the most frequently reported rules were those most frequently broken. Consequences for breaking rules were, like methods of conveying rules, largely verbal (Reminder, Rebuke, Discussion). When rules were followed parents most often praised the child or did nothing; overall positive consequences were twice as frequent as 'neutral' (did nothing) reactions.

Wahler and Graves (1983) acknowledge the role that setting events (e.g., stated rules, instructions) have in influencing parent–child interactions; they determine which stimulus–response interactions will become 'functional' for an individual, i.e., which will come to function *as if* they are discriminative stimuli. The targeted stimulus–response interaction need not display a contingent relationship with the setting event in order to become functional.

COMMANDS

We have seen that parents of children with conduct problems give more negative commands than parents of 'normal' youngsters. Parents with reasonably obedient children give more so-called 'alpha' commands. Alpha commands are characterized by being specific and direct, being given one at a time and being followed by a wait of five seconds.

Parents with noncompliant children characteristically employ more *stop* and 'beta' commands — chain commands, vague commands, question commands, 'lets ...' commands, and commands followed by a rationale or other verbalization (Forehand and McMahon, 1981; Peed, Roberts and Forehand, 1977; Williams and Forehand, 1984). The ineffectiveness of beta commands was convincingly demonstrated by Williams and Forehand (1984) when they found that beta commands were the best predictor of the child's noncompliance. Even though the mothers of oppositional children were aware that beta commands were less effective, they reported feeling unable to control the frequency of issuing such commands (Peed, Roberts and Forehand, 1977).

Parent training programmes attending to both antecedent and consequence sides of the ABC equation produce better generalization of effects; each side provides the parent with constructive skills (Forehand and McMahon, 1981).

DAILY ROUTINES AND PARENT–CHILD CONFRONTATIONS

Confrontations between disobedient children and their parents tend to be associated particularly with bedtime, bathtime and mealtime routines.

Eating and mealtime difficulties

Typical mealtime activities that cause concern are refusing food, fiddling with it, leaving the table, tantruming, crying and complaining. The mealtime setting should provide an important opportunity for children to learn social interactive skills and yet it seems a prime time for preschool children to engage in disruptive behaviour. Home based training programmes (based upon behavioural methods) for parents whose children display high rates of disruptive behaviour at mealtimes are few and far between. Nevertheless, the effectiveness of a range of behavioural treatment procedures has been demonstrated for reducing disruptive activity and the duration of meals, while increasing food intake (Ireton and Guthrie, 1972).

McMahon and Forehand (1978) found that improvements in the inappropriate mealtime behaviours of three preschool children and their mothers were associated with the provision of a brochure to parents. The brochure described a way in which behaviour management procedures could be applied to children's disruptive actions during meals. The subjects in the study were children from middle class families with behaviour problems limited to the mealtime setting. The provision of written information alone is often sufficient to produce behaviour change for problems which are not severe, long standing or present across a range of stimulus conditions (Clark, Risley and Cataldo, 1976; Hudson, 1980). (A useful review of treatment manuals is provided by Turvey, 1985.)

Research evidence indicates that more intensive training procedures might be needed when children have generalized behaviour problems (Bernstein, 1982; Iwata, et al., 1983; Koegel, Glahn and Nieminen, 1978; Nay, 1975).

Bedtime and sleeping difficulties

The effect of the exhaustion and stress on parents of intensive night-time disturbance on the part of their young children should not be underestimated or treated in a complacent manner. Richman's survey of 771 children with sleep disruption found that 10% in the 1–2-year age range had severe, that is to say, problematic, rates of waking (Richman, 1981). There are differences, of course, in the annoyance or tolerance threshold of their hapless parents; some become very distressed and angry, others seem resilient and/or forbearing. An unending series of sleepless nights can bring some parents to the point of abusing their children. Among the many causes of sleep disturbance, particularly in toddlers and older children, are factors associated with behavioural problems in general, some of which present themselves alongside the bedtime problems. Extreme disobedience is a noteworthy example.

Behavioural management techniques applied to settling and waking difficulties have been found to be successful in 90% of children between 1 and 5 years old (Richman et al., 1985). Douglas and Richman (1984) have produced a manual which has been successfully used by health visitors (68% improvement rate) (Farnes and Wallace, 1987) and in a community clinic (Thornton et al., 1984).

Part Four

The School-Going Child and Early Adolescent

INTRODUCTION

Children of 5 are said to lose some of their confidence and exuberance temporarily, as their capacity for being self-critical develops (Gesell, 1950). For a while they depend somewhat more upon adult emotional support. This dependency declines as their social horizons (at school and elsewhere) widen. The process of becoming a self-directed individual continues through *middle childhood* and on to *adolescence* as children attempt to achieve the goals society expects of them.

LIFE TASKS

These goals are communicated through parents, the school, and their peer group. They include:

- Developing a new individuality.
- Establishing relations with peers.
- Refining existing skills and acquiring new ones (physical, social and mental).

According to Elkind (1980), school-aged children tend to be ambivalent about attaining the ultimate status, control and power of adulthood. On the one hand they strongly desire to enter the fascinating world of adults, whose skills and abilities are admired; they are aware of the power and respect commanded by adults and wish for their approval. On the other hand — and this is the source of ambivalence about growing up and achieving these skills — there is a realization that adults may not have as much fun as they themselves enjoy.

MIDDLE CHILDHOOD (5–11)

It can be argued that the primary task of childhood is to develop ways of exerting control over the environment. Success in mastering a wide variety of physical, social and cognitive skills helps children to realize their own uniqueness and potential in the world of adults. The experiences that a child encounters in mastering this range of skills prepares him or her for eventual acceptance into the adult world.

Erikson (1965) has this to say:

> Children at this stage do like to be mildly but firmly coerced into the adventure of finding out that one can learn to accomplish things which one would never have thought of oneself, things which owe their attractiveness to the very fact that they are not the product of fantasy but the product of reality, practicability, and logic; things which thus provide a token sense of participation in the real world of adults.

The child is probably as amenable at this stage as he or she is ever likely to be to learning, direction and inspiration by others. What gets in the way of such readiness or subsequent achievements is the presence of emotional disorder, excessive competition, personal limitations, or other conditions which lead to repeated failure, resulting in feelings that one's behaviour does not work, and/or poor work habits.

RULES AND VALUES AT SCHOOL

Schools are in a powerful position to exert influence on their students; children spend almost as much of their waking life at school as at home. They enter an environment providing work and play for nearly a dozen years. The school introduces boys and girls to social and working relationships and to various forms of authority which they would not experience in the family. The areas of academic success, social behaviour, moral values and occupational choice represent major spheres of influence by teachers as well as parents in the socialization of young people. Rutter and a team of researchers, in their 1979 study of London secondary schools, found that children and adolescents are more likely to show socially acceptable behaviour and good scholastic attainment if they attend certain schools (regardless of their catchment area) rather than others (Rutter *et al.*, 1979).

The strong 'message' to emerge was that school values and norms appear to be more effective if it is clear to all that they have widespread support. Discipline is easier to maintain if the pupils appreciate that it relates to generally accepted approaches and does not simply represent the whims of the individual teacher. The particular rules which are set and the specific disciplinary techniques which are used are probably much less important than the establishment of some principles and guidelines which are clearly recognizable, and accepted by the school as a whole.

Problem areas

The school-going phase of a child's life is not without its problems; the demands of school seem to highlight, indeed exacerbate, the difficulties of vulnerable children. Garmezy (1983), considering the reactions of children to the major stressors of childhood, pointed to the age bracket of 5–10 as the most vulnerable age grouping, particularly if the stressor involved a period exceeding six months of separation from parents, siblings and the family home. Emotional disorders constitute just under half of the overall prevalence rate of children in their middle school years and adolescents; conduct disorders constitute a similar proportion (Rutter, Tizard and Whitmore, 1970). Yule (1981) provides a useful guide to the prevalence and type of childhood problems of the school-going period (see Table 12). These figures are helpful in the planning of a comprehensive strategy of child service delivery; it also provides a picture of the areas where the clinical child psychologist's expertise can usefully be enlisted.

Yule notes that handicapping problems are very common in the 9–11 age range. In the studies of over 2000 children in this bracket in the Isle of Wight in the early 1960s (Rutter, Tizard and Whitmore, 1970) there was a very strong relationship between school failure and behavioural problems. By the end of their junior schooling, 16 % in the 9–11-year age group were handicapped to a significant extent. In an epidemiological longitudinal study (Esser, Schmidt and Woerner, 1990), 356 out of 399 8-year-old German children were re-examined at age 13. The authors found that prevalence rates for psychiatric disorders in 8- and 13-year-olds lay in the range of 16–18 %. Between one quarter and one third of these children manifested serious disturbances definitely

Table 12. Prevalence rates of childhood disorders. Adapted from Yule, 1981, by permission of Plenum Publishing Corp.

		Rate per 1000
Hyperkinesis or Attention Deficit Disorder with Hyperactivity		1 (UK) to 30 (USA)
Conduct disorders		40–80
Emotional disorders	age 10–11 years	25–50
	$14\frac{1}{2}$ years	40–50
Phobias		3–6
Anxiety disorder		20
Depressive disorder	age 10	1.5
	age $14\frac{1}{2}$	15
Elective mutism	age $4\frac{1}{2}$–$5\frac{1}{2}$	7
	age 7	1
Anorexia Nervosa	age 12–18	4
Tics	age 6–7	100
	age 10	1
Stuttering		45
Enuresis	age 7	30 (girls), 70 (boys)
	age 10	20 (girls), 30 (boys)
	age 14	5 (girls), 10 (boys)
Encopresis	age 7–8	7 (girls), 23 (boys)
	age 10–11	3 (girls), 13 (boys)
Specific reading retardation	age 10–11	37

requiring professional treatment. The prevalence rates are lower than those reported (25 %) by Rutter *et al.*, (1975) for a large city (Inner London Borough) and higher than the rates (12 %) on the Isle of Wight (Rutter, Tizard and Whitmore, 1970). At the younger age level, only boys are found in this seriously affected group. Although the overall rates did not — in contrast to the Isle of Wight study — increase during adolescence, considerable shifts were seen in the relative frequency of individual diagnoses. Emotional disorders and developmentally related syndromes prevailed at the age of 8. Five years later, conduct disorders represented the most common category, even among girls. The observed stability of psychiatric disorders amounted to approximately 50 % — nearly the same as in the Isle of Wight (60 %) — but was demonstrated to vary remarkably across different types of disturbances. The course of emotional disorders gave rise to a very promising prognosis, which turned out to be even better than in the Isle of Wight study, whereas a highly unfavourable prospect was noted for conduct disorders. A study of 14-year-olds living in the Isle of Wight suggested a prevalence rate of 20 % of psychological problems in this age group. Leslie (1974) reported a similar rate for 13- to 14-year-olds living in a Northern English city. These findings bring us to a consideration of adolescence.

EARLY ADOLESCENCE

The notions of childhood and adulthood are clear enough. Children are wholly dependent upon their parents for love, nurturance and guidance; adults are required to be independent and able to care for themselves. Somewhere between the immaturity and the hoped-for maturity of adulthood lie the six or seven years referred to as adolescence. Seven years is far too long to reify adolescence into a homogeneous 'entity'. For this reason I will be taking the child only as far as *early* adolescence. It is sensible to distinguish between early, middle and late adolescence: the first (from about 11 to 13 years of age) being closer to childhood in its ramifications, the third (the late teens) overlapping with adulthood. Childhood ends, loosely speaking, with adolescence; the term 'adolescence' refers to the *psychological* developments which are related broadly to the physical growth processes defined by the term 'puberty'. Figure 12 provides some of the markers for the transition from one stage of development to another. Of course, the professional responsibility of clinical child psychologists transcends these somewhat arbitrary 'frontiers'. Indeed many clinical (psychology and psychiatry) posts are advertised in terms of combined child/adolescent specialisms.

By the time puberty arrives, triggered by an interaction between the sex hormones and certain cells of the brain, psychosexual development and differentiation between males and females in their identity with their gender, are well developed and largely irreversible.

Immense changes occur in puberty, and the maturing of the sex glands is of great consequence at this stage. Even more important, however, is the covergence of critical emotional and social developments which have been taking place since childhood, and which reach maturity now. The attainment of sexual maturity has a profound effect upon adolescents' status among those of their own age (see Herbert, 1987a; Rutter, 1979b, for reviews). Early-maturing boys and girls look grown up for their age and are thus given more responsibility by adults. They are likely to become leaders and to participate widely in school clubs and activities. They find it easier to compete and win at sport. Their self-confidence is boosted, and so is their popularity. Yet sometimes the strain of being different, of being expected to behave in a 'grown-up' manner, begins to tell.

Problem areas

Boys tend to cope with early maturing more easily than girls; their early maturity puts them on a par with girls of the same age. Girls, in particular, may find that their early maturity is perceived as sexually provocative by some. They may be self-conscious about their precocious sexual development, especially their body image and the fact of menstruation. Premature sexual development seldom means premature sexual outlets of

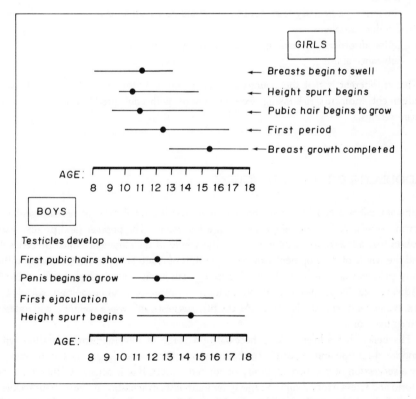

Figure 12. The age *range* for the onset of physical developments at puberty (● = average age).

an adult kind. In general, premature puberty leads to an increase in sexual arousal, but psychosexual behaviour tends to remain roughly in line with the child's actual age and social experience.

Late maturers look childlike for their age. They are more likely to be teased by their peers and thus beset by feelings of inferiority and a sense of social isolation. Girls are likely to suffer less than boys because they are on a par with most boys of their own age, but they may worry about late breast development and the onset of their periods, particularly if under pressure from their more physically advanced peers. Boys who are late developers seem to feel the most pressure and lack most in self-confidence.

As a major period of transition and change it would be surprising if there were not more serious problems than these, associated with adolescence; there are, but what is really surprising is that contrary to popular opinion (see page 195) adolescence does not, in fact, appear to be a markedly more vulnerable stage of development than others. Nevertheless, about one in five adolescents do experience significant psychological problems. Among these problems are:

- Depression (and suicide attempts, a much later phenomenon, with a peak at 15–19 years).
- Anxieties (particularly fears about school and social situations).
- Conduct problems.
- Eating disorders (anorexia nervosa, bulimia nervosa).
- Substance abuse.

What *is* different is that the youngster is at greater risk; the implications of errors of judgement, foolhardy risk-taking, experimentation with adult predilections, tend to be more serious.

ADOLESCENCE: FACT AND FICTION

Why, it must be asked, has adolescence been 'insulated' from the rest of development and given — relative to other stages — such a bad name? The popular (and professional) notion that adolescence is different from the whole of development which precedes it, and the whole of development which follows it, is of relatively recent origin. Among the early proponents of this view was G. Stanley Hall in his 1904 treatise on the subject: 'Adolescence: Its psychology and its relation to physiology, anthropology, sociology, sex, crime, religion and education'. As the title suggests, this was a weighty, and indeed, influential work.

His belief that adolescence is necessarily a stage of development associated with emotional turmoil and psychic disturbance was to become so deeply rooted, reinforced by a succession of psychoanalytically orientated writers, that it persists to this day. The 'storm and stress' story (built on eagerly by journalists in sensational items about feckless teenage hooligans and vandals) has filtered down to street level as a veritable 'demonological' theory of adolescence. Small wonder that so many parents await their child's adolescence with foreboding, and given the potency of self-fulfilling prophecies, the 'confirmation' for some of their worst predictions.

Certainly, the professional had tended to take a jaundiced view of adolescence, attention being drawn to neurotic- or psychotic-like features: hysteria, regression, mood swings and disintegration. Hutter in the 1930s described adolescence in Alice in Wonderland terms as a period of development 'in which normally abnormalities so often happen it is abnormal that everything passes normally' (Hutter, 1938).

Not much had changed by the 1950s. Anna Freud writing on adolescence in 'Psychoanalytic study of the child' said it was 'abnormal' if a child kept a 'steady equilibrium during the adolescent period ... The adolescent manifestations come close to symptom formation of the neurotic, psychotic or dissocial order and merge almost imperceptibly into ... almost all the mental illnesses' (Freud, 1958). In the 1960s, in 'Foundations of child psychiatry', the child psychiatrist, Gillespie, wrote that 'the astonishing contrasts and contradictions which are so characteristic of adolescence produce so strong an impression of instability as to lead sometimes to a mistaken suspicion of a schizophrenic illness' (Gillespie, 1968).

As a final illustration of the medical view of adolescence as pathology and one which almost brings us up to date, we have Van Krevelen writing in the 1970s that 'adolescence is a period of life, which by its disintegrative character may seem a psychosis in itself ... it is difficult to discern in this stage a pathological process from normal development' (Van Krevelen, 1971).

But are psychiatric symptoms, alienation, the generation gap, and identity crises really the norm? Take the storm and stress view of adolescence: this phase, although certainly not immune from its share of pain for those growing up (and for those guiding the growing-up process), is not unusually characterized by severe emotional disturbance. Although there may be problems, their overall significance and extensiveness have been exaggerated. Psychological problems are probably a little more common during adolescence than during middle childhood, but the difference is not very great (Graham and Rutter, 1973; Rutter, Graham, Chadwick, and Yule, 1976).

Alienation between generations

The much beloved (by the media) and feared (by parents) 'generation gap' is not as pervasive in adolescence as is generally thought (Herbert, 1987a). Distancing is not a typical pattern. Most adolescents are still attached to their homes in a positive way, and they continue to depend upon the emotional support, goodwill and approval of their parents. The family continues to be of critical importance to them as it was in earlier, less mature years; indeed, concern and supervision (as long as it is not oppressive, or too intrusive) can be demonstrated to be vital during a phase when youngsters are experimenting with life by 'trying on' different personae.

It is exceptional for teenagers to feel torn between their two 'worlds' of parents and peers, certainly on the more important issues of life. There are more likely to be differences of opinion on minor issues such as hairstyle, fashion, social habits and privileges, where parental views are likely to be rejected in favour of the standards of their offspring's friends. Where major issues are concerned, it seems that only a minority of adolescents radically depart from their parents' views; there is little evidence that secondary or higher education in itself causes changes in the political attitudes that young people absorb from their parents (Herbert, 1987a; Rutter, 1979b).

A majority of adolescents share their parents' attitudes towards moral and political issues, and are prepared (by and large) to accept their parents' guidance on academic, career and personal issues. If anything, it could be said that the generations are drawing together rather than apart (Hill and Aldous, 1969). Teenagers and their parents tend to agree on the important issues more than do parents and *their* parents (grandparents). Although the evidence is meagre, it does appear that rebelliousness and alienation are more likely in young persons who, in spite of considerable maturity, remain dependent on their parents economically or in other ways — such as students in higher education (Rutter, 1979b).

Another popular belief about adolescence is that an inevitable crisis over personal identity occurs, producing all or some of the symptoms of stress: anxiety, depression, a sense of frustration, conflict and defeatism. The development of identity does not always proceed smoothly, but what evidence we have calls into question the belief of Erikson (1965), that adolescents usually suffer a crisis over their identity. Most teenagers actually have a positive but not unrealistically inflated self-image and this view of themselves tends to be fairly stable over the years (Coleman, Wolkind and Ashley, 1977a).

Although adolescents have become more accepting in their attitudes to premarital sex, this does not imply, as the media like to suggest, a massive rise in casual sexual relationships. Young people, and particularly girls, continue to emphasize the importance of love and stable emotional attachment in premarital sex, although intended marriage or an engagement is not so often seen as a prerequisite of such relationships. The emphasis tends to be on a stable relationship with one sexual partner at a time — so-called 'serial monogamy' (Rutter, 1979b). Girls do, however, display more conservative attitudes to these issues than boys (see Chapter 12).

Most young people wish to get married and have children. Certainly, a committed relationship is generally thought to be essential for the rearing of children, and, although a majority of British adolescents would wish such a longstanding commitment to take the form of marriage, a substantial minority reject such a view (Rutter, 1979b; Schofield, 1973). An American study, by Sorensen in 1973, indicated that a majority of teenagers expect sexual fidelity after marriage, even though they do not expect it before then.

Cognitive development

It is during adolescence (roughly the years from 11 or 12 to 15) that the child begins to free his or her thinking from its roots in their own *particular* experience. They become capable of *general* propositional thinking, i.e., they can propose hypotheses and deduce consequences. Language is now fast, versatile, and extensive in its use. It is public, so that adolescents not only gain from their own thoughts but also from the articulated thoughts of many others. Their world has become larger and richer, socially, intellectually and conceptually. Both opportunity and training are essential to the development of logical and rational thinking and problem solving. It is not an innate characteristic; it depends upon the right sort of environmental stimulation and encouragement (particularly in the preschool period) and it also depends on natural growth processes. Logical thinking or rationality is an important requirement for adjusting to life's demands; it is also a vital criterion of mental health. It can also constitute a 'trial' for parents as teenagers flex their intellectual 'muscles' by asking 'why?' or 'why not?', and questioning parental social and moral values.

PARENTAL ATTRIBUTIONS

Why have parents been so prepared to believe the worst of teenagers? Doubtless the reasons are many and varied. Certainly, the context of raising teenagers is an important factor; parents are facing shifts at this time in their own personal development, from youthful maturity to early middle age. We cannot consider adolescents and their problems without considering the manner in which they interact with their parents (see Family Life Map, page 32), who are not without their own preoccupations and anxieties. Most parents are over 30-years-old when their first child reaches puberty. Indeed, there are many parents whose children reach their teens when they are in their forties or even fifties. Parents sometimes feel vulnerable as they survey their own bodily changes, reappraise their identity and achievements and look forward, with some apprehension, to the future. To some extent their preoccupation with self- and body-image, their changing, sometimes disturbing, thoughts about the meaning of life, the directions they have taken, and the choices put upon them, converge with those of their teenage children. This may well contribute to the ambivalence of parent–adolescent relationships.

For many parents, this parallel in developmental life tasks serves to sensitize them to their children's attempts to cope with change; it enhances their tolerance and understanding. For others, it is too sensitive and constitutes a threat. Selective amnesia seems to cloud some parents' judgement of young people.

Chapter 11

Problems of Middle Childhood
(from about 5 to 11 or 12 years of age)

DEVELOPING A NEW INDIVIDUALITY

The years of middle childhood are notable as a period in which youngsters' interactions with the people in their home and school environments help them to shape their personality, their individuality. The seriousness with which life is approached through work, and a preoccupation with what can be achieved, assist them to develop a sense of industry. In Erikson's framework of psychosocial development, the theme of this period of life is in a sense of duty and accomplishment — laying aside fantasy and play and undertaking real tasks, developing academic and social competencies. Crises are likely to be related to attitudes pertaining to 'industry' as opposed to feelings of 'inferiority'. The culture of childhood at this time in life is geared to a preoccupation with 'making things', especially with other children. Toys, which are still acceptable and desired, are of the type that help children to achieve a sense of success and accomplishment in making things. Not surprisingly, construction kits are especially popular.

Elkind (1967) describes the pragmatic-optimistic nature of school-aged children. The pragmatism shows itself in their concern with how things work and how to produce things of meaning and value that will receive the approval of others. Success in small endeavours feeds a sense of optimism about mastering new skills and acquiring new abilities. A source of this optimism for children according to Elkind, is their belief that there is an unlimited number of years in which to attain their goals and master the skills necessary to become an adult. The pragmatism that accompanies this optimism about themselves results in an attitude that persistent effort at a task eventually ends in its accomplishment. Achievement motivation is one of the earliest and most stable attributes displayed by children (McClelland, 1961).

The ever-increasing importance of social and extra-familial influences in the child's life has been discernible in the earlier developmental phases described in previous chapters. In order to achieve trust, autonomy and initiative it was necessary for the child to mix with an increasing number of people. Now, by going to school, his or her social universe is significantly extended. Where previously the parents and family were the main agents of socialization, in middle childhood, teachers, friends and peers now become important social influences. There are fairly crucial implications in the balance of power between parents and peer-group in the socializing of the child, as he or she grows older. Children at this stage tend to choose friends from those who live in the same neighbourhood or who are in the same class at school, also those who are about the same age. Even at this tender age children tend to choose friends who have the same status as themselves. In choosing friends, primary school children (after the age of 8 or so) prefer members of their own sex.

PROBLEMS IN THE CLASSROOM

Lippitt and Gold (1959) suggest that each classroom has its own social and emotional structure; children find their position in the structure of the class, and this position is thought to have a bearing on their social and academic adjustment. Glidewell et al. (1964) find that children who to do well in the classroom tend to possess the following attributes: they are middle class, with vigorous health, intelligence, and well-developed social skills. They are likely to have a good opinion of themselves, and the ability to gauge accurately their effect on others, to judge sensitively other people's approaches and responses of others to them. As skilful children gain more acceptance, power, and competence in the classroom, their self-esteem is enhanced. Under some conditions, they also develop more willingness to take risks by trying new approaches to people and tasks. Their new approaches can change their position in the system. As the risks — large and small — turn out to be fruitful, their self-esteem is further enhanced, and their status in the social system becomes even more gratifying. What Glidewell et al, call a 'circular, self-perpetuating process' thus becomes established. In plain English: 'success breeds success'.

At the other extreme, according to the findings there tend to be children with lower socio-economic status, who enter the classroom with less vigorous health, with limited intellect, and inadequate social skills. They are likely to be relatively anxious and to have low self-esteem. The evidence indicates that they tend to make awkward overtures to their peers and the teacher, and they are likely to provoke reactions which are, at best, restrained embarrassment, or at worst, hostile ridicule. They may feel humiliated, and are quite likely to react with either aggression or withdrawal, or both in alternation. If they respond aggressively, they are likely to invite some form of passive rejection or counterwithdrawal. The 'low-status' boys (often aggressive and troublesome) invite more criticism from the teacher than do their 'high-status' classmates, whereas the 'low-status' girls (often overdependent and passive) receive more emotional support from their teacher. The teacher's reaction tends to increase a boy's hostility and a girl's dependency.

The response of the other members of the classroom to the awkward child's social overtures are not likely to boost his or her self-esteem or social skills. Rejection breeds defensiveness and perceptual distortions; this leads to a reaction of further aggression or withdrawal from the other children, which in turn reduces the child's self-esteem. They do not make use of their full intellectual capacity. Again, a self-sustaining circular process is established. Failure breeds failure. Symptoms of emotional conflict and disturbance may also follow.

Cognition

Getting on toward 7 years of age children begin to solve problems concretely, using a variety of cognitive strategies which indicate the working of what Lazerson (1971) likens to a rational second-order as compared with lower-order 'computer' of earlier years. It is no accident that the child can cope with school at about the same time as the rational computer takes the dominant responsibility role so that he or she can see events from different perspectives and think conceptually about complex relationships (see Inhelder and Piaget, 1964).

Another significant finding is that developmental changes on a variety of intellectual tasks indicate that between 5 and 7 years of age there is a dramatic increase in the quality of performance on problems requiring focused and sustained attention. This generalization seem to hold for several cultures (Mussen, Conger and Kagan, 1984). The child under 5 years of age seems easily distracted and lacks the ability to select, shift and direct his or her focus like the over-fives. By the end of middle childhood we begin to see the fundamental difference between concrete operational thinking and the cognitive capabilities of the next stage which Piaget calls 'formal propositional thinking'.

The slow developer

We know that children develop at different rates in a variety of spheres of life; there is a wide range of differences which is quite normal. However, the really slow developer — be it physically, intellectually or emotionally — may face special difficulties in adjusting to school life. And these difficulties of adjustment are not necessarily confined to the opening phases of school life. The school environment is one which, all the time, is evolving towards greater complexity. It therefore continually increases its demands upon the child, demands of greater and wider mastery of intellectual, social and physical skills.

SPECIFIC LEARNING DISABILITIES

This is a major group of disorders which includes language, attentional and other deficits, and specific learning disabilities (such as reading) that appear to be associated and, in many cases, causally related (Rourke, 1983). In the past many of the brain-behaviour studies of problems such as these (currently among the concerns of clinical child neuropsychology) were linked to the concept of 'minimal brain damage' (or minimal cerebral dysfunction). A list of the dysfunctions commonly associated with brain damage in children typically included the following (Herbert, 1964):

- Language and other communication problems.
- Motor incoordination.
- Hyperactivity.
- Problems of attention.
- Perceptual difficulties.
- Specific learning difficulties (e.g., reading).
- Intellectual difficulties.

The concept of brain damage and the attempts to detect it with batteries of tests have lost favour, having been called into question by many (e.g., Herbert, 1964). The concept of 'learning difficulty or disability' covers the topics listed above but reflects psychological and educational rather than medical criteria. The term, like its predecessor, has proved to be overinclusive, imprecise and potentially misleading; nevertheless it endures and is probably to be preferred as a superordinate, umbrella term.

In the USA the legal definition is as follows:

> Specific learning disability means a disorder in one or more of the basic psychological processes involved in understanding or in using language, spoken or written, which may manifest itself in an imperfect ability to listen, think, speak, read, write, spell, or to do mathematical calculations. The term includes such conditions as perceptual handicaps, brain injury, minimal brain dysfunction, dyslexia, and developmental aphasia. The term does not include children who have learning problems which are primarily the result of visual, hearing, or motor handicaps, of mental retardation, or environmental, cultural, or economic disadvantage (1975, Section 5 (b)(4) Public Law 94–142).

The definition reflects its legal origins in its broadness, required as it is to have a good deal of generality in its application. What it lacks is behavioural referents which are specific to *learning difficulties* or rather (as it is a portmanteau term) the specific problems that come under its rubric.

Developmental factors appear to have a significant role in many of the conditions which I shall be discussing. Children suffering from language and learning disabilities tend to display a lag in neurological development. They differ most markedly in their skills from their normal counterparts when they are very young. Some catch up with time; others do not lose their neurological 'immaturities' and continue to show skill deficits as they get older (Denckla, 1979; Rourke, 1976a). Many children with learning disabilities display these deficits in a very uneven repertoire of abilities.

The Halstead-Reitan Neurological Test Battery (Boll, 1981) is a set of tests which is often used as part of a routine assessment. It includes classifications such as 'brain damage', 'normal', 'learning disabled' (Selz and Reitan, 1979). Telling criticisms have been levelled at the validity of the battery (e.g., Chadwick and Rutter, 1984), thus it is wise for the clinician (and this caveat applies to all classificatory tests in neuropsychology) to err on the side of conservatism when making an individual 'diagnosis'. It is worth considering what the requirements are for a diagnostic category to have scientific meaning. For Rutter (1978) it must be shown to be *distinctive* in terms of aetiology, course, response to treatment, or some variable *other than the symptoms that define it*. Not many of our clinical categories fulfil these criteria. Many are tautological descriptions that lack causal or treatment implications.

LANGUAGE AND OTHER COMMUNICATION PROBLEMS

The prevalence of language disorders (expression and understanding) is about 6 % of the child population (Cantwell and Baker, 1985a). These were dealt with in Chapter 8. It should be added that two tests of language ability have been developed on the basis of Osgood's theory of linguistic behaviour: The Illinois Test of Psycholinguistic Abilities (ITPA) (Kirk and McCarthy, 1962) and the Differential Language Facility Test (DLFT) (Sievers, 1959).

The authors of the ITPA (Kirk and McCarthy, 1962) make it explicit that their test (consisting of nine subtests which were standardized on 700 children between the ages of $2\frac{1}{2}$ and 9) is not presented as an instrument of classification, i.e., for the purpose of labelling a child as belonging to the particular group, type, or category, but as an instrument which assesses a child in such a way that an educational or remedial programme can be initiated. The test describes deficits in various psycholinguistic functions found particularly among cerebral palsied, brain-injured and some emotionally disturbed children. (Stephens and Montgomery, 1985, provide a critique of recent standardized language-function tests.)

MOTOR-INCOORDINATION

Poor motor coordination — a discrepancy between the mind's intention and the body's execution — is commonly found in children described as learning-disabled. Annell (1953) studied children with difficulties in fine motor function. She reports that it was not uncommon for their difficulties to remain unremarked or misunderstood at home. Direct inquiries disclosed that these children had been able to sit up and walk at the usual age but had been late in learning to dress themselves — in many cases they were unable to do so independently when they started school. Their table manners were frequently bad; they spilt liquids and ate clumsily. Articulatory difficulties of speech were often present as were writing difficulties. At school, hand-writing and drawing were particularly troublesome. Many of these children were enuretic and encopretic. It is difficult to determine whether these symptoms are due primarily to lack of sphincter control associated with general difficulties in fine motor functions, or whether they are part of a secondary psychogenic reaction. As a rule these two influences were thought to be jointly responsible.

Annell is concerned that disturbances in fine motor function may be overlooked or misinterpreted. The Gollnitz revision of the Oseretzky Test of Motor Ability has been used for research and clinical assessment (Stott, Meyes and Headridge, 1966).

HYPERACTIVITY

We have all known active, indeed 'overactive' children. But when do they become 'hyperactive' in the clinical sense, with all that that label implies? Hyperactive children are usually assessed as such because they display a pattern of persistent restlessness and inattentiveness that began early in their lives. Having said that, these children are not simply more active than most other children; they appear to have particular problems in controlling their behaviour in situations requiring concentration and relative immobility, e.g., mealtimes, classroom activities. Their parents (and teachers) complain about how exhausting, even demoralizing, they are to care for and teach. Rutter (1967), on the basis of his studies of hyperactive children, had this to say:

> These children are the despair of the school teacher. They are usually of below-average intelligence and may show any of the other developmental abnormalities ... delay in speech, clumsiness, difficulty in learning to read, poor perception and understanding of shape relationships and difficulties in differentiating right from left. Often, too, the children have fits. In middle and later childhood this over-active pattern of behaviour is often gradually replaced by an inert under-activity in which the children seem to lack drive and initiative, poor relations with other children continue and anti-social behaviour may develop.

This last feature has caused me to examine the problem in more detail under the heading of 'antisocial disruptive' problems in Chapter 16. It also has implications for the child's ability to achieve at school. Between 40 and 50 % of hyperactive children have learning problems (poor academic and test performance) (Weiss et al., 1971) and about 80 % have been reported as behaving very badly at school. Figures like these must be treated cautiously. This problem area is confusing; ambiguities over the definition abound because it has had so many names, including hyperkinesis, minimal brain dysfunction and more recently, Attention-Deficit Disorder with Hyperactivity (see below). Here the focus has shifted from excessive motor activity to poor attending skills.

Rutter (1984) states that the issue is not whether hyperactivity/attentional deficit syndromes differ from normality, which obviously they do, but rather whether they differ in any meaningful way from *other* psychiatric conditions. In his view there is no good support for the broad notion of a ubiquitous hyperactive or attentional deficit syndrome that accounts for half the cases seen at child psychiatric clinics. But there are pointers that there may be a less common syndrome definable in terms of overactivity and inattention that is manifested across a range of situations and circumstances.

PROBLEMS OF ATTENTION

The DSM-III posits a specific ADHD syndrome (APA, 1980). This is an attention deficit plus hyperactivity disorder. The number of symptoms specified is for children between the ages of 8 and 10, the peak age for referral. In younger children, more severe forms of the symptoms and a greater number of symptoms are usually present. The opposite is true of older children. The criteria include:

A   *Inattention.* At least three of the following symptoms:
   (i)   Often fails to finish things he or she starts.
   (ii)   Often doesn't seem to listen.
   (iii) Easily distracted.
   (iv)   Has difficulty concentrating on schoolwork or other tasks requiring sustained attention.
   (v)   Has difficulty sticking to a play activity.
B   *Impulsivity.* At least three of the following symptoms:
   (i)   Often acts before thinking.
   (ii)   Shifts excessively from one activity to another.
   (iii) Has difficulty organizing work (not due to cognitive impairment).
   (iv)   Needs a lot of supervision.
   (v)   Frequently calls out in class.
   (vi)   Has difficulty awaiting turn in games or group situations.
C   *Hyperactivity.* At least two of the following symptoms:
   (i)   Runs about or climbs on things excessively.
   (ii)   Has difficulty sitting still or fidgets excessively.
   (iii) Has difficulty staying seated.
   (iv)   Moves about excessively during sleep.
   (v)   Is always 'on the go' or acts as if 'driven by a motor'.
D   Onset before the age of 7.
E   Duration of at least six months.
F   Not due to schizophrenia, affective disorder, or severe profound mental retardation.

Teachers frequently report that children with learning disabilities are unable to sustain attention to tasks of some duration or they are ineffective at filtering out, i.e., ignoring, irrelevant aspects of a learning situation. There is evidence to suggest that learning-disabled children do not apply 'selective attention' to the same degree as non-disabled children (e.g., Cruickshank, 1977); they recall less central information in a situation and more irrelevant information.

Attention deficit disorders can be diagnosed either with or without hyperactivity according to the DSM-III-R classification system; in the latter case it is referred to as 'Undifferentiated Attention Deficit Disorder'. What is interesting about this group is the consistent findings with regard to its behavioural characteristics. The children display poor academic functioning and tend to be perceived as sluggish, drowsy, and apathetic, and do not have conduct problems. They may also be anxious, shy and socially withdrawn (see review of evidence by Carlson, Lahey and Neeper, 1986).

The two attention deficit groups — with or without hyperactivity — should differ in clinically important ways. The prognosis for the group without hyperactivity (and manifesting little in the way of aggression or other conduct problems) is likely to be more benign because of the absence of aggressive behaviour. Aggression is highly correlated with poor teenage outcome (Loney, Kramer and Milich, 1981); children who have conduct disorders are likely to display antisocial behaviour later in life (August, Stewart and Holmes, 1983).

PERCEPTUAL DIFFICULTIES

Two broad theoretical perspectives have dominated the explanations offered for the various learning disabilities: 'academic instruction theory' and 'perceptual deficit theory'. In the former theory it is suggested that learning disabilities represent problems of teaching rather than learning. It is a case of teachers having failed to instruct adequately rather than children being incapable of learning subjects like reading, writing and number work. There is little support for this proposition as a *general* explanatory principle.

The perceptual deficit theory suggests that children have extensive difficulties in particular areas of learning because they make errors in perceiving and processing sensory stimuli (Cruikshank, 1977). Certainly many children described ('diagnosed') as having learning disabilities are frequently reported as suffering from a disturbance in the awareness of objects, relations or qualities involving the interpretation of sensory stimulation. But are these factors sufficient or necessary causes of such a condition? The answer is probably no; there has been a failure to isolate perceptual deficits in many learning disabled children.

Nevertheless it is important to be aware of those that do occur.

Visual perception

Some 50 years ago it was reported that brain-injured children suffer from perceptual disturbances (such as a tendency to be attracted to the details of a stimulus), and consequently have an ability to conceptualize and respond to the gestalt. Perceptual anomalies in which the subject confuses, reverses or fails to discriminate figure and background were also reported in the research that ensued (Werner and Strauss, 1941).

These distortions have been studied by means of the Marble Board Test (Strauss and Lehtinen, 1947). On this test, the subject is required to copy designs set out by the examiner on a marble board. An incoherent, disconnected or disorganized type of copying procedure is said to be characteristic of brain-damaged children. A perceptual test like the Marble Board Test can be misleading. It is possible that the test's ability to detect brain damage is an artefact of, or inflated by, criterion contamination. Criterion contamination occurs when the type of information which is central to the test being validated is used in the selection of the criterion groups against which the test will be validated. In constructing a diagnostic test it is essential to have an adequate independent criterion of brain injury. However, there is no discussion of the proportion of brain-damaged children in the standardization sample who were diagnosed as such according to an independent criterion of injury.

By and large (as we have seen) the diagnosis of 'brain damage' per se in children has been abandoned and tests are used descriptively and for their implications in constructing rehabilitative or remedial programmes. Cruickshank (1977) contends that perceptual factors are the key to defining learning disabilities. Furthermore he has claimed that irrespective of the presence or absence of diagnosed neurological dysfunction, learning disabilities are essentially and almost always the result of perceptual problems based on the neurological system.

Since visual stimuli constitute a substantial source of information for the child in the classroom, abnormalities of visual perception are the source of significant performance handicap in this setting. Figure-ground discrimination (the Marble Board Test), visuo-motor performance (Bender Visual-Motor Test; Minnesota Percepto-Diagnostic Test); visual retention (Benton Visual Retention Test; Memory for Designs Test) and visual discrimination figure among the visual modalities in which learning-disabled children find particular difficulties in processing sensory information.

Auditory perception

Auditory perception involves the ability to recognize, organize, and interpret stimuli that are received through the sense of hearing. Learning-disabled children tend to have difficulties in one or more of four different components of auditory perception: discrimination, association, memory, and blending (Bryan, 1977). As with visual perception, the auditory modality is vital in school life for the reception of information. So it can be devastating if children (a) cannot distinguish between the sounds of certain syllables or words, (b) cannot make simple associations between ideas that are presented visually, (c) are unable to recall information presented in that modality, or (d) cannot blend the phonemic element (e.g., c–a–t) together into a whole (cat).

When an assessment uncovers problems in the auditory and or visual sensory systems, it may be necessary to teach, say, reading, through alternative modalities.

SPECIFIC LEARNING DIFFICULTIES (READING PROBLEMS)

This problem is fairly common and is usually found in boys. Using a criterion of two standard deviations (or about two years retarded) below expected reading age, specific retardation of reading has been found in some 10 % of inner-London children (Berger, Yule and Rutter, 1975). In the Isle of Wight survey (Rutter, Tizard and Whitmore, 1970) 4 % of the children were found to be reading at least 28 months below the level expected on the basis of their age and intelligence. They were all children of normal intelligence. Many backward readers were found to be clumsy and delayed in their speech. The backward readers showed difficulties in telling right from left. They also suffered from what is called motor impersistence. That is to say they couldn't hold any movement, such as shutting their eyes, for very long. They also had general difficulties in concentrating. Reading backwardness often goes hand in hand with difficulties in arithmetic and spelling, and it is not uncommon for there to be a family history of reading difficulties. The causes are probably multifactorial and include (notably) poor home situation, inadequate teaching, lack of home–school cooperation and genetic factors. Emotional problems are fequently associated with backwardness in reading; a third of the children with severe reading backwardness also exhibited marked antisocial behaviour.

INTELLECTUAL DIFFICULTIES

I.Q. level is obviously important in learning difficulties (see page 201), but in itself it is of little diagnostic value in detecting cerebral pathology. The entire range of intelligence will be found in a large sample of brain-damaged children (Meyer and Simmel, 1947). Some of these children produce superior performance. However, there is an overall negative correlation between I.Q. and brain injury (Pond, 1961).

Psychologists have studied the patterns of successes and failures obtained by brain-injured children on tests of general intelligence. This approach is based upon the hypothesis that brain-injured children often show selective impairment of intellectual functioning. For example, it is postulated that verbal items are more resistant to deterioration than performance items. This has been the basis of the popular 'verbal minus performance' index of brain damage. The Wechsler Intelligence Scale for Children (WISC-R) is particularly suited to this type of analysis as it is possible to estimate the statistical significance of an abnormal discrepancy between verbal and performance scales. Unfortunately, the interpretation of this index is complicated by the possibility that a spuriously high or low verbal score may be the partial result of home background factors. In addition, large discrepancies have been obtained from patients with no brain damage, and an absence of discrepancies found in children with demonstrable brain damage (Herbert, 1964). There are tables which allow the significance of any given verbal-performance discrepancy to be calculated according to its frequency in the general population. Among children aged $10\frac{1}{2}$ years, 25 % have discrepancies of 13.8 or more and 10 % obtain discrepancies of 19.7 or more.

Norris (1960) could not confirm the validity of this index. The explanation given for the allegedly poor performance ability of brain-damaged children is that they suffer from a visuo-spatial defect. Norris used 'Maxwell's (1961) WISC 'factor scores', on the assumption that a 'purer' visuo-spatial measure could give better discrimination. An analysis of the records of 198 children referred to a psychiatric hospital demonstrated that the 'verbal minus performance' index did not differentiate brain-damaged from non-brain-damaged patients.

An analysis of the pattern or scatter of subtest scores on tests like the Stanford-Binet

Test, the Cattell Infant Intelligence Scale and WISC, has been used to discern a typical profile of subtest scores, diagnostic signs which are pathognomonic of brain damage. An extensive literature (e.g., Rowley, 1961) has demonstrated, theoretically and empirically, the difficulties inherent in the diagnostic use of subtests. Their reliability coefficients (where published) are seldom high enough to bear the weight of diagnosis. The factorial composition of subtests is often not fully understood, or its implications for diagnosis, that is the changing factorial composition of subtests for different age groups, are not appreciated. A complicating factor in assessing the significance of subtest deviations in brain-damaged subjects, is the demonstration of greater dispersions of test scores in neurotic children than in normal controls (Maxwell, 1961) and the apparent sensitivity of certain subtests said to be pathognomonic of brain damage (e.g., block designs) to psychopathology (Caputo et al. 1962).

SEQUELAE OF ACADEMIC FAILURE

Failure to make progress in basic academic skills during adolescence can produce severe, long-term handicapping effects. It is rare to identify academic failure in adolescence in isolation from a range of other problems, particularly disruptive activities in the school setting and/or disturbance in relationships between the adolescent and other members of the family. Although the learning problems of adolescents in the school setting may sometimes be causally linked to attentional and other specific learning deficits, academic failure arising from such problems is much more likely to be manifested during the infant primary school years (Torgesen, 1975). Studies (e.g., Trites and Fidorowicz, 1976; Peter and Spreen, 1979) indicate that specific deficits in reading persist through adolescence into adulthood with the youth falling further and further behind. These effects seem to be most marked for female adolescents.

BEHAVIOUR PROBLEMS

Children with specific difficulties in learning manifest a variety of emotional and conduct problems, ranging from aggressive and disruptive behaviour, to anxiety, poor motivation and low self-esteem (Yule and Rutter, 1985). These are referred to by staff in many care and educational establishments as 'challenging' behaviours. There is also evidence that many such children fail to develop appropriate social skills (LaGreca, 1981).

Assessment

Because educational failure tends to have so many repercussions, the extent of the difficulties should be assessed in interviews with the young person, the parents and

teachers. School reports, giving details of the student's work and examination performance, may have to be augmented with a psychometric assessment of cognitive and
attainment skills, direct observation of the youngster's academic behaviour in the
classroom, and assessment of his or her social behaviour in the educational setting. In the
UK it is most likely an educational psychologist who will carry out such an investigation.

Intervention

The role of clinical child psychologists lies in the planning of interventions designed to
help the child, parents and teachers understand the nature and implications of the
problem. There may well be some overlap here with the work of the educational
psychologist, a matter to be resolved with diplomacy and consultation.

There is as yet no clear remedial or therapeutic procedure for specific learning
difficulties and the outcome is not a very optimistic one. Nevertheless a clinical
psychologist may well be able to offer valuable assistance with the associated behaviour
and management problems (Fontana, 1986; Shapiro, 1987). LaGreca's 1981 findings on
the poor social skills of children with learning difficulties have obvious implications for
social skills training, targetting especially positive verbal interactions, conversation skills,
non-verbal behaviour and pro-social behaviour. Studies that have investigated role-taking
abilities and skills in comprehending non-verbal communication, suggest that the
learning-disabled would benefit from specific skill training in these areas.

If unrealistic standards are set at home or school, it is not long before children become
self-conscious about the discrepancy between their performance and the level of
aspiration set for them by adults. After all, they are supposed to know best. A sense of
failure very often manifests itself in a 'don't care', obstinate facade behind which the child
hides. For many children who have been condemned at school, the great release comes
when they go out into the workaday world and have to earn a living and perhaps support
a family. They find new incentives and rewards for their efforts, and they surprise
themselves with their capacity for hard work and application.

They can no longer be labelled 'backward' — they cope with life's demands. This is
also the case for those many worthy children who are a little short on the much prized
(and somewhat over-rated) quality 'brightness'.

Chapter 12

Problems Related to Identity and the Self-concept

SELF-ATTITUDES

A reasonable agreement between the self-concept ('myself as I am') and the concept of the ideal self ('myself as I would like to be') is one of the most important conditions for a favourable psychological adjustment — at school and in other aspects of the child's life (Ausubel *et al.*, 1954). Marked discrepancies (i.e., negative self-concepts) are likely to arouse anxiety, unhappiness and a sense of dissatisfaction with life (Crandall and Bellugi, 1954). Under-achievers at school have been found to have poorer self-concepts than normal achievers and reflect feelings of defensiveness, loneliness, and being unduly restricted in their freedom (Ausubel *et al.*, 1954). It is clear that self-attitudes — as central and organizing aspects of personality — provide a gauge of the child's adaptation to his or her life-situation; they involve their meaning for others, how they want to be seen by others, and also what they wish to be like. Positive self-attitudes are the basic ingredients of positive mental health, and negative self-concepts among the critical predispositions to maladjustment (Coopersmith, 1967).

Assessment

The DSM-III-R has a category for problems relating to identity (see below). The essential feature of what is called 'identity disorder' (Code 313.82) is an inability to integrate various aspects of the self into a coherent and acceptable sense of self, causing considerable subjective distress, e.g., depression, anxiety or self-doubt.

The diagnostic criteria for identity disorder include the following:

A   Severe subjective distress regarding uncertainty about one or more issues related to identity, including at least *three* of the following:
   (i)   Long-term goals.
   (ii) Career choice.
   (iii) Friendship patterns.
   (iv) Sexual orientation and behaviour.

    (v)   Religious identification.

    (vi)   Moral value systems.

    (vii) Group loyalties.

B   Impairment in social or occupational (including academic) function as a result of the above symptoms.

C   Duration of at least three months.

D   Does not occur exclusively during the course of a Mood Disorder or a Psychotic Disorder.

E   Not sufficiently pervasive and persistent to warrant a diagnosis of Borderline Personality Disorder.

The term adjustment as it applies to personality and self has multiple meanings. The notion of integration is one of these. We speak of a well-integrated personality when the many facets of personality — different attitudes, opinions and beliefs which make for a harmonious self-concept — are organized into a smoothly functioning and congruent whole; that is, when internal conflicts and contradictions are at a minimum, the person enjoys a unifying outlook on life (see Allport, 1937; Jahoda, 1958).

Autonomy is another criterion of adjustment and refers to the extent to which the individual is capable of independent or self-directed behaviour. Obviously this notion of self-containment can only be applied in a relative sense to children, as they are dependent to a large extent on adults at this stage of life. Nevertheless, growing up consists largely of learning to do things for oneself and having confidence in one's ability and competence.

SELF-ESTEEM

Coopersmith (1967) conducted a series of studies of self-esteem, applying the techniques of clinical, laboratory and field investigation. The subjects consisted of a representative sample of normal boys aged 10–12 years, who were followed from this pre-adolescent stage to early adulthood. Various indices of self-esteem were used. Coopersmith provides evidence that the optimum conditions required for the achievement of high self-esteem in children are a combination of firm enforcement of limits on the child's behaviour, together with a marked degree of freedom or autonomy within these limits. As long as the parentally imposed constraints are backed up by social norms outside the home, this provides the youngster with a clear idea of an orderly and trustworthy social reality which, in turn, gives him a solid basis for his own actions.

Coopersmith found that children with a high degree of self-esteem are active, expressive individuals who tend to be successful both academically and socially. They initiate, rather than merely listen passively, in discussions, are eager to express opinions, do not evade disagreement, are not particularly sensitive to criticism, are very interested in public affairs, showed little destructiveness in early childhood, and are little troubled by feelings of anxiety. They seem to trust their own perceptions and reactions, and are confident in the likelihood of success in their endeavours. The approach to other persons is based upon the expectations that they will be well received. Their general optimism is not misplaced, but founded upon accurate assessments of their own abilities, social skills, and personal qualities. They are not self-conscious or obsessively preoccupied with personal problems. They are much less frequently affected with psychosomatic disorders (insomnia, headaches, fatigue, intestinal upset) than are youngsters of low self-esteem.

Those with low self-esteem presented a picture of discouragement and depression. They tended to feel isolated, unlovable, incapable of expressing or defending themselves and too weak to confront or overcome their deficiencies. They were anxious about angering others and shrank from exposing themselves to the limelight in any way. In the presence of a social group, be it school or elsewhere, they remained in the shadows as audience rather than participants, sensitive to criticism, self-conscious, preoccupied with inner problems. This dwelling on their own problems not only exacerbated their feelings of malaise but also isolated them from opportunities for the friendly relationships such persons need for emotional support.

The boys tended to gauge their individual worth primarily by their achievement and treatment in their own interpersonal environment, rather than by more general and abstract norms of success. A correlation of $+0.36$ was found between positive self-concept and school achievement. Self-esteem and popularity correlated $+0.37$. The teachers, in the main, judged these youngsters very much as they judged themselves.

ADOLESCENT IDENTITY

We have seen, in an earlier chapter, that there is a popular but erroneous belief in an almost inevitable adolescent identity crisis which is accompanied by symptoms of stress, such as anxiety, depression, frustration and defeatism. Erik Erikson's views on the development of identity have been very influential. In his 1965 and 1968 studies he sees adolescence as a stage in the life-cycle with a particular challenge or task to be met. For the teenager it is the challenge between 'identity' and 'identity diffusion' — in a sense, one set against the other (see Figure 13 which is an adaptation of Erikson's ideas about the vicissitudes of identity development, put in the form of a flow chart). In leaving behind their childish roles (stage 1), adolescents are thought to become preoccupied with finding for themselves a satisfactory answer to the question 'Who am I?'. They may 'try out' a variety of identities in their search for answers; they seek experience in different roles and through a variety of relationships (stage 2). It is self-exploration through experimentation. Some settle for an immature self too soon ('foreclosure'). Others are too late; thus it is suggested that if boys and girls fail to clarify and give substance to their personal identity they are likely to experience depression and even despair. These feelings, plus a sense of meaninglessness and self-depreciation, are the indications of what Erikson calls 'identity diffusion'. Of course, many of us never cease questioning our

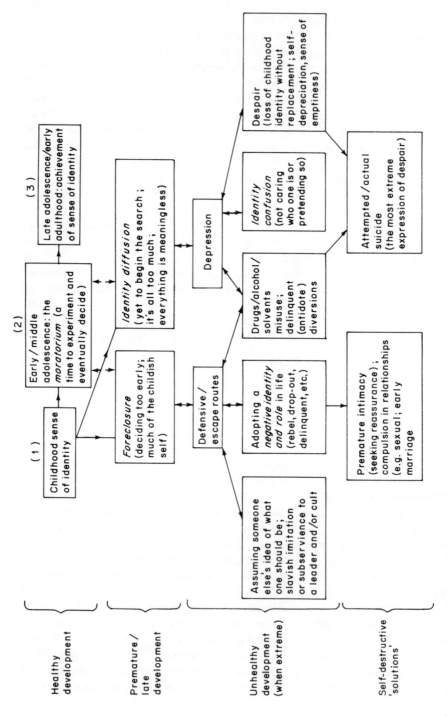

Figure 13. Stages of identity development (based upon Erikson, 1965.)

identity and elaborating or reshaping our personalities, but we enjoy the security of a clear sense of who we are (stage 3).

Depression figures a good deal in this theory of identity crisis and, as a relatively common feature of adolescence, is a possibility requiring vigilance on the part of the psychologist carrying out an assessment.

DEPRESSION

Depressive reactions are often mentioned in the literature as concomitants of school refusal and truancy; they also figure in discussions of problems such as failure-to-thrive, substance abuse and delinquency. But depression has only recently achieved the status of a problem of childhood in its own right, a syndrome rather than a predictable response to loss or deprivation (Cantwell and Carlson, 1983). Because of its undermining effects and the risk of suicide, childhood (and, indeed, adolescent) depression has become an increasing concern of people in the helping professions (Kazdin, 1990).

Assessment (see Finch, Saylon and Edwards, 1985; Kazdin, 1989; Kovaks, 1980)

Anxiety and depression — which both come under the 'internalizing problems' category — have nevertheless been treated, generally, as separate disorders in young people. But they can, and do, occur together. Depression is more likely to be manifested in children and adolescents with severe symptoms of anxiety (Bernstein and Garfinkel, 1986). This means that any assessment must be comprehensive enough to allow for the possible coexistence of depression and anxiety.

The checklist below contains the main signs of depression:

- A demeanour of unhappiness and misery (more persistent and intense than 'the blues' which we all suffer from now and then).
- A marked change in eating and/or sleeping patterns.
- A feeling of helplessness, hopelessness and self-dislike.
- An inability to concentrate and apply oneself to anything.
- Everything (even talking and dressing) seen as an effort.
- Irritating or aggressive behaviour.
- A sudden change in school work.
- A constant search for distractions and new activities.
- Dangerous risk-taking (e.g., with drugs/alcohol; dangerous driving; delinquent actions).
- Friends being dropped or ignored.

The milder form of depression may show itself as a lack of physical energy and well-being. In its more severe manifestations children and adolescents tend to be irritable and bad-tempered, and, when it is at its worst, they sleep poorly, lack an appetite, and are always dejected, apathetic and lifeless. Adolescents who are (for whatever reason) depressed feel helpless, sad and useless and find it sometimes impossible to meet the challenges of life. They cease to strive and to use their full effectiveness in whatever sphere of activity they find themselves.

The apathy of a young person with depression is often mistaken for laziness. Depression can be masked (particularly in adolescence) by frenetic, often antisocial, risky activities, and thus not easily detected. Another difficulty for the clinician is that any item in the list above can occur normally in adolescence without in any way indicating a depressive disorder.

The questions below are useful supplementaries:

● Are there several of the signs (listed above) present?
● Do they occur frequently?
● Have they persisted for a long time?
● Do they cause extensive suffering to him or her?
● Do they stand in the way of his or her development towards maturity?
● Do they get in the way of his or her relationships with (a) peers, (b) adults?
● Do they cause distress in others?

A range of assessment instruments is listed in Appendix II.

Causation

It seems paradoxical that the high standards which many pre-adolescents and adolescents set themselves also create problems for them. The evidence indicates that many young people who are highly self-critical tend to be anxious, insecure, depressed and somewhat cynical. Sometimes they lapse into feelings of despair (Herbert, 1987a).

There is a bewildering number and variety of aetiological models to sift through in the quest to understand and explain the phenomenon of childhood and adolescent depression. They range from the biological (biochemical, neuroendocrinal and genetic), through the psychosocial (behavioural, cognitive, family process, learned helplessness), to the psychodynamic. (See Kazdin, 1990, for an excellent guide to this complex literature.)

Bereavement

Clinical child psychologists are often called upon to provide bereavement counselling. The loss of a parent is one of the foremost precursors of depressive problems. To illustrate this theme it is worth looking at the work of Van Eerdewegh *et al.* (1982) who studied a sample of children of young widows and widowers, and the children of controls. The children's reactions to the parental death were recorded one month and thirteen months after the event in a structured interview with the surviving parent. They found the persistence of a minor form of depression; an increase in bed wetting; and a significant degree of impairment in school performance for older children. There were no significant increases in behavioural problems. Losing a parent of the same sex (particularly for boys) appeared to be a significant risk factor for depression.

Their results suggested several risk factors, including the following: mental illness in the surviving parent; financial deterioration of the family after the death of the parent; the sex of the child and of the surviving parent; the stability of the home environment prior to or after the death, the quality of the marital relationship before the death, the coping capacity of the surviving parent, and the quality of the support system of the family after the death.

In a more recent investigation, Van Eerdewegh, Clayton and Van Eerdewegh (1985) found that dysphoria, falling school performance and withdrawn behaviour were significantly increased in bereaved children of both sexes at all ages, while temper tantrums, bed wetting and depressive syndromes only increased in the age and sex categories normally associated with these conditions. The highest scores for both sexes were associated with having a mentally ill (more often than not depressed) mother. They found that bereaved daughters of mentally ill mothers had the highest scores. The investigators suggest that the delay between the time of the death and the onset of psychiatric difficulties in the child makes it less likely that the death itself is the sole factor leading to psychiatric problems.

In depression one of the most important risk factors is the absence of a close confiding relationship. Such a factor seems also to be of importance in taking up drug use. There is some evidence to suggest that drug takers, especially those who develop a problematic use, exhibit common characteristics such as low self-esteem, high levels of anxiety and depression (see Herbert, 1987a; Weiner, 1970).

SUICIDE AND ATTEMPTED SUICIDE

Suicide is extremely rare in young children. The rate in early childhood per thousand appears to be around 0.001 per 1000 at age 10 (Shaffer, 1974). However, it merits a brief mention here as it begins to appear in puberty, and increases in prevalence, reaching its highest levels in the late teens (Lumsden Walker, 1980). *Attempted* suicide has a much higher incidence; it has also a female–male ratio of around 3 : 1 (Weiner, 1970).

A survey by Hawton (1982) of a sample of 50 adolescents admitted to hospital after self-poisoning revealed that suicide attempts commonly follow episodes of ill-health (such as asthma or juvenile arthritis), rows with parents, friends or teachers, or admission into care of the Social Services Departments. Of these 50 adolescents, fewer than 20 % made a repeated self-poisoning attempt in the same year.

The aetiology of suicidal behaviour in adolescents is similar to that for adults. The most common pattern of influence is the setting of an example of suicidal behaviour by family members or friends (Toolan, 1975).

Intervention

The need for a broad-based intervention with depressive problems seems to be the conclusion of recent studies (e.g., Puig-Antich *et al.*, 1985a,b). Tricyclic medication, counselling, psychotherapy, behaviour therapy, cognitive therapy and group therapy are the main options, singly or in combination. In serious cases the young person may have to reside in an adolescent psychiatry unit or a social services home. (A useful account of the pros and cons of pharmacotherapy is given by Campbell *et al.*, 1989.)

Depression in older children (and adolescents) lends itself to a cognitive-behavioural approach. Most depressed clients manifest a high rate of intrusive negative thoughts, including selective ruminations about past negative events, and thoughts about the hopelessness of the future and their helplessness in the face of their perceived dilemma (Seligman, 1975).

Seligman's formulation of clinical depression is in terms of learned helplessness — a feature of many hard-pressed parents with difficult children (Herbert, 1988). A sense of helplessness, it is posited, leads to cognitive and motivational deficits and emotional disturbance. These learned helplessness effects are determined in large part by the attribution which the client makes when he or she experiences a persistent 'disconnection' (independence) between their behavioural responses and their outcomes (see also Abramson, Seligman and Teasdale, 1978). What a person tells himself or herself about their experience affects their behaviour. For example, some clients may tend to attribute the causes of what happens to them to forces beyond their control, while others may see themselves as having a major influence and say on the unfolding events of their life.

This notion ('locus of control') generates practice methods which have proved very promising with, for example, parents with low perceived self-efficacy — methods (e.g., 'cognitive restructuring') that include the attempt to alter overt behaviour by modifying thoughts, assumptions, and interpretations. Multi-faceted or integrative cognitive-behavioural interventions have proved successful for treating childhood depression (Kaslow and Rehm, 1983; Kendall, 1984; Reynolds, 1984). Reynolds and Coats (1986), following an initial screening of high school students, randomly assigned 30 moderately depressed adolescents to one of three conditions: cognitive-behavioural therapy, relaxation training, or waiting-list controls. Students on medication for depression or related disorders were excluded. In addition to the initial screening, subjects were tested on three occasions, i.e., pretreatment assessment, post-treatment assessment, and at a five-week follow-up assessment.

The cognitive-behavioural programme stressed training in self-control skills including self-monitoring, self-evaluation, and self-reinforcement. The relaxation training condition involved progressive muscle relaxation exercises, and the application of relaxation skills to tension-provoking situations. Both treatments were administered to small groups of subjects for 10 × 50 minute sessions over a five-week period. The interventions were evaluated on measures of depression (self-report and interview), self-concept (general and academic), and anxiety (State-Trait Anxiety Inventory-Trait Scale).

Both cognitive behaviour therapy and relaxation training were found to be effective in the treatment of the depressed adolescents. Compared to the waiting list control condition, both treatments resulted in a significant reduction in depressive symptomatology. Further, these improvements were maintained at the five-week follow-up assessment. Of interest were the findings in relation to measures of anxiety. On this criterion the greatest changes occurred for the relaxation training subjects, especially from post-treatment to follow-up assessment. In relation to general self-concept, there were no significant differences between the groups at post-test and follow-up. Both treatment groups, however, reported higher levels of academic self-concept at post-treatment relative to the control group. Yet at follow-up, only the cognitive-behavioural group showed a significantly greater level of academic self-concept compared to the waiting list control group.

Social skills training has been successfully applied to depressed children who often exhibit poor social skills. Frame *et al.* (1982) focused on behaviours such as inappropriate body position, lack of eye contact, and poor speech, in their treatment of a depressed boy.

SEXUAL ORIENTATION AND IDENTITY (see Money and Ehrhardt, 1972)

This is one of the areas of childhood and adolescent development capable of causing extreme distress — anxiety, depression and uncertainty — and, not surprisingly, it is listed as one of the DSM-III-R criteria of an identity disorder. The 'problems' related to sex, in the secondary school, are likely to be due to sexual curiosity and ignorance. Even in our supposedly enlightened age, one is impressed by the anguish and disappointment caused by widespread misinformation, misconceptions, myths, fears and inhibitions about sex.

In pre-adolescent individuals, sexual interest and behaviour are intermittent, casual and not very intense. Sexual experimentation, mainly sex play between children of the same sex, rises in incidence as youngsters get older. Homosexual play usually takes the form of handling each other's genitals. This occurs in roughly 30% of 13-year-olds (Herbert, 1987a). We know from surveys that about one in two adults is likely to have had one or more sexually tinged experiences involving someone of the same sex, and that at least half of those who haven't, have felt some sexual attraction to someone of their own sex. Usually the attraction or contact is a 'one-off' or transient matter which mainly occurs during adolescence.

CROSS-GENDER BEHAVIOUR

This can be a matter of concern for parents. Cross-gender behaviour in young children (DSM-III-R code 302.60) refers to the fact that there are youngsters whose actions, preferences, likes and dislikes do not fit neatly into society's expectations of what is an appropriate sexual identity for the sexes. There is persistent and intense distress about being a girl (or boy), and a desire to be mistaken for the opposite sex. It is not merely a matter of voicing the advantages of girlhood or boyhood. They are seen as very 'feminine' boys or extremely 'masculine' girls. This area of clinical concern is fraught with value judgements, stereotyping and confusion of terminology.

Training of sexual impulses and the nuances of 'correct' gender behaviour appear to be among the life-tasks that are universal in child-rearing. The vital process by which children learn the behaviour and attitudes culturally appropriate to their sex is called 'sex-typing'. Children learn certain sex-role standards, those psychological characteristics which are considered appropriate to one sex in contrast to the other. Physical gender is decided at conception. But the evidence suggests that, from a psychological point of view, the newborn human is not, in any essential sense, sexually differentiated. Gender identity and sexual role standards are acquired during childhood; in fact, by the age of 6 children are committed to shaping their behaviour to the cultural mould of what is 'appropriate' to their biological sex. They manifest anxiety, and even anger when accused of acting in ways regarded as characteristic of the opposite sex.

As early as the second year of life, children begin to distinguish between what is 'masculine' and 'feminine'. Preference for one sex role or the other also begins to emerge early, probably the third year. By school-going age, they have thoroughly learned the concepts 'male' and 'female'; they divide the world into male and female people and are preoccupied with boy-girl distinctions (Kagan, 1958b). Studies (Hampson and Hampson, 1961; Money, 1965) have shown that it is difficult to bring about a major realignment of sex role and gender identity after three years of age. Once the standards of sex-role behaviour are learned, they are not easily altered. The die is cast, pretty well, by the age of 6, if not earlier.

Biological influences

Studies of abnormalities of physiology and anatomy suggest that prenatal (or postnatal) genetic or hormonal influences play only a secondary part in the process; upbringing and indoctrination into a sex role have the overriding influence (Hampson and Hampson, 1961). Girls whose mothers took synthetic progestins during pregnancy to prevent uterine bleeding, were reported as being 'tomboyish' during their preschool years (Ehrhardt and Money, 1967). They had genitalia with male characteristics. Young boys whose mothers ingested female hormones when they were pregnant were reported as being less athletic as young children and less interested in rough-and-tumble play than their peers (Yalom, Green and Fisk, 1973). They were not necessarily abnormal in their gender identity but there was an associated higher than usual level of cross-gender behaviours and interests.

Psychosocial influences

There is evidence to support the claim that upbringing and societal indoctrination play the major part in shaping gender identities (Hampson and Hampson, 1961). Theories designed to account for the way in which the child acquires sex-typed patterns of behaviour have emphasized the role of identification, referring to the processes whereby one person models himself or herself upon another. It differs from the concept of imitation in certain ways. It suggests a relatively long-lasting relationship between subject and model, and focuses attention on the fact that some models exert more influence over the subject than others — although the reasons why they do so are not adequately explained in the literature.

A subject is said to be identified with a model if he or she is more likely to match that model's behaviour than other models' behaviour. Also, the matching behaviour is more extensive than that implied in the notion of imitation. The subject behaves as if he or she were the model in situations other than those in which he or she has seen the model, and in a relatively comprehensive manner. That is to say, he or she adopts the model's values, beliefs, attitudes and style of life, as well as matching particular forms of behaviour. According to the anaclitic theory of identification, the child imitates and identifies with the behaviour of the parent who is warm and nurturant.

The view of many social learning theorists (e.g., Bandura, 1969; Kagan, 1958a; Mischel, 1970) is that children's experience with parents (particularly same-sex parents) critically determines the nature of their subsequent learning of social roles. The empirical results of the many studies which have been carried out present a somewhat confusing picture, and there is not space to review the theoretical debates in detail here.

The question of a boy's or girl's gender-identity is sometimes of concern to men who rear girls, or women who bring up boys, in the absence of a partner. What they are worried about is the possibility of an inappropriate indentification. They may also worry about their child being homosexual. It is here that confusion arises because the issues of gender-identity problems and homosexuality are often mistakenly thought of as one and the same thing.

Homosexuality, transvestism and sexual inversion are independent (although sometimes overlapping) phenomena, and the failure to draw this distinction causes much misunderstanding. For example, only a small percentage of adult transvestites are homosexual (Randall, 1970), and only a minority of homosexuals are transsexuals. The direction of the individual's sexual interest — the choice of a sexual partner — is very rarely explained by chromosomal or hormonal anomalies. Early life experiences seem to play a part in many cases of homosexual inclination; poor relationships with parents, particularly the parent of the same sex, are thought to be a contributory factor (Bancroft, 1970). When one considers how many strongly heterosexual individuals have had poor relationships of this kind, such a theory is robbed of most of its explanatory value. Nevertheless, there remains strong evidence that early family relationships are, in some way, involved in homosexuality, but the precise 'hows' and 'whys' remain a mystery.

Transsexualism refers to the persistent discomfort and sense of inappropriateness about one's assigned sex. There is a preoccupation with ridding himself or herself of their primary and secondary sexual characteristics, while acquiring those of the opposite sex.

SEXUAL INTERCOURSE IN ADOLESCENCE

Having boyfriends or girlfriends can be the source of feelings of insecurity, not only for a lot of young people, but also for parents, who may worry about some of the implications of their offspring's newly awakened sexual feelings. Parents in general express more conservative, traditional attitudes than their adolescent sons or daughters on such topics as petting and, notably, premarital sexual intercourse, whether the couple intend to marry or not. The majority of adolescents appear to have their first experience with other adolescents. The majority of boys do so in a relationship they describe as emotionally unimportant. This is in clear contrast to girls. There also appear to be gender differences in the salience of the audience of sexual experience; boys talk to other people about their experiences whilst girls talk mostly to their partner about how they felt and what happened (Herbert, 1987a).

Parents are not necessarily boring, hypocritical or puritanical if they disapprove of (or have reservations about) teenagers having sex. Many are afraid that young people might be hurt or exploited if they embark on a sexual relationship too soon. It can be difficult to sustain a sexual relationship if the adolescent — who, by definition, is short on experience — has not yet learned to maintain intimacy in a non-sexual attachment. Parents are also likely to be concerned about unwanted pregnancies and sexually transmitted disease (notably AIDS). In fact, the number of teenage pregnancies has certainly increased markedly, despite innovations in contraception. The incidence of venereal disease among young people has also gone up.

Unfortunately, there is a lack of really satisfactory comparative data which might be used to assess changes in sexual attitudes and behaviour over time. Nevertheless, as Rutter's 1979 review of studies indicates, there is little doubt that in the UK and the USA adolescents engage in sexual activity at a younger age than their predecessors (Rutter, 1979b). Empirical studies of the development of sexual behaviours (Kinsey, Pomeroy and Martin, 1948; Schofield, 1973; Sorenson, 1973) have suggested that a substantial proportion of adolescents have their first sexual intercourse during the mid-teenage years.

Coital experience continues to be somewhat exceptional amongst younger adolescents. Studies in the early 1970s suggest that fewer than 1 in 10 of boys and girls younger than the age of 15 engage in sexual intercourse and the modal period of those experiences occurred during periods of 15–18 years for both sexes. There appear not to have been any major changes for boys in the age at which intercourse was first experienced or in the number of adolescent boys becoming involved in intercourse since the 1960s. However among girls there appears to be a significant increase in the number who have sexual intercourse, and girls appear to experience intercourse at increasingly earlier ages. In all of the studies quoted (see Herbert, 1987a) there appears to be a strong correlation between early coital experience and behaviours such as drug use, delinquency, smoking, alcohol use and solvent abuse.

Those not having sexual intercourse during their teens are not necessarily unhappy about their lack of experience although males and females tend to give different reasons for not engaging in coitus. Girls tend to quote parental disapproval and fear of losing social reputation while boys give lack of opportunity as a major reason.

Although adolescents have become more accepting in their attitudes to premarital sex, this does not imply a massive rise in casual sexual relationships. Young people, and particularly girls, continue to emphasize the importance of love and stable emotional attachment in premarital sex, although intended marriage or an engagement is not so often seen as a prerequisite of such relationships (Rutter, 1979b). The emphasis on a stable relationship with one sexual partner at a time is referred to as 'serial monogamy'. Girls do, however, display more conservative attitudes to these issues than boys.

Most youngsters wish to get married and have children. Certainly, a committed relationship is generally thought to be essential for the rearing of children, and, although a majority would wish such a longstanding commitment to take the form of marriage, a substantial minority reject such a view. An American study by Sorensen in 1973 indicated that a majority of teenagers expect sexual fidelity after marriage, even though they do not expect it before then. There is no evidence that this view has changed.

Clinical evidence suggests that teenagers are as secretive and wary about sex as ever. Most adolescents (according to surveys) believe that they have sexual problems of one kind or another, and many comment on the intense anxiety they suffer. Harmonious sexual relationships are relatively infrequent. Even today there are teenagers who worry about masturbation; nearly all boys and two-thirds of girls will masturbate by the age of 16. Rutter (1979b) reminds us that sexual competence and experience can be hard won. There is certainly a place for sexual counselling in the clinical child psychologist's repertoire of skills.

Chapter 13

Health Care Problems of Childhood
(see Sarafino 1990)

It may be a statement of the obvious to say that good health enhances the possibility of success at school. It is more than that of course; it engenders a sense of well-being and enjoyment of life. But a large number of children miss out on these benefits. The fact is that we face a daunting health care and educational problem; the total prevalence of children with chronic illness of one kind or another is estimated to be as high as 10 % (Pless and Douglas, 1971). Good health is the prerequisite for the stamina required by long hours of concentration in the classroom. Regular attendance at school depends upon it, and effective learning, in turn, depends upon a reasonably consistent presence at lessons. But even regular attenders may not be able to learn efficiently if they are tired, apathetic or if their physical systems are impaired in some way. Physical problems are not only responsible for undermining scholastic endeavours; they may also lead to low perceived self-efficacy, and perhaps emotional disturbance.

HEALTH CARE PSYCHOLOGY

Health care psychology for children has a longer history than its adult counterpart. Clinical child psychologists have found a niche for their skills in primary care (general practice), paediatric departments, child development and assessment centres and intensive care units. Psychologists are able to respond to a variety of illness-related problems (Lask and Fosson; 1989) e.g., encopresis, failure-to-thrive, anorexia nervosa, allergic conditions, meningitis and other diseases with behavioural sequelae, obesity, intractable or psychogenic pain, orthopaedic complications, and a whole array of previously baffling disorders are now being treated with a high degree of success. The move into this area marks a shift in emphasis from the secondary and tertiary preventative health care which is characteristic of the clinical child psychologist's more traditional concern with psychopathology (e.g., neurotic and psychotic conditions), to the *primary* prevention which engages much of the attention of general practitioners, community doctors and paediatricians (Caplan, 1964). Primary prevention aims at reducing the *incidence* or the number of new cases or disorders in a population. Secondary prevention or treatment has as its goal the reduction of the *prevalence* (the number of existing cases) of disorders or dysfunctions. Tertiary prevention focuses on reducing the sequelae resulting from established disorder or dysfunction.

A double-barrelled question which is often, and legitimately, put to psychologists is 'What is the role of clinical psychology in health care; what do clinical psychologists do that other health care personnel do not do? The answer provided by the Manpower Advisory Service, following a study of psychologists' roles in the UK National Health service (MAS Review, 1989) is that clinical psychologists aim:

> to improve, either directly or indirectly, the standard and quality of life of people who are served by and provide health services, and to alleviate disability through the application of appropriate psychological theories. The *process* is unique to the profession: the *outcomes* are shared with other health care professions.

There are (they suggest) three levels of psychological skill and knowledge used in health care:

Level 1:   basic psychology, such as establishing relationships with patients and relatives, maintaining and supporting a relationship, interviewing and using some simple, often intuitive techniques, such as counselling and stress management.

Level 2:   undertaking circumscribed psychological activities, such as behaviour modification. These activities may be described by protocol. At this level there should be awareness of the criteria for referral to a psychologist.

Level 3:   a thorough understanding of varied and complex psychological theories and their application.

Almost all health care workers use Level 1 and 2 skills. In particular, medical, nursing, occupational therapy, speech therapy and social work staff make varying use of them. Some have well developed specialist training in Level 2 activities. Health care psychologists possess skills and knowledge at all three levels. Their particular contribution is in their rounded knowledge of psychological theories and their application.

Fielding (1985) provides a good example of this; she draws attention to the importance of developmental factors in children's concept of illness, and the corollary that an understanding of the child patient's level of cognitive development underpins effective communication with him or her. She presents Table 13 as an aid to assessment.

Clinical child psychologists in community settings, in primary care settings and general hospitals are likely to find themselves involved in the following activities:

● The preparation of children for hospitalization and surgery (Vernon *et al.*, 1965; Zabin and Melamed, 1980) and for dentistry (Melamed, 1979).
● Encouraging compliance with treatment regimes (Henneborn and Cogan, 1975; Varni, 1983).
● Symptomatic control (Creer et al., 1982; Rose *et al.*, 1983).
● Preventative work on coping with stress (Ayalon, 1988; Meichenbaum, 1976).

Table 13. Developmental stages of children's concepts of illness. (Source: Fielding, 1985, reproduced by permission of the British Psychological Society.)

Approximate age range	Cognitive level	Concept of illness	Examples
	0 Incomprehension	0 No answer or response unrelated to question 1 Don't know	
	1 Phenomenism ⌐ ⌐ PRELOGICAL	2 Circular, magical or global response	'How do people get colds?' 'From the sun.' 'How does the sun give you a cold?' 'It just does.'
4–7 years	2 Contagion ⌐ 3 Contamination ⌐ CONCRETE ⌐ LOGICAL	3 Concrete rules: concrete rigid response with parrot-like quality — little comprehension by children	'How do people get colds?' 'By going out without a coat in cold weather.' 'By eating junk food.'
7–11 years	4 Internalization ⌐	4 Internalization and relativity: increased generalization with some indication of child's contribution to response — quality of invariant causation remains	'What is a cold?' 'You sneeze a lot, you talk funny and your nose gets clogged up.' 'How do people get colds?' 'In winter they breathe in too much air into their noses and it blocks up the nose.' 'How does this cause colds?' 'The bacteria gets in by breathing. Then the lungs get too soft (child exhales), and it goes to the nose.' 'How does it get better?' 'Hot fresh air, it gets in the nose and pushes the cold air back.'
		5 Generalized principles Beginning use of underlying principles — greater delineation of causal agents or illnesses	
11 years and over	5 Physiologic ⌐ FORMAL 6 Psychophysiologic ⌐ LOGICAL	6 Physiologic processes and mechanisms	'What is a cold?' 'It's when you get all stuffed up inside, your sinuses get filled up with mucus. Sometimes your lungs do, too, and you get a cough.' 'How do people get colds?' 'They come from viruses, I guess. Other people have the virus and it gets into your bloodstream and it makes you ill'.

- Treating (directly or indirectly) specific illnesses: e.g., recurrent abdominal pain (Apley, 1975), cancer (Dolgin and Jay, 1989), headaches (Williamson, Davis and Kelley, 1987), atopic dermatitis.
- Helping children to cope with the ramifications of accidents and illness (pain injections, nausea, epileptic fits, burns) e.g., Elliott and Olson, 1983).
- Facilitating effective communication with children and their families (Ley, 1977).
- Counselling families facing terminal illness or experiencing bereavement (Lansdown and Goldman, 1988; Parkes, 1973); helping families to come to terms with chronic illness (Lask and Fosson, 1989).

Family needs

With regard to the last item, there are few reports on the impact of illness on the family, and the value of those that have been published tends to be reduced because of methodological inadequacies such as the absence of control groups. Family therapists point out the importance of two characteristics when dealing with families and illness: (a) family group life and its regulatory mechanisms, and (b) family growth and development. Chronic illnesses have the capacity to alter both of these profoundly. A process often unfolds in which family life becomes increasingly organized around illness-generated needs and demands, to the detriment of the development of individual members and the family as a group. The ultimate consequence of this can be the suppression of those family priorities which are not related to illness, and a neglect of matters that are part of a normal family's development. During the crisis phase of an illness life plans are frequently put on 'hold' by the family in order to accommodate its adaptation to the illness; in the transition to the chronic phase a renegotiation takes place during which a clinical psychologist can help them to ensure that important individual and family interests are not unnecessarily sacrificed.

PSYCHOPHYSIOLOGICAL ILLNESS

Psychosomatic (psychophysiological) medicine was the first medical discipline to acknowledge wholeheartedly the influence of psychological processes in disease. Its approach encompasses research into relationships between biological, psychological and psychosocial factors in health and disease, a holistic approach to patient care, and the use of methods developed at the interface between medicine and the behavioural sciences. Psychophysiological illnesses consist of bodily (somatic) symptoms — such as bronchial asthma, hayfever, skin complaints (eczema), ulcerative colitis, migraine and others — which are associated in some children with psychological complications. These bodily disturbances are not limited to any particular age or phase of development. But they do occur frequently in school-age children. Next to acute respiratory illnesses they are the commonest cause of repeated absence from school.

It has been found that in many of these conditions, particular attacks or phases of the illness can be precipitated or prolonged by psychological stresses, such as conflict, anxiety and anger, as well as physical stresses (e.g., dietary factors, allergies, infections, etc.). Treatment of the symptoms by physical means alone is often ineffective. The advance brought about by a psychophysiological perspective in medicine is due to the reinstatement of the person into the consideration of his or her illness. There is space for three examples only: bronchial asthma, diabetes and anorexia; however, they illustrate the range of work being carried out by clinical psychologists these days.

Bronchial asthma (see Creer, 1982)

This is one of the most common childhood ailments; it can be serious in its implications, sometimes leading to death. Bronchial asthma illustrates general principles which are (or have been) thought to apply to psychophysiological conditions in general.

The emphasis on the personality of the sick individual (in systematic clinical studies) was very much a post-second-world-war phenomenon. The revolutionary advances made in the early part of this century in medical technology, particularly in physical methods of diagnosis and treatment and the uncovering of hitherto unseen physical agents (microorganisms) which cause certain illnesses, tended to reinforce a one sided organic approach to disease. For a long time, in keeping with the prevailing medical bias, asthma was considered almost solely as a physical (an allergic and infective) illness, and physical desensitization and the use of drugs became the main methods of treatment. However, an analysis of the literature of the 1940s and 1950s in particular reveals a considerable shift in orientation.

Crucial to this approach was the assumption that some illnesses represent, in certain circumstances, an individual's specific reaction to his or her life-situation — almost what one might call a mode of behaviour. Patients were no longer regarded simply as collections of separate bodily organ systems, each of which is subject to breakdown, but rather as unique individuals living in certain types of environment, subject to a variety of physical and psychological stresses to which they react as *whole* persons. Thus, in disease, causation is sought both in the nature of the individual and his or her environment; it is the child who has a particular illness; not just a disease that 'has' the child.

The context — the 'body language' and meanings associated with physiological functioning — are considered in a psychological assessment. The effects of emotion upon physical states, have long been implicit in language and folklore and confirmed in laboratories (Wolff and Goodell, 1968). Our language contains numerous metaphorical expressions for the effects of emotions upon respiratory functioning: sighing in sadness and in grief and fear; the rapid breathing of excitement and anticipation; the 'breathtaking' quality of wonder and amazement; the expansion of the chest in joy and in the choking of anxiety. Speech and crying which are closely related to respiratory functioning are also complex expressive phenomena.

An important consideration in the relationship of emotion to asthma may be the profound significance of attitudes related to breathing. For example, there is the fundamental anxiety caused by the asthma attack. Asthma involves a frightening disturbance of the normal breathing pattern, and the reasons for the anxiety — not least in a parent — are deep seated and probably have to do with the fact that breathing is the first and last act of life.

Some researchers — particularly those with a psychodynamic background — have tried to check on the popular notion that there is a very specific asthmatic 'personality type'. They have attempted experimentally to correlate personality profiles with specific psychosomatic illnesses. The present author and other investigators have been unable to substantiate the claims that there is a personality structure characteristic of asthmatics only (Herbert, 1965). Neuhaus (1958) found that the members of his group of asthmatic children were significantly more maladjusted or neurotic than were the children of a normal control group. They were characterized by traits of anxiety, insecurity and dependency. But he also found that a control group of children with cardiac disease exceeded normals in degree of neuroticism and dependency feelings. Neuhaus concluded that the lack of significant differences in test results between the asthmatic and cardiac patients indicates that the personality picture of the asthmatic child cannot wholly be ascribed to the nature of the asthmatic disorder. He is of the opinion that not only do the data clearly refute the concept of differential personality patterns for asthmatic and cardiac children, but, on the contrary, the presence of personality traits common to both illnesses are possibly common to protracted illnesses in general. Rees (1963), too, was unable to find any evidence of specificity of personality type in a large-scale study of 388 asthmatic children and a control group of accident cases. However, the incidence of factors such as maternal overprotection, insecurity and emotional tension in this group of asthmatics was found to be substantial.

What makes asthma so interesting from the aspect of learned behaviour is the fact that breathing, while largely an involuntary activity, is also subject to voluntary control. This implies that specific attacks of asthma might be conceptualized in classical conditioning and/or operant learning terms.

Intervention

Creer, Renne and Chai, (1982) describe a successful five-component treatment package which contains these elements:

- The first stage consists of detecting the onset of the attack by reporting shortness of breath and wheezing.
- If these symptoms have been a reliable predictor of an asthmatic attack, the child then has to restrict his or her physical activity especially if that is normally a trigger, as is reported in about 80% of children.

- Practising relaxation can counteract feelings of panic. Progressive muscular relaxation can be practised beforehand together with imaginary rehearsal of the experience of the onset of the attack. Children as young as 5 may be able to make use of relaxation (see Herbert, 1987c).
- The next step consists of drinking warm liquid, a full cup every 15 minutes.
- The use of a bronchodilator is the next procedure. Some children have difficulty in reporting the warning symptoms, so it may be appropriate to give them some practice in reporting what they experience when peak expiratory rates are low. This is done by frequent daily measurement of peak expiratory rates. Sampling of respiratory performance in this way may indicate which flow rates are critical for the onset of an attack.

A careful assessment (see page 64) may uncover the presence of reinforcement from various sources: such as avoidance of social activities which are feared or unpleasant school activities. Unacceptable behaviours (e.g., temper tantrums) may become reinforced by parents who are afraid of provoking an asthmatic episode. Single-case experimental investigation is a valuable aid in elucidating possible causal relationships (Morley, 1989).

School refusal can be reinforced in a similar manner by parents. Frequent absences from school are likely to undermine a child's attainment there; this may lead to further reluctance to go to school.

Diabetes mellitus

There has been a substantial research interest in the social, psychological and behavioural ramifications of diabetes in children (Shillitoe, 1988). Although this disease cannot be cured, it can be *controlled*; and it is here that a clinical child psychologist may be required to exercise all his or her skill, helping with the management of the child's treatment regimen. Diabetes results from a failure of the pancreas to produce sufficient insulin to metabolize glucose which then appears in the patient's urine from which it would normally be absent. If this abnormally high level of blood glucose (hyperglycaemia) continues untreated the person experiences excessive hunger and thirst and output of urine. Children may wet the bed. A marked loss of weight and lassitude are also characteristic. The illness, if unchecked, leads to widespread destruction of body tissue producing heart disease and circulatory problems which may result in the amputation of limbs. Neurological impairment and blindness may also occur.

These, then, are the physical ramifications of diabetes. But the disease affects all areas of functioning. Shillitoe (1988) makes the point that 'it affects family, friends and social roles. It can disrupt day-to-day living and future plans. It requires lasting changes to be made in such fundamental aspects of life as what is eaten and drunk, and in what quantities. Such things as how far family members are supportive, what attitudes they hold toward diabetes and how daily stress is dealt with are all central to the control of the disorder. These have little to do with disease processes and everything to do with psychology' (see Chapter 14).

Treatment

Treatment of the condition involves dietary care and the administration of insulin usually by injection. In most cases, treatment and management are administered by the patient or his or her parents. Rates of nonadherence to treatment regimes are very high. Some of the methods of dealing with this practical problem with its serious implications have been explored quite thoroughly; behavioural methods have been put to work to increase adherence to treatment plans, and to good effect (see review by Fonagy, Moran and Higgitt, 1989). Ioannou (Chapter 19) sets out some of the principles and practical strategies for helping parents and children to cope with fear and pain surrounding physical treatments, including dialysis.

Glucose levels are influenced by environmental variables, including psychological stress which gives scope for the psychologist's stress management packages (Rose *et al.*, 1983).

Anorexia nervosa

Efforts to restrict intake of foods and to use other substances in order to lose weight usually begins in adolescence. The fairly uncommon disorder of anorexia nervosa is most frequently seen in young women of ages 16 or 17, but can also occur in pre-pubertal children. An increasing, but small, number of male anorexics are beginning to make their presence felt. The anorexic individual deliberately starves herself. Indeed, she does not want to eat at all, because she believes she is fat and wishes to lose weight.

Assessment (see page 63)

The word 'anorexia' means loss of appetite. However, the absence of hunger or appetite is not a crucial feature of anorexia nervosa. Anorexia nervosa is essentially about weight rather than eating. Body weight is abnormally low for the age, height and sex of the person. There is a further crucial feature: the individual's attitude to her weight. What makes life difficult for parents and other would-be helpers is that someone with anorexia nervosa will not always be open or truthful about her feelings. If she is, she will say that she is ashamed and very frightened of the thoughts of being heavier. She may suffer in various ways through being thin, even emaciated, but compared with putting on weight it is seen as the lesser evil (see Palmer, 1980).

There is a variation in symptomatology called bulimia nervosa in which the individual has binges — rather joyless, guilt-ridden episodes of excessive eating — followed by self-induced vomiting and the abuse of laxatives. This problem peaks in the twenties.

Causation

There appear to be different patterns of causation, rather than one fixed path to anorexia nervosa (Palmer, 1980). Cultural factors may have a predisposing role. Slimming is an obsession in our culture today. People (women in particular) are bombarded with propaganda based upon the achievement of health and beauty. Being overweight is stigmatized, and the condition is viewed both as a physical deformity and as a behavioural aberration. Obese people tend to be 'chastised' for their lack of self-control and held responsible for their voluntary, self-inflicted disability. Many fat people, mortified and shamed, full of self-disparagement, are further disadvantaged because not only are they discriminated against but are made to feel that they deserve such discrimination.

It has been suggested (McCrea, 1986) that because they come to accept their treatment as just, a self-fulfilling prophecy develops. Self-fulfilling prophecies come true because the characteristics presented become part of the victim's picture of themselves; the way we imagine ourselves to appear to another person is an essential element in our conception of ourselves. Fat people who are repeatedly told that they are endangering their health are being told, in effect, 'We expect you to be sick.' Eventually the role of sick person becomes second nature to them. Similarly, the disturbed fat person may begin to condemn himself or herself and experience a disturbed body image (McCrea, 1986). The main feature of disturbance of the body image in obesity is a preoccupation with obesity, often to the exclusion of any other personal characteristic. It may make no difference whether the person is talented, wealthy or intelligent; weight is his or her overriding concern, and he or she sees the world in terms of body weight.

The anorexic individual is similarly obsessed, and tends to have a distorted perception of her body image — consistently exaggerating negative factors of size, shape and weight. There is evidence (Palmer, 1980) that families of anorexic individuals place greater than average stress upon food and eating. They may unwittingly reinforce or initiate tendencies in the make-up of the youngster which give peculiar importance and meaning to food, the act of eating, and the image of her self and body.

Intervention

Behaviour therapy

Those who advocate the use of operant methods for the treatment of anorexia nervosa claim that they produce faster and larger weight gains during hospitalization than do the medically oriented or psychiatrically oriented techniques. Swann Van Buskirk (1989) in her review of therapeutic approaches in anorexia nervosa, states that it is sometimes difficult to evaluate these claims, because the empirical results have often been complicated by the inclusion of various other forms of psychotherapy.

The operant paradigm generally includes restricting the patient to her room and making activities and privileges contingent on weight gain. Studies utilizing an operant technique as the only treatment dimension achieved average weekly weight gains of a little over 3lbs (e.g., Garfinkle, Kline and Stamcer, 1973; Halmi, Powers and Cunningham, 1975). The time spent in hospital was 8 and 6.2 weeks respectively. Systematic desensitization has been used to alleviate the weight phobia element (Schnurer, Rubin and Roy, 1973).

This 'eclectic' approach illustrates a problem in evaluating the effectiveness of specific approaches. Because anorexia nervosa is potentially fatal, therapists are ethically bound to give the immediate needs of their patients more priority than the integrity of their research designs. It is for this reason that they often combine different treatment modalities, using whatever methods they consider effective. Any attempt to compare different treatments is thus complicated by the lack of studies that isolate a treatment approach, measure its effects, and then replicate it using the same treatment again. There were other problems with the research designs utilized, according to Swann Van Buskirk (1989):

(a) If outpatient therapy is utilized, there are usually no follow-up data on the patients after the outpatient treatment is completed. Thus the effects beyond treatment cannot be determined;

(b) It is difficult to compare treatments because of the differential diagnostic criteria used by different authors. Some diagnosed a patient as anorexic only if she had lost 25 % or more of her original body weight;

(c) Some researchers applied diagnostic restrictions, e.g., an absence of other psychiatric disorders, others did not. So it cannot be easily determined if these patients were a homogeneous group or what effects different psychiatric disorders had on the results;

(d) The severity of the patient's condition differed, both within and between different studies. Some of the patients had been sick for a few months, others for several years. Consequently, it is difficult to ascertain what effect this had on the success rates of different treatment programmes;

(e) Authors also disagreed on improvement criteria. Even when evaluating weight gain, the authors often did not give their results in terms of how the patient compared with her ideal weight. When using amount of weight gained as a criterion for improvement, the authors disregarded normal growth and increases in height that would have been expected during adolescence. Thus, the patient may have gained 15lbs. but still have been underweight, because she also had grown 4 inches

It would seem that despite modest claims from combined therapies, milieu therapy (Eckert et al., 1979); family therapy (Rosman et al., 1976); cognitive-behaviour therapy (Garner, 1986) and behaviour therapy (Leon, 1979), the fact is that we are still floundering when it comes to the provision of a rational (i.e., theory based, empirically proven) therapy for this disorder. Brownell and Foreyt (1986) offer a valuable review of the literature on obesity, anorexia nervosa and other eating disorders.

Part Five

Clinical Psychology Interventions

The task of helping a family — following a formulation of the causes and implications of their problems — can be a daunting one, encompassing a wide range of concerns stretching from, say, the need for day care for a child, developmental or marital counselling for parents, to systematic desensitization for a phobic child. The clinical psychologist's role can vary from case to case, including that of resource-mobilizer (which implies a knowledge of available facilities, also when and where to refer), adviser, teacher, therapist, counsellor and problem-solver.

Such diversification calls for a remarkably flexible professional response on the part of the practitioner; it also requires a clear-headed grasp of what goals are salient to the client. The scope of the analysis and level of intervention can also range widely, from the large grouping (the community) through the small group (the family), the couple (parents and partners) to the particular individual (say, child). It might also involve working with managers in monitoring policy, getting involved in planning and increasingly, of late, teaching other professionals (e.g., nurses, care staff) psychological skills where applicable to their work. The latter is of great significance. The number of children and adolescents requiring help is extremely large; the number receiving psychological therapy is relatively small.

Gould's review of several epidemiological studies in the UK and USA estimated the prevalence of clinical dysfunction in children at 12 %, with a range in the various studies stretching from as low as 6 % to as high as 37 % (Gould *et al.*, 1980). A major evaluation conducted in the USA by the President's Commission on Mental Health (1978) concluded that 5 to 15 % (which means 3 to 10 million) of American children and adolescents were in need of some form of mental health service. What evidence there is suggests that only 20 to 33 % of British and American youngsters with significant psychological problems receive the treatment they require (e.g., Knitzer, 1982; Rutter, Tizard and Whitmore, 1970); worse still, children with less serious difficulties are more likely to receive the scarce resource of therapy than those with the more worrying disorders (Sowder, 1975).

The consequences of a mismatch between the need for help for children with these problems and the available provision are serious enough in the short term; one thinks of the distress that goes unalleviated for so many young people. But there is another concern: the possibility (especially in the case of those disorders with a poor prognosis) of blighted futures over the longer term, because of the paucity of therapeutic resources directed at secondary and tertiary preventative work. What and where are these scarce resources? Let us look at the settings in which children with special needs and their families can seek help, and where they are likely to find psychologists at work.

PROVISION OF SERVICES

Emotional and behaviour problems tend to be identified by parents and teachers. From home the child is likely to be referred to a general practitioner. There is likely to be a substantial proportion of cases (perhaps a quarter of child consultations with GPs) with a psychological component to the presenting problem. If the problem is serious the doctor will refer to a child and family psychiatric clinic either in the community or situated in a hospital department.

Psychiatric provision

Here they will find a multi-disciplinary team consisting of psychiatrists, psychologists, social workers and (in the London area) a psychotherapist.

Children with severe problems can be referred to a psychiatric day centre or to an in-patient unit. There are in-patient units specifically available for the treatment of pre-adolescent children, but also taking some adolescents of school age and older adolescents. There are also residential psychiatric units in England and Wales which cater specifically for adolescents. Regional adolescent teams also provide specialist back-up to other services (Hollin, Wilkie and Herbert, 1987).

Educational provision

From school the child is likely to be referred to an educational psychology service. In some areas this service will be part of a multi-disciplinary team, in others it may liaise with a hospital service (e.g., paediatric units). There is a wide range of special educational provision for children with emotional and behaviour problems, including tutorial classes, units for disruptive children (e.g. persistent truants), special day and residential schools for maladjusted children, and day and residential schools for autistic children.

Severe retardation in reading ability in children of normal intelligence is usually provided for in part-time remedial classes in ordinary schools. However, some local education authorities run separate remedial education units which children usually attend on a part-time basis.

Social welfare provision

There is also a range of social welfare provision for children with emotional and behavioural problems, especially intermediate treatment centres and Community Homes with education. Attendance at these facilities usually follows criminal or care proceedings in a juvenile court.

MOBILIZING HUMAN RESOURCES

Professional resources are not the only source of help. A psychologist can put his or her clients in touch with people, clubs and specialized self-help groups. As social networks, personal ties and contacts promote psychological well-being, it is important for the psychologist to identify their presence or absence for the client (see Brown and Harris, 1978). Intimate or close relationships of the type provided by primary groups (those people with whom one has face-to-face interaction and a sense of commitment) are the most significant sources of support (Brown and Harris, 1978). The supportiveness of relationships is reflected by the availability of:

- Emotional support (the expression of liking, respect, etc.).
- Aid (material assistance, services, guidance, advice).
- Social companionship.
- Affirmation (the expression of agreement).
- Social regulation (appropriate role-related support such as mothering, fathering, partnership — husband/wife/companion, etc.).

COUNSELLING AND GIVING ADVICE

Counselling has, as its main aim, the production of constructive behavioural and attitudinal change. Such change emerges from a relationship of trust and confidentiality, one which emerges from empathetic non-judgemental conversations between the professionally trained counsellor and the client. Professionals have recently shown more interest in preparing couples for parenthood as a means of preventing later difficulties that flow from faulty child management (e.g., Hawkins 1972; Herbert, 1985b). This may be utopian but it does reflect a fruitful area of intervention (see Chapter 15).

Crisis counselling

Children are referred often to Child and Family Psychiatric Clinics at times of crisis for themselves and their families. Skilled counselling and/or therapy have been shown to be invaluable following traumatic situations such as surgery, bereavement, sexual abuse, divorce and, increasingly, major disasters (see Chapter 20).

People are most susceptible to help during periods of rapid change, and adolescence is a period of transition and dramatic change. At times of crisis parents too, are particularly receptive to advice. Yet high on their list of complaints about professionals are failures of communication. These failures involve:

- Insufficient information.
- Inaccurate information.
- An indigestible overload of information at any one time.
- Information that is difficult to comprehend because of technical jargon or poor presentation.

Of particular value to clients is the provision of the factual data, or know-how about how to get access to information that helps them to make informed choices and decisions. There are many stages throughout parenthood during which well-founded psychological advice, developmental and personal counselling can help to alleviate distress and prevent the development of further difficulties. An example is pregnancy; some mothers-to-be can be shown to be at high risk of having a handicapped child. Sophisticated obstetric techniques (e.g., ultra-sound scanning, amniocentesis, and various blood tests) contribute to screening for handicaps such as Down's syndrome, spina bifida, or anencephaly. Where a disability is detected, the mother might be offered a therapeutic termination of her pregnancy. Many women are not psychologically prepared to deal with the conflicts that surround these decisions and moral issues. The availability of psychological advice is likely to enhance the quality of the service being offered to them. This also applies where a couple already have a handicapped child; there is a need for genetic counselling and advice on appropriate contraception.

Hospitals have run ante-natal classes for years. Parents appear to benefit from good preparation for labour and delivery. In addition to educating prospective parents about what to expect during labour, most classes teach some form of relaxation as an aid to delivery. There is evidence that systematic desensitization may be even more effective than general psychoprophylactic methods in shortening labour and lowering the intensity of pain (Kondaš and Sčentricka, 1972). A good preparation during pregnancy is associated with easier deliveries, the use of fewer drugs in labour, and fewer complications (Doering and Entwistle, 1975; McNeil and Kaij, 1977). A psychologist may know people who can offer objective, matter-of-fact information or guidance to the client. Giving clients an understanding of the *stages* of adaptation that follow particular crises (e.g., bereavement) can facilitate the restoration of personal equilibrium, especially when accompanied by a sympathetic hearing (Parkes, 1973).

A major theoretical and practical contribution by psychologists to the alleviation of suffering and solution of problems has been the development and evaluation of psychological therapies. This is the subject of the next chapter.

Chapter 14

Psychological Therapies

Psychological therapies can be differentiated, first of all, on two major dimensions:

- A passive versus an active role on the part of the therapist.
- The method (technique) versus relationship as the main agent for change.

They can further be distinguished in terms of four attributes:

- The goals (or purpose) of therapy: e.g., supportive, prescriptive, or exploratory.
- The means by which goals are sought. This encompasses the theoretical rationale, e.g., behavioural, cognitive, client-centred or psychodynamic. (In child therapy these approaches may be mediated by talking to, playing with, rewarding the child or rehearsing skills with him or her.)
- The modality of therapy, e.g., individual, group, couple or family.
- The level of expertise of the therapist.

Among the most durable and popular therapies are relationship therapy (e.g., Allen); play therapy (e.g., Virginia Axline); child analysis (e.g., Anna Freud, Melanie Klein); behaviour therapy/modification (e.g., Patterson) and the relative newcomers: cognitive behaviour therapy (e.g., Kendall) and family therapy (e.g., Minuchin).

THERAPEUTIC GOALS

Not surprisingly, there is some overlap in goals and process. For Kazdin (1988), the *goals* consist of improving adjustment and functioning in both intrapersonal and interpersonal spheres and reducing maladaptive behaviours and various psychological (also physical) complaints. Even when there are differences of emphasis in therapeutic goals all treatments share the objective of producing change. They all probably contain a learning element. Indeed, Goldstein, Heller, and Sechrest (1966) propose the following definition of psychotherapy:

> Whatever else it is, psychotherapy must be considered a learning enterprise. We need not specify too narrowly just what it is to be learned in psychotherapy; it may be specific

behaviours or a whole new outlook on life, but it cannot be denied that the intended outcome of psychotherapy is a change in an individual that can only be termed a manifestation of learning.

Any form of therapy (be it psychotherapy or behaviour therapy) involves psychological influence — implicit or explicit — deployed in the setting of a relationship between client and therapist. The dichotomy drawn between interpersonal and relationship factors on the one hand, and technique on the other, seems somewhat forced; also false, because it is doubtful whether these two major components in the therapeutic enterprise can ever be isolated in pure and separate cultures.

SOURCES OF THERAPEUTIC CHANGE

Therapeutic change depends (inter alia) upon:

(a) *Persuasion*, which rests on practical knowledge or practice wisdom. It offers reasons why the client should change his or her beliefs and/or behaviour. It is (subject to ethical constraints and the process of negotiating goals with clients) important to voice clear opinions based upon valid information, knowledge of the developmental literature, an understanding of children's rights, and of hard-gained practice wisdom and experience. Clients should be informed when they are being offered facts (based on scientific studies) as opposed to personal opinions (e.g., value judgements).

(b) *Teaching*, which entails the offering of information and training in skills of acting. The client (or a staff group) may not be able to act without instruction, training and monitoring. Because some actions (e.g., child-training techniques) are so ingrained in parents' repertoires (anchored as they are by ideology or habit, or constrained by lack of skill), it is not usually good enough simply to advise them to change. Demonstrations, discussions, rehearsals, instructions and practice may be required in order to provide clients with the wherewithal for change.

(c) *Insight*, which is believed by many to be a facilitative influence in any therapeutic endeavour. Yelloly (1972) says:

> Awareness may operate in a number of ways. The sheer provision of accurate information may correct a false and erroneous belief and bring about considerable change in behaviour. Prejudice, for instance, may be diminished by new information which challenges the prejudiced belief. And in human beings (pre-eminently capable of rational and purposive action) comprehension of a situation, knowledge of cause and effect sequences and of one's own behaviour and its consequences, may have a dramatic effect on manifest behaviour. Thus to ignore the role of insight is just as mistaken as to restrict attention wholly to it.

(d) *Increasing perceived self-efficacy*. According to Bandura (1977) all psychological procedures designed to bring about change, whatever their type, are mediated through a system of beliefs about the level of skill required to bring about an outcome and the likely end result of a course of action. Efficacy expectations are thought to be the most important component. This notion is explored on page 218.

(e) *Technical therapeutic input.* There is an agnostic school of thought (the members tend to be eclectic) that is of the opinion that the technical claims of the diverse schools have never been adequately vindicated. Such a view, that there are minimal differences between therapeutic approaches with regard to outcome, is disputed by other researchers/practitioners — especially when it comes to *child psychotherapy* (Kazdin, 1988; Kolvin, *et al.*, 1981; Yule, 1989).

Nevertheless it is the kind of assumption put forward by Bergin and Lambert (1978), that led Jerome Frank (1973) in his book, 'Persuasion and healing', to argue that the 'active ingredients' — the effective 'therapeutic processes' — are the same for all treatment paradigms. He identifies as the common components of all types of influence and healing: warmth, respect, kindness, hope, understanding, and the provision of 'explanations'. These attributes are stressed in the Rogerian client-centred literature and their effect is related to fairly global aspects of the client's well-being (e.g., self-esteem) (see Axline, 1947; Truax and Carkhuff, 1967).

Whether a trained professional has special access to these qualities (or some unique deployment of them) is thrown into doubt (surely even for those who give most weight to the relationship factor in therapy) by the absence of substantive differences in the results of professional as opposed to non- or para-professional therapists (Durlak, 1979).

The arguments and counter-arguments about effectiveness are confounded by individual differences in the therapeutic qualities and skills of therapists. In addition, some are antitherapeutic, indeed noxious, in their effects upon clients. Another difficulty arises from the sheer number of experimental comparisons that would be required if all of 230 alternative psychosocial treatments (an estimate by Kazdin, 1988, of what is available to children and adolescents) were to be evaluated.

It would be only too easy for the 'hardheaded' manager of clinical services, husbanding scarce resources, to dismiss the claims of child therapists as rhetoric. Where is the evidence that a massive injection of therapeutic (notably psychotherapy) services directed at children's problems would do anything to dent the prevalence rates? Which of the many available treatments — be they physical (pharmacological) or psychological — is most deserving of support? Are there 'horses for courses' in the sense that we can match specific therapies to particular problems? If so, is this confidence based on hard evidence rather than wishful thinking and special pleading?

THE EFFECTIVENESS OF PSYCHOLOGICAL THERAPIES

Reviews of multiple techniques bearing the superordinate title 'psychological therapy' or 'psychotherapy' (e.g., Hersen and Van Hasselt, 1987; Tuma, 1989; Weisz *et al.*, 1987) certainly suggest that *psychotherapy is better than no treatment* for a large number of childhood problems, including anxiety, hyperactivity, social withdrawal and aggression (see Kazdin, 1988 for an excellent review). This may be reassuring to know, even if it has to be hedged in with many reservations; but it is still far too crude and ambiguous a generalization. There is a more specific set of requirements which is put in the following way in Paul's much quoted question: '*what* treatment, by *whom*, is more effective for *this* individual with *that* specific problem, under *which* set of circumstances?' (Paul, 1967). We still cannot provide precise answers to this question posed over two decades ago; yet it continues to be relevant, especially if we maintain that psychotherapy is a general term that encompasses many different treatments.

VARIETIES OF TREATMENT

The task of making a case for more resources, to increase the psychological input for children with problems is not made easy (and this is also the case in adult work) when there are so many competing claims from so many different approaches, to be the true faith. There is also, often, an implied suggestion that a particular approach can be applied to all problems. Sadly, faith, rather than evidence, is mostly what is on offer to support the more panglossian prospectuses.

What also tends to undermine confidence is the fact that there are considerable variations in the theoretical ideas that inform even similarly named treatments. Different theories of family processes generate different schools of family therapy (see Herbert, 1988; Vetere and Gale, 1987). Behavioural work is no longer a monolithic enterprise built upon a narrow reading of experimentally based learning theory. Kazdin (1978) observes, in his history of behaviour therapy, that behaviour therapy has become so variegated in its conceptualizations of behaviour, research methods, and techniques, that no unifying schema or set of assumptions can incorporate all extant techniques. The importance of 'private events' or the cognitive mediation of behaviour is more generally recognized as a vital feature in programme planning. Cognitive therapy and cognitive behaviour therapy take account of cognitions per se, and cognitive mediators such as causal attributions, control-related beliefs (perceived contingency), locus of control and cognitive level, all of which have been shown to affect therapeutic outcomes (Weisz and Weiss, 1989).

There is evidence — albeit still somewhat tentative — that differences in treatment effects, when apparent, tend to favour behavioural rather than non-behavioural approaches (Kazdin, 1988).

Play therapy is another therapeutic method that draws on different nuances of childhood psychopathology theory, and thus takes different forms (e.g., active play therapy, release therapy and the play interview) and can be applied on a dyadic basis (e.g., Axline's approach) or in a group format (e.g., Filial therapy). The range of choice of *individual psychotherapies* — notably in the case of adolescents — almost rivals the choice available to adults: psychodynamic, client-centred, behaviourally-orientated psychotherapy, communication, drama, role-construct, social system, multimodal, provocative, transactional, existential, gestalt, to mention a few. These are relatively broad approaches or perspectives. When we come down to techniques, as we saw earlier, there are dozens to choose from (Corsini, 1981; Hersen and Van Hasselt, 1987; Schaefer et al., 1986; Tuma, 1989).

What does such profusion mean? The sceptic might say that when so many treatments are in use, applied often to the same kinds of problem, it means that we lack a firm conceptual grasp of causation and/or have yet to develop valid methods to meet the problems we face in clinical child psychology. This is our cue to evaluate the effectiveness of that part of the therapeutic armamentarium that relies primarily on concepts of systemic and psychosocial causation.

FAMILY THERAPIES

There is no one 'family therapy' but several 'schools' or 'paradigms', such as analytic, structural, strategic and behavioural family approaches. Some versions of family therapy have explicit roots in psychological theories, such as the application of social learning principles to the resolution of family problems (e.g., Patterson, 1982). Some have been influenced by psychoanalytic theory; others by programmes of psychological research into family processes (e.g., Haley, 1976; Jackson and Weakland, 1961).

All therapies tend to be concerned with helping families to move from entrenched habits — individual behaviours and patterns of interaction — which preclude them from finding solutions to the problems that confront them. The members are encouraged by a variety of therapeutic strategies and homework tasks to think, feel and act differently. In order to understand the family across the generations (the extended family) and the alliances, conflicts and attachments within the family unit, clients are encouraged to look at themselves from a fresh perspective and to seek alternative solutions to their dilemmas.

The family systems approach

The structural approach to producing family change is particularly associated with Salvador Minuchin, and the Philadelphia Child Guidance Clinic. The focus of attention is very much on the developmental tasks faced by the family and its members, at various stages of its (and their) life-span. Day-to-day nuances and patterns of relationship — communication and interaction — between members, are inferred from highly charged or repetitive sequences observed and analysed in the therapy room.

The therapeutic task is defined in broader terms than the individual — be it parent or child. The child — brought to the clinic as the 'patient' or 'client' by the parents — is viewed as one part of a complex network of personal and family relationships. Family therapists see the total network of family transactions as part of a 'system' which is greater than the sum of its parts, hence their rejection of the parents' exclusion of themselves from the arena by referring to the problem as 'my son's/daughter's problem'. The family system is viewed as the critical context for an assessment and intervention. The system is made up of the functioning of three sub-systems (spouses; parents and children; children alone) all contained within a defined boundary and, in turn, operating within a social-cultural context. A most important person not be left out is the referrer (Palazzoli *et al.*, 1978) — the one who has identified the problem as needing a solution now. This could be a parent or spouse, but is often another concerned individual who feels responsible in some way, such as a teacher or general practitioner.

Assessment (see Lask, 1980, 1987)

Typically, an assessment by a family therapist might concern itself with whether there is:

- Too great a distance between members of the family leading potentially to emotional isolation and physical deprivation.
- Excessive closeness between members of the family leading potentially to over-identification and loss of individuality.
- An inability to work through conflicts, solve problems or make decisions.
- An inability on the part of parents to form a coalition and to work together, with detrimental effects on the marriage and/or the children.
- An alliance across the generations disrupting family life as when a grandparent interferes with the mother's child-rearing decisions.
- Poor communication between members.
- A failure to respond appropriately to each other's feelings.

Some of the ways in which a child may contribute (wittingly or unwittingly) to a family's inability to cope with conflict have been described by Lask (1980):

- *Parent-child coalition*, where one parent attacks the other, using one of the children as an ally.
- *Triangulation*, where both parents attempt to induce a child to take *their* side.
- *Go-between*, where a child is used to transmit messages and feelings.
- *Whipping-boy*, where one parent, instead of making a direct attack on the other, uses their child as a whipping-boy.
- *Child as weapon*, where one parent attacks the other using the child as a weapon.
- *Sibling transfer*, where the children agree to divert the parents from arguing.

The family is thought of as dynamic; it is seen to change continuously. Children grow into adolescents and bring new interests, ideas, values and friends into the family system. The peer group gains more influence. The child, becoming adolescent, learns that friends' families work by different standards and rules. The teenage culture introduces its values with regard to sex, religion, politics and drugs. Parents, too, are changing in ways that I described in Chapter 1.

STRUCTURAL FAMILY THERAPY

With all this in mind the structural family therapist's first step is to 'join' with the family, to participate in its transactions and observe members' roles, their communications, and the boundaries within the family and between the family system and other systems. The family 'organism', like the individual person, is thought to move between two poles: one representing the security of the known, and other being the exploration necessary for adaptation to changing conditions. When the family comes to treatment, it may be in difficulty because it is figuratively stuck, trying to maintain old ways which no longer meet the needs of a changed and changing set of circumstances.

The therapist takes a family (according to Minuchin, 1974) along the developmental spiral and creates a crisis that will push the family in the direction of their own evolution. The approach involves the therapist as an energetic intruder. He or she works actively to restructure family organization and channels of communication by modelling, direction and the use of 'action techniques'. The techniques for creating crisis or 'creative turmoil' and for putting the family on to a new and harmonious path (thus enhancing the potential for growth of each of its members) are many and varied. They might include:

Enactments

This is the direct illustration by the clients (as opposed to mere description) of the problems that exist between them. Clients are encouraged, where appropriate, to talk directly to one another rather than to (or through) the therapist.

Boundary clarification

The creation or clarification of boundaries between family members is a feature of structural work. A mother who babies her teenager may hear with surprise her daughter's reply to the question 'How old do you think your mother treats you as — three or thirteen?'

Reframing

This is an important method in fulfilling the objective of helping clients change in a covert, less directed manner. It involves an alteration in the emotional or conceptual viewpoint within which a situation is experienced. That experience is placed in another 'frame' which fits the facts of the situation as well (or more plausibly), thereby transforming its entire meaning. Giving people different 'stories' to tell themselves about themselves or about events — stories that are less self-defeating or destructive — is also a feature (under the name of cognitive restructuring) of behavioural work.

Changing space

Asking clients in the therapy room to move about can intensify an interaction or underline an interpretation being made about a relationship. For example, if a husband and wife never confront one another directly, but always use their child as a mediator or channel of communication, the therapist blocks than manoeuvre (called triangulation) by moving the child from between the parents. He or she may comment, 'Let's move Sara from the middle so you can work it out together'.

There is said to be a basic sequence through which family therapy passes. Treacher (1984) describes it as follows:

The Joining Phase. The family and the therapist are originally isolated from each other. But therapists use their skills so that they become absorbed into the family through a process of accommodation. This process creates a new system — family and therapist. It may take several sessions to create the new system, but since it is essentially a transitory one therapists carefully monitor any signs that family members are going to drop out of therapy and thus disrupt the new system.

The Middle Therapy Stage. This is the phase during which the major restructuring 'work' occurs. Restructuring interventions are made during sessions, and consolidating home-work tasks are set between sessions.

The Termination Stage. This phase involves testing the family's ability to 'fire' the therapist and go it alone. The 'ghost' of the therapist is left behind by getting the family to simulate or rehearse its ability to solve new problems and to deal with old problems if they recur.

The Follow-up. A follow-up session after three months, six months or a year enables the therapist to evaluate the impact of therapy and test whether it has been successful in achieving second order change, which means the facilitation of changes in family rules and family functions such that the family generates effective solutions to its own problems.

Improving relationships within the family

It is difficult to specify criteria for terminating therapy with families as such — a problem which does not loom so large in the case of specific target goals for individual members. When it comes to the family, they tend to be somewhat vague. The concept of cohesion provides a useful checklist of therapeutic objectives. The presence of family cohesion has a marked effect on the psychological well-being of family members (Orford, 1980).

- Members spend a fair amount of time in shared activity.
- Withdrawal, avoidance and segregated (separate) activities are rare.

- Interactions that are warm are common and interactions that are hostile are infrequent among members.
- There is full and accurate communication between members of the family.
- Valuations of other members of the family are generally favourable; critical judgements are rare.
- Individuals tend to perceive other members as having favourable views of them.
- Members are visibly affectionate.
- They show high levels of satisfaction and morale, and are optimistic about the future stability of the family group.

When these features are absent, the family members who are particularly at risk are those already vulnerable for other reasons: the young, the elderly, those coping with stress such as hospitalization, alcohol dependence, or caring for a large number of children. Contingency contracting — discussed in Chapter 15 — is also claimed to facilitate family cohesion.

Evaluations of effectiveness

Family therapy has been subjected to fewer evaluation studies than behaviour therapy. There is very little evidence from controlled trials to show that it is effective (Rutter, 1982). Nevertheless, there are some positive indications for the value of family therapy, both when compared with no intervention and with a variety of other treatments. For example, there is encouraging evidence for the use of family therapy with conduct disorders, though some of the more successful studies have used a behavioural version of family therapy (e.g., Christensen et al., 1980). A major concern about family therapy (and it also applies to training programmes) is that when the programme is terminated, the motivation to apply its precepts and techniques diminishes (Christensen et al., 1980).

The question of whether family therapy 'works' is too general; more research is needed on the effectiveness of specific well-defined forms of family intervention for specific clinical problems. A major difficulty is the lack of agreement on how to assess family interactions in a reliable and valid manner. There are aspects of the method (the one-way screen, the telephone, the consultations) that are worrying or distasteful to some clients, especially if not explained properly to them. An over-emphasis on formalism — the uncharitable call it 'mystique' — is the enemy of all therapies.

Treacher and Carpenter (1984), in their exploration of family therapy and its various applications, criticize some family therapists for their failure to consider the significance of wider social systems. Such therapists, by their concentration on therapy with nuclear families within clinical settings have allowed their vision of family therapy to become 'myopic'. The family replaces the individual as the locus of pathology; its social context is ignored, and it is 'assumed that all its problems can be easily revealed to the gaze of a group of therapists who cluster behind a one-way screen'. These authors maintain that such a narrow approach to understanding change within a family system cannot be defended at a theoretical level. As they put it:

> Change is often best effected by an intervention at another system level. For example, a worker who is attempting to produce change in a family which is experiencing many problems may be better advised to assist in the formation of a housing action group, designed to influence the housing department, than to concentrate on a more limited goal of defining boundaries between the members of a family who are crowded into a small, damp and decaying flat at the top of a tower block with no working lifts.

They go on to make the important point that family therapy and individual counselling and psychotherapy have been unhelpfully polarized. The skills of working individually with members of a family are often indispensable to the systems approach — especially when the therapeutic task is to help an individual detach himself or herself from the family system.

BEHAVIOURAL FAMILY THERAPY (see Griest and Wells, 1983)

During the late 1960s and early 1970s behaviour therapists established that parents could be taught to use behavioural principles to bring about positive change in the behaviour of their conduct-problem children (the subject of Chapter 16). The work of Gerald Patterson in Oregon was part of, and the inspiration for, a rapid proliferation of family-orientated research. In view of the relatively high levels of clinical affectiveness claimed for the approach it is necessary to elaborate the discussion on behavioural methods to be found in Chapter 3 by considering their application as a family therapy paradigm. This approach is in large part about the assessment and recruitment of naturally-occurring environmental influences, specifically those occurring within the family between parents, siblings and child, in order to modify deviant behaviour and teach new skills and behaviour repertoires. Behavioural family therapy — as its name implies — tends to operate much more at a *systemic* level than the parent training described in Chapter 15, where the main emphasis is on the parent–child (which usually means the mother–child) dyad rather than the family. Being mainly home-based it reduces — in theory — the problem of generalizing improvements from the consulting room to the outside world. The issue of temporal generalization remains a difficult technical problem; nevertheless, parents and teachers — as primary mediators of change — are in situ most of the time, and are in a position to apply contingencies and inductive methods of training, in a variety of situations and over the 'long haul' required especially in treating anti-social, aggressive children.

The triadic model (Herbert, 1985a)

The conceptual framework for our work at the Centre for Behavioural Work with Families (Herbert, 1987c) provides an illustration of the 'triadic model', which underpins behavioural family therapy, at work. The child, parents (or other members of the family) plus therapist (or consultant) make up the triad. The parents, generally speaking, are the main mediators of change. But other members of the family may well be involved in a therapeutic programme (Herbert, 1987c, 1988). The child is likely to be interviewed, tested and consulted by the therapist, but a dyadic therapeutic relationship is not central to this approach.

During the initial interview with the child and both parents (a crucial therapeutic configuration where there are two parents) we explain who we are and how we work. It is the Centre's policy to raise some of the major issues generated by a triadic behavioural approach: the concept of a therapeutic partnership; our desire to share our knowledge and thinking with the family; to take into account their own expertise based on long-standing knowledge of each other and the child; to involve the family system and/or subsystems in the assessment and treatment; and also to communicate the commitment we have to negotiate with them treatment goals which are explicit (see Herbert, 1987c and 1988 for case illustrations). It is vital to look at the ethical implications of any plans to institute changes within the family. There is a technical pay-off in sharing information, a reduction in the number of drop-outs from treatment (Baekeland and Lundwall, 1975). There may, of course, be other variables such as the style of training (e.g., didactic versus a participant approach) which influence drop-out rates.

Parents frequently tells us at debriefing interviews that this information and the 'insights' they gain from a more rigorous definition (and tracking) of anti-social and pro-social behaviour mark the beginning of change for many of them, in their interactions with their child and (for some) a growing sense of competence (Holmes, 1979; Iwaniec, Herbert and McNeish, 1985; Sutton, 1988). The clinical formulation is very much (but not exclusively) focused on a functional analysis — the ABC sequence. (See Figure 5, page 46.) A comprehensive history is a feature of the early stages of assessment (see Chapter 4).

The earlier literature on behaviour modification reflected a relative neglect of antecedent events. In their preoccupation with consequences of behaviour and, hence, operant procedures in the past, practitioners sometimes overlooked environmental controlling stimuli and the possibilities of ameliorating and restructuring the child's environment. The more recent parent-training research has done much to correct this omission.

It is helpful to observe what behaviours the parents or others in the family model (consciously or unconsciously) for the child to imitate or the confusing or weak verbal signals (instructions) they give. There are other factors to be taken into account (for example, parents' attributions and child-rearing and disciplinary ideologies), but there is insufficient space here to elaborate them (see Herbert, 1988).

Effective individual programmes depend upon a thorough behavioural analysis leading to a formulation. This includes a specification of the child's and family's behaviour, a picture of the family rules and roles, an understanding of distal influences which might still, via current attitudes and attributes, be an active influence on events. Treatment is also based on hypotheses about the contemporary factors that influence the instigation and maintenance of maladaptive interactions. It is useful in family work to negotiate a contract which specifies goals and behavioural objectives that are mutually agreeable to the child, the adults caring for him or her, and perhaps other people or agencies (e.g., school, social services or a court of law). The treatment plan provides the therapist with a strategy of intervention, but his or her personal ingenuity and experience are the main resources for its practical implementation.

An intensive input at the beginning of a programme (providing prompts, cues, moral support, modelling, etc.) is undoubtedly crucial in facilitating the work. Therapeutic conversations and developmental counselling are an almost invariable and central part of the work.

Contracts

The communication, negotiation, compromise and formulation of agreements implicit in working contracts, make family discussions an important feature of our work. It is helpful, as children get older, to hold family meetings in order to settle differences or decide important family concerns, such as discipline, rules, pocket money or bedtime. These methods can be translated to the other major natural environment of children — their schools and classrooms. Here again meetings with teachers and/or teachers/pupils, with a view to working out agreements about such matters as rules, appropriate behaviours and contingencies, can be initiated (Fontana, 1986; O'Leary and O'Leary, 1977).

Organizing interventions

The methods elaborated at the Centre for Behavioural Work with Families (Herbert, 1987c) involve a multimodal package depending for its final constituents on the behavioural and developmental-social assessment. It might involve developmental and/ or personal counselling. Variations in family values and attitudes and individual differences in children require the flexibility of individualized programmes; thus techniques are not applied in a cookbook fashion. It is only too easy, given the multilevel nature of so many child and family interventions, for the programme to become fragmented.

Evans (1989) suggests a simple conceptual framework as a means of organizing the many types and categories of treatment used in child behaviour therapy. They contend that in order for clinical treatment to be effective over the long term, at least four basic levels of intervention need to be implemented in concert:

(a) manipulating the immediate consequences of the undesirable behaviour;
(b) reducing the behaviour's probability by rearranging the environment;
(c) facilitating (teaching, reinforcing, shaping) the emergence of alternative skills;
(d) designing long-term prevention through imparting new patterns of behaviour.

Controlling natural consequences

This refers to externally and self-imposed rewards and punishments; the objective is to ensure that the density of reinforcement available for appropriate behaviour is greater than that available for pathological and socially unacceptable behaviour. This is based on the observation that negative, undesirable behaviours work for children — they serve some function. In a very real sense a child does not *have* a problem; he or she is trying to solve a problem — although in a self-defeating manner. It is these functional relationships that behaviour therapy seeks to adjust (see Chapter 3).

Ecological manipulations

A major function of ecological manipulation is to create productive environments that not only reduce the antecedents for undesirable behaviour but also maximize the opportunities for new learning to occur. The model also includes tactics that physically prevent undesirable behaviour from occurring. The approach excludes contingency management, but includes increasing the amount of reinforcement available, as well as such methods as preventing an overweight child's access to fattening foods by putting them out of reach.

There is no real need for ecological manipulations to be temporary or superficial as can be seen in such examples as changing the atmosphere in a ward or classroom setting, designing programmes whereby juvenile offenders spend their free time in a boys' club rather than on the streets, or fostering a child out of an abusive home situation; all require careful inter-agency and therapeutic planning, and clinical skills.

Teaching alternative behaviours

An important goal in therapy is to develop more acceptable alternatives to deviant behaviour. The methods used include shaping, reinforcing, providing feedback and modelling.

Long-term prevention

The need for certain types of reinforcement can itself indicate response deficits of a more fundamental kind. For example, in order to effect a more permanent change in an aggressive child, behaviour therapy might need to focus on *both* alternative social skills and more positive cognitions about self-worth and self-competence. These latter skills should also serve to prevent related problems from developing in the future and are thus thought of as long-term prevention strategies. Phobic conditions provide a good illustration. The general behavioural strategy is to try to extinguish the inappropriate emotional response. Abnormal fears can be reduced through direct exposure (see Chapter 18). However, unless the origin of the fear was unequivocally some unique traumatic conditioning experience, it is unlikely that this will remedy those deficits in coping which may be part of the origin of the fearful behaviour. Evans points out that there are two broad types of alternative to anxiety: one is its emotional antithesis, such as being calm and relaxed, reinterpreting cues as non-threatening, and so on; the other is the set of attitudinal and practical skills that permit coping in any stressful situation. Thus, the child who fears school may lack the skills that are required to cope with peer interactions, teacher demands, and being separated from a nurturing parent. Which of these possible skill deficits needs to be addressed in a given case is a matter for individual assessment; but the general principle is that there is a treatment dimension which should include the acquisition of both immediate alternatives and longer term preventative skills (see Kendall, Howard and Epps, 1988).

FAMILY-STYLE RESIDENTIAL HOMES

There are programmes which have been designed to take into account several of the behavioural methods described in Chapter 3, and to apply them systematically in planned environments. There has been a trend in the United States and elsewhere, away from the use of large penal institutions toward the establishment of small family-style residential units. An outstanding example of such a unit employing token economy principles with delinquent and predelinquent boys is Achievement Place.

The rationale for this work is that the delinquent behaviour of these boys is the product of inadequate social learning experiences. As Phillips *et al.* (1971) put it:

> The cause of this disturbing behaviour is that the past environment of youths has failed to provide the instructions, examples, and feedback necessary to develop appropriate behaviour ... and this general behavioural failure often forces the youth to become increasingly dependent upon a deviant peer group which provides inappropriate instructions, models and reinforcement that further expand the behaviour problems.

In trying to reverse such developments, the most important role of teaching-parents is educational. They teach youths a variety of social, academic, vocational, and self-help skills to equip them with alternative, more adaptive behaviours. The aim is to increase their chances of survival and success in the community. A very powerful and comprehensive token reinforcement system is established to develop specific social skills such as manners and communication, academic skills, and personal hygiene habits. Unlike many treatment programmes with global objectives, the specific treatment aims are specified in great detail.

An advantage of operating a community-based programme is that it allows the teaching-parents to work directly with a young person in natural settings, such as the home (to which they typically return on weekends) and the school (which they continue to attend). It is hoped that this increases the likelihood that prosocial behaviours acquired in these settings will persist even when they leave the programme. Being community-based, this approach also allows the teaching-parents to monitor and, if necessary, to provide additional treatment for the youth after they move away from the programme.

The evaluation of procedures has played a significant part in the development and refinement of the Achievement Place model. The majority of the original research publications evaluating Achievement Place were intraindividual reversal designs (ABAB) or variations on this theme.

An evaluation of the Achievement Place model has been carried out at the programme level (Fixsen *et al.*, 1972). Pre- and post-treatment comparisons were made post hoc, between the first 16 youths treated at Achievement Place and 28 other youths who, in the opinion of the probation officer, could have been candidates for Achievement Place. Of these, 13 youths had been placed on formal probation and 15 had been placed in the state industrial school (Kansas Boys School, an institution for 250 boys). It should be noted that these data are only suggestive since these youths were not randomly assigned to the two groups. The preliminary follow-up results indicated that youths who participated in the Achievement Place programme were progressing better than comparable youths who were placed on probation or sent to the state training school. For example, only 20 % of the Achievement Place youths required further treatment within one year after their release as compared to 44 % of the training school youths and 55 % of the probation youths.

Achievement Place youths and youths assigned to the Kansas School for Boys were most similar in terms of their prior offences, whereas the boys placed on probation had fewer offences than those assigned to Achievement Place or Kansas Boys School. While it is possible that other differences may have existed between boys assigned to the latter two facilities, the post-treatment differences in their recidivism and school attendances was dramatic — a tenfold difference in their school attendance.

Hoefler and Bornstein (1975) provide an evaluative review of the work carried out at Achievement Place. The model of 'teaching parents' and a family-style (but, nevertheless, controlled) environment has proved to be an evolving system. Achievement Place has provided a refreshingly detailed account of procedural details so that other communities can establish similar facilities utilizing principles based on empirical data rather than arbitrary decisions. It should be possible to replicate the work and evaluate whether other 'teaching-parents' can produce beneficial changes. This is a crucial matter because, although a good relationship between the youths and their teaching-parents is important, it can also be argued that this is not enough. Half-way house, family-style living arrangements, foster homes, and variations thereof have existed for years, but their efficacy with delinquents has not been demonstrated.

Chapter 15

Parent and Child Skills Training

The advantages of training parents and other caregivers are notably in the areas of primary prevention (Hawkins, 1972); therapeutic effectiveness (Topping, 1986) and cost effectiveness (Johnson and Katz, 1973). In the light of such a claim it seems appropriate to look more closely at the way it works. I will restrict this review to behavioural or applied social learning approaches to parent training. They have been the primary focus of research efforts; emphasizing as they do the observable behaviour of both parent and child, their reciprocal interactions, and the environmental variables that maintain specific behaviour patterns (Tavormina, 1974). Parents and significant others are trained (most often in group settings) in the provision of appropriate attention, in how to give instructions, use reinforcement effectively and many other skills.

COMPONENTS OF PARENT TRAINING

Efforts have been made to 'tease out' the specific components which contribute to a successful outcome (e.g., Christensen *et al.*, 1980; Forehand and Atkeson, 1977; McMahon, Forehand and Griest, 1981; Webster-Stratton, 1989a,b; Webster-Stratton, Hollinsworth and Kalpacoff, 1989).

Training formats

An important issue is how best to train parents. Walder *et al.* (1969) describe three broad approaches to parent training: individual consultation, a controlled learning environment and using educational groups.

In the *individual* consultation approach, the parent complaining of specific problems is instructed in how to behave towards the child under various contingencies. Individual programmes can range from enabling parents to carry out simple instructions in contingency management to a full involvement as co-therapists in all aspects of observation, recording, programme planning, and implementation.

The *controlled* learning environment, another variant of parent training, involves *highly structured* individual instruction, with the consultant directly shaping or modelling parent–child interactions. Sophisticated signalling and feedback devices are used while the parent interacts with the child.

Another means of training parents is within *educational groups*. Courses vary in duration, intensity, and structure. Various aids to learning such as lectures, guides, manuals, role-playing, videotape feedback, modelling, discussion, and home exercises have been used. Parents have been successfully trained in groups (e.g., O'Dell, Flynn and Benlolo, 1977).

Christensen *et al.* (1980) directly compared these three formats. Although parents in all three approaches perceived their children as significantly improved at the end of treatment, behaviour observations recorded by parents demonstrated that the individual and group formats were superior to the consultation only approach. Parents found the individual treatment format most satisfying. However, this format was most costly in therapist time. There are advantages and disadvantages in all of these approaches. Rose (1972) found that group sessions were more cost-efficient then either individual or family sessions, a finding not confirmed by Mira (1970) or Kovitz (1976).

There are several advantages in working with a group manifesting similar difficulties. They include the following functions:

(a) experiential;
(b) dynamic;
(c) social;
(d) didactic.

Many adults feel that they have failed miserably as parents, and that their child is uniquely difficult to understand and manage. Sharing experiences with other parents can be comforting, indeed reassuring. Swapping 'horror stories' is fine up to a point, but must not go on too long, thus engendering a mood of pessimism. The opportunity to express feelings of apprehension, resentment and anger (the latter aimed — not uncommonly — at the helping agencies) in a group setting, can be beneficial if handled sensitively by the group organizer. According to Johnson and Johnson (1975), a group intervention will be effective if it meets the following criteria:

● The group climate should be warm, accepting and nonthreatening — vital if people are to engage in controversy, expose their vulnerability, show their ignorance, take risks with touchy subjects.
● Learning should be conceived as a cooperative enterprise — impossible if the participants 'come over' as hostile, competitive, ridiculing, arrogant or judgemental.
● Learning should be accepted as the primary purpose of the group — a desideratum that requires painstaking and imaginative preparation of the material and sensitive but firm management of the group.
● Every member of the group should participate in discussions — a function, again, of a skilful, facilitative group leader.
● Such leadership functions might usefully be shared out for certain themes and/or sessions.

- Group sessions don't have to be endlessly solemn or heavy-going. They should be stimulating and thus pleasurable, and (at times) sheer fun.
- Evaluation should be viewed as an integral part of the group's activities. Group skills can be improved by constructive, critical evaluation.
- Members should attend regularly and come prepared — and the importance of mutual responsibility for the well-being of the group may be underlined by drawing up contracts with participants.

Sutton (1988) — a member of the Centre for Behavioural Work with Families — compared an individual and group approach and minimal contact bibliotherapy (booklets plus phone and postal contact) using standard content in each of the programmes. The British mothers of under 5-year-old children with conduct problems reported a significant improvement in their children compared with a waiting list control: there were no marked differences between the three modalities of training. Improvements were maintained over several years.

Course content

Horton (1982) has provided a comprehensive review of comparison studies which have examined the *content* of parent training programmes. She makes a distinction between 'broad-focus training' which is concerned with teaching general behavioural principles as well as skills for changing the child's particular behavioural problems, and 'specific-focus training' which includes only skills training for the problem in question (e.g., McMahon and Forehand, 1983).

Studies of broad-focus content (e.g., Christensen, *et al.*, 1980; Sutton, 1988) indicate that parents can learn general principles of behaviour change simply from reading a manual, although individual and group training appear to facilitate actual implementation of skills. It is hypothesized that audio- or videotaped instruction would make the acquisition of broad-focus skills even more effective. Studies of specific-focus training (e.g., Nay, 1975; O'Dell *et al.*, 1979) suggest that, in general, parents can be trained to use a specific behavioural procedure with very little professional time, and that this occurs equally well with all methods of training, though modelling and behaviour rehearsal may increase the parents' ability to actually perform the skill.

Research studies investigating the relative merits of broad-focus behavioural principles versus specific behavioural change techniques have arrived at mixed results. Ollendick and Cerny (1981) conclude a review of the evidence on content and formal aspects of parent training by concluding that although training in behavioural principles may not significantly increase parents' intellectual comprehension of child management techniques in the behavioural modality, or their attitudes toward parent training, a grounding in these basic principles does seem to facilitate the implementation and generalization of the newly acquired skills in non-training situations.

Horton (1982) has highlighted several methodological difficulties which may account for inconsistencies in studies: they include varying lengths of treatment involved, differing sampling procedures (some parents responding to media ads, some being paid to attend, while others were asked for a security-deposit), also variations in outcome measures.

Negative findings may reflect an erroneous clinical formulation; at the individual casework level this is always what we should check out first. At the more general level, failure may result from a lack of *ability* on the part of parents to conceptualize learning principles or a resistance to perceiving improvement in their children's behaviour. Some practitioners suggest that failure is sometimes a reflection of great stress (social and economic) undermining parents with worry, exhaustion and despair (Herbert, 1988). The absence of change may relate to the parents' own previous experiences of parenting and to ideologies of child-care and discipline (in particular, punishment) that are at odds with the assumptions of parent 'trainers'. The somewhat poor outcome reported for parents of lower socio-economic status, for parents with strong ideologies (Holmes, 1979), or single parents (Webster-Stratton, 1985) could be due to a lack of perceived relevance, an absence of face validity, in the applied social learning approach. Perhaps such parents, who have tried for many years to manage an intractable child, are looking for 'better' (i.e., more effective) ways to punish their child rather than a long, drawn-out programme that emphasizes rewards and the positive side of their offspring. In other words there is an ideological mismatch; they are sometimes looking for more immediate (and punishment-led) results.

All of this is rather hypothetical, but the issue of what family characteristics affect successful parent training outcome is very much of current concern. Webster-Stratton (1985, 1989a,b) has suggested that the failure of many parent training programmes to hold up over time is related to extrafamilial stressors such as adverse life-events and socioeconomic status; intrafamilial influences such as single parent status and marital conflict; and personal factors including depression. Longitudinal studies certainly bear out her own findings. Olendick and Cerny (1981) indicate on the basis of their review how programmes are liable to fail due to parents' marital problems or other conflicts within the family. Children from low socio-economic families generally display more antisocial behaviours and poorer school adjustment (Robins, 1966), which require longer treatment periods, and are less likely to benefit from treatment (Holmes, 1979) than children from higher socio-economic families Reviews (Cobb and Medway, 1978; O'Dell, 1974) claim that parental drop-out from training programmes may be linked to factors such as income level and educational background, also the demands made of already debilitated parents — the need for increased consistency, patience and hard work. Practical support (e.g., child-minding facilities) and social support, in the form of self-help parent groups, are of great benefit.

Casework skills

Herbert and Iwaniec (1981) stress the importance of the following casework skills: clarifying problems, listening sympathetically and indicating empathetic understanding and acceptance. Alexander, Corbett and Smigel (1976), in examining therapist skills, found that relationship skills (affection, warmth and humour) and structuring skills accounted for approximately 60 % of the outcome variance in treated cases, relationship skills being of greatest significance.

The therapist should (it is suggested by Johnson, 1980) adopt a positive attitude to change in discussing a person's problems. In this way they become more clearly defined. An important factor to consider is the stability of the problem implied by the explanation given to clients. People feel less demoralized when they attribute their problems to unstable causes. Explanations in terms of inappropriate attitudes, learned habits of thinking and behaving, or environmental stresses, all imply instability. Attributions of difficulties to fixed personality traits or to a malignant destiny imply stability. As Johnson (1980) puts it:

> All too often demoralized people fear that their personality make-up has a permanent defect. Others feel that they have been singled out and fated to endure a painful existence. Neither of these attributions lead to change and health.

It would appear that the involvement of fathers in parent training programmes is important (Webster-Stratton, 1985). Self-control training for mothers increases the likelihood of temporal generalization of beneficial change (Wells, Griest and Forehand, 1980).

EFFECTIVENESS

Several years of evaluating parent training at the Centre for Behavioural Work with Families has convinced us that there is encouraging evidence of the ability of parents to help themselves and their 'problematic' children over a wide range of difficult problems, ranging from conduct disorders (Herbert, 1980; Holmes, 1979); hyperactivity (Sutton, 1988); developmental disorders such as enuresis and encopresis (Herbert and Iwaniec, 1981); child abuse and failure-to-thrive (Iwaniec, 1983; Iwaniec, Herbert and McNeish, 1985); to maternal rejection (Herbert and Iwaniec, 1977) and mental handicap (Dean *et al.*, 1976).

It is necessary to find out the most economical and effective methods of training parents, and techniques for changing maladaptive behaviours, and to know what range of problems can be tackled by this approach. It is safe to say that it is particularly promising for parents with conduct disordered youngsters or chronically handicapped children, who are likely to need a strategy for coping with novel problems, or at least a succession of teaching tasks, in the future.

THE MAINTENANCE OF CHANGE (GENERALIZATION)

Long-term maintenance of change is a major consideration when examining the cost-effectiveness of parent training. Patterson and Fleischman (1979) and Wells, Griest and

Forehand (1980) amongst others demonstrated reasonable levels of temporal generality of therapeutic gains, but others have reported discouraging returns to baseline behaviour (e.g., Wahler and Fox, 1980). Christensen et al. (1980) also report positive maintenance and suggest that the timing of the follow-up measure may be crucial; they recorded a 64 % success rate at one year compared with 41 % at one month follow-up.

LIFE SKILLS TRAINING (see Combs and Slaby, 1977)

Social skills training (SST)

Programmes and packages have been applied in profusion to behaviourally disordered children; delinquent youth; developmentally delayed or retarded children; non-clinic-attending children; socially insulated and withdrawn children; unpopular, rejected or neglected children; and aggressive-impulsive youngsters (Herbert, 1986; Ladd, 1984). Who is most likely to benefit from SST is stilll a matter of doubt.

The majority of studies evaluating the effectiveness of SST have been conducted on children with behavioural problems such as unassertiveness, excessive aggression, and social withdrawal (e.g., Allen et al., 1964; Hart et al., 1968; Michelson and Wood, 1980). The results are encouraging (see Beck and Forehand, 1984 for an invaluable critical review).

There have been few, but promising, studies of developmentally delayed or retarded children (Apolloni, Cooke and Cooke, 1977; Whitman, Mercurio and Caponigri, 1970); other work has focused specifically on skills training in school (e.g., McPhail, Middleton and Ingram, 1978).

Helping unpopular, rejected children to improve the quality and quantity of relationships with peers has also been a matter of concern (Bornstein, Bellack and Hersen, 1977; Gresham and Nagle, 1980; Ladd and Mize, 1983; Oden and Asher, 1977). Here again we find an increase in positive peer interactions and 'social standing' in the experimental situation, although as usual the generalization (situational and temporal) issue remains unresolved.

There is something of a 'hit and miss' feeling to many of these studies, a lack of a precise rationale as an underpining to the training programme chosen, In establishing a curriculum for SST, many researchers tend to rely on empirical criteria of behaviours that are associated with success in peer relations, e.g., behaviours associated with peer popularity, those judged competent by teachers or valued by peers (Ladd, 1981). For all that, there is no agreement in the literature on what children should be taught during SST. It may be that an emphasis on facilitating active social-problem-solving processes, rather than teaching static social skills, will produce the longer-term gains that have so far evaded most interventions.

Problem-solving therapies

The rationale for these methods is succinctly provided by D'Zurilla and Goldfried (1971):

> Much of what we view clinically as 'abnormal behaviour' or 'emotional disturbance' may be
> viewed as ineffective behaviour and its consequences, in which the individual is unable to
> resolve certain situational problems in his life and his inadequate attempts to do so are having
> undesirable effects, such as anxiety, depression, and the creation of additional problems.

Although some of the therapeutic procedures commonly used in adult cognitively-orientated work can be understood by adolescents, many of them would not be suitable for children. Nevertheless, youngsters can be taught rational thinking, stress-inoculation techniques and problem-solving strategies.

The aim of training children in problem-solving skills is to provide them with a general coping strategy for a variety of difficult situations. The method has been used to help parents, children and adolescents deal more effectively with a variety of conflict situations (e.g., arriving at mutually acceptable decisions with parents, developing cooperation with the peer group). Its prime advantage as a training method is the provision of principles, so that the individual can function as his or her own 'therapist'. It is a variant of self-control training, directed towards the objective of encouraging clients to think and work things out for themselves (see Spivack, Platt and Shure, 1976).

George Spivack and his colleagues have defined a number of differing interpersonal cognitive problem-solving skills. They suggest a series of skills rather than a single (unitary) ability. The significance of each of these abilities in determining the degree of social adjustment is said to differ as a function of age.

The interpersonal cognitive problem-solving skills include the following:

Problem-sensitivity

This is the ability to be aware of problems which arise out of social interactions and a sensitivity to the kinds of social situations out of which interpersonal difficulties may arise. It also involves the ability to examine relationships with others in the here and now.

Alternative solution thinking

A close parallel to this is 'brain-storming'. The key feature is the ability to generate a wide variety of potential solutions to the problem. Judgement about what is best is suspended and the skill is to draw from a repertoire of ideas representing differing categories of solutions to a given problem.

Brainstorming

This is the creative art of generating the greatest number of ideas in the shortest possible time. It is ideally suited to group participation as well as individual application.

Means-ends thinking

This reflects the ability to articulate the step-by-step means necessary to carry out the solution to a given interpersonal problem. The skill encompasses the ability to recognize obstacles, the social consequences deriving from these solutions and a recognition that interpersonal problem solving takes time.

Consequential thinking

This involves being aware of the consequences of social acts as they affect self and others and includes the ability to generate alternative consequences to potential problem solutions before acting.

Causal thinking

This reflects the degree of appreciation of social and personal motivation and involves the realization that how one felt and acted may have been influenced by (and, in turn, may have influenced) how others felt and acted.

BEHAVIOURAL MARITAL WORK (BMW)

There has been a lot of research into the adjustments required of married couples, into the conflicts, dysfunctional communications, manipulations and changes that take place in the course of a marital relationship (see Bornstein and Bornstein, 1988; Noller and Guthrie, 1989). The emphasis on conflict and manipulation is somewhat misleading. The evident fact is that in many ongoing marriages there is a great deal of interaction which is playful, complementary and joyous, as well as much that is hostile. However, marital problems loom large in work with problematic children (Patterson, 1982).

Social exchange theory

A process of bargaining may underlie some of the similarities in succesful marriages of long duration. It is one of the great platitudes — part of popular wisdom — that marriage is a matter of give and take. In marital interactions the social exchange model helps us to assess (in part) what is going wrong with a partnership. People initiate and prolong relationships of intimacy as long as those relationships are reasonably satisfactory with regard to what are called the 'rewards' and 'costs'. For example, immature individuals are not always able to manage the give-and-take of friendship. Exchange theory provides a pointer to why this should be so; it also provides one method of improving people's social attractiveness and their relationships. In this model, social interactions and relationships are compared to economic bargains or the exchange of gifts. All activities carried out by one individual, to the benefit of another, are termed 'rewards', while detrimental activities — hostility and anxiety — are seen as 'costs' (Beech, 1985; Behrens, Halford and Sanders, 1989).

A notable feature of a partnership that is 'working' is the balance in the relationship that exists between the partners, often called 'status symmetry'. It concerns the mutual respect and lack of dominance and exploitation which characterize intimate and lasting relationships. In friendly or loving relationships there is an overall balance in the influence of each of the participants.

It is useful to draw up a balance sheet. On the debit side, the term 'cost' is applied to deterrents that may be incurred in the course of interactions with another person — such as criticism, neglect, hostility, anxiety, embarrassment, and the like. For attraction to another individual to occur (or to be maintained) the reward-cost outcome must be above the 'comparison level', a standard against which satisfaction is judged.

In this model, marital discord is dealt with by redistributing (with the help of a contract) prevailing rates of reinforcement (satisfaction) and punishment (dissatisfaction) within the relationship. Individuals are encouraged — following discussion, negotiation and (hopefully) compromise — to maximize satisfactions (the positives) while minimizing the dissatisfaction (mutually irritating behaviours) provoked by the couple. This is where contracts can be very useful, not only for marital work but for other family relationships (e.g., between parents and teenagers) that are tense and unhappy. Encouraging high rates of exchange of positive behaviours, plus training in communication and problem-solving — as the main foci of BMW — have produced behaviour change. But many marriages do not improve with this sort of therapy (see Behrens, Halford and Sanders, 1989; Noller and Guthrie, 1989).

Part Six

Five Major Clinical Problems of Childhood and Early Adolescence

This section deals with the assessment and treatment of five problems of major concern to contemporary clinical child psychologists: antisocial, disruptive disorders; fears and phobias; delinquent behaviour; acute pain; and psychological trauma following major disasters. These clinical issues take us from the child and family psychiatric clinic, the forensic centre and general hospital, to the community arena. All are linked conceptually by a viewpoint rooted in empirical psychology: in particular, the fields of learning and development. Each is a self-contained chapter.

Part Six

Major Clinical Problems of Childhood and
Early Adolescence

Chapter 16

Antisocial, Disruptive Behaviour Disorders

There is a mounting tide of public concern about violence and disruptive behaviour in homes, classrooms and on the streets. Accounts in the media of violence at school (bullying and blackmail of peers, attacks on teachers), the flouting (or lack) of authority at home, not to forget vandalism and hooliganism on the streets, sound a note of hysteria and moral panic. A glance through old newspaper archives may reassure us that there is nothing new about such phenomena, but will not appease the apocalyptic school of thought which detects a feral quality in the sheer mindlessness of much contemporary antisocial behaviour.

A representative of this pessimistic viewpoint is Patricia Morgan (1975) who paints a sombre picture of growing numbers of poorly socialized individuals who have scarcely acquired the rudiments of human culture. As she puts it:

> The most alarming aspect is probably the sharp increase in crime, violence and aimless destruction of all kinds, with larger proportionate increases as one goes down the age scale. Also much crime, often of a highly dangerous and serious nature, is committed by those well under the age of criminal responsibility ... Actually, to use the expression 'crime' for much modern anti-social behaviour is rather misleading, since it has no end beyond the most transitory titillation. The delinquent is frequently far too unsocialized to control his pursuit of instant excitement for rational gain.

What does a more objective, clinical perspective tell us about disruptive antisocial problems in children and adolescents?

DEFINING DISRUPTIVE BEHAVIOUR

In large part, what teachers (or parents) define as 'disruptive' activity depends upon their view of the essential nature of children in general, and pupils in particular. Teachers' perspectives range over a wide spectrum and often seem polarized: at one extreme is the view of the 'good' student as deferential and docile — one who passively receives the wisdom of, and correct answers from, the teachers. At the other extreme, the pupil is regarded as an active partner in the learning process — figuratively speaking, the 'fire to be lit' rather than the 'vessel to be filled'. In this child-centred (as opposed to teacher-centred) approach, the child may be thought of as deviant if passive, whereas, in the other view, passive-receptivity is the desideratum of the good pupil. Not surprisingly what one teacher calls disruptive may not be so for another.

The perceptions of parents must also be taken into account. In order to bring young children to the professionals' attention, one or more of his or her parents must come to the view that their problems merit such a referral. However, mothers may inaccurately label their children as deviant due to their own problems of adjustment (e.g., marital dissatisfaction, depression, anxiety) (Webster-Stratton, 1988, 1989a).

DEVELOPMENTAL-BEHAVIOURAL ASSESSMENT

Behaviour that is disruptive at school tends to occur in particular situations, between:

- Pupil and authority (lateness, absenteeism, truancy, non-compliance).
- Pupil and work (repeated failure to do homework or produce written work, opposition to projected work).
- Pupil and teacher (the use of abusive and foul language, persistent interruption of the teacher, refusal to carry out instructions, disruptions of the teaching situation).
- Pupil and pupil (bullying, intimidation, violent assault, extortion, theft).

Specificity

In many respects disruptive actions tend to occur at certain times, in certain settings, towards certain objects or individuals and in response to certain forms of provocation; children rarely show antisocial behaviour, be it aggression or defiance in blind, indiscriminate ways. There are two categories of contributary influence to consider in an assessment leading to a formulation and eventually treatment: contemporary circumstances and early learning.

Contemporary circumstances

For instance, physical or verbal attacks, deprivation, frustration, conflict and exposure to disruptive models which *instigate*, or *maintain* (by direct, vicarious and self-reinforcement) antisocial activities. An account of instruments for the assessment of disruptive, antisocial behaviour is provided in Appendix II.

The interactions between parents and child go a long way (as we have seen) towards shaping disruptive actions in the home, because of the reinforcing consequences inherent in their nature. Children are likely to generalize what they learn about the utility and benefits of being 'difficult' with parents to other persons and situations. In these circumstances they put to the test the consequences of being antisocial and disruptive.

For example, they may try being aggressive because it produced results (e.g., much needed kudos) with siblings or with the peer group in the playground at school. Of course, deviant behaviour which has been acquired as part of the child's repertoire, may not necessarily be performed often, either because appropriate instigating conditions do not occur, or because the consequences of such acts are likely to be unrewarding or aversive.

Early learning

But it is not only the 'here-and-now', current influences that must be taken into account in a clinical assessment. Early learning and development are important and knowledge of such factors may well influence the line taken in planning an intervention (see Part 2).

We know that continuity or stability varies according to *type* of behavioural disturbance. This is highlighted by the findings of Fischer *et al.* (1984) (see page 19). The longitudinal investigation, by Robins (1966) of American children, suggests that by ages 7 or 8 the child with *extreme* antisocial aggressive patterns of behaviour is at quite considerable risk of continuing on into adolescence and indeed adulthood with serious deviancy of one kind or another. Knowledge of the long 'incubation' period for many of the more serious antisocial childhood manifestations has implications for policy with regard to preventative work and for the credibility of applied social learning theory. Can this approach break through and interrupt the pattern of persistent antisocial behaviour?

The implication of a long and gradual (as opposed to relatively 'acute') onset of problems, is often that of a 'long-haul' intervention and a clinical formulation that includes the family system (not only the child) as client. I shall return to this theme shortly. First, let us look at some of the behavioural components of the disruptive 'syndrome'.

Disruptive behaviour disorder in the DSM-III-R is something of a diagnostic ragbag; it includes the following:

(a)   oppositional defiant behaviour;
(b)   conduct disorder;
(c)   Attention-Deficit Hyperactivity Disorder (ADHD).

OPPOSITIONAL DEFIANT DISORDER (code 313.81)

The behaviour of a young child is assessed to be 'oppositional' if parents or teachers regard it as representing an unacceptably low level of cooperation with their authority (Green, Forehand and McMahon, 1979). This generally means disobedience of adult commands and requests, rule-breaking in the home or school, and resistive temper tantrums. Gross and Wixtead (1987) make the point that it is unfortunate and confusing that children who exhibit such behaviour are variously referred to as oppositional, conduct disordered, or deviant. Although the term 'deviancy' appears to have no clearly defining criteria the terms 'oppositional behaviour' and 'conduct disorder' can be distinguished: the former is characterized primarily by obstreperous disobedience, while the latter is characterized by physical aggression and serious flouting of conventions and social norms. In practice, a younger child is more likely to be referred to as oppositional, though this problem can occur in late childhood and adolescence as well (APA, 1980). Oppositional problems were dealt with in a developmental context in Chapter 7.

CONDUCT DISORDERS

Conduct disorders of childhood and adolescence entail far too many diverse problems, not to mention a long and eventful developmental timespan, for any one chapter to cover fully (see Kazdin, 1987). In the USA some two-thirds of all young children who are referred to mental health agencies are eventually classified as antisocial, oppositional, or conduct disordered. These problems are on the increase and demand for help outstrips available personnel and resources (President's Commission on Mental Health, 1978).

Assessment

As with the generic term 'disruptive behaviour' any definition of conduct disorder must involve a consideration of the social and subjective judgements that lead to a child being assessed in this way. This is an important caveat given the attempts that have been made to treat the label as a precise diagnostic category.

In the tenth edition of the 'International Classification of Disease' (ICD-10) (World Health Organization, 1988) conduct disorders are defined as 'repetitive and persistent patterns of antisocial, aggressive or defiant conduct. Such behaviour when at its most extreme for the individual, should amount to major violations of age-appropriate social expectation; and is therefore more severe than ordinary child's mischief or adolescent rebelliousness.' (p. 163). In DSM-III-R (code 312 xx) conduct disorders are characterized as a 'persistent pattern of conduct in which the basic rights of others or major age-appropriate social norms or rules are violated. The behaviour pattern typically is present in the home, at school, with peers, and in the community.' (p. 53). These descriptions beg many questions; they certainly lack precision. The list of behaviours making up this pattern (see below) demonstrates the permeable boundary between conduct disorders and what society adjudicates as 'delinquent' activities.

The child must have at least three of the following:

- Two or more incidents of stealing without confronting the victim (including forgery).
- Running away from home overnight at least twice (or once without returning).
- Frequent lying (other than to avoid physical or sexual abuse).
- Deliberate firesetting.

- Frequent truancy or absence from work.
- Breaking into others' property.
- Deliberate destruction of others' property (other than by firesetting).
- Physically cruel to animals.
- Forced sexual activity.
- More than one fight in which a weapon has been used.
- Frequent initiation of physical fights.
- Stealing with confrontation of the victim (e.g., mugging).
- Physically cruel to people.

A diagnostic criterion in DSM-III-R is that conduct disorders should be pervasive in all major situations of home, school and community. A drawback of this specification is that is excludes the situation specific characteristics of children's psychological problems: *persistence* of antisocial behaviour is also seen as a major diagnostic characteristic of conduct disorders. In DSM-III-R, this is defined as at least six months duration.

Central to all of these problems is the child's or adolescent's unwillingness and/or inability to conform to the rules that operate at different levels and in different settings in the community. This means house-rules, parental expectations, classroom rules, social norms and, in the end, the law of the land. In the light of such problems it is perhaps not surprising that such children have been shown to be at increased risk of being abused by their parents (Wolfe, 1987).

DELINQUENT BEHAVIOUR (see Morris and Braukmann, 1987)

This mention of law-breaking introduces the concept of delinquency. The trouble with a term like 'juvenile delinquency' is that it is not possible to draw a clearcut line of demarcation between delinquents and non-delinquents. Recent surveys have shown that it is not only, or even usually, children known to the police who have committed acts contrary to the law. A large number of English grammar-school boys were asked (Gibson, 1967) about their delinquencies. About one-half of them admitted committing some sort of antisocial act. A large proportion of them, moreover, said that they had committed an act which could have landed them in a Juvenile Court had they been found out.

Over half of the boys had stolen money, two-thirds had shop-lifted and nine out of ten had stolen something from school. In a survey (Elmhorn, 1965) of 1000 school children aged 9–14 carried out in Norway and Sweden, 89 % confessed to petty illegal offences, 39 % ordinary theft, 17 % breaking in and 14 % wilful damage to property. In a Polish study (Malewska and Muszynski, 1970) of children aged 12–13, over 63 % admitted that they had taken other people's property.

The term 'delinquent' is a very flexible one, being in part a function of a particular set of laws *and* law enforcement policies. Although many children commit 'delinquent' acts at one time or another, certain children (particularly those from privileged homes and schools) are more likely than others to avoid detection. The concept of a 'delinquent' is essentially an administrative rather than a clinical one. It is important to bear in mind that not all conduct disordered children become delinquent, nor do all delinquent youngsters display clinical features of a conduct disorder. Nevertheless delinquent activities figure to a worrying extent in the repertoire of conduct disordered youngsters (see DSM-III-R).

The range of delinquent acts is enormous, as is the list of personal attributes attributed to delinquents. So unsuccessful have been the attempts to differentiate sharply between those who commit 'delinquent' acts and non-offenders, in terms of intelligence, physique, personality, social background, and the like, that some theorists have abandoned the search for general hypotheses to explain 'delinquency' as such.

An exception is Trasler (1966, 1973). His ideas on the evolution of antisocial, delinquent problems begin with the observation made by Walker (1965) that most crimes take the form of acquisitive, violent or sexually-aggressive behaviour which may, with reason, be attributed to basic and universal human motives. The delinquent range of acts is separated from non-criminal behaviours by the fact that they are prohibited by the criminal law and often (but not necessarily) by the mores or norms of society. Most delinquent acts do not depend upon special skills or techniques. It follows, Trasler argues, that the fundamental problem in explaining delinquency or criminality is not to discover the manner in which criminal habits are acquired, but to explain why certain individuals fail to inhibit those activites that society formally proscribes, and which the majority of the population has learned to repudiate.

On reflection the behaviour of small children is often antisocial and judged by literal adult criteria, 'delinquent'. Toddlers lash out at each other inflicting pain; they 'steal' each other's possessions, and what is more, show no remorse after transgressing the rules. They do not need to learn antisocial behaviours or attitudes. These tendencies occur quite spontaneously and to the child they have a logic of their own. What happens, as children mature, is that they must learn to avoid certain actions; that is to say they must be trained to check certain impulses and to regulate their behaviour in terms of certain informal and formal rules of conduct. The basic question to be answered for theorists like Trasler is 'Why are most children eventually law-abiding, given that in early childhood they were so asocial or antisocial?'

Ryall (1968) states that;

> One possible answer is that as we grow up we learn the nature of the law, that if we perform certain acts we may be punished. This answer suggests that we balance the benefit from doing the forbidden act against the risk of being caught and the probable punishment that would follow. If we do not fancy the penalty, even at the small risk of being caught, we do not commit the offence. This calculation almost certainly occurs in the minds of many motorists before they park in a no-parking zone or before they drive having had too much to drink. However, where acts of dishonesty are concerned for most people this calculating process does not take place. Even if the circumstances are such that the chance of detection is nil, they still do not steal. Most people have an aversion to stealing which cannot simply be' explained as being caused by a fear of the consequences.

This strong aversion to dishonest acts is variously explained in terms of conscience development (in psychoanalytic terminology 'super-ego') or in terms of avoidance learning. According to the latter, children have to learn *not* to be antisocial. We have already seen (Chapter 2) the role of conditioning in training the child to avoid certain acts. When a child is trained or conditioned not to do something the underlying process is known as 'passive avoidance conditioning'; responses of fear and anxiety are elicited automatically in the youngster when he or she contemplates transgressing the rules. These emotions persist throughout his or her life if the early conditioning processes have been effective (Eysenck, 1967).

The question of why there should be such dramatic individual differences in social 'conditioning' usually finds an answer in the Eysenckian version of learning theory, in terms of personality factors (in part inherited) and different constellations of environmental factors (e.g., particular patterns of child-rearing) (see page 99). Specific defects in avoidance learning due to an inability to form anticipatory fear responses is another theme in the explanations of extreme, i.e., psychopathic, antisocial persons. Eysenck (1967) postulates the existence of stable individual differences in conditionability, i.e., in speed of acquisition and resistance to extinction of conditioned responses of all kinds. These differences are thought to be a function of personality (extraversion–introversion). There is less of an emphasis on individual differences in constitutional determinants and more on the variations in the social context of learning in other accounts (e.g., Patterson, 1982) (see page 277).

It has always seemed a problem to the author, that the relatively simple conditioning (in Eysenck's theory) of reflexes (as in eye-blink conditioning) has to bear an enormously heavy burden in its extrapolation to such complex processes as are implied in social training. It is not self-evident that the personality factors relevant to eye-blink experiments are also pivotal to the many-sided (notably cognitive) story of socialization. While it may prove to be an important theme, its centrality is questionable. In any event, several investigators have failed to demonstrate differences between psychopaths (who manifest a dramatic failure to be socialized) and others, in terms of eye-blink conditioning (e.g., Miller, 1966). The generality of conditionability as a personality variable has also been disputed (see Trasler, 1973). Another problem arises from the observation that this version of learning theory does not predict the relatively late entry of some children into the delinquent ranks. Many young offenders do not make their first court appearance until after they have turned twelve; and their previous history is unremarkable for deviant acts.

Dishonest behaviour

The term 'conduct disorders' has an archaic ring to it, redolent of the value judgements about 'good' or 'reprehensible' conduct which children used to get (perhaps still get) in their school reports. It has moralistic overtones. But then we *are* dealing, inter alia, with moral problems, notably social value judgements to do with unrestrained aggressive, dishonest and acquisitive activities (e.g., theft and fraud).

Moral awareness

As many as four facets make up moral awareness and behaviour:

- Resistance to temptation: the 'braking' or inhibitory mechanism against misdemeanours that work even when the child is not being observed.
- Guilt, or the acute emotional discomfort that follows transgression and may lead to confession, reparation, or self-blame.
- Altruism, representing various prosocial acts of kindness, helpfulness, generosity, sympathy, empathy and service to others.
- Moral belief and insight, covering all aspects of what people think and say about morality, including their willingness to blame others who do wrong.

Each of these components is complex, and related one to the other in a complex manner. The evidence (Herbert, 1974) concerning resistance to temptation in private, for example, suggests a personality trait of some generality; but it is also clear that situational factors exert a powerful influence. According to Wright (1971), the evidence suggests that moral self-restraint is one aspect of a broader control factor — a generalized capacity to check or suppress one's impulses in situations that do not necessarily raise moral issues.

Cognitive processes contribute significantly to these moral and more general control mechanisms. As children grow older they are better able to conceptualize right and wrong; they gradually learn sets of rules taught them by parents and teachers. These developments are facilitated by an interaction with authority figures who behave rationally, and who explain the reasons for their requirements, and by the individual's own experience in taking the role of authority.

Piaget (1932) has demonstrated how the logic of children's moral reasoning changes radically from the age of 4 until adolescence. During the early stages of moral development the rules are felt to be absolute; morality is a unilateral system based, essentially, upon authority and, as such, external to the child. From the age of about 7 years onwards, children increasingly experience relationships which involve mutual respect — relationships between individuals of equal status, thus they meet other children who do not always share their views. By the age of 10 years the system of morality had undergone considerable change so that children now perceive rules to be manmade. Morality is very much a matter of negotiation and compromise; the rules *can* be changed if agreement can be obtained.

Piaget believes that the mature understanding of rules goes with an ability to keep them. On this point Kohlberg (1976) is particularly critical of both learning and psychoanalytic approaches to moral development. In his view behavioural psychology and psychoanalysis have always upheld what he sees as a Philistine view that fine moral words are one thing and moral deeds another. Kohlberg suggests that morally mature reasoning is quite a different matter and does not really depend on 'fine words'. The person who understands justice is more likely to practise it.

With adolescence the young person enters the final phase of moral development when morality is seen as a matter of individual principles. Young adults — or, at least, many of them — begin to appreciate that without certain basic principles there would be no morality at all. They usually understand that, although there may be endless debates and arguments over how these principles should be applied in particular circumstances. Notions of right and wrong based on adult authority have been replaced by internalized principles of conscience. When a child has developed a conscience it is generally thought that he or she is able to refrain from doing wrong much of the time, even when no one is present to prompt or check them.

It is often asked whether any particular stage of moral development is characteristic of delinquent adolescents. Kohlberg believes that the majority of adolescent offenders are preconventional (with attitudes of the 4- to 10-year-old) in their moral reasoning, as compared with the mainly coventional reasoning of nonoffending adolescents. A review of 15 studies (Blasi, 1980) supports the hypothesis that moral reasoning differs between delinquents and nondelinquents. Delinquent individuals tend to use developmentally lower modes of moral reasoning than do matched nondelinquents — as measured mainly by Kohlberg's scale (Kohlberg, 1976; 1978). Nevertheless the empirical findings are somewhat mixed and inconsistent and not easy to interpret or summarize. Several investigations in the Blasi review indicate that 80 % of the delinquent group were at Kohlberg's Level 1 (Stages 1 and 2), where moral and self-serving values are not differentiated. Modes of reasoning are characterized here by the primacy of one's concrete self-interests, reward and punishment; pragmatism, relativism, and opportunism rule the day. These are preconventional moral attitudes. But other studies found substantial numbers of delinquents who scored at Kohlberg's conventional Level 2 where moral values are defined in terms of maintaining the social order. Social conformity, mutual interpersonal expectations, and interdependent relationships are emphasized.

However, Jurkovic (1980) concludes, following an extensive review of structural-developmental studies of moral immaturity in juvenile delinquents, that preconventional reasoning does not represent a necessary component in the development of delinquency; nor does conventional morality inoculate the individual against delinquency. Jurkovic states that:

> On the most general level, it appears that adolescents who have failed to relinquish a premoral orientation in Kohlberg's framework at a time when their peers are moving to higher stages are at risk of behaviour problems, whereas those performing along more conventional lines may or may not be at a similar risk.

As pointed out earlier, moral judgement and moral behaviour intercorrelate in a complex manner; nowhere is this fact more apparent than in the conduct disorders and juvenile delinquency, where a plethora of situational variables and nonmoral personality factors can be inculpated in the aetiology of the disorders. To the extent that premoral reasoning is conducive to delinquent actions, it is not clear whether preconventional delinquents are 'fixated' in their moral development or are progressing at slower rates.

Incidentally, attempts to modify and enhance the moral maturity of juvenile offenders have produced ambiguous findings. Changes that have been brought about seem superficial. The methods used do not appear to stimulate a reorganization of moral reasoning at more advanced stages of sophistication (see Jurkovic, 1980). (Hollin, in

Chapter 17, explores this and other aspects of the cognitive behaviour modification of delinquent behaviours and attitudes.) At a more macro- (child rearing) level of social training, the factors that facilitate the development of moral and social awareness and behaviour include (Hoffman, 1970):

- Strong ties of affection between parents and children.
- Firm moral demands made by parents on their offspring.
- The consistent use of sanctions.
- Techniques of punishment that are psychological rather than physical (i.e., methods that signify or threaten withdrawal of love and approval), thus provoking anxiety or guilt rather than anger.
- An intensive use of reasoning and explanations (inductive methods).
- Giving responsibility.

Family influences

A variety of social and family conditions preclude the operation of these factors in the lives of some children. Disharmonious, rejecting home backgrounds, the breakdown of discipline, parental loss, and broken homes are examples of *distal* life variables that are often linked aetiologically to conduct disorders (Herbert, 1986). When the family fails the child seems to be particularly vulnerable to the development of conduct and delinquent disorders, a fact reflected in empirical studies (e.g., West and Farrington, 1973). Some of these influences are reflected in Figure 14.

Although a large number of young people commit crimes, few develop into adult offenders. After a steady increase in the frequency of delinquent acts during childhood, reaching a peak in later adolescence, there is a fairly sharp decline in the delinquency rates in the early twenties (Rutter and Madge, 1976). The large majority of 'delinquents' gradually merge with the more-or-less law-abiding population, settled down perhaps by leaving school, the source often of unremitting criticism and irrelevance, and by the responsibilities (and rewards) of a job, marriage and family life. Fortunately, most do not appear before the courts again. There is much to be said for trying heroically to keep the less dangerous adolescents out of the penal institutions which, despite their good intentions, provide a higher education in crime, or perpetuate a delinquent career which, otherwise might have been aborted.

The notion that delinquency is maintained by reinforcers located in the individual's social and physical environment, and becomes extinguished when these are withdrawn, is at variance with the view that antisocial behaviour is primarily a characteristic of persons rather than situations. Much delinquent behaviour seems to be a response to a particular set of circumstances — opportunities, frustrations, periods of boredom, social and material rewards — which the individual will not encounter in other circumstances or at other periods of his life. Regrettably there is a hard core of future recidivists which gradually emerges during the years of adolescence and becomes distinguished from those

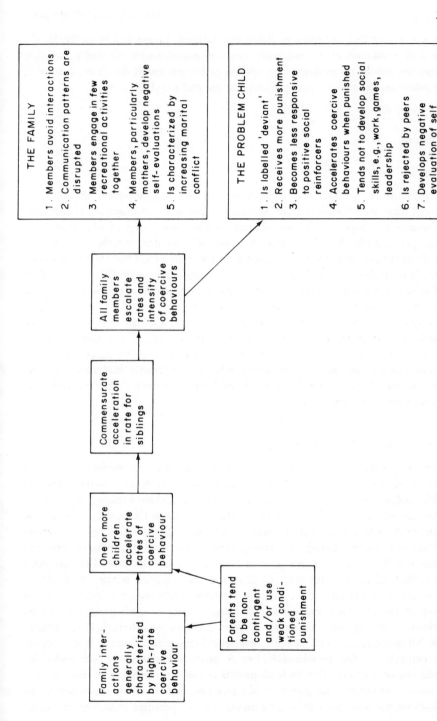

THE FAMILY

1. Members avoid interactions
2. Communication patterns are disrupted
3. Members engage in few recreational activities together
4. Members, particularly mothers, develop negative self-evaluations
5. Is characterized by increasing marital conflict

THE PROBLEM CHILD

1. Is labelled 'deviant'
2. Receives more punishment
3. Becomes less responsive to positive social reinforcers
4. Accelerates coercive behaviours when punished
5. Tends not to develop social skills, e.g., work, games, leadership
6. Is rejected by peers
7. Develops negative evaluation of self and others

All family members escalate rates and intensity of coercive behaviours

Commensurate acceleration in rate for siblings

One or more children accelerate rates of coercive behaviour

Family interactions generally characterized by high-rate coercive behaviour

Parents tend to be non-contingent and/or use weak conditioned punishment

Figure 14. Coercive family interactions. (Source: Patterson, 1982, reproduced by permission of the Castalia Publishing Company.)

who will discard their antisocial or delinquent patterns (Knight and West, 1975). The gradual differentation of the recidivists from the majority who eventually assimilate themselves with the mainstream of law-abiding citizenry is mainly discernible in terms of their misdemeanours — for example, carrying out thefts on their own.

Treatment

Residential

Not infrequently, children and adolescents with conduct/delinquent disorders are removed from their homes and are ostensibly exposed to treatment or rehabilitation programmes in a variety of residential settings. The success rates of what used to be called 'approved schools' in England differ considerably one from the other; nevertheless, overall rates of success in the UK — based on a three-year period free from reconviction — reach no higher than 30 % to 35 % (Her Majesty's Stationery Office, 1972). One explanation for the failure of institutional programmes is a model of human deviance that places the main source of behavioural variance within the individual. The primary thrust of therapy is in changing the individual; the hope is that a change in behaviour in the institutional setting represents a fundamental change (e.g., in character formation, maturity, or self-discipline) which will therefore remain with the individual upon his or her return to the community — no matter what its temptations, frustrations or other disadvantages. (A more productive form of residential treatment — Achievement Place — is described in Chapter 14.)

Parent training (see Wahler, 1976)

Parent training, on an individual or group basis, has proved a more fruitful enterprise. As a reaction, in part, to the large numbers of conduct disordered children and the shortfall of professional personnel, agencies have looked increasingly to parent training. In a sense all parents are informal behaviour modifiers; certainly all are in the business of changing behaviour by using homespun applications of 'learning theory'. They use various methods — rewarding, punishing, ignoring, time-out and fines — familiar to behaviour modifiers to train, influence, and change the children in their care. The systematic investigation of parents and other caregivers as more formal, primary mediators of behavioural change began in the 1960s (e.g., Patterson, 1965; Wahler, 1969). Many of the studies of the feasibility and efficacy of using parents — particularly for conduct problems — have appeared in the last 20 years. Reviews (e.g., Herbert, 1987b; Dumas, 1989; Moreland et al., 1982) suggest that behavioural parent training is an effective intervention for conduct disordered children. A variety of methods have been used, either individually or in combination, to teach parents contingency management and contracting, conflict resolution skills, parent–child interaction, and household organization. The methods include oral and written instructions, live and videotape modelling, and direct prompting, shaping, and feedback by the trainer; some or all of the training has occurred in either the clinic or the home.

Today, there is less emphasis on the contingency management of specific target behaviours, and more on broad principles of child management, the interpersonal interactions of members of the family, the marital relationships (which are often poor in the parents of problematic children — e.g., Webster-Stratton, 1989a), and the perceived efficacy of parents — e.g., Bandura, 1987. What we are talking about is a *multimodal* treatment/training package. Examples of the use of these methods appear in Chapters 14 and 15.

Many of the problems dealt with in families with conduct disordered children are eminently capable of modification, even if the task is a difficult one (Moreland *et al.*, 1982). Parents of deviant children display a significantly greater proportion of commands and criticisms and high rates of threats, anger, nagging and negative consequences than parents of non-referred children (Delfini, Bernal and Rosen, 1976; Lobitz and Johnson, 1975). There is frequently a lack of contingent consequences among the distressed family members. The probability of receiving a positive, neutral or aversive consequence for coercive behaviour seems to be independent of the behaviour — a gross inconsistency. Indeed, there may be positive consequences for deviant behaviour and punishment for those rare prosocial actions (Patterson, 1977; Snyder and Brown, 1983). Patterson and Fleischman (1979) hypothesize that the disturbed social interactions among the members of the family induce powerful feelings of frustration, anger and helplessness.

Parent training programmes therefore emphasize methods designed to reduce confrontations and antagonistic interactions among the family members, to increase the effectiveness of positive interactions and moderate the intensity of parental punishment (see Chapter 1).

The need to train parents of non-compliant children to give clear instructions has been well documented in the literature (e.g., Roberts *et al.*, 1978). The focus has been on the content of what is said, and also the non-verbal aspects of instruction giving. In a study by Hudson and Blane (1985) eight clinic and eight non-clinic mother child pairs were observed. The non-verbal elements of (i) distance from child, (ii) body orientation of mother, (iii) eye contact between mother and child, (iv) tone of voice, and (v) mother's orientation towards objects involved in the instruction, were all related to the rate of child compliance.

Patterson and his colleagues at the Oregon Research Institute have been a prolific source of ideas and data on the subject (inter alia) of children's conduct disorders, notably aggression and stealing. They have developed a treatment package that involves training parents (and teachers) in child management skills (Patterson *et al.*, 1975); also methods for addressing the marital problems of parents. It is difficult to summarize such an extensive contribution, but it is worth reporting the team's results with 27 conduct disordered boys referred to them and accepted for treatment from January 1968 to June 1972. Training the families took an average of 31.5 hours of professional time. The treatment programme (parents read a semi-programmed text followed by a multiple choice test; staff teach parents to pinpoint problem areas and learn appropriate change techniques; home visits occur where necessary) lasted on average from three to four months. Most parents opted to work on reducing their children's noncompliance to requests, but overall a further 13 behaviours in the conduct disorder syndrome were also pinpointed for treatment.

With regard to criterion measures such as the targeted deviant behaviours of the boys, an average 60 % reduction from baseline level to termination was achieved. In 75 % of cases, reductions exceeded 30 % from baseline levels. In six cases the rate of problematic behaviour deteriorated. On another criterion — total deviant scores — the 27 boys showed a reduction from higher than normal overall rates (scores computed for normal boys over 14 'problem areas') to within normal limits. According to parental daily reports there was a significant drop in the level of reported problems during follow-up (data were obtained here on 14 families only). About two-thirds of the families reported marked reductions in the problems for which they were originally referred. Follow-up data were obtained monthly for the first six months after termination of treatment, and every two months after that until a year after termination. Booster treatment programmes during follow-up took an average of 1.9 hours of professional time.

It was soon discovered that improvements at home did not generalize to school, so a separate but parallel package was prepared for use in classroom settings (Patterson, Cobb and Ray, 1972). Patterson (1975) found, as we have at the Centre for Behavioural Work with Families (Herbert, 1987b), that a substantial proportion of families (approximately one-third in his sample) requires much more in the way of intervention than child management skills: the parents need help with social problems, negotiation skills, depression, and resolving marital conflict. Despite the attractiveness (in earlier years) of a clinical intervention which was clearly underpinned by assessments and formulations drawn from the learning theory canon and the move towards working in the triadic model in which parents were trained to be 'therapists' for their own children, it soon became obvious that teaching behavioural principles to parents was not always sufficient to improve child behaviour. The narrower behavioural model which attributed child conduct problems solely to deficient parenting skills in the parents ignored other aspects of parents' functioning such as parental attitudes to child-rearing; parental attributions and psychopathology; and interpersonal (marital and sibling) relationships. Failures in treatment began to be associated with difficulties in these and other areas; social and cognitive factors were identified as moderating variables influencing the outcome of behavioural parent-training. Consequently, conduct-problems in children could no longer be conceptualized in such relatively simple terms as the child's response to maladaptive environmental contingencies. Rather, conduct-problems needed to be viewed in a much wider systemic context in which many other aspects of family functioning have to be assessed.

In recent years the work of Carolyn Webster-Stratton (among others) has helped to identify active change-inducing ingredients of parent training programmes. For example Webster-Stratton, Kolpacoff and Hollinsworth (1988) carried out a programme based on therapist-led group discussion and videotape modelling (GDVM). They randomly assigned families with conduct-problem children to one of four conditions: an individually self-administered videotape modelling treatment (IVM), a group discussion videotape modelling treatment (GDVM), a group discussion treatment (GD), and a waiting-list control group (CON). Results immediately post-treatment suggested that all three treatment programmes resulted in significant parent–report and parent–child behavioural improvements compared with waiting-list control families. There were relatively few differences between the three treatment conditions, although the differences found consistently favoured the combined GDVM treatment. The results relative to the IVM treatment also suggested the potential power of parents to learn how to change their own behaviours, as well as their children's behaviours, from self-administered videotape programmes. However, it was unclear whether the IVM treatment programme that did not have skilled therapist feedback or group support would be able to sustain its effectiveness, whether the GDVM programme would be able to sustain its effectiveness or whether the GDVM programme would be able to maintain its superiority over the other two treatment approaches over time. In a further study Webster-Stratton, Hollinsworth and Kolpacoff (1989) evaluated the long-term effectiveness of three cost-effective parent training programmes for conduct-problem children. One year post-treatment, 93.1% of families (94 mothers and 60 fathers) were assessed on the basis of teacher and parent reports and home observations. Results indicated that all the significant improvements reported immediately post-treatment were maintained one year later. Moreover, approximately two thirds of the entire sample showed 'clinically significant' improvements. There were few differences between the three treatment conditions except for the 'consumer satisfaction' measure indicating that the treatment combining group discussion and videotape modelling was superior to treatments without both components.

A framework for assessment (one of many) designed to take into account social, developmental and cognitive-behavioural factors is implicit in Parts 1 and 2 of this book; it has been explicated in a more focused way in Herbert, 1987c. (See also Ollendick and Hersen, 1984; Patterson, 1982).

AGGRESSION

After non-compliance, the flouting of authority, which I dealt with in Chapter 10, aggression is one of the most common complaints of adults who have to rear, care for, or teach children with a conduct disorder.

Assessment

Aggressive behaviour includes destructiveness, physical attack, and verbal assault. Interpretations of aggressive behaviour vary with the age of the child, thus aggressive activities in 2- and 3-year-old boys lead less often than at later ages, to a call for professional help. Most people have heard of the 'terrible' twos and threes. Parents tend to make allowances for the child's cognitive immaturity and distinguish between his or her actions and intentions. At that tender age the child does not 'mean' to hurt the other child when he or she hits out. Parents whose attributions are more sinister ('It's his bad blood'; 'She has the devil in her') are quite likely to be among those who physically abuse their children when they are aggressive and disobedient.

Social and cultural attitudes will also determine which actions are labelled 'aggressive' as opposed, say, to more socially acceptable 'assertive' behaviour. Precise specifications of aggression in overt behavioural terms are a desideratum of research and therapy because of such possibilities of disagreement over inferential and abstract social definitions. Various measures are discussed in Appendix II.

Prevalence

There is no problem of definition in the mind of the child who is the victim of bullying. Smith (1990) carried out a survey of bullying in schools in South Yorkshire. Of the 1000 children questioned, 18.3 % of secondary and 17.1 % of middle school pupils claimed to have been bullied. Many said they were regularly bullied — 8 % of secondary pupils at least once a week, and 5.5 % of middle school children several times a week. More than half kept their suffering from their parents and teachers. I have taken only one example of the prevalence of an aggressive activity to illustrate how widespread, and how far-reaching in its consequences, interpersonal violence can be.

Continuity

Lefkowitz et al. (1977) followed a group of New York children from the age of 8 to age 19 years, the study having a particular focus on the persistence of aggression. Aggression was much less common in girls than in boys but in both sexes children who were highly aggressive at age 8 years tended also to be unduly aggressive at 19 years (correlations of 0.38 for boys and 0.47 for girls). In West and Farrington's study of London boys, substantial continuity was again evident (West and Farrington, 1973). Of the youths rated most aggressive at 8 to 10 years, 50 % were in the most aggressive group at 12 to 14 years (compared with 19 % of the remaining boys) and 40 % were so at 16 to 18 years (compared with 27 % of the remainder). The boys who were severely aggressive at 8 to 10 years were especially likely to become violent delinquents (14 % vs 4.5 %).

The same study demonstrated the very considerable extent to which troublesome, difficult and aggressive behaviour in young boys was associated with later juvenile delinquency. Both the measure at age 8 to 10 years of 'combined conduct disorder', which was based on combined ratings of teachers and social workers, and that of 'troublesomeness' at the same age, which was a combined rating of peers and teachers, proved to be powerful predictors of delinquency. This was especially so with respect to severe and persistent delinquency going on into adult life. Some half of such individuals showed deviant ratings on these measures compared with only one-in-six of non-delinquent boys.

Causation: a social learning perspective

There is convincing evidence (see Bandura, 1973) of the importance of reinforcement in shaping up and maintaining aggressive behaviour. Several theorists (e.g., Patterson, 1982) have also looked at aggression in terms of the concept of coercive power. There is fairly good agreement in the clinical literature that there are two major types of aggressive reponse: 'hostile aggression', in which the only objective of the angry individual is to harm another person by inflicting some injury; and 'instrumental aggression', in which the occurrence of harm or injury to another person is only incidental to the individual's aim of achieving some other goal. Bandura (1973) points out that hostile aggression is also instrumental, except that the actions are used to produce injurious outcomes rather than to gain status, power, resources, or some other goal. In either case, the 'aggressor' exercises coercive power against another person.

The coercion hypothesis

This hypothesis formulated and tested, notably, by Patterson (1982) illuminates the manner in which children's noxious, antisocial behaviours can serve as punishment or negative reinforcement for the behaviour of other family members. The essential idea is that an aversive stimulus such as hitting, teasing or crying is applied contingently and repeatedly to increase or decrease certain behaviours displayed by the other member of a parent–child, sibling–sibling dyad. The impact of these aversive behaviours is reflected in changes in the ongoing behaviours of both members of the dyad involved in the coercive interchanges. Probably it is the immediate shift in the ongoing behaviour of one individual that is reinforcing for the other. Wahler and Dumas (1986), asking how coercive mother–child interactions are maintained and escalate, formulate two hypotheses to explain how some parent–child dyads ratchet up their aversive exchanges into progressively more 'painful', coercive interactions: the compliance hypothesis, and the predictability hypothesis. The compliance hypothesis proposes that the mother's caving in to her child's aversive behaviour acts as a positive reinforcer and therefore is a major influence for the maintenance of his kind of behaviour. She complies — gives in, gives way — to 'turn off' her child's temper tantrum, hitting, screaming, or whatever. The payoff — relief from painful stimuli, with its escape and avoidance implications, makes further compliance more and more likely (negative reinforcement). The predictability hypothesis suggests that aversive behaviour of conduct disordered children may be maintained by mother's consistent aversive reactions to it. Children know where they stand because reactions to their deviant behaviour is always punitive, whereas the response to their positive behaviour is extremely unpredictable; they never know what to expect — indifference, praise or punishment. For some youngsters, the predictable response seems preferable to the unpredictable.

Observations suggest that mothers and siblings are the most affected in these coercive spirals because their rates of noxious behaviour are significantly higher than those manifested by their counterparts in non-problem families (Patterson, 1982). He suggests that inspection of observational data suggests that such behaviours tend to come in bursts. For example, given the occurrence of one response, there tends to be a significant increase in the probability that the same response will recur or persist. Children who are described as highly aggressive are characterized by a longer duration of such behavioural bursts and also by shorter time intervals between these behavioural bursts. Comparing non-problem boys with socially aggressive children, the latter are more likely to come up with a second noxious response, having just presented one perhaps only a few seconds ago. To summarize: noxious behaviours tend to be exhibited by socially aggressive boys not only more frequently and with greater intensity than non-problem children, but such behaviours are likely to be emitted with fairly high probability in extended 'runs' of aversive behaviours.

Patterson (1982) lists the following possibilities for children's failure to substitute more adaptive, more mature behaviours for their infantile and primitive coercive repertoire:

(i)   The parents might neglect to condition pro-social skills (e.g., they seldom reinforce the use of language or other self-help skills).
(ii)   They might provide rich schedules of positive reinforcement for coercive behaviours.
(iii) They might allow siblings to increase the frequency of aversive stimuli which are terminated when the target child uses coercive behaviours.
(iv)   They may use punishment inconsistently for coercive behaviours, and/or
(v)   They may use weak-conditioned punishers as consequences for coercion.

Previous learning experience

There is a confidently expressed consensus that aggressive behaviour in children can be related to broader (long-term) attitudes and child-rearing practices. To summarize the findings (see Herbert, 1987b), a combination of lax discipline (especially with regard to the offsprings' acts of aggression) combined with hostile attitudes in the parents produces very aggressive and poorly controlled behaviour in the offspring. Parents with hostile attitudes are mainly unaccepting and disapproving of children: they fail to give affection, understanding or explanations to children, and tend to use a lot of physical punishment, but not give reasons when they do exert their authority — something applied erratically and arbitrarily.

Intervention

The methods which have been evaluated at the Centre for Behavioural Work with Families (Herbert and Iwaniec, 1981; Herbert, 1987b,c, 1989a; Holmes, 1979; Sutton, 1988) involve a multimodal package depending for its final constituents on a comprehensive behavioural-developmental and social assessment. It might involve (in addition to child-management work) marital therapy, developmental and/or personal counselling. Variations in the complexity of problems, in family values and attitudes, and individual differences in the temperament of the children concerned, require often the flexibility of individualized programmes. However, *group training* and the use of the phone plus manuals, have proved equally effective (Sutton, 1988).

Antecedent control

We have found, as have others, that there are several methods for reducing aggression based on a modification of the antecedent side of the ABC 'equation' (see page 66):

- *Stimulus change: reducing discriminative stimuli for aggression.* Certain stimulus conditions provide signals to the child that aggressive behaviour is likely to have rewarding consequences. Treatment programmes are planned to reduce *discriminative stimuli* for such aggression.
- *Providing models for non-aggressive behaviour.* Acceptable alternatives to aggression may be enhanced by exposing youngsters to prestigious or influential children or adolescents who manifest alternative non-hostile behaviours, especially when they are instrumental in obtaining pleasing outcomes for the models.
- *Reducing the exposure to aggressive models.* Exposure to other people behaving aggressively may facilitate the imitation of such behaviour by the observer. An attempt to reduce the exposure of children to such models (e.g., aggressive peers) is likely to decrease the likelihood of their behaving similarly.
- *Reducing aversive stimuli.* Violent reactions may be instigated by a large variety of aversive stimuli: it is reasonable to expect that a reduction of such aversive stimuli might be accompanied by a decrease in aggression. One technique is to resolve conflicts before they flare up into violence. Another involves the defusing of aversive stimuli by diminishing their power to arouse anger in the child. This can be achieved by using humour, by cognitive restructuring (reframing 'provocative' stimuli), or by using desensitization procedures.
- *Conflict resolution.* ('settling differences') There are two broad approaches to conflict resolution: (a) arbitration or mediation of specific conflicts, and (b) modification of communication processes (see Herbert, 1988). Behavioural contracting is the most common example of the negotiation and arbitration approach; it involves the therapist in the role of a mediator or arbitrator who facilitates discussions to seek compromises and mutual agreements between opposing parties. Contracts about

reciprocal exchanges of specific behaviours and reinforcers can be drawn up to enhance the likelihood of a positive outcome (see Kirschenbaum and Flanery, 1983).

- *Desensitization.* O'Donnell and Worell (1973) provide examples of the effectiveness of three procedures applied in order to reduce anger: systematic desensitization, desensitization with cognitive relaxation and desensitization in the absence of relaxation training. (Chapter 17 contains further discussion of these techniques.)

- *Communication training.* Verbal instructions, practice and feedback are the major techniques used to modify communication processes (Kifer *et al.*, 1974). Their emphasis is more on learning new adaptive behaviours rather than eliminating problem behaviours; the techniques are primarily educational rather than therapeutic. Much of the misunderstanding, 'sound and fury', and negative messages, that abound in the homes of conduct-disordered children can be traced to extremely poor or faulty communication skills.

- *Self-instruction.* Self-instruction training — the development of children's skills in guiding their own performance by the use of self-suggestion, comments, praise and other directions — has proved invaluable with hyperactive, aggressive (impulsive) children (Meichenbaum and Goodman, 1971; Schneider, 1973).

  More cognitively orientated methods have proved useful with older children and adolescents, e.g., self-control training (assertion and relaxation training, role-play, behaviour rehearsal (Craighead *et al.*, 1983).

- *Cognitive change (with regard to antecedent events).* The instigation of aggression may be influenced by antecedent cognitive events such as aversive thoughts (e.g., remembering a past grudge), being aware of the probable consequences of aggressive actions or being capable of solving problems mentally instead of 'lashing out' reflexly.

  The youngster's search for various possible courses of action in the face of provocation and frustration can be made more flexible by attention to the thinking processes that precede, accompany and follow violent actions. A skill that hostile children sometimes lack is the ability to identify (i.e., label) the precursors, physiological, affective and cognitive, to an aggressive outburst, so that they can bring into play more adaptive solutions to their problems.

- *Skills training.* (see Herbert, 1986; also Chapter 15). Children often lack (due to a variety of experiences of social deprivation) the skills to choose between alternative courses of action in person-to-person situations, and, in addition, knowledge of actions ('solutions') which they can take, plus some means of choosing between those they do have. Alternatively, they are locked into narrow, rigid and perhaps self-destructive modes of action, aggression being a classic example. Thus the therapeutic aim is to increase the child's or caregiver's repertoire of possible actions in person-to-person situations, making their relationships with others both more constructive and more creative.

- *The problem-solving model.* The assumption here is that some children are unskilled or deskilled (i.e., lose proficiency at problem-solving) due to lack of opportunity to practise them in various situations (see Bornstein and Kazdin, 1985; Spivack, Platt and Shure, 1976). It is crucial to unravel the situational factors that operate in (say) a social deficit problem (a complicated social interaction), to analyse it and to generate alternative solutions to the self-defeating strategies so far adopted. Those adopting a cognitive-social learning model view effective social functioning as being dependent upon the client's (a) knowledge of specific interpersonal actions and how they fit into different kinds of person-to-person situation; (b) ability to convert knowledge of social nuances into the skilled performance of social actions in various interactive contexts; (c) ability to evaluate skilful and unskilful behaviour accurately and to adjust one's behaviour accordingly.

Outcome control

Extinction

There is sound evidence that procedures based on reduction of reinforcement identified as maintaining aggressive behaviour, can reduce its frequency and/or intensity. In some studies, aggressive behaviour is consistently ignored; in others it is ignored while a competing pattern of pro-social conduct is rewarded. In other cases pro-social behaviour is positively reinforced, but aggression is punished (Herbert, 1989a).

Planned ignoring, time-out and response cost have been systematically applied in programmes designed to provide stimulus conditions which signal to the child that his or her aggressive behaviour will not only fail to have rewarding consequences but, indeed, will result in punitive consequences. The provision of such discriminative stimuli brings aggression under control while more acceptable alternative behaviour is being encouraged. (Herbert and Iwaniec, 1981.)

Punishment

Aversive consequences (punishments) are another contemporary influence on the performance of aggressive behaviour and a contentious issue in any treatment repertoire. In general, punishment tends to decrease aggression but the effects are complex and often paradoxical.

Modifying self-perceptions/reinforcers

Given the low self-esteem and underachievement commonly found in aggressive, conduct-disordered youngsters, it is worth bearing in mind potent sources of reinforcement for aggressive behaviour — the aggressors themselves. To some extent, children regulate their actions by self-produced consequences. They tend to repeat behaviour which has given them feelings of satisfaction and worth. Conversely, they tend to refrain from behaviour that produces self-criticism or other forms of self-devaluation. Irrational beliefs about oneself may be acquired through the remarks and teaching of other people or may be self-generated. These fictional reinforcement contingencies can be even more powerful than real external reinforcing conditions.

ATTENTION-DEFICIT HYPERACTIVITY DISORDER (ADHD) (code 314.01)

Hyperactivity and disruption tend to go together in formidable tandem. The first written record of the disruptive qualities of a hyperactive child is quite likely to be the one in a poem about 'fidgety Phil who wouldn't sit still', written in 1854 by a German physician named Hoffman (see Opie and Opie, 1973). And the first representation on film of this kind of child could well be one who drives Charlie Chaplin to distraction in one of his early silent movies. Hyperactive children had to wait until the early 1960s to be studied systematically. This scholarly concern was long overdue as hyperactive children are notorious for their knack of generating very special learning and management problems at home and in the classroom. It has aptly been said that when referring to hyperactive children we enter a 'semantic jungle'. The hyperactive child is like the proverbial elephant: difficult to define, but, by golly, we know one when we see one. The frenetic and wilful approach to life is unmistakable.

Prevalence

Hyperactivity (identified as a narrow-band disorder in Achenbach and Edelbrock, 1978) is one of the primary reasons for referral to school psychologists and mental health clinics (Patterson, 1964) in the US. Given the problem of definition mentioned earlier (notably a less conservative specification in the US than the UK) epidemiological findings have to be treated with caution.

Assessment

The most important change in the diagnosis of ADHD in the DSM-III-R (see page 204) is the primacy given to inattention and impulsivity which tend to persist into adulthood. Overactivity tends to reduce in adolescence (Weiss et al., 1971). Assessment is difficult for several reasons. There is the issue of situation-specificity to begin with. Many hyperactive children who present badly at school and/or at home show exemplary behaviour in the clinic consulting room. There are no necessary and sufficient criteria for the diagnosis of hyperactivity. Neurological signs, when they exist, are 'equivocal'. Attempts (see Barkley, 1982) have been made to quantify and objectify the activity dimension. The clinical psychologist can now choose from several instruments which have been designed as aids to assessment. Generally ADHD children are rated two standard deviations or more above the mean for their age on the different screening scales (see Appendix II).

It is important to remember that there is a sizeable overlap in what many theorists think of as independent syndromes, namely hyperactivity and conduct disorder. Factor analytic studies indicate a high positive correlation between hyperactive behaviour and conduct disorder. Sandberg, Rutter and Taylor, (1978) divided clinic-attending conduct-disordered children into those scoring high or low on measure of hyperactivity — parent and teacher questionnaires (Rutter and Conners scales) — and found that the groups, so classified, did not differ in such factors as pre- and perinatal complications, neurological abnormalities, social class, or psychiatric status of the mother. Furthermore, the prognosis for hyperactive children was not demonstrably different from the general run of conduct disorders. A later epidemiological study (Sandberg, Wieselberg and Shaffer, 1980) of 226 boys, aged 5 to 9, confirmed and extended the results of this clinic survey. These were children in ordinary junior schools. A high correlation was found between hyeractive behaviour and conduct problems as measured by both the parent and teacher question-naires (Rutter and Conners scales). The 'disturbed' groups — the children scoring in the top 10 % of the hyperactivity and conduct disorder scales — could not be distinguished from one another in biological or psychosocial background variables.

Causation

What is one to make of the diverse problems shown by hyperactive children? Is there an underlying organic condition or some other unifying process? It is not clear whether some of the behaviours these children exhibit are primary or secondary to other problems. For example, hyperactivity, lack of attention, and distractibility could represent the random response pattern of an over-aroused individual who has not found the operant that terminates aversive stimulation. In the case of a child, the stressful event may be the social pressure to learn difficult academic and social skills. The reason for failure to produce the appropriate behaviour might be an inability to perceive the relevant discriminative stimuli, or an inability to make the responses in the manner demanded by the environment. It could also be argued that lack of attention, distractibility, and hyperactivity themselves provide the reasons why the child is unable to attend to discriminative stimuli, thus failing to learn. This hypothesis begs a further question: why, in the first place, is the child distractible and hyperactive?

Organic factors

Various aetiological theories have been offered for the disturbed motor and attentional behaviour, but the cause or, more probably, causes are unknown. Explanatory theories include brain damage, biochemical disorders, minor congenital physical anomalies, abnormal central nervous system arousal, genetic disorders, food allergies or simply a biological variation made manifest by universal compulsory education. All these theories are rather speculative (see Barkley, 1982). It is quite likely that hyperactive/attentional problems represent the final common pathway for the expression of various disorders; this implies several treatment options.

Treatment

The absence of a full understanding of the causes of ADHD is no reason to abandon the search for remedies or palliatives. Aspirin has eased the pain of many headaches of mysterious origin. Observations of hyperactive children suggest that many of their hyperactive behaviours can usefully be conceived of as operants. Patterson *et al.* (1965) has successfully employed operant techniques to reduce the high rates of behaviour associated with the syndrome.

Werry (1968) conceptualizes the hyperactivity problem as follows: each of the child's days consists of an infinite number of successive learning trials in which hyperactivity is being strengthened or weakened. Thus, it follows that a successful behaviour modification programme for hyperactivity should utilize at least a majority of these learning trials. Werry maintains that this can be achieved only by a substantial and significant alteration of the eliciting stimuli and response-reinforcement contingencies — by restructuring the child's environment where these problem behaviours are displayed and by involving those persons who ordinarily dispense rewards and punishments and who have control over eliciting stimuli.

Promoting prosocial behaviour

Therapists and educators have utilized principles of operant conditioning to supplant inattentive (and disruptive motor) behaviours by strengthening incompatible but socially acceptable alternatives. It is assumed (Patterson *et al.*, 1965) that both environmental and internal stimuli have become discriminative for the emission of such behaviours as pinching, squirming, looking around, tapping, and walking about the room. Theoretically, it should be possible to condition a set of responses to these same stimulus configurations that would interfere with the occurrence of these hyperactive behaviours.

Teacher attention

To give one example of the potency of attention in influencing disruptive behaviour, Thomas, Becker and Armstrong (1968) were able (by systematically varying teacher attention) to change an initially well-behaved class with an average rate of disruptiveness of only 8.7 % to one in which disruptiveness reached a level (on average) of 25.5 %. This was achieved by seeing that approval was not given to attending behaviour. It went down to 12.0 % on reversal to baseline, increased again to 19.4 % on return to the non-approval condition and rose higher to 31 % when frequent disapproval was given to disruptive behaviours. Disruptiveness went to 25.9 % in the third no-approval condition and fell to 13.2 % on the final return to baseline conditions.

Behavioural approaches using reinforcement of desired behaviour in the classroom and home-based reinforcement, have been repeatedly demonstrated (K. D. O'Leary, 1980) to lead to beneficial changes in a direction away from disruptive behaviour, poor cooperation with peers, and poor attention — all features of hyperactive and conduct-disordered children. Academic performance also responds to classroom- or home-based reinforcement programmes (see O'Leary and O'Leary, 1977). Although those studies that emphasize self-instructional or self-control approaches with hyperactive/conduct-disordered children have not led to improvements in social behaviour in the classroom (K. D. O'Leary, 1980), there is evidence that they do improve academic performance (e.g., Kent and O'Leary, 1976). It has been possible to modify social behaviour with more complex, multifaceted programmes (e.g., Filipczak, Archer and Friedman, 1980).

Cognitive-behavioural approaches

Rapport (1987) believes that findings with regard to cognitive behaviour therapy applied to ADHD — used alone or in combination with behavioural or psychostimulant drug therapies — are as yet equivocal. He is scathing about the popularity of the self-concept in such work. As he puts it: 'Unfortunately, the excess conceptual baggage implied in the term "self-control" obscures the underlying controlling variables in these treatments and should be discarded if this area is to advance'. Rapport's strictures, like his pessimism about the value of this approach, are controversial, to say the least, but certainly worth debating.

Medication

Pharmacological agents — notably psychostimulants — have been used since the 1930s to control hyperactivity. Here is another controversial area with enthusiasts for and against (see Achenbach, 1982; Barkley, 1982; 1987; for painstaking reviews of what are complex *and* emotive issues). Their use has been a matter of considerable public debate in the US (e.g., Schrag and Divoky, 1975), where the diagnosis of hyperactivity is somewhat popular. All these compounds carry their risks of side-effects. Perhaps the greatest risk is the psychological one for clinicians — that these are so easy to prescribe in the context of a busy general, psychiatric, or paediatric practice. Their availability may short-circuit the necessary detailed analysis of the child's motor, attentional, and behavioural problems. In the absence of such care, drug therapy can degenerate into a facile and dangerous method of social control in the home and the classroom. A behavioural approach can make the use of drugs unnecessary or may, in combination with medication (Herbert, 1987b) make prolonged drug dependence and the abdication from personal/parental responsibility less likely.

Another risk is also psychological in the sense that the patient is likely to attribute change to an outside agent (the drug or 'the pill') rather than to himself or herself. In view of the side-effects, the ineffectiveness of medication with many ADHD children, and the reluctance of many parents to use medication, physicians may in many cases have to look to alternative treatments.

SUMMARY

In this chapter I have examined the major components of antisocial disruptive disorder: conduct disorder, ADHD and aggression. This review has adopted a developmental and social learning perspective. Although the prognosis of these problems is far from benign, I have attempted to indicate that clinical child psychologists have the methods to intervene — especially early on by training parents — in a way that can (in an encouraging number of cases) break the 'chain' of continuity that links childhood, adolescent and adult deviancy. In the course of this discussion I touched briefly on delinquency and, as with the other problems, described some of the main issues of assessment and treatment.

Chapter 17

Cognitive Behaviour Modification With Delinquents

CLIVE R. HOLLIN

The use of cognitive-behavioural interventions with delinquents is becoming increasingly prevalent in both clinical practice and the experimental-clinical literature. In this present overview my aim is to look at the empirical basis for such interventions, to review the clinical studies, and to offer a broad critique including wider policy issues to inform future clinical programmes. However, before beginning this agenda, it is important to make some clear statements regarding the use of clinical techniques with offenders.

CLINICAL APPROACHES TO CRIMINAL BEHAVIOUR

While part of the argument concerns which type of treatment approach is to be preferred, this is almost secondary to the debate about the appropriateness of a clinical approach to criminal behaviour. At the heart of the conflict stand two opposing explanations of criminal behaviour. *Classical* theories hold central the concept of free will in explaining crime: according to this view, when the opportunity for crime arises each individual is free to choose between criminal and non-criminal behaviour. If the payoffs for the crime are greater than the chances of being caught and suffering the subsequent retribution, so the probability of choosing the criminal option is increased. On the other hand, *positivist* theories maintain that influences outside the realm of free will can be identified as the causes of crime. As theories have advanced and fallen so the determinants of crime have been hypothesized to be genetic, biological, psychological, and social in origin (Hollin, 1989; Siegel, 1986).

Classical and positivist views of crime also lead to very different responses to crime. Classical theories hold that punishment, retribution, and deterrence are the appropriate strategies for dealing with criminals and reducing the crime rate (e.g., Van Den Haag, 1982). While classical theories were not popular, among theorists at least, during the earlier part of this century, the 1970s and 1980s saw many political changes and the forceful re-emergence of 'neoclassical' or 'conservative' theories of crime. It would be true to say that this punishment orientated approach, and the associated 'justice model' (Hudson, 1987), presently holds sway in many countries, including Britain and America.

Alternatively, positivist theories, which are generally seen as more liberal in political orientation, maintain that the response to crime should be to 'put right' the conditions which produced the crime. Thus strategies for reducing crime take the form of some type of intervention, such as social welfare or individual treatment, to help offenders to cope with and overcome the causes of their criminal behaviour.

There are many criticisms of clinical criminology, some justified others not (West, 1980): while the arguments cannot be rehearsed here, it is perhaps important to make the point that clinicians in this field are not, as a generalization, opposed to social reform: there is no reason why modification of social and legal systems and individual change should be incompatible. However, while theoretical debate is important, the efficacy of a clinical approach is in part an empirical question: does treatment work? A number of studies are frequently cited in support of the 'nothing works' position regarding clinical intervention with offenders (e.g., Bailey, 1966; Brody, 1976; Lipton, Martinson and Wilks, 1975; Martinson, 1974). While the conclusions from some of these studies may well go beyond the data (Thornton, 1987), recent advances in statistics, principally the technique of meta-analysis, have provided strong evidence that treatment can be effective (Garrett, 1985; Gendreau and Andrews, in press). Indeed, Gendreau and Ross (1987) have the confidence to state that 'It is downright ridiculous to say "Nothing works" ... much is going on to indicate that offender rehabilitation has been, can be, and will be achieved' (p. 395). The unanswered question is, of course, what works best, for whom, and under what conditions.

In the final analysis it is left to each individual to make an informed decision based on his or her own experience and reading and interpretation of the evidence. My own position is that it would be foolish to suggest that clinical treatment, of any type, is a remedy for crime: crime is a multidimensional concept and its amelioration requires change at legal, political, social, and individual levels. However, given that individual change is part of the equation, it is here that a clinical approach may have most to offer. What can be said of the contribution of cognitive behaviour modification to this turmoil?

Before trying to answer this question, it is important to define two crucial terms — 'cognitive behaviour modification' and 'delinquency'.

COGNITIVE BEHAVIOUR MODIFICATION

As is clear from the recent text edited by Fishman, Rotgers, and Franks (1988), there is no one simple definition of cognitive behaviour modification. Many writers use the term in a number of different senses, sometimes interchangeably with cognitive behaviour *therapy*, drawing on varying theoretical positions. For the purpose of moving toward a working definition, it is useful to distinguish three theoretical views. The first is *radical behaviourism*, most closely associated with operant theories of learning (e.g., Skinner, 1974). This position, while not neglecting cognition, maintains an emphasis on environmental influences on behaviour. The second is *cognitive theory*, with its contemporary beginnings owing much to Neisser (1967, 1976), and more recently to the work of writers such as Anderson (1980), Eysenck (1984), and Mandler (1985). Cognitive theories hold that the key to understanding human behaviour lies in knowledge about 'inner' processes such as thoughts, beliefs, memory, attributions, and perception. The third view is *cognitive-behavioural* theory, perhaps most closely allied with social learning theory (Bandura, 1977, 1986). This theoretical view acknowledges the importance of the environment while seeking to incorporate 'inner' forces and processes. Thus cognitions may be afforded a mediational role between the outside world and overt behaviour: for example, what we attend to in the environment and our decision-making following perception, mediate between environmental cues and behavioural response.

These three theoretical positions are each associated with different styles of clinical practice: learning theories are aligned with behaviour modification (Bellack, Hersen and Kazdin, 1982); cognitive theory with cognitive therapy (Brewin, 1988); and, of course, cognitive-behavioural theory with cognitive behaviour modification (Meichenbaum, 1977). It would be overstating the case to suggest that there are clinical techniques which are the sole province of any one style of intervention: although it is fair to say that, depending on their theoretical view, practitioners use the techniques and explain their effects in very different ways.

DELINQUENCY

Turning to delinquency, it is important to make the distinction between delinquent and anti-social behaviour. While some delinquency is anti-social in nature, its distinguishing characteristic — as compared to, say, noncompliance, school disruption, or other conduct disorders — is that it involves acts by young people ('young' as defined by a given legal system) expressly forbidden by law. In addition, the young person should not be suffering from mental disorder (again as legally defined).

The three theoretical positions discussed above have all been used in attempts to understand delinquency (Hollin, 1989). In terms of clinical intervention with delinquents, however, it is the techniques associated with behaviour modification and cognitive behaviour modification which predominate: the recent enthusiasm for cognitive therapy appears, from the literature at least, not to have infected those who work with young offenders. The use of behavioural techniques with offenders generally (Morris and Braukmann, 1987) and young offenders specifically (Hollin, 1990; Stumphauzer, 1986) is well documented in the literature. There are reviews of interventions with young offenders based specifically on social learning theory (Nietzel, 1979); indeed this is a field which has received a great deal of attention, both from researchers and clinicians, over the past few years.

COGNITION AND CRIME

While the study of cognitive ability as assessed by performance on tests of intelligence is a traditional area in the study of delinquency, it is social cognition in delinquents which has been of recent interest to researchers. Social cognition can be defined as that part of cognition concerned with people and their actions and our social functioning. A variety of styles and characteristics of social cognition have been associated with delinquency (Hollin, 1990; Ross and Fabiano, 1985).

Empathy and role-taking

The ability to see things from the other person's point of view and to empathize with them is an important part of social cognition: a number of studies have looked at this cognitive ability in relation to delinquent samples. Several studies have suggested that delinquents score low on measures of empathy and role-taking (e.g., Chandler, 1973; Kaplan and Arbuthnot, 1985); although other studies have not found any systematic or consistent difference in empathy between delinquents and non-delinquents (e.g., Ellis, 1982; Lee and Prentice, 1988). Such discrepant findings may be attributable to a number of causes such as the types of measure used in different studies, the subjects' age, sex and length of criminal career, and the type of offence (DeWolfe, Jackson and Winterberger, 1988; Kendall, Deardorff and Finch 1977).

Locus of control

Locus of control refers to the degree to which individuals perceive their behaviour to be under their own *internal* control, or controlled by *external* factors such as luck, fate, or people in authority. A number of studies have suggested that delinquents tend to external control, that is, they see their behaviour as being controlled by factors outside their own personal control (Beck and Ollendick, 1976; Kumchy and Sayer, 1980). However, some studies have failed to find any difference between delinquents and non-delinquents (Groh and Goldenberg, 1976). This may be due to variations within delinquent samples: for example, violent young offenders tend toward greater external control than non-violent young offenders (Hollin and Wheeler, 1982).

Moral reasoning

Kohlberg (1978) argues that moral development progresses through a number of levels, with different stages at each level. At the lower stages moral reasoning is characterized by its concrete nature and egocentricity; at the higher stages moral reasoning is guided by abstract notions such as 'justice' and 'rights' and is much more social in orientation. Following this model, offending is said to be associated with a delay in moral reasoning development so that, given the opportunity for crime, the delinquent does not have the ability to control and resist temptation. A body of research studies has examined this proposition and reviews are available (Blasi, 1980; Jennings, Kilkenny and Kohlberg, 1983; Jurkovic, 1980). The broad consensus is that these experimental studies are equivocal: some suggest that delinquents use less mature reasoning than non-offenders; others fail to show any difference between offenders and non-offenders. Two procedural explanations have been offered to account for the varied empirical findings: the first is that moral reasoning is correlated with other cognitive developmental processes which, in an experimental study, should be controlled in order to determine true between-group differences in moral development; the second is the heterogeneity of the offender population, which may mean that there are *within*-group differences which should be taken into account when searching for differences *between* offenders and non-offenders.

The force of the first point is seen in a study of sociocognition in delinquents reported by Lee and Prentice (1988). This study assessed a range of indices of cognitive functioning — including empathy, role-taking ability, logical cognition, and moral reasoning — in both delinquent and non-delinquent samples. Comparing across groups, it was found that the delinquents scored significantly lower on role-taking, logical cognition, and moral reasoning; but not empathy. However, when the inter-relation of these measures of sociocognition was calculated, it was found that there were significant correlations between role-taking, logical cognition, and moral development. Further analysis suggested that role-taking plays a mediating role between logical cognition and moral reasoning. Thus the position is rather more complex than just that of differences between delinquents and non-delinquents in level of moral reasoning. The importance of the second procedural point, the effect of within-group differences in the offender population, is shown in studies by Thornton and Reid (1982) and by DeWolfe, Jackson and Winterberger (1988). Thornton and Reid found that convicted offenders who had committed crimes without financial gain (assault, murder, sex offences) showed more mature moral judgement than those who offended for money (robbery, burglary, theft, fraud). DeWolfe *et al.*, with a sample of (adult) convicted criminals, found that male offenders showed higher levels of moral reasoning than female offenders.

It appears therefore that the link between moral development and delinquency is unlikely to be either simple or direct. While there are indications that young offenders use less mature moral reasoning than non-offenders, this difference is probably mediated by the level and functioning of other sociocognitive abilities; by variables such as sex, age, and type of offence; and by experimental procedures such as type of moral problem and the selected measure of moral development — with the contrast between moral *content* and the *process* of moral reasoning being of particular importance.

Self-control

Low self-control, characterized by impulsive behaviour, is described by Ross and Fabiano (1985) as the omission of thought between impulse and action: it is manifest by a failure to stop and think, a failure to learn effective ways of thinking about social situations, and a failure to generate alternative courses of action. The empirical evidence is equivocal with respect to impulsivity in delinquent samples. Some studies have found higher levels of impulsivity in delinquents (e.g., Rotenberg and Nachshon, 1979), others no difference between delinquent and non-delinquent samples (e.g., Saunders, Reppucci and Sarata, 1973). The conflicting findings are once again most probably due to the use of different definitions and measures of impulsivity across studies, and to the heterogeneity of the delinquent population (Arbuthnot, Gordon and Jurkovic, 1987).

Social problem solving

Social problem solving refers to the process, in a given social situation, of generating feasible courses of action, considering the various outcomes that might follow, and planning how to achieve the preferred outcome. In a typical study with young offenders Freedman, et al., (1978) compared the social problem solving ability of delinquents and non-delinquents using the Adolescent Problem Inventory (API). The API consists of a series of social problems, such as being asked by peers to join in with a delinquent act: the respondents say what they would do in the various situations. Freedman et al. found that the offenders' verbal responses to the API items were rated as less socially competent than the responses of the matched non-delinquent group. The delinquents used a more limited range of alternatives to solve interpersonal problems, and relied more on verbal and physical aggression. In another study using the API, Veneziano and Veneziano (1988) found that delinquents scored lower than non-delinquents on this inventory (although there were considerable within-group differences in API performance for the delinquent sample). Similar findings have been reported by Higgins and Thies (1981) and, specifically with female young offenders, by Gaffney and McFall (1981) and Ward and McFall (1986).

COGNITIVE-BEHAVIOURAL PROGRAMMES

From the evidence discussed above there are grounds, although by no means certain grounds, for suggesting that delinquents show less well developed social cognition than non-delinquents. A number of clinical programmes with delinquents have therefore attempted to modify social cognition using cognitive-behavioural techniques.

Moral reasoning development

On the basis of the evidence discussed above suggesting that delinquents are character-ized by delayed or impaired moral reasoning, a number of attempts have been made to modify moral reasoning with offender groups. In a typical study, Gibbs et al., (1984) evaluated a sociomoral reasoning development programme for male and female institutionalized young offenders. The programme took the form of a number of small group discussions on various sociomoral dilemmas: the young offenders were encouraged to give their views and opinions on their moral choice, but were also required to justify their thoughts and to engage in the process of reaching a group consensus on the best solution. Compared to a no-treatment control group, the intervention produced a significant upward movement in moral reasoning as assessed by Kohlberg's stages of moral judgement. A similar study, although carried out with adolescents 'at risk' for delinquency, also reported beneficial effects following a moral reasoning development programme (Arbuthnot and Gordon, 1986). This programme not only showed improved moral reasoning following intervention, but also improvement on a number of behavioural measures including academic performance and police/court contact.

Role-taking

The single intervention designed to modify role-taking ability with delinquents was reported by Chandler (1973). The design compared three groups: a role-taking skills training group, a placebo treatment control group, and a no-treatment control group. The role-taking skills group took part in exercises such as drama and film making to develop and enhance their ability both to see themselves from another perspective and to appreciate the views of other people. The outcome data showed that role-taking abilities were enhanced and, at an 18-month follow-up, the role-taking skills group had committed fewer offences than the controls. While as Gordon and Arbuthnot (1987) comment, 'Role-taking abilities may perhaps best be viewed as necessary but not sufficient for delinquency prevention and treatment' (p. 301), it is nevertheless remarkable that Chandler's work has not been replicated.

Self-control and self-instruction

The developmental of self-control in childhood has been described as following three discrete stages: (1) the child's behaviour is controlled by the verbal community; (2) the child's own overt speech regulates his or her behaviour; (3) the child's covert or 'inner' speech governs his or her actions (Luria, 1961). A failure to progress through this developmental sequence results in maladaptive regulatory self-statements, with a concomitant lack of self-control and impulsive behaviour. In order to train or modify self-control, techniques have been developed to change the individual's private speech or self-statements; 'self-instructional training' has become particularly popular, especially with child and adolescent populations (Dush, Hirt and Schroeder, 1989; Meichenbaum, 1977). Following the developmental model described above, training moves through a series of stages: initially a model performs a task making appropriate overt self-statements, the trainee then practises the same behaviour, gradually moving to whispered self-instruction, and finally progresses to covert, silent self-instruction. The trainee is encouraged to use self-statements to self-observe, self-evaluate, and self-reinforce appropriate overt behaviours (Kanfer, 1975).

A number of studies have used such cognitive behaviour modification procedures with young offenders (Snyder and White, 1979; Williams and Akamatsu, 1978). In a well-designed study Snyder and White (1979) used self-instructional training with aggressive adolescents with a history of criminal behaviour, living in a residential establishment. Initially the programme identified the delinquents' self-statements prior to an aggressive episode, then explored, with the trainee, the consequences of such statements and the actions which followed. In the second stage of the intervention more appropriate, less aggressive, verbalizations were modelled, rehearsed, and practised first overtly then covertly: the new verbalizations included self-reinforcing statements for successful behaviour. In the third and final stage of the programme homework assignments were used to develop further self-monitoring and self-reinforcement skills. The experimental evaluation of this programme compared the cognitive self-instruction group with two control groups; one control participated in discussion of problem behaviour but without the use of training, the other was a no-treatment control. On all three evaluative measures — absence from class, completion of social and self-care duties, and frequency of impulsive behaviour — the self-instruction group showed superior performance to both controls both post-training and at an eight-week follow-up. As Snyder and White suggest, these findings clearly show that the cognitive behaviour modification was a valuable addition to the institutional token economy in which all the trainees, treatment and control groups alike, were participating.

Anger control

An extension of self-control procedures lies in the development of techniques specifically designed for the control of anger. Owing much to the work of Novaco (1975, 1979, 1985), anger management has become a popular clinical technique generating a large experimental-clinical literature over the past few years. Anger management does not seek to remove anger but rather seeks to encourage self-regulation of cognition, emotion, and behaviour through the application of methods of self-control. A typical anger management programme has three components: first 'cognitive preparation' to educate the individual about their anger and its causes and effects; then 'skill acquisition' in which coping strategies — including self-statement modification, relaxation and assertion skills — are trained; finally 'application training' in which the newly acquired skills are put to the test in a range of supervised in vivo and role-play settings. Considerable expertize is available in the design of anger management programmes for adolescents (Feindler and Ecton, 1986; Goldstein and Heller, 1987).

Anger control has been widely used with offenders, particularly violent offenders, of all ages (Howells, 1989). A number of these programmes have been with young offenders. Schlichter and Horan (1981) compared the use of anger management, relaxation, and no-treatment with groups of aggressive institutionalized delinquents. On self-report and role-play measures of aggression both treatment groups showed significant change compared to the no-treatment group. However, there was no comparable treatment effect on institutional ratings of behaviour. Fiendler, Marriott and

Iwata (1984) evaluated the effects of an anger management programme with young people suspended from school because of offending. Again using a no-treatment control, the anger control group showed a number of improvements: these positive changes included less aggressive behaviour, improved problem-solving skills, and an increase in observer-rated self-control. As was the case with the Snyder and White (1979) study discussed previously, Feindler et al. suggest that their anger management programme was a valuable addition to the token economy in which all the delinquents were participating. Finally, McDougall et al., (1987) evaluated the effectiveness of an anger management course at a secure establishment for young offenders. It was found that compared to a waiting-list control, the anger management group showed a significant drop in aggressive offences within the establishment.

Social problem solving

A number of problem solving skills are necessary for successful social interaction: these include sensitivity to interpersonal problems, the ability to see the consequences of one's actions, the ability to generate solutions to social problems, and means-end thinking in planning the steps towards successful outcomes (Spivack, Platt and Shure, 1976). In problem solving skills-training, cognitive techniques (particularly self-instructional training) are blended with modelling, role-play, and discussion to train skills such as problem recognition, problem definition, generating solutions, and planning outcomes (Camp and Bash, 1981).

This type of training has been used successfully with a variety of client groups, including heroin addict offenders (Platt, Perry and Metzger, 1980). As shown by Hains (1984), problem solving training can be successful in increasing the ability of young offenders to generate solutions to hypothetical problems. However, as Hains notes, the difficulty seems to be in maintaining this improvement in order that the skills are applied to real-life social problems. However, a later study by Hains and Hains (1987) did provide some indication of generalization of problem solving skills. A group of five institutionalized delinquents were trained in social problem solving skills: all five showed an immediate improvement in problem solving ability, but two then immediately returned to baseline levels after the initial training. The remaining three continued at follow-up to show an improvement over baseline performance. Informal data collection on other aspects of institutional behaviour suggested an improvement in institutional performance following the problem solving skills-training.

MULTIMODAL PROGRAMMES

As seen in several of the studies discussed above, cognitive-behavioural techniques seem particularly effective when used alongside other behavioural methods such as the token economy. A number of studies have investigated the potency of 'multimodal programmes' which incorporate both cognitive-behavioural and behavioural styles of intervention.

Gross et al., (1980) used a combination of social skills training (SST), behaviour therapy, and self-management training with female young offenders. They found that the programme was successful in increasing self-control, lowering the number of social problems, and reducing school absenteeism and suspensions. DeLange, Barton and Lanham (1981) designed a programme, called the WISER Way, which combined problem solving skills training and SST. The acronym WISER denotes the aims of the programme, which are to train the person to Wait, Identify the problem, generate Solutions, Evaluate consequences and self-Reinforce. An evaluation of the programme was reported by DeLange, Lanham and Barton (1981) in which the WISER Way method was compared to both standard skills training and to a no-treatment control. The outcome data showed that all three groups, including the control group, improved on a role-play measure of behavioural change; there were no differences between groups on changes on self-report measures of assertiveness and self-concept; and all three groups shifted, to a similar degree, towards greater internal locus of control. Similarly, Hollin et al., (1986) compared the effectiveness of SST plus self-instructional training with traditional SST. The two training groups were compared with attention-placebo and no-treatment control groups. The two training groups both improved significantly on a role-play measure of social skills; neither of the control groups showed this improvement. All three trainer-contact groups — i.e., both training groups and the attention-placebo group — showed an improvement in institutional behaviour, in contrast to the no-treatment control which deteriorated markedly on this measure. At post-intervention all four experimental groups showed no significant change from their pre-intervention scores on measures of personality, locus of control, and staff ratings of institutional behaviour.

Bowman and Auerbach (1982) used a range of techniques, including relaxation training, problem solving skills-training, self-statement modification, and behaviour rehearsal, with a group of male young offenders. Compared to a no-treatment control, the treatment group showed a significant improvement in institutional behaviour and on a measure of cognitive reasoning ability. However, there was no significant training effect on measures of impulsive behaviour, social problem solving, and locus of control. McDougall, Thomas and Wilson (1987) successfully used a combination of role-play, role-taking skills-training, and discussion in a programme to modify the attitudes towards violence of a group of violent young offenders.

The Reasoning and Rehabilitation programme detailed by Ross and Fabiano (1985) provides an excellent model for conducting a cognitively orientated intervention with offenders. An empirical evaluation of the programme demonstrated that it was effective in significantly lowering recidivism (Ross, Fabiano and Ewles, 1988). However, this evaluation was conducted with adult offenders: the effectiveness of the programme with young offenders therefore awaits investigation.

Aggression Replacement Training (ART) is one of the most recent and comprehensive multimodal programmes (Goldstein et al., 1989). ART uses a range of cognitive-behavioural and behavioural methods clustered into three categories: 'Structured learning training' which includes both SST and social problem-solving training; 'anger control training'; and 'moral education'. An evaluation of ART with male young offenders was reported by Glick and Goldstein (1987). The programme was successful with less serious young offenders (theft, drug use): compared to controls, these young offenders showed improvements in skill acquisition and institutional behaviour, and after discharge improved ratings from probation and parole officers. More serious young offenders (murder, sex offences, violent crime) showed less change as assessed by institutional performance; although they did display an improvement in moral reasoning which was not evident with the less serious offenders.

OUTCOME: A CRITICAL OVERVIEW

Before looking critically at the outcome studies it is important to emphasize the point made by Roberts (1987) that, despite the large-scale professional and financial commitment to rehabilitation with juvenile offenders, remarkably few research and follow-up studies have been reported. While, in those cases where research is undertaken, delinquent behaviour is often omitted from the evaluation (Blakely and Davidson, 1984). It follows that the studies which appear in the literature are but a sample, perhaps only a small sample, of the efforts in this field. The reasons for this state of affairs form part of the following discussion.

Clinical measures

The outcome studies discussed above have used a wide range of cognitive and behavioural measures of the efficacy of the various cognitive-behavioural interventions. In terms of *clinical* outcome such measures make obvious sense as dependent variables in an experimental investigation. As would be anticipated, the majority of studies show substantial improvements on such clinical measures, clearly testifying to the efficacy of cognitive-behavioural techniques. This can be taken, rightly so, as a success in purely clinical terms and as evidence for an effective means of intervention with young people who commit crimes. However, in one sense clinical efficacy is not the issue: the crucial point to make is that these studies were carried out with *delinquents*. What relevance do clinical outcome measures have with offending as the central cause of concern? Emery and Marholin (1977) argued strongly that the literature in this field is dominated by a strategy of 'targeting behaviours that are believed to be incompatible with delinquency' (p. 867). Such a strategy contains two related assumptions: that the clinical target is functionally related to the offending; and that modifying the clinical target will, in turn, change the offending.

Establishing a functional relationship between the clinical target (in any clinical approach) and delinquent behaviour is an empirical concern. As discussed previously, the evidence does suggest that as a group delinquents may be characterized by certain types and levels of social cognition. (Having said that, the importance of individual differences within the delinquent population cannot be overstated.) It is, however, an inferential leap to suppose that sociocognitive functioning *causes* offending; and a further leap to assume that modifying such cognitive functioning will have any effect on offending behaviour. This same point has, indeed, been made previously with respect to behavioural interventions with delinquents (Blakely and Davidson, 1984; Emery and Marholin, 1977). Blakely and Davidson (1984) take matters a stage further in theoretical terms in arguing that in those programmes that targeted behaviours *associated* with delinquency, it is implicit that '... temporal, setting, and behavioural generalization were hypothesized in suggesting that behavioural procedures would affect delinquency rates' (p. 261). The experimental strategy of using criminal behaviour as a measure of generalization from cognitive-behavioural (or, indeed, any other) programmes is not without problems.

In discussing this issue, Hollin and Henderson (1984) suggested that the important distinction to consider is between *stimulus generalization* and *response generalization*. Stimulus generalization refers to the generalization of a trained response to situations other than those in which training occurred; response generalization, on the other hand, occurs when changing one response directly influences other responses in an individual's behavioural repertoire. Thus, for example, if an institutionalized young offender is trained in anger management skills and on release applies these skills in a family setting, then stimulus generalization has occurred. However, to monitor the criminal behaviour of the young offender after release implies that the researcher expects response generalization: that modifying anger control will, in turn, modify delinquency. It is not impossible to formulate a hypothesis which causally links anger management with offending, but, and this is the crucial point, such a hypothesis awaits empirical verification. It follows that by conducting clinical programmes without empirical support — either at a general theoretical level or by appropriate individual assessment — clinicians are playing the percentages in gambling that the hypothesized link exists and that a given intervention with a particular young offender will be successful.

A ready example of the uncertainty of relating social cognition to delinquency is to be found with social problem solving. As noted previously, Freedman *et al.* (1978) found that delinquents gave less competent responses on the Adolescent Problem Inventory (API). Hunter and Kelley (1986) tested the hypothesis that the degree of impaired performance, as assessed using the API, should be related to the level of offending. With a sample of 60 young offenders, API score was correlated with various measures of offending such as type of offence, number of arrests, and so on. The API score failed to correlate significantly with any of the measures of delinquency. Veneziano and Veneziano (1988) also reported that no relationship was found between number and type of offence and API performance. However, Ward and McFall (1986) did find that scores of female delinquents on a similar inventory, the Problem Inventory for Adolescent Girls (Gaffney and McFall, 1981), correlated significantly with self-reported delinquency. This whole issue points to the general lack of any theoretical understanding of the role of social cognition in the aetiology and maintenance of delinquency.

Criminological measures

As well as problems with generalization, the use of criminological measures poses a particular set of problems for the experimental clinician. Criminological data can be gathered in a number of forms: self-report, police cautions, reconviction rates, time to reconviction, and offence type. There are problems with both self-report and official measures of crime as exemplified by two recent studies with delinquents. Spence and Marzillier (1981) used both types of measure — police arrest rate and self-reported offending — following social skills training with young offenders. They reported that 'The most noticeable finding was the large discrepancy between the number of police convictions . . . and the number of offences reported by the boys' (p. 362). The young offenders who had participated in the social skills programme had the lowest level of official crime but the largest number of self-reported offences. Similarly, Davidson *et al.*, (1987), evaluating the effects of a diversionary programme for young offenders, found lower rates of recidivism after the intervention as measured by official indices such as police records and court petitions, but that self-report delinquency data failed to show any treatment effect.

When we consider cognitive-behavioural programmes in this light it quickly becomes apparent that there is little to say regarding their effects on offending. There are very few such studies which have included offending as a measure of the effectiveness of the programme: in a meta-analysis of residential treatment, Garrett (1985) noted only two cognitive behaviour modification studies which had included measures of recidivism. Indeed, as the reviews of behavioural interventions with delinquents note with consistent regularity, the literature is sorely lacking in follow-up data (Blakely and Davidson, 1984; Braukmann and Fixsen, 1975; Hollin, 1990). It appears that cognitive-behavioural programmes are setting off on the same path.

Follow-up

Why have follow-up studies not been conducted? Emery and Marholin (1977) have strong views on this failure:

> Because most researchers produce frequent permanent products (articles, chapters, books) in order to receive reinforcement in the form of raises, tenure, social acknowledgement by peers, editorships, and job offers, they are likely to avoid any delay in terminating a particular research effort, especially if the delay is as long as the one or two years often required to collect adequate follow-up data. (p. 869)

However, there are other reasons for the failure of researchers to collect follow-up data. While it is comparably easy to collect data while running a treatment programme —

which is typical of most studies — follow-up data demands the time, funding, and resources to track down offenders when they are no longer easily accessible. Needless to say, most practitioners and researchers are denied access to the funding which would make it possible to conduct extensive and thorough follow-up studies.

MAXIMIZING SUCCESS: MINIMIZING FAILURE

The outcome evidence with delinquents shows that cognitive-behavioural techniques can be effective in changing behaviour: a number of strategies can be identified to build on this success.

Treatment delivery

Good programme design will, of course, include selection of suitable motivated clients, treatment integrity, rigorous assessment distinguishing between clinical and criminological targets, and appropriate evaluation measures. In addition, strategies for increasing the chances of generalization should be built into the programme (Burchard and Harrington, 1986; Huff, 1987). In the field of clinical criminology not all programmes are run by trained psychologists; very often the intervention is conducted by trained personnel from another profession. Thus, for example, in the evaluation of the Reasoning and Rehabilitation programme noted above (Ross, Fabiano and Elwes, 1988), the intervention was conducted by probation officers trained in the use of cognitive-behavioural methods. Ross et al. commented that the probation officers varied greatly in their competence as trainers: some 'became rather good trainers' while others were 'not suited' for the demands of clinical work of this type. Quay (1987) has similarly commented on this issue of treatment integrity, citing the example of one published study in which 'the majority of those responsible for carrying out the treatment were not convinced that it would affect recidivism ... and the group leaders (not professional counsellors) were poorly trained (see Quay, 1977)' (p. 246). As might be expected, this treatment programme was not successful and another 'failure' entered the literature. It is therefore important to have some knowledge of the strength and integrity of training in order to assess the merits of a study: it is encouraging that some researchers are beginning to build such a measure into their evaluations (Davidson et al., 1987).

Other problems can arise: Laws (1974) and Cullen and Seddon (1981) describe the obstacles to setting up behavioural programmes within an institution when resistance is set up by both staff and members of other professional groups. Similarly, Schlichter and Horan (1981) noted that their self-control programme, conducted in a residential establishment, was undermined by staff members who 'modeled aggressive behaviour in response to anger provocations (and) encouraged the subjects to experience and express their "pent-up" anger' (p. 364). Experiences such as these suggest that to be effective programmes must attend to the sources of resistance. A number of strategies can be used: clear communication with all concerned about the programme; good staff training; and tackling misconceptions and prejudice about clinical approaches to criminal behaviour. With respect to the latter point, Perkins (1987) has formulated the tactic of costing, in financial terms, the relative cheapness of clinical intervention in preventing future offences and lowering recidivism with adult sex offenders. (Unfortunately, cognitive-behavioural programmes with delinquents await an empirical base from which to launch this claim.)

Influencing policy

Burchard (1987a) makes the distinction between therapeutic contingencies and social and/or political contingencies. The former are designed by therapists, the latter — generally known as rules, regulations, policies, or laws — are established by administrators and legislators. As Burchard argues, social and political contingencies have a profound influence on the work of those who seek to design therapeutic contingencies. It is administrators who decide on funding of research projects (including expensive follow-up research), on equipment, on disposal of young offenders, and ultimately on what the therapist can achieve. Burchard (1987b) points out that therapists and administrators come from very different worlds: therapists are concerned with individual clients, administrators with large-scale social policies affecting large numbers of people. Clearly the power lies with the administrators, a state of affairs which Burchard (1987a) suggests must change: 'Behavior analysts must broaden their focus. Social/political contingencies should be brought into the realm of behavior analysis and behavior therapy' (p. 88). As administrators are unlikely to rush to psychologists for advice, it follows that we should be devising strategies to engage the attention of policy makers in order to make our voice heard. This requires new skills in lobbying, commenting on policy papers, and educating administrators to use psychological expertise properly. It seems unlikely that this can be accomplished on an individual level and it is therefore incumbent on our professional bodies — in which behaviour analysts surely must have a say — to develop the structures and mechanisms to allow work of this type to develop.

SUMMARY

I wish to conclude with a summary of what I believe to be the most important points raised in this chapter, and which are crucial to the successful growth of cognitive behaviour modification with delinquents:

● Carry out assessments on an individual basis in order to allow for heterogeneity in the delinquent population.

- Make a clear distinction between clinical and criminological targets for change.
- Use multimodal programmes aimed at both cognition and overt behaviour.
- Ensure treatment integrity.
- Build strategies for generalization into cognitive-behavioural programmes.
- Monitor and adapt to the rapidly changing theoretical developments in both criminology and cognitive-behavioural theory and practice.
- Counter the 'nothing works' myth.
- Develop the skills to influence social policy makers.

This may seem a great deal but it all demands attention if we are to build successfully on the promise of cognitive behaviour modification with delinquents.

Chapter 18

Fears and Phobias of Childhood

Thomas H. Ollendick & Neville J. King

Although the fears and phobias of children have been studied for a number of years, considerable controversy remains about the distinction between fears and phobias, their role in child development, and their long-term course across development. Do fears have an adaptive function, and do they facilitate development? Or are they maladaptive, and do they lead to negative consequences for the growing child? Are they short-lived? Or do they, under some circumstances, persist into adolescence and adulthood? Do fears differ from phobias? These questions and others related to the understanding, assessment and treatment of children's fears and phobias will be explored in this chapter.

Fear is a normal response to a wide variety of threatening situations or objects. In its simplest form, fear is the state or condition of being afraid or apprehensive when exposed to threatening stimuli. All children experience fear during their development; it is a part of normal development that serves to ensure children's safety and, ultimately, their survival. From a practical standpoint, it is easy to see that a 'healthy' fear of heights, snakes, or the sight of blood is appropriate and adaptive. Usually, these fears are mild, age-specific, and transitory (Ollendick, 1979a). Moreover, children experience a wide variety of 'normal' fears over their development and these fears appear to be related to their level of cognitive development (King, Hamilton and Ollendick, 1988; Morris and Kratochwill, 1983). Young infants are afraid of loss of support, loud noises and strangers, as well as sudden, unexpected, and looming objects. One- and two-year-olds show a range of fears including separation from parents and fear of strangers. During the third and fourth years, fears of the dark, being left alone, small animals and insects emerge. Fears of wild animals, ghosts and monsters come to the foreground during the fifth to sixth years; and fears of school, supernatural events, and physical danger emerge in the seventh and eighth years. During the ninth to eleventh years, social fears and fears of war, health, bodily injury, and school performance become more prominent.

Several authors have commented on the developmental progression of these 'normal' fears and have shown how they emanate from increasingly sophisticated cognitive development in the growing child (e.g., Bauer, 1976; Ferrari, 1986). As is evident, infants and very young children show fear to things that occur in their immediate environment (e.g., loud noises, strangers, separation from parents). Their level of cognitive development limits the range of stimuli to which they can experience fear to those stimuli which are in the here and now and in their immediate presence. Preschool children, on the other hand, are capable of showing fear to more global and imaginary stimuli such as ghosts, monsters, and the dark. Older children, able to differentiate 'internal representations from objective reality' (Bauer, 1976, p. 71), begin to show more realistic and specific fears including fears related to physical injury, health, and school performance.

Types of fears children experience at different ages was illustrated in a study by Bauer (1976) in which he examined the fears of 4–6, 6–8, and 10–12-year-old children. The children were interviewed individually and told that all children were afraid but that some children were more afraid of some things than others. They were then asked, 'What are you afraid of most?' and then allowed to draw a picture while describing their fears. Other questions probed the presence of nighttime fears and scary dreams. Seventy-four percent of the 4- to 6-year-olds, 53 % of the 6- to 8-year-olds, but only 5 % of the 10- to 12-year-olds reported fears of ghosts and monsters; on the other hand, only 11% of the 4- to 6-year-olds, but 53 % of the 6- to 8-year-olds and 55 % of the 10- to 12-year-olds described fears of bodily injury and physical danger. These age-related differences were also reflected in the description of scary dreams reported by the younger and older children. The younger children reported that the appearance of the monster itself (e.g., 'His face looks ugly' or 'He has big ears') were sufficient to induce fear, while the older children imputed harmful actions to the monster (e.g., 'They wanted to cut my head off' or 'Guess he would have choked me or something'). Such differences reflect general developmental trends in cognition toward separation of internal representation from objective reality (Bauer, 1976).

Recently, we have shown that both the number and intensity of fears reported by children and adolescents *decreases* with age (King *et al.*, 1989; Ollendick, King and Frary, 1989). Using the Fear Survey Schedule for Children–Revised (Ollendick, 1983), we found that 7- to 10-year-old children reported significantly more fears than 11- to 13-year-olds or 14- to 16-year-olds, who did not differ from one another. The Fear Survey Schedule for Children–Revised consists of 80 stimuli to which the children are asked to indicate the extent of their fear: 'none', 'some', or 'a lot'. The younger children, on average, reported having a lot of fear to 17 of the stimuli, whereas the two older groups reported a lot of fear, on average, to 13 of the items. When we examined the kinds of fears that the children were reporting, we were surprised to learn that eight of the ten most feared objects or situations were the same regardless of age: being hit by a car or truck, not being able to breathe, bombing attacks, fire — getting burned, falling from a high place, a burglar breaking into our house, earthquakes and death. For 7- to 10-year-old children, the remaining two most frequently reported fears were getting lost in a strange place and being sent to the (school) principal. For older children and adolescents, however, the remaining two fears consisted of getting poor grades and failing a test. Overall, it is evident that children and adolescents between 7 and 16 years of age reported realistic and specific fears and that eight of the top ten fears were the same across these age ranges. Consistent with Bauer's (1976) developmental analysis, however, it is clear that the additional fears reported by younger children were of separation and punishment whereas those of the older children and adolescents were of a social-evaluative nature.

This pattern of fears was found for both Australian (King *et al.*, 1989) and American (Ollendick *et al.*, 1989) children. More recently, we have documented a similar pattern for British school children (Ollendick, Yule and Ollier, in press).

In addition to age-related differences, several studies have shown gender and socioeconomic differences in the number and kinds of fears reported by children and adolescents. Girls have been shown to report more fears than boys and lower socioeconomic status children to report more fears than upper socioeconomic status children (see Ferrari, 1986, for a review of these findings). The exact meaning and significance of these findings is unclear, however. For example, it is not at all clear that girls actually *have* more fears than boys, even though they report more fears. It is possible that boys are less likely to acknowledge their fears than girls because of the stigma attached to such self-reports or, conversely, that girls are more likely to report the full extent of their fears than boys due to current socialization practices. Observational studies, documenting or refuting the oft-found self-reported sex differences, remain to be conducted and will help clarify the meaning of such findings.

Let us now turn our attention from 'normal' fears to clinical fears or phobias. Phobias can be defined as intense fears that are out of proportion to the degree of danger or threat posed by the threatening stimuli. Specifically, when fears (a) are excessive to the situation, (b) cannot be reasoned away, (c) are beyond voluntary control, (d) lead to avoidance of the threatening object or situation, (e) persist over time, (f) are maladaptive, and (g) are not age-specific, they can be labeled phobias (Marks, 1987; Miller, Barrett and Hampe, 1974). In understanding children's phobias, it is important to keep these characteristics in mind because, as we have seen, it is quite normal for children to express a variety of mild fears throughout their development.

Children's phobias may be quite debilitating and create severe living problems for children and their parents. For example, a 10-year-old child's phobia of darkness manifests itself in tantrums and panic at bedtime. Frequently, such a child insists on sleeping with his or her parents and refuses to sleep overnight with friends or relatives because of embarrassment about the phobia (Graziano *et al.*, 1979). A 7-year-old child's phobia of medical procedures may be so severe that it is impossible to conduct routine diagnostic and treatment practices which may be necessary for the child's well-being. A 12-year-old child's phobia of school, especially if it results in prolonged absenteeism, may hinder the child's social and academic development (Hersov, 1960; King and Ollendick, 1989). Phobic reactions to specific activities or events at school, such as tests or speaking in front of class, can also interfere with optimal performance and self-esteem. An 8-year-old child's phobia of dogs can be so extreme that the child takes an inordinate amount of time to get from home to school and back again (Lazarus and Abramovitz, 1962). In fact, the parents may have to drive the child to school in order to avoid the fear stimulus. On a family outing, the dog-phobic child may become panic-stricken at the sight of an oncoming dog and possibly run into the street to avoid the dog (King, Hamilton and Ollendick, 1988). Thus, childhood phobias may produce a great deal of personal anguish and unhappiness on the part of the child, possibly impede social and academic development, at times create danger for the child, and may be disruptive for the child's parents and family. Unlike the 'normal' fears of childhood, phobias are likely to be intense, durable, and not age-specific.

Determining an accurate estimate of the prevalence of phobias in children is difficult due to the various ways of determining such figures. On the basis of test questionnaires, observations and interviews, Agras, Sylvester and Oliveau (1969) retrospectively classified the fears of children as common fears, intense fears, and phobias. Common fears were abundant; however, the rate of intense fears was about 8 % while the rate of phobias was about 2 %. In an extensive survey of 9- to 11-year-old children on the Isle of Wight, Rutter, Tizard and Whitmore (1970) found fewer than 1 % of the children to have clinically significant phobias. However, as noted by King, Hamilton and Ollendick (1988), this may be an underestimate since children with single phobias were not included in these estimates. Based on these studies and others, it appears that Miller, Barrett and Hampe's (1974) suggestion that 'the most typical response pattern approximates a J-curve in which 84 % or more of the children show no fear of the stimuli, while 5 to 15 % show what parents consider to be normal fear, and 0 to 5 % show excessive fear' (p. 104) is supported. Such a conclusion is consistent with the finding that phobic disorders in children account for about 5 % of referrals to child psychiatrists and psychologists (Graham, 1964; Graziano and DeGiovanni, 1979).

Before examining the assessment and treatment of intense childhood fears and phobias, a comment about the natural course of fears and phobias is in order. There exists an impression in the literature that children's phobias are benign and that they have a good prognosis with or without treatment. However, as we have noted elsewhere (King, Hamilton and Ollendick, 1988; Ollendick, 1979a), this impression is based more on the retrospective account of adults than on follow-up and follow-through studies of anxious and phobic children. In one of the few longitudinal studies, for example, Fischer et al., (1984), following preschoolers through junior high school, found positive relationships in the presentation of internalizing, fearful-anxious behavior over time. Similarly, the pioneering work by Kagan and his associates (1984) has affirmed the long-term relationship between anxious-inhibited behavioral styles in infancy and similar disposi- tions in adolescence. While it may be the case that some highly fearful and phobic children 'outgrow' their condition over time (e.g., Agras, Chapin and Oliveau, 1972), it is probable that many do not and that, for those children, fears persist and develop into phobias. Such a conclusion is borne out by the reports of phobic adults who frequently indicate that their animal phobias started in early childhood (Agras, Chapin and Oliveau, 1972) and that their social phobias began in early adolescence (Francis and Ollendick, 1986). Clearly, follow-up studies are needed to confirm these retrospective reports and to document the course from mild fears to phobias.

DEVELOPMENTAL-BEHAVIORAL ASSESSMENT

Comprehensive assessment of childhood phobias requires measures of behavioral, cognitive, and physiological responding (Barrios, Hartmann and Shigetomi, 1981), as well as a determination of the social and cultural context in which the phobias occur. Our strategy is to begin with broad-based assessment of the child and his or her environment (e.g., family, school, peers) and then to obtain information regarding specific stimulus features, response modes, antecedents and consequences, severity, duration, and pervasiveness of the particular phobias. The assessment begins with a behavioral interview and utilizes a multimethod, problem-solving approach to obtain as complete a picture of the child and his or her family as is possible (Mash and Terdal, 1988; Ollendick and Hersen, 1984).

Behavioral interviews

The behavioral interview is the initial step in the assessment process. The purposes of the interview are to establish rapport with the child and family, obtain information as to the nature of the phobic behavior as well as its antecedents and consequences, assess the child's developmental level, determine the broader sociocultural context in which the phobic behavior occurs, and to formulate treatment plans (Bierman and Schwartz, 1986; Murphy et al., 1982; Ollendick and Cerny, 1981).

Interviewing a phobic child and his or her family requires an understanding that such a child may be timid, shy, fearful, anxious, and relatively unresponsive to interview questions. It also demands an appreciation of the child's developmental level and how his or her cognitive development places constraints on the types of questions that can be asked and how they should be phrased. It is frequently necessary to phrase questions in specific, direct terms so that the child will understand them and to provide the child with additional support and encouragement to respond. Generally, open-ended questions such as 'How do you feel?' or 'How are things going in school?' result in unelaborated responses such as 'OK' or 'I don't know'. Specific questions such as 'What kinds of things do you get scared about?', 'What do your parents do when you tell them you are afraid?' and 'What about getting an injection (dogs, high places) worries you?' are more easily and readily responded to by the child. In addition, it is helpful to use the child's own words when discussing these fears. For example, children may distinguish 'nervous' feelings (scared, upset) from 'anxious' (eager, anticipatory) ones. In order to assist the child in describing the antecedents and consequences of the phobia, it may be beneficial to instruct the child to imagine the fear-producing situation and to describe exactly what is happening. At this time the child can be observed for overt signs of fear such as crying, tremors, or flushing. This procedure has been described in detail by Smith and Sharpe (1970) and Ollendick and Gruen (1972).

During the initial interview, it is also important to obtain information from the family regarding their perceptions of the child's phobic behavior, as well as information regarding its antecedents and consequences. Again, it is helpful to ask specific questions such as 'What does Martin do that leads you to say he is afraid of meeting someone for the first time?' Sometimes it is also useful to interview the child in the setting in which the phobia occurs. This approach is illustrated in the work of Blagg and his associates (Blagg, 1987; Blagg and Yule, 1984); an advocate of rapid assessment and treatment,

Blagg suggests that the child and parents be interviewed in the school with the onus on the parents to get the child to school (by force if necessary) for the interview. A number of practical advantages are seen to be associated with this tactic. For example, it minimizes parent and child collusion from the beginning, demonstrates the parent's desire to get the child to school under protest and ability to act as an escort, and gives information on whether the child's problem is largely that of separation from parents and leaving home or a phobic avoidance of school.

With interviews, as well as other assessment procedures, there are psychometric concerns. Often, children and parents are inconsistent and unreliable reporters of behavior, particularly past behavior. That is, parents and children may not agree on the occurrence of behaviors, particularly anxious or phobic behaviors, and whether such behaviors are a significant problem. One way to maximize the reliability of reporting is to assess current behaviors and the conditions under which they occur (e.g., Herjanic et al., 1975; Ollendick and Cerny, 1981; Rutter and Graham, 1968). Thus the focus of the interview should be on the phobic behavior and its antecedents and consequences in the here and now.

Self-report instruments

A wide variety of self-report instruments are available to supplement information obtained from the interview. In general, they consist of fear survey schedules that provide lists of fear-evoking stimuli and anxiety measures that provide the child a set of responses with which to describe subjective experiences felt in the fear-producing situations.

Fear Survey Schedules

Scherer and Nakamura (1968) developed the Fear Survey Schedule for Children (FSSC), modeled after the Wolpe-Lang Fear Survey Schedule for Adults (Wolpe and Lang, 1964). On this scale, children are asked to rate their fear of each of 80 items on a five-point scale. Factor-analytic studies of the FSSC show that this scale taps major types of fear: fear of death, fear of the dark, and home and school fears (Scherer and Nakamura, 1968). It was developed for children between 9 and 12 years of age.

Modified versions of the FSSC have been developed by Ryall and Dietiker (1979) and Ollendick (1983). The Children's Fear Survey Schedule (Ryall and Dietiker, 1979) is a short form of the FSSC that contains 48 specific fear items and two blanks for children to indicate additional fears if desired. Each item is rated on a three-point scale ranging from 'not scared or nervous or afraid' to 'a little scared' to 'very scared'. It was modified in order to be used with younger children and is reported to be useful with children between 5 and 12 years of age. Although no information is available as to the validity of this revised Children's Fear Survey Schedule, it possesses good test-retest reliability and internal consistency.

The revision of the Fear Survey Schedule for Children undertaken by Ollendick (FSSC–R; Ollendick, 1983) is another potentially useful tool for determining specific fear stimuli related to children's phobias. School-aged children are instructed to rate their fear of the 80 items on a three-point scale ranging from being frightened by the item 'none', 'some', or 'a lot'. Normative data for children between 7 and 16 years of age are available. Further, the instrument has been used in cross-cultural studies in Australia, England, and the United States (King et al., 1989; Ollendick, Matson and Helsel, 1985; Ollendick, King and Frary, 1989; Ollendick, Yule and Ollier, in press). Initial examination of the scale suggests that it is a reliable and valid revision of the FSSC. For example, high scores on the survey are positively related to measures of anxiety and negatively related to internal locus of control and positive self-concept. Further, Ollendick and Mayer (1984) reported that it discriminated between 'school phobic' children whose fears were related to separation anxiety and school phobic children whose fears were related to specific aspects of the school situation itself. In addition, the scale has discriminated reliably between the fears of normally sighted children and blind children (Ollendick, Matson and Helsel, 1985), possesses acceptable test-retest reliability, and is internally consistent (Ollendick, 1983). In general, as we noted earlier, girls report a greater number of fears and a greater intensity of fears than do boys, and younger children report more fears than do older children and adolescents.

Finally, the instrument has been found to possess factorial invariance across wide age ranges and diverse cultures. A five-factor solution has been obtained: Fear of Failure and Criticism, Fear of the Unknown, Fear of Minor Injury and Small Animals, Fear of Danger and Death, and Medical Fears. Interestingly, the five most common fears in boys and girls between 7 and 16 years of age can be found on the Fear of Danger and Death factor: 'A burglar breaking into our house', 'Bombing attacks', 'Being hit by a car or truck', 'Falling from high places', and 'Not being able to breathe'.

Anxiety measures

In contrast to fear survey schedules, measures of anxiety have been used to determine the subjectively experienced effects of being in phobic or anxiety-producing situations. The Children's Manifest Anxiety Scale (CMAS; Casteneda, McCandless and Palmero, 1956), a scaled-down version of the Manifest Anxiety Scale for Adults (Taylor, 1951), consists of 42 anxiety items and 11 lie items that assess a child's report of pervasive anxiety. Reynolds and Richmond (1978) developed a revised version of the CMAS titled 'What I Think and Feel' (CMAS-R). The purpose of this 37-item revision was to clarify the wording of items, decrease administration time, and lower the reading level of the items. The CMAS-R is suitable for children and adolescents between 6 and 18 years of age; normative information for a variety of child groups is available (Ollendick and Yule, 1990; Reynolds and Paget, 1982). The scale yields three anxiety factors: physiological, worry/oversensitivity, and concentration (Reynolds and Richmond, 1978).

In brief, fear survey schedules and anxiety measures appear useful as instruments to identify specific fear sensitivities and anxiety responses in children, as normative instruments for selecting children for treatment, and as outcome measures of therapeutic efficacy. Of course, they also possess limitations attendant to self-report instruments (Finch and Rogers, 1984).

Parent and teacher measures

A variety of parent- and teacher-rating scales and checklists have been used in the assessment of fears and anxieties in children. Among the more frequently used are Achenbach's Child Behavior Checklist and Quay and Peterson's Behavior Problem Checklist. Both of these rating forms have been developed and standardized for use with children between 4 and 16 years of age.

The Child Behavior Checklist (CBCL; Achenbach, 1978; Achenbach and Edelbrock, 1979) has been used extensively in factor-analytic studies by Achenbach and his colleagues. Parents or teachers are asked to fill out this 138-item scale that taps both behavior problems and social competence. Social competency items assess the child's participation in social organizations, activities, and school. The behavior problem items are rated on a three-point scale as to how well each describes the child. The inclusion of social competency and behavior problem items allows for a comprehensive assessment of the child's strengths and weaknesses. In addition, the scale allows for identification of children who display a variety of behaviors including withdrawal, depression and somatic complaints. Specific anxiety items include 'clings to adults', 'school fears', and 'shy, timid'. This scale has been found to be reliable and valid and provides important normative data for boys and girls of varying ages (see Achenbach, 1985, for additional detail regarding the use of the CBCL with anxious and fearful children).

The Revised Behavior Problem Checklist (Quay & Peterson, 1983) consists of 89 problem behaviors that are also rated on a three-point scale ranging from 'not a problem' to 'mild problem' to 'severe problem'. Factor analysis of the scale yields the following six dimensions: conduct problem, socialized aggression, attention problem–immaturity, anxiety-withdrawal, psychotic behavior, and motor excess. Like the CBCL, the Problem Behavior Checklist is a reliable and valid tool with which to assess significant-other reports of children's anxious behavior and its relationship to other deviant or pathological behavior.

Thus, a variety of parent and teacher report measures are available for use. Although they generally possess sound test-retest and interjudge reliability, their validity, in terms of how closely they correspond to other measures such as self-reports and behavioral observation, is in need of empirical examination.

Behavioral observations

The most direct way to assess fearful and anxious behaviors in children is to observe these behaviors in the situations in which they occur. In behavioral observation systems, specific behaviors indicative of fear are defined, observed, and recorded. Oftentimes these systems are highly individualized and tailored to the measurement of specific phobias. For example, Graziano and Mooney (1980) detailed a set of operationally defined behaviors reflective of nighttime fears in 6- to 12-year-old children. The behaviors included the number of minutes the child required to get to bed after being asked; the number of minutes the child took to fall asleep; the avoidance and delay behavior displayed, such as crying, getting out of bed, arguing, and asking for a glass of water; and an overall rating of the child's willingness to go to bed.

More general behavioral observation systems for childhood fears and anxieties have also been described. Among them is the Preschool Observation Scale of Anxiety (POSA; Glennon and Weisz, 1978). The POSA includes 30 behavioral indices of anxiety which are observed using a standard time-sampling procedure. Among the behavioral indices are nail biting, avoidance of eye contact, silence to questions, and fearful facial expressions. Although more information is needed regarding its reliability and validity, this scale appears to be a promising clinical tool. We are currently using a variant of this system to code the fearful behaviors of children called to the principal's office. (Being sent to the principal is one of the ten most common fears in American children.) In addition to the actual route and time taken to arrive at the principal's office, a trembling voice, lip licking, and gratuitous hand movements are being reliably recorded and associated with high levels of reported fear about going to the principal's office.

More important, developmental differences in the fear response itself might be discovered through direct observation procedures. As one example, Katz, Kellerman and Siegel (1980) reported important age differences in children with cancer in response to bone marrow aspirations. Children under 6 years of age expressed their anxiety by crying, screaming, needing to be physically restrained, and expressing pain verbally (e.g., 'That hurts', 'Stop hurting me'). The intermediate age group, children between 6 and 10 years of age, did not require physical restraint but did express their pain predominantly verbally. In addition, muscular rigidity appeared in this intermediate age group. The oldest children and adolescents, those between 10 and 18 years of age, evinced only two high-rate modes of anxiety expression: verbal expression of pain and muscular rigidity. Thus Katz *et al.* observed and documented a developmental tendency toward less diffuse vocal protest (screams, cries) and skeletal activity (motor excess) and greater emphasis on verbal expression and muscle tension with age. The general picture was that of increased body control accompanied by constriction of the musculature with progressive age. Such findings may have important implications for treatment; specifically, muscle relaxation procedures might be more useful for older children and adolescents, whereas operant-based procedures to help moderate motor excess behaviors might be more appropriate for younger children.

The use of Behavioral Avoidance Tests (BAT) in simulated settings is another frequently used device for measuring phobic responses in children (Lang and Lazovik, 1963). Typically, this procedure involves having the child enter a room containing the fear-producing stimulus and approach, ultimately handling, the feared object. As noted by Kazdin (1973), the BAT provides specific behavioral measures of avoidance such as the amount of time spent in the presence of the anxiety-provoking object, distance from the object, and number and latency of approach responses. However, a significant number of limitations accompany the use of behavioral avoidance tests, including (a) the procedures and instructions are not well standardized, (b) there are few data available regarding the influence of procedural variations and demand characteristics on children's BAT performance, and (c) there are presently no data available as to the reliability and validity of such tests with phobic children (see King, Hamilton and Ollendick, 1988; Morris and Kratochwill, 1983).

Self-monitoring procedures

Although less frequently used, the self-monitoring of both avoidance responses and the cognitions accompanying those responses is a potentially useful source of information as well, at least for older children. With self-monitoring, the child is required to discriminate and record the occurrence of an actual behavior, or the thoughts that accompany the behavior as it occurs. In this respect, self-monitoring is a direct measure of the phobic response and is distinct from self-report measures of fear and anxiety, which involve the report of behaviors that occurred at some earlier time. Particularly intriguing at this time is the rapidly developing use of self-statement tests to monitor the cognitions that accompany fearful or anxious behaviors.

Self-statement tests are usually administered following participation in a simulated or real-life anxiety-producing situation. Such tests consist of a list of statements; the child is instructed to indicate which thoughts he or she was thinking during the task. Although this means of assessing the cognitions of children has been advocated by some (e.g., King, Hamilton and Ollendick, 1988; Morris and Kratchowill, 1983), there are few examples of self-statement tests available for phobic children at this time. An exception is Zatz and Chassin's (1983, 1985) assessment of the self-statements of test-anxious children. The Children's Cognitive Assessment Questionnaire (CCAQ) taps the self-statements of test-anxious children and contains four subscales: positive evaluation, negative evaluation, on-task thoughts, and off-task thoughts. The authors report that highly test-anxious children endorse more negative evaluation and off-task thoughts than do low test-anxious children.

In a similar vein, Stefanek et al. (1987) examined children's inhibiting and facilitating self-statements in response to role-play situations in which the child was in conflict with, or was to initiate an interaction with, a peer. They reported that fearful, socially withdrawn children endorsed more inhibiting and fewer facilitating self-statements than did their well-adjusted peers.

As noted above, the use of self-statement tests with fearful and phobic children is relatively new. A productive area of research might be to replicate studies such as Zatz and Chassin (1983) and Stefanek et al. (1987) in order to establish the psychometric properties of the procedure and to examine limitations related to its use, especially with different age groups. Assessing the specific cognitions of anxious children of varying ages may provide vital information to the treatment of such children. That is, more reliable information would be made available as to the content of the cognitions to be modified as well as the extent to which coping cognitions are already existent in the children's repertoire.

Physiological assessment

Principles and procedures of the physiological assessment of children are in their infancy (Beidel, 1988; King, in press). Little normative information is available as to children's physiological responding in general, let alone physiological distinctions among the emotional responses. In two of the few discussions of the physiological assessment of childhood fears and phobias, King (in press) and Barrios, Hartmann and Shigetomi, (1981) acknowledge that little is known about the effects of laboratory or clinic settings, ambient noise, or instructional set on physiological responding in children.

The most commonly used measures of physiological responding in children are those that assess cardiovascular and electrodermal responding (Morris and Kratochwill, 1983). Cardiovascular responding can be assessed by measures of heart rate, blood pressure, and peripheral blood flow. Typically, heart rate has been the more common measure, because it is measured easily and is least sensitive to measurement artifacts (Nietzel and Bernstein, 1981). Recently, Beidel (1988) examined the cardiovascular responses of test-anxious children when engaged in two social-evaluative tasks, namely, a timed vocabulary test and an oral reading session. The anxious children displayed significantly higher heart rates on these tasks than their non-anxious peers; however, there were no differences between the groups on systolic and diastolic blood pressure. Unfortunately, it is difficult to differentiate specific heart rate patterns in children. For example, although Tal and Miklich (1976) reported increased heart rate in children asked to imagine a fearful situation, Johnson and Melamed (1979) reported similar increases in heart rate in children asked to pretend that they were angry. Moreover, Sternbach (1962) found a low correlation between heart rate and self-report of fear. Thus, a change in heart rate in and of itself may be indicative of general emotional responding and provide little information as to the specific nature of emotional arousal. Further, it might not be related to actual self-reports of fear. Finally, Nietzel and Bernstein (1981) have cautioned that (a) heart rate is overly sensitive to motor and perceptual activity (a problem especially relevant for children) and that it may be confounded easily with stress, and (b) heart rate can be idiosyncratic in that it may increase or decrease or remain stable in response to anxiety-provoking stimuli.

Electrodermal responding is assessed typically through measures of skin conductance and skin resistance. Two examples of such measures are Palmar Sweat Prints (PSP) and Finger Sweat Prints (FSP). Melamed and her colleagues (e.g., Melamed and Siegel, 1975) reported electrodermal responding to be correlated with both self-report and observations of dental fears and anxiety in children. Barrios, Hartmann and Shigetomi (1981) caution, however, that electrodermal responding is highly reactive and, as such, is responsive to a number of environmental and psychological artifacts.

In sum, although the investigation of the relationship between childhood anxiety and physiological responding holds promise, few conclusions can be drawn at this time. Given the lack of systematic, normative data regarding physiological responding in children and the expense (monetarily and timewise) of physiological assessment, it seems premature to advocate regular use of such assessment techniques in clinical practice at this time. Rather, it might prove more fruitful to explore more fully the parameters of physiological responding in children in general before excursions into the clinical world are encouraged (Ollendick and Francis, 1988).

TREATMENT

In this section, we will review behavioral strategies that are frequently used in the treatment of fears and phobias in children. Conceptually, these strategies are derived from principles of classical, vicarious, and operant conditioning, as well as recent advances in information processing theory. Although strategies based on each of these principles and theories will be presented separately, it should be understood from the onset that the most effective and durable treatments draw on all of these principles and theories in a complex interactive fashion. The use of such integrated approaches recognizes that fears and phobias, from the behavioral perspective, are acquired and maintained through an interactive combination of conditioning and mediational processes.

Before proceeding to a review of specific treatment procedures, however, it is instructive to recall the early treatments recommended by Watson and Rayner (1920) and Jones (1924). It will be recalled that Watson and Rayner (1920) demonstrated the early principles of conditioned emotional reactions in the now-famous case of 'Albert B'. Although Albert was discharged from the hospital before the deconditioning of his fear of white rats and other related stimuli could be undertaken, Watson and Rayner recommended the following potential treatments: (a) constantly confront the child with those stimuli that elicit the response in the anticipation that habituation would occur, (b) recondition the child by presenting objects that produce the fear response and simultaneously stimulate 'the erogenous zones' (p. 12), (c) recondition the child by feeding candy or some other food just as the animal is presented, and (d) build up 'constructive' activities around the feared object by imitation and by putting the lad through the motions of manipulation. Jones (1924) recommended similar treatments, including 'social imitation'. This latter procedure essentially relied on the principles of modeling. Thus, as can be seen, many current behavioral treatments have been in vogue for some time. More recently, it has been shown that such procedures are *acceptable* to both children and caregivers, an important issue given the need for their cooperation during intervention (King and Gullone, 1990).

Systematic desensitization

Systematic desensitization procedures evolved from the early writings of Pavlov, Watson, Jones, and Masserman. Subsequently, Wolpe (1958) expanded on these works and formulated the systematic desensitization procedure. In this paradigm, fears and phobias are viewed as classically conditioned responses that can be unlearned through specific counterconditioning procedures. In counterconditioning, the fear-producing stimuli are presented (either imaginally or in vivo) in the presence of other stimuli that elicit responses incompatible with fear. In this manner, the fear is said to be counterconditioned and inhibited by the incompatible response.

The first and most often-cited account of counterconditioning is that of Jones's early treatment of Peter (Jones, 1924). She successfully treated Peter's fear of rabbits by exposing him to the actual feared rabbit in a systematic manner and in the presence of food (a stimulus that produced a positive response). Aside from this early demonstration, systematic desensitization has relied primarily on the relaxation response as the competing, inhibiting response (Wolpe, 1958). In its most basic form, systematic desensitization consists of three components: (a) induction of relaxation, (b) development of a fear-producing stimulus hierarchy, and (c) the systematic, graduated pairing of items in the hierarchy with relaxation. Generally, the fear-producing stimuli are presented imaginally (in order of least to most fear-producing) while the child is relaxed. This aspect of treatment is the desensitization proper and is thought to lead to the direct inhibition of the fear response. As noted by Wolpe, it is imperative that the counterconditioning response (i.e., relaxation) be sufficient to inhibit fear at each step of the hierarchy. Although studies have questioned the active mechanisms and the necessary ingredients of systematic desensitization (see review of Hatzenbuehler and Schroeder, 1978), there is little doubt that it is a frequently used procedure with children and adolescents.

As noted, systematic desensitization has typically involved imaginal representation of the fear-producing stimuli and has employed muscular relaxation as the competing, inhibiting response. Although these procedures appear to work reasonably well with adolescents and older children (e.g., Ollendick, 1979b; Van Hasselt et al., 1979), younger children appear to have difficulty in acquiring the muscular relaxation response and in being able to image clearly the fear-producing stimuli (Kissel, 1972; Rosenstiel and Scott, 1977). As a result, in vivo desensitization (as originally used by Jones, 1924) and emotive imagery (as suggested by Lazarus and Abramowitz, 1962) have become increasingly popular, at least with younger children (Hatzenbuehler and Schroeder, 1978; Ollendick, 1979a). Illustrative of the emotive imagery approach is the treatment of a five-year-old child with extreme fears of the dark, noises, and shadows (Jackson and King, 1981). Having determined that the child was fond of the comic character Batman (the boy reportedly wore his Batman cape and mask around the house, watched reruns of the Batman series on television, and possessed several toys associated with Batman, including puzzles and a batmobile), Jackson and King created a fear hierarchy and then asked the child to imagine that 'he and Batman had joined forces and that he was appointed as a special agent'. Next he was asked to close his eyes and to imagine the fear-producing stimuli in a graduated fashion, while accompanied by Batman. Altogether, there were four sessions of emotive imagery. Treatment, albeit uncontrolled, was highly successful. In this case study, muscular relaxation had been attempted and was unsuccessful, leading Jackson and King to use the child's favorite character as the fear-inhibiting agent. More recently, King and his colleagues have provided a controlled, multiple baseline analysis of the effects of emotive imagery on the treatment of children's nighttime fears (King, Cranstoun and Josephs, 1989). The children showed marked behavioral improvement on a test for darkness toleration as well as reduced fear on the Revised Fear Survey Schedule for Children (Ollendick, 1983).

Other uncontrolled and controlled case studies have illustrated the potential efficacy of systematic desensitization and its variants in the treatment of a variety of childhood fears (e.g., dogs, dark, dentists, water, school, bees, and loud noises). In one particularly interesting and well-controlled study, Van Hasselt et al. (1979) treated an 11-year-old multiphobic child (blood, heights and test-taking) with standard systematic desensitization procedures in a multiple-baseline fashion. Fear of heights was treated first, followed by fear of blood, and then fear of taking tests. In addition, consistent with the tripartite assessment of fear, measures of motoric, cognitive, and physiological measures were obtained for each of these fears. Results indicated that relaxation alone had little or no effect on the three response modes; however, the pairing of items in the graduated hierarchy with relaxation led to a significant reduction in both the motoric and cognitive aspects of the anxiety but not the physiological ones. These changes occurred for each fear only when systematic desensitization was applied specifically to that fear. Such results affirm the controlling effects of the desensitization procedure.

In addition to controlled and uncontrolled single-case studies, at least seven group studies evaluating systematic desensitization have been reported with children and adolescents (Barabasz, 1973, 1975; Kondaš, 1967; Little and Jackson, 1974; Mann and Rosenthal, 1969; Miller et al., 1972; Ultee, Griffiaen and Schellekens, 1982). In all of these studies, systematic desensitization was found to be more effective than no-treatment or waiting-list control conditions. Subjects ranged from 5 to 15 years of age; fears ranged from specific phobias to interpersonal anxieties. Consistent with our earlier observations, one study (Ultee, Griffiaen and Schellekens, 1982) found that in vivo desensitization was more effective than imaginal desensitization with 5- to 10-year-olds. At older ages, imaginal and in vivo procedures appeared to be equally effective. Although systematic desensitization procedures were shown to be more effective than no-treatment or waiting-list control conditions in these studies, in only one study (Miller et al., 1972) were these procedures compared to other therapeutic procedures. Unfortunately, methodological problems precluded a clear test of the differential effectiveness of systematic desensitization and the more traditional therapeutic procedure (Ollendick and Francis, 1988).

In summary, systematic desensitization and its variants represent reasonably effective and clinically useful procedures for the treatment of phobic disorders in children and adolescents. It should be noted, however, that it is frequently necessary to alter the standard procedures for younger children. Moreover, it should be acknowledged that well-controlled studies comparing the effectiveness of these procedures are lacking (Ollendick, 1986).

Modeling-based procedures

Treatments based on classical conditioning principles emphasize the role of direct learning experiences in the acquisition, maintenance and reduction of fears and phobias. In contrast, treatments based on vicarious conditioning principles focus on modeling or observational learning: learning and behavior change that occur as a result of observing another person's behavior and its consequences (Bandura, 1968, 1969).

Modeling involves demonstrating nonfearful behavior in the fear-producing situation *and* showing the child appropriate responses to use in the fearful situation. Thus fear is reduced and appropriate skills are learned. After the demonstration, the child is instructed to model or imitate performance of the model. Following repeated rehearsals of the observed behaviors, the child is provided feedback and reinforcement for performance that matches that of the model. Thus operant principles are used to maintain the desired behaviors once they are acquired through the modeling process.

Three types of modeling have been described in the literature: filmed modeling, live or in vivo modeling, and participant modeling. Filmed modeling consists of having the child observe a film in which a model (usually of similar characteristics to the targeted child) displays progressively more intimate interaction with the feared object or setting, whereas live modeling entails having the child observe a *live* model (again, usually of similar characteristics to the fearful child) engage in graduated interactions with a *live* feared object or actually participate in real-life situations found to be fear-producing. Participant modeling, on the other hand, consists of live modeling *plus* contact with a therapist (or fearless peer) who physically guides the child through the fearful situation. Thus, in addition to observing another interact fearlessly, the child is provided with physical and psychological support and direct contact with the therapist *while* performing the appropriate behavior. Ritter (1968) refers to this procedure as 'contact desensitization'.

Based on an earlier review of modeling studies with fearful children and adolescents, Ollendick (1979a) concluded that filmed modeling is effective in about 25% to 50% of cases, live modeling in about 50% to 67%, and participant modeling in 80% to 92%. A clear ordering of effectiveness was evident in these studies, filmed modeling being least effective, live modeling intermediate, and participant modeling most effective.

Illustrative of these procedures, Ross, Ross and Evans (1971) used modeling (along with social reinforcement) to treat a 6-year-old boy whose fear and avoidance of interactions with age-mates was so extreme that he actively avoided peers and refused to even watch filmed presentations featuring young children. Treatment consisted of establishing generalized imitation, participant modeling, and social reinforcement. Following treatment, the child was observed to interact positively with his peers and to display few avoidant behaviors. On follow-up, two months after cessation of treatment, he was observed to 'join ongoing play groups, initiate verbal contacts, and sustain effective social interactions, all with children who were complete strangers to him' (Ross, Ross and Evans, 1971, p. 277). Clearly, significant clinical improvement was noted in this case study.

In addition to fearful and withdrawn children, modeling procedures have been used for the reduction of anticipatory anxiety and fear in children about to undergo hospitalization or surgical procedures. Based on an early study by Melamed and Siegel (1975), in which children undergoing surgery were shown a film depicting a child who gradually comes to cope with his fears of an operation, a host of studies have been conducted (e.g., Melamed et al., 1980; Peterson et al., 1984; Peterson and Shigetomi, 1981). In general, these studies have found that children who were shown films of the preparation and conduct of surgery (in comparison to attention control or no-treatment control group children) were less fearful and posed fewer behavior problems postsurgery. In addition, the number of medical complications and the duration of hospitalization were reduced as well (see review by King, Hamilton and Murphy, 1983).

In sum, modeling procedures have been used frequently and productively in the treatment of anxious and fearful children and adolescents. In addition, a number of studies have begun to delineate specific parameters of modeling that appear to enhance its efficacy. These include the use of models similar in age and sex, the use of multiple models instead of only one model, and the use of coping models (e.g., Bandura and Menlove, 1968; Kornhaber and Schroeder, 1975; Meichenbaum, 1971). These characteristics are reviewed in detail by Graziano et al. (1979), especially as they apply to the treatment of fearful or anxious children. As with systematic desensitization and its variants, modeling-based procedures have received some empirical support for their utility, at least with mild to moderate fears. As noted by O'Leary and Carr (1982), however, most of these studies have been analogue in nature, and the efficacy of these procedures with clinically referred youngsters is in need of additional empirical support. Further, studies comparing modeling procedures with other behavioral procedures, as well as traditional psychotherapeutic ones, are needed.

Operant-based procedures

In contrast to systematic desensitization and modeling, both of which assume that anxiety must be reduced or eliminated before approach behavior will occur, procedures based on principles of operant conditioning make no such assumption. Briefly, operant conditioning refers to a type of learning in which behaviors are altered by the consequences that follow them (Kazdin, 1975). For fear reduction, operant-based procedures assert that acquisition of approach responses to the fear-producing situation is sufficient and that anxiety reduction, per se, is not necessary. This model most forcefully calls for a thorough assessment of the positive and negative reinforcing stimuli that produce or maintain anxious and fearful behaviors (Ayllon, Smith and Rogers, 1970; Hersen, 1970).

Operant-based programs have been the most useful in the modification of school phobic behavior (e.g., Ayllon, Smith and Rogers, 1970; Blagg and Yule, 1984; Doleys and Williams, 1977; Hersen, 1970; Kennedy, 1965; Rines, 1973). Illustratively, Ayllon, Smith and Rogers, (1970) treated an 8-year-old girl through a home-based operant approach. Following collection of baseline data in the home and school, a shaping procedure was implemented. The girl was taken to school toward the end of the school day by an assistant who remained with her until school was dismissed. Each successive day, she was taken to school earlier. By the seventh day of this procedure, she was able to remain in school all day. Contingent on each step, the young girl was reinforced by the assistant and her mother. Similarly, Rines (1973) presented a case study in which a school-based contingency management program was implemented with a 12-year-old girl who was described as 'unmanageable' in the school setting. Although she did not refuse to attend school entirely, she made numerous phone calls from school to her mother who invariably made arrangements to have her sent home from school. To reverse this trend, school personnel were instructed not to let her call home, and her teachers were advised as to how to ignore her crying behaviour in the classroom. Additionally, teachers and mother were instructed to reinforce positive behaviors in both school and home settings. On follow-up, she was attending school regularly and achieving satisfactory grades.

Operant procedures have also been used in the treatment of socially avoidant children (e.g., Allen et al., 1964; Clement and Milne, 1967) and children who display mild fears, such as fear of the dark, dogs, riding on school buses, and sitting on the toilet (e.g., Leitenberg and Callahan, 1973; Luiselli, 1977, 1978; Obler and Terwilliger, 1970; Pomerantz et al., 1977). In the Leitenberg and Callahan study, fear of the dark was studied in otherwise normal kindergarten children. Children were assigned to either a treatment or no-treatment group. Following eight sessions of treatment (consisting of practice in staying in the darkened room, feedback, and reinforcement), children in the treatment group were able to stay longer in the darkened room than control children. Obler and Terwilliger (1970), on the other hand, examined the use of reinforced practice and exposure to the fear-producing stimuli in the treatment of neurologically impaired children who were reported to be phobic of dogs and/or riding on a bus. Ten weekly sessions of a five-hour duration each were held. Although aspects of systematic desensitization were present (i.e., exposure to the stimuli was graded and the therapist served as a 'buffer' between the child and the fear-producing stimuli), this study seems best conceptualized as one in which reinforced practice was the active treatment ingredient. In any event, the treatment was effective, at least as ascertained by parent and therapist reports.

In sum, support for the utility of operant-based procedures in the treatment of anxious and withdrawn behaviors in children and adolescents is evident. As with systematic desensitization and modeling, however, this conclusion is based solely on comparisons to no-treatment or waiting-list control conditions. Considerably more comparative evaluations with other behavioral procedures, as well as more traditional ones, are also necessary.

Cognitive-based procedures

According to Ledwidge (1978), a cognitive-based intervention can be defined as a 'treatment approach that aims at modifying behavior and emotion by influencing the client's pattern of thought' (p. 356). In such procedures, an attempt is made to alter specific perceptions, images, thoughts, and beliefs through direct manipulation and restructuring of faulty, maladaptive cognitions. Although a variety of procedures has been described, they all share a common focus: the direct modification of faulty cognitions (as assessed through verbal behavior) in order to produce behavior change. Basically, it is assumed that maladaptive thinking leads to maladaptive behavior. Thus 'self-statements' or 'self-talk' are believed to be perceived by the individual as plausible and logically related to the situation at hand. For example, a child exhibiting intense fear of social evaluation might think, 'If I make a mistake, the teacher and the other kids might laugh at me' and 'I know they think I'm dumb, everyone says so anyway'. These self-statements inhibit the child from emitting appropriate approach responses and, in turn, serve to bolster the child's convictions and reinforce him or her for the avoidant behavior. The presence of self-statements such as these have been clearly identified in the literature. For example, Zatz and Chassin (1983) have documented the cognitions of test-anxious children. Anxious children not only endorse more debilitating statements (e.g., 'I'm doing poorly; I don't do well on tests like this; everyone usually does better than I'), they also ascribe to fewer facilitative, coping statements (e.g., 'I am bright enough to do this; I am doing the best that I can; I do well on tests like this'). Stefanek *et al.* (1987) have affirmed a similar pattern of self-statements in fearful, socially withdrawn children.

Probably the most frequently used cognitive approach with anxious and fearful children is verbal self-instruction training (Graziano and Mooney, 1980, 1982; Graziano *et al.*, 1979, Kanfer, Karoly and Newman, 1975). In the first laboratory application of this approach, Kanfer, Karoly and Newman, (1975) treated 5- to 6-year-old children who were afraid of the dark. Three groups of children were formed. The first group rehearsed active control or competence-mediating statements (e.g., 'I am a brave boy (girl) and I can handle the dark'); the second group rehearsed statements aimed at reducing the aversive quality of the stimulus situation itself (e.g., 'The dark is not such a bad place to be'); and the third group rehearsed neutral statements (e.g., 'Mary had a little lamb'). When later exposed to a darkness tolerance test, both the competence and stimulus groups surpassed the neutral instruction group in duration. The competence and stimulus groups did not differ significantly from each other, suggesting that adaptive statements were acquired under both conditions.

Subsequent to this laboratory study, Graziano and his colleagues conducted a series of studies with clinically phobic children (Graziano and Mooney, 1980; Graziano *et al.*, 1979), including a two- to three-year follow-up (Graziano and Mooney, 1982). Forty children between 6 and 13 years of age were treated. The children were severely nighttime fearful, displaying panic behaviors (e.g., frequent crying and frightened calling out to the parents) that had disrupted the families nearly every night for a mean of five years. Children were randomly assigned to the treatment and waiting-list control group. The treatment rationale, illustrative of the cognitive approach, was as follows:

> All of you have told us you are afraid of the dark or of being alone. As you know, some kids are afraid in the dark and others are not. The main difference between you and those other kids who are not afraid is that those other kids know how to *make* themselves not be afraid. In this class, we are going to teach you how to make yourselves less afraid. We are going to teach you how to relax, *think pleasant thoughts*, and *say special words*, all of which will help you become braver (p. 209, italics added).

Results clearly attested to the efficacy of this approach. Significant changes were noted for the treatment group on a host of variables including number of minutes to get in bed and time to fall asleep, self-reported willingness to go to sleep, and proportion of days that delay tactics (e.g., ask for water, light on) were used. Following treatment the waiting-list group was also treated. In total, 39 of the 40 children showed significant change in behavior as judged against a strict criterion: ten consecutive nights of fearless nighttime behaviors. Long-term follow-up information was obtained two to three years after treatment from 34 of the 40 families using a mail questionnaire and extensive telephone contacts. Maintenance of improvement was noted for 31 of the 34 children.

Unfortunately, this clinically significant study included three shortcomings: *first*, treatment was not solely cognitive in nature, precluding the possibility of evaluating this study as a true test of the cognitive position. Both relaxation training and social reinforcement were used in the treatment phase. *Second*, evidence of the long-term maintenance of the gains would have been more convincing had multiple sources of information been obtained (e.g., child self-report, direct behavioral observation). As it is, the authors relied solely upon parental report. *Third*, an attention-control group was not used, making it difficult to determine whether attention alone might have been efficacious. Recently, Friedman and Ollendick (1989) included an attention-control group in an attempt to systematically replicate the findings of Graziano and his colleagues. Although the sample size was small, findings indicated that at least part of the effects of this treatment package were due to therapist attention variables and reactivity to intervention efforts. Still more recently, we have attempted to disentangle the self-instructional and reinforcement components of the procedure (Ollendick, Hagopian and Huntzinger, in press). Our initial results suggest that the operant components may be more beneficial to younger children and the cognitive components to older children. Nonetheless, the studies by Graziano and his colleagues approach the type of studies that need to be undertaken in order to substantiate the utility of these procedures, as well as others.

Cognitive-restructuring procedures have been used less frequently with children and adolescents. Nonetheless, they too appear to be useful. In a well-controlled single-case study, Ollendick (1979b) demonstrated the use of such procedures with a 16-year-old anorectic male. Initially, systematic desensitization was used and was found to be effective in altering excessive fear of eating and gaining weight. However, its effects were short-lived; and when treatment was withdrawn, substantial weight was lost. In an effort to gain greater control over the youngster's behavior, additional assessment was conducted and revealed that he was frequently observed saying, 'I can't eat, I'll get fat again'. It was hypothesized that this self-statement (along with several similar ones) served to maintain poor eating habits, heightened anxiety, and low body weight. Accordingly, his cognitions were addressed in greater detail. Specifically, the five categories of weight-relevant thoughts proposed by Mahoney and Mahoney (1975) were examined: (a) thoughts about pounds gained ('I've tried to eat that food but haven't gained a pound'), (b) thoughts about capabilities ('There's no way I can gain weight again'), (c) excuses about not gaining weight ('If those other kids liked me, I could gain weight'), (d) thoughts about inappropriate standard setting ('I threw up this morning, there's no use to try. I may as well give up'), and (e) thoughts about how peers would perceive him ('Nobody will like me if I gain weight'). Between treatment sessions, he was asked to self-monitor and record 'self-statements' about these areas. During sessions, this 'homework' was reviewed and his thoughts were 'restructured' to be more realistic and adaptive (e.g., 'If I gain weight, it is true that some kids might not like me. Other kids will like me, however. Besides, what difference will it make whether they like it or not. I will feel better'). With the introduction of cognitive restructuring, weight gain was realized and maintained over a two-year period. It should be noted, however, that treatment was prolonged and that it followed a successful trial of systematic desensitization. Whether cognitive restructuring alone would have been effective is unclear. Certainly, this procedure warrants additional study with children of younger ages and across different anxieties and fears. Kane and Kendall (1989) have recently undertaken just such an analysis for anxious children and found a similar procedure to be effective.

In sum, the new cognitive-based procedures show considerable promise in the treatment of anxious and fearful children. Although initial findings suggest that effects produced in such programs may be long term and generalizable, a clear and well-controlled demonstration of such effects is not yet available (Kendall, Howard and Epps, 1988). As with the other procedures reviewed, considerably more investigation is necessary before use of these procedures can be said to be firmly supported, however.

SUMMARY

In this chapter we have explored the fears and phobias of childhood from a developmental-behavioral perspective and have reviewed a variety of assessment and treatment strategies flowing out of that perspective. Many childhood fears are mild, age-specific, and transitory. However, other fears are more extensive and persist beyond normal developmental periods. These intense fears are labeled phobias, and they present major distress for the growing child. They are in need of systematic assessment and treatment.

We have presented an assessment strategy that is best described as multi-modal. A variety of sources of information is required in order to obtain as complete and accurate a picture of the phobic child as is possible. No one source of information is sufficient nor is one source better than another. For the assessment of children, however, it is always important to keep developmental considerations in the foreground. Some measures may be more useful than others depending on the child's age and cognitive level.

Similar attention to developmental factors must be evident when selecting treatments to reduce clinical fear and phobia in children and adolescents. Standard behavioral procedures need to be altered to take such factors as the age of the child into consideration. We have illustrated this process with treatments based on classical, vicarious and operant conditioning principles as well as information processing strategies and the more recently developed cognitive procedures.

Finally, it should be concluded that although the available assessment and treatment strategies show considerable promise, they are in need of continued refinement, elaboration, and evaluation. For example, little is known about the extent to which treatment strategies are consistent with the coping skills of children and caregivers in their natural environments. A related concern is the long-term effectiveness of behavioral strategies and their ecological validity. Importantly, behavioral strategies are in their own state of childhood, or at best, adolescence. Additional experience with these procedures may help them mature into the sophisticated strategies we need to truly benefit anxious, fearful and phobic youth.

Chapter 19

Acute Pain in Children

CHRISSI IOANNOU

INTRODUCTION

Pain in children has received a considerable amount of attention in recent years, culminating in the arrival of three textbooks (McGrath, 1987; McGrath and Unrah, 1987; Ross and Ross, 1988). The area has been extensively reviewed by several authors (Anderson and Masur, 1983; Bush, 1987; Eland and Anderson, 1977; Jay, 1988; Zeltzer and LeBaron, 1986). Since Eland and Anderson's (1977) review of the medical literature on pain which highlighted the relatively cursory attention paid to childhood pain in contrast to adult pain, there has been increased interest in the problem of pain in children, in both its psychological assessment and management. Much progress has been made regarding procedural pain in children, associated with invasive medical procedures. These involve penetration of tissue or body orifices, for diagnostic or treatment purposes (Anderson and Masur, 1983). Such invasive procedures constitute a significant threat for many children, particularly for children with chronic illness who have to undergo invasive procedures on a regular basis. These procedures often evoke anxiety and fear, which may compound the child's perception of pain. It is not uncommon for children to also develop conditioned generalized anxiety to acute medical situations.

This chapter will focus on acute pain in children and begins with a discussion on the nature of pain and reviews different assessment methods. Psychological interventions are then discussed in relation to the following invasive procedures: surgery, burns, bone marrow aspirations and lumbar punctures, dental procedures, and injections and venipunctures.

THE NATURE OF PAIN

According to the gate control theory of pain (Melzack and Wall, 1965), pain is multidimensional with sensory-discriminative, motivational-affective, and cognitive-evaluative aspects. In the literature pain has been conceptualized as a trimodal behavioural construct involving an interaction of behavioural, cognitive-affective and physiological responses, produced by tissue damage or irritation; however, it may also be produced and maintained by antecedent and consequent conditions (Sanders, 1979). Behavioural (overt) pain responses refer to observable verbal and nonverbal behaviours such as crying, screaming and physical resistance. Cognitive-affective (covert) responses refer to the child's perceptions, imagery and thoughts during invasive procedures. Physiological responses may include autonomic and biochemical reactions, such as elevated blood pressure and heart rate. Assessment and intervention of pain should take into account the interaction of behavioural, cognitive-affective and physiological responses.

ASSESSMENT

Effective management of pain in children depends on accurate assessment (Beales, 1983; Varni, 1983). The major dependent variables assessed during acute clinical situations have been the child's experience of anxiety, pain and distress. These can be very difficult to assess and distinguish and led a number of investigators to use the term 'distress' to refer to both anxiety and pain in acute situations (Jay and Elliott, 1984; Jay et al., 1985; Katz, Kellerman and Siegel, 1980). The relation between anxiety and the sensory components of pain has been reviewed by Sternbach (1968) and Hilgard and Hilgard (1983). Assessment measures are classified according to behavioural, cognitive and physiological responses. These measures are all essential to provide an adequate assessment of pain and anxiety because of the multidimensional nature of pain (Hilgard and LeBaron, 1984; LeBaron and Zeltzer, 1984; Varni, 1983). There is no evidence, however, that any one response system reflects pain more than any other. One difficulty is that measures may not necessarily correlate *between* or even *within* response systems (Jay et al., 1984; Lang, Melamed and Hart, 1970). An example of this discordance between measures would be a child reporting low anxiety or pain by pointing to a happy face, which may be inconsistent with the child's behaviour during the procedure (e.g., crying and screaming). Advantages and disadvantages of self-report and observer ratings have been discussed in the literature (Glennon and Weisz, 1978; McReynolds, 1968) as well as the tendency for observers to rate adolescents' pain lower than the children do themselves (Hilgard and LeBaron, 1982; Winer, 1982) suggesting older children learn to control their overt behaviours although they still feel anxious.

Before considering medical or psychological intervention, it is important to assess the intensity of pain and anxiety: what makes the child's pain better or worse; the child's coping strategies; the meaning of pain; and the social and environmental factors which many influence pain. The choice of assessment methods will depend on the nature of the pain, and whether the data are required for clinical or research purposes. If the latter, multidimensional assessment is recommended. The next section reviews behavioural, cognitive-affective and physiological assessment and the assessment of clinical variables.

Behavioural measures

Three types of techniques have been reported to measure behavioural, overt pain responses: (a) behavioural observation scales, (b) global rating scales, and (c) indirect measures.

Behavioural rating scales

These are the most reliable observation scales for assessing behavioural distress (Jay, 1988). They consist of a checklist of operationally defined behaviours indicative of anxiety and pain (crying, screaming, muscle tension, anxiety and pain verbalized etc.). Observers record the occurrence of these behaviours during a stressful procedure for a specified time and many also rate their intensity. Several scales have been reported in the literature. Venham *et al.* (1980) developed the Anxiety Scale and the Uncooperative Behaviour Scale, both valid and reliable scales, to assess children's behavioural responses in dental settings. Three observational scales have been developed on a paediatric oncology population, to measure distress during bone marrow aspirations and lumbar punctures. Katz, Kellerman and Siegel (1980) developed the Procedure Behaviour Rating Scale (PBRS) which consisted of 25 operationally defined behaviours, later reduced to 13 items. Strong reliability data was reported, but little validity data. Jay and Elliott (1984) and Elliott, Jay and Woody (1987) developed the Observation Scale of Behavioural Distress (OSBD) an 11-item revision of the PBRS which included two methodological refinements: (a) continuous recording in 15-second intervals, and (b) a weighting scale of severity of distress. There were no significant differences in validity measures with or without these methodological refinements. The OSBD was found to be a reliable and valid scale in measuring acute pain in children with cancer (Elliott, Jay and Woody, 1987; Jay *et al.*, 1985; Jay and Elliott, 1984; Jay, Ozolins, Elliott and Caldwell, 1983). LeBaron and Zeltzer (1984) developed the Procedure Behaviour Checklist (PBCL) also based on the PBRS, but consisting of eight behaviours. Although these scales have been developed to measure distress during bone marrow aspirations (BMA's) and lumbar punctures, they would also be useful for assessing procedure related distress during venipunctures, injections and debridement for burns.

Further scales have been developed for children undergoing dental treat-ment (Melamed *et al.*, 1975), bloodtest and pulse assessment (Russell, 1984), surgery (Melamed and Siegel, 1975) and nonmedical situations (Glennon and Weisz, 1978).

The advantages of behavioural scales are that target behaviours or variables can be operationally defined and are reliably observable; also the cost effectiveness of the intervention can be shown by documenting behaviours which affect the efficient running of a clinic (Zeltzer and LeBaron, 1986). The disadvantages are: (1) behavioural checklists do not differentiate between pain and anxiety responses (Sacham and Daut, 1983); (2) behavioural expressions of pain and anxiety reflect a number of individual differences

(Abu-Saad, 1984; Ross and Ross, 1984), which are presumed to indicate distress, but may be adaptive coping responses for some children (Zeltzer and LeBaron, 1986); (3) they are less useful for adolescents who are likely to display fewer overt pain responses (Jay, Elliott and Varni, 1986); and (4) observers' characteristics such as experience and attitude can affect observation scores (Ross and Ross, 1988). Disadvantages of relying solely on a behavioural checklist have been discussed by LeBaron and Zeltzer (1984).

Global rating scales

These are similar to scales used with adults, and enable direct comparisons between observer and child reports (Hilgard and LeBaron, 1982; Katz, Kellerman and Siegel, 1980; LeBaron and Zeltzer, 1984). Commonly used observer scales are based on Likert ratings, for example, on a 1 to 5 continuum (1 = no distress; 5 = extreme distress). These ratings may be used for clinical as well as experimental purposes. Although subjective and gross, several studies have shown high correlations between behaviour observation scales and observer ratings of behavioural distress (Katz, Kellerman and Siegel, 1980; LeBaron and Zeltzer, 1984). Subjective rating scales are discussed in more detail in the section to follow.

Indirect measures

These may include recording behaviours presumed to be indicative of pain or absence of pain. For example, documenting 'well' behaviours such as the time the child spends playing or does not request medication (Fordyce, 1976). These measures may not be reliable, however, as children may play despite experienced pain and may be reluctant to request further medication for fear of needles (Eland and Anderson, 1977). The main difficulty with indirect measures is that there are no behavioural indicators solely accounting for paediatric pain (Ross and Ross, 1988). Behaviours suggestive of pain such as increased or decreased activity may in fact be adaptive coping mechanisms.

Cognitive-affective assessment

Self-report rating scales are the most common approach to assessment of pain (Ross and Ross, 1988) and have varied across studies from impressionistic to quantifiable (Zeltzer and LeBaron, 1986). Self-reports provide information about a child's perception of his or her own pain and anxiety, cognitions, imagery and emotional reactions. Their advantage is of obtaining information from the child who is experiencing the pain (Hilgard and LeBaron, 1982, 1984; Ross and Ross, 1984). Examples of quantifiable scales include visual analogue scales (Abu-Saad, 1984; Abu-Saad and Holzemer, 1981; Varni, Thompson and Hanson, 1987), numerical scales (Hilgard and LeBaron, 1982; Zeltzer and LeBaron, 1982), picture assortment (Lollar, Smits and Patterson, 1982), and questionnaires (Varni, Thompson and Hanson, 1987). Numerical scales are the most frequently reported scales in the paediatric literature. They consist of numbers reflecting increasing severity of pain (or anxiety). There are a number of permutations of these, including the pain thermometer, 'faces' scales and tangible objects such as poker chips. These are noted for their simplicity and clarity. Both the pain thermometer (Jay et al., 1983; Katz, Kellerman and Siegel, 1980) and 'faces' scales (Katz, Kellerman and Siegel, 1982; LeBaron and Zeltzer, 1984; Kuttner, 1984) are the most popular assessment methods used with children (Jay, 1988). The pain thermometer is a visual representation of a thermometer on a numerical scale (0–10, or 0–100) where 0 represents no pain and 10 or 100 represents pain as bad as it can be. The child is asked to indicate on the thermometer how much the procedure hurt. Faces scales usually consist of about five faces representing differing degrees of pain or anxiety, from smiling (no anxiety or pain) to crying (intense anxiety or pain). The child is asked to point to the face which shows how much 'hurting' they felt, or how scared they felt, during the medical procedure.

Although visual analogue scales have often been used with adults, they are also used with children. This scale is simply a vertical or horizontal line with labels at either end such as no pain and severe pain. The child places a mark on the line to indicate the level of pain or anxiety. Variations of this would be a numerical scale (e.g., 0–7) with similar descriptions at either end (Hilgard and LeBaron, 1982, 1984).

Children as young as 5 years can understand and use a rating scale (Zeltzer et al., 1988) with clear instruction and practice (Ross and Ross, 1988) and are able to think conceptually about the differences between pain and anxiety (LeBaron and Zeltzer, 1984). Generally, studies have shown self-report to be valid for children over the age of 6 years (Abu-Saad and Holzemer, 1981; Hilgard and LeBaron, 1982; Jay et al., 1983; LeBaron and Zeltzer, 1984) but problematical and less reliable for younger children. The difficulty is in translating personal experience into visual representations such as those used on a numerical scale, or verbal representations (no pain, mild pain, severe pain) useful in assessing adult pain.

An alternative way of assessing cognitive-affective pain responses is to undertake a cognitive-functional analysis (Meichenbaum, 1976, 1977; Meichenbaum and Turk, 1976). This involves asking the child to report thoughts, images, feelings and fantasies, while imagining a stressful procedure, during the painful procedure itself, or to 'think out loud' during rehearsal. This process can be very helpful in identifying dysfunctional thoughts, misconceptions, and positive and negative coping strategies, which may then be used to plan a psychological intervention. The method may be useful with older adolescents who are able to express themselves verbally but less useful for children.

Other assessment methods reported in the paediatric pain literature include projective techniques (Eland, 1974; Lollar, Smits and Patterson, 1982), use of poker chips to represent pieces of hurt (Hester, 1979), pain colour scales (Scott, 1978; Eland, 1981), and perceptions of pain relating to dimensions of colour, pattern, shape, texture and continuous versus intermittent quality (Scott, 1978). Reliability and validity data are however limited on most of these methods.

Physiological assessment

There is both clinical (Eland and Anderson, 1977) and empirical evidence (Melamed *et al.*, 1978) that physiological responses may be elevated by psychological factors such as fear, pain, expectancy and social reinforcement. Physiological measures which have been found to relate to pain experience include increased pulse rate, systolic and diastolic blood pressure, skin resistance, respiration rate, and muscular tension (Sanders, 1979; Sternbach, 1968). Although physiological measurement is useful in assessing pain and anxiety, there are a number of methodological problems in such assessment which make interpretation difficult. One problem is the variability of response and the individual differences in response elicited by painful stimuli (Sternbach, 1968). Further, the behavioural (overt), cognitive (covert) and physiological systems do not tend to correlate highly with one another and it is not clear which measure most reflects anxiety or pain (Epstein, 1976).

Studies with older children have focused on pulse rate as an index of anxiety during invasive procedures (Jay, Elliott and Varni, 1986; Peterson and Shigetomi, 1981; Shapiro, 1975), however the results are not clear. The Palmar Sweat Index has been found to be a useful measure of anxiety related to surgery and dental procedures (Melamed and Siegel, 1975; Melamed *et al.*, 1978). It involves the use of a plastic impression method that allows measurement of sweat gland activity in the finger (Johnson and Dabbs, 1967). The Palmar Sweat Index can be sensitive to nonrelevant sources of sweat production, such as room temperature, and highlights the problem of extraneous variables in natural clinical environments (Barrios, Hartman and Shigetomi, 1981). Clinical and experimental observations highlight the need for physiological as well as self-report measures for older children and adolescents, who may be highly anxious but do not exhibit their distress overtly (Hilgard and LeBaron, 1982, 1984; Jay *et al.*, 1983). Barrios, Hantmann and Shigetomi (1981) provide a brief overview on physiological assessment in children.

Biochemical assessment of changes accompanying stress and anxiety has been reported in the literature (Mason, 1975; Selye, 1976). There are highly sensitive laboratory procedures (e.g., radioimmunoassays and chromatography) which can measure biochemical variables linked to the neuroendocrine system (Katz, Varni and Jay, 1984). Endogenous opiates (endorphins and encephalins) have been identified as important in pain modulation, acting in pain pathways in the brain and spinal cord (Varni, Katz and Dash, 1982). Although complex, biochemical assessment is relevant in assessing children's reactions to pain and could further our understanding of individual differences in pain response.

Assessment of clinical variables

The assessment of pain in children should take into account clinical variables which may influence coping with invasive medical procedures, such as age and developmental factors, previous experience, parental behaviour, and cognitive coping styles. These variables are discussed in detail by Ross and Ross (1988) and Jay (1988).

Age and developmental factors

Age is an important variable as it is likely to affect the meaning of pain for the child. Younger children have been shown to exhibit more distress than older children during highly painful procedures. For example, Jay *et al.* (1983) found distress levels in children under the age of 7 years were five to ten times higher than older children. This distress is probably due to the meaning of pain for the child, his or her immature cognitive processes and difficulty in understanding cause and effect, which may result in distorted conceptions and misattributions about pain and illness (Simeonsson, Buckley and Monson, 1979; Willis, Elliott and Jay, 1982). For example, some children believe it is possible to bleed to death from bloodtests (Sheridan, 1975), and perceive pain and illness as punishment for bad thoughts and behaviour and transgression of the rules (Perrin and Gerrity, 1981). Children's understanding of illness follows a predictable developmental sequence, consistent with Piaget's stages of cognitive development (Bibace and Walsh, 1980; Perrin and Gerrity, 1981). Chronically ill children's understanding of their illness has not been systematically studied however.

Previous experience

The effects of previous experience are unclear. This issue has been addressed by various investigators regarding children's distress during bone marrow aspirations (Jay *et al.*, 1983; Jay *et al.*, 1984; Katz, Kellerman and Siegel, 1980). The question is whether children habituate or get 'used' to painful procedures over time. Katz, Kellerman and Siegel (1980) reported that children did not habituate to procedures over time. However, Jay *et al.* (1983) did find that children became less distressed over time. Habituation was found to take as long as two years (at least 12 procedures) for children under 7 years. Little is known about habituation to other medical procedures. There is some evidence that burned children show less rather than more tolerance of painful stimuli as their treatment progresses (Savedra, 1976).

Parental anxiety and behaviour

This is an important variable to assess as parental attitudes and expectations may mediate children's perceptions and reactions (Jay, 1988). Parental anxiety and parental presence have been discussed in the literature in relation to children's distress during medical procedures. Jay *et al.* (1983) found parental anxiety was one of three variables most highly predictive of children's distress during bone marrow aspirations. She suggested that children who cope more effectively have parents who do not reinforce pain behaviours, or display their own personal anxiety, who are supportive and expect them to cope well (Jay, 1988). Zabin and Melamed (1980) found children who had lower hospital- and surgery-related anxiety had parents who tended to use modelling, positive reinforcement and reassurance in stressful medical situations. Some studies have provided evidence that parental presence can exacerbate, disinhibit or reinforce children's distress during less painful procedures such as bloodtests and injections (Shaw and Routh, 1982; Gross *et al.*,

1983). Parental presence may conversely be a discriminative stimulus for coping. In a study by Ross and Ross (1984) 99% of 720 children aged 9–12 years, reported that having their parent present was what helped the most, regardless of the type of painful experience. It is unclear what specific parenting behaviours intensify children's responses to medical stressors. It is likely that what is important is what the parent does during the medical procedure. Bush, Melamed, Sheras and Greenbaum (1986) investigated mother–child patterns of coping with anticipatory medical stress and found that mothers who supported their children's coping skills rather than emphasizing emotional expression, had children who coped better. Further research is required examining the effect of parental presence on behavioural, cognitive-affective and physiological responses.

Cognitive style

Assessment of individual coping styles is important before planning an intervention. Most psychological interventions are based on the assumption that preparation is helpful for all children. However, some children become more distressed during preparation and respond by closing their eyes and covering their ears to avoid receiving information about forthcoming stressful procedures (Ross and Ross, 1984). Three cognitive styles have been described in the adult literature which all describe a similar construct: repression-sensitization, (Byrne, 1964), minimization-vigilant focusing (Lipowski, 1970), and monitor-distractor (Miller, 1979). Sensitizers, vigilant focusors and monitors actively seek information, and focus on details and practise coping skills. In contrast, repressors, minimizers and distractors avoid information, use denial, repression and rationalization about the stressful event. The implications of such coping styles for intervention have been discussed by Shipley *et al.* (1978) who suggested extensive preparation for sensitizors and no preparation for repressors, except preparations which would support their defences.

The literature contains only a few studies on coping style in children. Burstein and Meichenbaum (1979) found two classes of 'copers' in children undergoing surgery: a 'low defensive' group who engaged in the 'work of worrying' by playing with stress-related toys before hospitalization; and a second 'high defensive' group who avoided stress-related toys. The low-defensive group showed less distress and better post-surgery emotional adjustment than the high-defensive group. In another study Knight *et al.* (1979) found that children who used a mixed pattern of defences and intellectualization coped better with hospitalization and surgery than children who used denial and displacement. Studies therefore suggest that children who actively seek information are able to cope better with a stressful medical situation (Siegel, 1981; Peterson and Toler, 1986).

Internal-external locus of control is another cognitive dimension (Neuhauser *et al.*, 1978), and refers to a person's perception of whether events are controlled by oneself (internal) or by external forces such as luck and fate (external). Children who have high internal locus of control perceive themselves as being more in control of the healing process (Neuhauser *et al.*, 1978). Jay *et al.* (1983) did not find a correlation between locus of control and children's distress levels during BMAs. Locus of control is one of several variables being assessed by the author in diabetic children and children who have undergone kidney transplants (Ioannou, in progress). Further research is required to investigate coping styles in children, for painful and less painful medical procedures and their implications for psychological intervention.

PSYCHOLOGICAL INTERVENTION

Varni (1983) categorized interventions for paediatric pain into two categories: (a) pain perception regulation methods which involve altering the child's *perception* of pain through self-regulatory processes as hypnosis, guided imagery, meditation, relaxation and biofeedback, and, (b) pain behaviour regulation methods (e.g., contingency management) which identify and modify socioenvironmental factors which may influence pain expression. Pain perception regulation is the primary treatment modality for acute pain in children, while pain behaviour regulation is utilized in the treatment of chronic pain. Interventions are aimed at reducing anxiety as well as pain. Most studies of pain perception have used a combination of techniques which tend to capitalize on children's fantasy and imagery following progressive relaxation or hypnotic induction (Fielding, 1985). The most common interventions described in the literature will be reviewed below in relation to acute pain associated with surgery, burns, dentistry, BMAs, lumbar punctures and injections. These interventions include preparation, hypnosis, behavioural therapy and cognitive therapy.

Surgery

Preparation for surgery or hospitalization has been shown to be effective in reducing pre- and post-surgical distress and post-surgical pain (Melamed and Siegel, 1975). Preparation is a generic term including a range of interventions such as doll play, hospital tours, and modelling films. Its purpose is to provide children with information about the forthcoming medical procedure, encourage emotional expression and establish a trusting relationship with hospital staff (Vernon *et al.*, 1965). It is predicated on the belief that surgery and hospitalization are stressful and painful experiences which may lead to transient or long-term psychological disturbance, especially if the child is not sufficiently prepared (Melamed and Siegel, 1980).

Preoperative instruction is the most frequently used method of preparation for children. It involves helping the child understand the purpose and meaning of the procedure, correcting misconceptions, and helping the child master the experience (Melamed and Siegel, 1975). Preparatory information is either *sensory* or *procedural* (Johnson, Kirchoff and Endress, 1975). Sensory information provides details concerning sensations the child will experience during the procedure, such as smells and kinesthetic awareness. Procedural information describes the steps of the procedure. A combination of procedural and sensory preparation is the most effective (Anderson and Masur, 1983).

Puppet therapy (Cassell, 1965) and play therapy (Dimock, 1960) have been used as preparatory methods for surgery. These techniques enable children to carry out the 'work of worrying' (Janis, 1958), to act out, express their fears, while also providing information about medical procedures.

Research studies investigating preoperative preparation suffer from a number of methodological flaws such as uncontrolled variables and inadequate measurement, which make interpretation difficult (Melamed and Siegel, 1975). Results are therefore equivocal in showing differences between prepared and unprepared children on a number of measures. More controlled and sophisticated outcome studies can be found in the recent literature (Melamed and Siegel, 1975; Melamed et al., 1976; Wolfer and Visintainer, 1975). Many studies demonstrate the efficacy of filmed modelling, which is the most commonly investigated technique, but not the most commonly used procedure (Peterson and Ridley-Johnson, 1980) possibly because practitioners are not in touch with the literature. Findings suggest that regardless of the type of modelling procedure used (filmed, videotaped or puppet) a model is an effective preparation for children (Peterson and Mori, 1988). There is some evidence, however, to suggest this is contraindicated for young 'experienced' children (Melamed and Siegel, 1980; Melamed, Dearborn and Hermecz, 1983) who may be sensitized by viewing modelling preparation (Faust and Melamed, 1984). Melamed and Siegel (1975) conducted a well controlled study on the efficacy of filmed modelling in reducing children's anxiety over elective surgery. Children were shown either a peer modelling film 'Ethan has an operation', or a control — unrelated — film. Children who viewed the model film showed fewer anxiety related behaviours and medical concerns at preoperative and postoperative assessment.

Peterson and Shigetomi (1981) found a combination of coping techniques (deep muscle relaxation, imagery distraction and self-instruction) and filmed modelling to be more effective than modelling or coping techniques alone in preparing children for surgery. Previous work suggests that older children benefit from a longer time interval between preparation and surgery, while younger children benefit from preparation closer to the procedure (Dimock, 1960; Melamed et al., 1976). Wolfer and Visintainer (1975) found any preparation to be better than routine hospital practice although the effects of intervention did not generalize beyond surgery.

Research into preparing children for surgery has largely focused on minor (short stay) surgery such as tonsillectomies. For extensive reviews of this area see McCue (1980) and Peterson and Mori (1988). There is a need, however, to develop methods of preparation for the chronically sick child undergoing surgery. For example, little attention has been paid to preparing chronically ill children undergoing kidney, liver or heart and lung transplants.

Burns

The problem of pain relief for burns has received little attention in the literature (Bonica, 1980). The burned child poses a difficult management problem to hospital personnel. In addition to the pain caused by injury, the child must undergo highly painful treatment of his or her wounds involving hydrotherapy, debridement and dressing changes. Such procedures have been reported as the most painful aspects of hospitalization for burned victims (Savedra, 1976). Burned children do not habituate to these treatments, rather they tend to become less tolerant over time (Savedra, 1976). Factors influencing expectation of pain have been discussed by Beales (1982) and include beliefs about therapy and recovery, and exposure to the sight of instruments and the injured area. Respondent and operant conditioning play an important part in children's pain behaviour (Fordyce, 1976; Varni et al., 1983). The child learns to experience pain in the presence of particular conditioned stimuli.

The experience of pain is often misunderstood by medical staff; physicians' fear of creating addiction in children and lack of knowledge of narcotic analgesics lead to undermedication of children's pain. Perry and Heidrich (1982) surveyed 151 US burn units and found that children were frequently undermedicated even though their level of pain was assessed as being the same as adults (i.e., moderate to severe). Pain was rated as most severe by staff who provided most analgesia before the procedure and by staff who had spent less time on the job.

Crasilneck et al. (1955) first demonstrated the effectiveness of hypnosis in the management of burned victims. The majority of studies, however, consist of a series of case studies rather than controlled research (Bernstein, 1963, 1965; Gardner and Olness, 1981; LeBau, 1973). Wakeman and Kaplan (1978) conducted a methodologically sound study of hypnosis for burns in children and adults and found that children (aged 7–18 years) did significantly better than adults in managing pain regardless of burn size (0–30 % or 31–60 %) and used significantly less medication. Although hypnotic susceptibility was probably the significant predictor variable, it was unfortunately not assessed. Elliott and Olson (1983) developed a stress management programme to reduce distress in burned children undergoing painful treatment of their injuries. The package included the following components: attention-distraction, relaxation, emotive imagery, and reinforcement. The intervention was moderately effective for three of the four children and the presence of the therapist was essential as distress levels increased when the therapist was absent.

Kelly et al. (1984) evaluated a multicomponent behavioural package involving cartoon viewing and star feedback chart in two severely burned children. The results suggested decreases in pain behaviour during physical therapy, but cartoon viewing without the star chart produced only slight decreases in pain behaviour.

Other methods which may be effective for pain relief for burn related pain include filmed modelling and training in specific coping techniques (e.g., Melamed and Siegel, 1975; Peterson and Shigetomi, 1981; Turk, 1978). Modifying the child's beliefs about the healing process and the role of burn treatments, involving the child in therapy and achieving distraction from the pain source, have all been suggested as important in increasing compliance with medical procedures (Beales, 1983). Empirically based treatment of burned children is difficult from a clinical and methodological perspective, as pain responses tend to increase over time such that stable baselines cannot be obtained (Kelly *et al.*, 1984). Other difficulties regarding research include the stressful nature of observing children's suffering, which may partly explain why little research has been conducted in this area (Kelly *et al.*, 1984). For a recent review of children's burns see Miller *et al.* (1988).

Bone marrow aspirations and lumbar punctures

Children with cancer frequently undergo bone marrow aspirations and lumbar punctures (spinal taps), both highly painful and distressing procedures. Studies have shown the behavioural distress associated with these medical procedures is virtually ubiquitous in paediatric cancer patients, particularly in young children (Katz, Kellerman and Siegel, 1980; Jay *et al.*, 1983). These procedures are often perceived as worse than the disease itself. Bone marrow aspirations involve the insertion of a needle into the hip bone (posterior ileac crest) in order to withdraw bone marrow to be examined for the presence or absence of cancer cells. Lumbar punctures are similar and involve inserting a needle into the spinal column, spinal fluid is then withdrawn to be examined for cancer cells. Sometimes chemotherapeutic drugs are injected into the spinal column for therapeutic purposes.

Hypnosis is the most frequently used intervention for acute procedure related distress and pain in paediatric cancer patients. Its efficacy for reducing pain and discomfort has been reported in the literature (Gardner and Olness, 1981; Hilgard and Hilgard, 1983; Zeltzer and LeBaron, 1986; Hart, in press; Ioannou, in press). Imaginative involvement and dissociation are essential components of the hypnotic experience. Some studies which do not refer to their approach as hypnotherapy nevertheless share some features with hypnosis, such as use of imagery. While formal hypnotic procedures have not been reported to be effective with children under the age of 6 years undergoing BMAs and lumbar punctures (Hilgard and Morgan, 1976), older children have been found to be responsive (Kellerman *et al.*, 1983; Zeltzer and LeBaron, 1982). Recently, Kuttner (1988) has provided support for the efficacy of hypnotic pain reduction (story techniques) for children as young as three years old. This work is important as children under age 6 have been documented as being in most need of psychological intervention (Jay *et al.*, 1983).

Katz, Kellerman and Siegel (1980), in a controlled study of 36 children aged 6–11 years, found hypnosis to be more helpful for girls and supportive play to be more helpful for boys. Hilgard and LeBaron (1982) found hypnosis effective in reducing self-reported pain in 24 children undergoing BMAs. Hypnotic treatment was individualized but followed a standard pattern in which rehearsal played a prominant part. For a detailed description of this study the reader is referred to Hilgard and LeBaron's excellent book 'Hypnotherapy of Pain in Children with Cancer' (1984), which also has many case examples.

Gardner and Olness (1981) describe several methods of hypnoanalgesia in their book 'Hypnosis and Hypnotherapy with Children', an excellent and comprehensive text on paediatric problems. The approaches are as follows: (1) direct suggestions — 'just imagine painting numbing medicine on your hand'; (2) distancing suggestions —

'imagine yourself in the mountains'; (3) suggestions for feelings antithetical to pain —
such as relaxation or thinking of the funniest thing that ever happened; (4) distraction
techniques such as story telling; and (5) distracting attention to the pain itself.

Case studies and uncontrolled reports provide support for the efficacy of hypnosis in
reducing procedural anxiety and pain in children with cancer (Ellenberg et al., 1980;
Gardner, 1976; LaBaw et al., 1975; Olness, 1980). The methodological shortcomings of
many reports on hypnosis have been described as follows: (1) objective measures of
distress are rarely used; (2) lack of control groups; and (3) hypnotic procedures are
vaguely specified (Jay, 1988). Two controlled outcome studies have, however, been
reported in the literature (Zeltzer and LeBaron, 1982; Kuttner, Bowman and Teasdale,
1988). Kuttner, Bowman and Teasdale, (1988) reported that imaginative involvement was
most effective for younger children (aged 3–6 years), while older children were helped by
both imaginative involvement and distraction.

Jay and colleagues (Jay and Elliott, 1983; Jay et al., 1985; Jay et al., 1987) developed a
cognitive behavioural package for children undergoing BMAs and lumbar punctures. The
package is partly based on a stress inoculation model described by Meichenbaum (1976)
which involves providing information about the stressful event, teaching coping skills
such as distraction and relaxation, and practising coping skills. The cognitive-behavioural
intervention consists of five components: filmed modelling, breathing exercises, positive
reinforcement, emotive imagery and behavioural rehearsal. The intervention was found
to be effective in reducing behavioural distress in paediatric cancer patients in a pilot
study (Jay et al., 1985) and further validated in a more recent comparative study (Jay et al.,
1987).

Dental procedures

Behavioural interventions for anxiety related to dentistry have been reviewed by several
investigators (Melamed, 1979; Winer, 1982; Siegel, 1988). Three intervention approaches
have been used for dental fear: information approaches, coping skills training and
modelling techniques (Siegel, 1988).

Information approaches

These provide the child with information about the dental procedure such as information
about its purpose, procedural information, sensory information and information about
specific coping strategies (Cohen and Lazarus, 1979). Siegel and Peterson (1980) found an
informative treatment as effective as a cognitive-behavioural one for children with no
previous experience with dental restorations. Children were provided with sensory and
procedural information or taught coping skills including relaxation, pleasant imagery, and
calming self-talk. Compared to a placebo group, both groups showed better adjustment
on behavioural and physiological measures.

Coping skills training

This involves training in the use of self-control procedures (Melamed, Klingman and Siegel, 1984). Perceived control is important as it may influence the level of pain experienced by an individual (Corah, 1973; Thompson, 1981). Nocella and Kaplan (1982) taught coping skills to young children aged 5–13 years with prior dental experience scheduled to have dental restorations or extractions. Coping strategies included identification of anxiety provoking events, deep breathing exercises, muscle relaxation, in vitro desensitization (imagining using coping strategies at next dental visit) and positive self statements ('I'm doing good, I can handle this'). The coping skills group had significantly fewer anxiety related and disruptive behaviours during dental procedures compared to attention-control and no treatment groups. Self-generated coping strategies which children use in response to stressful procedures have received some attention (Curry and Russ, 1985; Hilgard and LeBaron, 1984).

Modelling procedures

Controlled studies support the efficacy of modelling procedures in reducing anxiety related behaviours in children during dental treatment, especially children with no prior experience of the dental setting (Melamed, 1979; Melamed and Siegel, 1980; Melamed *et al.*, 1975; Melamed *et al.*, 1978). Modelling interventions involve observing a live or filmed model coping with a dental procedure. Some studies, however, have not found modelling helpful for children with previous dental treatment or for children who viewed a mastery versus coping model (Ginther and Roberts, 1983) or covert modelling (Chertok and Bornstein, 1979). The efficacy of modelling depends on such factors as the use of coping versus mastery models, previous experience with dental treatment, and age of the child (Melamed, 1979).

Other approaches

Ayer (1973) found imagery effective in reducing injection fears in three children requiring dental extraction. Children held their mouths open and imagined they were barking dogs. They were also reinforced for cooperative behaviour and given control over the procedure. Neiburger (1978) gave suggestions to paediatric dental patients that a teeth cleaning instrument would tickle and make some children laugh. Such suggestions given for limited effect can be helpful and are described in detail by Hilgard and LeBaron (1984). Descriptions of hypnotherapeutic procedures for dental fears can be found in the literature (Crasilneck and Hall, 1975; Gardner and Olness, 1981; Hilgard and LeBaron, 1984).

Injections and venipunctures

Injections are critical and stressful events for most children and are viewed as a bodily invasion (Lewis, 1978). Some investigators noted children perceive injections and venipunctures as the most anxiety provoking experiences in the hospital (Eland and Anderson, 1977; Fernald and Corry, 1981; Poster and Betz, 1983). Medical and injection phobias have not been extensively studied in children. Agras, Sylvester and Oliveau (1969) found a prevalence rate of 14 % of needle phobias in a population of 20-year-olds. No data exists on prevalence of injection phobias in children, but one could expect a higher proportion of children who would be fearful of needles, given their immature cognitive processes and misconceptions about invasive procedures (Willis, Elliott and Jay, 1982).

Prior preparation is the most common method of intervention for injections. Preparations involve some or all of the following: providing information about the procedure, letting the child handle equipment, having the child practise on a doll, introducing the child to medical personnel, and discussion of fears (Jay, 1988). Fernald and Corry (1981) studied empathic versus directive preparations for bloodtests in 39 children aged three to nine years. The empathic group were told 'it's going to hurt a little bit' and 'I don't mind if you cry' while the directive group were told to 'be big, brave, not cry and hold still'. The children in the directive group cried more in anticipation of the needle and many felt the technician had intentionally tried to hurt them. In contrast, Hedberg and Schlong (1973) found children who were not given instructions were more likely to faint or vomit in a mass inoculation clinic, than children who were given stern instructions to 'stand on their feet and not be silly'.

There is little consensus on how best to prepare a child for injections. While preparation is helpful it does not directly teach the child a coping skill (Varni, Katz and Dash, 1982). Techniques used successfully with children include participant modelling, hypnosis, imagery, cognitive-behavioural strategies, and in vivo systematic desensitization (Ayer, 1973; Dash, 1981; Katz, 1974; Poster and Betz, 1983; Rainwater et al., 1988; Ross, 1984). However, empirical validation of these techniques is required. These uncontrolled studies provide a useful source for further research into managing children's anxiety of injections.

Although injections and venipunctures are the most common invasive procedures which children undergo, little attention has been paid to these, particularly in chronically ill children. A three year study of psychological assessment and intervention in diabetic children for acute pain associated with bloodtests is being completed at Addenbrooke's Hospital, Cambridge (Ioannou, in progress). The intervention study is comparing the effectiveness of hypnotherapy versus cognitive behavioural management with a control waiting treatment group. Preliminary results suggest both hypnotherapy and behavioural methods to be helpful for reducing behavioural distress associated with bloodtests.

Ioannou (1988) reported on the efficacy of a cognitive behavioural intervention in reducing acute pain and anxiety during regular bloodtests, following kidney transplantation in ten children aged 4–7 years. The intervention was adapted from Jay et al. (1985) and consisted of four phases: breathing exercises, reinforcement, superhero imagery and behavioural rehearsal.

The preparation was administered shortly before the bloodtest, and lasted approximately 20 minutes. Parents were always present and were encouraged to act as coaches

Figure 15. Gemma, a six-year-old diabetic, practises giving a doll a bloodtest.

during preparation and the procedure itself. (Figures 15a and b demonstrate the behavioural rehearsal component used with both kidney transplant and young diabetic children.) The results of the study showed significant reductions in children's anxiety and pain responses, following a single session, according to both nurse and parent global ratings and a behaviour checklist. Further work is required with a larger group of children to isolate which components are most effective. As doll play features strongly in this intervention, this may be appropriate for hospital play specialists to administer and would be cost effective. The author is currently training playstaff at Addenbrooke's Hospital in these pain management methods to pilot on the children's wards. Further work is required in this area, because of the large number of children who undergo injections and venipunctures for immunization, preoperative sedation and monitoring and treatment of illness.

SUMMARY AND FUTURE DIRECTIONS

This chapter reviewed the literature on assessment and intervention of acute pain in children. The first section addressed the multidimensional nature of pain and its conceptualization as an interaction of behavioural, cognitive-affective and physiological responses. Assessment measures were described to assess behavioural, cognitive and physiological pain responses. Assessment of clinical variables, such as age, previous experience, parental anxiety and cognitive style were also discussed. Psychological interventions for various paediatric pain problems were reviewed. Interventions which have been helpful in reducing children's distress include types of preparation, cognitive-behavioural interventions and hypnosis, but unfortunately few have been empirically validated.

Advances are being made in the area of pain in children, particularly over the last few years. However, much of the controlled work is still in the area of paediatric oncology. Injections and venipunctures are the most common invasive procedures children undergo, yet little attention has been paid to these. Much work remains to be done in developing more sophisticated reliable and valid assessment methods. Controlled outcome studies are required to evaluate the effectiveness of different interventions, and to assess which interventions are most appropriate for which type of children, and under what conditions. Issues of treatment maintenance and generalization also need to be addressed in future studies.

Chapter 20

Work with Children Following Disasters

WILLIAM YULE

SUMMARY

Following major disasters, a high proportion of children experience a number of distressing reactions, including anxiety, fear, depression. Evidence is mounting that many show Post Traumatic Stress Disorder (PTSD) and that without treatment such disorders can last for considerable time. Implications for identification and treatment are discussed.

INTRODUCTION

Just after school started on the morning of 21st October 1966, a huge coal tip slid down a mountainside in Wales and engulfed the primary school in Aberfan, killing 116 children and 28 adults. One hundred and forty-three primary school children survived. Scarcely a family in the tightly knit community was unaffected by the disaster. Offers of help poured in, but plans to study the psychological effects of the disaster were strongly resisted. Lacey (1972) reports how 56 children were treated at the local child guidance clinic over the following four years:

'Symptoms varied but the commonest were sleeping difficulties, nervousness, lack of friends, unwillingness to go to school or out to play, instability and enuresis. Some of the children, too, had shown some of these symptoms before the disaster, but they were said to be very much worse after it. Broadly speaking, the children who were most affected were those with other anxiety creating situations in their backgrounds.' (Lacey, 1972, p. 259).

Some anxious parents became overprotective of their children. Fears of the dark and nightmares caused sleep problems. Bad weather upset the children as a period of bad weather had preceded the tip slide. Children rarely spoke spontaneously of their experiences. Three children played games of 'burying' in the sand.

Twenty-two years later to the day on 21st October 1988, the cruise ship, *Jupiter*, sailed from Athens to take a party of around 400 British school children and their teachers on an educational cruise of the eastern Mediterranean. As they left harbour, it was beginning to get dark. Some of the groups were lining up for the evening meal, some were attending a briefing lecture on what they were to see on the trip. Just out of the harbour, the *Jupiter* was struck amidships by an Italian tanker and holed.

At first, no one realized the seriousness of their predicament, but very quickly the *Jupiter* shipped water and began listing badly to the port and aft. Children were told to assemble in a lounge on an upper deck, but many were unfamiliar with the layout of the ship. As the vessel listed at 45° and then worse, they found it very difficult to get around. Children became separated from friends and teachers. Many were able to jump across to tugs that had come alongside, but sadly two seamen assisting in the transfer were fatally crushed between the ship and the tug. Many children saw their dead bodies.

Other children, some of whom were non-swimmers, clung to the railings on the topmost deck under the lifeboats and had to jump in the water as the *Jupiter* went down, its funnel hissing and spurting out soot and smoke. Children and staff clung to wreckage in the dark oily water until rescued. Some of those swimming in the water were terrified lest they were run down by the rescue craft. It was many hours before it was realized that all but one child and one teacher had survived. After spending a sleepless night on a sister ship moored in Piraeus harbour, the children were flown back to a barrage of publicity the next day. Although the tour company offered to arrange counselling for any of the children who requested it, schools varied enormously in how they dealt with the aftermath. Some were very sympathetic and arranged individual and group help; others wanted to forget the whole episode and discouraged children from even talking about it.

The purpose of this chapter is to examine how far our understanding of the effects of disasters on children has progressed in the 22 years between the tragedy at Aberfan and the sinking of the *Jupiter*. What do we know about the phenomenology of the psychological sequelae? How can we identify those survivors at most risk of developing major problems? What is known about intervention and treatment? It will be argued that it is no coincidence that research was resisted at Aberfan or that some schools tried to put the shutters down after the *Jupiter* sinking. It is now well documented that adults deny the severity of the effects of disasters on children and that problem must be borne in mind when evaluating the evidence presented below.

SOME DISASTERS INVOLVING CHILDREN

There are very few systematic studies of the effects of major trauma on children, and most of the published ones suffer major methodological weaknesses (Garmezy, 1986). Garmezy and Rutter (1985) concluded that following a variety of stressors, ' ... behavioural disturbances appear to be less intense than might have been anticipated; a majority of children show a moderate amount of fear and anxiety but this subsides; regressive behaviour marked by clinging to parents and heightened dependency on adults appears and then moderately mild sleep disturbance persists for several months; a later less severe stressor such as a storm may lead to a temporary increase in emotional distress, although this is variable; enuresis occurs in some cases, while hypersensitivity to loud noises may be evident in others' (Garmezy and Rutter, 1985, p. 162). In their view, severe acute stressors such as occur in major disasters result in socially handicapping emotional disorders in some children, but in the majority of those cases, the disturbances are short lived. Because children tend not to show amnesia for the event, nor to show 'psychic numbing' or intrusive flashbacks, they argue that there is no need for a specific diagnostic category for stress reactions in children parallel to PTSD in adults.

The difficulty with these conclusions is that the studies themselves have rarely dealt with the aftermath of major disasters in which the children have been exposed to life threatening factors. For example, Handford et al.'s (1986) detailed study of 35 children aged 5 to 19 years one-and-a-half years after the Three Mile Island nuclear accident is important in establishing that parents under-report the extent and severity of their children's reactions and in demonstrating that the widely used Quay and Peterson (1979) Behavior Problem Checklist completed by parents is insensitive to the children's reactions. However, it must be seriously questioned whether this is really a study of the effects of a major disaster in that, as the authors put it, Three Mile Island was a silent disaster with no apparent physical damage to people or property, and the children were not separated from their parents during the time of the evacuation that some of them experienced.

Galante and Foa (1986) studied children badly traumatized by the massive earthquakes in a remote mountainous region of central Italy in November 1980. They set up treatment groups for 300 first to fourth grade children who were first rated on an Italian translation of the Rutter (1967) behaviour rating scale for completion by teachers. Many of the predictions relating the teachers ratings to indices of trauma and bereavement were not substantiated in the data. However, the Rutter scales were developed as screening instruments for use in general population studies and were not intended to screen out rare conditions nor can teachers be expected to report on the subjective experiences of the children.

Rutter's screening scales were also favoured by McFarlane in his large scale studies of the effects of the February 1983 bush fires on children in South East Australia (McFarlane, 1987; McFarlane, Policansky and Irwin, 1987). Many teachers were unwilling to participate fully and while McFarlane tried to get repeated measures two, eight and twenty-six months after the fire, the attrition rate in his sample was very high.

In the immediate aftermath of the fire at two months, the children were rated as less disturbed than a comparison group. However, by eight months, both parents and teachers report significant increases in the numbers of children at high risk of psychiatric disorder and these high rates maintained at 26 months. Teachers lagged behind parents in reporting problems and overall the study demonstrates a consistent increase in reported morbidity from eight months after the disaster. McFarlane et al. (1987) concluded that the delayed recognition of problems suggests that many problems do not spontaneously resolve.

In a related paper, McFarlane (1987) reports his investigations of family reactions and functioning and their relationship to children's adjustment. Again keeping the caveats about sample attrition, inappropriate measures and doubts about the strength of the trauma in mind, the questions he poses are very apposite in trying to understand why some children are affected more than others and why some remain affected for longer. He concludes that at the 8 month follow-up. the families showed increased levels of conflict, irritability and withdrawal, with maternal overprotection being quite common. The adjustment of the parents themselves was an important determinant of the adjustment of the children. In particular, he comments that '... families who did not share their immediate reactions to disaster may have had more trouble with their long-term adjustment ... and experienced a greater degree of estrangement'. Equally important, the child's reactions to the fire affected the adjustment of the family, emphasizing the reciprocal interactions among members of a family system.

There are many other, mainly descriptive, studies of the effects of various disasters on children. Terr (1979, 1983) worked with children who were kidnapped in a school bus and imprisoned underground for 27 hours. All the children were badly affected and, despite help, remained affected over four years later. Terr's studies were influential in focusing on such phenomena as distortions in time perception, re-enactment of the trauma in play, and sense of foreshortened future. Among children who survived the bursting of a dam at Buffalo Creek, Newman (1976) noted that many had a precocious awareness of their own mortality and of the fragility of life. Two years after the disaster, Newman (1976) and Edwards (1976) reported considerable disturbance in the children's behaviour.

Bloch, Silber and Perry (1956) reported the effect of a tornado in Vicksburg, Mississippi. Many children played 'tornado games'. Fifty-six out of 183 children who were evaluated showed mild to severe reactions. Frederick (1985) developed a Post Traumatic Stress Reaction Index to study the effects of trauma on children. He reports that 60% of disaster victims, 100% of children who were sexually molested, and 70% of those who were physically abused, showed PTSD as defined by DSM-III. Frederick (1985) describes the adverse effects of the April 1974 tornado on schools in Xenia, Ohio. He also comments on the difficulties in eliciting evidence of 'psychic numbing' in children.

Blom (1986) discusses the effects of the collapse of a pedestrian skywalk on school children who were either on the walkway at the time or who witnessed the accident from the school playground. Thirteen days after the accident, 19 families indicated considerable distress. Four to six weeks after the accident, 17 children (11%) were still noticeably upset; seven months later, only three children were mildly upset. Children mainly showed anxiety about walking near walkways. Boys took longer to recover, and they showed more sleep disturbance, fighting and fears; girls, in contrast, showed more startle reactions and thought more frequently about the accident. Five to 8 year olds seemed less stressed than older children, showing a predominance of phobias and somatic problems; 9 to 12 year olds showed more sleep disturbances, worry about their friends and thoughts about the accident.

Martini et al. (1990) describe the effects of the Pittsburgh Regatta accident on five young children. A power boat went out of control and ploughed into the crowds. These five children were among those hit by the boat. Using Frederick's PTSD Reaction Index, four of the five children aged 3 to 9 years reported scores that indicated the children suffered PTSD, although only three of the children satisfied DSM-III-R criteria. This report is interesting in noting the disagreement in reporting symptoms between parents and children, and in illustrating that even 3 year olds can provide detailed information on their own symptomatology following a trauma, provided that they are asked.

Sugar (1989) describes the seven children aged 3 to 12 years who were traumatized when a Pan Am airplane crashed on their community in Kenner, Louisiana in July 1982, killing 146 people on board and six children and two adults on the ground. Sugar believes that child survivors need individualized treatment post-disaster, but reports no outcome data on treatment.

Frederick (1985) reports data suggesting that 100 % of 50 children who had been sexually abused suffered PTSD. Wolfe, Gentile and Wolfe (1989) go further, and conceptualize the impact of sexual abuse on children in PTSD terms. They make the important point that children will not tell you about their subjective distress until you ask the right questions. When they did just that, they found that sexual abuse victims did not score above the norms on depression and anxiety, but did so on PTSD items, particularly those involving intrusive thoughts about what had happened to them.

Children who are caught up in bloody wars also suffer emotionally and behaviourally. The historical reports of children surviving the London blitz unscathed emotionally, provided they were not separated from their parents, does not accord with recent studies of the effects of local wars on children (Macksoud, 1990; Macksoud, Dyregrov and Raundalen, 1990). Richman, Ratilal and Aly (1990) report their findings on 50 Mozambican children aged 7 to 15 years who had been brutalized by kidnapping or witnessing murder or other atrocities. Forty of the children suffered psychological symptoms related to the war; 25 % were markedly affected. As Richman et al. comment, while such children may well require specialist psychological services to help them readjust, what is really needed is a political solution to end such wars.

Martin and Little (1986) are the only people so far to attempt to assess the effects of a disaster on children's academic attainment. They tried to study the effects of a tornado that devastated part of Wichita Falls in April 1979, but their analysis of school records is difficult to interpret and they made no attempt to obtain direct ratings of the emotional effects on the children.

Pynoos and his colleagues have undertaken among the most systematic studies of children suffering Post Traumatic Stress Disorders following a variety of trauma from witnessing a parent being murdered or raped to themselves surviving an attack from a sniper in their school playground (Pynoos and Eth, 1986; Pynoos et al., 1987; Pynoos and Nader, 1988). To avoid the weaknesses of previous studies, they sampled 159 children (14.5 % of those attending the school) who were exposed to a sniper attack on the school in which one child and a passer-by were killed and 13 other children were injured. Many children were trapped in the playground under gunfire and others were trapped in classrooms. Many were separated from siblings and, of course, parents. The siege lasted a number of hours.

Pynoos and his collaborators used a structured interview to obtain information on the children's reactions and codified this into a PTSD Reaction Index. On average the children were 9.2 years old at the time of the trauma. Nearly 40 % of the children were found to have moderate to severe PTSD approximately one month after the event. A particularly striking finding in this study was the very strong relationship between exposure and later effects in that those children who were trapped in the playground scored much higher than those who had left the vicinity of the school before the attack or were not in school that day.

At fourteen-month follow-up, Nader et al. (1990, in press) report that 74 % of the most severely exposed children in the playground still report moderate to severe levels of PTSD, contrasted with 81 % of the unexposed children reporting no PTSD. Earlier PTSD Reaction Index scores were strongly related to those obtained at follow-up. Nader et al. (1990) found that only among the less exposed children did greater knowledge of the victim increase the strength of the emotional reaction to the trauma. In other words, the level of exposure to the life threatening trauma was more important than other factors such as knowledge of the victim. In this study, the moderating effects of families' reactions was not reported but the strength of the relationships noted challenges McFarlane's (1987) claim that most effects are mediated by parental reaction.

Yule and Williams (1990a) report on children who survived the capsize of the Herald of Free Enterprise in Zeebrugge harbour in March 1987. They assessed 13 of the then known 22 surviving children under the age of 16 years. At six to nine months post accident, over half the children were reported by parents to be showing significant disturbance, while only two of eight children rated by teachers were said to be disturbed. The authors used the Rutter parent and teacher rating scales and, despite the small numbers, concluded that these screening scales were not sensitive to the subjective distress that is the hallmark of PTSD. In interviews, children revealed much more pathology than was known to parents or teachers.

Later, the children completed Horowitz's Revised Impact of Events Scale (Horowitz, Wilner and Alvarez, 1979). Children as young as 8 years found the scale meaningful and it was concluded that the children scored higher than adult patients attending Horowitz's clinic for treatment. At twelve to fifteen months post accident, the children repeated their ratings and it was found that the overall level had scarcely dropped.

Yule and Udwin (in press) offered to help the survivors of the Jupiter at one school. An account of the preliminary, 'debriefing' work is given below. They screened all 24 survivors on three scales — the Impact of Events Scale, Birleson's Depression Scale (Birleson, 1981; Birleson et al., 1987) and the Revised Children's Manifest Anxiety Scale (Reynolds and Richmond, 1978). On the basis of their scores 10 days after the sinking, ten girls aged 14 years were thought to be at high risk of developing problems. When help was offered on an individual or group basis, eight of the ten high risk group came forward for help on the first day. The other two attended the second meeting. Only five others ever attended any group meeting. This was a highly significant relationship between scores on the screening scales and later help-seeking, and the authors conclude that the battery shows considerable promise in identifying children who most need help after a disaster.

Few studies have attempted to use the opportunity to test theories relevant to emotional processing in children or to evaluate different approaches to treatment. Dollinger, O'Donnell and Staley (1984) studied the effects of a lightning strike on 27 soccer players and two spectators all aged 10–13 years. All had been knocked flat by a lightning strike in which one boy was killed and six required immediate medical treatment. The survivors later completed the Louisville Fear Survey for Children (Miller *et al.*, 1972; Staley and O'Donnell, 1984). A respondent conditioning theory of children's fears predicts that ' ... (a) a high-intensity stimulus can result in a conditioned fear, and (b) this conditioned fear can generalize to other similar stimuli' (Dollinger, O'Donnell and Staley, 1984, p. 1028). The investigators found that the children on the soccer field showed more fears of storms than did matched controls, and these fears were more intense. Detailed analyses of their responses showed a clear generalization gradient effect, in keeping with the theoretical prediction, with fears of storms being strongest, followed by fears related to sleep, noise/disasters, death and dying, while there was no effect on fears of people or embarrassment. Thus, Dollinger *et al.* have shown how a carefully conducted study of children who survive a disaster can contribute to our understanding of the conditioning theory of children's fears.

Following on this model, Yule, Udwin and Murdoch (1990) asked all fourth year girls in one school which had had a party of 24 aboard the *Jupiter* when it sank, to complete the Revized Fear Survey Schedule for Children (Ollendick, Yule and Ollier, in press). Effectively, there were three subgroups of girls — those who went on the cruise and were traumatized, those who had wanted to go but could not get a place, and those who showed no interest in going in the first place. However, this latter group could not be considered as an unaffected control group as the whole school was badly affected by the aftermath of the disaster. Accordingly, fourth year girls in a nearby school also completed the fear schedule, along with the depression and anxiety scales.

The girls on the cruise were significantly more depressed and anxious than the other groups five months after the disaster. Indeed, there is a strong suggestion of an exposure/ effect gradient on these two measures, reminiscent of that reported by Pynoos *et al.* (1987). Eleven of the fear items were judged to be related to the sinking and 33 were unrelated. There were no differences across the four exposure groups on unrelated fears. By contrast, on related fears, only the girls who experienced the traumatic events showed a significant increase in reported fears. Thus, the effects of the disaster on children's fears are specific to stimuli present and this provides more confirmatory evidence of the conditioning theory of fear acquisition.

The adult PTSD literature is increasingly full of examples of the successful application of behaviour therapy to reduce intrusive thoughts, startle reaction and phobic and avoidance behaviour. The child literature is so sparse that there appears to be only one published report by Saigh (1986) of the in vitro flooding treatment of PTSD exhibited by a 6-and-a-half-year-old Lebanese boy who had been traumatized by a bomb blast. Two years after the event, he suffered nightmares, intrusive thoughts and avoided areas associated with the bombing. Four scenes were successively worked on in therapy and rapid improvement was obtained in ten sessions, and improvement was maintained over six months. Saigh (1986) notes that earlier attempts to treat other children with systematic desensitization failed, and in this case, each session began with fifteen minutes relaxation followed by 24 minutes of in vitro flooding. This extended exposure to the fear inducing stimuli fits in well with Rachman's (1980) views on factors that accelerate successful emotional processing.

This review of the scattered but relevant literature indicates that after major disasters, a high proportion of children are likely to suffer from a variety of post traumatic stress disorders. As many as 30 to 50 % of children will show significant symptomatology, at least when carefully assessed. Sadly, their problems are not always recognized by their parents and teachers (Earls *et al.*, 1988). The three studies that have followed children over a year post trauma agree in finding that there is only a slow resolution of the problems in that time. Two of the studies find that the initial level of reported distress is highly predictive of later adjustment, and they also report a strong linear relationship between the level of exposure to life threatening situations and subsequent psychopathology. Before going on to consider how services should respond to these identified needs, let us look at the phenomenology presented by children in greater detail, paying particular attention to the question of the developmental changes that may occur in the expression of the distress.

COMMON STRESS REACTIONS IN CHILDREN

Both from the literature reviewed above and from working with children who have survived the capsize of the *Herald of Free Enterprise*, the terrorist attack on the cruise ship, *City of Poros*, the sinking of the cruise ship, *Jupiter*, the crushing disaster at the Hillsborough football stadium, and a variety of other personal trauma of similar life-threatening magnitude, I can now describe more fully some of the commonest stress reactions that children show.

Sleep disturbance Almost all children had major sleep problems in the first few weeks. They reported fears of the dark, fear of being alone, intrusive thoughts when things are quiet, bad dreams, nightmares, waking through the night. Problems persisted over many months. Use of music to divert thoughts helped.

Separation difficulties Initially, most wanted to be physically close to their surviving parents, often sleeping in the parental bed over the first few weeks. Some distressed parents found their clinginess difficult to cope with.

Concentration difficulties During the day, children had major problems concentrating on school work. When it was silent in the classroom they had intrusive memories of what had happened to them.

Memory problems They also had problems remembering new material, or even some old skills such as reading music.

Intrusive thoughts All were troubled by repetitive thoughts about the accident. These occurred at any time, although often triggered off by environmental stimuli — e.g., movement on a bus, noise of glass smashing, sound of rushing water, sight of tables laid out like the ship's cafeteria. Thoughts intruded when they were otherwise quiet.

Talking with parents Many did not want to talk about their feelings with their parents so as not to upset the adults. Thus, parents were often unaware of the details of the children's suffering, although they could see they were in difficulty. There was often a great sense of frustration between parents and children.

Talking with peers At some points, survivors felt a great need to talk over their experiences with peers. Unfortunately, the timing was often wrong. Peers held back from asking in case they upset the survivor further; the survivor often felt rejected.

Heightened alertness to dangers Most were wary of all forms of transport — not willing to put their safety into anyone else's hands. They were more aware of other dangers. They were affected by reports of other disasters.

Foreshortened future Many felt they should live each day to the full and not plan far ahead. They lost trust in long-term planning.

Fears Most had fears of travelling by sea and air. Many had fears of swimming, of the sound of rushing water.

Irritability Many of the children found themselves much more irritable than previously, both with parents and peers. Some found that they got much more angry than before the disasters.

Guilt 'Survivor guilt' has long been discussed as a paradoxical reaction following a disaster. Inexplicably, this symptom, so characteristic of post traumatic disorders, is not considered in DSM-III-R although it was regarded as a central feature of the earlier definition. Child and adolescent survivors often feel guilty that they are alive when others have died. They feel guilt that they might have done more to help others during the disaster. Less frequently discussed, but present nevertheless, they sometimes also feel guilty about things they did during the crisis in order to survive. Guilt has been a particularly strong theme among adolescents surviving the *Jupiter* sinking.

Depression As noted earlier, adolescents from the *Jupiter* report significantly higher rates of depression than do controls of the same age. Whilst those figures refer to self-report on questionnaires, similar findings are confirmed on detailed clinical interviews. A small, but significant number of children became clinically depressed and some had suicidal thoughts and even took overdoses in the year after the accident.

Bereavement Particularly in the *Herald of Free Enterprise* disaster, a number of children were bereaved and no treatment plan could ignore the children's grief. Bereavement reactions complicate the presenting picture of symptoms, but must be attended to.

Anxiety and panic A significant number of children became very anxious after the accidents, although it is our impression that the appearance of panic attacks was sometimes considerably delayed. Usually, it is possible to identify stimuli in the child's immediate environment that trigger off panic attacks, hence the need to get very detailed accounts of the impact of the trauma on all the child's senses.

These commonly occurring symptoms are almost identical with those recognized by the American Psychiatric Association in its Diagnostic and Statistical Manual, 3rd Edition Revised (APA, DSM-III-R, 1987) as comprising Post Traumatic Stress Disorder. The defining characteristics of this are: persistent re-experiencing of the traumatic event in thoughts or dreams; persistent avoidance of stimuli associated with the trauma; and a variety of signs of increased physiological arousal such as sleep disturbance and difficulty in concentration. It should be noted that there is not complete agreement on how best to define PTSD, especially as it manifests in children. Indeed, the World Health Organization in its International Classification of Diseases, 10th Edition (WHO, ICD-10, 1988) regards numbing of affect as a frequent but not necessary component of PTSD.

There is now no longer any doubt that significant proportions of children are emotionally upset by major, life-threatening trauma. Such reactions are not simply mild adjustment reactions, but persist in many cases for two to four years or more, significantly interfering with children's social and emotional adjustment. Children from 8 years upwards display a syndrome that is virtually identical to that described as PTSD in adults. Some younger children also manifest distress in ways that closely resemble PTSD.

However, research studies at present are in danger of getting into circular arguments. A number of workers are accepting the DSM-III-R criteria as proven as a result of empirical research rather than having been decided on by a committee. They then base a semi-standard interview around these 'criteria' and think they have developed an instrument to measure and diagnose PTSD. As is clear from the above review, children react to disasters in a very varied way and to restrict one's assessment only to the currently official list of symptoms would be to do the children a great disservice. It is far too early to foreclose on descriptions of PTSD or other similar reactions in children.

Many older children and adolescents fear that they are going mad when they begin experiencing intrusive thoughts and the other symptoms listed earlier. They are often frightened by what they see as inexplicable panic attacks. At the first assessment interview or debriefing session, the child psychologist should use the assessment in part as educative and therapeutic. By anticipating some of the child's symptoms and worries and by stressing that other people react similarly, it is then possible to reconstrue many of the presenting symptoms as being normal reactions to a very abnormal experience, one which anyone would have found frightening.

It is vital to obtain very detailed accounts from the child as to the precise manner that each of the senses was assailed during the disaster. Children usually have vivid, but very specific, memories of sights, sounds, smells, movement sensations and so on of the particular disaster. Thus, following the capsize of the *Herald*, children reported being scared when vehicles they were travelling on tilted as they rounded corners.

INDIVIDUAL DIFFERENCES

It is implicit from much of the literature reviewed that there are individual differences in children's reactions to disasters, both in who develops significant reactions and, having done so, how quickly they improve or respond to treatment. Unfortunately, these have not been formally studied.

Developmental perspectives are discussed more fully elsewhere (Yule and Williams, 1990b). While young children's lack of cognitive development may protect them from understanding the extent of the life-threatening nature of disasters, on the other hand it also hinders their ability to make sense of what happened to them, particularly if parents and other adults do not discuss it with them. Parents find it hard to talk to children about what happens in a major disaster, and teenagers find it hard to confide in parents. Often, they fear that they will upset their parents by discussing it, especially if the parents were also involved and distressed.

The evidence on the specificity of fears fairly clearly indicates that children do suffer direct effects of disasters. Some writers (Bloch, Silber and Perry, 1956; McFarlane, 1987) have stressed the indirect effects of disasters and argued that such children's reactions as there are are mediated by effects on parents. Clearly, where parents are themselves adversely affected, this will impair their ability to cope with the children's reactions. Parents may convey some of their own anxieties to their children. Thus, in trying to understand what factors make some children more vulnerable than others, and, conversely, what factors act as protection against the effects of the disaster, family functioning needs to be considered.

Rachman (1980) summarizes those factors that make for difficulties in processing emotions engendered by traumatic events. Although his theory addresses emotional processing in adults, it is a useful guide to understanding how children may also be affected. Thus, the personality factors that he associates with difficulties in emotional processing are neuroticism, introversion and a sense of incompetence. While not yet tested empirically in relation to major disasters, there are good grounds from related research to expect these factors to operate in children as well.

TREATMENT

Beverley Raphael's (1986) book, 'When Disaster Strikes' is an excellent introduction to the whole area of disasters and their emotional aftermath. Unfortunately, little is written about treating child survivors. In many cases of natural disasters — flooding, fires, tornadoes, earthquakes — people emphasize the need to facilitate the rebuilding of the community, to treat people in groups in which children can participate. In the case of mass transport disasters, there is no natural group and with survivors scattered over thousands of square miles, it is difficult to get useful groups established. In the case of school journey disasters, there are clear groups to work with. So what work needs to be done?

In the immediate aftermath, children usually need to be reunited with their parents and family. Even teenagers may go back to sleeping in their parents' bed. Tolerance and understanding are called for. Survivors need to talk over what happened so as to get the sequence of events clear in their minds as well as to master the feelings that recall engenders. Repetitive retelling is not enough alone. Professionals can help by creating a relatively safe environment in which such recounting can take place. Experiencing that the world does not come to an end when feelings are shared between parent and child can be very facilitating. Learning that other survivors share similar, irrational guilt about surviving can help to get things in perspective. Learning how to deal with anxiety attacks, how to identify trigger stimuli, how to take each day as it comes — all are important therapeutic tasks.

However, these things should not be left to chance. Mental health professionals are rapidly learning that formal psychological debriefing can help adult victims of disaster (Dyregrov, 1988). Yule and Udwin (in press) describe debriefing girls who survived the sinking of the *Jupiter* suggesting that this can also be helpful with teenagers.

Ten days after the accident, they met with the teachers, the pupils, and many of the parents initially in separate groups throughout an afternoon. The pupils were encouraged to describe and share their reactions, and by anticipating some of these, the therapists were able to emphasize that the reactions were understood and were normal reactions to an abnormal experience. At the end of the afternoon, the pupils and parents were brought together to share publicly some of their feelings. Hopefully, that gave permission for such discussions to take place more readily at home. Subsequently, the more seriously affected girls were seen in small groups to treat more specific fears, panic disorders and depression.

Whereas most professionals who have worked with recent disasters are convinced of the value of early debriefing, there is little published evidence to support this claim. There are differences of opinion about when such debriefing of victims should take place, with a consensus emerging that during the first 48 hours or so most survivors are too numb to benefit from such intervention. Somewhere around seven to fourteen days after the disaster seems right, but again there have been no studies of this. Again, one must assume that there are individual differences in response to debriefing and that not all children will benefit to the same extent or to intervention at the same point in time.

Rachman (1980) lists a number of factors that promote emotional processing after it has got stuck following a disaster. Relaxation figures prominently, as does a low level of arousal. Presentation of distressing scenes should be both vivid and long, the very characteristics that most adults in the child's everyday surroundings shy away from. Agitated rehearsals which stress a lack of coping skills only make things worse. Where distressing scenes are badly organized or presented too briefly, as may happen when a child spontaneously tells an adult what happened, this is likely to be associated with poor recovery.

Saigh's (1986) flooding treatment proved very successful, but longer exposure sessions than normal were needed. Ayalon (1988) provides sensible suggestions culled from a variety of theoretical perspectives. She emphasizes the need to help children make sense of what happened to them and to gain mastery over their feelings. To this end, many practitioners agree that children should be treated in small groups. They should be asked to write detailed accounts of their experience and be helped to cope with the emotions that brings up. They should be given specific treatment for fears, phobias and any other avoidant behaviours. Given that intrusive thoughts seemed worse at night just before dropping off to sleep, many children have been advised to use portable tape-recorders to play music to distract them and blot out the thoughts. With better sleep, they were better able to face the thoughts in the safety of daylight.

Yule and Williams (1990b) describe some of the difficulties encountered in engaging children and parents who survived the *Herald of Free Enterprise* sinking. The groups they ran were open to any survivor to attend and met initially at monthly intervals over about one year, tailing off to every 6 to 8 weeks thereafter. They seem to be drawing to a natural close some three years after the disaster. The children appreciated an opportunity to share their feelings with others who had been there, without having to explain everything to outsiders. They took advantage of the cognitive-behavioural, problem-solving approach whereby efforts were made to help them identify things they were finding difficult, to place these within a framework that suggested that most of the problems were understandable reactions to abnormal circumstances, and to use the resources of the group to develop solutions to the identified problems. The therapist working directly with the children also acted as a go-between with the parents' group.

The parallel group with parents had the dual task of addressing the parents' and other relatives' own distress as well as discussing how best they could support the children. As with the children, the adults were very supportive of each other and the group quickly became very cohesive. Two years after the disaster, it was deemed appropriate to organize a group crossing of the channel by ferry. Two weeks before the due date, in September 1989, the pleasure boat, *Marchioness*, sank in the Thames with considerable loss of life. Not surprisingly, most of the families called off and only one family crossed to Calais. The ferry company were very sensitive to the family's needs and the trip was very successful. The ten-year-old who had previously been unable to face up to a crossing showed some signs of anxiety but was quickly calmed by his parents and the welfare officer. He felt a great sense of achievement at the end of the day.

As children spend a great deal of their life in school and as some disasters involve schools directly, it is important that school personnel are better advised and supported in dealing with child victims. It is understandable that many teachers wish to underplay the effects of disasters on children, but such denial can often add to the children's burdens. It is clear that many post disaster problems manifest at school and so teachers need support from mental health professionals to ensure that they can cope with these problems.

It is possible to identify high risk groups at an early post trauma stage, and the scores of high risk groups on measures of distress remain remarkably stable over a one year period (Nader *et al.*, 1990; Yule and Udwin, submitted). Thus, even at present, it is possible to do some screening and ensure that services are delivered to the most needy.

Health, education and social services should cooperate in planning the best use of increasingly scarce resources to deal with the emotional aftermath of disasters involving children. This does not mean that all personnel should be trained at a high level of readiness for a disaster that never happens, but rather that lines of responsibility are clearly identified before the fateful event. All personnel, from whatever background, should be trained to screen for serious problems and know when to refer on. Clinical child psychologists will be among those coordinating treatment and dealing with complex cases.

Although the foregoing has rather emphasized how much we do not know about the effects of disasters on children, I would like to finish by emphasizing how much we do know in treating children — how many skills clinical child psychologists have that are very relevant.

Firstly, we know how to talk with children and the value of this must not be underplayed. In my experience, the initial diagnostic interview is often the first time that anyone has sat down with the child to allow them to talk at length about what happened and how they feel about it. Secondly, with children who are anxious, we have a whole armamentarium of techniques for inducing relaxation and reducing anxiety. These can be applied in both individual and group settings. Thirdly, we can liaise with schools and families to help them better support the children in everyday life.

It stands to reason that if a child is having difficulty sleeping over many months, then that child will find coping in the daytime more problematic. Hence, it is vital to tackle sleep problems early on. A careful analysis will reveal whether the problem is mainly one of getting off to sleep or in waking because of intrusive nightmares related to the disaster. In the former case, implementing relaxing routines before bed and masking thoughts with music may help. In the latter, there are now some promising cognitive behavioural techniques for alleviating nightmares.

Palace and Johnston (1989) successfully treated a long-standing nightmare in a 10-year-old boy who had been traumatized by two separate accidents involving motor cars. They combined relaxation and systematic desensitization with teaching positive self-coping statements with story line alteration. This latter component has previously been used successfully with adults (Halliday, 1987; Marks, 1978, 1987) and consists, in essence, of getting the patient to recount the dream with a different, happy ending. Palace and Johnston's (1989) dream reorganization package worked very well with the boy who ceased having nightmares altogether and remained symptom free at six-months follow-up. Clearly, this approach, which has theoretical underpinnings in Seligman and Yellen's (1987) theory of dream construction, offers considerable promise to all who have to treat the frightening nightmares of children who survive disasters.

DISCUSSION

Children are the victims of both major and individual disasters, and it is now clear that such traumas have wide ranging and relatively long lasting effects. The work of the past few years has improved the ability of psychologists to assess these effects and it is now possible to screen victims of major disasters and be reasonably confident that one can identify high risk groups. Once the particular phenomena are identified, it becomes more obvious that psychologists already have many techniques which can help alleviate distress.

Having said that, it is still important to recognize just how distressing such work can be. When children have witnessed their parents being sucked out of portholes to a certain death, but a death that was not confirmed for many weeks, or where they were dumped in the sea thousands of miles from their loved ones at home and did not know for hours whether they would survive, such distress is difficult for professionals to cope with. It is important that all who get involved in disaster work have adequate support themselves.

Many psychological questions remain unanswered, but the work summarized above highlights some of the main issues. The question of clarifying the phenomenology is clearly posed. Individual differences, factors of vulnerability and resilience, continuities and discontinuities of psychopathology over time — all these areas call out for careful investigation. That sort of study is now feasible because useful measures are now beyond the pilot stage. Above all, we now need more carefully controlled treatment studies, both of individual cases and of groups.

Many of the recent advances have grown out of a fruitful collaboration between clinical psychologists and lawyers representing the survivors who were suing for compensation. Any clinical child psychologist entering this field is likely to get involved in such legal work. This is not the place to detail the different ways that the law and psychology has in considering the whole question of the emotional effects of disasters. These issues are considered elsewhere (Yule, 1990). Preparing an assessment in a litigation case sharpens one's thinking considerably and this has benefits both for the client and for our understanding of the effects of disasters on children.

ACKNOWLEDGEMENTS

I should like to thank my colleagues in the psychology department of the Institute of Psychiatry who have shared with me the task of assessing the survivors. My thanks are also due to the solicitors who referred the clients and took the initial load of obtaining written statements. But, above all, I should like to thank the survivors themselves for agreeing to allow me to use this material in order to advance all our understanding.

Appendix I

Recording and Assessment

(1) MONITORING CHANGE

Without an objective assessment and record-keeping system, it is not possible to evaluate accurately and reliably the progress made by the child (or parent) in the therapeutic situation. It is clear that many children's problems are transient and change can occur often as a function of time and non-specific placebo effects. For these reasons, a controlled evaluation of the therapeutic process is essential. Objective data make possible two important goals: determining whether a child in treatment is changing, and the direction and extent of change. They also make possible an assessment of the relationship between different kinds of intervention within the overall therapeutic programme. Intrasubject ($N = 1$) and control group research designs provide the means to fulfil these objectives (Herbert, 1990; Morley, 1989). An example of a typical record of treatment is displayed in Figure 16.

(2) ASSESSMENT/DIAGNOSIS

A large variety and number of methods have been employed to assess children's level of developmental and behavioural adjustment:

(a)   questionnaires or checklists;
(b)   structured or unstructured interviews;
(c)   structured and unstructured observations.

The contributors to these assessment methods include parents, teachers, peers, siblings, children, and clinicians — all potentially valuable sources of information. The context of assessment may vary from naturalistic observations to structured play situations in laboratory or clinical settings.

In a review of assessment issues in child psychopathology, Achenbach (1978) concluded that the most accurate observations of children's behaviour are related to the context in which they were made. Parental reports, based on either interviews or

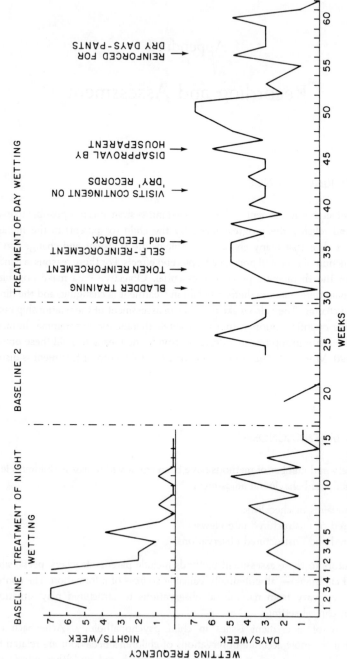

Figure 16. A typical ABC design graph. Elizabeth aged 10 years. Frequency of nocturnal and of diurnal enuresis.

questionnaire responses, constitute the primary source of clinical and research information about children's behavioural attributes.

Observational techniques have also been developed for the assessment of individual children (e.g., Johnson and Bolstad, 1973) or parent–child interactions (e.g., Browne, 1986; Dowdney *et al.*, 1984; Martin and Beezley, 1977). Bates and Bayles (1984) are of the opinion that parental reports of children's behaviour consist of objective, subjective, and error components. They found support for an objective component through significant mother-father and parent-observer convergences in ratings of children's behaviour. Moderately high inter-parental correlations are found in most studies in the literature. Maternal reports of children's behavioural dysfunction have been found to exhibit higher congruence with clinician's ratings in structured play sessions than paternal reports (Earls, 1980).

In a meta-analysis of 119 studies, Achenbach, McConaughy and Howell (1987) examined the degree of consistency between different informants (parents, teachers, observers, peers, self) on ratings of children's behavioural and emotional adjustment. They found mean correlations of around 0.6 between similar informants (e.g., pairs of parents) and 0.28 between different types of informants (e.g., parent-teacher). There were generally higher levels of agreement for the younger group, and for undercontrolled than for overcontrolled problems.

Achenbach and his colleagues suggest that variations in assessment between different informants can be viewed as a function of different experiences with children, and that multiaxial assessments could account for situational variability in children's behaviour.

The form of any assessment approach involves some important assumptions about behavioural attributes. Behaviourally orientated psychologists tend to view behaviours with, say, aggressive or anxiety attributes, as instances or samples of response classes rather than as outward and visible signs of internal or underlying dispositions. The language of personality, to the extent that it is used by behaviourists, is employed descriptively rather than inferentially. Conventional trait attributions are thought by critics to represent nothing more than giving two names to the same class of behaviour. Thus, if a child is seen to hit another child, there is no reason to infer that the child who does the striking is not only aggressive but also has a 'need for aggression'. Behaviours with aggressive attributes would be classified in terms of their frequency, intensity and duration. Diverse attributes would be considered to be members of the same response class if it could be shown that such attributes enter into the same functional relationships with antecedent, concurrent and consequent stimulus conditions, rather than because they co-exist or co-vary in a group of persons. Wiggins (1973) notes that:

> ... issues of stability and generality become empirical questions rather than assumptions. Given a change in stimulating conditions, particularly conditions of reinforcement, the frequency, intensity, or duration of the response class of interest should be predictable from a knowledge of the functional relationships between these attributes and the stimulus conditions which control them. Under these circumstances, it is more important to determine whether or not an individual is capable of performing a response, rather than trying to estimate the typical or characteristic level at which he responds.

Because of research demonstrating the relative independence of the three major systems involved in human functioning: cognitive (subjective), motor, and physiological, a comprehensive assessment should target in on all of them (see page 48).

Measures (Most chapters, particularly those in Part 6, detail specialized tests and techniques)

Below is a *small* cross-section of instruments (and reviews of assessment measures) which have been applied to particular disorders:

Anorexia Nervosa

Garner, D. M., Olmstead, M. P., and Polivy, J. (1983). Development and validation of a multidimensional eating disorder inventory for anorexia nervosa and bulimia. *International Journal of Eating Disorders*, **2**, 15–34.

Anger

Finch, A. J., and Rogers, T. R. (1984). Self report instruments. In T. Ollendick and M. Hersen (eds), *Child behavioural assessment*. New York: Pergamon.

Attention deficit with hyperactivity

Abikoff, H., Gittelman, R., and Klein, D. F. (1980). Classroom observation code for hyperactive children: A replication of validity. *Journal of Consulting and Clinical Psychology*, **48**, 555–565.

Barkley, R. A. (1982). Specific guidelines for defining hyperactivity in children. In B. Lahey and A. Kazdin (eds), *Advances in clinical child psychology* (Vol. 5). New York: Plenum.

Douglas, V., and Peters, K. (1979). Toward a clearer definition of the attentional deficit in hyperactive children. In G. Hale and M. Lewis (eds), *Attention and the development of cognitive skills*. New York: Plenum.

Ullmann, R. K., Sleator, E. K., and Sprague, R. L. (1984). A new rating scale for diagnosis and monitoring of ADD children. *Psychopharmocology Bulletin*, **20**, 169–177.

Werry, J., Sprague, R., and Cohen, M. (1975). Conners Teacher Rating Scale for use in drug studies with children — An empirical study. *Journal of Abnormal Child Psychology*, **3**, 217–229.

Conduct/antisocial/disruptive behaviours

Achenbach, T. M., and Edelbrock, C. (1983). *Manual for the Child Behavior Checklist and Revised Child Behavior Checklist*. Vermont: Queen City Printers.

Mann, R. A. (1976). Assessment of behavioural excesses in children. In M. Hersen and A. S. Bellack (eds), *Behavioural assessment: A practical handbook*. New York: Pergamon.

Quay, H. C. (1983). A dimensional approach to behavior disorder: The Revised Behavior Problem Checklist. *School Psychology Review*, **12**, 244–249.

Fears and phobias (see Chapter 16)

Depression

Boyle, G. J. (1985). Self-report measures of depression: Some psychometric considerations. *British Journal of Clinical Psychology*, **24**, 45–59.

Cytryn, L., McKnew, D. H., and Bunney, W. E. (1980). Diagnosis of depression in children: A reassessment. *American Journal of Psychiatry*, **137**, 22–25.

Kazdin, A. E. (1982). Self-report and interview measures of childhood and adolescent depression. *Journal of Child Psychology and Psychiatry*, **23**, 437–457.

Kovacs, M., and Beck, A. T. (1977). An empirical clinical approach toward a definition of childhood depression. In J. G. Schutterbrandt and A. Raskin (eds), *Depression in childhood*. New York: Raven Press.

Nowicki, S., and Strickland, B. R. (1973). A locus of control scale for children. *Journal of Consulting and Clinical Psychology*, **40**, 148–154.

Saylor, C. F., Finch, H. J., Spirito, A., and Bennett, B. (1984). The children's depression inventory: A systematic evaluation of psychometric properties. *Journal of Consulting and Clinical Psychology*, **52**, 955–967.

Seligman, M. E. P., and Peterson, C. (1986). A learned helplessness perspective on childhood depression: Theory and research. In M. Rutter, C. E. Izaro and P. B. Bead (eds), *Depression in young people*. New York: Guilford Press.

Mental handicap

Kazdin, A. E., and Straw, M. L. (1976). Assessment of behavior of the mentally retarded. In M. Hersen and A. S. Bellack (eds), *Behavioral assessment: A practical handbook*. New York: Pergamon.

Pervasive developmental disorder

Parks, S. L. (1983). The assessment of autistic children: a selective review of available instruments. *Journal of Autism and Developmental Disorder*, **13**, 255–267.

Social competence

Dodge, K. A., and Murphy, R. R. (1984). The assessment of social competence in adolescents. *Advances in Child Behavioral Analysis and Therapy*, **3**, 61–96.

Greenwood, C. R., Walker, H. M., Todd, N. M., and Hops, H. (1979). Selecting a cost-effective screening measure for the assessment of preschool social withdrawal. *Journal of Applied Behavior Analysis*, **12**, 639–652.

Jessness, C. F. (1972). *Manual for the Jessness Inventory*. Palo Alto, CA: Consulting Psychologist Press, Inc.

Michelson, L., Andrasik, F., Vucelic, I., and Coleman, D. (1981). Temporal stability and internal reliability of measures of children's social skill. *Psychological Reports*, **48**, 678.

Rathus, S. A. (1973). A 30-item schedule for assessing assertive behavior. *Behavior Therapy*, **4**, 398–406.

Van Hasselt, V. B., Hersen, M., and Bellack, A. S. (1981). The validity of role play tests for assessing social skills in children. *Behavior Therapy*, **12**, 202–216.

Walker, H. M. (1976). *Problem Behavior Identification Checklist*. Los Angeles, CA: Western Psychological Services.

(3) PSYCHOMETRIC TESTING

To test or not to test; that is the question faced by clinical child psychologists, especially when it comes to the issue of assessing I.Q. It has been, and remains, a controversial issue. Part of the problem is that people (including some psychiatrists) tend to equate assessment with psychological tests only; tests designed to measure anything and everything from brain damage and maladjustment to personality atributes such as extraversion, self-esteem and fantasy life.

Anastasi (1982), doyenne of writers about psychometrics, defines a psychological test as 'essentially an objective and standardized measure of a sample of behaviour'. Tests of intelligence, personality and academic achievement in children are *standardized* on the assumption that the tester will be able to make comparisons between the child being tested and the sample of children on whom the test was developed. The conditions and procedures by which the test is administered, scored and interpreted are held constant for all test-takers. Such tests are called 'normative' and such comparative approaches are referred to as 'nomothetic'.

There have been debates about the extent to which tests measure *traits* and *states* which are generalized attributes, stable across time and situations, or *situational*, the person varying in his or her behaviour depending upon different contextual factors or situations (see Mischel, 1968). Rejecting polarized positions are the *interactionalists* (e.g., Bowers, 1973) who propose that people do manifest trait characteristics that determine their behaviour, but that situations always exert a strong influence to modify or moderate the effects of traits.

(a) I.Q. testing

Child clinical psychologists are sometimes put under pressure to provide — for a variety of reasons — a statement about a child's 'intelligence' and its implications. Many refuse, or are very reluctant, to put a numerical answer to such a request. Berger (1986) in a valuable and novel review of the issues, puts two main reasons for the negative ethos surrounding the measurement of I.Q.:

> First, there is the now well-documented historical and contemporary association between I.Q. testing and allegations of discrimination, racial, educational, or otherwise ... Second, philosophers, many psychologists — especially those in the developmental and cognitive fields — as well as others are, to say the least, sceptical if not contemptuous and dismissive of I.Q. tests being paraded as devices that can generate a measure that in turn encompasses something as remarkable, complex, and subtle as human intelligence.

Berger passes judgement on this last point. He argues, from the evidence, that I.Q. tests do not index intelligence, or at least 'not the type of intelligence that any self-respecting person would like to lay claim to'. Furthermore, he argues that I.Q. tests do not *measure* in any meaningful sense of the term measurement. You might well ask: what is left? What remains is that they provide a numerical expression of performances; and tests, in his view, are useful insofar as they provide data that can be interpreted in ways that are relevant to clinical problems. Psychological tests are administered not because psychologists wish to produce a score, but because knowledge of the score enables certain clinically relevant statements to be made or hypotheses to be formulated or validated. And, of course, it is useful to have instruments that produce reasonably robust scores. The question of the suitability of a test for indexing performance and interpreting scores can usually be decided on the basis of expectancy tables or regression equations (see page 312).

What kind of performance, then, is indexed by some of the popular tests? We know that I.Q.s are quite good predictors of school achievement for *older* children. There is a direct association between a child's I.Q. score and later adjustment (prognosis) for infantile autism (DeMyer, Hingten and Jackson, 1981) and mental handicap. When combined with other variables such as socioeconomic status, family conditions and the presence of learning disabilities, I.Q. is an important factor in predicting academic success and adult outcome, for children with attention deficit disorder (see Wing, 1971a). Rutter and Yule (1970) have found high correlations between academic deficits and the conduct disorders.

For very young children, intelligence tests are helpful in uncovering developmental delays but have little predictive validity for school performance or the likelihood of behaviour problems.

There is sufficient evidence — and the examples mentioned above represent only a few — that I.Q.s have non-chance (i.e., statistically reliable) associations, concurrent and predictive, with a wide range of behavioural phenomena that are important in clinical practice in elucidating developmental, academic and behavioural problems. This, Berger (1986) acknowledges. The question for him is not *whether* to use I.Q. tests but *how* to do so.

(b) Classical test (reliability) theory

For critics of the mystique of scientific respectability that attaches to psychological testing as symbolized by statistical paraphernalia (e.g., standard errors of measurement, reliability coefficients, validity coefficients), *specificity* has been the 'trojan horse' to subvert classical test theory, especially with regard to the repeatability of scores *and* their interpretation. As Berger (1986) points out, general statements (e.g., reliable or unreliable) about any test are inappropriate, mainly because altering one aspect of a reliability estimation study can lead to marked variations in the reliability coefficients (and the same can be said for validity coefficients) as *specific* to the sample test, circumstances of testing, and computational procedure. The implication is that the robustness of scores must be ascertained at least for each major variation in application.

Expectancy tables, it is argued, can be constructed from any investigation that generates numerical data. With appropriate studies it is possible to draw up expectancy tables which provide the information required to decide whether a test is *suitable* as a procedure and as an instrument allowing interpretations that are relevant to the purpose of testing. There need to be no recourse to reliability theory or dubious assumptions about what tests 'measure' (see Kaufman, 1980).

(4) PAEDIATRIC NEUROPSYCHOLOGICAL TESTING

In a significant proportion of children with learning and behavioural problems it is possible to discern a neurodevelopmental aetiology, a factor given added poignancy given the increase in the number of children surviving neurological trauma. As we saw in Chapter 4, the advances in neonatal intensive care in the last 15 years or so has resulted in the survival of many more low birthweight infants. These children are at risk of neurological complications, including hydrocephalus and intraventricular haemorrhage.

These and other developments have led to an increasing interest in paediatric neuropsychological assessment (see Hynd, Snow and Becker, 1986).

Appendix II

Interviewing Children and Parents

Interviewing is a vital skill for clinical child psychologists as it is a primary source of information in the various tasks they carry out. Parents, teachers and other caregivers, adolescents and children, are most often the subjects of the clinical interview. In order to learn about the behaviour and problems of other persons, the three principal methods are through observation and questioning, and giving them a sympathetic 'hearing'.

Interviewing, because of the opportunity it gives to 'see them', 'question them' and, by no means least, 'listen to them', becomes a prime instruction of assessment, investigation, intervention and evaluation. Verbal report, based upon clinical conversations, may be a fairly good predictor of real-life behaviour, but it can also be very misleading, and therefore, unreliable. Do not rely entirely on it (and that means the interview) for your data. Clients may not notice things, they may misperceive events, they may forget significant details and emphasize irrelevant points. Embarrassment or guilt may lead to errors of commission and omission in information-giving. If the crucial behaviour consists of overlearned responses, the client may be quite unaware ('unconscious') of his or her actions. So go and look for yourself and/or train the clients to observe so that you can see things through their informed eyes.

It sounds deceptively simple and straightforward to say, 'I am going to interview the Smith family to find out what lies behind the referral by their GP'. But you need to be clear about the answers to several questions before you (in essence) intrude on the privacy of a home and its family.

- Do I have the right (and the family's permission) to conduct this and subsequent interviews? This can be a significant problem for those workers who frequently have to wear two hats called 'care' and 'control', and whose intervention may be unwelcome.
- What do I wish to find out (what are my objectives) in this interview?
- Who do I need to speak to in order to fulfil my objectives? (All the family members; parents only; the child alone; his or her brothers and sisters?)
- Do I invite them to meet me as a full family group? Do I speak to the mother first? Both parents together? Should the child be present initially?
- How do I begin the interview?

- How do I best express some quite complex and potentially threatening ideas?
- How do I reassure them about confidentiality?
- What is the best way of eliciting reliable and relevant information? How do I deal with their tendency to digress or to get an agenda which avoids key issues?
- Indeed, what is relevant (salient) information?
- How do I terminate the interview, without leaving clients feeling 'up in the air' or threatened?

These are psychological questions as they have a bearing on psychological issues such as the development of rapport with clients, clear communication, summarizing and memory skills, obtaining accurate and relevant (meaningful) information; maintaining a good working relationship; conducting one's business in a professional (which also means ethical) manner; and so on.

The guided (semi-structured) interview is the main vehicle for the preliminary assessment. Such interviews provide chiefly two kinds of information:

(i)   They afford an opportunity for direct observation of a rather limited sample of behaviour manifested during the interview situation itself (e.g., the individual's speech, his or her style of thinking, competence, poise and manner of relating to the child).

(ii) The interviewer seeks to secure directly as much information of a factual or personal nature from the client as is relevant to the purpose of the interview (e.g., information about the problem, opinions, relationships, parental skills, experience). A particularly important function in a clinical or social work setting is to elicit life-history data. What the individual has done in the past is thought to be a good indicator of what he or she may do in the future.

Interviewing children (see Kovacs, 1978; Murphy *et al.*, 1982)

Young children tend to be talkative but are limited in their ability to reflect insightfully about their experiences; adolescents are usually introspective (reflective) but have a way of becoming monosyllabic when asked personal questions. This poses a problem for the would-be interviewer.

Children are not always very good at expressing their fears, frustrations or uncertainties. They cannot always tell their parents, let alone a comparative stranger, how they feel, but they have a language that adults can learn to translate — the language of behaviour and fantasy. What they do (in a direct sense in everyday life) and say (indirectly through play or story-telling) can be most revealing.

It is easy to forget that children are not simply little adults and it can therefore come as a surprise when they don't interview like adults. They often fidget, become alarmingly restless in their movements, tic, look out of the window, or fiddle endlessly with a button, when they find the interview uncomfortable. And there may be many good, objective reasons for their discomfort, and for the series of blank looks or 'don't knows' that meet the interviewer's queries. Style is important. A patronizing, insincere tone will soon be picked up and responded to negatively. An artificial ('this is my voice for children') style is also counterproductive.

The child may not comprehend the question, especially when he or she is cognitively immature, and the question is abstract and global. The double-barrelled (two-in-one) question, laced in jargon, is also likely to floor the older child. The child may simply not know the answer to the question. Interviewers and questionnaire designers often assume that clients must know the answers to their questions, if only they'd speak out.

Children, especially those with low self-esteem, may be afraid to give their opinions because they think the interview is like a test, with right or wrong answers. They may be afraid to say anything out of loyalty to their family and/or fear of the consequences of their answers for themselves and their parents.

They may put too literal an interpretation on questions, and their egocentricity, when young, may prevent them from seeing another's point of view. Then again, cognitive immaturity may not allow them to see or understand the causal connections you are seeking.

Shyness about the topic of investigation may also inhibit responses to questions. All of these emotions: fear, embarrassment, loyalty, and others, require a delicate approach in the interview, the establishment of rapport, and carefully judged reassurance where necessary.

Adjuncts to the child interview

The advantage of using projective techniques (which include play, puppets, dramatic creations, completing stories or sentences) for assessment, is that they involve relatively unstructured tasks that permit an almost unlimited variety of responses. The client has to fall back on his or her own resources rather than stereotyped, socially desirable answers. The techniques (as psychometric instruments) have their critics, but are invaluable if used cautiously as aids to communicating with children. The caution refers to interpreting the protocols — the statements about feelings and attitudes toward various members of the family. It is thought that children identify with the central characters in their stories, project their own feelings (especially unacceptable or difficult-to-acknowledge impulses or attitudes) into the fantasy figures, and attribute various motives and ideas that are essentially their own, into the play or other creative situations and plots.

Where the child is too loyal, too frightened or ashamed, or too inarticulate to speak about feelings (or painful events in the family) it may be possible to express these things in the evolving story (you can make up the basic structure, leaving spaces for the child to fill in) about a boy or girl of similar age. Thus the therapist begins, 'Once upon a time there was a boy/girl. What did he/she most like doing?' ... 'What did he/she not like doing?' ... (The therapist gradually introduces, among neutral themes, topics such as secrets, fears, worries, preoccupations, family tensions, parental behaviours, and so on.)

Sentence completions are useful:

'I like to ....'
'What I most dislike..'
'My best friend...'
'I wish ....'
'My dad ....'
'My mum..'
'If only...'
'In my home the nicest thing is..'
'The worst thing is ....'

With stories told as a response to pictures the therapist needs (as always) to be cautious about their interpretations. There is a tendency to find what one hopes to find or to superimpose our 'theories' onto the projective protocols. The safest use of these instruments is not as psychometric devices — they are too unreliable — but as a means of eliciting *clues* to important themes, which are then investigated further. With these caveats in mind, play, drama (with puppets or miniatures) or stories are undoubtedly an invaluable adjunct to work with children. The psychologist would do well to have a store of miniatures, drawing materials and pictures available.

Interviewing parents

There are many investigations (e.g., Yarrow, 1960; Yarrow, Campbell and Burton, 1968) which point to the consistent and persistent biasing of maternal reports in the direction of cultural stereotypes. The idealized picture of the happy family is one of the most potent in modern society and any failure to live up to that image rebounds on the parents, particularly on the mother. Sigmund Freud ensured that the sins of the children would be visited on the parents. Not surprisingly, parents complaining about 'deviant' behaviours of their children are very conscious that the complaints reflect back on them. Yarrow (1960) makes the point that, stripped of all elaboration, mother's interview responses represent self-description by extremely ego involved reporters.

The finding of bias in maternal reports is particularly high when they are giving retrospective reports; the passage of time dims the memory and what memory cannot provide imagination elaborates, an elaboration that is in a direction that is socially desirable. Reports of *current* beliefs and practices are more accurate and reliable. The parent presumably finds it more difficult (certainly not impossible) to falsify the present; it is much easier to rewrite history.

Reliability studies (e.g., Yarrow, 1960) have shown that there are wide discrepancies between the reports of the same mother at different times: of the same mother with a different interviewer. When data is obtained from more than one source there is again a lack of consensus. How, then, can one improve the reliability of parental reports? According to the evidence, if the mother is asked for a statement on *current* beliefs and practices, then the reports reach a satisfactory level of validity and reliability. When parents are asked to describe rather than interpret, reliability and validity measures can reach satisfactory levels of accuracy (Yarrow, 1960). Yarrow also suggests that as a check on the maternal report, clinicians and researchers should systematically seek out information from different sources, noting areas of concordance and discordance.

Child abuse interviews (parents and children)

Interviews with children and parents, when a case of suspected child abuse comes to light, can be particularly difficult for professionals, and require a mixture of great delicacy and assurance. The feelings of the psychologist (who may be working alongside a social worker) may get in the way of these requirements. Jones *et al.* (1987), in an excellent guide to the interview, list the following common reactions that beset all professionals:

'Denial: that anything is wrong, often presented as "all children in that area have those sort of bruises — if we react to this case we shall have all the children on the estate in care"; or "I have known these people for years and they are really very nice — I don't know what happened but I'm sure they couldn't do anything like that". Such comments are often valid but do not always fit the facts.

Anger: with the family for having let the worker down. "I gave them all that time and helped them in so many ways yet still they go and do this — well that's all they're getting from me" or with a colleague for not having done more.

Guilt: that more should have been done to help before the incident, or that the worker should have been more skilful or perceptive: "It's all my fault."

Fear: of personal and professional criticism for not having prevented what has happened and of possible damage to future career prospects (often associated with guilt) of getting caught up in procedures over which nobody has control and which may swamp family and worker.

Despair: that all seems so bleak with nothing apparently possible by way of help; occasionally justified, but such feelings can defeat systematic appraisal of alternatives.

Horror: that such serious and possibly permanent injuries can be inflicted on a child, freezing consideration of future action.

Jealousy: of professional colleagues now more intimately involved with a family known for a long time; perhaps associated with:

Resentment: that somebody else is doing the investigation and formulating an assessment, possibly disturbing a carefully nurtured, long-term relationship in the process.

Omnipotence: a belief that "I know best", "I have the best relationship with the family", or "I alone know how to deal with this — leave it all to me". In practice a multidisciplinary approach is essential, even if one person has most contact with the family.'

The authors advise workers to listen more than talk, and to avoid selective gathering of information; they need to keep calm and alert and should not confront. It is vital to maintain a neutral, objective attitude. The authors add that 'it is important to remember that this "neutral" approach must never imply acceptance of ill-treatment of a child nor condoning of such behaviour. It is quite possible to convey empathy and understanding of behaviour which is still unacceptable, even illegal, but the objective stand of the worker must be honestly stated and never forgotten'.

Appendix III

Race, Gender and Creed in Clinical Child Psychology

Living and working, as we do, in a multi-ethnic society it is of critical importance that psychologists should be sensitive, not only to the norms, sensibilities and sensitivities of people from different cultures but also the stressful life experiences they endure in a sadly racist society. Racism extends, far too often, into service delivery.

It is not only in matters of race, nationality and creed where prejudice has its corrosive influence; it affects women and female children in many subtle and unsubtle ways. In many senses of the word they are 'disabled' in our society and demeaned in the way that those of our clients to whom we attach the label 'disabled' are patronized and robbed of their self-fulfilment.

I have listed several references below. These books and articles should provide a useful introduction to the literature on these important themes.

Ahmed, S. (1986). *Social work with black children and their families*. London: Batsford.

Broverman, I. K., Broverman, D. M., Clarkson, F. E., Rosenkrantz, P. S., and Vogel, S. R. (1970). Sex role stereotypes and clinical judgements of mental health. *Journal of Consulting and Clinical Psychology*, **34**, 1–7.

Chevannes, M. (1989). Child rearing among Jamaican families in Britain. *Health Visitor*, February, 222–223.

Dominelli, L. (1988). *Anti-racist social work*. London: Macmillan.

Hess, R. D. (1970). Social class and ethnic influences on socialization. In P. H. Mussen (eds), *Carmichael's manual of child psychiatry*, (3rd edn). New York: John Wiley.

Leiderman, P. H., Tulkin, S. R., and Rosenfeld, A. (1977). *Culture and infancy: Variations in the human experience*. New York: Academic Press.

Maxime, J. (1986). *Black like me*. London: Emani Publications.

Stubbs, P. (1989). Developing anti-racist practice: Problems and possibilities. In C. Wattam, J. Hughes, and H. Blagg (eds), *Child sexual abuse: Listening, hearing and validating the experiences of children*. London: Longman.

Walker, J., Noble, C. A., and Self, P. A. (1983). Cross-cultural research with children and families. In C. E. Walker and M. C. Roberts (eds), *Handbook of clinical child psychology*. New York: John Wiley.

Ward, R. (Ed.). *A descriptive bibliography of articles and books on black and ethnic community mental health in Britain*. Mind, South East (available from Mind mail order department, 24–32 Stephenson Way, London NW1 2HD).

References

Abramson, L. Y., Seligman, M. E. P., and Teasdale, J. D. (1978). Learned helplessness in humans: Critique and reformulation. *Journal of Abnormal Psychology*, **87**, 49–74.

Abu-Saad, H. (1984). Cultural components of pain. The Arab-American child. *Issues in Comprehensive Pediatric Nursing*, **7**, 91–99.

Abu-Saad, H., and Holzemer, W. L. (1981). Measuring children's self-assessment of pain. *Issues in Comprehensive Pediatric Nursing*, **5**, 337–349.

Achenbach, T. M. (1974). *Developmental psychopathology*. New York: Ronald Press.

Achenbach, T. M. (1978). The child behavior profile: I. Boys aged 6–11. *Journal of Consulting and Clinical Psychology*, **46**, 478–488.

Achenbach, T. M. (1982). *Developmental psychopathology* (2nd ed). New York: Wiley.

Achenbach, T. M. (1985). Assessment of anxiety in children. In A. H. Tuma and J. Maser (eds), *Anxiety and the anxiety disorders*. Hillsdale, NJ: Lawrence Erlbaum.

Achenbach, T. M., and Edelbrock, C. S. (1978). The classification of child psychopathology: A review and analysis of empirical efforts. *Psychological Bulletin*, **85**, 1275–1301.

Achenbach, T. M., and Edelbrock, C. S. (1979). The child behavior profile: II. Boys aged 12–16 and girls aged 6–11 and 12–16. *Journal of Consulting and Clinical Pyschology*, **47**, 223–233.

Achenbach, T. M., and Edelbrock, C. S. (1983). Taxonomic issues in child psychology. In T. Ollendick and M. Hersen (eds), *Handbook of child psychopathology*. New York: Plenum.

Achenbach, T. M., and Edelbrock, C. S. (1989). Diagnostic taxonomic, and assessment issues. In T. H. Ollendick and M. Hersen (eds), *Handbook of child psychopathology* (2nd ed). New York: Plenum.

Achenbach, T. M., McConaughy, S. H., and Howell, C. T. (1987). Child/adolescent behaviors and emotional problems: Implications of cross-informant correlations for situational specificity. *Psychological Bulletin*, **101**, 213–232.

Ager, A. (1985). Alternatives to speech for the mentally handicapped. In F. N. Watts (ed.). *New developments in clinical psychology*. Leicester: British Psychological Society/Wiley.

Agras, W. S., Chapin, H. H., and Oliveau, D. (1972). The natural history of phobias: Course and prognosis. *Archives of General Psychiatry*, **26**, 315–317.

Agras, W. S., Sylvester, D., and Oliveau, D. (1969). The epidemiology of common fears and phobias. *Comprehensive Psychiatry*, **10**, 151–156.

Ainsworth, M. D. (1969). Object relations, dependency and attachment: A theoretical review of the infant–mother relationship. *Child Development*, **40**, 969–1025.

Ainsworth, M. D. (1970). Attachment and dependency: A comparison. In J. L. Gewirtz (ed.), *Attachment and dependence: The utility of the concepts*. London: Academic Press.

Ainsworth, M. D. S., Behar, M. C., Walters, E., and Wall, S. (1978). *Patterns of attachment: A psychological study of the strange situation*. Hillsdale, NJ: Erlbaum.

Alexander, R. N., Corbett, T. F., and Smigel, J. (1976). The effects of individual group consequences on school attendance and curfew violations with predelinquent adolescents. *Journal of Applied Behaviour Analysis*, **9**, 221–226.

Allen, D. A., and Affleck, G. (1985). Are we stereotyping parents? A postscript to Blacher. *Mental Retardation*, **23**, 200–202.

Allen, F. H. (1942). *Psychotherapy with children*. New York: Norton.

Allen, K. E., Hart, B. M., Buell, J. S., Harris, F. R., and Wolf, M. M. (1964). Effects of social reinforcement on isolate behavior of a nursery school child. *Child Development*, **35**, 511–518.

Allport, G. W. (1937). *Personality: A psychological interpretation*. London: Constable.

American Psychiatric Association. (1980). *Diagnostic and statistical manual of mental disorders* (3rd ed). Washington, DC: APA.

American Psychiatric Association. (1987). *Diagnostic and statistical manual of mental disorders* (3rd ed revised). Washington, DC: APA.

Anastasi, A. (1982). *Psychological testing*. New York: Collier Macmillan.

Anderson, J. R. (1980). *Cognitive psychology and its implications*. San Francisco, CA: W. H. Freeman.

Anderson, K. O., and Masur, F. T. (1983). Psychological preparation for invasive medical and dental procedures. *Journal of Behavioural Medicine*, **6**, (1), 1–37.

Andrews, G., and Harris, M. (1964). *The syndrome of stuttering. Clinics in developmental medicine*, **17**, Heinemann Medical Books.

Annell, A. L. (1953). Pertussis in infancy as a cause of behaviour disorders in children. *Boktrycheri, A.B.*, **3**, 49. Almquist and Wiksells, Uppsala.

Anthony, E. J. (1957). An experimental approach to the psychopathology of childhood: Encopresis. *British Journal of Medical Psychology*, **30**, 146–175.

Anthony, E. J. (1959). An experimental approach to the psychopathology of childhood sleep. *British Journal of Medical Psychology*, **32**, 19–37.

Apley, J. (1975). *The child with abdominal pain*. Oxford: Blackwell Scientific.

Apolloni, T., Cooke, S. A., and Cooke, T. P. (1977). Establishing a normal peer as a behavioral model for developmentally delayed toddlers. *Perceptual and Motor Skills*, **44**, 231–241.

Arbuthnot, J., and Gordon, D. A. (1986). Behavioral and cognitive effects of a moral reasoning development intervention for high risk behavior-disordered adolescents. *Journal of Consulting and Clinical Psychology*, **34**, 208–216.

Arbuthnot, J., Gordon, D. A., and Jurkovic, J. G. (1987). Personality. In H. C. Quay (ed.), *Handbook of juvenile delinquency*. New York: Wiley.

Aries, P. (1973). *Centuries of childhood: A social history of family life*. Harmondsworth: Penguin.

Aronfreed, J. (1968). *Conduct and conscience*. New York: Academic Press.

Aronfreed, J., and Leff, R. (1963). *The effects of intensity of punishment and complexity of discrimination upon the learning of internalized suppression*. Unpublished manuscript. University of Pennsylvania.

Aronfreed, J., and Reber, A. (1965). Internal behavioural suppression and the timing of social punishment. *Journal of Personality and Social Psychology*, **1**, 3–16.

Asch, S. E. (1956). Studies of independence and conformity: I. A minority of one against a unanimous majority.. *Psychological Monographs*, **70**, (9), No. 416.

August, G. J., Stewart, M. A., and Holmes, C. S. (1983). A four-year follow-up of hyperactive boys with and without conduct disorder. *British Journal of Psychiatry*, **143**, 192–198.

Austin, J. (1811). *Sense and sensibility*. London: Collins Clear Type Press.

Ausubel, D. P., and Sullivan, E. V. (1954). *Theory and problems of child development* (2nd ed). London: Grune & Stratton.

Ausubel, D. P., Balthazar, E. E., Rosenthal, I., Blackman, L. S., Schpoont, S. H., and Welkowitz, J. (1954). Received parent attitudes as determinants of children's ego structure. *Child Development*, **25**, 173–183.

Axline, V. M. (1947). *Play therapy*. Boston: Houghton-Mifflin.

Ayalon, O. (1988). *Rescue! Community oriented preventive education for coping with stress*. Haifa: Nord Publications.

Ayer, W. (1973). Use of visual imagery in needle-phobic children. *Journal of Dentistry for Children,* **40**, 41–43.

Ayllon, T., Smith, D., and Rogers, M. (1970). Behavioral management of school phobia. *Journal of Behavior Therapy and Experimental Psychiatry,* **1**, 125–138.

Bach, R., and Moyland, J. J. (1975). Parents administer behavior therapy for inappropriate urination and encopresis: A case study. *Journal of Behavior Therapy and Experimental Psychiatry,* **6**, 239–241.

Baekeland, F., and Lundwall, L. (1975). Dropping out of treatment: A critical review. *Psychological Bulletin,* **82**, 738–783.

Baer, D. M., Wolf, M. M., and Risley, T. R. (1968). Some current dimensions of applied behavior analysis. *Journal of Applied Behavior Analysis,* **1**, 91–97.

Bailey, W. (1966). Correctional outcome: An evaluation of 100 reports. *Journal of Criminal Law, Criminology and Police Science,* **57**, 153–160.

Baldwin, S. (1985). No silence please. *Times Educational Supplement,* **679**, (8th November), p.25.

Baller, W. R. (1975). *Bedwetting: Origins and treatment.* New York: Pergamon.

Baltes, P. B., Reese, H. W., and Lipsitt, L. P. (1980). Life-span developmental psychology. *Annual Review of Psychology,* **31**, 65–110.

Bancroft, J. H. (1970). Homosexuality in the male. *British Journal of Hospital Medicine,* **3**, 168–181.

Bandura, A. (1968). Modeling approaches to the modification of phobic disorders. In R. Porter (ed.), *Ciba Foundation Symposium: The role of learning in psychotherapy.* London: Churchill.

Bandura, A. (1969). *Principles of behavior modification.* New York: Holt, Rinehart & Winston.

Bandura, A. (1973). *Aggression: A social learning analysis.* Englewood Cliffs, NJ: Prentice-Hall.

Bandura, A. (1977). *Social learning theory.* Englewood Cliffs, NJ: Prentice-Hall.

Bandura, A. (1986). *Social foundations of thought and action: A social cognitive theory.* Englewood Cliffs, NJ: Prentice-Hall.

Bandura, A., and Menlove, F. L. (1968). Factors determining vicarious extinction of avoidance behavior through symbolic modeling. *Journal of Personality and Social Psychology,* **8**, 99–108.

Bandura, A., and Walters, R. H. (1963). *Social learning and personality development.* New York: Holt, Rinehart & Winston.

Bannister, D., and Fransella, F. (1980). *Inquiring man.* Harmondsworth: Penguin.

Barabasz, A. F. (1973). Group desensitization of test anxiety in elementary school. *Journal of Psychology,* **83**, 295–301.

Barabasz, A. F. (1975). Classroom teachers as paraprofessional therapists in group systematic desensitization of test anxiety. *Psychiatry,* **38**, 388–392.

Barkley, R. A. (1982). *Hyperactive children: A handbook for diagnosis and assessment.* Chichester: Wiley.

Barkley, R. A. (1987). *Defiant children: A clinican's manual for parent training.* New York: The Guilford Press.

Barrios, B. A., Hartmann, O. P., and Shigetomi, C. (1981). Fears and anxieties in children. In E. J. Nash and L. G. Terdal (eds), *Behavioral assessment of childhood disorders.* New York: Guilford Press.

Barron, A., and Earls, F. (1984). The relation of temperament and social factors to behaviour problems in three year old children. *Journal of Child Psychology and Psychiatry,* **25**, 23–32.

Bartak, L., Rutter, M., and Cox, A. (1975). A comparative study of infantile autism and specific developmental receptive language disorder. I. The children. *British Journal of Psychiatry,* **126**, 127–145.

Bates, J. E., and Bayles, K. (1984). Objective and subjective components in mothers' perceptions of their children from age 6 months to 3 years. *Merrill-Palmer Quarterly,* **30**, 111–130.

Bauer, D. H. (1976). An exploratory study of developmental changes in children's fears. *Journal of Child Psychology and Psychiatry,* **17**, 69–74.

Baumrind, D. (1966). Effects of authoritative parental control on child behaviour. *Child Development,* **37**, (4), 887–907.

Baumrind, D. (1971). Current patterns of parental authority. *Developmental Psychology Monograph,* **4**, (1), Pt. 2, 1–103.

Beales, J. G. (1983). Factors influencing the expectation of pain among patients in a children's burns unit. *Burns*, **9**, 187–192.

Beck, S. J., and Forehand, R. (1984). Social skills training for children: A methodological and clinical review of behaviour modification studies. *Behavioural Psychotherapy*, **12**, 17–45.

Beck, S. J., and Ollendick, T. H. (1976). Personal space, sex of experimenter, and locus of control in normal and delinquent adolescents. *Psychological Reports*, **38**, 383–387.

Becker, W. C. (1964). Consequences of different kinds of parental discipline. In M. L. Hoffman and L. W. Hoffman (eds), *Review of child development research*. New York: Russell Sage Foundation.

Bee, H. (1981). *The developing child* (3rd edn). New York: Harper & Row.

Beech, H. R. (1981). Creating change. In M. Herbert (ed.), *Psychology for social workers*. London: McMillan & British Psychological Society.

Beech, H. R. (1985). *Staying together*. Chichester: Wiley.

Beech, R., and Fransella, F. (1968). *Research and experiment in stuttering*. Oxford: Pergamon.

Behrens, B. C., Halford, W. K., and Sanders, M. R. (1989). Behavioural marital therapy: An overview. *Behaviour Change*, **6**, 112–113.

Behrens, M. L. (1954). Child rearing and the character structure of the mother. *Child Development*, **25**, 225–238.

Beidel, D. C. (1988). Psychophysiological assessment of anxious emotional states in children. *Journal of Abnormal Psychology*, **97**, 80–82.

Beidel, D. C. (1989). Assessing anxious emotion: A review of psychophysiological assessment in children. *Clinical Psychology Review*, **9**, 717–736.

Bell, R. A. (1971). Stimulus control of parent or caretaker behaviour by offspring. *Developmental Psychology*, **4**, 63–72.

Bell, R. Q., and Harper, L. V. (1977). *Child effects on adults*. Hillsdale, NJ: Erlbaum.

Bell, R. Q., and Waldrop, M. F. (1982). Temperament and minor physical anomalies. In Ciba Foundation Symposium No. 89. *Temperamental differences in infants and young children*. London: Pitman.

Bellack, A. S., Hersen, M., and Kazdin, A. E. (eds). (1982). *International handbook of behavior modification and therapy*. New York: Plenum Press.

Bellman, M. (1966). Studies on encopresis. *Acta Paediatricia Scandanavia*, Supplement 170.

Belsky, J. (1984). The determinants of parenting: A process model. *Child Development*, **55**, 83–96.

Belsky, J., and Nezworski, T. (1988). Clinical implications of attachment. In J. Belsky and T. Nezworski (eds), *Clinical implications of attachment*. Hillsdale: Lawrence Erlbaum.

Belsky, J., Rovine, M., and Fish, M. (1989). The developing family system. In M. Gunnar (ed.), *Systems and development: Minnesota symposium on child development* Vol. 22, pp. 119–166. Hillside, NJ: Erlbaum.

Belson, W. A. (1975). *Juvenile theft: The causal factors*. London: Harper & Row.

Bender, L. (1969). The nature of childhood psychosis. In J. G. Howells (ed.), *Modern perspectives in international child psychiatry*. Edinburgh: Oliver & Boyd.

Berenda, R. W. (1950). *The influence of the group in judgements of children*, New York: King's Crown Press.

Berg, I. (1979). Annotation: Day wetting in children. *Journal of Child Psychology and Psychiatry*, **20**, 167–173.

Berger, M. (1986). Toward an educated use of IQ tests: A reappraisal of intelligence testing. In B. B. Lahey and A. E. Kazdin (eds), *Advances in clinical child psychology* Vol. 9, New York: Plenum.

Berger, M., Yule, W., and Rutter, M. (1975). Attainment and adjustment in two geographical areas. II: The prevalence of specific reading retardation. *British Journal of Psychiatry*, **126**, 510–519.

Bergin, A. E., and Lambert, M. J. (1978). The evaluation of therapeutic outcomes. In S. L. Garfield and A. E. Bergin (eds), *Handbook of psychotherapy and behavior change: an empirical analysis*. New York: Wiley.

Berkowitz, L., Parke, R. D., Leyens, J. P., West, S., and Sebastian, R. J. (1978). Experiments on the reactions of juvenile delinquents to filmed violence. In L. A. Hersov and M. Berger (eds), *Aggression and antisocial behaviour in childhood and adolescence*. Oxford: Pergamon.

Bernstein, G. A., and Garfinkel, B. D. (1986). School phobia: The overlap of affective and anxiety disorders. *Journal of the American Academy of Child Psychiatry*, **25**, 235–241.

Bernstein, G. S. (1982). Training behavior change agents: A conceptual review. *Behavior Therapy*, **13**, 1–23.

Bernstein, M. R. (1965). Significant values of hypnoanesthesia: Three clinical examples. *American Journal of Clinical Hypnosis*, **7**, 259–260.

Bernstein, N. R. (1963). Management of burned children with the aid of hypnosis. *Journal of Child Psychology and Psychiatry*, **4**, 93–98.

Bertalanffy, L. (1968). *General system theory*. Harmondsworth: Penguin.

Bibace, R., and Walsh, M. E. (1980). Development of children's concepts of illness. *Pediatrics*, **66**, (6), 912–917.

Bidder, T. R., Bryant, G., and Gray, O. P. (1975). Benefits to Down's syndrome children through training their mothers. *Archives of Disease in Childhood*, **50**, 383–386.

Bierman, K. L., and Schwartz, L. A. (1986). Clinical child interviews: Approaches and developmental considerations. *Journal of Child and Adolescent Psychotherapy*, **3**, 267–278.

Bijou, S. W. (1968). Child behavior and development: A behavioral analysis. *International Journal of Psychology*, **3**, 221–238.

Birleson, P. (1981). The validity of depressive disorder in childhood and the development of a self-rating scale: A research report. *Journal of Child Psychology and Psychiatry*, **21**, 83–88.

Birleson, P., Hudson, I., Buchanan, D. G., and Wolff, S. (1987). Clinical evaluation of a self-rating scale for depressive disorder in childhood (Depression Self-Rating Scale). *Journal of Child Psychology and Psychiatry*, **28**, 43–60.

Blacher, J. (1984). Sequential stages of parental adjustment to the birth of a child with handicaps: Fact or artifact? *Mental Retardation*, **22**, 55–68.

Black, D., and Urbanowicz, M. A. (1987). Family intervention with bereaved children. *Journal of Child Psychology and Psychiatry*, **28**, 467–476.

Blackwell, B., and Currah, J. (1973). The psychopharmacology of noctural enuresis. In I. Kolvin, R. C. MacKeith and S. R. Meadow (eds), *Bladder control and enuresis*. London: Heinemann.

Blagg, N. (1987). *School phobia and its treatment*. London: Croom Helm.

Blagg, N. R., and Yule, W. (1984). The behavioural treatment of school phobia: A comparative study. *Behaviour Research and Therapy*, **22**, 119–127.

Blakely, C. H., and Davidson, W. S. (1984). Behavioral approaches to delinquency: A review. In P. Karoly and J. J. Steffen (eds), *Adolescent behavior disorders: Foundations and contemporary concerns*. Lexington, MA: Lexington Books.

Blasi, A. (1980). Bridging moral cognition and moral action: A critical review of the literature. *Psychological Bulletin*, **88**, 1–45.

Bloch, D. A., Silber, E., and Perry, S. E. (1956). Some factors in the emotional reactions of children to disaster. *American Journal of Psychiatry*, **133**, 416–422.

Blom, G. E. (1986). A school disaster — intervention and research aspects. *Journal of the American Academy of Child Psychiatry*, **25**, 336–345.

Boll, T. J. (1981). The Halstead-Reitan Neuropsychology Battery. In S. B. Silskov and T. J. Bell (eds), *Handbook of clinical neuropsychology*. New York: Wiley.

Bonica, J. J. (1980). Pain. *Research publications: Association for research in nervous and mental diseases*, **58**. New York: Raven Press.

Bornstein, P. H., and Bornstein, M. T. (1988). *Marital therapy: A behavioral-communications approach*. Oxford: Pergamon.

Bornstein, P. H., and Kazdin, A. E. (eds). (1985). *Handbook of clinical behavior therapy with children*. Homewood, IL: Dorsey Press.

Bornstein, M., and Sigman, M. (1986). Continuity in mental development from infancy. *Child Development*, **57**, 251–274.

Bornstein, M. R., Bellack, A. S., and Hersen, M. (1977). Social skills training for unassertive children: A multiple baseline analysis. *Journal of Applied Behavior Analysis*, **10**, 183–195.

Boucheau, L. D., and Jeffry, C. D. (1973). Stuttering treated by desensitization. *Journal of Behavior Therapy and Experimental Psychiatry*, **4**, 209–212.

Boulton, M. G. (1983). *On being a mother*. London: Tavistock.

Bower, T. G. R. (1977). *The perceptual world of the child*. Cambridge, Mass: Harvard University Press.

Bowers, K. S. (1973). Situationism in psychology: An analysis and a critique. *Psychological Review*, **80**, 307–336.

Bowlby, J. (1969). *Attachment and loss* Vol. 1. London: Hogarth Press.

Bowman, P. C., and Auerbach, S. M. (1982). Impulsive youthful offenders: A multimodal cognitive behavioral treatment program. *Criminal Justice and Behavior*, **9**, 432–454.

Brackbill, Y. (1958). Extinction of the smiling response in infants as a function of reinforcement. *Child Development*, **29**, 115–124.

Braukmann, C. J., and Fixsen, D. L. (1975). Behavior modification with delinquents. In M. Hersen, R. M. Eisler, and P. M. Miller (eds), *Progress in behavior modification*, Vol. 1. New York: Academic Press.

Bremner, J. G. (1988). *Infancy*. Oxford: Basil Blackwell.

Bretherton, I. (1985). Attachment theory: Retrospect and prospect. In I. Bretherton and E. Waters (eds), *Growing points in attachment theory and research*. Monographs of the Society for Research in Child Development (pp. 3–36) Vol. 50, No. 209.

Brewin, C. R. (1988). *Cognitive foundations of clinical psychology*. London: Lawrence Earlbaum.

Brim, O., and Kagan, J. (eds). (1980). *Constancy and change in human development*. Cambridge, Mass: Harvard Educational Press.

Brody, S. (1976). *The effectiveness of sentencing: A review of the literature*. London: HMSO.

Brown, G., and Harris, T. (1978). *Social origins of depression: A study of psychiatric disorder in women*. London: Tavistock.

Brown, B. J., and Lloyd, H. (1975). A controlled study of children not speaking at school. *Journal of the Association of Workers for Maladjusted Children*, **3**, 49–63.

Browne, K. D. (1986). Methods and approaches to the study of parenting. In W. Sluckin and M. Herbert (eds), *Parental behaviour*. Oxford: Basil Blackwell.

Brownell, K. D., and Foreyt, J. P. (eds). (1986). *Handbook of eating disorders*. New York: Basic Books.

Bryan, T. H. (1977). Learning disabled children's comprehension of non-verbal communication. *Journal of Learning Disabilities*, **10**, 36–41.

Bruner, J. S. (1975). *Beyond the information given*. London: Allen & Unwin.

Bruner, J. S. (1977). Early social interaction and language acquisition. In H. R. Schaffer (ed.), *Studies in mother–infant interaction*. London: Academic Press.

Burchard, J. D. (1987a). Social policy and the role of the behavior analyst in the prevention of delinquent behavior. *The Behavior Analyst*, **10**, 83–88.

Burchard, J. D. (1987b). Social and political challenges to behavioral programs with delinquents and criminals. In E. K. Morris and C. J. Braukmann (eds), *Behavioral approaches to crime and delinquency: A handbook of application, research and concepts*. New York: Plenum Press.

Burchard, J. D., and Harrington, W. A. (1986). Deinstitutionalization: Programmed transition from the institution to the community. *Child and Family Behavior Therapy*, **7**, 17–32.

Burns, D., and Brady, J. P. (1980). The treatment of stuttering. In A. Goldstein and E. B. Foa (eds), *Handbook of behavioral interventions*. New York: Wiley.

Burstein, S., and Meichenbaum, D. (1979). The work of worrying in children undergoing surgery. *Journal of Abnormal Psychology*, **7**, 121–132.

Bush, J. P. (1987). Pain in children: A review of the literature from a developmental perspective. *Psychology and Health*, **1**, 215–236.

Bush, J. P., Melamed, B. G., Sheras, P. L., and Greenbaum, P. E. (1986). Mother–child patterns of coping with anticipatory medical stress. *Health Psychology*, **5**, (2), 137–157.

Byrne, D. (1964). Repression-sensitization as a dimension of personality. In B. A. Maher (ed.), *Progress in experimental personality research* Vol. 1. New York: Academic Press.

Caldwell, B. M. (1964). The effects of infant care. In M. L. Hoffman and L. N. Hoffman (eds), *Review of child development research*. New York: Russell Sage Foundation.

Cameron, J. R. (1978). Parental treatment, children's temperament, and risk of childhood behavior problems. *American Journal of Orthopsychiatry*, **48**, 140–147.

Camp, B. W., and Bash, M. B. (1981). *Think aloud: Increasing social and cognitive skills — a problem-solving program for children*. Champaign, IL: Research Press.

Campbell, M., Cohen, I. L., Perry, R., and Small, M. (1989). Psychopharmocological treatment. In T. H. Ollendick and M. Hersen (eds), *Handbook of child psychopathology*. New York: Plenum.

Campbell, S. (1989). Developmental perspectives. In T. H. Ollendick and M. Hersen (eds), *Handbook of child psychopathology*. New York: Plenum.

Cantwell, D. P. (1985). Organization and use of DSM III. In D. Shaffer, A. A. Erhardt, and L. L. Greenhill (eds), *The clinical guide to child psychiatry*. New York: The Free Press.

Cantwell, D. P., and Baker, L. (1985a). Psychiatric and learning disorders in children with speech and language disorders. A descriptive analysis. *Advances in Learning and Behavioral Disabilities*, **4**, 29–47.

Cantwell, D. P., and Baker, L. (1985b). Speech and language: Development and disorders. In M. Rutter and L. Hersov (eds), *Child psychiatry: Modern approaches* (2nd ed). Oxford: Blackwell.

Cantwell, D. P., and Carlson, G. A. (eds). (1983). *Affective disorders in children and adolescence: An update*. New York: Spectrum.

Caplan, G. (1964). *Principles of preventive psychiatry*. New York: Basic Books.

Caputo, D. V., Edmonton, W. E., L'Abate, L., and Rondberg, S. R. (1962). *Extended report: Type of brain-damage and intellectual functioning in children*. Paper read at Midwestern Psychological Association meeting in Chicago, May 5. University School of Medicine Publication, Washington.

Carlson, C. L. (1986). Attention deficit disorder without hyperactivity: A review of preliminary experimental evidence. In B. B. Lahey and A. E. Kazdin (eds), *Advances in clinical child psychology* (Vol. 12). New York: Plenum Press.

Carlson, C. L., Lahey, B. B., and Neeper, R. (1986). Direct assessment of the cognitive correlates of attention deficit disorders with and without hyperactivity. *Journal of Psychopathology and Behavioral Assessment*, **8**, 69–86.

Carr, J. (1975). *Young children with Down's Syndrome: Their development, upbringing and effect on their families*. London: Butterworth.

Case, H. W. (1960). Therapeutic methods in stuttering and speech blocking. In H. J. Eysenck (ed.), *Behaviour therapy and neuroses*. pp. 207–220. Oxford: Pergamon Press.

Cassell, S. (1965). Effects of brief puppet therapy upon the emotional responses of children undergoing cardiac catherization. *Journal of Consulting and Clinical Psychology*, **29**, 1–8.

Casteneda, A., McCandless, B. R., and Palmero, D. S. (1956). The children's form of the Manifest Anxiety Scale. *Child Development*, **16**, 317–326.

Chadwick, O. F. D., and Rutter, M. (1984). Neurological assessment. In M. Rutter (ed.), *Developmental Neuropsychiatry*. Edinburgh: Churchill Livingstone.

Chandler, M. J. (1973). Egocentrism and anti-social behavior: The assessment and training of social perspective-taking skills. *Developmental Psychology*, **9**, 326–332.

Chazan, M., and Jackson, S. (1974). Behaviour problems in the infant school: Changes over two years. *Journal of Child Psychology and Psychiatry*, **15**, 33–46.

Cherry, C., and Sayers, B. Mc. A. (1956). Experiments upon the total inhibition of stammering by external control and some clinical results. *Journal of Psychosomatic Research*, **1**, 233–246.

Chertok, S. L., and Bornstein, P. H. (1979). Covert modeling treatment of children's dental fears. *Child Behaviour Therapy*, **1**, 249–255.

Chess, S. (1964). Editorial: 'Mal de mere', *American Journal of Orthopsychiatry*, **34**, 613–614.

Chess, S., and Thomas, A. (1984). *Origins and evolution of behavior disorders*. New York: Brunner/ Mazel.

Christensen, A., Johnson, S. M., Phillips, S., and Glasgow, R. E. (1980). Cost effectiveness in parent consultation. *Behaviour Therapy*, **11**, 208–226.

Cicchetti, D. (1984a). The emergence of developmental psychopathology. *Child Development*, **55**, 1–7.

Cicchetti, D. (1984b). *Developmental psychopathology*. Chicago: University of Chicago Press.

Cicchetti, D., Toth, S., and Bush, M. (1988). Developmental psychopathology and incompetence in childhood: Suggestions for intervention. In B. B. Lahey and A. E. Kazdin (eds), *Advances in Clinical Child Psychology* (Vol. II). New York: Plenum.

Clark, H. B., Risley, T. R., and Cataldo, M. F. (1976). Behavioral technology for the normal middle-class family. In E. J. Mash, L. A. Hamerlynck and L. C. Handy (eds), *Behavior modification and families*. New York: Brunner/Mazel.

Clark, P., and Rutter, M. (1981). Autistic children's responses to structure and to interpersonal demands. *Journal of Autism and Developmental Disorders*, **11**, 201–217.

Clarke, R. G. V. (1977). Psychology and crime. *Bulletin of the British Psychological Society*, **30**, 280–283.

Clarke, A. M., and Clarke, A. D. B. (1976). *Early experience: Myth and reality*. London: Open Books.

Clarke, A. M., and Clarke, A. D. B. (1986). Thirty years of child psychology: A selective review. *Journal of Child Psychology and Psychiatry*, **27**, 719–759.

Clement, P. W., and Milne, D. C. (1967). Group play therapy and tangible reinforcers used to modify the behavior of 8-year-old boys. *Behaviour Research and Therapy*, **5**, 301–312.

Clements, J. C. (1987). *Severe learning disability and psychological handicap*. Chichester: Wiley.

Clements, J. C., Bidder, R. T., Gardner, S., Bryant, G., and Gray, O. P. (1979). A home advisory service for pre-school children with developmental delays. *Child: Care, Health and Development*, **6**, 25–33.

Cobb, D. E., and Medway, F. J. (1978). Determinants of effectiveness in parent consultation. *Journal of Community Psychology*, **6**, 229–240.

Coddington, R. D. (1972). The significance of life events as etiologic factors in the diseases of children. *Journal of Psychosomatic Research*, **16**, I. A survey of professional workers pp. 7–18; II. A study of a normal population pp. 205–213.

Cohen, F., and Lazarus, R. S. (1979). Coping with stress of illness. In G. C. Stone, F. Cohen and N. Adler (eds), *Health psychology*. San Francisco: Jossey-Bass.

Cohn, J. F., and Tranick, E. L. (1983). Three-month-old infant's reactions to simulated maternal depression. *Child Development*, **54**, 185–193.

Coleman, J. C., Herzberg, J., and Morris, M. (1977). Identity in adolescence: Present and future self-concepts. *Journal of Youth and Adolescence*, **6**, 63–75.

Coleman, J., Wolkind, S., and Ashley, L. (1977). Symptoms of behaviour disturbance and adjustment to school. *Journal of Child Psychology and Psychiatry*, **18**, 201–210.

Collins, R. W. (1973). Importance of the bladder cue contingency in the conditioning treatment for enuresis. *Journal of Abnormal Psychology*, **82**, 299–308.

Collins, L. F., Maxwell, A. E., and Cameron, C. (1962). A factor analysis of some child psychiatric clinic data. *Journal of Mental Science*, **108**, 274–285.

Combs, M. L., and Slaby, D. A. (1977). Social skills training with children. In L. Lahey and A. Kazdin (eds), *Advances in clinical child psychology* (Vol. 1). New York: Plenum.

Cone, J. D. (1987). Behavioral assessment with children and adolescents. In M. Hersen and V. B. Van Hasselt (eds), *Behavior therapy with children and adolescents*. New York: Wiley.

Conger, R. D., McCarty, J. A., Yang, R. K., Lahey, B. B., and Kropp, J. P. (1984). Perception of child, child-rearing values, and emotional distress as mediating links between environmental stressors and observed maternal behaviour. *Child Development*, **55**, 2234–2247.

Coopersmith, S. (1967). *The antecedents of self-esteem*. San Francisco: W. H. Freeman.

Corah, N. L. (1973). Effect of perceived control on stress reduction in pedodontic patients. *Journal of Dental Research*, **52**, 1261–1264.

Corsini, R. J. (ed.). (1981). *Handbook of innovative psychotherapies.* New York: John Wiley.

Craighead, W. E., Meyers, A., Wilcoxon-Craighead, L., and McHale, S. M. (1983). Issues in cognitive-behaviour therapy with children. In M. Rosenbaum, G. M. Franks and Y. Joffe (eds), *Perspectives on behavior therapy in the eighties.* New York: Springer-Verlag.

Crandall, V. J., and Bellugi, U. (1954). Some relationships of interpersonal and intrapersonal conceptualizations to personal-social adjustment. *Journal of Personality,* **23**, 224–232.

Crasilneck, H. B., and Hall, J. A. (1975). *Clinical hypnosis: Principles and applications.* New York: Grune and Stratton.

Crasilneck, H. B., Stirman, J. A., Wilson, B. J., McCranie, E. J., and Fogelman, M. J. (1955). Use of hypnosis in the management of patients with burns. *Journal of the American Medical Association,* **158**, 103–106.

Creak, E. M. (1961). Schizophrenic syndrome in childhood: Progress report of a working party. (April 1961). *Cerebral Palsy Bulletin,* **3**, 501–504.

Creer, T. L. (1982). Asthma. *Journal of Consulting and Clinical Psychology,* **50**, 912–921.

Creer, T. L., Renne, C. M., and Chai, H. (1982). The application of behavioural techniques to childhood asthma. In D. C. Russo and J. W. Varni (eds), *Behavioural pediatrics: Research and practice.* New York: Plenum.

Crittendon, P. M. (1988). Relationships at risk. In J. Belsky and T. Nezworski (eds), *Clinical implications of attachment.* Hillsdale, NJ: Lawrence Erlbaum.

Crowell, J. A., and Feldman, S. S. (1988). Mothers' internal models of relationships and children's behavioral and developmental status: A study of mother–child interaction. *Child Development,* **59**, 1273–1285.

Cruickshank, W. M. (1977). Myths and realities of learning disabilities. *Journal of Learning Disabilities,* **10**, 51–63.

Cruickshank, W. M., Hallahan, D. P., and Brice, H. V. (1976). The evaluation of intelligence. In W. M. Cruickshank (ed.), *Cerebral palsy: A developmental disability.* New York: Syracuse University Press.

Cullen, J. E., and Seddon, J. W. (1981). The application of a behavioral regime to disturbed young offenders. *Personality and Individual Differences,* **2**, 285–292.

Cunningham, C. E., Cataldo, M. F., Mallion, C., and Keyes, J. B. (1983). A review and controlled single case evaluation of behavioral approaches to the management of elective mutism. *Child and Family Behavior Therapy,* **5**, 25–49.

Curry, S. L., and Russ, S. W. (1985). Identifying coping strategies in children. *Journal of Clinical Child Psychology,* **14**, 61–69.

Dalali, I. D., and Sheehan, J. G. (1974). Stuttering and assertion training. *Journal of Communication Disorders,* **7**, 97–111.

Daley, B., Addington, J., Kerfoot, S., and Sigston, A. (1985). *Portage: The importance of parents.* Windsor: NFER/Nelson.

Damon, W. (1989). *The Social World of the Child.* San Francisco: Jossey-Bass.

Danziger, K. (1971). *Socialization.* Hardmondsworth: Penguin.

Darwin, C. (1877). A biographical sketch of an infant. *Mind,* **2**, 286–294.

Dash, J. (1981). Rapid hypno-behavioural treatment of a needle phobia in a five-year-old cardiac patient. *Journal of Pediatric Psychology,* **6**, 37–42.

Davidson, W. S., Redner, R., Blakely, C. H., Mitchell, C. M., and Emshoff, J. G. (1987). Diversion of juvenile offenders: An experimental comparison. *Journal of Consulting and Clinical Psychology,* **55**, 68–75.

Day, D. E., and Roberts, M. W. (1983). An analysis of the physical punishment component of a parent training program. *Journal of Abnormal Child Psychology,* **11**, 141–152.

Dean, G., Gannoway, K., Jagger, D., Jehu, D., Morgan, R. T. T., and Turner, R. K. (1976). Teaching self-care skills to the mentally handicapped in children's homes. *Child Treatment Research Unit.* Paper No. 6. University of Leicester (Clinical Psychology Section).

Delange, J. M., Barton, J. A., and Lanham, S. L. (1981). The WISER way: A cognitive-behavioural model for group social skills training with juvenile delinquents. *Social Work with Groups,* **4**, 37–48.

Delange, J. M., Lanham, S. L., and Barton, J. A. (1981). Social skills training for juvenile offenders: Behavioural skill training and cognitive techniques. In D. Upper and S. Ross (eds), *Behavior group therapy: An annual review,* (Vol. 3). Champaign, IL: Research Press.

Delfini, L., Bernal, M., and Rosen, P. (1976). Comparison of deviant and normal boys in home settings. In E. Marsh, L. Hamerlynck and L. Handy (eds), *Behaviour Modification and Families.* New York: Brunner/Mazel.

De Myer, K. K., Hingten, J. N., and Jackson, R. K. (1981). Infantile autism reviewed. A decade of research. *Schizophrenia Bulletin,* **7**, 338–351.

Denckla, M. B. (1979). Childhood learning disabilities. In K. M. Heilman and E. Valenstein (eds), *Clinical Nueropsychology.* Oxford: Oxford University Press.

Dennis, W. (1960). Causes of retardation among institutional children in Iran. *Journal of Genetic Psychology,* **6**, 47–59.

DeWolfe, T. E., Jackson, L. A., and Winterberger, P. (1988). A comparison of moral reasoning and moral character in male and female incarcerated felons. *Sex Roles,* **18**, 583–593.

DHSS (1984). *Helping mentally handicapped people with special problems.* DHSS Report.

Di Lorenzo, T. M., and Matson, J. L. (1981). Stuttering. In M. Hersen and V. B. Van Hasselt (eds). *Behaviour Therapy with Children and Adolescents.* Chichester: John Wiley.

Dimock, H. G. (1960). *The child in the hospital: A study of his emotional and social well-being.* Philadelphia: Davis.

Dix, T. H., Ruble, D., Grusec, J., and Nixon, S. (1986). Social cognition in parents: Inferential and affective reactions to children of three age levels. *Child Development,* **57**, 879–894.

Doering, S. G., and Entwistle, D. R. (1975). Preparation during pregnancy and ability to cope with labor and delivery. *American Journal of Orthopsychiatry,* **45**, 825–837.

Doleys, D. M. (1977). Behavioral treatments for nocturnal enuresis in children: A Review of the recent literature. *Psychological Bulletin,* **8**, 30–54.

Doleys, D. M. (1978). Assessment and treatment of enuresis and encopresis in children. In M. Hersen, R. M. Eisler and P. M. Miller (eds), *Progress in Behavior Modification,* **6**, 85–121. New York: Academic Press.

Doleys, D. M., and Williams, S. C. (1977). The use of natural consequences and a make-up period to eliminate school phobic behavior: A case study. *Journal of School Psychiatry,* **15**, 44–50.

Dolgin, M. J., and Jay, S. M. (1989). Childhood cancer. In T. H. Ollendick and M. Hersen (eds). *Handbook of Child Psychopathology* (2nd ed). New York: Plenum.

Dollinger, S. J., O'Donnell, J. P., and Staley, A. A. (1984). Lightning-strike disaster: Effects on children's fears and worries. *Journal of Consulting and Clinical Psychology,* **52**, 1028–1038.

Douglas, J., and Richman, N. (1984). *My Child Won't Sleep.* Harmondsworth: Penguin.

Dowdney, L., Mrazek, D., Quinton, D., and Rutter, M. (1984). Observations of parent-child interaction with two- to three-year olds. *Journal of Child Psychology and Psychiatry,* **25**, 379–407.

Dreger, R. M. (1982). The classification of children and their emotional problems: An overview. *Clinical Psychology Review,* **2**, 239–386.

Drillien, C. M. (1964a). *The Growth and Development of the Prematurely Born Infant.* Baltimore: Williams and Wilkins.

Drillien, C. M. (1964b). The effect of obstetrical hazard on the later development of the child. In D. Gardner (ed.). *Recent Advances in Pediatrics.* London: Churchill.

Dubin, R., and Dubin, E. R. (1965). Children's social perceptions: A review of research. *Child Development,* **36**, (3), 809–838.

Dumas, J. E. (1989). Treating anti-social behavior in children: Child and family approaches. *Clinical Psychology Review,* **9**, 197–222.

Dunn, J. B. (1975). Consistency and change in styles of mothering. In *Parent-Infant Interactions.* CIBA Foundation Symposium. **33**, 155–176. Elsevier-Excerpta Medica-North Holland, Amsterdam.

Dunn, J. (1988). *The Beginnings of Social Understanding.* Oxford: Basil Blackwell.

Dunn, J., and Kendrick, C. (1982). *Sibling: Love, Envy and Understanding.* Cambridge, MA: Harvard University Press.

Dunn, J. B., and Richards, M. P. (1977). Observations on the developing relationship between mother and baby in the neonatal period. In H. R. Schaffer (ed.). *Studies in Mother–Infant Interactions.* London: Academic Press.

Dunn, J., Kendrick, C., and MacNamee, R. (1981). The reaction of first-born children to the birth of a sibling: mothers' reports. *J. Child Psychology and Psychiatry,* **22**, 1–18.

Durlak, J. A. (1979). Comparative effectiveness of paraprofessional and professional helpers. *Psychological Bulletin,* **86**, 80–92.

Dush, D. M., Hirt, M. L., and Schroeder, H. E. (1989). Self-statement modification in the treatment of child behavior disorders: A meta-analysis. *Psychological Bulletin,* **106**, 97–106.

Dyregrov, A. (1988). Critical incident stress debriefings. Unpublished manuscript, Research Center for Occupational Health and Safety, University of Bergen, Norway.

D'Zurilla, T. J., and Goldfried, M. R. (1971). Cognitive processes, problem-solving and effective behaviour. In M. R. Goldfried and M. Merbaum (eds). *Behaviour change through self-control.* New York: Holt, Rinehart & Winston.

Earls, F. (1980). Prevalence of behavior problems in 3-year-old children: A cross maternal replication. *Archives of General Psychiatry,* **37**, 1153–1157.

Earls, F. (1981). Temperamental characteristics and behavior problems in three-year-old children. *The Journal of Nervous and Mental Disease,* **169**, 367–374.

Earls, F., and Richman, N. (1980a). The prevalence of behavior problems in three year old children of West Indian-born parents. *Journal of Child Psychology and Psychiatry,* **21**, 99–106.

Earls, F., and Richman, N. (1980b). Behavior problems in preschool children of West Indian parents: A re-examination of family and social factors. *Journal of Child Psychology and Psychiatry,* **21**, 107–117.

Earls, F., Smith, E., Reich, W., and Jung, K. G. (1988). Investigating psychopathological consequences of a disaster in children: A pilot study incorporating a structured diagnostic approach. *Journal of the American Academy of Child and Adolescent Psychiatry,* **27**, 90–95.

Eckert, E. D., Goldberg, S. C., Halmi, K. A., Casper, R. C., and Davis, J. M. (1979). Behavior therapy in anorexia nervosa. *British Journal of Psychiatry,* **134**, 55–59.

Edwards, J. G. (1976). Psychiatric aspects of civilian disasters. *British Medical Journal,* I, 944–947.

Ehrhardt, A., and Money, J. (1967). Progestin-induced hermaphroditism: IQ and psychosexual identity in a study of ten girls. *Journal of Sex Research,* **3**, 83–100.

Eisenberg, L., and Kanner, L. (1956). Early infantile autism. *American Journal of Orthopsychiatry,* **26**, 556–566.

Eisser, C. (1985). *The Psychology of Childhood Illness.* New York: Springer.

Eland, J. M. (1974). Children's communication of pain. Unpublished master's thesis, University of Iowa.

Eland, J. M. (1981). Minimizing pain associated with pre-kindergarten intramuscular injections. *Issues in Comprehensive Pediatric Nursing,* **5**, 361–372.

Eland, J. M., and Anderson, J. E. (1977). The experience of pain in children. In: A. Jacox (ed.), Pain: a source book for nurses and other health professionals. Boston: Little, Brown, Mass.

Elkind, D. (1967). Egocentrism in Adolescence. *Child Development,* **38**, 1035–1044.

Elkind, D. (1980). Strategic interactions in early adolescence. In J. Adelson. (ed.). *Handbook of adolescent psychology.* New York: Wiley.

Ellenberg, L., Kellerman, J., Dash, J., Higgins, G., and Zeltzer, L. (1980). Use of hypnosis for multiple symptoms in an adolescent girl with leukemia. *Journal of Adolescent Health Care,* **1**, 132–136.

Elliott, C. H., and Olson, R. A. (1983). The management of children's distress in response to painful medical treatment for burn injuries. *Behaviour Research and Therapy,* **21**, (6), 675–683.

Elliott, C. H., Jay, S. M., and Woody, P. C. (1987). An observation scale for measuring children's distress during medical procedures. *Journal of Pediatric Psychology*, **12**, (4), 543–551.

Ellis, P. L. (1982). Empathy: A factor in antisocial behavior. *Journal of Abnormal Child Psychology*, **2**, 123–133.

Elmhorn, K. (1965). Study in self-reported delinquency among school children. In *Scandinavian Studies in Criminology*. London: Tavistock.

Emery, R. E., and Marholin, D. (1977). An applied behavior analysis of delinquency: The irrelevancy of relevant behavior. *American Psychologist*, **6**, 860–873.

Emmerich, W. (1969). The parental role: A functional-cognitive approach. *Monographs of the Society for Research in Child Development*, **34**. (8, Serial No. 132).

Epstein, L. (1976). Psychophysiological measurement in assessment. In M. Hersen and A. S. Bellack (eds), *Behavioural Assessment: A practical handbook*. New York: Pergamon.

Erickson, M., Sroufe, A., and Egeland, B. (1985). The relationship between quality of attachment, and behaviour problems in preschool in a high-risk sample. In I. Bretherton and E. Waters. *Growing Points of Attachment Theory and Research. Monographs of the Society for Research in Child Development*, **50**, 147–166.

Erikson, E. (1965). *Childhood and Society*. (Rev. ed). Harmondsworth: Penguin.

Erikson, E. (1968). *Identity, Youth and Crisis*. New York: Norton.

Eron, L. D., Walder, L. O., Toigo, R., and Lefrowitz, M. M. (1963). Social class, parental punishment for aggression, and child aggression. *Child Development*, **34**, 849–867.

Erwin, E. (1979). *Behaviour Therapy: Scientific, Philosophical and Moral Foundations*. Cambridge: Cambridge University Press.

Esser, G., Schmidt, M. I., and Woerner, W. (1990). Epidemiology and course of psychiatric disorders in school-age children. *Journal of Child Psychology and Psychiatry*, **31**, 243–263.

Evans, I. M., (1989). A multi-dimensional model for conceptualizing the design of child behavior therapy. *Behavioural Psychotherapy*, **17**, 237–251.

Evans, I. M., and Meyer, L. H. (1985). *An Educative Approach to Behavior Problems: A Practical Decision Model for Intervention with Severely Handicapped Learners*. Baltimore: Paul H. Brookes.

Evers, W. L., and Schwartz, J. C. (1973). Modifying social withdrawal in preschoolers: The effects of filmed modeling and teacher praise. *Journal of Abnormal Child Psychology*, **1**, 248–256.

Eysenck, H. J. (1964). *Crime and Personality*. London: Routledge.

Eysenck, H. J. (1967). *The biological basis of personality*. Springfield, IL: C. C. Thomas.

Eysenck, H. J., and Rachman, S. (1965). *The Causes and Cures of Neurosis*. London: Routledge & Kegan Paul.

Eysenck, M. W. (1984). *Handbook of cognitive psychology*. London: Lawrence Earlbaum.

Farnes, J., and Wallace, C. (1987). Pilot study for a sleep clinic. *Health Visitor*, **60**, 41–43.

Farrell, B. A. (1970). Psychoanalysis: The method. In S. G. Lee and M. Herbert (eds), *Freud and psychology*. Harmondsworth: Penguin.

Farrell, P. T. (1982). An evaluation of an EDY course in behaviour modification: techniques for teachers and care staff in an ESN(S) school. *Special Education: Forward Trends*, **9**, 21–25.

Farrington, D. P. (1978). The family backgrounds of aggressive youths. In L. A. Hersov and M. Berger (eds), *Aggression and Anti-social Behaviour in Childhood and Adolescence*. Oxford: Pergamon.

Faust, J., and Melamed, B. G. (1984). Influence of arousal, previous experience, and age on surgery preparation of same day of surgery and in-hospital pediatric patients. *Journal of Consulting and Clinical Psychology*, **52**, 359–365.

Feindler, E. L., and Ecton, R. B. (1986). *Adolescent anger control: Cognitive-behavioral techniques*. Elmsford, NY: Pergamon Press.

Feindler, E. L., Marriott, S. A., and Iwata, M. (1984). Group and control training for junior high school delinquents. *Behaviour Therapy and Research*, **8**, 299–311.

Feldman, M. P. (1977). *Criminal Behaviour: A Psychological Analysis*. Chichester: John Wiley.

Fergusson, D. M., and Horwood, L. J. (1987). The trait and method components of ratings of conduct disorder. Part 1. Maternal and teacher evaluations of conduct disorder in young children. *Journal of Child Psychology and Psychiatry*, **28**, 249–260.
Part 2. Factors related to the trait component of conduct disorder scores. *Journal of Child Psychology and Psychiatry*, **28**, 261–272.

Fergusson, D. M., and Horwood, L. J. (1989). Estimation of method and trait variance in ratings of conduct disorder. *Journal of Child Psychology and Psychiatry*, **30**, 365–378.

Fernald, C., and Corry, J. (1981). Empathic versus directive preparation of children for needles. *Child: Health, Care and Development*, **10**, 44–47.

Ferrari, M. (1986). Fears and Phobias in childhood: some clinical and developmental considerations. *Child Psychiatry and Human Development*, **17**, 75–87.

Ferrari, M., and Harris, S. L. (1981). The limits and motivating potential of sensory stimuli as reinforcers for autistic children. *Journal of Applied Behavior Analysis*, **14**, 339–343.

Ferster, C. B., and Skinner, B. F. (1957). *Schedules of reinforcement*. New York: Appleton.

Fielding, D. (1983). Adolescent services. In A. Liddell (ed.), *The practice of clinical psychology in Great Britain*. Chichester: Wiley.

Fielding, D. (1985). Chronic illness in children. In F. Watts (ed.), *New developments in clinical psychology*. Leicester: British Psychological Society/Wiley.

Fielding, D. (1987). Working with children and young people. In J. S. Marzillier and J. Hall (eds), *What is clinical psychology?* Oxford: Oxford University Press.

Filipczak, J., Archer, M., and Friedman, R. (1980). In-school skills training use with disruptive adolescents. *Behavior Modification*, **4**, 243–263.

Finch, A. J. Jr., and Rogers, T. R. (1984). Self-report instruments. In T. H. Ollendick and M. Hersen (eds), *Child behavior assessment: Principles and procedures*. New York: Pergamon Press.

Finch, A. J., Saylor, C. F., and Edwards, G. L. (1985). Children's Depression Inventory: Sex and grade norms for normal children. *Journal of Consulting and Clinical Psychology*, **53**, 424–425.

Fischer, M., Rolf, J. E., Hasazi, J. E., and Cummings, L. (1984). Follow-up of a preschool epidemiological sample: Cross-age continuities and predictions of later adjustment with internalizing and externalizing dimensions of behavior. *Child Development*, **55**, 137–150.

Fishman, D. B., Rotgers, F., and Franks, C. M. (eds) (1988). *Paradigms in behavior therapy: Present and promise*. New York: Springer.

Fixsen, D. L., Phillips, E. L., Harper, T., Mesigh, C., Timbers, G., and Wolf, M. M. (1972). *The teaching-family model of group home treatment*. Paper read at the American Psychological Association, Honolulu, Hawaii.

Flament, M. F., Koby, E., Rapoport, J. L., Berg, C. J., Zahn, T., Cox, C., Denckla, M., and Lenane, M. (1990). Childhood obsessive–compulsive disorder: a prospective follow-up study. *Journal of Child Psychology and Psychiatry*, **31**, 363–380.

Flanagan, B., Goldiamond, I., and Azrin, N. (1958). Operant stuttering: The control of stuttering behavior through response-contingent consequences. *Journal of Experimental Analysis of Behavior*, **1**, 173–178.

Fonagy, P., Moran, G. S., and Higgitt, A. C. (1989). Insulin dependent diabetes mellitus in children and adolescents. In S. Pearce and J. Wardle (eds), *The practice of behavioural medicine*. Leicester: British Psychological Society/Oxford University Press.

Fontana, D. (1986). *Classroom control*. Leicester: British Psychological Society/Methuen.

Fordyce, W. (1976). *Behavioral methods for chronic pain and illness*. St Louis: Masby.

Forehand, R. (1977). Child non-compliance to parental requests: Behavioural analysis and treatment. *Progress in Behaviour Modification*, **5**, 111–147.

Forehand, R., and Atkeson, B. M. (1977). Generality of treatment effects with parents as therapists: A review of assessment and implementation procedures. *Behavior Therapy*, **8**, 575–593.

Forehand, R., and King, H. E. (1977). Noncompliant children: Effects of parent training on behavior and attitude change. *Behavior Modification*, **1**, 93–108.

Forehand, R., and McMahon, R. J. (1981). *Helping the noncompliant child: A clinician's guide to effective parent training*. New York: Guilford.

Forehand, R., and Peed, S. (1979). Training parents to modify noncompliant behavior of their children. In A. J. Finch, Jr. and P. C. Kendall (eds), *Treatment and research in child psychopathology*. New York: Spectrum.

Forehand, R., and Scarboro, M. E. (1975). An analysis of children's oppositional behaviour. *Journal of Abnormal Child Psychology*, **3**, 27–31.

Forehand, R., Gardner, H., and Roberts, M. (1978). Maternal response to child compliance and noncompliance: Some normative data. *Journal of Clinical Child Psychology*, **7**, 121–123.

Forehand, R., Wells, K. C., and Griest, D. L. (1980). An examination of the social validity of a parent training program. *Behavior Therapy*, **11**, 488–502.

Frame, C., Matson, J. L., Sonis, W. A., Fialkov, M. J., and Kazdin, A. E. (1982). Behavioral treatment of depression in a prepubertal child. *Journal of Behavior Therapy and Experimental Psychiatry*, **3**, 239–243.

Francis, G., and Ollendick, T. H. (1986). Anxiety disorders. In C. L. Frame and J. L. Matson (eds), *Handbook of assessment in child psychopathology: Applied issues in differential diagnosis and treatment evaluation*. New York: Plenum Press.

Frank, J. (1973). *Persuasion and healing*. The John Hopkins University Press: Baltimore.

Frankenburg, W., and Dodd, J. B. (1967). The Denver Developmental Screening Test. *Journal of Pediatrics*, **71**, 181–191.

Frederick, C. J. (1985). Children traumatized by catastrophic situations. In S. Eth and R. Pynoos (eds), *Post-traumatic stress disorder in children*. Washington: American Psychiatric Press, pp. 73–99.

Freedman, B. J., Rosenthal, L., Donahue, C. P., Schlundt, D. G., and McFall, R. M. (1978). A social-behavioral analysis of skill deficits in delinquent and non-delinquent adolescent boys. *Journal of Consulting and Clinical Psychology*, **46**, 1448–1462.

Freud, A. (1946). *The psychoanalytic treatment of children*. New York: International Universities Press.

Freud, A. (1958). *Adolescence: Psychoanalytic study of the child*. New York: International Universities Press.

Freud, S. (1905/1953). Three essays on the theory of sexuality. In J. Strachey (ed.) *The standard edition of the complete psychological works of Sigmund Freud*, (Vol. 7). London: Hogarth Press.

Freud, S. (1917). Mourning and melancholia. In J. Strachey, (ed.) *The standard edition of Sigmund Freud's works*, (Vol. 14). London: Hogarth Press.

Friedman, A. G., and Ollendick, T. H. (1989). Treatment programs for severe night-time fears: A methodological note. *Journal of Behavior Therapy and Experimental Psychiatry*, **20**, (2), 171–178.

Fry, P. S. (1985). Relations between teenagers' age, knowledge, expectations and maternal behaviour. *British Journal of Developmental Psychology*, **3**, 47–55.

Fryers, T. (1984). *The epidemiology of intellectual impairment*. London: Academic Press.

Furman, W. (1980). Promoting appropriate social behavior. In B. Lahey and A. Kazdin (eds), *Advances of Clinical Child Psychology*, Vol. 3. New York: Plenum.

Gabel, S. (ed.). (1981). *Behavioral problems in childhood: A primary care approach*. New York: Grune & Stratton.

Gaffney, L. R., and McFall, R. M. (1981). A comparison of social skills in delinquent and nondelinquent girls using a role-playing inventory. *Journal of Consulting and Clinical Psychology*, **49**, 959–967.

Gaines, R., Sandgrund, A., Green, A. H., and Power, E. (1978). Etiological factors in child maltreatment: A multivariate study of abusing, neglecting, and normal mothers. *Journal of Abnormal Psychology*, **87**, 531–540.

Galante, R., and Foa, D. (1986). An epidemiological study of psychic trauma and treatment effectiveness after a natural disaster. *Journal of the American Academy of Child Psychiatry*, **25**, 357–363.

Garbarino, J. (1978). The elusive crime of emotional abuse. *Child Abuse and Neglect*, **2**, 89–99.

Garbarino, J. (1988). *A note on children and youth in dangerous environments: The Palestinian situation as a case study.* Unpublished paper, Erikson Institute for Advance Study in Child Development, Chicago.

Gardner, F. (1987). *Observation study of preschool children with behaviour problems.* Unpublished PhD thesis, University of Oxford, Oxford.

Gardner, G. G. (1976). Childhood death, and human dignity: Hypnotherapy for David. *International Journal of Clinical and Experimental Hypnosis,* **24,** 122–139.

Gardner, G. G., and Olness, K. (1981). *Hypnosis and hypnotherapy with children.* New York: Grune & Stratton.

Garfinkle, P. E., Kline, S. H., and Stamcer, H. C. (1973). Treatment of anorexia nervosa using operant conditioning techniques. *Journal of Nervous and Mental Disease,* **157,** 428–433.

Garmezy, N. (1977). DSM-III: Never mind the psychologists — Is it good for the children? *The Clinical Psychologist,* **31,** 3–4.

Garmezy, N. (1983). Stressors of childhood. In N. Garmezy and M. Rutter (eds), *Stress coping and development in children.* New York: McGraw-Hill.

Garmezy, N. (1986). Children under severe stress: Critique and comments. *Journal of the American Academy of Child Psychiatry,* **25,** 384–392.

Garmezy, N. (1987). Stress, competence and development: The search for stress-resistant children. *American Journal of Orthopsychiatry,* **57,** 159–174.

Garmezy, N., and Rutter, M. (1985). Acute reactions to stress. In M. Rutter and L. Hersov (eds), *Child and adolescent psychiatry: Modern approaches* (2nd ed). Oxford: Blackwell, pp. 152–176.

Garmezy, N., Masten, A. S., and Tellegen, A. (1984). The study of stress and competence in children: A building block for developmental psychopathology. *Child Development,* **55,** 97–111.

Garner, D. (1986). Cognitive therapy for anorexia nervosa. In K. D. Brownell and J. P. Foreyt (eds), *Handbook of eating disorders.* New York: Basic Books.

Garrett, C. J. (1985). Effects of residential treatment on adjudicated adolescents: A meta-analysis. *Journal of Research in Crime and Delinquency,* **25,** 463–489.

Gath, A. (1972). The mental health of siblings of congenitally abnormal children. *Journal of Child Psychology and Psychiatry,* **13,** 211–218.

Gelber, H., and Meyer, V. (1965). Behaviour therapy and encopresis: The complexities involved in treatment. *Behaviour Research and Therapy,* **2,** 227–231.

Gelfand, D. M., Jenson, W. R., and Drew, C. J. (1988). *Understanding child behavior disorders* (2nd ed). New York: Holt, Rinehart and Winston.

Gendreau, P., and Andrews, D. A. (In press). What the meta-analyses of the offender treatment literature tell us about 'what works'. *Canadian Journal of Criminology.*

Gendreau, P., and Ross, R. R. (1987). Revivifaction of rehabilitation: Evidence from the 1980s. *Justice Quarterly,* **4,** 349–407.

Gesell, A. (1950). *The first five years of life: A guide to the study of the preschool child.* London: Methuen.

Gesell, A., and Ilg, F. L. (1943). *Infant and child in the culture of today.* New York: Harper & Row.

Gibbs, J. C., Arnold, K. D., Cheesman, F. L., and Ahlborn, H. H. (1984). Facilitation of sociomoral reasoning in delinquents. *Journal of Consulting and Clinical Psychology,* **52,** 37–45.

Gibson, H. B. (1967). Self-reported delinquency among schoolboys and their attitudes to the police. *British Journal of Social and Clinical Psychology,* **6,** 168–173.

Gil, D. G. (1970). *Violence against children: Physical child abuse in the United States.* Cambridge, MA: Harvard University Press.

Gillespie, W. H. (1968). The psychoanalytic theory of child development. In E. Miller (ed.), *Foundations of child psychiatry.* Oxford: Pergamon.

Gillison, T. H., and Skinner, J. L. (1958). Treatment of nocturnal enuresis by the electric alarm. *British Medical Journal,* **2,** 1268–1272.

Ginther, L. J., and Roberts, M. C. (1983). A test of mastery versus coping modeling in the reduction of children's dental fears. *Child and Family Behaviour Therapy*, **4**, 41–52.

Glennon, B., and Weisz, J. R. (1978). An observational approach to the reassessment of anxiety in young children. *Journal of Consulting and Clinical Psychology*, **46**, 1246–1257.

Glick, B., and Goldstein, A. P. (1987). Aggression replacement training. *Journal of Counseling and Development*, **65**, 356–367.

Glicklich, L. B. (1951). An historical account of enuresis. *Paediatrics*, **8**, 859–876.

Glidewell, J. C., Kantor, M. B., Smith, L. M., and Stringer, L. A. (1964). Socialization and social structure in the classroom. In L. W. Hoffman and M. L. Hoffman (eds), *Review of child development research*, (Vol. 2). New York: Russell Sage Foundation.

Goddard, K. E., Brodge, G., and Wenar, C. (1961). Special article — reliability of pediatric histories, a preliminary study. *Paediatrics*, **28**, 321–324.

Goetz, E. M., Holmberg, M. C., and Le Blanc, J. M. (1975). Differential reinforcement of other behaviour and non-contingent reinforcement as control procedures during the modification of a preschooler's compliance. *Journal of Applied Behavioral Analysis*, **8**, 77–82.

Goldstein, A., and Foa, E. B. (eds.). (1987). *Handbook of behavioural interventions*. New York: Wiley.

Goldstein, A. P., and Heller, H. (1987). *Aggressive behavior: Assessment and intervention*. Elmsford, NY: Pergamon Press.

Goldstein, A. P., Heller, H., and Sechrest, L. B. (1966). *Psychotherapy and the psychology of behavior change*. New York: John Wiley.

Goldstein, A. P., Glick, B., Irwin, M. J., Pask-McCartney, C., and Rubama, I. (1989). *Reducing delinquency: Intervention in the community*. Elmsford, NY: Pergamon Press.

Goodnow, J. J. (1984). Parents' ideas about parenting and development. A review of issues and recent work. In M. E. Lamb, A. L. Brown and B, Rogoff (eds), *Advances in developmental psychology*, (Vol. 3). Hillsdale, NJ: Erlbaum.

Goodnow, J. J. (1988). Parents' ideas, actions and feelings: Models and methods for developmental and social psychology. *Child Development*, **59**, 286–320.

Goodnow, J. J., Cashmore, J., Cotton, S., and Knight, R. (1984). Mothers' developmental timetables in two cultural groups. *International Journal of Psychology*, **19**, 193–205.

Goodyer, I. M. (1990). Family relationships, life events and childhood psychopathology. *Journal of Child Psychology and Psychiatry*, **31**, 161–192.

Goodyer, I. M., Wright, C., and Altham, P. M. E. (1989). Recent friendships in anxious and depressed school-age children. *Psychological Medicine*, **19**, 165–174.

Gordon, D. A., and Arbuthnot, J. (1987). Individual, group and family intervention. In H. C. Quay (ed.), *Handbook of juvenile delinquency*. New York: Wiley.

Gould, M. S., Wunsch-Hitzig, R., and Dohrenwend, B. P. (1980). Formulation of hypotheses about the prevalence, treatment and prognostic significance of psychiatric disorders in children in the United States. In B. P. Dohrenwend, B. S. Dohrenwend, M. S. Gould, B. Link, R. Neugebaur and R. Wunsch-Hitzig (eds), *Mental illness in the United States: Epidemiological estimates*. New York: Praeger.

Graham, D. T., Rutter, M., and George, S. (1973). Temperamental characteristics as predictors of behaviour disorders in children. *American Journal of Orthopsychiatry*, **43**, (3), 328–339.

Graham, P. (1964). *Controlled trial of behavior therapy vs conventional therapy: A pilot study*. Unpublished dissertation. University of London.

Graham, P. (1980). Epidemiological studies. In H. C. Quay and J. C. Werry (eds), *Psychopathological disorders of childhood* (2nd ed). New York: Wiley.

Graham, P., and Rutter, M. (1973). Psychiatric disorders in the young adolescent: A follow-up study. *Proceedings of the Royal Society of Medicine*, **66**, 1226–1229.

Gray, J. (1982). *The neuropsychology of anxiety: An enquiry into the function of the septi-hippocampal system*. New York: Oxford University Press.

Graziano, A. M., and DeGiovanni, I. S. (1979). The clinical significance of childhood phobias: A note on the proportion of child-clinical referrals for the treatment of children's fears. *Behaviour Research and Therapy*, **17**, 161–162.

Graziano, A. M., and Mooney, K. C. (1980). Family self-control instruction for children's night-time fear reduction. *Journal of Consulting and Clinical Psychology*, **48**, 206–213.

Graziano, A. M., and Mooney, K. C. (1982). Behavioral treatment of 'night-fears' in children: Maintenance of improvement at 2- to 3-year follow-up. *Journal of Consulting and Clinical Psychology*, **50**, 598–599.

Graziano, A. M., Mooney, K. C., Huber, C., and Ignaziak, D. (1979). Self-control instruction for children's fear reductions. *Journal of Behavior Therapy and Experimental Psychiatry*, **10**, 221–227.

Green, K., Forehand, R., and McMahon, R. (1979). Parental manipulation of compliance and non-compliance in normal and deviant children. *Behaviour Modification*, **3**, 245–266.

Green, R. (1974). *Sexual identity conflict in children and adults*. New York: Basic Books.

Greenacre, Y. (1945). The biological economy of birth. In *The psychoanalytic study of the child*, pp. 31–51. New York: International University Press.

Greenberg, M., and Morris, N. (1974). Engrossment: The newborn's impact upon the father. *American Journal of Orthopsychiatry*, **44**, 520–531.

Greenberg, M. T., and Speltz, M. L. (1988). Attachment and the ontogeny of conduct problems. In J. Belsky and T. Nezworski (eds), *Clinical implications of attachment*. Hillsdale, NJ: Erlbaum.

Gresham, F. M., and Nagle, R. J. (1980). Social skills training with children: Responsiveness and coaching as a function of peer orientation. *Journal of Consulting and Clinical Psychology*, **48**, 718–729.

Griest, D. L., and Wells, K. C. (1983). Behavioural family therapy with conduct disorders in children. *Behavior Therapy*, **14**, 37–53.

Griest, D. L., Forehand, R., and Wells, K. C. (1981). Follow-up assessment of parent behavioral training: An analysis of who will participate. *Child Study Journal*, **4**, 221–229.

Griest, D. L., Forehand, R., Wells, K. C., and McMahon, R. F. (1980). An examination of the differences between nonclinic and behavior problems clinic referred children and their mothers. *Journal of Abnormal Psychology*, **89**, 497–500.

Groh, T. R., and Goldenberg, E. E. (1976). Locus of control with subgroups in a correctional population. *Criminal Justice and Behavior*, **3**, 169–179.

Gross, A. M. (1983). Conduct disorders. In M. Hersen (ed.), *Outpatient behavior therapy: A clinical guide*. New York: Grune & Stratton.

Gross, A. M., and Wixtead, J. T. (1987). Oppositional behavior. In M. Hersen and V. B. Van Hasselt (eds), *Behavior therapy with children and adolescents*. Chichester: John Wiley.

Gross, A. M., Brigham, T. A., Hopper, C., and Bologna, N. C. (1980). Self-management and social skills training: A study with pre-delinquent and delinquent youth. *Criminal Justice and Behavior*, **7**, 161–184.

Gross, A. M., Stern, R. M., Levin, R. B., Dale, J., and Wojnilower, D. A. (1983). The effect of mother-child separation on the behaviour of children experiencing a diagnostic medical procedure. *Journal of Consulting and Clinical Psychology*, **51**, 783–785.

Grusec, J. E. (1982). The socialization of altruism. In N. Eisenberg (ed.), *The development of prosocial behaviour*. New York: Academic Press.

Hagman, E. R. (1932). A study of fears of children of preschool age. *Journal of Experimental Education*, **1**, 110–130.

Hains, A. A. (1984). A preliminary attempt to teach the use of problem solving skills to delinquents. *Child Study Journal*, **14**, 271–285.

Hains, A. A., and Hains, A. H. (1987). The effects of a cognitive strategy intervention on the problem-solving abilities of delinquent youths. *Journal of Adolescence*, **10**, 399–413.

Haley, J. (1976). *Problem Solving Therapy*. New York: Warper Colophon.

Hall, S. (1904). *Adolescence: Its psychology and its relation to physiology, anthropology, sociology, sex, crime, religion, and education* (Vols. I and II). New York: D. Appleton.

Halliday, G. (1987). Direct psychological therapies for nightmares: A review. *Clinical Psychology Review*, **7**, 501–523.

Halmi, K. A., Powers, P., and Cunningham, S. (1975). Treatment of anorexia nervosa with behavior modification. *Archives of General Psychiatry*, **32**, 93–95.

Hampson, J. L., and Hampson, J. G. (1961). The ontogenesis of sexual behavior in man. In W. C. Young and G. W. Corner (eds), *Sex and internal secretions* Vol II (3rd ed). Baltimore: Williams & Wilkins.

Handford, H. A., Mayes, S. O., Mattison, R. E., Humphrey, F. J., Bagnato, S., Bixler, E. O., and Kales, J. D. (1986). Child and parent reaction to the TMI nuclear accident. *Journal of the American Academy of Child and Adolescent Psychiatry*, **25**, 346–355.

Harré, R. (1979). *Social being*. Oxford: Blackwell.

Harris, S. L., and Handleman, J. S. (1987). Autism. In M. Hersen and V. B. Van Hasselt (eds), *Behavior therapy with children and adolescents*. Chichester: John Wiley.

Hart, B. B. (1991) Hypnosis and pain. In M. Heap and W. Dryden (eds), *Handbook of hypnotherapy in Britain*. Open University Press.

Hart, B. M., Reynolds, N. J., Baer, D., Brauley, E. R., and Harris, F. R. (1968). Effects of contingent and noncontingent social reinforcement on the cooperative play of pre-school children. *Journal of Applied Behavior Analysis*, **1**, 73–78.

Hartshorne, H., and May, M. A. (1928–30). *Studies in the nature of character*. New York: Macmillan.

Hartup, W. W. (1974). Aggression in childhood: Developmental perspectives. *American Psychologist*, **29**, 336–341.

Haswell, K., Hook, E., and Wener, C. (1981). Oppositional behaviour of pre-school children. Theory and intervention. *Family Relations*, **30**, 440–446.

Hatzenbuehler, L. C., and Schroeder, H. E. (1978). Desensitization procedures in the treatment of childhood disorders. *Psychological Bulletin*, **85**, 831–844.

Hawkins, R. P. (1972). It's time we taught the young how to be good parents (and don't you wish we'd started a long time ago?). *Psychology Today*, November, 28–32.

Hawton, K. (1982). Motivation aspects of deliberate self-poisoning in adolescents. *British Journal of Psychiatry*, **141**, 286–291.

Haymari, E. (1932). A study of fears of children of preschool age. *Journal of Experimental Education*, **1**, 110–130.

Haynes, S. N. (1978). *Principles of behavioral assessment*. New York: Gardner Press.

Hedberg, A. G., and Schlong, A. (1973). Eliminating fainting by school children during mass inoculation clinics. *Nursing Research*, **22**, 352–353.

Heinicke, C. M. (1989). Psychodynamic psychotherapy with children. In B. B. Lahey and A. E. Kazdin (eds), *Advances in clinical child psychology* (Vol. 12). New York: Plenum Press.

Hellman, I. (1962). Sudden separation and its effects followed over twenty years: Hampstead nursery follow-up studies. *Psychoanalytic study of the child*, **17**, 159–174.

Hemsley, R., Howlin, P., Berger, M., Hersov, L., Holbrook, D., Rutter, M., and Yule, W. (1978). Treating autistic children in a family context. In M. Rutter and E. Schopler (eds), *Autism: Reappraisal of concepts and treatment*. New York: Plenum.

Henneborn, W. J., and Cogan, R. (1975). The effect of husband participation in reported pain and the probability of medication during labor and birth. *Journal of Psychosomatic Research*, **19**, 215–222.

Herbert, E. W., Pinkston, E. M., Hayden, M. L., Sajwaj, T. E., Pinkston, S., Cordua, G., and Jackson, C. (1973). Adverse effects of differential parental attention. *Journal of Applied Behavior Analysis*, **6**, 15–30.

Herbert, M. (1964). The concept and testing of brain-damage in children: A review. *Journal of Child Psychology and Psychiatry*, **5**, 197–216.

Herbert, M. (1965). Personality factors and bronchial asthma: A study of South African Indian children. *Journal of Psychosomatic Research*, **8**, 353–356.

Herbert, M. (1966). The development of the self-image and ego identity. *Common Factor Monographs*, **4**, 61–68.

Herbert, M. (1974). *Emotional problems of development in children*. Academic Press: London and New York.

Herbert, M. (1980). Socialization for problem resistance. In P. Feldman and J. Orford (eds), *Psychological problems: The social context*. Chichester: Wiley.

Herbert, M. (1985a). Triadic work with children. In F. Watts (ed.), *Recent developments in clinical psychology*. Chichester: John Wiley.

Herbert, M. (1985b). *Caring for your children: A practical guide*. Oxford: Basil Blackwell.

Herbert, M. (1986). Social skills training with children. In C. R. Hollin and P. Trower (eds), *Handbook of social skills training. Volume 1: Applications across the life-span*. Oxford: Pergamon Press.

Herbert, M. (1987a) *Living with teenagers*. Oxford: Basil Blackwell.

Herbert, M. (1987b). *Conduct disorders of childhood and adolescence: A social-learning perspective* (revised ed). Chichester: John Wiley.

Herbert, M. (1987c). *Behavioural treatment of children with poblems: A practice manual*. London: Academic Press.

Herbert, M. (1988). *Working with children and their families*. Leicester: British Psychological Society/ Routledge.

Herbert, M. (1989a). Aggressive and violent children. (The use of triadic interventions). In K. Howells and C. R. Hollin (eds), *Clinical approaches to violence*. Chichester: Wiley.

Herbert, M. (1989b). *Discipline: A positive guide for parents*. Oxford: Basil Blackwell.

Herbert, M. (1990). *Planning a research project: A guide for trainees and the helping professions*. London: Cassell.

Herbert, M., and Iwaniec, D. (1977). Children who are hard to love. *New Society*, **40**, (759), 111–112.

Herbert, M., and Iwaniec, D. (1981). Behavioural psychotherapy in natural home-settings: An empirical study applied to conduct disordered and incontinent children. *Behavioural Psychotherapy*, **9**, 55–76.

Herbert, M., and Kemp, M. (1969). The reliability of the brain. *Science Journal*, **5a**, 47–52.

Herbert, M., and Sluckin, A. (1985). A realistic look at mother-infant bonding. In M. L. Chiswick (ed.), *Recent advances in perinatal medicine* No. 2. Edinburgh: Churchill Livingstone.

Herbert, M., Sluckin, W., and Sluckin, A. (1982). Mother-to-infant bonding. *Journal of Child Psychology and Psychiatry*, **23**, 205–221.

Herjanic, B., Herjanic, M., Brown, F., and Wheatt, T. (1975). Are children reliable reporters? *Journal of Abnormal Child Psychology*, **3**, 41–48.

Her Majesty's Stationery Office. (1972). *Statistics relating to approved schools, remand homes and attendance centres in England and Wales for the year 1970*. London: HMSO.

Hermelin, B. (1963). Response behaviour of autistic children and subnormal controls. *Paper to the XVII International Congress of Psychology*, Washington.

Hermelin, B. (1966). Psychological research. In J. K. Wing (ed.), *Childhood autism: Clinical, educational and social aspects*. Oxford: Pergamon.

Hermelin, B., and O'Connor, N. (1964). Crossnodal transfer in normal, subnormal and autistic children. *Neuropsychologica*, **2**, 229–232.

Hersen, M. (1970). Behavior modification approach to a school phobia case. *Journal of Clinical Psychology*, **26**, 128–132.

Hersen, M., and Van Hasselt, V. B. (1987). *Children and adolescents*. New York: Wiley.

Hersov, L. A. (1960). Refusal to go to school. *Journal of Child Psychology and Psychiatry*, **1**, 137–145.

Hester, N. K. O. (1979). The preoperational child's reaction to immunization. *Nursing Research*, **28**, 250–255.

Hetherington, E. M. (1979). Divorce: A child's perspective. *American Psychologist (Special Issue)*. **34**, (10), 851–858.

Hetherington, E. M., Cox, M., and Cox, R. (1979). Play and social interaction in children following divorce. *Journal of Social Issues*, **5**, 26–49.

Hewett, S. (1970). *The family and the handicapped child*. London: Allen & Unwin.

Hewstone, M. (1989). *Causal attribution*. Oxford: Blackwell.

Higgins, J. P., and Thies, A. P. (1981). Social effectiveness and problem-solving thinking of reformatory inmates. *Journal of Offender Counseling, Services and Rehabilitation*, **5**, 93–98.

Hilgard, E. R., and Hilgard, J. R. (1983). *Hypnosis in the relief of pain*. Los Altos, CA: William Kaufman, Inc.

Hilgard, J. R., and LeBaron, S. (1982). Relief of anxiety and pain in children and adolescents with cancer: Quantitative measures and clinical observations. *International Journal of Clinical and Experimental Hypnosis*, **4**, 417–442.

Hilgard, J. R., and LeBaron, S. (1984). *Hypnotherapy of pain in children with cancer*. Los Altos, CA: Kaufman.

Hilgard, J. R., and Morgan, A. H. (1976). *Treatment of anxiety and pain in childhood cancer through hypnosis*. Paper presented to the 7th International Conference of Hypnosis and Psychosomatic Medicine, Philadelphia.

Hill, R., and Aldous, J. (1969). Socialization for marriage and parenthood. In D. A. Goslin (ed.), *Handbook of socialization*.

Hinde, R. A. (1979). *Towards understanding relationships*. London: Academic Press.

Hobbs, S. A., and Forehand, R. (1977). Important parameters in the use of time-out with children: A re-examination. *Journal of Behaviour Therapy and Experimental Psychiatry*, **8**, 365–370.

Hoefler, S. A., and Bornstein, P. H. (1975). Achievement Place: An evaluative review. *Criminal Justice and Behaviour*, **2**, 146–168.

Hoffman, M. L. (1970). Moral development. In P. H. Mussen (ed.), *Carmichael's manual of child psychology*. Chichester: Wiley.

Hoffman, M. L., and Saltzstein, H. D. (1967). Parent discipline and the child's moral development. *Journal of Personality and Social Psychology*, **5**, 45–57.

Hollin, C. R. (1989). *Psychology and crime: An introduction to criminological psychology*. London: Routledge.

Hollin, C. R. (1990). *Cognitive-behavioral interventions with young offenders*. Elmsford, NY: Pergamon Press.

Hollin, C. R., and Henderson, M. (1984). Social skills training with young offenders: False expectations and the 'failure of treatment'. *Behavioural Psychotherapy*, **12**, 331–341.

Hollin, C. R., and Wheeler, H. M. (1982). The violent young offender: A small group study of a Borstal population. *Journal of Adolescence*, **5**, 247–257.

Hollin, C. R., Wilkie, J., and Herbert, M. (1987). Behavioural social work: Training and application. *Practice*, **1**, 297–304.

Hollin, C. R., Huff, G. J., Clarkson, F., and Edmondson, A. C. (1986). Social skills training with young offenders in a Borstal: An evaluative study. *Journal of Community Psychology*, **14**, 289–299.

Holmes, A. (1979). *The development and evaluation of a programme for hyperactive and conduct disordered children*. Unpublished PhD thesis, University of Leicester.

Holmes, F. (1935). An experimental study of fear in young children. In A. Jersild and F. Holmes *Children's fear*. *Child Development Monographs*, No. 20.

Horowitz, M. J., Wilner, N., and Alvarez, W. (1979). Impact of event scale: A measure of subjective stress. *Psychosomatic Medicine*, **41**, 209–218.

Horton, L. (1982). Comparison of instructional components in behavioural parent training: A review. *Behavioural Counselling Quarterly*, **2**, 131–147.

Houts, A., and Peterson, J. K. (1986). Treatment of a retentive encopretic child using contingency management and diet modification. *Journal of Pediatric Psychology*, **11**, 375–383.

Howells, K. (1989). Anger-management methods in relation to the prevention of violent behaviour. In J. Archer and K. Browne (eds), *Human aggression: Naturalistic approaches*. London: Routledge.

Howlin, P. (1984). Parents as therapists: A critical review. In D. Muller (ed.), *Remediating children's language: Behavioural and naturalist approaches*. London: Croom Helm.

Hudson, A. (ed.). (1980). *Behaviour analysis and the problems of childhood*. Victoria, Australia: PIT Publishers.

Hudson, A. (1982). Training parents of developmentally handicapped children: A component analysis. *Behavior Therapy*, **13**, 325–333.

Hudson, A. (1988). *Helping children to learn to be obedient*. Unpublished manuscript.

Hudson, A., and Blane, M. (1985). The importance of non-verbal behaviour in giving instructions to children. *Child and Family Behaviour Therapy*, **7**, 1–10.

Hudson, B. (1987). *Justice through punishment: A critique of the 'justice' model of corrections*. London: Gower.

Huff, G. J. (1987). Social skills training. In B. J. McGurk, D. M. Thornton, and M. Williams (eds), *Applying psychology to imprisonment: Theory and practice*. London: HMSO.

Hunter, N., and Kelley, C. K. (1986). Examination of the validity of the Adolescent Problem Inventory among incarcerated juvenile delinquents. *Journal of Consulting and Clinical Psychology*, **54**, 301–302.

Hutt, C. (1972). *Males and females*. Harmondsworth: Penguin.

Hutter, A. (1938). Endegene ein Functionelle Psychosen bei Kindern in den Pubertatsjahren. *A. Kinderpsychiat.*, **5**, 97–102.

Hyman, C. A. (1980). Families who injure their children. In N. Frude (ed.), *Psychological approaches to child abuse*. London: Batsford.

Hynd, G. W., Snow, J., and Becker, M. G. (1986). Neurological assessment in clinical child psychology. In B. B. Lahey and A. E. Kazdin (eds), *Advances in clinical child psychology* (Vol. 9). New York: Plenum.

Inhelder, B., and Piaget, J. (1964). *The early growth of logic in the child*. London: Routledge & Kegan Paul.

Ioannou, C. (1988). *Helping young children cope with bloodtests following transplantation*. Paper presented at the 19th European conference on the study of psycho-social aspects of children with chronic renal failure, Cardiff.

Ioannou, C. (in progress). Psychological assessment and intervention of acute pain in chronically ill children. PhD.

Ireton, C. L., and Guthrie, H. A. (1972). Modification of vegetable eating behavior in preschool children. *Journal of Nutrition Education*, **4**, (3), 100–103.

Iwaniec, D. (1983). *Social and psychological investigation of the aetiology and management of children who fail to thrive*. Unpublished PhD thesis. University of Leicester.

Iwaniec, D., Herbert, M., and McNeish, S. (1985). Social work with failure-to-thrive children and their families. Part I: Psychosocial factors. Part II: Behavioural casework. *British Journal of Social Work*, **15**, Nos 3 (June) and 4 (August) respectively.

Iwaniec, D., Herbert, M., and Sluckin, A. (1988). Helping emotionally abused children who fail to thrive. In K. Browne, C. Davies and P. Stratton (eds), *Early prediction and prevention of child abuse*. Chichester: Wiley.

Iwata, B. A., Riordan, M. M., Wohl, M. K., and Finney, J. W. (1983). Paediatric feeding disorders: Behavioural analysis and treatment. In P. Accardo (ed.), *Early infancy and early childhood: A multi-disciplinary team approach*. Baltimore: University Park Press.

Jackson, D. (1957). The question of family homeostasis. *Psychiatry Quarterly Supplement*, **31**, 79–80.

Jackson, D. D., and Weakland, J. (1961). Conjoint family therapy: Some considerations on theory, technique and results. *Psychiatry*, **24**, 30–45.

Jackson, H. J. E., and King, N. J. (1981). The emotive imagery treatment of a child's trauma-induced phobia. *Journal of Behavior Therapy and Experimental Psychiatry*, **12**, 325–328.

Jahoda, M. (1958). *Current concepts of positive mental health*. New York: Basic Books.

Jampala, V. C., Sierles, F. S., and Taylor, M. A. (1986). Consumers' views of DSM-III. Attitudes and practices of U.S. psychiatrists and 1984 graduating residents. *American Journal of Psychiatry*, **143**, 148–153.

Janis, I. L. (1958). *Psychological stress*. New York: Wiley.

Jay, S. M. (1988). Invasive medical procedures: Psychological intervention and assessment. In D. K. Routh (ed.), *Handbook of pediatric psychology*. New York: Guilford Press. pp. 401–425.

Jay, S. M., and Elliott, C. H. (1984). Behavioural observation scales for measuring children's distress: The effects of increased methodological rigor. *Journal of Consulting and Clinical Psychology*, **52**, 1106–1107.

Jay, S. M, Elliott, C. H., and Varni, J. W. (1986). Acute and chronic pain in adults and children with cancer. *Journal of Consulting and Clinical Psychology*, **54**, 5, 601–607.

Jay, S. M., Elliott, C. H., Katz, E. R., and Siegel, S. E. (1984). Assessment of children's distress during painful medical procedures. Paper presented at the meeting of the *Society of Behavioural Medicine*, Philadelphia.

Jay, S. M., Elliott, C. H., Katz, E., and Siegel, S. E. (1987). Cognitive-behavioural and pharmacologic interventions for children's distress during painful medical procedures. *Journal of Consulting and Clinical Psychology*, **55**, 6, 860–865.

Jay, S. M., Ozolins, M., Elliott, C. H., and Caldwell, S. (1983). Assessment of children's distress during painful medical procedures. *Health Psychology*, **2**, 133–147.

Jay, S. M., Elliott, C. H., Ozolins, M., Olson, R. A., and Pruitt, S. D. (1985). Behavioural management of children's distress during painful medical procedures *Behaviour Research and Therapy*, **23**, 513–520.

Jeffree, D. M., McConkey, R., and Hewson, S. (1977). A parental involvement project. In P. Mittler (ed.), *Research to practice in mental retardation, Vol 1, Care and Intervention*. Baltimore: University Park Press.

Jehu, D., Morgan, R. T. T., Turner, R. K., and Jones, A. (1977). A controlled trail of the treatment of nocturnal enuresis in residential homes in children. *Behaviour Research and Therapy*, **15**, 1–16.

Jennings, W. S., Kilkenny, R., and Kohlberg, L. (1983). Moral development theory and practice for youthful and adult offenders. In W. S. Laufer and J. M. Day (eds), *Personality theory, moral development, and criminal behavior*. Toronto: Lexington Books.

Joffe, J. M. (1968). *Prenatal determinants of behaviour*. Oxford: Pergamon.

Johansson, S., Johnson, S. M., Wahl, G., and Martin, S. (undated). *Compliance and noncompliance in young children: A behavioral analysis*. University of Oregon. Eugene: Oregon.

Johnson, C. A., and Katz, C. (1973). Using parents as change agents for children: A review. *Journal of Child Psychology and Psychiatry*, **14**, 181–200.

Johnson, D. W. (1980). Attitude modification methods. In F. H. Kanfer and A. P. Goldstein (eds), *Helping people change*. (2nd ed) Oxford: Pergamon.

Johnson, D. H., and Johnson, F. R. (1975). *Joining together*. New York: Prentice-Hall.

Johnson, J. E., and Dabbs, J. M. Jr. (1967). Enumeration of active sweat glands: A simple physiological indicator of psychological changes. *Nursing Research*, **16**, 273–276.

Johnson, J., Kirchoff, K., and Endress, M. (1975). Altering children's distress behaviour during orthopedic cast removal. *Nursing Research*, **24**, 404–410.

Johnson, J. H., and McCutcheon, S. M. (1980). Assessing life stress in older children and adolescents. In I. G. Sarason and C. D. Spielberger (eds), *Stress and anxiety* (Vol. 7). Washington, DC: Hemisphere.

Johnson, S. M., and Bolstad, L. G. (1973). Methodological issues in naturalistic observation: Some problems and solutions for field research. In L. A. Hamerlynck, L. C. Handy and E. J. Mash (eds), *Behavior change: Methodology, concepts and practice*. IL: Research Press.

Johnson, S., and Lobitz, G. (1974). Parental manipulation of child behavior in home observations. *Journal of Applied Behavior Analysis*, **7**, 23–31.

Johnson, S. B., and Melamed, B. G. (1979). The assessment and treatment of children's fears. In B. Lahey and A. E. Kazdin (eds), *Advances in clinical child psychology* (Vol. 12). New York: Plenum Press.

Johnson, S. M., Wahl, G., Martin, S., and Johansson, S. (1973). How deviant is the normal child? A behavioural analysis of the preschool child and his family. In R. D. Rubin, J. P. Brady, and J. D. Henderson (eds), *Advances in behaviour therapy (4)*. New York: Academic Press.

Johnson, W. (1956). Stuttering. In W. Johnson, S. J. Curtis, J. J. Edney, and K. Keaster (eds). *Speech handicapped schoolchildren*. New York: Harper.

Jones, D. N., Pickett, J., Oates, M. R., and Barber, P. (1987). *Understanding child abuse* (2nd edn). London: Macmillan.

Jones, M. C. (1924). The elimination of children's fears. *Journal of Experimantal Psychology*, **7**, 382–390.

Jurkovic, G. J. (1980). The juvenile delinquent as moral philosopher: A structural-developmental approach. *Psychological Bulletin*, **88**, 709–727.

Kagan, J. (1958a). The concept of identification. *Psychological Review*, **65**, 296–305.

Kagan, J. (1958b). Acquisition and significance of sex-typing and sex-role identity. In M. L. Hoffman and L. W. Hoffman (eds). *Review of Child Development Research*. (Vol. 1). New York: Russell Sage Foundation.

Kagan, J. and Moss, H. A. (1962). *Birth to Maturity; A study in Psychological Development*. New York: Wiley.

Kagan, J., Reznick, J. S., Clarke, C., Snidman, N., and Garcia-Coll, C. (1984). Behavioural inhibition to the unfamiliar. *Child Development*, **55**, 2212–2225.

Kallarackal, A. and Herbert, M. (1976). The happiness of Indian immigrant children. *New Society*, **35**, 422–424.

Kane, M. T. and Kendall, P. C. (1989). Anxiety disorders in children: A multiple baseline evaluation of a cognitive-behavioral treatment. *Behavior Therapy*, **20**, 499–508.

Kanfer, F. H. (1975). Self-management methods. In F. H. Kanfer and A. P. Goldstein (eds). *Helping people change: A textbook of methods*. Elmsford, NY: Pergamon Press.

Kanfer, F. H., Karoly, P., and Newman, A. (1975). Reduction of children's fear of the dark by competence-related and situational threat-related verbal cues. *Journal of Consulting and Clinical Psychology*, **43**, 251–258.

Kanner, L., (1953). *Child Psychiatry*. Springfield, IL: Thomas.

Kanner, L. (1943). Autistic disturbances of affective contact. *Nervous Child*, **2**, 217–250.

Kaplan, P. J. and Arbuthnot, J. (1985). Affective empathy and cognitive role-taking in delinquent and nondelinquent youth. *Adolescence*, **20**, 323–333.

Kaslow, N. J. and Rehm, L. P. (1982). Childhood depression. In R. J. Morris and T. R. Kratochwill (eds). *The practice of child therapy*. 27–51. New York: Pergamon Press.

Katz, E., Kellerman, J., and Siegel, S. (1980). Behavioural distress in children with cancer undergoing medical procedures: developmental considerations. *Journal of Consulting and Clinical Psychology*, **48**, 356–365.

Katz, E., Kellerman, J., Siegel, S. (1982). Self-report and observational measures of acute pain, fear, and behavioural distress in children with leukemia. Paper presented at the 3rd annual meeting of the Society of Behavioural Medicine, Chicago.

Katz, E., Varni, J., and Jay, S. M. (1984). Behavioural assessment and management of pediatric pain. In: M. Hersen, R. M. Eisler, and P. M. Miller (eds). *Progress in behaviour modification*. New York: Academic Press.

Katz, R. C. (1974). Single session recovery from a hemodialysis phobia: A case study. *Journal of Behaviour Therapy and Experimental Psychiatry*, **5**, 205–206.

Kaufman, A. S. (1980). Issues in psychological assessment. In B. B. Lahey and A. E. Kazdin (eds). *Advances in Clinical Child Psychology*, (Vol. 3). New York: Plenum.

Kaye, B. (1962). *Bringing up Children in Ghana*. London: George Allen & Unwin.

Kaye, K. (1982). *The Mental and Social Life of Babies: How Parents Create Persons*. London: Methuen.

Kazdin, A. E. (1973). The effectiveness of suggestion and pretesting on avoidance reduction in fearful subjects. *Journal of Behavior Therapy and Experimental Psychology*, **4**, 213–222.

Kazdin, A. E. (1975). *Behavior modification in applied settings*. Homewood, IL: Dorsey Press.

Kazdin, A. E. (1977). Assessing the clinical or applied significance of behaviour change through social validation. *Behaviour Modification*, **1**, 427–552.

Kazdin, A. E. (1978). *History of Behavior Modification: Experimental Foundations of Contemporary Research*. Baltimore: University Park Press.

Kazdin, A. E. (1987). *Conduct Disorders in Childhood and Adolescence*. Newbury Park, CA: Sage.

Kazdin, A. E. (1988). *Child Psychotherapy: Developing and Identifying Effective Treatments*. Oxford: Pergamon.

Kazdin, A. E. (1989). Developmental differences in depression. In B. B. Lahey and A. E. Kazdin (eds). *Advances in Clinical Child Psychology*, Vol 12. New York: Plenum.

Kazdin, A. E. (1990). Childhood depression. *Journal of Child Psychology & Psychiatry*, **31**, 121–160.

Kellerman, J., Zeltzer, L., Ellenberg, L., and Dash, J. (1983). Adolescents with cancer: Hypnosis for the reduction of the acute pain and anxiety associated with medical procedures. *Journal of Adolescent Health Care*, **4**, 85–90.

Kelly, E. W, (1973). School phobia: A review of theory and treatment. *Psychology in the Schools*, **10**, 33–42.

Kelly, G. A. (1955). The Psychology of Personal Constructs. Norton, New York.

Kelly, M. L., Jarvie, G. J., Middlebrook, J. L., McNeer, M. F., and Drabaman, R. S. (1984). Decreasing burned children's pain behaviour: Impacting the trauma of hydrotherapy. *Journal of Applied Behavioral Analysis*, **17**, 147–158.

Kendall, P. C. (1981). Cognitive-behavioural interventions with children. In B. Lahey and A. E. Kazdin (eds). *Advances in Child Clinical Psychology*, (Vol. 4), New York: Plenum Press.

Kendall, P. C. (1984). Cognitive-behavioural self-control therapy for children. *Journal of Child Psychology & Psychiatry*, **25**, 173–179.

Kendall, P. C., Deardorff, P. A., and Finch, A. J. (1977). Empathy and socialization in first and repeat juvenile offenders and normals. *Journal of Abnormal Psychology*, **5**, 93–97.

Kendall, P. C., Howard, B. L., and Epps, J. (1988). The anxious child: Cognitive-behavioral treatment strategies. *Behavior Modification*, **12**, 281–310.

Kennedy, W. A. (1965). School phobia: Rapid treatment of fifty cases. *Journal of Abnormal Psychology*, **70**, 285–289.

Kent, R. N., and O'Leary, K. D. (1976). A controlled evaluation of behavior modification with conduct problem children. *Journal of Counsulting and Clinical Psychology*, **44**, 594.

Kerpowitz, D. H., and Johnson, B. M. (1981). Stimulus control in child-family interaction. *Behavioural Assessment*, **3**, 151–171.

Kiernan, C. C. (1983). The exploration of sign and symbol effects. In J. Hogg and P. J. Mittler (eds). *Advances in Mental Handicap Research, Vol. 2. Aspects of Competence in Mentally Handicapped People*. Chichester: Wiley.

Kifer, R. E., Lewis, M. A., Green, D. R., and Phillips, E. L. (1974). Training predelinquent youths and their parents to negotiate conflict situations. *Journal of Applied Behavior Analysis*, **7**, 357–364.

King, N. J. (1991). Physiological assessment. In T. H. Ollendick and M. Hersen (eds). *Handbook of child and adolescent assessment*. New York: Pergamon Press.

King, N. J., and Gullone, E. (1990). Acceptability of fear reduction procedures with children. *Journal of Behavior Therapy and Experimental Psychiatry*, **21**, 1–8.

King, N, J., and Ollendick, T. H. (1989). School refusal: Graduated and rapid behavioural treatment strategies. *Australian and New Zealand Journal of Psychiatry*, **23**, 213–223.

King, N. J., Cranstoun, F., and Josephs, A. (1989). Emotive imagery and children's night-time fears: A multiple baseline design evaluation. *Journal of Behavior Therapy and Experimental Psychiatry*, **20**, 125–135.

King, N. J., Hamilton, D. I., and Murphy, G. C. (1983). The prevention of children's maladaptive fears. *Child and Family Behavior Therapy*, **5**, 43–57.

King, N. J., Hamilton, D. I., and Ollendick, T. H. (1988). *Children's phobias: A behavioural perspective.* London: Academic Press.

King, N. J., Ollier, K., Iacuone, R., Schuster, S., Bays, K., Gullone, E., and Ollendick, T. H. (1989). Child and adolescent fears: An Australian cross-sectional study using the Revised Fear Survey Schedule for Children. *Journal of Child Psychology and Psychiatry*, **30**, 775–784.

Kinsey, A. C., Pomeroy, W. B., and Martin, C. E. (1948). *Sexual Behaviour in the Human Male.* Philadelphia: W. B. Saunders.

Kirk, S. A., and McCarthy, J. J. (1962). The Illinois Test of Psycho-linguistic Abilities: An approach to differential diagnosis. *American Journal of Mental Deficiency*, **66**, 399–412.

Kirschenbaum, D. S., and Flanery, R. C. (1983). Behavioural contracting: outcomes and elements. *Progress in Behavior Modification*, **15** 217–275.

Kissel, S. (1972). Systematic desensitization therapy with children: A case study and some suggested modifications. *Professional Psychology*, **3**, 164–169.

Klaus, M. H., and Kennell, J. H. (1976). *Maternal-infant Bonding.* St. Louis, C.V.: Mosby.

Klein, M. (1932). *Psychoanalysis of Children.* New York: Norton.

Klorman, R., Hilpert, P. L., Michael, R., LaGana, C., and Sveen, O. B. (1980). *Behaviour Therapy*, **11**, 156–168.

Knight, B. J., and West, D. J. (1975). Temporary and continuing delinquency. *British Journal of Criminology*, **15**, 43–50.

Knight, R. B., Atkins, A., Eagle, C. J., Evans, N., Finkelstein, J., Fukushima, D., Katz, J., and Wener, H. (1979). Psychological distress, ego defenses, and cortisol production in children hospitalized for elective surgery. *Psychosomatic Medicine*, **41**, 40–49.

Knitzer, J. (1982). *Unclaimed Children: The Failure of Public Responsibility to Children and Adolescents in Need of Mental Health Services.* Children's Defense Fund: Washington, D.C.

Knoblock, H., and Pasamanick, B. (1966). Perspective studies on the epidemiology of reproductive casualty: Methods, funding and some implications. *Merrill Palmer Quarterly of Behavior and Development*, **12**, 27–43.

Koegel, R. L., Glahn, T. J., and Nieminen, G. S. (1978). Generalization of parent training results. *Journal of Applied Behavior Analysis*, **11**, 95–109.

Kohlberg, L. (1974). Moral stages and moralization. In T. Lickona (ed.). *Moral Development and Behavior: Theory, Research and Social Issues.* New York: Holt, Rinehart & Winston.

Kohlberg, L. (1976). *Moral Development.* New York: Holt, Rinehart & Winston.

Kohlberg, L. (1978). Revisions in the theory and practice of moral development. In W. Damson (ed.). *New directions in child development: Moral development.* San Fransisco, CA: Jossey-Bass.

Kolvin, I. (1973). Feature clustering and prediction of improvement in nocturnal enuresis. In I. Kolvin, R. C. MacKeith and S. R. Meadow (eds). *Bladder control and enuresis.* London: Heinemann.

Kolvin, I., and Fundudis, T. (1981). Elective mute children: Psychological development and background factors. *Journal of Child Psychology and Psychiatry*, **22**, 219–233.

Kolvin, I., MacKeith, R. C., and Meadows, S. R. (eds). (1973). *Bladder Control and Enuresis.* London: Heinemann.

Kolvin, I., Garside, R. F., Nicol, A. R., MacMillan, A., Wolstenholme, F., and Leitch, I. M. (1981). *Help Starts Here: The Maladjusted Child in the Ordinary School.* London: Tavistock.

Kondaš, O. (1967). Reduction of examination anxiety and stagefright by group desensitization and relaxation. *Behaviour Research and Therapy*, **5**, 275–281.

Kondaš, O., and Ščentricka, B. (1972). Systematic desensitization as a method of preparation for childbirth. *Journal of Behaviour Therapy and Experimental Psychiatry*, **3**, 51–54.

Kornhaber, R. C., and Schroeder, H. E. (1975). Importance of model similarity on extinction of avoidance behavior in children. *Journal of Consulting and Clinical Psychology*, **5**, 601–607.

Kovacs, M. (1978). *Interview Schedule for Children* (ISC) (10th rev.). University of Pittsburgh School of Medicine, Pittsburgh.

Kovacs, M. (1980). Rating scales to assess depression in school-aged children. *Acta Paedopsychiatrica*, **46**, 305–313.

Kovitz, K. E. (1976). Comparing group and individual methods for training parents in child management techniques. In E. J. Mash, L. C. Handy and L. A. Hammerlynk (eds). *Behaviour Modification Approaches to Parenting*. New York: Brunner/Mazel.

Kratochwil, T. (1981). Selective mutism: Implications for research and treatment. New Jersey: Lawrence Erlbaum Associates.

Kumchy, C., and Sayer, L. A. (1980). Locus of control and delinquent adolescent populations. *Psychological Reports*, **46**, 1307–1310.

Kuttner, L. (1984). Psychological treatment of distress, pain and anxiety for young children with cancer. Unpublished doctoral dissertation, Simon Fraser University.

Kuttner, L. (1988). Favorite stories: a hypnotic pain-reduction technique for children in acute pain. *American Journal of Clinical Hypnosis*, **30**, 289–295.

Kuttner, L., Bowman, M., and Teasdale, M. (1988). Psychological treatment of distress, pain and anxiety for young children with cancer. *Developmental and Behavioural Pediatrics*, **9**, 374–381.

LaBaw, W., Holton, C., Tewell, K., and Eccles, D. (1975). The use of self-hypnosis by children with cancer. *American Journal of Clinical Hypnosis*, **17**, 233–238.

Labbe, E. E., and Williamson, D. A. (1984). Behavioral treatment of elective mutism: A review of the literature. *Clinical Psychology Review*, **4**, 273–292.

Lacey, G. N. (1972). Observations on Aberfan. *Journal of Psychosomatic Research*, **6**, 257–260.

Lacey, J. I. (1964). Somatic response patterning and stress: Some revisions of activation theory. In M. Appley and R. Trumball (eds), *Psychological stress: Issues in research*. New York: Appleton-Century-Crofts.

Lacey, J. I., and Lacey B. C. (1958). Verification and extension of the principle of autonomic response stereotopy. *American Journal of Psychology*, **71**, 50–73.

Lacey, J. I., and Lacey, B. C. (1962). Law of initial values in the longitudinal study of autonomic constitution: Reproducibility of autonomic responses and response patterns over a 4-year interval. *Annals of the New York Academy of Science*, **98**, 1257–1290.

Ladd, G. W. (1981). Effectiveness of a social learning method for enhancing children's social interaction and peer acceptance. *Child Development*, **52**, 171–178.

Ladd, G. W. (1984). Social skills training with children: Issues in research and practice. *Clinical Psychology Review*, **4**, 317–337.

Ladd, G. W., and Mize, J. (1983). A cognitive-social learning model of social skill training. *Psychological Review*, **90**, 127–157.

LaGreca, A. (1981). Social behaviour and social perception in learning-disabled children: A review with implications for social skills training. *Journal of Pediatric Psychology*, **6**, 385–416.

Lamb, M. E. (1981). *The role of the father in child development*. New York: Wiley.

Lamb, M. E., Pleck, J. H., and Levine, J. A. (1985). The role of the father in child development: The effects of increased paternal involvement. In B. B. Lahey and A. E. Kazdin (eds), *Advances in Clinical Child Psychology*, (Vol. 18). New York: Plenum.

Lang, P. J., and Lazovik, A. D. (1963). Experimental desensitization of phobias. *Journal of Abnormal and Social Psychology*, **66**, 519–525.

Lang, P. J., Melamed, B. G., and Hart, J. (1970). Psychophysiological analysis of fear motivation used in automated desensitization procedure. *Journal of Abnormal Psychology*, **76**, 220–234.

Lansdown, R., and Goldman, A. (1988). Annotation: The psychological care of children with malignant disease. *Journal of Child Psychology and Psychiatry*, **29**, 555–567.

Lapouse, R., and Monk, M. A. (1958). An epidemiologic study of behaviour characteristics in children. *American Journal of Public Health*, **48**, 1134–1144.

Lask, B. (1980). Evaluation, why and who. *Journal of Family Therapy*, **2**, 119–210.

Lask, B. (1987). Family therapy. *British Medical Journal*, **294**, 203–204.

Lask, B., and Fosson, A. (1989). *Childhood illness: The psychosomatic approach*. Chichester: Wiley.

Last, C. G., Strauss, C. C., and Francis, G. (1987). Comorbidity among childhood anxiety disorders. *Journal of Nervous and Mental Disease*, **175**, 726–730.

Laws, D. R. (1974). The failure of a token economy. *Federal Probation*, **38**, 33–38.

Lazarus, A. A., and Abramowitz, A. (1962). The use of 'emotive imagery' in the treatment of children's phobias. *Journal of Mental Science*, **108**, 191–195.

Lazerson, A. (ed.) (1971). *Developmental psychology today*. DelMar, CA: C.R.M. Brooks.

LeBaron, S., and Zeltzer, L. (1984). Assessment of acute pain and anxiety in children and adolescents by self-reports, observer reports, and a behaviour checklist. *Journal of Consulting and Clinical Psychology*, **52**, (5), 690–701.

LeBau, W. L. (1973). Adjunctive trance therapy with severely burned children. *International Journal of Child Psychotherapy*, **2**, 80–92.

Ledwidge, B. (1978). Cognitive behavior modification: Step in the wrong direction? *Psychological Bulletin*, **85**, 353–375.

Lee, M., and Prentice, N. M. (1988). Interrelations of empathy, cognition, and moral reasoning with dimensions of juvenile delinquency. *Journal of Abnormal Child Psychology*, **16**, 127–139.

Lee, S. G., and Herbert, M. (1970). *Freud and psychology*. Harmondsworth: Penguin.

Lee, S. G., Wright, D. S., and Herbert, M. (1972). *Aspects of the development of social responsiveness in young children*. Report to the Social Science Research Council, U.K.

Lefkowitz, M. M., Eron, L. D., Walder, L. O., and Heussmann, L. R. (1977). *Growing up to be violent: A longitudinal study of aggression*. Oxford: Pergamon.

Leitch, I. M. (1981). *Help starts here: The maladjusted child in the ordinary school*. London: Tavistock.

Leitenberg, H., and Callahan, E. J. (1973). Reinforced practice and reduction of different kinds of fears in adults and children. *Behaviour Research and Therapy*, **11**, 19–30.

Leon, G. (1979). Cognitive-behavior therapy for eating disturbances. In P. Kendall and S. Hollon (eds), *Cognitive behavioural interventions: Theory, research and procedures*. New York: Academic Press.

Leon, G., and Dinklage, D. (1989). Childhood obesity and anorexia nervosa. In T. H. Ollendick and M. Hersen (eds), *Handbook of child psychopathology*. New York: Plenum.

Leslie, S. A. (1974). Psychiatric disorders in the young adolescents of an industrial town. *British Journal of Psychiatry*, **125**, 113–124.

Lewis, C. (1986). The role of the father in the human family. In W. Sluckin and M. Herbert (eds), *Parental behaviour*. Oxford: Basil Blackwell.

Lewis, N. (1978). The needle is like an animal: How children view injections. *Children Today*, January–February, 18–21.

Lewis, V. (1987). *Development and handicap*. Oxford: Basil Blackwell.

Lewis, M., Feiring, C., McGuffog, C., and Jaskir, J. (1984). Predicting psychopathology in six-year-olds from early social relations. *Child Development*, **55**, 123–136.

Ley, P. (1977). Psychological studies of doctor-patient communication. In S. Rachman (ed.), *Contributions to medical psychology*, (Vol. 1). Oxford: Pergamon.

Liddiard, M. (1928). *The mothercraft manual*. London: Churchill.

Lidz, T. (1968). *The person*. New York: Basic Books.

Lipowski, Z. J. (1970). Physical illness, the individual, and the coping process. *Psychological Medicine*, **1**, 91–102.

Lippitt, R., and Gold, M. (1959). Classroom social structure as a mental health problem. *Journal of Social Issues*, **15**, 40–49.

Lipton, D., Martinson, R., and Wilks, D. (1975). *The effectiveness of correctional treatment.* New York: Praeger.

Little, S., and Jackson, B. (1974). The treatment of test anxiety through attentional and relaxation training. *Psychotherapy: Theory, Research and Practice,* **11,** 175–178.

Lobitz, G. K., and Johnson, S. M. (1975). Normal versus deviant children: A multimethod comparison. *Journal of Abnormal Child Psychology,* **3,** 353–374.

Lock, A., and Fisher, E. (1984). *Language development.* London: Routledge.

Lockyer, L., and Rutter, M. (1969). A five to fifteen year follow-up study of infantile psychoses: II psychological characteristics. *British Journal of Psychiatry,* **115,** 865–882.

Loevinger, J. (1966). The meaning and measurement of ego development. *American Psychologist,* **21,** 195–206.

Logan, C. H. (1979). Evaluation research in crime and delinquency: A reappraisal. *Journal of Criminal Law, Criminology and Police Science,* **63,** 378.

Lollar, D. J., Smits, S. J., and Patterson, J. (1982). Assessment of pediatric pain: An empirical perspective. *Journal of Pediatric Psychology,* **7,** (3), 267–277.

Loney, J., Kramer., and Milich, R. (1981). *The hyperkinetic child grows up, Prediction of symptoms, delinquency, and achievement at follow-up.* American Association for the Advancement of Science, Houston, TX.

Lotter, V. (1966). Epidemiology of austistic conditions in young children: Prevalence. *Social Psychiatry,* **1,** 124–137.

Lovaas, O. I. (1977). *The autistic child: Language development through behavior modification.* New York: Wiley.

Lowe, G. R. (1972). *The growth of personality: From infancy to old age.* Harmondsworth: Penguin.

Luiselli, J. K. (1977). Case report: An attendant-administered contingency management program for the treatment of a toileting phobia. *Journal of Mental Deficiency Research,* **21,** 283–288.

Luiselli, J. K. (1978). Treatment of an autistic child's fear of riding a school bus through exposure and reinforcement. *Journal of Behavior Therapy and Experimental Psychiatry,* **9,** 169–172.

Lumsden Walker, W. (1980). Intentional self-injury in school age children: A study of 50 cases. *Journal of Adolescence,* **3,** 217–228.

Luria, A. R. (1961). *The role of speech in the regulation of normal and abnormal behavior.* New York: Liveright.

Lutzker, J. R., McGinsey, J. F., McRae, S., and Campbell, R. V. (1983). Behavioural parent training: There's so much more to do. *Behavioural Therapist,* **6,** 110–112.

Lynch, M. A., Roberts, J., and Gordon, M. (1976). Predicting child abuse: Signs of bonding failure in the maternity hospital. *British Medical Journal,* **1,** 624–626.

Lytton, H., and Zwirner, W. (1975). Compliance and its controlling stimuli observed in a natural setting. *Developmental Psychology,* **11,** 766–799.

Maccoby, E. E. (1984). Socialization and developmental change. *Child Development,* **55,** 317–328.

Maccoby, E. E., and Martin, J. P. (1983). Socialization in the context of the family: Parent-child interaction. In P. Mussen (ed.), *Handbook of child psychology* (Vol. 4). New York: Wiley.

MacFarlane, A. (1977). *The psychology of childbirth.* London: Fontana/Open Books.

MacFarlane, J. W., Allen, L., and Honzik, M. P. (1954). *A developmental study of the behavior problems of normal children between twenty-one months and fourteen years.* Berkeley: University of California Press.

MacKeith, R. C. (1973). The causes of nocturnal enuresis. In I. Kolvin, R. C. MacKeith and S. R. Meadow (eds), *Bladder control and enuresis.* London: Heinemann.

MacKinnon, O. E., and Arbuckle, B. S. (1989). *The relation between mother-son attributions and the coerciveness of their interactions.* Paper read at the April meeting of the Society for Research in Child Development. Kansas City, Missouri.

Macksoud, M. S. (in press). The war traumas of Lebanese children. *Journal of Traumatic Stress.*

Macksoud, M. S., Dyregrov, A., and Raundalen, M. (1990), Traumatic war experiences and their effects on children. In J. P. Wilson and B. Raphael (eds), *International handbook of traumatic stress syndromes.* New York: Plenum.

Mackworth, H. N., and Bruner, J. S. (1970). How adults and children search and recognize pictures. *Human Development,* **13**, 149–177.

Maddox, B. (1980). *Step-parenting: How to live with other people's children.* London: Unwin.

Mahler, M. S. (1952). On childhood psychoses and schizophrenia: Autistic and symbiotic infantile psychoses. *Psychoanalytic Study of the Child,* **7**, 286–305.

Mahoney, M. J., and Mahoney, K. (1975). Treatment of obesity: A clinical exploration. In B. J. Williams (ed.), *Obesity: behavioural approaches to dietary management.* New York: Brunner/ Mazel.

Malewska, H. E., and Muszynski, H. (1970). Children's attitudes to theft. In K. Danziger (ed.), *Readings in child socialization.* Oxford: Pergamon.

Mandler, G. (1985). *Cognitive psychology: An essay in cognitive science,* Hillsdale, NJ: Erlbaum.

Mann, J., and Rosenthal, T. L. (1969). Vicarious and direct counter-conditioning of test anxiety through individual and group desensitization. *Behaviour Research and Therapy,* **7**, 359–367.

Margison, F. R. (1982). The pathology of the mother-child relationship. In I. F. Brockington and R. Kumar (eds), *Motherhood and mental illness.* London: Academic Press.

Marks, I. (1978). Rehearsal relief of a nightmare. *British Journal of Psychiatry,* **133**, 461–465.

Marks, I. (1987). Nightmares. *Integr. Psychiatry,* **5**, 71–73.

Marks, I. M. (1987). *Fears, phobias and rituals.* New York: Oxford University Press.

Martin, H., and Beezley, P. (1977). Behavioral observations of abused children. *Developmental Medicine and Child Neurology,* **19**, 373–387.

Martin, S., and Little, B. (1986). The effects of a natural disaster on academic abilities and social behavior of school children. *B.C.J. Special Education,* **10**, 167–182.

Martini, D. R., Ryan, C., Nakayama, D., and Ramenofsky, M. (1990). Psychiatric sequelae after traumatic injury: The Pittsburgh Regatta accident. *Journal of the American Academy of Child and Adolscent Psychiatry,* **29**, 70–75.

Martinson, R. (1974). Who works? Questions and answers about prison reform. *The Public Interest,* **35**, 22–54.

M.A.S. Review (1989). Sharing skills and care. (Summary of the major findings by B. Kat). *The Psychologist,* October, 434–438.

Mash, E. J., and Terdal, L. G. (1988). *Behavioral assessment of childhood disorder.* New York: The Guilford Press.

Maslow, A. H. (1954). *Motivation and personality.* New York: Harper & Row.

Mason, J. (1975). Emotion as reflected in patterns of endocrine integration. In L. Levi (ed.), *Emotions: Their parameters and measurement.* New York: Raven Press.

Masters, J. C., Burish, T. G., Hollon, S. D., and Rimm, D. C. (1987). *Behavior therapy: Techniques and empirical findings* (3rd edn). New York: Harcourt Brace Jovanovich.

Maxwell, A. E. (1961). Discrepancies between the pattern of abilities for normal and neurotic children. *Journal of Mental Science,* **107**, 300–307.

McCabe, R. J. R., and Green, D. (1987). Rehabilitating severely head-injured adolescents: Three case reports. *Journal of Child Psychology and Psychiatry,* **28**, 111–126.

McClelland, D. (1961). *The achieving society.* Princeton: Van Nostrand.

McCrea, C. (1986). *Modified video feedback in the study of body image distortion in obese and pregnant women.* Unpublished PhD thesis, Birkbeck College, University of London.

McCue, K. (1980). Preparing children for medical procedures. In J. Kellerman (ed.), *Psychological aspects of childhood cancer.* Springfield: Charles C. Thomas.

McCune, Y. D. (1985). Psychosocial health issues in pediatric practices: Parent's knowledge and concerns. *Pediatrics,* **74**, 183–190.

McDougall, C., Barnett, R. M., Ashurst, B., and Willis, B. (1987). Cognitive control of anger. In B. J. McGurk, D. M. Thornton and M. Williams (eds), *Applying psychology to imprisonment: Theory and practice*. London: HMSO.

McDougall, C., Thomas, M., and Wilson, J. (1987). Attitude change and the violent football supporter. In B. J. McGurk, D. M. Thornton and M. Williams (eds), *Applying psychology to imprisonment: Theory and practice*. London: HMSO.

McFarlane, A. C. (1987). Family functioning and overprotection following a natural disaster: The longitudinal effects of post-traumatic morbidity. *Australian and New Zealand Journal of Psychiatry*, **21**, 210–218.

McFarlane, A. C., Policansky, S., and Irwin, C. P. (1987). A longitudinal study of the psychological morbidity in children due to a natural disaster. *Psychological Medicine*, **17**, 727–738.

McGrath, P. A. (1987). *Pain in children: The perception, assessment and control of childhood pain*. New York: Guilford Press.

McGrath, P. J., and Unrah, A. M. (1987). *Pain in children and adolescents*. Amsterdam: Elsevier.

McGuffin, P., and Gottesman, I. (1985). Genetic influence on normal and abnormal development. In M. Rutter and L. Hersov (eds), *Child and adolescent psychiatry: Modern approaches*. Oxford: Blackwell.

McIndoe, R. (1989). *A pilot study of child compliance to rules*. Unpublished dissertation, Graduate Diploma of Applied Child Psychology. Phillip Institute of Technology, Melbourne, Australia.

McMahon, R. J., and Forehand, R. (1978). Non-prescription behavior therapy: Effectiveness of a brochure in teaching mothers to correct their children's inappropriate mealtime behaviors. *Behavior Therapy*, **9**, 814–820.

McMahon, R. J., and Forehand, R. (1983). Parent training for the noncompliant child: Treatment outcome, generalization, and adjunctive therapy procedures. In R. F. Dangel and R. A. Polster (eds), *Behavioral parent training: Issues in research and practice*. New York: Guilford.

McMahon, R. J., Forehand, R., and Griest, D. L. (1981). Effects of knowledge of social learning principles on enhancing treatment outcome and generalization in a parent training program. *Journal of Consulting and Clinical Psychology*, **49**, 526–532.

McNeil, T. F., and Kaij, L. (1977). Prenatal, perinatal and post-partum factors in primary prevention of psychopathology. In G. W. Albee and J. M. Joffe (eds), *Primary prevention of psychopathology: Vol. I. The issues*. Hanover, New Hampshire: University of New England Press.

McPhail, P., Middleton, D., and Ingram, D. (1978). *Moral education in the middle years*. London: Longman.

McReynolds, P. (1968). The assessment of anxiety: A survey of available techniques. In P. McReynolds (ed.), *Advances in psychological assessment* (Vol. 1). Palo Alto: Science and Behaviour Books.

Meichenbaum, D. (1971). Examination of model characteristics in reducing avoidance behavior. *Journal of Personality and Social Psychology*, **17**, 298–307.

Meichenbaum, D. H. (1976). A self-instructional approach to stress management: A proposal for stress inoculation training. In *Stress and anxiety in modern life*. New York: Winston and Sons.

Meichenbaum, D. (1977). *Cognitive behavior modification*. New York: Plenum Press.

Meichenbaum, D. H., and Goodman, J. (1971). Training impulsive children to talk to themselves: A means for developing self-control. *Journal of Abnormal Psychology*, **77**, 115–126.

Meichenbaum, D. H., and Turk, K. (1976). *The cognitive-behavioural management of anxiety, anger and pain*. New York: Brunner/Mazel.

Melamed, B. G. (1979). Behavioural approaches to fear in dental settings. In M. Hersen, R. M. Eisler and P. M. Miller (eds), *Progress in behaviour modification*. New York: Academic Press.

Melamed, B. G., and Siegel, L. G. (1975). Reduction of anxiety in children facing hospitalization and surgery by use of filmed modeling. *Journal of Consulting and Clinical Psychology*, **43**, 511–521.

Melamed, B. G., and Siegel, L. G. (1980). *Behavioural medicine: Practical applications in health care.* New York: Springer.

Melamed, B. G., Dearborn, M., and Hermecz, D. A. (1983). Necessary considerations for surgery preparation: Age and previous experience. *Psychosomatic Medicine*, **45**, 517–525.

Melamed, B. G., Klingman, A., and Siegel, L. J. (1984). Childhood stress and anxiety: Individualizing cognitive behavioural strategies in the reduction of medical and dental stress. In A. W. Meyers and W. E. Craighead (eds), *Cognitive behaviour therapy with children.* New York: Plenum.

Melamed, B. G., Hawes, R. R., Heiby, E., and Glick, J. (1975). Use of filmed modeling to reduce uncooperative behaviour of children during dental treatment. *Journal of Dental Research*, **54**, 797–801.

Melamed, B. G., Meyer, R., Gee, C., and Soule, L. (1976). The influence of time and type of preparation on children's adjustment to the hospital. *Journal of Pediatric Psychology*, **1**, 31–37.

Melamed, B., Robbins, R., Smith, S., and Graves, S. (1980). *Coping strategies in children undergoing surgery.* Paper presented at the American Psychological Association, Montreal.

Melamed, B. G., Weinstein, D., Hawes, R., and Katin-Borland, M. (1975). Reduction of fear-related dental management problems with use of filmed modeling. *Journal of the American Dental Association*, **90**, 822–826.

Melamed, B. G., Yurcheson, R., Fleece, E. L., Hutcheson, S., and Hawes, R. (1978). Effects of filmed modeling on the reduction of anxiety-related behaviours in individuals varying in levels of previous experience in the stress situation. *Journal of Consulting and Clinical Psychology*, **46**, 1357–1367.

Melzack, R., and Wall, P. D. (1965). Pain mechanisms: A new theory. *Science*, **150**, 971–979.

Meyer, E., and Simmel, N. (1947). Psychological appraisal of children with neurological defects. *Journal of Abnormal Social Psychology*, **42**, 193–205.

Michelson, L., and Wood, R. (1980). Behavioral assessment and training of children's social skills. In M. Hersen, R. Eisler and P. M. Miller (eds), *Progress in behavior modification*, (Vol. 9). New York: Academic Press.

Miller, J. G. (1966). Eyeblink conditioning of primary and neurotic psychopaths. *Dissertation Abstracts*, **27b**, III.

Miller. L. C., Barrett, C. L., and Hampe, E. (1974). Phobias in children in a prescientific era. In A. Davids (ed.), *Child personality and psychopathology: Current topics* (Vol. 1). New York: John Wiley.

Miller, L. C., Barrett, C. L., Hampe, E., and Noble, H. (1972a). Comparison of reciprocal inhibition, psychotherapy and waiting list control of phobic children. *Journal of Abnormal Psychology*, **79**, 269–279.

Miller, L. C., Barrett, C. L., Hampe, E., and Noble, H. (1972b). Factor structure of children's fears. *Journal of Consulting and Clinical Psychology*, **39**, 264–268.

Miller, M. D., Elliott, C. H., Funk, M., and Pruitt, D. G. (1988). Implications of children's burns injuries. In D. K. Routh (ed.), *Handbook of pediatric psychology*, pp 426–447. New York: Guilford Press.

Miller, N. E., and Dollard, J. (1941). *Social learning and imitation.* New Haven: Yale University Press.

Miller, S. A. (1986). Parents' beliefs about their children's cognitive abilities. *Developmental Psychology*, **22**, 276–284.

Miller, S. M. (1979). Coping with impending stress: Psychophysiological and cognitive correlates of choice. *Psychophysiology*, **16**, 572–581.

Minuchin, S. (1974). *Family and family therapy.* Cambridge, Mass: Harvard University Press.

Mira, M. (1970). Results in a behaviour modification training program for parents and teachers. *Behaviour Research and Therapy*, **8**, 309–311.

Mischel, W. (1968). *Personality and assessment.* New York: Wiley.

Mischel, W. (1970). Sex-typing and socialization. In P. H. Mussen (ed.), *Carmichael's manual of child psychology* (3rd edn). New York: Wiley.

Mitchell, S., and Shepherd, M. (1966). A comparative study of children's behaviour problems at home and at school. *British Journal of Educational Psychology*, **36**, 248–254.

Money, J. (1965). Psychosexual differentiation. In J. Money (ed.), *Sex research: New developments*. London: Holt, Rinehart & Winston.

Money, J., and Ehrhardt, A. (1972). *Man and Woman: Boy and girl*. Baltimore: Johns Hopkins University Press.

Montagu, M. F. A. (1964). *Life before birth*. New York: The New English Library.

Moreland, S. R., Schwebel, A. L., Beck, S., and Wells, K. C. (1982). Parents as therapists: a review of the behaviour therapy parent training literature 1975 to 1981. *Behavior Modification*, **6**, 250–276.

Morgan, P. (1975). *Child care: Sense and fable*. London: Templesmith.

Morgan, R. T. T., and Young, G. C. (1972). The conditioning treatment of childhood enuresis. *British Journal of Social Work*, **2**, 503–509.

Morgan, R. T. T. (1984). *Behavioural treatments with children*. London: Heinemann Medical Books.

Morley, S. V. (1989). Single case methodology in behaviour therapy. In S. J. E. Lindsay and G. E. Powell (eds), *An introduction to clinical child psychology*. Aldershot: Gower.

Morris, E. K., and Braukmann, C. J. (eds). (1987). *Behavioral approaches to crime and delinquency: A handbook of application, research and methods*. New York: Plenum Press.

Morris, R. J., and Kratochwill, T. R. (1983). *Treating children's fears and phobias: A behavioural approach*. New York: Pergamon Press.

Mowrer, O. H. (1960a). *Learning theory and behaviour*. New York: Wiley.

Mowrer, O. H. (1960b). *Learning theory and the symbolic processes*. New York: Wiley.

Mowrer, O. H., and Mowrer, W. (1938). Enuresis: A method for its study and treatment. *American Journal of Orthopsychiatry*, **8**, 436–447.

Murphy, G. C., Hudson, A. M., King, N. J., and Remenyi, A. (1982). An interview schedule for use in the behavioural assessment of children's problems. *Behaviour Change*, **2**, 6–12.

Mussen, P. H. (1963). *The psychological development of the child*. New Jersey: Prentice-Hall.

Mussen, P. H., Conger, J. J., and Kagan, J. (1984). *Child development and personality* (6th ed). London: Harper & Row.

Nader, K., Pynoos, R. S., Fairbanks, L., and Frederick, C. (in press). *Childhood PTSD reactions one year after a sniper attack*.

Nay, W. R. (1975). Systematic comparison of instructional techniques for parents. *Behavior Therapy*, **6**, 14–21.

Neiburger, E. J. (1978). Child response to suggestion. *Journal of Dentistry in Children*, **45**, (5), 52–58.

Neisser, U. (1967). *Cognitive psychology*. New York: Appleton-Century-Crofts.

Neisser, U. (1976). *Cognition and reality*. San Francisco, CA: Jossey-Bass.

Neisworth, J., Madle, R., and Goeke, K. (1975). 'Errorless' elimination of separation anxiety: A case study. *Journal of Behavior Therapy and Experimental Psychiatry*, **6**, 79–82.

Nelson, K. (1973). Structure and strategy in learning to talk. *Monographs of the Society for Research in Child Development*, **38**, No. 149.

Neuhaus, E. C. (1958). A personality study of asthmatics and cardiac children. *Psychosomatic Medicine*, **20**, 181–183.

Neuhauser, C., Amsterdam, B., Hines, P., and Steward, M. (1978). Children's concepts of healing: Cognitive development and locus of control factors. *American Journal of Orthopsychiatry*, **48**, 335–341.

Newman, C. J. (1976). Children of disaster: Clinical observation at Buffalo Creek. *American Journal of Psychiatry*, **133**, 306–312.

Nietzel, M. T. (1979). *Crime and its modification: A social learning perspective*. Elmsford, NY: Pergamon Press.

Nietzel, M. T., and Bernstein, D. A. (1981). Assessment of anxiety and fear. In M. Hersen and A. S. Bellack (eds), *Behavioural assessment: A practical handbook* (2nd ed). New York: Pergamon Press.

Ninio, A. (1979). The naive theory of the infant and other maternal abilities in two subgroups in Israel. *Child Development*, **50**, 976–980.

Nocella, J., and Kaplan, R. M. (1982). Training children to cope with dental treatment. *Journal of Pediatric Psychology*, **7**, 175–178.

Noller, P., and Guthrie, D. (1989). Assessment of and modification of marital communication. *Behaviour Change*, **6**, 124–136.

Norris, H. (1960). The WISC and diagnosis of brain damage. Unpublished dissertation, University of London Diploma in Abnormal Psychology.

Novaco, R. W. (1975). *Anger control: The development and evaluation of an experimental treatment*. Lexington, MA: Heath.

Novaco, R. W. (1979). The cognitive regulation of anger and stress. In P. Kendall and S. Hollon (eds), *Cognitive-behavioral interventions; Theory, research and procedures*. New York: Academic Press.

Novaco, R. W. (1985). Anger and its therapeutic regulation. In M. A. Chesney and R. H. Rosenman (eds), *Anger and hostility in cardiovascular and behavioral disorders*. New York: Hemisphere.

Oates, J., and Sheldon, S. (1987). *Cognitive development in infancy*. Milton Keynes: Open University/ Lawrence Erlbaum.

Obler, M., and Terwilliger, R. F. (1970). Pilot study on the effectiveness of systematic desensitization with neurologically impaired children with phobic disorders. *Journal of Consulting and Clinical Psychology*, **34**, (1), 314–318.

O'Brien, T. P., and Budd, K. S. (1982). A comparison of methods for assessing child compliance during behavioural parent training. *Journal of Behavioural Assessment*, **4**, No. 2, 153–164.

O'Dell, S. (1974). Training parents in behaviour modification: A review. *Psychological Bulletin*, **81**, (7), 418–443.

O'Dell, S., Flynn, J., and Benlolo, L. (1977). A comparison of parent training techniques in child behaviour modification. *Journal of Behaviour Therapy and Experimental Psychiatry*, **8**, 261–268.

O'Dell, S., Mahoney, N. D., Horton, W. G., and Turner, P. E. (1979). Media assisted parent training: Alternative models. *Behaviour Therapy*, **10**, 94–102.

Oden, S., and Asher, S. R. (1977). Coaching children in social skills for friendship making. *Child Development*, **48**, 495–506.

O'Donnell, C. R., and Worell, L. (1973). Motor and cognitive relaxation in the desensitization of anger. *Behaviour Research and Therapy*, **11**, 473–481.

O'Leary, K. D. (1980). Pills or skills for hyperactive children? *Journal of Applied Behavior Analysis*, **13**, 191–204.

O'Leary, K. D., and Carr, E. G. (1982). Childhood disorders. In G. T. Wison and C. Franks (eds), *Contemporary behavior therapy*. New York: Guilford Press.

O'Leary, K. D. and O'Leary, S. G. (1977). (Rev. ed). *Classroom management: The use of behavior modification*. Oxford: Pergamon.

Ollendick, D. G., and Matson, J. L. (1983). Stereotypic behaviors, stuttering, and elective mutism. In T. H. Ollendick, and M. Hersen (eds), *Handbook of child psychopathology*. New York: Plenum Press.

Ollendick, T. H. (1979a). Fear reduction techniques with children. In M. Hersen, R. M. Eisler, and P. M. Miller (eds), *Progress in behaviour modification*. New York: Academic Press.

Ollendick, T. H. (1979b). Behavioral treatment of anorexia nervosa. *Behavior Modification*, **3**, 124–135.

Ollendick, T. H. (1983). Reliability and validity of the Revised Fear Survey Schedule for Children (FSSC-R). *Behaviour Research and Therapy*, **21**, 685–692.

Ollendick, T. H. (1986). Behavior therapy with children and adolescents. In S. L. Garfield and A. E. Bergen (eds), *Handbook of psychotherapy and behaviour change* (3rd ed). New York: John Wiley.

Ollendick, T. H., and Cerny, J. A. (1981). *Clinical behavior therapy with children*. New York: Plenum Press.

Ollendick, T. H., and Francis, G. (1988). Behavioral assessment and treatment of childhood phobias. *Behavior Modification*, **12**, (2), 165–204.

Ollendick, T. H., and Gruen, G. E. (1972). Treatment of bodily injury phobia with implosive therapy. *Journal of Consulting and Clinical Psychology*, **38**, 389–393.

Ollendick, T. H., and Hersen, M. (1984). *Child behavior assessment: Principles and procedures*. New York: Pergamon Press.

Ollendick, T. H., Hagopian, L. P., and Huntzinger, R. M. (in press). Cognitive behavior therapy with nighttime fearful children. *Behavior Therapy*.

Ollendick, T. H., and Mayer, J. (1984). School phobia. In S. M. Turner (ed.), *Behavioral treatment of anxiety disorders*. New York: Plenum Press.

Ollendick, T. H., and Yule, W. (in press). Depression in British and American children and its relationship to anxiety and fear. *Journal of Consulting and Clinical Psychology*.

Ollendick, T. H., King, N. J., and Frary, R. B. (1989). Fears in children and adolescents: Reliability and generalizability across gender, age, and nationality. *Behaviour Research and Therapy*, **27**, 19–26.

Ollendick, T. H., Matson, J. L., and Helsel, W. J. (1985). Fears in children and adolescents: Normative data. *Behaviour Research and Therapy*, **23**, 465–467.

Ollendick, T. H., Yule, W., and Ollier, K. (in press). Fears in British children and their relation to manifest anxiety and depression. *Journal of Child Psychology and Psychiatry*.

Olness, K. (1981). Imagery (self-hypnosis) as an adjunct therapy in childhood cancer. *American Journal of Pediatric Hematology-Oncology*, **3**, 313–321.

Olness, K., Wain, H., and Ng, N. (1980). A pilot study of blood endorphin levels in children using self-hypnosis to control pain. *Journal of Developmental and Behavioural Pediatrics*, **1**, 187–188.

Opie, I., and Opie, P. (eds). (1973). *The Oxford Book of Children's Verse* contains the story of Fidgety Phil from Der Struwwelpeter oder lusige Ges chichten und drollige Bilder (1944). Oxford: Clarendon Press.

Orford, J. (1980). The domestic context. In P. Feldman and J. Orford (eds), *Psychological problems: The social context*. Chichester: Wiley.

Palace, E. M., and Johnston, C. (1989). Treatment of recurrent nightmares by the dream reorganization approach. *Journal of Behaviour Therapy and Experimental Psychiatry*, **20**, 219–226.

Palazzoli, M. S., Boscolo, L., Cechinn, G., and Prata, G. (1978). *Paradox and counterparadox*. New York: Aronson.

Palmer, R. (1980). *Anorexia Nervosa*. Harmondsworth: Penguin.

Parke, R. D. (1972). The modification of the effectiveness of punishment training by a cognitive-structuring procedure. *Child Development*, **40**, 213–235.

Parke, R. D. (1978). Parent–infant interaction: Progress, paradigms and problems. In G. P. Sackett *Observing Behaviour Vol. I. Theory and Applications in mental retardation*. Baltimore: University Park Press.

Parkes, C. M. (1973). *Bereavement*. London: Tavistock.

Parry, P. A., and Douglas, V. A. (1983). Effects of reinforcement on concept identification in hyperactive children. *Journal of Abnormal Child Psychology*, **11**, 327–340.

Pasamanick, B., and Knoblock, H. (1961). Epidemiologic studies on the complications of pregnancy and the birth process. In G. Caplan (ed.), *Prevention of mental disorders in childhood*. New York: Basic Books.

Patterson, G. R. (1964). An empirical approach to the classification of disturbed children. *Journal of Clinical Psychology*, **20**, 326–337.

Patterson, G. R. (1965). Responsiveness to social stimuli. In L. Krasner and L. P. Ullmann (eds), *Research in behavior modification*. New York: Holt, Rinehart & Winston.

Patterson, G. R. (1974). A basis for identifying stimuli which control behavior in natural settings. *Child Development*, **45**, 900–911.

Patterson, G. R. (1975). *A social learning approach to family intervention. Vol. I. Families with aggressive children*. Eugene, Oregon: Castalia.

Patterson, G. R. (1977). Accelerating 'stimuli' for two classes of coercive behaviors. *Journal of Abnormal Child Psychology*, **5**, 334–350.

Patterson, G. R. (1979). A performance theory for coercive family interaction. In R. B. Cairns (ed.), *The analysis of social interaction: Methods, issues and illustrations*. Hillsdale, NJ: Erlbaum.

Patterson, G. R. (1982). *Coercive family process*. Eugene, Oregon: Castalia.

Patterson, G. R., and Bank, L. (1986). Boot strapping your way on the normological ticket. *Behavioral Assessment*, **8**, 49–73.

Patterson, G. R., and Fleischman, M. J. (1979). Maintenance of treatment effects: Some considerations concerning family systems and follow-up data. *Behavior Therapy*, **10**, 168–185.

Patterson, G. R., Cobb, J. A., and Ray, R. S. (1972). Direct intervention in the classroom: A set of procedures for the aggressive child. In F. Clark, D. Evans and L. Hamerlynck (eds), *Implementing behavioral programs for schools and clinics*. Champaign, IL: Research Press.

Patterson, G. R., Jones, R., Whittier, J., and Wright, M. A. (1965). A behaviour modification technique for the hyperactive child. *Behaviour Research and Therapy*, **2**, 217–226.

Patterson, G. R., Reid, J. B., Jones, J. J., and Conger, R. E. (1975). *A social learning approach to family intervention. Vol. I. Families with aggressive children*. Eugene: Castalia.

Paul, G. L. (1967). Outcome research in psychotherapy. *Journal of Consulting Psychology*, **31**, 109–118.

Pavlov, I. (1927). *Conditional reflexes*. (Translation by G. V. Anrep). Oxford: Clarendon Press.

Peed, S., Roberts, M., and Forehand, R. (1977). Evaluation of the effectiveness of a standardised parent training program in altering the interactions of mothers and their noncompliant children. *Behaviour Modification*, **1**, 323–350.

Penfield, W., and Roberts, L. (1959). *Speech and brain mechanisms*. New Jersey: Princeton University Press.

Perkins, D. E. (1987). A psychological treatment programme for sex offenders. In B. J. McGurk, D. M. Thornton, and M. Williams (eds), *Applying psychology to imprisonment: Theory and practice*. London: HMSO.

Perrin, E. C., and Gerrity, P. S. (1981). There's a demon in your belly: Children's understanding of illness. *Pediatrics*, **67**, 6, 841–849.

Perry, S., and Heidrich, G. (1982). Management of pain during debridement: A survey of U.S. burns units. *Pain*, **13**, 267–280.

Peter, B. M., and Spreen, O. (1979). Behavior rating and personal adjustment scales of neurologically and learning handicapped children during adolescence and early adulthood. Results of a follow-up study. *Journal of Clinical Neuropsychology*, **1**, 75–92.

Peterson, D. R. (1961). Behaviour problems of middle childhood. *Journal of Consulting Psychology*, **25**, 205–209.

Peterson, L. J., and Mori, L. (1988). Preparation for hospitalization. In D. K. Routh (ed.), *Handbook of pediatric psychology*, pp. 460–491. New York: Guilford Press.

Peterson, L., and Ridley-Johnson, R. (1980). Pediatric hospital response to survey on prehospital preparation for children. *Journal of Pediatric Psychology*, **5**, 1–7.

Peterson, L., and Shigetomi, C. (1981). The use of coping techniques to minimize anxiety in hospitalized children. *Behavior Therapy*, **12**, 1–14.

Peterson, L., and Toler, S. (1986). An information-seeking disposition in child surgery patients. *Health Psychology*, **5**, 343–358.

Peterson, R. A., Wright, R. L. D., and Hanlon, C. C. (1969). The effects of extending the CS-UCS interval on the effectiveness of the conditioning treatment for nocturnal enuresis. *Behaviour Research and Therapy*, **7**, 351–357.

Peterson, L., Schultheis, K., Ridley-Johnson, R., Miller, D. J., and Tracy, K. (1984). Comparison of three modeling procedures on the presurgical and postsurgical reactions of children. *Behavior Therapy*, **15**, 197–203.

Phaire, T. (1553). *The boke of chyldren*. (Reprinted 1965). London: Livingstone.

Phillips, E. L., Phillips, E. A., Fixsen, D. L., and Wolf, M. M. (1971). Achievement Place: Modification of the behaviors of pre-delinquent boys within a token economy. *Journal of Applied Behavior Analysis*, **4**, 45–59.

Piacentini, J. C. (1987). Language dysfunction and childhood behavior disorders. In B. B. Lahey and A. E. Kazdin (eds), *Advances in clinical child psychology* Vol.10. New York: Plenum.

Piaget, J. (1932). *The moral judgement of the child*. New York: Harcourt & Brace.

Piaget, J. (1953). *Origins of intelligence in the child*. London: Routledge & Kegan Paul.

Piaget, J. (1954). *The construction of reality in the child*. New York: Basic Books.

Platt, J. J., Perry, G., and Metzger, D. (1980). The evaluation of a heroin addiction treatment program within a correctional setting. In R. Ross and P. Gendreau (eds), *Effective correctional treatment*. Toronto: Butterworths.

Pless, I. B., and Douglas, S. W. B. (1971). Chronic illness in childhood: Part 1. Epidemiological and clinical characteristics. *Pediatrics*, **47**, 405–414.

Pollitt, E., and Eichler, A. W. (1976). Behavioural disturbances among failure-to-thrive children. *American Journal of Diseases of Children*, **130**, 24–29.

Pollitt, E., Eichler, A. W., and Chan, C. K. (1975). Psychosocial development and behaviour of mothers of failure-to-thrive children. *American Journal of Orthopsychiatry*, **45**, 525–537.

Pomerantz, P. B., Peterson, N. T., Macholin, D., and Stern, S. (1977). The in vivo elimination of a childhood phobia by a paraprofessional interventionist at home. *Journal of Behavior Therapy and Experimental Psychiatry*, **8**, 417–421.

Pond, D. A. (1961). Psychiatric aspects of epileptic and brain-damaged children. *British Medical Journal*, 1377–1382; 1454–1459.

Poresky, R. H., and Hendrix, C. (1989). Parenting priorities: Stability, change and impact on young children. Paper read at the April meeting of Society for Research on Child Development. Kansas, Missouri.

Porrino, C. J., Rapoport, J. I., Behar, D., Sceery, W., Ismond, D. R., and Bunney, W. E. (1983). A naturalistic assessment of the motor activity of hyperactive boys. *Archives of General Psychiatry*, **40**, I Comparison with normal boys pp. 681–687; II Stimulant drug effects, pp. 688–693.

Poster, E. C., and Betz, C. L. (1983). Allaying the anxiety of hospitalized children using stress immunization techniques. *Journal of Comprehensive Pediatric Nursing*, **6**, 227–233.

Pratt, K. C. (1954). The neonate. In L. Carmichael (ed.), *Manual of child psychology* (2nd ed). New York: Wiley.

President's Commission on Mental Health. (1978). *Report to the President* Vols. 1–4, Washington, DC: US Government Printing Office.

Pringle, M. L. K., Butler, N., and Davie, R. (1966). *11,000 seven-year-olds*. London: Longmans Green.

Proven, L. (1990). Personal communication.

Public Law 94–142 (USA) (1975) Section 5(b) (4).

Puckering, C. (1987). Deprived mothers, depressed mothers, and distressed children. Paper given at the British Psychological Society Conference, York.

Puckering, C. (1989). Annotation: Maternal depression. *Journal of Child Psychology and Psychiatry*, **30**, 807–817.

Puig-Antich, J. (1986). Psychobiological markers: The effects of age and puberty. In M. Rutter, C. E. Izzard, and P. B. Read (eds), *Depression in young people: Development and clinical perspectives*. New York: Guilford Press.

Puig-Antich, J., Lukens, E., Davies, M., Goetz, D., Brennan-Quattrock, J., and Todak. (1985a/b). Psychosocial functioning in prepubertal major depressive disorders. *Archives of General Psychiatry*, **42**, I Interpersonal relationships during the depressive episode, pp. 500–507, II Interpersonal relationships after sustained recovery from affective episode, pp. 511–517.

Pynoos, R. S., and Eth, S. (1986). Witness to violence: The child interview. *Journal of the American Academy of Child Psychiatry*, **25**, 306–319.

Pynoos, R. S., and Nader, K. (1988). Psychological first aid and treatment approach for children exposed to community violence: Research implications. *Journal of Traumatic Stress*, **1**, 243–267.

Pynoos, R. S., Frederick, C., Nader, K., Arroyo, W., Steinberg, A., Eth, S., Nunez, F., and Fairbanks, L. (1987). Life threat and post-traumatic stress in school-age children. *Archives of General Psychiatry*, **44**, 1057–1063.

Quay, H. C. (1977). The three faces of evaluation: What can be expected to work? *Criminal Justice and Behaviour*, **4**, 341–354.

Quay, H. C. (1984). A critical analysis of DSM-III as a taxonomy of psychopathology in childhood and adolescence. Unpublished manuscript, University of Miami.

Quay, H. C. (1987). Institutional treatment. In H. C. Quay (ed.), *Handbook of juvenile delinquency*. New York: Wiley.

Quay, H. C., and Peterson, D. R. (1979). Manual of the Behavior Problem Checklist (unpublished).

Quay, H. C., and Peterson, D. R. (1983). Manual for the Revised Behavioral Problem Checklist (unpublished manuscript).

Quay, H. C., Routh, D. K., and Shapiro, S. K. (1987). Psychopathology of childhood: From description to validation. *Annual Review of Psychology*, **38**, 491–532.

Quinton, D., and Rutter, M. (1976). Early hospital admissions and later disturbances of behaviour: An attempted replication of Douglas' findings. *Developmental Medicine and Child Neurology*, **18**, 447–459.

Rachman, S. (1962). Learning theory and child psychology: Therapeutic possibilities. *Journal of Child Psychology and Psychiatry*, **3**, 149–163.

Rachman, S. (1978). *Fear and courage*. San Francisco: Freeman.

Rachman, S. (1980). Emotional processing. *Behaviour Research and Therapy*, **18**, 51–60.

Radke-Yarrow, M., Campbell, J., and Burton, R. V. (1964). Reliability of maternal retrospection: A preliminary report. *Family Process*, **3**, 207–218.

Rainwater, N., Sweet, A. A., Elliott, L., Bowers, M., McNeill, J., and Stump, N. (1988). Systematic desensitization in the treatment of needle phobias for children with diabetes. *Child and Family Therapy*, **10**, (1), 19–31.

Randall, J. (1970). Transvestism and trans-sexualism. *British Journal of Hospital Medicine*, **3**, 211–213.

Raphael, B. (1986). *When disaster strikes: A handbook for the caring professions*. London: Hutchinson.

Rapoport, R., Rapoport, R. N., and Strelitz, Z. (1977). *Fathers, mothers and others*. London: Routledge & Kegan Paul.

Rapport, M. D. (1987). Hyperactivity and attention deficit disorders. In V. B. Van Hasselt, P. S. Strain and M. Hersen (eds), *Handbook of developmental and physical disabilities*. New York: Pergamon.

Rapport, M. D., Murphy, A., and Bailey, J. S. (1982). Ritalin vs response-cost in the control of hyperactive children: A within-subject comparison. *Journal of Applied Behavior Analysis*, **15**, 205–216.

Reed, G. F. (1963). Elective mutism in children. A reappraisal. *Journal of Child Psychology and Psychiatry*, **4**, 99–107.

Rees, L. (1963). The significance of parental attitudes in childhood asthma. *Journal of Psychosomatic Research*, **7**, 181.

Reid, W. H., and Wise, M. G. (1989). *DSM-III-R Training guide*. New York: Brunner/Mazel.

Reitan, R. M., and Davison, L. A. (eds). (1974). *Clinical neuropsychology: Current status and applications*. New York: Wiley.

Revill, S., and Blunden, R. (1979). A home training service for pre-school developmentally handicapped children. *Behaviour Research and Therapy*, **17**, 207–214.

Reynolds, C. R., and Paget, K. D. (1982). National normative and reliability data for the Revised

Children's Manifest Anxiety Scale. Paper presented at the annual meeting of the National Association of School Psychologists, Toronto.

Reynolds, C. R., and Richmond, B. O. (1978). 'What I think and feel': A revised measure of children's manifest anxiety. *Journal of Abnormal Child Psychology*, **6**, 271–280.

Reynolds, M. M. (1982). Negativism of preschool children: An observational and experimental study. *Contributions to Education*, No. 228. Bureau of Publications, Teachers College, Columbia University, New York.

Reynolds, W. M. (1984). Depression in children and adolescents: Phenomenology, evaluation and treatment. *School Psychology Review*, **13**, 171–182.

Reynolds, W. M., and Coats, K. I. (1986). A comparison of cognitive-behavioral therapy and relaxation training for the treatment of depression in adolescents. *Journal of Consulting and Clinical Psychology*, **54**, 653–660.

Rheingold, H. L., and Eckerman, C. O. (1970). The infant separates himself from his mother. *Science*, **168**, 78–83.

Richards, M., and Dyson, M. (1982). *Separation, divorce and the development of children: A review*. Cambridge: Child Care and Development Group.

Richman, N. (1981). A community survey of characteristics of one- to two-year-olds with sleep disruptions. *Journal of the American Academy of Child Psychiatry*, **20**, 280–291.

Richman, N. (1988). The family. In N. Richman and R. Lansdown (eds), *Problems of preschool children*. Chichester: Wiley.

Richman, N., Ratilal, A., and Aly, A. (submitted). The psychological effects of war on Mozambican children.

Richman, N., Stevenson, J., and Graham,. P. (1975). Prevalence and patterns of psychological disturbance in children of primary age. *Journal of Child Psychology and Psychiatry*, **16**, 101–103.

Richman, N., Stevenson, J., and Graham, P. (1982). *Preschool to school: A behavioural study*. London: Academic Press.

Richman, N., Douglas, J., Hunt, H., Lansdown, R., and Levere, R. (1985). Behavioural methods in the treatment of sleep disorders — a pilot study. *Journal of Child Psychology and Psychiatry*, **26**, 581–590.

Rimland, B. (1964). *Infantile autism*. New York: Appleton-Century-Crofts.

Rimm, D. C., and Masters, J. C. (1989). *Behavior therapy: Techniques and empirical findings*. New York: Academic Press.

Rines, W. B. (1973). Behavior therapy before institutionalization. *Psychotherapy: Theory, Research and Practice*, **10**, 281–283.

Ritter, B. (1968). The group desensitization of children's snake phobias using vicarious and contact desensitization procedures. *Behaviour Research and Therapy*, **6**, 1–6.

Roberts, A. R. (1987). National survey and assessment of 66 treatment programs for juvenile offenders: Model programs and pseudomodels. *Juvenile and Family Court Journal*, **38**, 39–45.

Roberts, G., Block, J. H., and Block, J. (1984). Continuity and change in parents' child-rearing practices. *Child Development*, **55**, 586–597.

Roberts, M. U., Hatzenbuehler, L. C., and Bean, A. W. (1981). The effects of differential attention and time-out on child noncompliance. *Behaviour Therapy*, **12**, 93–99.

Roberts, M. U., McMahon, R. J., Forehand, R., and Humphreys, L. (1978). The effects of parental instruction-giving on child compliance. *Behavior Therapy*, **9**, 793–798.

Robins, L. N. (1966). *Deviant children grown up*. Baltimore: Williams & Wilkins.

Robins, L. N. (1981). Epidemiological approaches to natural history research: Anti-social disorders in children. *Journal of the American Academy of Child Psychiatry*, **20**, 566–580.

Robson, K. M., and Powell, E. (1982). Early maternal attachment. In I. F. Brockington and R. Kumar (eds), *Motherhood and mental illness*. London: Academic Press.

Rose, M. I., Firestone, P., Heick, H. M. C., and Fraught, A. K. (1983). The effects of anxiety on the control of juvenile diabetes mellitus. *Journal of Behavioural Medicine*, **6**, 382–395.

Rose, S. D. (1972). *Training children in groups: A behavioural approach.* San Francisco: Jossey-Bass.

Rosenstiel, S. K., and Scott, D. S. (1977). Four considerations in imagery techniques with children. *Journal of Behavior Therapy and Experimental Psychiatry,* **8,** 287–290.

Rosman, B. L., Minuchin, S., Liebman, R., and Baker, L. (1976). Input and outcome of family therapy in anorexia nervosa. In J. L. Cleghorn (ed.), *Successful psychotherapy.* New York: Brunner/Mazel.

Ross, D. M. (1984). Thought-stopping: A coping strategy for impending feared events. *Issues in Comprehensive Pediatric Nursing,* **7,** 83–89.

Ross, D. M., and Ross, S. A. (1984). Childhood pain: The school aged child's viewpoint. *Pain,* **20,** 179–191.

Ross, D. M., and Ross, S. A. (1988). *Childhood pain: Current issues, research and management.* Maryland: Urban & Schwarzenberg.

Ross, D., Ross, S., and Evans, T. A. (1971). The modification of extreme social withdrawal by modification with guided practice. *Journal of Behavior Therapy and Experimental Psychiatry,* **2,** 273–279.

Ross, R. R., and Fabiano, E. A. (1985). *Time to think: A cognitive model of delinquency prevention and offender rehabilitation.* Johnson City, TN: Institute of Social Sciences and Arts.

Ross, R. R., Fabiano, E. A., and Ewles, C. D. (1988). Reasoning and rehabilitation. *International Journal of Offender Therapy and Comparative Criminology,* **20,** 29–35.

Rotenberg, M., and Nachshon, I. (1979). Impulsiveness and aggression among Israeli delinquents. *British Journal of Social and Clinical Psychology,* **18,** 59–63.

Rourke, B. P. (1976a). Issues in the neuropsychological assessment of children with learning disabilities. *Canadian Psychological Review,* **17,** 89–102.

Rourke, B. P. (1976b). Reading retardation in children. Developmental lag or deficit? In R. M. Knights and D. J. Bakker (eds), *Neuropsychology of learning disorders: Theoretical approaches.* Baltimore: University Park Press.

Rourke, B. P. (1983). Outstanding issues in research on learning disabilities. In M. Rutter (ed.), *Developmental neuropsychiatry.* Edinburgh: Churchill Livingstone.

Routh, D. K. (1985). Training clinical child psychologists. In B. B. Lahey and A. E. Kazdin (eds), *Advances in clinical child psychology* (Vol. 8). New York: Plenum.

Rowley, V. N. (1961). Analysis of the WISC performance of brain-damaged and emotionally disturbed children. *Journal of Consulting Psychology,* **20,** 343–350.

Russell, S. W. (1984). *Development of a behavioural coding system for pain expression of children.* Unpublished doctoral dissertation, University of Utah.

Rutter, M. (1966). *Children of sick parents: An environmental and psychiatric study.* Institute of Psychiatry Maudsley Monographs No. 16. London: Oxford University Press.

Rutter, M. (1967a). A children's behaviour questionnaire for completion by teachers: Preliminary findings. *Journal of Child Psychology and Psychiatry,* **8,** 1–11.

Rutter, M. (1967b). Brain-damaged children. *New Education,* **3,** 10–12.

Rutter, M. (1971). Parent–child separation: Psychological effects on the children. *Journal of Child Psychology and Psychiatry,* **12,** 233–260.

Rutter, M. (1977). Speech delay. In M. Rutter and L. Hersov (eds), *Handbook of child psychiatry: Modern approaches.* Oxford: Blackwell Scientific.

Rutter, M. (1978). Diagnosis and definition of childhood autism. *Journal of Autism and Developmental Disorder,* **8,** 139–161.

Rutter, M. (1979a). Protective factors in children's responses to stress and disadvantage. In M. W. Kent and J. E. Rolfe (eds), *Primary prevention of psychopathology: Vol. 3. Social competence in children,* pp. 49–74. Hanover: University Press of New England.

Rutter, M. (1979b). *Changing youth in a changing society.* The Nuffield Provincial Hospitals Trust.

Rutter, M. (1980a). Raised lead levels and impaired cognitive behavioural functioning: A review of the evidence. *Developmental Medicine and Child Neurology,* **22** (Suppl. 1).

Rutter, M. (1980b). The long-term effects of early experience. *Developmental Medicine and Child Neurology*, **22**, 800–815.

Rutter, M. (1981a). *Maternal deprivation revisited*. Harmondsworth: Penguin.

Rutter, M. (1981b). Stress, coping and development: Some issues and some questions. *Journal of Child Psychology and Psychiatry*, **22**, 323–356.

Rutter, M. (1981c). Social/emotional consequences of day care for pre-school children. *American Journal of Orthopsychiatry*, **51**, 4–28.

Rutter, M. (1982). Psychological therapies in child psychiatry: Issues and prospects. *Psychological Medicine*, **12**, 723–740.

Rutter, M. (1983). Cognitive deficits in the pathogenesis of autism. *Journal of Child Psychology and Psychiatry*, **24**, 513–531.

Rutter, M. (ed.). (1984). Developmental neuropsychiatry. Edinburgh: Churchill Livingstone.

Rutter, M. (1988). Psychiatric disorder in parents as a risk factor for children. *Commissioned Review for the American Academy of Child Psychiatry*.

Rutter, M., and Graham, P. (1968). The reliability and validity of the psychiatric assessment of the child: Interview with the child. *British Journal of Psychiatry*, **114**, 563–579.

Rutter, M., and Madge, N. (1976). *Cycles of disadvantage*. London: Heinemann.

Rutter, M., and Shaffer, D. (1980). DSM-III: A step forward or backward in terms of the classification of child psychiatric disorders? *Journal of the American Academy of Child Psychiatry*, **19**, 371–394.

Rutter, M., and Yule, W. (1970). Reading retardation and antisocial behaviour — the nature of the association. In M. Rutter, J. Tizard, and K. Whitmore (eds), *Education, health and behaviour*. London: Longmans.

Rutter, M., Chadwick, O., and Shaffer, D. (1984). Head injury. In M. Rutter (ed.), *Developmental neuropsychiatry*. Edinburgh: Churchill Livingstone.

Rutter, M., Graham, P., and Yule, W. (1976). A neuropsychiatric study in childhood. *Clinics in Developmental Medicine* Nos 35 and 36. London: Spastics International Publ., Heinemann.

Rutter, M., Tizard, J., and Whitmore, K. (eds). (1970). *Education, health and behaviour*. London: Longmans,. (Reprinted, Krieger, New York, 1980).

Rutter, M., Graham, P., Chadwick, O. F. D., and Yule, W. (1976). Adolescent turmoil: Fact or fiction. *Journal of Child Psychology and Psychiatry*, **17**, 35–56.

Rutter, M., Cox, A., Tupling, C., Berger, M., and Yule, W. (1975). Attainment and adjustment in two geographical areas. I. The prevalence of psychiatric disorder. *British Journal of Psychiatry*, **126**, 493–509.

Rutter, M., Maughan, B., Mortimore, P., Ouston, J., and Smith, A. (1979). *Fifteen thousand hours: Secondary schools and their effects on children*. Open Books, London: Harvard University Press.

Rutter, M., Bolton, P., Harrington, R., Le Couteur, A., Macdonald, H., and Simonoff, E. (1990a). Genetic factors in child psychiatric disorders — I A review of research strategies. *Journal of Child Psychology and Psychiatry*, **31**, 3–37.

Rutter, M., Macdonald, H., Le Couteur, A., Harrington, R., Bolton, P., and Bailey, A. (1990b). Genetic factors in child psychiatric disorders — II Empirical findings. *Journal of Child Psychology and Psychiatry*, **31**, 39–84.

Ryall, M. R., and Dietiker, K. E. (1979). Reliability and clinical validity of the CFFS. *Journal of Behavioral Therapy and Experimental Psychology*, **10**, 303–309.

Ryall, R. (1968). Delinquency: The problem for treatment. *Social Work Today*, **5**, 98–104.

Rycroft, C. (1970). Causes and meaning. In S. G. Lee and M. Herbert (eds), *Freud and psychology*. Harmondsworth: Penguin.

Sacham, S., and Daut, R. (1983). Anxiety or pain: What does the scale measure? *Journal of Consulting and Clinical Psychology*, **49**, 468–469.

Sacks, S., and De Leon, G. (1973). Conditioning two types of enuretics. *Behaviour Research and Therapy*, **11**, 653–654.

Saigh, P. A. (1986). In vitro flooding in the treatment of a 6-year-old boy's posttraumatic stress disorder. *Behaviour Research and Therapy*, **24**, 685–688.

Sandberg, S. T., Rutter, M. L., and Taylor, E. (1978). Hyperkinetic disorder in psychiatric clinic attenders. *Developmental Medicine and Child Neurology*, **20**, 278–289.

Sandberg, S. T., Wieselberg, M., and Shaffer, D. (1980). Hyperkinetic and conduct problem children in a primary school population: Some epidemiological considerations. *Journal of Child Psychology and Psychiatry*, **21**, 293–310.

Sanders, S. (1979). Behavioural assessment and treatment of clinical pain: Appraisal of current status. *Progress in Behaviour Modification*, **8**, 249–291.

Sandler, J. (1980). Aversion methods. In F. H. Kanfer and A. P. Goldstein (eds), *Helping people change* (2nd ed). Oxford: Pergamon.

Sanok, R. L., and Ascione, F. R. (1978). The effects of reduced time limits on prolonged eating behavior. *Journal of Behavior Therapy and Experimental Psychiatry*, **9**, 177–179.

Sanok, R. L., and Stiefel, S. (1979). Elective mutism: Generalization of verbal responding across people and settings. *Behavior Therapy*, **10**, 357–371.

Sarafino, L. P. (1990). *Health psychology*. Chichester: Wiley.

Saunders, J. T., Reppucci, N. D., and Sarata, B. P. (1973). An examination of impulsivity as a trait characterizing delinquent youth. *American Journal of Orthopsychiatry*, **43**, 789–795.

Savedra, A. (1976). Coping with pain: Strategies of severely burned children. *Maternal Child Nursing Journal*, **5**, 197–203.

Scaife, J., and Frith J. (1988). A behaviour management and life-stress course for a group of mothers incorporating training for health visitors. *Child Care, Health & Development*, **14**, 25–50.

Scaife, J. M., and Holland, A. (1987). *An evaluation of the Leicestershire Portage training scheme*. In R. Hedderley and K. Jennings (eds), *Extending and developing Portage*. Windsor: NFER-Nelson.

Schachter, F. F., and Strage, A. A. (1982). Adults' talk and children's language development. In S. G. Moore and C. R. Cooper (eds), *The young child: Reviews of research*, Vol. 3. Washington, DC: National Association for the Education of Young Children.

Schaefer, C. E., Millman, H. L., Sichel, S. M., and Zwilling, J. R. (1986). *Advances in therapies for children*. San Francisco, CA: Jossey-Bass.

Schaefer, E. S. (1959). A circumplex model for maternal behavior. *Journal of Abnormal and Social Psychology*, **59**, 226–235.

Schaffer, H. R., and Crook, C. K. (1980). Child compliances and material control techniques. *Developmental Psychology*, **6**, 54–61.

Schaffer, R., and Collis, G. (1986). Social responsiveness and child behaviour. In W. Sluckin and M. Herbert (eds), *Parental behaviour*. Oxford: Basil Blackwell.

Scheinfeld, A. (1967). *The basic facts of human heredity*. London: Pan Books.

Scherer, M. W., and Nakamura, C. Y. (1968). A fear survey schedule for children (FSSC): A factor analytic comparison with manifest anxiety (CMAS). *Behavior Research and Therapy*, **6**, 173–182.

Schlichter, K. J., and Horan, J. J. (1981). Effects of stress inoculation on the anger and aggression management skills of institutionalized young offenders. *Cognitive Therapy and Research*, **5**, 359–365.

Schneider, M. (1973). Turtle technique in the classroom. *Exceptional Children*, **42**, 201.

Schnurer, A. T., Rubin, R. R., and Roy, A. (1973). Systematic desensitization of anorexia nervosa seen as a weight phobia. *Journal of Behavior Therapy and Experimental Psychiatry*, **4** 149–153.

Schofield, M. (1973). *The sexual behaviour of young adults*. London: Longman.

Schrag, P., and Divoky, D. (1975). *The myth of the hyperactive child*. New York: Pantheon.

Schutze, V. (1987). The good mother: The history of the normative model 'mother-love'. *Sociological Studies of Child Development*, **2**, 39–78.

Schwartz, S., and Johnson, J. H. (1985). *Psychopathology of childhood: A clinical-experimental approach* (2nd ed). Oxford: Pergamon.

Scott, R. (1978). 'It hurts red': A preliminary study of children's perception of pain. *Perceptual and Motor Skills*, **47**, 787–791.

Sears, R. R., Maccoby, E. E., and Levin, H. (1957). *Patterns of child rearing*. Evanston, IL: Row, Peterson.

Seligman, M. E. P. (1975). *Helplessness*. San Francisco: Freeman.

Seligman, M. E., and Yellen, A. (1987). What is a dream? *Behaviour Research and Therapy*, **25**, 1–24.

Selman, R. L. (1980). *The growth of interpersonal understanding: Developmental and clinical analyses*. New York: Academic Press.

Selye, H. (1976). *Stress in health and disease*. Reading MA: Butterworths.

Selz, M., and Reitan, R. M. (1979). Rules for neuropsychological diagnosis: Classification of brain function in older children. *Journal of Consulting and Clinical Psychology*, **47**, 258–264.

Shaffer, D. (1973). The association between enuresis and emotional disorder: A review of the literature. In I. Kolvin, R. C. MacKeith and S. R. Meadow (eds), *Bladder control and enuresis*. London: Heinemann.

Shaffer, D. (1974). Suicide in childhood and early adolescence. *Journal of Child Psychology and Psychiatry*, **15**, 275–279.

Shaffer, H. R. (1977). *Mothering*. London: Fontana/Open Books.

Shaner, J. M. (1985). Older adolescent females' knowledge of child development norms. *Adolescence*, **20**, 53–59.

Shapiro, A. H. (1975). Behaviour of kibbutz and urban children receiving an injection. *Psychophysiology*, **12**, 79–82.

Shapiro, E. S. (1987). Academic problems. In M. Hersen and V. B. Van Hasselt (eds), *Behavior therapy with children and adolescents: A clinical approach*. New York: Wiley.

Shaw, E. G., and Routh, D. K. (1982). Effect of mother presence on children's reaction to aversive procedures. *Journal of Pediatric Psychology*, **7**, 33–44.

Shepherd, M., Oppenheim, B., and Mitchell, S. (1971). *Childhood behaviour and mental health*. London: University of London Press.

Sheridan, M. D. (1975) *From birth to five years: Children's developmental progress* (3rd ed). Windsor, Berks: NFER-Nelson.

Sheridan, M. S. (1975). Talk time for hospitalized children. *Social Work*, **20**, 40–44.

Shillitoe, R. W. (1988). *Psychology and diabetes: Psychosocial factors in management and control*. London: Chapman & Hall.

Shipley, R. H., Butt, J. H., Horwitz, B., and Farbry, J. (1978). Preparation for a stressful medical procedure: Effect of amount of stimulus pre-exposure and coping style. *Journal of Consulting and Clinical Psychology*, **46**, 499–507.

Shope, J. T. (1981). Medication compliance. *Pediatric Clinics of North America*, **28**, 5–21.

Siegel, L. J. (1981). *Naturalistic study of coping strategies in children facing medical procedures*. Paper presented at the meeting of the Southwestern Psychological Association, Atlanta.

Siegel, L. J. (1986). *Criminology* (2nd ed). St. Paul, MN: West Publishing.

Siegel, L. J. (1988). Dental treatment. In D. K. Routh (ed.), Handbook of pediatric psychology, pp. 448–459. New York: Guilford Press.

Siegel, L. J. and Peterson, L. (1980). Stress reduction in young dental patients through coping skills and sensory information. *Journal of Consulting and Clinical Psychology*, **46**, 499–507.

Siegler, R. S., and Richards, (1982). In R. J. Sternberg (ed.), *Handbook of human intelligence*. Cambridge: Cambridge University Press.

Sievers, D. J. (1959). A study to compare the performance of brain-injured mentally-retarded children in the Differential Language Facility Test. *American Journal of Mental Deficiency*, **63**, 839–847.

Simeonsson, R., Buckley, L., and Monson, L. (1979). Conceptions of illness causality in hospitalized children. *Journal of Pediatric Psychology*, **4**, 77–84.

Sines, J. O. (1987). Influence of the home and family environment on childhood dysfunction. In B. B. Lahey and A. E. Kazdin (eds), *Advances in clinical child psychology*. Vollo, New York: Plenum.

Skinner, B. F. (1969). *Contingencies of reinforcement: A theoretical analysis*. New York: Appleton.

Skinner, B. F. (1974). *About behaviorism*. London: Cape.

Slater, E., and Cowie, V. (1971). *The genetics of mental disorder*. Oxford: Oxford University Press.

Sluckin, A. (1973). Social work intervention in cases of encopresis: A behavioural and cognitive approach. (personal communication).

Sluckin, A. (1989). Behavioral social work treatment of childhood nocturnal enuresis. *Behavior Modification*, **13**, 482–497.

Sluckin, W., and Herbert, M. (eds). (1986). *Parental behaviour*. Oxford: Basil Blackwell.

Sluckin, A., Foreman, N., and Herbert, M. (in press). Behavioural treatment programmes and selectivity of speaking at follow-up in a sample of 25 selective mutes. *Australian Psychologist*.

Sluckin, W., Herbert, M., and Sluckin, A. (eds). (1983). *Maternal bonding*. Oxford: Basil Blackwell.

Smith, P. K. (1990). The silent nightmare: Bullying and victimization in school peer groups. Paper read to British Pychological Society London Conference. (Submitted to *The Psychologist*).

Smith, P. S., and Smith, L. J. (1987). *Continence and incontinence*. London: Croom Helm.

Smith, R. E., and Sharpe, T. M. (1970). Treatment of school phobia with implosive therapy. *Journal of Consulting and Clinical Psychology*, **35**, 239–243.

Snyder, J. J. (1977). Reinforcement analysis of interaction in problem and non-problem families. *Journal of Abnormal Psychology*, **86**, 528–535.

Snyder, J., and Brown, K. (1983). Oppositional behaviour and noncompliance in pre-school children. Environmental correlates and skill deficits. *Behavioural Assessment*, **5**, 333–348.

Snyder, J. J., and White, M. J. (1979). The use of cognitive self-instruction in the treatment of behaviorally disturbed adolescents. *Behavior Therapy*, **10**, 227–235.

Sontag, L. W. (1966). Implications of fetal behavior and environment for adult personalities. *Annals of the New York Academy of Science*, **134**, 782–786.

Sorensen, R. C. (1973). *Adolescent sexuality in contemporary America*. New York: World Publishing.

Sowder, B. J. (1975). *Assessment of child mental health needs* (Vols I–VIII). McLean, VA: General Research Corporation.

Spence, S. H., and Marzillier, J. S. (1981). Social skills training with adolescent male offenders: II. Short-term, long-term and generalized effects. *Behaviour Research and Therapy*, **19**, 349–368.

Spinetta, J. J., and Maloney, L. J. (1975). Death anxiety in the outpatient leukemic child. *Pediatrics*, **56**, 1034–1037.

Spitz, R. A. (1945). Hospitalism: An enquiry into the genesis of psychiatric conditions in early childhood. *Psychoanalytic Study of the Child*, **1**, 53–74.

Spitz, R. (1946). Anaclitic depression. *Psychoanalytic Study of the Child*, **2**, 313–342.

Spivack, G., Platt, J. J., and Shure, M. B. (1976). *The problem-solving approach to adjustment*. San Francisco: Jossey-Bass.

Sroufe, L. A., and Fleeson, J. (1988). The coherence of family relationships. In R. Hinde and J. Stevenson-Hinde (eds), *Relationships within families*. Oxford: Oxford University Press.

Sroufe, L. A., and Rutter, M. (1984). The domain of developmental psychopathology. *Child Development*, **55**, 17–29.

Staats, A. W. (1971). *Child learning, intelligence and personality*. London: Harper & Row.

Staley, A. A., and O'Donnell, J. P. (1984). A developmental analysis of mother's reports of normal children's fears. *Journal of Genetic Psychology*, **144**, 165–178.

Staub, E. (1975). *The development of prosocial behavior in children*. Morrison, NJ: General Learning Press.

Stayton, D., Hogan, R., and Ainsworth, M. D. S. (1971). Infant obedience and maternal behavior: The origins of socialization reconsidered. *Child Development*, **42**, 1057–1069.

Stefanek, M. E., Ollendick, T. H., Baldock, W. P., Francis, G., and Yaeger, N. J. (1987). Self-statements in aggressive, withdrawn, and popular children. *Cognitive Behavior Therapy and Research*, **2**, 229–239.

Stein, L., and Mason, S. E. (1968). Psychogenic and allied disorders of communication in childhood. In E. Miller *Foundations of Child Psychiatry*. Oxford: Pergamon.

Steinhausen, H. C., and Spohr, H. L. (1986). Fetal alcohol syndrome. In B. B. Lahey and A. E. Kazdin (eds), *Advances in clinical child psychology*, Vol. 9. New York: Plenum.

Stendler, C. B. (1952). Critical periods in socialization and over-dependency. *Child Development*, **23**, 3–12.

Stephens, M. I., and Montgomery, A. A. (1985). A critique of recent relevant standardized tests. *Topics in Language Disorders*, **5**, 21–45.

Stern, D. (1977). *The first relationship: Infant and mother*. London: Fontana/Open Books.

Stern, D. N. (1985). *The interpersonal world of the infant*. New York: Basic Books.

Sternbach, R. (1962). Assessing differential autonomic patterns in emotions. *Journal of Psychosomatic Research*, **6**, 87.

Sternbach, R. A. (1968). *Pain: A psychophysiological analysis*. New York: Academic Press.

Stevenson, J. (1984). Predictive value of speech and language screening. *Developmental Medicine and Child Neurology*, **26**, 528–538.

Stiffman, A. R. (1983). Assessing child compliance-noncompliance. *Child and Family Therapy*, **4** 141–149.

Stott, D. H., Moyes, F. A., and Headridge, S. E. (1966). *Test of motor impairment.*. Department of Psychology, University of Glasgow.

Strauss, A. A., and Lehtinen, L. E. (1947). *Psychopathology and education of the brain-injured child*. New York: Grune & Stratton.

Stroh, G., and Buick, D. (1964). Perceptual development in childhood psychosis. *British Journal of Medical Psychology*, **37**, 291–299.

Stumphauzer, J. S. (1986). *Helping delinquents change: A treatment manual of social learning approaches*. New York: Haworth Press.

Sugar, M. (1989). Children in disaster: An overview. *Child Psychiatry and Human Development*, **19**, 163–179.

Sullivan, H. S. (1953). *The interpersonal theory of psychiatry*. New York: Norton.

Sutton, C. (1988). *Behavioural parent training: A comparison of strategies for teaching parents to manage their difficult young children*. Unpublished PhD thesis, University of Leicester.

Swann van Buskirk, S. (1989). Two-phase perspective on the treatment of anorexia nervosa. *Psychological Bulletin*, **84**, 529–538.

Tal, A., and Miklich, D. C. (1976). Emotionally induced decreases in pulmonary flow rates in asthmatic children. *Psychosomatic Medicine*, **38**, 190–200.

Tams, V., and Eyberg, S. M. (1976). A group treatment program for parents. In E. J. Mash, L. C. Handy and L. A. Hamerlynck (eds), *Behaviour modification approaches to parenting*. New York: Brunner/Mazel.

Tanner, J. M. (1978). *Foetus into man: Physical growth from conception to maturity*. London: Open Books.

Tavormina, J. B. (1974). Basic models of parent counselling: A critical review. *Psychological Bulletin*, **81**, 827–835.

Taylor, J. A. (1951). The relationship of anxiety to the conditioned eyelid response. *Journal of Experimental Psychology*, **42**, 183–188.

Terr, L. C. (1979). The children of Chowchilla. *Psychoanalytic Study of the Child*, **34**, 547–623.

Terr, L. C. (1983). Chowchilla revisited: The effects of psychic trauma four years after a schoolbus kidnapping. *American Journal of Psychiatry*, **140**, 1543–1550.

Thomas A., and Chess, S. (1977). *Temperament and development*. New York: Brunner/Mazael.

Thomas, A., Chess, S., and Birch, H. G. (1968). *Temperament and behaviour disorders in children.* University of London Press: London.

Thomas, D. R., Becker, W. C., and Armstrong. (1968). Production and elimination of disruptive classroom behavior by systematically varying teacher's behaviour. *Journal of Applied Behavior Analysis,* **1**, 35–45.

Thompson, S. C. (1981). Will it hurt less if I can control it? A complex answer to a simple question. *Psychological Bulletin,* **90**, 98–101.

Thornton, D. M. (1987). Treatment effects on recidivism: A reappraisal of the 'nothing works' doctrine. In B. J. McGurk, D. M. Thornton, and M. Williams (eds), *Applying psychology to imprisonment: Theory and practice.* London: HMSO.

Thornton, D. M. and Reid, R. L. (1982). Moral reasoning and type of criminal offence. *British Journal of Social Psychology,* **21**, 231–238.

Thornton, P., Walsh, J., Webster, J., and Harris, C. (1984). The sleep clinic. *Nursing Times,* 14 March, 40–43.

Toolan, J. M. (1975). Suicide in children and adolescents. *American Journal of Psychotherapy,* **79**, 339–344.

Topping, K. J. (1986). *Parents as educators: Training parents to teach their children.* London: Croom Helm.

Torgersen, A. M., and Kringlen, E. (1978). Genetic aspects of temperament differences in infants. *Journal of the American Academy of Child Psychiatry,* **17**, 433–444.

Torgesen, J. (1975). Problems and prospects in the study of learning disabilities. In E. M. Hetherington (ed.), *Review of Child Development Research,* Vol. 5. Chicago: University of Chicago Press.

Trasler, G. (1966). *The explanation of criminality.* London: Routledge & Kegan Paul.

Trasler, G. (1973). Criminal behaviour. In H. J. Eysenck (ed.), *Handbook of abnormal psychology.* London: Pitman Medical.

Treacher, A. (1984). Family therapy with children: The structural approach. In G. Edwards (ed.), *Current issues in clinical psychology,* Vol. 4. London: Plenum.

Treacher, A., and Carpenter, J. (eds) (1984). *Using family therapy.* Oxford: Basil Blackwell.

Trevarthen, C. (1977). Descriptive analysis of infant communicative behavior. In H. R. Schaffer (ed.), *Studies in mother-infant interaction.* London: Academic Press.

Trites, R., and Fidorowicz, C. (1976). Follow-up study of children with specific or primary reading disability. In R. Knights and D. Bakkar (eds), *The neuropsychology of reading disorders.* Baltimore: University Park Press.

Truax, C. F., and Carkhuff, H. R. (1967). *Toward effective counseling and psychotherapy.* Chicago: Aldine.

Trueman, D. (1984). What are the characteristics of school phobic children? *Psychological Reports,* **54**, 191–202.

Tuma, J. M. (1989). Traditional therapies with children. In T. H. Ollendick and M. Hersen (eds), *Handbook of child psychopatholgy* (2nd ed). New York: Plenum.

Turk, D. (1978). Cognitive behavioural techniques in the management of pain. In *Cognitive behaviour therapy.* New York: Plenum.

Turner, R. K., and Taylor, P. D. (1974). Conditioning treatment of nocturnal enuresis in adults: Preliminary findings. *Behaviour Research and Therapy,* **12** 41–52.

Turner, R. K., Young, G. C., and Rachman, S. (1970). Treatment of nocturnal enuresis by conditioning techniques. *Behaviour Research and Therapy,* **8**, 367–381.

Turvey, A. (1985). Treatment manuals. In F. Watts (ed.). *New developments in clinical psychology.* Leicester: British Psychological Society/Wiley.

Ultee, C. A., Griffiaen, D., and Schellekens, J. (1982). The reduction of anxiety in children: A comparison of the effects of systematic desensitization in vitro and systematic desensitization in vivo. *Behaviour Research and Therapy,* **20**, 61–67.

Vandenberg, S. G., and Crowe, L. (1989). Genetic factors in childhood psychopathology. In B. B. Lahey and A. E. Kazdin (eds), *Advances in clinical child psychology*, Vol. 12. New York: Plenum.

Van Den Haag, E. (1982). Could successful rehabilitation reduce the crime rate? *Journal of Criminal Law and Criminology*, **73**, 1022–1035.

Van Eerdevegh, M. M., Bieri, M. D., Parrilla, R. H., and Clayton, P. J. (1982). The bereaved child. *British Journal of Psychiatry*, **140**, 23–29.

Van Eerdewegh, M., Clayton, P., and Van Eerdewegh, P. (1985). The bereaved child: variables influencing early psychopathology. *British Journal of Psychiatry*, **147**, 188–194.

Van Hasselt, V. B., Hersen, M., Bellack, A. S., Rosenbloom, N., and Lamparski, D. (1979). Tripartite assessment of the effects of systematic desensitization in a multiphobic child: An experimental analysis. *Journal of Behavior Therapy and Experimental Psychiatry*, **10**, 57–66.

Van Krevelen, D. A. (1971). Psychoses in adolescence. In J. G. Howells (ed.), *Modern perspectives in adolescent psychiatry*. Edinburgh: Oliver & Boyd.

Varni, J., Bessman, B. A., Russo, D. C., and Cataldo, M. F. (1980). Behavioural management of chronic pain in children: Case study. *Archives of Physical Medicine and Rehabilitation*, **61**, 375–379.

Varni, J. W. (1983). *Clinical behavioural pediatrics*. New York: Pergamon.

Varni, J. W., Katz, E., and Dash, J. (1982). Behavioural and neurochemical aspects of pediatric pain. In D. C. Russo and J. W. Varni (eds), *Behavioural pediatrics: Research and practice*. New York: Plenum.

Varni, J. W., Thompson, K. L., and Hanson, V. (1987). The Vanni/Thompson Paediatric Pain Questionnaire. I. Chronic musculoskeletal pain in juvenile rheumatoid arthritis. *Pain*, **28**, 27–38.

Veneziano, C., and Veneziano, L. (1988). Knowledge of social skills among institutionalized juvenile offenders: An assessment. *Criminal Justice and Behavior*, **15**, 152–171.

Venham, L., Gaulin-Kremer, E., Munster, E., Bengston-Audia, D., and Cohan, J. (1980). Interval rating scales for children's dental anxiety and uncooperative behaviour. *Pediatric Dentistry*, **2**, 195–202.

Vernon, D. T., Foley, J. M., Sipowicz, R. R., and Schulman, J. L. (1965). *The psychological responses of children to hospitalization and illness*. Springfield: Charles C. Thomas.

Vernon, P. E. (1964). *Personality assessment: A critical survey*. London: Methuen.

Vetere, A., and Gale, A. (1987). *Ecological studies of family life*. Chichester: Wiley.

Wahler, R. G. (1969). Oppositional children: A quest for parental reinforcement control. *Journal of Applied Behavior Analysis*, **2**, 159–170.

Wahler, R. G. (1976). Deviant child behaviour within the family. Development speculations and behaviour change strategies. In H. Leitenberg (ed.), *Handbook of behaviour modification and behaviour therapy*. Englewood Cliffs, N.J.: Prentice-Hall.

Wahler, R. G., and Dumas, J. E. (1986). Maintenance factors in coercive mother–child interactions: The compliance and practicability hypothesis. *Journal of Applied Behavior Analysis*, **19**, 3–22.

Wahler, R. G., and Fox, J. J. (1980). Solitary toy play and time out: A family treatment package for children with aggressive and oppositional behaviour. *Journal of Applied Behaviour Analysis*, **13**, 23–39.

Wahler, R. G., and Graves, M. G. (1983). Setting events in social networks: Ally or enemy in child behaviour therapy? *Behaviour Therapy*, **14**, 19–36.

Wakeman, R. J., and Kaplan, J. Z. (1978). An experimental study of hypnosis in painful burns. *The American Journal of Clinical Hypnosis*, **21**, (1), 3–12.

Walder, L. O., Chen, S. L., Breiter, D. E., Darton, P., Hirsch, I., and Liebowitz, J. (1969). Teaching behavioral principles to parents of disturbed children. In B. Guerney Jr. (ed.), *Psychotherapeutic agents: New roles for non-professionals*. Parents and teachers, New York: Holt Rinehart & Winston.

Walker, H. M., Greenwood, C. R., Hops, H., and Todd, N. M. (1979). Differential effects of reinforcing topographic components of social interaction: Analysis and direct replication. *Behavior Modification*, **3**, 291–321.

Walker, N. D. (1965). *Crime and punishment in Britain*. Edinburgh: University Press.

Waller, D. L., Hobbs, S. A., and Caldwell, H. S. (1984). Sequencing of parent training procedures: Effects of child noncompliance and treatment acceptability. *Behaviour Modification*, **8**, 553–566.

Walsh, F. (1981). Conceptualizations of normal family functioning. In F. Walsh (ed.), *Normal family processes*. New York: Guilford.

Ward, C. I., and McFall, R. M. (1986). Further validation of the Problem Inventory for Adolescent Girls. Comparing caucasian and black delinquents and nondelinquents. *Journal of Consulting and Clinical Psychology*, **54**, 732–733.

Warnock, M. (1978). *Special education needs*. London: HMSO.

Wasserman, G., and Allen, R. (1985). Maternal withdrawal from handicapped toddlers. *Journal of Child Psychology and Psychiatry*, **26**, 381–387.

Watson, J. B., and Rayner, R. (1920). Conditioned emotional reactions. *Journal of Experimental Psychology*, **3**, 1–14.

Watts, F. N. (1990). *The efficacy of clinical applications of psychology: An overview of research*. Cardiff: Shadowfax Publishing.

Weatherby, B., and Baumeister, A. A. (1981). Mental retardation. In S. M. Turner, K. S. Calhoun and H. E. Adams (eds), *Handbook of Clinical Behavior Therapy*. New York: Wiley.

Webster-Stratton, C. (1985). Predictors of treatment outcome in parent training for conduct-disordered children. *Behavior Therapy*, **16**, 223–245.

Webster-Stratton, C. (1988). Mothers' and fathers' perceptions of child deviance: Roles of parent and child behaviors and parent adjustment. *Journal of Consulting and Clinical Psychology*, **56**, 909–915.

Webster-Stratton, C. (1989a). The relationship of marital support, conflict, and divorce to parent perceptions, behaviours and child conduct problems. *Journal of Marriage and the Family*, **51**, 417–430.

Webster-Stratton, C. (1989b). Comparing factors that predict long-term treatment success for families with conduct problem children. Unpublished manuscript.

Webster-Stratton, C., Hollinsworth, T., and Kolpacoff, M. (1989). The long-term effectiveness and clinical significance of three cost-effective training programs for families with conduct-problem children. *Journal of Consulting and Clinical Psychology*, **57**, 550–553.

Webster-Stratton, C., Kolpacoff, M., and Hollinsworth, T. (1988). Self-administered videotape therapy for families with conduct problem children. Comparison with two cost-effective treatments and a control group. *Journal of Consulting and Clinical Psychology*, **56**, 558–566.

Weiner, I. B. (1970). Depression and suicide. In I. B. Weiner (ed.), *Psychological disturbance in adolescence*. New York: Wiley.

Weiss, B. (1984). Food additive safety evaluation: The link to behavioral disorders in children. In B. B. Lahey and A. E. Kazdin (eds), *Advances in Clinical Child Psychology*, (Vol. 7). New York: Plenum.

Weiss, G., and Hechtman, L. (1979). The hyperactive child syndrome. *Science*, **205**, 1345–1354.

Weiss, G., Minde, K., Werry, J. S., Douglas, V., and Nemeth, E. (1971). Studies on the hyperactive child. VIII 5-year follow-up. *Archives of General Psychiatry*, **24** 409–414.

Weisz, J. R., and Weiss, B. (1989). Cognitive mediators of the outcome of psychotherapy with children. In B. B. Lahey and A. E. Kazdin (eds), *Advances in clinical child psychology*, Vol. 12. New York: Plenum Press.

Weisz, J. R., Weiss, B., Alicke, M. D., and Klotz, M. L. (1987). Effectiveness of psychotherapy with children and adolescents. A meta-analysis for clinicians. *Journal of Consulting and Clinical Psychology*, **55**, 542–549.

Wells, K. C., Griest, K. L., and Forehand, R. (1980). The use of a self control package to enhance temporal generality of a parent training programme. *Behaviour Research and Therapy*, **18**, 347–353.

Wender, P. H. (1971). *Minimal brain dysfunction in children*. New York: Wiley.

Werner, E., and Smith, R. S. (1977). *Kauai's children come of age*. Honolulu: University Press of Hawaii.

Werner, E. E., and Smith, R. S. (1982). *Vulnerable, but invincible: A longitudinal study of resiliant children and youth*. New York: McGraw-Hill.

Werner, H., and Strauss, A. A. (1941). Pathology of figure-background relation in the child. *Journal of Abnormal Social Psychology*, **36**, 236–248.

Werry, J. S. (1968). Developmental hyperactivity. *Pediatric clinics of North America*, **15**, 581–599.

West, D. J. (1980). The clinical approach to criminology. *Psychological Medicine*, **10**, 619–631.

West, D. J., and Farrington, D. P. (1973). *Who becomes delinquent?*. London: Heinemann Educational.

Whiting, B. (1963). *Six cultures: Studies of child rearing*. New York: John Wiley.

Whitman, T. L., Mercurio, J. R., and Caponigri, V. (1970). Development of social responses in two severely retarded children. *Journal of Applied Behavior Analysis*, **3**, 133–138.

Wiggins, J. S. (1973). *Personality and prediction: Principles of personality assessment*. Reading MA: Addison-Wesley.

Williams, C. A., and Forehand, R. (1984). An examination of predictor variables for child compliance and noncompliance. *Journal of Abnormal Child Psychology*, **12**, (3), 491–504.

Williams, D. Y., and Akamatsu, T. J. (1978). Cognitive self-guidance training with juvenile delinquents: Applicability and generalization. *Cognitive Therapy and Research*, **2**, 285–288.

Williamson, D. A., Davis, C. J., and Kelley, M. L. (1987). Headaches. In T. H. Ollendick and M. Hersen (eds), *Handbook of child psychopathology* (2nd ed). New York: Plenum.

Willis, D., Elliott, C., and Jay, S. M. (1982). Psychological effects of physical illness and its concomitants. In J. Tuma (ed.), *Handbook for the practice of pediatric psychology*. New York: Wiley.

Wilson, F. E., and Evans, I. M. (1983). The reliability of target-behavior selection in behavioral assessment. *Behavioral Assessment*, **5**, 15–23.

Winer, G. A. (1982). A review and analysis of children's fearful behaviour in dental settings. *Child Development*, **53**, 1111–1133.

Wing, L. (1971a). *Autistic children*. London: Constable.

Wing, L. (1971b). Perceptual and language development in autistic children: A comparative study. In M. Rutter (ed.), *Infantile autism: Concepts, characteristics and treatment*. Edinburgh: Churchill Livingston.

Winnicott, D. W. (1957). *Mother and child: A primer of first relationships*. New York: Basic Books.

Wolfe, D. A. (1987). *Child abuse: Implications for child development and psychopathology*. Newbury Park, LA: Sage.

Wolfe, V. V., Gentile, C., and Wolfe, D. A. (1989). The impact of sexual abuse on children: A PTSD formulation. *Behaviour Therapy*, **20**, 215–228.

Wolfe, V. V., Wolfe, D. A., Gentile, C., and LaRose, L. (1987). Children's impact of traumatic events scale. Unpublished manuscript, University of Western Ontario, London, Ontario, Canada.

Wolfensberger, W. (1980). The definition of normalization. In R. J. Flynn and K. E. Nitsch (eds). *Normalization, social integration and community service*. Baltimore: University Park Press.

Wolfer, J., and Visintainer, M. (1975). Pediatric surgical patients' and parents' stress responses and adjustment. *Nursing Research*, **24**, 244–255.

Wolff, S. (1981). *Children under stress*. Penguin: England.

Wolff, S., and Goodell, G. (eds) (1968). *Harold G. Wolff's stress and disease*. Springfield, IL: Charles C. Thomas.

Wolkind, S., and Rutter, M. (1985). Separation, loss and family relationships. In M. Rutter and L. Hersov (eds), *Child and adolescent psychiatry: Modern approaches* (2nd ed). Oxford: Blackwell.

Wolpe, J. (1958). *Psychotherapy by reciprocal inhibition*. Stanford, CA: Stanford University Press.

Wolpe, J., and Lang, P. J. (1964). A Fear Survey Schedule for use in behavior therapy. *Behaviour Research and Therapy*, **2**, 27–30.

Woolston, T. L. (1984). Eating disorders in infancy and early childhood. *Journal of the American Academy of Child Psychiatry*, **22**, 112–121.

World Health Organization (1980). *International Clarification of Impairments, Disabilities and Handicaps*. Geneva: WHO.

World Health Organization (1988). *International Classification of Diseases: 10th Edition*. (ICD-10). Geneva: WHO.

Wright, D. (1971). *The psychology of moral behaviour*. Harmondsworth: Penguin.

Wright, H. F. (1960). Observational child study. In P. H. Mussen (ed.), *Handbook of research methods in child development*. New York: Wiley.

Yalom, I. D., Green, R., and Fisk, N. (1973). Prenatal exposure to female hormones: Effect on psychosexual development in boys. *Archives of General Psychiatry*, **28**, 554–561.

Yarrow, L. J. (1960). Interviewing children. In P. Mussen (ed.), *Handbook of research in child development*. New York: Wiley.

Yarrow, M. R., Campbell, J. D., and Burton, R. V. (1968). *Child rearing: an inquiry into research and methods*. San Francisco: Jossey-Bass.

Yates, A. J. (1970). *Behaviour therapy*. Chichester: Wiley.

Yelloly, M. A. (1972). The concept of insight. In D. Jehu (ed.), *Behaviour modification in social work*. Chichester: Wiley.

Young, G. C. (1973). The treatment of childhood encopresis by conditioned gastro-ileal reflex training. *Behaviour Research and Therapy*, **11**, 499–503.

Young, G. C., and Morgan, R. T. T. (1973). Rapidity of response to the treatment of enuresis. *Developmental Medicine and Child Neurology*, **15**, 488–496.

Yule, W. (1981). The epidemiology of child psychopathology. In B. B. Lahey and A. E. Kazdin (eds), *Advances in clinical child psychology* (Vol. 4). New York: Plenum.

Yule, W. (1983). Child health. In A. Liddell (ed.), *The practice of clinical psychology in Great Britain*. Chichester: Wiley.

Yule, W. (1989). An introduction to investigation in clinical child psychology. In S. J. E. Lindsay and G. E. Powell (eds), *An introduction to clinical child psychology*. Aldershot: Gower.

Yule, W. (1990). *The psychological sequelae of disasters and resulting compensation: Practical reviews in psychiatry*. Practical Reviews in Psychiatry, Series 2 (No. 9), 6–8, 12.

Yule, W., and Carr, J. (1980). *Behaviour modification for people with mental handicaps* (2nd ed). London: Croom Helm.

Yule, W., and Rutter, M. (1985). Reading and other learning difficulties. In M. Rutter and L. Hersov (eds), *Child psychiatry: Modern approaches* (2nd ed). Oxford: Blackwell.

Yule, W., Udwin, O., and Murdoch, K. (1990). The 'Jupiter' sinking: Effects on children's fears, depression and anxiety. *Journal of Child Psychology and Psychiatry*, **31**, 1051–1061.

Yule, W., and Udwin, O. (in press). *Screening child survivors for post-traumatic stress disorders: Experiences from the 'Jupiter' sinking*. British Journal of Clinical Psychology.

Yule, W., and Williams, R. (1990a). Post traumatic stress reactions in children. *Journal of Traumatic Stress*, **3**, (2), 279–295.

Yule, W., and Williams, R. (1990b). The management of trauma following disasters: Therapeutic issues. In D. A. Lane and W. Dryden (eds), *Handbook of child and adolescent therapy in Britain*. Milton Keynes: Open University Press.

Zabin, M. A., and Melamed, B. G. (1980). Relationship between parental discipline and children's ability to cope with stress. *Journal of Behavioural Assessment*, **2**, 17–38.

Zatz, S., and Chassin, L. (1983). Cognitions in text-anxious children. *Journal of Consulting and Clinical Psychology*, **51**, 526–534.

Zatz, S., and Chassin, L. (1985). Cognitions of test-anxious children under naturalistic test-taking conditions. *Journal of Consulting and Clinical Psychology*, **53**, 393–401.

Zebrowitz-MacArthur, L. A., and Kendall-Tackett, K. A. (1989). Parental reactions to transgressions by baby-faced and mature-faced 4 and 11 year old children. Paper read at meeting of the *Society for Research in Child Development* (April), Kansas City.

Zeilberger, J., Sampen, S., and Sloane, H. (1968). Modification of a child's problem behaviours in the home with the mother as therapist. *Journal of Applied Behavior Analysis*, **1**, 47–53.

Zeltzer, L. (1980). The adolescent with cancer. In J. Kellerman (ed.), *Psychological aspects of childhood cancer*. Springfield IL: Thomas.

Zeltzer, L., and LeBaron, S. (1982). Hypnosis and non-hypnotic techniques for reduction of pain and anxiety during painful procedures in children and adolescents with cancer. *Journal of Pediatrics*, **101**, 1032–1035.

Zeltzer, L., and LeBaron, S. (1986). The hypnotic treatment of children in pain. *Advances in Developmental Paediatrics*, **7**, 197–234.

Zeltzer, L., LeBaron, S., Richie, D. M., and Reed, D. (1988). Can children understand and use a rating scale to quantify somatic symptoms? Assessment of nausea and vomiting as a model. *Journal of Consulting and Clinical Psychology*, **56**, (4), 567–572.

Index

Index compiled by John Gibson